Elementary
Applied
Symbolic Logic

Elementary Applied Symbolic Logic

Bangs L. Tapscott

University of Utah

Prentice-Hall, Inc.
Englewood Cliffs, New Jersey

Library of Congress Cataloging in Publication Data

TAPSCOTT, BANGS L   (date)
    Elementary applied symbolic logic.

    Bibliography: p. 485
    Includes index.
    1. Logic, Symbolic and mathematical.   2. Prop-
osition (Logic)   3. Identity.   4. Truth.   I. Title.
BC135.T27   511′.3   75-17642
ISBN 0-13-252940-8

10   9   8   7   6   5   4   3

Printed in the United States of America

PRENTICE-HALL INTERNATIONAL, INC., *London*
PRENTICE-HALL OF AUSTRALIA, PTY. LTD., *Sydney*
PRENTICE-HALL OF CANADA, LTD., *Toronto*
PRENTICE-HALL OF INDIA PRIVATE LIMITED, *New Delhi*
PRENTICE-HALL OF JAPAN, INC., *Tokyo*
PRENTICE-HALL OF SOUTHEAST ASIA (PTE.), *Singapore*

*To Christopher and Teresa
and to Fran*

contents

part II QUANTIFIER LOGIC
             (a) *Monadic Predicate Logic*

QUANTIFIER LOGIC
(b) *Polyadic Predicates, Identity,
and Definite Descriptions*

appendixes

preface

The writing of this text has been guided by two beliefs. One is that an introductory logic book should contain all of the relevant information, not just some of it. The other is that formal logic may be assimilated by any person of average abilities, provided it is taken in proper-size bites. The first of these has dictated the content of the book; the second has dictated its structure.

I have attempted to produce a text that will enable the reader to do as much of his own learning as possible. The explanations are as concise and thorough, and the content is as complete, as I could make them. Exercises are provided to cover each stage of development, and answers for many of them are furnished to enable the student to check on his or her own progress. A textbook earns its keep by doing all it can to anticipate questions and problems that would otherwise have to be answered on classroom time, thereby enabling the live instructor to concentrate upon those things which cannot be accomplished by printed words. A student learns logic without getting confused or overwhelmed by consuming it in small, individually manageable doses whose effects are cumulative.

This is a book in *applied* symbolic logic, in that it treats logic primarily as a system for the evaluation of statements and arguments, rather than as an abstract discipline in its own right. It is *elementary* in that its main course proceeds only through the standard ramifications of first-order quantification. Extensive coverage has been given to translation from English into symbols, at all levels. The proof procedure, after truth-tables, is standard natural deduction, since this is intuitively clearer in application than any of its present rivals. Principia notation with bracket punctuation has been used because of the visual perspicuity of its formulae. Arrow-and-bar notation for introducing and discharging assumptions has been used for the same reason, and because of the relative simplicity it lends to the formulation of the discharge rules. Substantial care has been taken to provide a conceptually clear groundwork for the instantiation and generalization rules, since the restrictions to them, in the usual stark presentation, are difficult for the average student either to understand or to memorize.

There are two natural breaking points in the book. Truth-functions are completely covered before taking up quantification, and monadic predicate logic (including invalidity proofs) is completely covered before taking up relations, identity, and descriptions.

Appendixes deal with a variety of matters usually not mentioned, or entirely outside the scope of standard elementary logic. For those wishing something beyond the elementary level, there are completeness and consistency proofs presented in a context which illustrates the purely formal development of a system, the logical equivalence of different systems, the distinction between primitive and derived rules, and similar matters none of which are touched upon in the body of the text.

Among the many persons who have contributed in one way or another to this book, I owe special thanks to the following: to Arnie, Ruth Anna, and David, who introduced me to logic; to Penny Tadman Zlutnick, who typed the original version of the manuscript, and to Denece Childs who typed the copy for the instructor's manual; to Fred Hagen, Pat Johnston, Peter Windt, and Robert Faaborg for their useful comments and encouragement; to David Bennett, for many conversations on topics logical and for permission to include a version of his completeness proof; to Hilda Tauber of Prentice-Hall, for being a patient and friendly production editor; to my wife Frances Tapscott, for her invaluable assistance in preparing the manuscript and in reading proofs; to the hundreds of students who have learned from earlier versions of this material, and who taught me much about how a logic book should be written; and especially to my friend and former student Ken Tohinaka, without whose unfailing enthusiasm this book might never have been published.

                                                   BANGS L. TAPSCOTT

Elementary
Applied
Symbolic Logic

PRELIMINARIES

Logic, for our purposes, may be characterized as the science of evaluating human reasoning. We employ logic in determining whether a given specimen of reasoning is correct or incorrect and in ascertaining the logical status of propositions which are or might be involved in it—that is, in discovering whether or not they are the sort of proposition that could conceivably be false, since these are the only propositions which require *evidence* for their truth or falsity.

A claim of ancient tradition is that logic is "the art of thinking" or "the art of producing correct reasoning," but this claim is not true. The art of *producing* correct reasoning cannot be taught but only learned. Mastery of the techniques of formal logic may sometimes help to produce correct reasoning, but this result is serendipitous: logic *per se* does not and cannot tell us what to infer from available information; it does tell us, after we have inferred something, whether or not the inference was correct. Thus the primary function of formal logical techniques is to assist us in avoiding the results of *in*correct reasoning; the techniques come into play after a piece of reasoning has been produced, to determine its correctness, rather than to deliver correct reasoning in the first place.

The kind of reasoning susceptible to logical evaluation is that which is expressed in language—in written or spoken assertions about what is or is not the case. If a type of reasoning exists that does not involve language at all (and this is unlikely), it is essentially non-logical; it is irrelevant to logic, and logic to it. Logic is concerned not with the psychological processes of reasoning but with the beginning- and end-points of those processes—that is, the propositions expressing the information reasoned about, and the conclusion reasoned to.

The purpose of all reasoning is to proceed from certain given pieces of information to conclusions based upon that information. The question of whether a given specimen of reasoning is *correct* is the question of whether

1

the conclusions follow from the given information in the manner asserted. This latter question is one of logic.

In logic, the linguistic expression of any piece of reasoning is called an **argument**. In ordinary discourse, the word 'argument' frequently designates a verbal dispute or disagreement between individuals. But in logic, an argument has nothing to do with disputation or disagreement. So far as logic goes, the word 'argument' may be defined as follows:

> *Argument.* An argument is a collection of (two or more) statements, one of which (the **conclusion**) is presented as being based upon the other(s) and the other(s) of which (the **premisses**) express the information upon which the conclusion is based.

Whenever a statement or several statements are presented as reasons for accepting a further statement, the whole collection of statements constitutes an argument. For example, should someone say: "Science has demonstrated that potassium cyanide is bad for hamsters; therefore, if you feed potassium cyanide to your hamster he will probably become ill," the speaker would be advancing an argument. The premiss of his argument is the statement "Science has demonstrated that potassium cyanide is bad for hamsters," and the conclusion of his argument is the statement "If you feed potassium cyanide to your hamster he will probably become ill." Similarly, if someone asserts: "Jenny owns a white female cat, and all white female cats are deaf; so Jenny owns a deaf cat," he will have presented an argument. Its conclusion is the statement "Jenny owns a deaf cat," and its premisses are the other two statements.

In this book we are concerned exclusively with deductive reasoning and with deductive arguments. But not all reasoning is deductive. For example, much of the reasoning that goes on in science and crime detection is nondeductive. In any species of reasoning an argument is a good one and constitutes an example of correct reasoning if its premisses give a sufficient ground for accepting its conclusion. But what constitutes a sufficient ground will vary, depending upon the particular argument and the circumstances and purposes of its presentation. In deductive logic the requirements are extremely rigorous, more so than in any other area of logic. A deductive argument is not acceptable unless it is **deductively valid**, defined as follows:

> *Deductive Validity.* An argument is deductively valid if, and only if, there is no *possible* way for its conclusion to be false while all of its premisses are true.

To apply this definition properly, one must understand the special notion of *possibility* involved. In ordinary discourse we sometimes say that a thing is not possible and mean only that it is extremely unlikely (as in "Rain tomorrow is not possible"); and we sometimes say that a thing is not possible meaning that the present state of knowledge or technology does not permit it ("It is impossible to build a pollution-free automobile"). But the concept of possibility in formal logic has nothing to do with likelihood, knowledge, or technology. Within logic, nothing is impossible unless it is literally *self-contradictory* (that is, unless it involves the simultaneous occurrence and non-occurrence of the same state of affairs). Thus, for example, it is logically possible for a man to have ten billion wives, since there is nothing self-contradictory in the supposition that someone might accomplish this extraordinary feat. (The supposition might contradict some other fact, such as the known female population of the earth, but it wouldn't contradict *itself*.) On the other hand, it is logically *im*possible for a *bachelor* to have even one wife, since if he did, he would not be a bachelor. To be a bachelor with a wife, one would have to be an unmarried man (bachelor) and a married man simultaneously, which is self-contradictory. Similarly, it is logically impossible for a person to be taller than himself, or for two people to be taller than each other, or for the following statement to be true:

> Clyde and Harvey are both seniors, but Clyde isn't one.

since its truth involves a self-contradiction.

Once these notions of "logical possibility" and "logical impossibility" are understood, we can see that there are a number of different ways of expressing the conditions for deductive validity. For example, we might say

> An argument is deductively valid if, and only if, it would be self-contradictory to suppose that its conclusion is false and all of its premisses true.

or

> An argument is deductively valid if, and only if, there is no way for its conclusion to be false without at least one of its premisses also being false.

or, perhaps most simply,

> An argument is deductively valid if, and only if, it satisfies the following description: If all of its premisses were true, its conclusion could not be false.

It should be clear, from these various explanations, that deductive validity has nothing to do with whether the premisses or conclusion of an argument are actually true. An argument does not need true premisses in order to be valid, nor does it need a false conclusion in order to be *in*valid. The only requirement for deductive validity is that if all the premisses *were* true (whether they actually are or not), then the conclusion would also have to be true (whether it actually is or not). If an argument satisfies this requirement, then it is deductively valid, even if its conclusion and/or premisses are false. Conversely, if an argument fails to satisfy this requirement (that is, if all its premisses can be true while its conclusion is false), then it is deductively invalid, even if its premisses and conclusion all happen to be true.* These

---

*An argument which is deductively valid, and which has all true premisses, is called a *sound argument*. Those who apply logic are normally interested in soundness, not merely validity. But logic itself is concerned only with validity.

facts may be illustrated by the following two extremely simple arguments:

1. Some antelope are students.	2. All birds are warm-blooded.
All students are freshmen.	All elephants are mammals.
Therefore some antelope are fresh-men.	Therefore all mammals are warm-blooded.

We should be able to recognize, on the basis of common sense, that argument (1) is valid even though it consists entirely of false statements, and that argument (2) is invalid even though it consists entirely of true statements.

A method often used (in science, law, and the like) for showing an argument to be faulty consists in showing that one or more of its premises is false. This procedure, useful as it is, is not a part of formal logic—because, in general, the question of the *actual* truth or falsity of statements is not a logical question and is not to be answered by logic but by extralogical procedures such as observation or experiment.

The validity or invalidity of simple arguments, such as (1) and (2), can often be determined on the basis of common sense (or "intuition") without the need for logical techniques of the sort contained in this book. However, most arguments are not that simple; and as arguments become more and more complex, common sense becomes less and less trustworthy. For example, it is not easy to tell, on the basis of intuition alone, whether the following argument is valid or not:

> If the defendant had nothing to hide, then he didn't wipe his fingerprints from the doorknob. If he wasn't trying to escape detection, then he stayed until after the police arrived. If he was at the scene of the crime, then he wiped his fingerprints from the doorknob. He was there all right, but he left before the police arrived. If he had something to hide and was trying to escape detection, he was frightened or guilty. Therefore, if he was innocent, he was frightened.

In fact, it is valid; but to determine this we need something more systematic than unaided common sense.

The General Nature of Applied Symbolic Logic

Symbolic logic* consists basically of two parts: (1) an artificially constructed symbolic language, complete with its own grammar and a vocabulary consisting of such symbols as '⊃', '∼', '≡', '*p*', '*q*', '*A*', '*B*', and (2) a set of testing procedures and operating rules for this language.

---

*Also referred to as formal logic. These labels are intended to differentiate the present discipline from the traditional logic of categorical propositions. They are labels, rather than descriptions, since traditional logic is equally *formal* and is equally susceptible to symbolization. A less contentious label is "mathematical logic," but this usually frightens away the student who is not mathematically oriented.

Natural languages, such as English, Japanese, or Bantu, are by their very nature unsuited to the precision required in logic. The words and expressions in a natural language are rich in peripheral overtones and subtle ambiguities which make them suitable vehicles for poetry and storytelling, as well as for descriptions of fact. But their very expressiveness makes them imprecise: one word or expression can do many different jobs, can evoke many different ideas, and for this reason can leave some doubt, on occasion, as to just what *is* being expressed. This richness makes natural languages useful for conversation and literature but impractical for logic. Logic is concerned not with beauty or subtlety of expression but with *accuracy*, with *clarity*, with what it would take to make a statement true or false, with absolute lack of ambiguity. Formal logic employs an artificial language designed specifically to have just these features.

The first stage in applying formal logic is learning how to translate statements out of our natural language (in the present case, English) into the language of symbolic logic. When translating from one natural language into another, the translator usually tries to reproduce the entire meaning of the original. But it is impossible to reproduce the entire meaning of English expressions in the sterile language of symbolic logic; so the goal is to reproduce the truth- and falsity-conditions of the original, since these are what is relevant to logic. (The conditions under which a statement would be true are its truth-conditions; those under which it would be false, its falsity-conditions. But logicians habitually speak simply of "truth-conditions," with the understanding that this refers to both.) Learning to translate properly is the hardest part of learning logic, since there are no absolute rules for it. There are some helpful guides and rules of thumb, which will be presented in due course. But, as in all translation, there is no substitute for understanding both languages.

The reason for translating into the symbolic language is that there are ironclad, exceptionless rules for operating on, and within, that language. Since the symbolic language is totally unambiguous (there is never any question as to what it means), these rules can be applied mechanically, without any fear of going wrong by them. They eliminate the need for intuition, with its notorious fallibilities, in evaluating arguments or statements. The second stage in applying formal logic consists in learning these rules and procedures.

part I

Propositional Logic

chapter 1

STATEMENTS; TRUTH-VALUES;
COMPOUNDS; ABBREVIATIONS

§1.1 Statements

The basic concept in logic is that of the **statement** or **proposition**. (These two terms are used interchangeably throughout the book.) A definition adequate for our purposes is the following:

> *Statement* (*Proposition*). A statement (or proposition) is what is expressed in uttering—vocally, or in writing, or in some other way—a declarative sentence on a particular occasion of normal discourse.*

While declarative sentences are the vehicles of statements, a statement is not the same thing as a sentence. Statements are abstractions, which cannot be equated with the sentences used to express them for two obvious reasons: First, any given sentence may be used, on different occasions, to make *different* statements. Second, different sentences may sometimes be used to make the *same* statement. For example, the sentence

1. John is bald.

uttered by someone in Detroit to say something about his brother, would on that occasion express one proposition, while the same sentence uttered by someone in Los Angeles to say something about his parrot would express a different proposition. Similarly, the two different sentences

2. Today is Wednesday.
3. Yesterday was Wednesday.

might be used to express the same proposition; for example, if (2) were uttered one day and (3) were uttered the next.

---

*See Appendix A for more on this subject. The appendices contain supplementary information for the interested reader. They need not be consulted to understand the text.

Sentences are identified and distinguished by the words they contain and their grammatical form. *Propositions* are identified and distinguished by their truth-conditions—that is, the conditions that would have to obtain in order for them to be true or to be false. Different truth-conditions indicate different propositions; and, for our purposes, identical truth-conditions indicate identical propositions. For example, returning to (1), let us suppose that the man in Detroit is named Jones and the man in Los Angeles is named Smith. Then, in order for Jones' statement to be true, Jones' brother would have to be bald; and in order for Smith's statement to be true, Smith's parrot would have to be bald. But the condition of Jones' brother being bald, and the condition of Smith's parrot being bald, are quite different. Hence the two statements are different statements. On the other hand, if (2) and (3) are uttered on consecutive days, so that the pronouns 'today' and 'yesterday' come to designate the same day, then both statements will be true if that day happens to be Wednesday and both will be false if it happens not to be Wednesday. The truth-conditions for the two statements are identical; hence, we can say the two statements are identical. In general, any pair of natural-language statements may be treated as identical if, and only if, they have the same truth-conditions.

Not every utterance of a declarative sentence expresses a proposition. Only those which are genuine portions of discourse do so. The sentence "John is bald" uttered above does not express a proposition; it was uttered simply as an example of a sentence, not as an attempt to communicate information to you about anyone named John. Most of the example-sentences in any logic book will fail to express propositions for the same reason. However, since it is virtually impossible to teach or learn logic without the help of examples, we shall treat our examples as if they were genuine portions of discourse, uttered by someone for the purpose of communication. Henceforth, every sentence employed as an example will (unless otherwise indicated) be treated as if it expressed a proposition.

Also, for purposes of simplicity and to avoid confusion, we shall stipulate two further conventions about sentences and statements, which will be adhered to throughout the remainder of the book.

"SAME SENTENCE SAME STATEMENT" CONVENTION. Unless otherwise stated, repeated occurrences of the same sentence, within a given context, will be regarded as repetitions of the same statement. (This means that we shall not allow a sentence to express different propositions in the same context.)

"SAME NAME SAME REFERENCE" CONVENTION. Unless otherwise stated, repeated occurrences of the same name within a given context will be regarded as references to the same thing. (This means, for example, that John Smith and John Jones cannot both be referred to simply as 'John' in the same context.)

§1.2 Truth-Values

Statements can be either true or false; that is, they have **truth-values**. There are two truth-values: True and False. A true statement has a truth-value of True; a false statement has a truth-value of False. There is no third truth-value in addition to these two.*

No statement can have both truth-values. No statement is both true and false. So far as truth-values go, a miss is as good as a mile. A baseball player who was "almost out" is safe, and one who was "almost safe" is out. Similarly, a proposition that is "almost true" is nevertheless false, and one that is "almost false" is nevertheless true.

So far as we are concerned, every statement has at least one of the two truth-values. It is a matter of some philosophical dispute whether or not all statements satisfy this condition: it has been argued that some statements (for example, those having to do with moral or religious matters) are neither true nor false. This dispute is irrelevant to elementary logic. If there are any statements lacking a truth-value, they fall entirely outside the scope of our discipline and are of no interest to us. So far as the *logic* of statements is concerned, it is regarded as an axiom that every statement up for logical consideration is either true or false.†

From the fact that every statement has a truth-value and no statement has both, it follows that every statement has just one of the two truth-values. A statement which is not true is false, and one which is not false is true. Likewise, a statement which is false is not true and one which is true is not false.

§1.3 Simple and Compound Statements

Any declarative sentence which contains another declarative sentence as an independent clause is referred to in logic as a **compound sentence**. The notion of an "independent" clause, as given in most grammar books, is rather vague; but for present purposes we may take it to mean a clause (that is, a grammatical unit of the sentence) whose truth-conditions could be specified in ignorance of the remainder of the sentence in which the clause occurs. For logical purposes, "function words" (prepositions, conjunctions, conjunctive adverbs, relative pronouns, and so on) preceding or following a clause are not regarded as part of the clause itself. This notion can best be explained

---

*Professional logicians sometimes study what are called "multiple-valued logics." But the values involved in addition to truth and falsity are not *truth*-values.

†This is sometimes called the "Law of Excluded Middle": There is no "middle ground" between truth and falsity.

with the help of examples. Consider

1. The boy who kicked Evangeline is a brat.

Even though the last four words of this sentence, 'Evangeline is a brat', have
the grammatical form of a declarative sentence, it would be a mistake to
regard (1) as a compound sentence on these grounds, since the last four
words do not constitute a *clause* within the sentence; rather, 'Evangeline' is
a portion of the subject-phrase, and 'is a brat' is the predicate of the whole
sentence. In sorting out the independent clauses within sentences it is often
helpful to enclose them in parentheses. But if we attempt to analyze (1) as

1a. The boy who kicked (Evangeline is a brat).

the result is not even a *sentence*; (1a) does not express anything with truth-
conditions. If (1) is analyzed as (1a) it does not make a coherent assertion,
which is sufficient to indicate that (1a) is the wrong analysis. We can state
this by saying that the sentence 'Evangeline is a brat' is not a *component* of
sentence (1), since it is not an independent clause within that sentence. As
another example, consider

2. It is true that turtles lay eggs.

which contains two declarative sentences as clauses:

2a. (It is true) that (turtles lay eggs).

However, only the second of these is an *independent* clause. 'It is true' is not
an independent clause, since one could not specify its truth-conditions without knowing *what it is* that is supposed to be true; that is, the remainder of
the sentence. On the other hand, 'turtles lay eggs' expresses a proposition
with independently specifiable truth-conditions, and so is an independent
clause which is a *component* of sentence (2). Similarly for

3. Clyde revealed that Harvey is a policeman.

Although this may be analyzed as

3a. (Clyde revealed) that (Harvey is a policeman).

the first clause in (3a) is not an independent clause. 'Reveal' is a transitive
verb, and there is no way to describe the truth-conditions of a statement
involving this verb without knowing its direct object, which in the present
case is the proposition that Harvey is a policeman—that is, the remainder of
the sentence. Thus (3) is a compound sentence with only one component: the
clause 'Harvey is a policeman'. As another example, in

4. Jones was fired by the company for embezzlement.

the clause 'Jones was fired by the company' is an independent clause and thus
is a component of (4). (Or, if we take the verb to be the intransitive 'fired',
rather than the transitive 'fired by', the clause 'Jones was fired' may also be
taken as an independent clause.) Although the adverbial phrase 'for embez-

zlement' modifies something within the independent clause, it is not *part* of the independent clause, since it is not part of the declarative sentence constituting that clause.

Clauses may be regarded as independent even though there is a pronominal overlap between them. For example, the sentence

5. Evangeline walked in and Percy kicked her.

should be regarded as containing two independent clauses 'Evangeline walked in' and 'Percy kicked her', even though the personal pronoun in the second clause has its antecedent in the first clause. A referential overlap of this sort does not destroy the independence of the two clauses. This is quite different from cases such as (2) and (3), in which we literally cannot understand what the dependent clause asserts until we understand (not merely the reference, but) the entire content of the independent clause. Thus (5) is a compound sentence with two components, as is

6. Either it will rain tonight or the weatherman is incompetent.

in which the two components 'it will rain tonight' and 'the weatherman is incompetent' are totally independent.

An independent clause in a compound sentence may itself be a compound sentence. For example, in the sentence

7. If it rained last night and the park is all wet then the picnic has been cancelled.

the independent clauses can be presented as

7a. If (it rained last night and the park is all wet) then (the picnic has been cancelled).

However, the first of these is itself a compound sentence whose component clauses are 'it rained last night' and 'the park is all wet'; thus, the full analysis of (7) will be

7b. If ((it rained last night) and (the park is all wet)) then (the picnic has been cancelled).

The statements expressed by compound sentences are called **compound statements**. A statement which is not compound is called a **simple statement**. Simple statements are expressed by sentences which are not compound.* Just as the independent clauses of a compound sentence are called its **components**, the propositions expressed by them are called the **components** of the compound statement expressed by the whole sentence.

In logic, **negative** statements are always regarded as compound—that is, as the denials of their affirmative counterparts. For example, the negative statement

8. It won't rain tonight.

---

*Cf. Appendix B.

is to be treated as if it said

    8a. It's not the case that it will rain tonight.

which is a compound whose component is the statement 'It will rain tonight'. This treatment is invariant and is employed even when (as in this illustration) the sentence expressing the negative statement is not phrased as a compound sentence.

Exercises I

Decide which of the following statements are simple and which are compound. For the compound ones, decide what their components are.

*□ **1.** They invited me to the party but I didn't go.

    2. If Harvey drank from that bottle he is going to die.

□ **3.** Today is Wednesday.

    4. Clyde believes that the earth is flat.

□ **5.** My car is better than yours.

    6. Thelma told Harvey that she had a headache.

□ **7.** The earth is not flat.

    8. Clyde pinched Edna for laughing too loud.

□ **9.** Anyone who can swim the Atlantic Ocean is a very athletic person.

    10. I won't go unless you beg me.

There are two different sorts of compound statements. On the one hand, some compound statements are such that the truth-values of their components make no difference at all to the truth-value of the whole compound. An example is

    9. Harvey says that there is life on Venus.

This is a compound whose component is the statement: 'There is life on Venus'. Now whether or not there is life on Venus is immaterial to the truth (or falsity) of (9). The only thing relevant to its truth-value is whether or not Harvey has said what is attributed to him.

    On the other hand, some compound statements are such that the truth-values of their components *do* make a difference to the truth-value of the whole compound. Compound statements of this sort are called **truth-dependent compounds**. An example would be

    10. Harvey hit Edna in order to make her shut up.

This is a compound whose component is 'Harvey hit Edna'. And if this component happened to be false (that is, if Harvey didn't hit Edna at all),

---

*An open square indicates that the answer to the problem may be found in the back of the book.

then the whole compound would also be false. Of course, if the component happened to be *true*, the whole compound might still be false (he might have hit her for some other reason); but nevertheless the truth-value of the component is, to a certain extent, relevant to the truth-value of the whole. Another example of a truth-dependent compound is

11. Clyde drinks a lot but Harvey is a teetotaler.

This is a compound whose components are 'Clyde drinks a lot' and 'Harvey is a teetotaler'. It is truth-dependent, since if either one of these (or both of them) happened to be false, then the whole compound would also be false. However, if both components happen to be *true*, then the whole compound will also be true. This means that the truth-value of (11) is *completely* determined by the truth-values of its components: if both of its components are true, then it is true; otherwise, it is false. A compound statement of this sort is said to be **truth-functional**, since its truth-value is a function of the truth-values of its components.

> *Truth-Function.* X is a truth-function of Y if and only if the truth-value(s) of Y completely determine(s) the truth-value of X. Thus every statement is, trivially, a truth-function of itself.

> *Truth-Functional Compound.* A compound statement is a truth-functional compound if and only if its truth-value is completely determined by the truth-values of its components. In such a circumstance, the compound statement is also said to be a truth-function of its components.

It should be obvious that every *negative* statement is a truth-functional compound, since the negative statement will be true if its component is false, and false if its component is true.

The first area of logic to be studied is called **truth-functional logic** (or **propositional logic**). It is concerned exclusively with truth-functional structures and the logical relationships that obtain between statements in virtue of their truth-functional makeup. Thus, the only compound statements that will be of logical interest will be the truth-functional compounds.* For this reason, in truth-functional logic all statements that are not truth-functional compounds are lumped together as "simple statements." A statement which is not a truth-functional compound is, from a logical point of view, simple. From now on we shall not bother to differentiate between *bona fide* simple statements and "simple" statements which are really some sort of non-truth-functional compound, and we shall use the word "compound" as a synonym for "truth-functional compound," unless there is a specific indication to the contrary.

---

*Appendix C gives procedures for treating certain non-truth-functional compounds.

§1.4 Abbreviating Simple Statements

In truth-functional logic no attention is paid to the internal structure or subject matter of simple statements. They are of interest only insofar as they can be spliced together into different kinds of truth-functional compounds. For this reason, it is standard practice to abbreviate simple statements as drastically as possible. This is done by abbreviating them down to a single *capital* letter—generally the initial letter of some key word in the statement, though this is not mandatory. One of the first preliminaries to all logical operations is to abbreviate the simple statements (including simple components of truth-functional compounds) being considered. For example, if we wish to "prepare"

  1. Thelma lives in the country but Harvey lives in town.

for logical treatment, we first identify its simple components. These are

  1a. Thelma lives in the country.

  1b. Harvey lives in town.

We then abbreviate these. For example, (1a) might be abbreviated as '*C*', and (1b) might be abbreviated as '*T*'. Applying these abbreviations to (1) we obtain the drastically shortened statement

  1c. *C* but *T*.

Occasionally, compound statements contain "hidden components," or components which are not explicitly presented by means of a fully articulated sentence. Before performing the abbreviations in such cases it is helpful to paraphrase the compound statement into a form which explicitly presents all components. For example, the statement

  2. Clyde was injured in the accident even though Harvey wasn't.

has, as its second component, the statement 'Harvey wasn't injured in the accident', though this statement isn't presented by means of a full sentence. Thus, it will be helpful to paraphrase (2) as

  2a. Clyde was injured in the accident even though Harvey wasn't injured in the accident.

The second component is negative and therefore compound. It is helpful to paraphrase negative statements to bring out explicitly their affirmative component. One way of doing this is to paraphrase 'Harvey wasn't injured in the accident' as 'It's not the case that Harvey was injured in the accident'. Following this procedure, we would paraphrase (2a) as

  2b. Clyde was injured in the accident even though it's not the case that Harvey was injured in the accident.

The simple components of (2b) are the two statements 'Clyde was injured in the accident' and 'Harvey was injured in the accident'. Abbreviating these, respectively, as '*C*' and '*H*', we obtain the full abbreviation of (2b):

2c. *C* even though it's not the case that *H*.

Similarly, the statement

3. We have no milk, but plenty of eggs.

might be successively paraphrased and abbreviated as

3a. We have no milk, but we have plenty of eggs.

3b. It's not the case that we have milk, but we have plenty of eggs.

3c. It's not the case that *M*, but *E*.

When abbreviating simple statements, there is one rule we *must* adhere to. It is an instance of the general rule of consistency: "Never try to make one symbol or expression do two jobs at once." Here, it may be stated as:

CONSISTENCY: NEVER use the same capital letter to abbreviate two *different* statements in the same context. Always choose a different capital letter for each different statement.

Exercises II

Abbreviate the following statements, using paraphrase as necessary.

☐ **1.** I didn't go to the party, even though I was invited.

2. Clyde will cry if his new paint job is scratched.

☐ **3.** Harvey has gone to either Canada or Sweden.

4. It's false that I can't swim.

☐ **5.** If Clyde wore his boots in, then he will drown whether or not he knows how to swim.

6. We sell cars and trucks.

☐ **7.** If it's raining or snowing we won't go on the picnic unless the weather improves.

8. Clyde and Thelma both moved to Argentina.

chapter 2

TRUTH-FUNCTIONAL OPERATORS; CONJUNCTION AND NEGATION; TRUTH-TABLE DEFINITIONS; PUNCTUATION

§2.1 Truth-Functional Operators

A **truth-functional operator** is an expression or symbol which, when suitably attached to a sentence or a pair of sentences, produces a larger sentence expressing a truth-functional compound of the original statement(s).* English contains a great many truth-functional operators, some of which we have already looked at briefly. For example, the common word 'not' is a truth-functional operator which, suitably placed within a sentence, produces a statement which is a truth-function of the original statement. Likewise, the word 'but' is a truth-functional operator which, when located between a pair of sentences, produces a compound which is a truth-function of the original statements.

Every truth-functional compound consists of a collection of simple components operated upon in various ways by truth-functional operators. As has already been noted, a truth-functional compound may have components which are themselves truth-functional compounds. But no matter how complex a truth-functional compound is, it ultimately consists of simple components hinged together by truth-functional operators.

The artificial symbolic language of truth-functional logic has a standing vocabulary which consists almost entirely of truth-functional operators. There are five such operators: ' ∼ ' (*tilde*), ' · ' (*dot*), ' ∨ ' (*wedge*), ' ⊃ ' (*horseshoe*), and ' ≡ ' (*triple bar*). Each corresponds (in a manner to be explained) to a number of English truth-functional operators. "Logical translation" consists in translating English operators into corresponding operators from the symbolic language. In order to do this accurately, it is necessary to understand what the symbolic operators mean and what it is for an English opera-

---

*Truth-functional operators are also called "truth-functional connectives," which tends to be confusing in the case of such operators as 'not', which don't serve to connect anything to anything. Suitably understood, however, either terminology is acceptable.

tor to correspond to a symbolic one. These matters are taken up in this and succeeding chapters.

§2.2 Conjunction

When the operator-word 'but' is used to connect two statements together, the resulting compound will be true if both of its components are true, and false otherwise (that is, false if either or both of the components are false). For example, the statement

    1. Harvey lives in Paraguay but his wife lives in Brazil.

is false unless *both* of its components are true; the whole compound is true only if it is true that Harvey lives in Paraguay and it is also true that his wife lives in Brazil.

A compound which is true if both its components are true and false otherwise is called a "truth-functional conjunction," or more simply a **conjunction**. Thus, (1) above is a conjunction. An operator which produces a conjunction is a **conjunctive operator**. Other conjunctive operators in English are 'and', 'however', and 'although', to mention a few. The components of a conjunction are called its **conjuncts**.

In logic there is only one conjunctive operator: the symbol '·', called **dot**. Whenever the dot is placed between two statements, abbreviated or otherwise, the result is a compound statement, a conjunction, whose components are the statements that the dot occurs between. The dot has no exact synonym in English; it is a *pure* truth-functional operator, which is to say that it has no meaning beyond its ability to hook statements together into conjunctions. Nevertheless, the dot corresponds to a great many expressions in English; namely, those expressions which are conjunctive operators.

The two English conjunctive operators 'and' and 'however' do not mean the same thing; there are situations in normal discourse when it would be proper to use the one and quite inappropriate to use the other. But logic is not concerned with subtle nuances of meaning; hence, when performing logical translation it is the standard practice to replace (translate) *all* conjunctive operators with the dot, effectively ignoring their differences of meaning and concentrating only upon the truth-conditions of the compounds formed with their assistance.

A logical translation of (1), then, would proceed as follows. First its simple components are isolated and abbreviated; perhaps 'Harvey lives in Paraguay' is abbreviated as '*P*' and 'his wife lives in Brazil' is abbreviated as '*B*', resulting in

    1a. *P* but *B*

The conjunctive operator 'but' is then translated as the dot, resulting in

    1b. *P · B*

which is the completed logical translation of (1). As another example, take the statement

    2. Although Harvey is quite ugly, he's not very intelligent.

This paraphrases as

    2a. Although Harvey is quite ugly, it's not the case that he's very intelligent.

which abbreviates to

    2b. Although *U*, it's not the case that *I*.

Finally, translating the conjunctive operator 'although' by the dot, we get

    2c. *U ·* it's not the case that *I*

The dot is a "word" in the symbolic language of formal logic. If a precise definition must be given, we can say:

> ***The dot*** *means that the compound formed by inserting it between two statements is true when both components are true, and false if either or both components are false.*

§2.3 Truth-Table Definitions

There is a more convenient way, however, to give the definition of the dot. This is by means of a diagram called a **truth-table**. Briefly stated, a truth-table is a diagram for displaying all possible combinations of truth-values of a set of statements and for showing how each such combination will affect the truth-value of a compound having those statements as components. The above "definition" of the dot says, in effect, that if p is a statement and q is a statement, then the compound statement $p · q$ is *true* if p is true and q is true; it is *false* if p is true and q is false; it is *false* if p is false and q is true; and it is *false* if p is false and q is false. All this is represented quickly and conveniently in the "truth-table definition" of the dot:

p	q	$p · q$
T	T	T
T	F	F
F	T	F
F	F	F

In this diagram the two columns to the left (called the **base columns**) display the four possible combinations of truth-values that a pair of statements can have: they may both be true (top row), or the first may be true and the second false (second row down), or the first may be false and the second true (third row down), or both may be false (bottom row). The column to the right shows how each of these possibilities will affect a compound formed by inserting the dot between the two statements—that is, that the compound will be true when both components are true, and false otherwise. Reading across the diagram one row at a time, we see that when the components are both True, the compound is True; when the first component is True and the second is False, the compound is False; and so on. Because the dot is a pure truth-functional operator, a truth-table definition is a *complete* definition: the information in the diagram completely exhausts the meaning of the dot.

When reading the symbolic language aloud, it is conventional to read the dot either as "dot" or as "and." However, it should be borne in mind that it is not intended to be a synonym for the English word "and," and that so reading it is merely a matter of convenience.

TRANSLATION AID

The following is a list of some of the more common English conjunctive operators:

and	not only . . . but also . . .
but	in spite of the fact that
although	but even so
however	plus the fact that
whereas	inasmuch as (*but not* 'insofar as')
also	while (*in the sense of* 'although', *not in the sense of*
besides	'during which time')
both . . . and . . .	since (*in the sense of* 'whereas', *not in the sense of*
nevertheless	'after')
even though (*but not*	as (*in the sense of* 'whereas')
'even if')	

§2.4 Negation

When the operator-word 'not' is appropriately inserted into a sentence, the result is a compound statement that will be true if its component is false, and false if its component is true. For example, the statement

   1. Harvey is not married.

will be true if the component statement 'Harvey is married' is false; but it will be false if the component 'Harvey is married' is true. Its truth-value is always the opposite of its component's truth-value.

A compound which is true if its component is false and false if its component is true is called a **negation**. The component of a negation is called its

negate. Thus, (1) is a negation, whose negate is the statement 'Harvey is married'. An operator which produces a negation when applied to a statement is called a **negative** (ne-GAY-tiv) **operator**. Thus, the word 'not' is a negative operator. Other negative operators in English are 'it is not the case that', 'it is false that', and 'no', to name a few.

In logic there is only one negative operator: the symbol '∼', called **tilde** (TIL-deh). Whenever the tilde is placed immediately to the left of a statement, abbreviated or otherwise, the result is a compound statement, a negation, whose component is the statement that the tilde is immediately to the left of. The tilde, like the dot, is a pure truth-functional operator which has no exact synonym in English. Rather, it corresponds to all of the various negative operators in English, and when performing logical translation it is standard practice to translate all negative operators by the tilde.

For example, the logical translation of (2c) from §2.2

2c. *U* · it is not the case that *I*

can be completed by translating the negative operator 'it is not the case that' by the tilde, to produce

2d. *U* · ∼*I*

Similarly, the logical translation of (1) might proceed as follows:

1. Harvey is not married.

paraphrases to

1a. It is not the case that Harvey is married.

which abbreviates to

1b. It is not the case that *M*.

which translates to

1c. ∼*M*

The truth-table definition of the tilde is:

p	∼*p*
T	F
F	T

When reading the symbolic language aloud, it is conventional to read the '∼' as "tilde," "not," or "it is false that." "Not" is perhaps most common.

There is an obvious but important difference between the conjunctive operator and the negative operator. The negative operator is a **unary** operator—it operates upon a *single* element (proposition) to negate it; the conjunctive operator is a **binary** operator—it operates upon a *pair* of elements (propositions) to conjoin them. In formal logic, a unary operator is normally placed immediately to the left of the element it operates on, with punctuation (discussed in the next section) to show how much of the following formula it governs. However, a binary operator is normally placed between the elements it operates on, with punctuation to show its "scope" in both directions.

§2.5 Punctuation

Punctuation marks belong almost uniquely to written languages. They serve in lieu of the inflections of voice and tone which operate in spoken language to inform the listener of how the speaker's phrases are jointed, of what is to be grouped with which. There are many notorious examples of the ambiguity that can result when we are not sure of how the parts of a sentence are to be grouped together. For example, the sentence

1. I saw him jump through the keyhole.

can express two completely different propositions (one absurd, the other plausible) if we group its elements in different ways:

1a. I saw him (jump through the keyhole).

1b. I saw him jump (through the keyhole).

Similarly, the sentence

2. Irishmen who are cowards are fortunately rare in prizefighting.

says one thing without internal punctuation and something quite different when punctuated as

2a. Irishmen, who are cowards, are fortunately rare in prizefighting.

In logic, as elsewhere, it is important to be able to avoid such ambiguities. Consider, for example, the sentence

3. It is false that there is life on Mars and there is life on Venus.

In the absence of punctuation, there is no way to tell whether the negative operator is applied to the whole conjunction or only to its lefthand conjunct. The same is true for the logical translation of (3):

3a. $\sim M \cdot V$

The ambiguities of (3) and (3a) are easily overcome, however, with an adequate system of punctuation and an appropriate set of conventions governing its application.

The only punctuation marks used in formal logic are parentheses of various shapes, such as curved parentheses ( ), square brackets [ ], and braces { }.* And while the conventions governing their use are much more easily

---

*Some alternative methods of punctuation are presented in Appendix D.

seen than said, a short explanation may nevertheless be helpful. In giving this, it will be necessary to revise a bit of terminology slightly.

The notion of a "logical unit" is as follows: a simple statement is a logical unit; a negation is a logical unit; a compound statement enclosed by a pair of parentheses is a logical unit. Truth-functional operators attach to logical units (single ones in the case of negation; pairs of them in the case of other operators) to form compounds. When a negative operator is attached to a logical unit to form a negation, what is negated is the *unit*, rather than anything concealed inside the unit (if such there be). Similarly, when a conjunctive operator is attached to a pair of logical units to form a compound, what are conjoined are the *units*, not anything sealed up inside the units.

Parentheses serve to package up compounds into units. Just as the wrappings are part of the package, so the parentheses are part of the unit. The general rules of logical punctuation may be stated as follows: a tilde (negative operator) applies to the whole of the first logical unit to its right, and nothing more (or less); any other operator applies to the whole of the two logical units on its immediate right and left, and nothing more (or less).

Given these conventions, (3a) as it stands is a conjunction, one of whose conjuncts is the negation 'It is false that there is life on Mars'. Thus, (3a) will be true only if there is life on Venus but none on Mars. The negation of the whole (compound) statement 'There is life on Mars and there is life on Venus' is written, not as (3a), but as

3b. $\sim (M \cdot V)$

which will be true if either or both planets are devoid of life—that is, if $(M \cdot V)$ is false.

§2.6   Mating Parentheses

As statements in the symbolic language become more complex, the punctuation tends to become more difficult to follow; it is sometimes not easy to tell, just by looking, which lefthand parenthesis mates with which righthand one. Should this difficulty arise, it can easily be overcome by "mating" the pairs—joining them with a line drawn from the one to the other. Properly done, this will provide a clear picture of the way the various components are nested one inside the other.

To mate parentheses, proceed along the formula* from left to right until you come to a righthand ("closing") parenthesis; backtrack to the last lefthand ("opening") parenthesis you passed, and mate the two. Then continue on through the formula. Each righthand parenthesis mates with the closest unmated lefthand parenthesis to its left. For example, consider the formula

---

*A *formula* is any series of (one or more) parentheses, letters, and/or operators.

$$\sim((A \cdot \sim(B \cdot C)) \cdot (((B \cdot D) \cdot \sim(A \cdot \sim D)) \cdot \sim B))$$

Proceeding from left to right, the first closing parenthesis we come to is the one after 'C'; we backtrack to the last opening parenthesis we passed (the one before the first 'B') and mate the two:

$$\sim((A \cdot \underset{\rule{1.2em}{0pt}}{\underline{\sim(B \cdot C)}}) \cdot (((B \cdot D) \cdot \sim(A \cdot \sim D)) \cdot \sim B))$$

Continuing rightwards, the next closing parenthesis (the second one after 'C') is mated to the last unmated opening parenthesis (the one before 'A') thus:

$$\sim(\,(A \cdot \sim(B \cdot C)\,) \cdot (((B \cdot D) \cdot \sim(A \cdot \sim D)) \cdot \sim B))$$

and so on throughout the formula, mating each closing parenthesis with the last unmated opening one until all are mated:

$$\sim(\,(A \cdot \sim(B \cdot C)\,) \cdot (\,(\,(B \cdot D) \cdot \sim(A \cdot \sim D)\,)\, \cdot \sim B)\,)$$

In this procedure there are two things to watch out for. (a) If any mating lines cross each other, you have done something wrong. (b) If any parentheses turn out to be "unmatable"—if you run out of closing (or opening) parentheses before using up all the opening (or closing) ones—then the formula is incorrectly written and must be changed, either by the addition of more parentheses or the deletion of excess ones.

Using alternating parentheses of different shapes can be helpful in laying out the structure of a complex formula; for example, the structure of the above is clearer when written

$$\sim\{[A \cdot \sim(B \cdot C)] \cdot [(\{B \cdot D\} \cdot \sim\{A \cdot \sim D\}) \cdot \sim B]\}$$

However, it is not a logical requirement that different-shaped parentheses be used. In the present book formulae are written sometimes with different-shaped parentheses and sometimes with only round ones.

When reading the symbolic language aloud, it is conventional to read lefthand parentheses as "pren" ("bracket," "brace," and so on) and right-hand parentheses as "close pren" ("close bracket," "close brace," and so on). For example, the statement

1. $\sim(M \cdot V) \cdot J$

would be read aloud as

1a. Not pren em and vee close pren and jay.

Similarly, the statement

2. $\sim((M \cdot V) \cdot J)$

would be read aloud as

2a. Not pren pren em and vee close pren and jay close pren.

Exercises I

Give a logical translation of each of the following statements. Paraphrase when
necessary, abbreviate all simple components, translate negative operators by the
tilde, conjunctive operators by the dot, and supply punctuation as needed. You
need not attempt translation further than this.

   1. Percy kicked his sister, but she didn't scream.

□ **2.** Percy didn't kick his sister, in spite of the fact that she was screaming.

   3. It's false that Percy kicked his sister even though she was screaming; but he
did kick her even though she *wasn't* screaming.

□ **4.** If Percy didn't kick his sister and she didn't scream, then either my ears aren't
very good or somebody is lying.

   5. It's not the case that it's false that Percy's sister didn't scream.

□ **6.** While Percy's sister didn't scream, he kicked her nevertheless.

   7. Percy didn't kick his sister, since she didn't scream.

Exercises II

Supposing that A and B are both true statements, and that X and Y are both false
statements, determine which of the following compound statements are true. It may
be helpful to mate the parentheses in some of the more complex examples.

□ **1.** $A \cdot X$

   2. $\sim A \cdot X$

   3. $\sim (A \cdot X)$

□ **4.** $A \cdot \sim Y$

   5. $\sim (A \cdot \sim Y)$

   6. $A \cdot B$

□ **7.** $\sim \sim A \cdot B$

   8. $\sim (\sim A \cdot B)$

   9. $\sim (\sim A \cdot \sim B)$

□ **10.** $\sim \sim (A \cdot \sim B)$

  11. $\sim [(A \cdot X) \cdot \sim (B \cdot Y)]$

  12. $\sim \sim [\sim (A \cdot B) \cdot \sim (\sim X \cdot \sim Y)]$

□ **13.** $A \cdot \sim A$

  14. $\sim (Y \cdot \sim Y)$

  15. $\sim \sim \sim \sim \sim (\sim Y \cdot B)$

□ **16.** $\sim (A \cdot \sim \{B \cdot \sim [X \cdot \sim (Y \cdot \sim A)]\})$

  17. $A \cdot [B \cdot (X \cdot Y)]$

  18. $A \cdot [(B \cdot X) \cdot Y]$

□ **19.** $(A \cdot B) \cdot (X \cdot Y)$

  20. $[(A \cdot B) \cdot X] \cdot Y$

  21. $[A \cdot (B \cdot X)] \cdot Y$

chapter 3

DISJUNCTION; BRACKETING AUXILIARIES; DOMINANCE AMONG OPERATORS

§3.1 Disjunction

As we have seen, a **conjunction** is a truth-functional compound which is true when both of its components are true and false otherwise. Another sort of truth-functional compound is the **disjunction** (also called **alternation**). A disjunction is a compound which is true if one or the other of its components is true, and false otherwise. The components of a disjunction are called its **disjuncts**. An operator which produces a disjunction when appropriately applied to a pair of statements is called a **disjunctive operator**. Perhaps the most commonly used English disjunctive operator is the word 'or', as in the statement

1. This soup contains too much salt or too little water.

There are two different types of disjunction, the "strong" or "exclusive" disjunction and the "weak" or "nonexclusive" disjunction. A **strong disjunction** is true if *one* of its disjuncts is true, but false otherwise (that is, is false if both disjuncts are false, and is false if they are both true). A **weak disjunction** is true if *one or both* of its disjuncts are true, but false otherwise (is false only if both disjuncts are false). English contains operators of both types. The most obvious example of a strong disjunctive operator is the expression 'or . . . but not both', as in the statement

2. We will go to the beach or to the mountains, but not both.

Similarly, the most obvious example of a weak disjunctive operator is the expression 'or . . . or both', as in the statement

3. Jones is sick or incompetent, or both.

But some operators are ambiguous or indifferent as to the strong/weak distinction. The word 'or' is a case in point. Is (1) above a strong disjunction or a weak one? Intuitively, we should probably regard it as a weak disjunction; that is, if the soup were both oversalted and underwatered we would

27

not regard that as grounds for calling (1) false. Nevertheless, there are conceivable circumstances in which 'or' might be used to form a strong disjunction. But it is standard practice in logic to treat all disjunctions as *weak* disjunctions unless they are clearly and explicitly strong ones—that is, unless they contain the operator 'or . . . but not both' or something very similar. In this connection two points must be made.

First, the character of the disjuncts does *not* dictate the sense in which a disjunctive operator is being used. There is a tendency to suppose that in a statement such as

4. Jones is, at this moment, in Spain or he is in Tibet.

the word 'or' must have the sense of strong disjunction, since it is impossible for both disjuncts to be true (Jones cannot simultaneously be in Spain and in Tibet). But this supposition is unwarranted, for, in the first place, the *fact* that both disjuncts cannot be true in no way shows that the *operator* explicitly denies their conjoint truth; and in the second place, the fact that both disjuncts *cannot* be true would seem to indicate that (4) is a perfect place to employ *weak* disjunction, since the situation which would otherwise be ruled out by strong disjunction (mutual truth of both disjuncts) is ruled out *de facto* by the nature of the case, without the need for any disclaimers to that effect.*

Second, the expression 'either . . . or' is *not* equivalent to 'or . . . but not both'. It is sometimes supposed that the auxiliary 'either' produces a strong disjunctive operator. However, the function of 'either' in 'either . . . or' is not to generate strong disjunction but to serve as a kind of bracket, indicating the beginning of the first disjunct of the disjunction. It is a verbal punctuation mark. For example, the statement

5. Old Williams is preparing to retire and Smith will become chairman or the company is headed for ruin.

as it stands is ambiguous; but suitable applications of 'either' eliminate the ambiguity in the same way that parentheses would. One interpretation of (5) is

5a. Either Old Williams is preparing to retire and Smith will become chairman or the company is headed for ruin.

The other interpretation of (5) is

5b. Old Williams is preparing to retire and either Smith will become chairman or the company is headed for ruin.

and both (5a) and (5b) are unambiguous. (5a) is clearly a *disjunction* whose first disjunct is a compound statement about Old Williams and Smith; (5b) is clearly a *conjunction* whose second conjunct is a compound statement

---

*This point is aptly made by Quine, *Methods of Logic*, 3d ed., p. 11.

about Smith and the company. So far as the strong/weak distinction goes, 'either . . . or' has the same status as 'or'.

In logic there is only one disjunctive operator, the symbol '∨', called **wedge**. The wedge is a weak disjunctive operator. Whenever it is placed between two statements, abbreviated or otherwise, the result is a weak disjunction whose disjuncts are the statements that the wedge occurs between. Like the dot and the tilde, the wedge is a pure truth-functional operator with no exact synonym in English. It is standard practice to translate all weak disjunctive operators, and all *indifferent* disjunctive operators, by means of the wedge. (The procedures for translating strong disjunctive operators are given later on.) For example, the logical translation of (1) above will proceed as follows:

    1. This soup contains too much salt or too little water.

becomes, by paraphrase,

    1a. This soup contains too much salt or this soup contains too little water.

which abbreviates to

    1b. *M* or *L*

which, translating 'or' by the wedge, becomes

    1c. *M* ∨ *L*

When reading the symbolic language aloud, the wedge is conventionally pronounced as "wedge" or as "or." The truth-table definition of the wedge is

p	q	$p \lor q$
T	T	T
T	F	T
F	T	T
F	F	F

which says that a disjunction formed with the wedge is false when both disjuncts are false, and true otherwise.

§3.2 Bracketing Auxiliaries

As has already been noted in the case of 'either . . . or . . .', some English truth-functional operators contain what might be called a **bracketing auxiliary**: a word which delimits the "left scope" of the operator. For example, in a sentence containing 'either . . . or . . .', the words 'either' and 'or' bracket the first (lefthand) disjunct of the disjunction: the first disjunct consists of everything between the auxiliary 'either' and the primary operator-word 'or'; and the second disjunct will normally be everything after the 'or', unless punctuation indicates otherwise. In such a case it is tacitly understood that operators coming *before* the bracketing auxiliary govern the entire compound (for example, the entire disjunction) rather than merely its first element.

This means that whenever there is a bracketing auxiliary, (i) it may initially be translated as an opening bracket whose mate falls just before the primary operator-word, and (ii) punctuation may be inserted to assure that any operators *before* the auxiliary govern the entire compound. Following this procedure, the logical difference between the two statements

1. Either it's not the case that Smith will become chairman or the company will be ruined.

2. It's not the case that either Smith will become chairman or the company will be ruined.

is quickly brought out as the difference between

1a. ((It's not the case that Smith will become chairman) or the company will be ruined).

and

2a. It's not the case that ((Smith will become chairman) or the company will be ruined).

which translate fully as

1b. $(\sim C \lor R)$

2b. $\sim (C \lor R)$

Another example of a bracketing auxiliary is the phrase 'not only' in the conjunctive operators 'not only . . . but . . .' and 'not only . . . but also . . .'.* As in the previous example, the difference between the two statements

3. It's false that not only will Smith become chairman but the company will be ruined.

4. Not only is it false that Smith will become chairman but the company will be ruined.*

comes out clearly, in translation, as the difference between

3a. It's false that ((Smith will become chairman) but the company will be ruined).

4a. (It's false that (Smith will become chairman)) but the company will be ruined.

which translate fully as

3b. $\sim (C \cdot R)$

4b. $\sim C \cdot R$

---

*An oddity of English grammar is that 'not only' usually leads to an inversion in the normal word order ('Smith will decide' but 'Not only will Smith decide . . .'). Such inversions are irrelevant to logic and may easily be eliminated by paraphrase in the course of translation.

As a further illustration of the translation of bracketing auxiliaries, the two statements

    5. Not only will Old Williams retire unless Smith advises against it, but the stockholders are prepared to rebel.

    6. Old Williams will retire unless not only Smith advises against it but the stockholders are prepared to rebel.

differ in precisely the same way as the following:

    5a. (Old Williams will retire unless Smith advises against it) but the stockholders are prepared to rebel.

    6a. Old Williams will retire unless (Smith advises against it but the stockholders are prepared to rebel).

or, fully translated,

    5b. $(W \lor A) \cdot S$

    6b. $W \lor (A \cdot S)$

When paraphrasing English statements as a preparation for translating them, it is sometimes quite helpful to supply bracketing auxiliaries if they do not appear in the original. Also, it sometimes happens that when the auxiliary is given, the primary operator-word is suppressed, as in the statement

    7. Not only is Smith incompetent, he is insane.

In such cases it is also helpful (if not downright necessary) to supply the missing operator-word, prior to translating. In the lists of English operators given as Translation Aids, the operators involving bracketing auxiliaries are given with a three-dot ellipsis ('either . . . or'; 'both . . . and').

    Bracketing auxiliaries, and the operators they go with, may be mated in the same way as parentheses. Doing this before attempting formal punctuation will usually show quite graphically how the various components of the statement are nested together. First, abbreviate all the simple components. Then go through the sentence from left to right and mate each operator with the first grammatically appropriate and unmated bracketing auxiliary to its left.* The result will be a picture of how the sentence is articulated. For example, the sentence

    8. Either both A and B or both either C or not only D but E and F.

contains a number of bracketing auxiliaries. When these are mated to the operators they go with, the result is

    8a. Either both A and B or both either C or not only D but E and F.

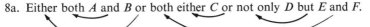

which shows that 'both A and B' is the first half of a disjunction, since it is sandwiched between a corresponding 'either' and 'or', so that the correct

---

*Except 'if' and 'then'; they can't be mated thus mechanically.

punctuation is

    8b. Either (both *A* and *B*) or both either *C* or not only *D* but *E* and *F*.

It also shows that 'either *C* or not only *D* but *E*' is the first half of a conjunction, since it is between a corresponding 'both' and 'and', so that the punctuation is

    8c. Either (both *A* and *B*) or both (either *C* or not only *D* but *E*) and *F*.

with what follows the 'and' being the second conjunct, so that the whole conjunction may be packaged up as

    8d. Either (both *A* and *B*) or (both (either *C* or not only *D* but *E*) and *F*).

Similarly, '*D*' is the first element of a conjunction (since it is between 'not only' and 'but'), and what follows 'but' is the second element, so that the whole conjunction brackets as

    8e. Either (both *A* and *B*) or (both (either *C* or (not only *D* but *E*)) and *F*).

which may now be translated easily into

    8f. $(A \cdot B) \vee ((C \vee (D \cdot E)) \cdot F)$

    A final remark about paraphrasing and punctuating: the whole process of giving paraphrases hinges upon *understanding* the English statements being paraphrased; there can be no formal rules for paraphrasing, since a given sentence may express different statements on different occasions, and when that happens different paraphrases may be required. Frequently, a statement which would be totally ambiguous in isolation has a meaning which is quite clear given the context of its utterance. However, when the context is not provided, or when there is otherwise no way of telling which of its possible meanings a given sentence may have, there are three alternatives open: (1) either ignore the statement altogether and go do something else, or (2) arbitrarily select one of the various possible meanings the sentence might have and translate in accordance with that, or (3) give different translations corresponding to *each* of the various possible meanings, and subject each of these in turn to whatever logical purposes you have in mind. The first of these alternatives is not available to the student of logic who is doing exercises for the purpose of learning; the third is normally too time-consuming for the student who is simply doing exercises. Hence, *unless otherwise indicated*, the second alternative is the one to take. It must be emphasized, however, that this is a last resort. One should never be too quick to judge a statement hopelessly ambiguous and give it an arbitrary interpretation. As an illustration, the two statements

> 9. Old Williams will retire tomorrow; and Smith will become chairman or the company is headed for ruin.
> 10. Old Williams will retire tomorrow and Smith will become chairman, or the company is headed for ruin.

contain no bracketing auxiliaries, but this doesn't mean that we are unable to distinguish between them, or to tell how they differ. Here, the English punctuation marks serve to indicate how the various clauses are grouped, telling us that the two are to be punctuated, respectively, as

> 9a. $W \cdot (C \lor R)$
> 10a. $(W \cdot C) \lor R$

without the need for any arbitrary decisions.

TRANSLATION AID

The following are some disjunctive operators in English.

or	otherwise
either . . . or . . .	with the alternative that
or else	unless
or, alternatively	

Exercises I

Give a logical translation of each of the following. Paraphrase as necessary, abbreviate all simple components, translate disjunctive operators by the wedge, conjunctive operators by the dot, negative operators by the tilde, and supply punctuation as needed. You need not attempt translation further than this.

☐ **1.** Percy has taken the car without telling us, or else someone has stolen it and we must inform the insurance company.

2. I shall blot out the sun and destroy your crops unless you release me immediately and return the magic ring to me.

☐ **3.** You will have to take the shortcut home; otherwise you'll be late and either you won't get any supper or you'll have to eat leftovers.

4. You will have to take the shortcut home; otherwise either you'll be late and you won't get any supper or you'll have to eat leftovers.

☐ **5.** If it doesn't rain or snow tomorrow and they get the car fixed in time, then we'll go to the mountains or to the beach and do some surfing.

6. If it rains and snows tomorrow or they don't get the car fixed in time, then we won't go to the beach or have a picnic.

Exercises II

Supposing that A and B are both true statements, and that X and Y are both false statements, determine which of the following compound statements are true:

☐ **1.** $\sim(A \lor X)$

2. $\sim A \lor \sim X$

   3. $A \lor (X \cdot Y)$

☐ **4.** $(A \lor X) \cdot Y$

   5. $(A \cdot B) \lor (X \cdot Y)$

   6. $(A \lor B) \cdot (X \lor Y)$

☐ **7.** $A \cdot [X \lor (B \cdot Y)]$

   8. $X \lor [A \cdot (Y \lor B)]$

   9. $X \lor {\sim} X$

☐ **10.** $A \lor {\sim} A$

   11. ${\sim}\{{\sim}[{\sim}(A \cdot {\sim} X) \cdot {\sim} A] \cdot {\sim} X\}$

   12. $[(A \cdot X) \lor {\sim} B] \cdot {\sim}[(A \cdot X) \lor {\sim} B]$

☐ **13.** $[(X \lor A) \cdot {\sim} Y] \lor {\sim}[(X \lor A) \cdot {\sim} Y]$

   14. $\{X \lor [Y \lor {\sim}(A \lor X)]\} \lor B$

§3.3   Translating "Strong" Disjunctions

When it becomes necessary to translate a strong disjunction, we may do so with the symbolism already at our disposal, with no need for anything new. Strong disjunctions assert "one or the other, but not both," and this is exactly the way they are translated. The strong disjunction

   1. Harvey visited Washington or Baltimore, but not both.

becomes, by repeated paraphrase:

   1a. Harvey visited Washington or Harvey visited Baltimore, but Harvey did not visit both Washington and Baltimore.

   1b. Harvey visited Washington or Harvey visited Baltimore, but it is not the case that Harvey visited both Washington and Baltimore.

   1c. Harvey visited Washington or Harvey visited Baltimore, but it is not the case that both Harvey visited Washington and Harvey visited Baltimore.

which abbreviates to

   1d. *W* or *B*, but it is not the case that both *W* and *B*.

which translates, step by step, as

   1e. $(W \lor B)$ but it is not the case that both *W* and *B*

   1f. $(W \lor B)$ but it is not the case that $(W \cdot B)$

   1g. $(W \lor B) \cdot$ it is not the case that $(W \cdot B)$

   1h. $(W \lor B) \cdot {\sim}(W \cdot B)$

(1h) is a conjunction whose first conjunct asserts "one or the other" and whose second conjunct asserts "not both"; thus (1h) asserts "one or the other, but not both." *Any* strong disjunction may be translated in this same way—that is, as a conjunction asserting "one or the other" and "not both."

Exercises III

Give a logical translation of the following statements.

1. Either Old Williams will retire or Smith will become chairman, but not both.
☐ 2. We'll go to the mountains and have a picnic or to the beach and do some surfing, but not both.
3. Either we'll go to the mountains and have a picnic, or else we'll go to the beach and do some fishing or some surfing but not both.
☐ 4. Either Old Williams won't retire or Smith won't become chairman, but not both.
5. Either we'll go to the mountains or have a picnic or both, or we'll go to the mountains or have a picnic but not both.

§3.4 Dominance and Subordination among Operators

When an operator attaches to a statement or a pair of statements to form a compound, the statement or statements to which the operator attaches are the components of that compound. However, for the sake of brevity, it is sometimes convenient to refer to them as components *to the operator* which generates the compound. Speaking in this loose fashion, we might say that in the statement

1. $\sim (A \lor B) \cdot C$

the components to the dot are the statements '$\sim (A \lor B)$' and 'C', while the components to the wedge are the statements 'A' and 'B', and the component to the tilde is the statement '$(A \lor B)$'.

One operator **dominates** another if the other occurs in a component to the one. Thus, in (1), the tilde dominates the wedge, and the dot dominates the tilde (and also the wedge). If one operator dominates another, the second is said to be **subordinate** to the first. In (1), the tilde is subordinate to the dot, and the wedge is subordinate to the tilde (and also to the dot).

An operator is the **dominant operator** in a formula if it dominates all other operators in the formula. In (1), the dominant operator is the dot. But in the first conjunct of (1) the dominant operator is the tilde.

Clearly, there are different levels of domination—a "pecking order" among the operators in compound statements. One operator **directly dominates** another if the second is the dominant operator in a component to the first. If one operator directly dominates another, the second is **directly subordinate** to the first. Thus, in (1), the dot directly dominates the tilde. The dot does *not* directly dominate the wedge, since the wedge is not the dominant operator in either of the components of (1). (Remember, '$(A \lor B)$' is *not* a component of (1)—is not a component to the dot—since '$(A \lor B)$' is not one of the conjuncts of the conjunction generated by the dot.)

If one operator dominates another, but does not directly dominate it, then it is a case of *indirect* domination. In (1), the dot indirectly dominates the wedge. We could, if necessary, coin a terminology to cover different levels of indirect domination. For example, we might say that in

2. $\sim(X \lor \sim Y) \cdot Z$

the dot exercises *first-level* indirect domination over the wedge and *second-level* indirect domination over the tilde in '$\sim Y$' (since the dot indirectly dominates the wedge, and the wedge dominates the tilde in '$\sim Y$'). But this terminology is ordinarily unneeded at the level of elementary logic.

A formula is not properly written in the symbolic language unless it contains a **dominant operator**, whose dominance is clearly shown by the punctuation.* For example, the formula

3. $A \cdot B \lor C$

is not a properly written statement in the symbolic language, since there is no way to tell whether its dominant operator is the dot or the wedge. And, perhaps needless to say, a formula is not properly written in the symbolic language unless its component or components are properly written.

The dominant operator in a statement defines the logical character of the statement. For example, if the statement contains no operators, then it is **simple**; if its dominant operator is a tilde, then it is a **negation**; if its dominant operator is a dot, then it is a **conjunction**; and so on. Hence, we might describe (1) by saying: it is a conjunction, whose second conjunct is simple and whose first conjunct is a negation whose negate is a disjunction whose disjuncts are simple. Another way of stating the points in the preceding paragraph is that a statement is not properly written in the symbolic language unless it can be given a complete description of this sort. Thus (3) is not a properly written statement, since we are stymied, at the very beginning, as to whether it is a conjunction or a disjunction.

Exercises IV

Pick out and circle the dominant operator in each of 1–14, Exercises II.

Exercises V

Give a complete logical description of each of statements 1–7 in Exercises II. As an illustration:

(1) A negation whose negate is a disjunction whose disjuncts are simple.

---

*The only exceptions are simple statements which contain no operators at all.

Exercises VI

Do the same for 8–14. As an illustration:

(12) A conjunction whose first conjunct is
      a disjunction whose first disjunct is
         a conjunction whose conjuncts are simple, and
      whose second disjunct is
         a negation whose negate is simple; and
   whose second conjunct is
      a negation whose negate is
         a disjunction whose first disjunct is
            a conjunction whose conjuncts are simple, and
         whose second disjunct is
            a negation whose negate is simple.

chapter 4

CONDITIONALS

§4.1 Conditionals

In everyday discourse we often find it worthwhile to assert that *if* some statement is true, then so is another. When such an assertion is made, the result is a compound statement, formed with the help of an operator such as 'if ... then ...'. Compound statements of this kind are called **conditional** statements, and the operator which generates the compound is called a **conditional operator**.

The logical treatment of conditionals is a more complicated affair than the treatment of conjunctions and disjunctions. For one thing, many conditionals are not even truth-dependent compounds, a matter discussed at some length later on. But even those conditionals which are truth-dependent compounds present difficulties when we try to fit them into the rigid structure of formal logic. Let us begin by considering some examples.

    1. If Harvey traveled to Spain, then he crossed the Atlantic Ocean.

First, it should be noted that conditionals are not "symmetrical" as conjunctions and disjunctions are: the order in which the components of a conditional occur makes a difference to what is said. Statement (1) says something quite different from

    2. If Harvey crossed the Atlantic Ocean, then he traveled to Spain.

even though they have the same components. Thus, instead of using a single word to designate the components of a conditional (as with the *conjuncts* of a conjunction or the *disjuncts* of a disjunction), a different designation is used for each of the two components. One of them is called the **antecedent** (or the **protasis**) of the conditional, and the other is called the **consequent** (or the **apodosis**) of the conditional. In a conditional formed with the operator 'if ... then ...', for example, the component occurring between the 'if' and the 'then' is the antecedent; the component occurring after the 'then' is the consequent. In (1) above, the antecedent is the statement 'Harvey traveled to Spain' and the consequent is 'He crossed the Atlantic Ocean'.

The first prerequisite for fitting conditionals into truth-functional logic is to decide what their *truth-conditions* are. Until this is done, it will not even be possible to translate them, since the purpose of logical translation is to swap English statements for formulae in the symbolic language which have the same truth-conditions.

It will be easiest to begin by seeking out the conditions under which a conditional statement is *false*. Normally, the way in which we *show* a conditional to be false is by showing that, although it has a true antecedent, it nevertheless has a false consequent. For example, if we could demonstrate that although Harvey did travel to Spain he did not cross the Atlantic (perhaps he went, and returned, via China), this would be sufficient to show that (1) is false. Similarly, the conditional

3. If that candle is left out in the sun, it will melt.

may be proven false by leaving the candle out in the sun and observing its failure to melt. This would prove (3) false by showing that even though its antecedent is true, its consequent is nevertheless false. In general, *whenever* the antecedent of a conditional is true but its consequent is false, then the conditional is false. This may be stated as

CONDITION ONE. A conditional is **false** if it has a true antecedent but a false consequent.

Do conditional statements have any other falsity-conditions besides this one? There is no *definitely* established answer; the semantics of conditional statements is still a subject of considerable study. But it is quite certain that there is no other *truth-functional* falsity condition for statements of this type. Hence, for purposes of formal logic Condition One is taken as the *only* falsity condition, and conditional statements are regarded as true unless they have a true antecedent and false consequent.

This decision is not *purely* arbitrary. It accords to a large extent with our standard attitude toward conditional statements. For example, from Condition One it follows that if a conditional is true, and has a true antecedent, it must also have a true consequent. If any conclusion is to be drawn from this, it is that one way for a conditional to be *true* is for it to have a true antecedent and also a true consequent. And this adheres very closely to one of our standard ways of verifying conditionals. Thus, (3) might be proven true by leaving the candle in the sun and seeing it melt. In that case, the person uttering (3) might say, "See? I was right." And we would no doubt admit that he was indeed right; what he said was true. We observe that the antecedent of his claim is true, and that its consequent is also true, and thus we admit the correctness of the claim. This can be phrased formally as

CONDITION TWO. A conditional is **true** if it has a true antecedent and also a true consequent.

In a similar fashion, the way we operate with conditionals in normal discourse also provides a basis for saying that a conditional can be true when its *consequent* is false, provided that its antecedent is also false. This may be brought out in several different, but related, ways.

First, when we accept a conditional as true we do not thereby commit ourselves to the truth of its consequent (for example, if we accept (1) as true we do not thereby commit ourselves to the belief that Harvey has ever crossed the Atlantic). Our commitment is only that its consequent is true *if* its antecedent is. A later discovery that its consequent is false will not, thereby, refute the original conditional. The discovery that a conditional's consequent is false only shows that its antecedent must also be false. Given the conditional statement

4. If Clyde is at home then he left the porch light on.

the discovery that Clyde's porch light is off will not entitle us to infer that (4) is false, but only that Clyde is not at home. It is an interesting (and logically important) feature of conditionals that they cut both ways. From Condition One it follows that a true conditional with a true antecedent must also have a true consequent; and likewise a *true* conditional with a false consequent must also have a false antecedent. (Otherwise the conditional would not be *true*.) And just as we sometimes confirm a conditional [as in the case of (3)] by first ascertaining that its antecedent is true and then discovering the truth of its consequent, so also we sometimes confirm a conditional the other way around, by first ascertaining the falsity of its consequent and then discovering the falsity of its antecedent. For instance, we might confirm (4) by first phoning Clyde (to make sure he's home) and then driving past his house and observing that the porch light is on. But we might also confirm (4) by first noticing that his porch light is off, and then breaking into his house to discover that he is absent. In either case, the person asserting (4) might say, "See? I was right." And in either case, we would no doubt agree.

In accepting a conditional as true, we are agreeing that *if* its antecedent is true, *then* its consequent is also true. But this is the same as agreeing that *if* its consequent is false, *then* so is its antecedent. Agreeing to (4) is the same as agreeing to

5. If Clyde didn't leave the porch light on then he's not at home.

In both cases, we are denying that Clyde is home with the porch light off. Two statements related as (4) and (5) are said to be *contrapositives*. The contrapositive of a conditional is formed by exchanging the two components and then negating them. Thus the antecedent of (5) is the negation of the consequent of (4), and the consequent of (5) is the negation of the antecedent of (4). A conditional and its contrapositive are, to all intents and purposes, equivalent statements. In normal discourse we quite often use them interchangeably, as mere stylistic variants of one another. For example, instead of (1) we might just as easily have said

6. If Harvey didn't cross the Atlantic, then he didn't travel to Spain.

And insofar as two statements are equivalent, they have exactly the same truth-conditions. Thus (4) and (5) have the same truth-conditions [as do (1) and (6)]. But each of the components of (5) is the negation of a component of (4), so when both components of (4) are true, both components of (5) are false. But also when both components of (4) are true, (4) is true—per Condition Two. And when (4) is true, (5) is true, since they are equivalent. Therefore, when both components of (5) are false, then (5) is true.

In general, the mutual falsity of the components of a conditional is on a logical par with their mutual truth. We can state this formally as

CONDITION THREE. A conditional is **true** if it has a false consequent and also a false antecedent.

This leaves us with one troublesome case: that of the conditional whose consequent is true but whose antecedent is false. Here, there are no standards within normal discourse for us to appeal to. If a conditional turns out to have a true antecedent but a false consequent, we accept that as proof that the conditional is false. If a conditional turns out to have a true consequent along with a true antecedent, or a false antecedent along with a false consequent, we (may) accept that as proof that the conditional is true. However, when a conditional turns out to have a false antecedent but a true consequent, we do not regard it either as true or as false, but simply as *pointless*. There is nothing in common practice to tell us which truth-value to ascribe to such conditionals, since it is just here that common practice is silent on the matter. Appeals to contrapositives are equally useless, since if a conditional has a false antecedent and a true consequent, so does its contrapositive. Thus, if a truth-value is to be ascribed to such conditionals, we are forced to choose one arbitrarily. In doing this, it is of some comfort to know that whatever choice we make, it cannot *conflict* with common usage, for the very good reason that common usage has nothing to say.

Thus, for purposes of logic, it is stipulated that a conditional with a false antecedent and a true consequent is to be regarded as *true*, which allows us to assert

CONDITION FOUR. A conditional is **true** if it has a false antecedent and a true consequent.

Although this choice has some curious-sounding consequences, which will be touched upon later, it is justified by the fact that it is the only choice which will allow conditionals into truth-functional logic.*

---

*If the opposite choice were made—if we elected to regard the "pointless" cases as *false*— this would have the effect of eliminating the distinction between conditionals and what are called *biconditionals* (cf. Chapter 5).

§4.2 Material Conditionals

A conditional statement which is true except when its antecedent is true and its consequent is false is called a **material conditional**. Thus, the effect of stipulating Condition Four is that every (truth-dependent) conditional will be interpreted, for logical purposes, as a material conditional.

Two facts about material conditionals have led some logicians to regard them as in some way "paradoxical." These facts are: (1) a material conditional whose antecedent is false will be true irrespective of the truth-value of its consequent, and (2) a material conditional whose consequent is true will be true irrespective of the truth-value of its antecedent. These facts are sometimes referred to as "the paradoxes of material implication."*

In logic, there is only one conditional operator; the symbol '⊃', called **horseshoe**. Whenever it is placed between two statements, abbreviated or otherwise, the result is a material conditional, whose antecedent is the statement to the left of the horseshoe, and whose consequent is the statement to the right of the horseshoe. The horseshoe, like the dot, wedge, and tilde, is a pure truth-functional operator which has no exact synonym in English. Rather, it is used to translate all of the various English conditional operators. The truth-table definition of the horseshoe is:

p	q	$p \supset q$
T	T	T
T	F	F
F	T	T
F	F	T

As illustrations of the way the horseshoe is used, the statement

1. If Harvey traveled to Spain, then he crossed the Atlantic Ocean.

becomes, by abbreviation,

1a. If S then C

which, translating 'if . . . then . . .' by the horseshoe, becomes

1b. $S \supset C$

Similarly, the statement

2. If Harvey visited Spain and Portugal, then he crossed the Atlantic or went the long way around.

---

*Material conditionals are sometimes called "statements of material implication," and practitioners of logic sometimes say that the antecedent of a material conditional "materially implies" its consequent.

paraphrases to

> 2a. If Harvey visited Spain and Harvey visited Portugal, then Harvey crossed the Atlantic or Harvey went the long way around.

which abbreviates to

> 2b. If S and P then C or L.

which translates, step by step, as

> 2c. If $(S \cdot P)$ then C or L
> 2d. If $(S \cdot P)$ then $(C \lor L)$
> 2e. $(S \cdot P) \supset (C \lor L)$

As a slightly more complex example, the statement

> 3. If Harvey visited Spain, then if he didn't cross the Atlantic then he went the long way around.

paraphrases to

> 3a. If Harvey visited Spain, then if it's not the case that Harvey crossed the Atlantic then Harvey went the long way around.

which abbreviates to

> 3b. If S then if it's not the case that C then L.

which translates, step by step, as

> 3c. If S then if $\sim C$ then L
> 3d. If S then $(\sim C \supset L)$
> 3e. $S \supset (\sim C \supset L)$

When reading the symbolic language aloud, we customarily read the '$\supset$' as "horseshoe" or as "if . . . then . . .," or sometimes as "implies," though the last can be misleading if taken to mean what the English word 'implies' usually means.

TRANSLATION AID

Unfortunately for the logical translator, English conditionals do not always come with the antecedent conveniently placed before the consequent. Half the time the English will give the consequent first, followed by its antecedent. Furthermore, the same operator is often capable of producing conditionals with the components in either order, as 'if' does in the two statements

> If you touch me, I'll scream.
> I'll scream if you touch me.

For this reason it is not sufficient to give a list of English conditional operators; it is necessary to indicate the forms of statement in which the antecedent is given first, and the forms of statement in which it is given last.

Structures in which the antecedent occurs first: $(A \supset B)$

> If . . . then . . . (If A then B)
> If . . . , . . . (If A, B)
> Given that . . . it follows that . . . (Given that A it follows that B)
> Not . . . unless . . . (Not A unless B)
> In case . . . , . . . (In case A, B)†
> Given that . . . , . . . (Given that A, B)
> Insofar as . . . , . . . (Insofar as A, B)
> . . . implies . . . (A implies B)*
> . . . leads to . . . (A leads to B)*
> Whenever . . . , . . . (Whenever A, B)
> . . . only if . . . (A only if B)
> . . . is a sufficient condition for . . . (A is a sufficient condition for B)
> . . . means that . . . (A means that B)
> So long as . . . , . . . (So long as A, B)

Structures in which the consequent occurs first: $(B \supset A)$

> . . . if . . . (A if B)
> . . . in case . . . (A in case B)†
> Unless . . . , not . . . (Unless A, not B)
> . . . whenever . . . (A whenever B)
> . . . insofar as . . . (A insofar as B)
> . . . follows from (A follows from B)*
> . . . is implied by . . . (A is implied by B)*
> . . . is a necessary condition for . . . (A is a necessary condition for B)
> Only if . . . , . . . (Only if A, B)
> . . . provided that . . . (A provided that B)
> . . . so long as . . . (A so long as B)

The following expressions are operators which, in English, always come directly *before* the *antecedent* of the conditional, regardless of the order of the components:

> if (but not 'only if' and not 'even if')
> given that
> in case
> whenever
> provided that

The operator 'only if' always comes directly before the *consequent* of the conditional, regardless of the order of the components.

The expression 'even if' is *not* a conditional operator. Its treatment will be explained later on.

---

*Cf. Appendix A and Appendix C.
†Cf. Appendix F.

The bracketing auxiliary 'then' (and 'it follows that') always comes immediately after the antecedent and immediately before the consequent. The expression 'then if' never occurs except in the middle of a conditional whose consequent is another conditional, as in the statement

> If today is Sunday, **then if** we go to the fair then we can watch the balloon go up.

The antecedent of this statement is 'today is Sunday' and the consequent is 'if we go to the fair then we can watch the balloon go up'. This statement will translate as

$$S \supset (F \supset W)$$

And it may be taken as an ironclad rule of thumb that the expression 'then if' will always translate as 'horseshoe pren', as in the emphasized portion of the above translation: 'If S **then if** F then W'.

Exercises I

Give the logical translation of each of the following.

□ **1.** Julia won't scream unless Percy kicks her.

2. Julia will scream only if Percy kicks her.

3. It will snow tonight, provided that it gets cold enough.

□ **4.** Whenever a candle is left in the sun, it melts and runs all over.

5. The candle won't melt, provided that you don't leave it in the sun or do something else foolish.

6. If Southwestern loses and doesn't get to be in the playoffs, Percy will cry and pout. $(S \cdot \sim P) \supset (C \cdot O)$

□ **7.** If the engine is all right, then if we aren't out of gas, then something must be wrong with the battery. $E \supset (\sim G \supset B)$

8. It will snow tomorrow, and if the kumquats are in blossom the crop will be ruined.

9. If it snows tomorrow and the kumquats are in blossom, the crop will be ruined.

10. If it snows or freezes tomorrow, then if the kumquats are in blossom and are unprotected, then the crop will be ruined unless a miracle occurs.

□ **11.** Given that it freezes only if it snows, and that it won't freeze unless the sky is clear, and that a clear sky is a sufficient condition for its not snowing, it follows that the crop is safe if the locusts don't get to it.

12. If, whenever the sky is cloudy it either rains or snows, and whenever the sky is not cloudy it freezes, then given that freezing will ruin the kumquats and that snow will ruin the mulberries, it follows that if you planted mulberries instead of kumquats, and the sky is clear, you have nothing to worry about unless freezing ruins mulberries.

Exercises II

Supposing that A and B are both true statements, and that X and Y are both false statements, determine which of the following compound statements are true.

☐ 1. $X \supset A$

   2. $A \supset X$

   3. $Y \supset Y$

☐ 4. $B \supset B$

   5. $X \supset (X \supset Y)$

   6. $(X \supset X) \supset Y$

☐ 7. $(A \supset X) \supset Y$

   8. $(X \supset A) \supset Y$

   9. $A \supset (B \supset Y)$

☐ 10. $(X \supset A) \supset (B \supset Y)$

  11. $(A \supset B) \supset (\sim A \supset \sim B)$

  12. $(X \supset A) \supset (\sim X \supset \sim A)$

☐ 13. $(X \supset \sim Y) \supset (\sim X \supset Y)$

  14. $((A \cdot X) \supset Y) \supset (B \supset X)$

  15. $((A \cdot X) \supset B) \supset (A \supset (B \supset X))$

  16. $((X \supset Y) \supset X) \supset X$

§4.3 Subjunctive Conditionals

It was mentioned before that not all conditionals are truth-dependent compounds. Some examples of conditionals which are not truth-dependent are:

> If I were you, I would take poison.
> If the South had won the Civil War, it would still have slavery.
> If Jupiter were a star, there would be only eight planets.
> You wouldn't dare insult me sir, if Jack were only here.
> The poison wouldn't have killed him if he hadn't taken such a large dose.
> If the general had been less cautious, he would have been more successful.

The common feature of such conditionals is that they are phrased in what grammarians call the "subjunctive mood." Their most usual identifying feature is the auxiliary 'would' attached to the main verb in the consequent. Subjunctive conditionals are also called "counterfactual conditionals" and "contrary-to-fact conditionals"; a more appropriate label, however, would be "speculative conditionals," since the subjunctive mood is one of speculation, and this *need* not involve any contrariness-to-fact.

Subjunctive conditionals are called "conditionals" because they are couched in sentences whose clauses are connected by conditional operators.

They are not truth-dependent compounds, since in the first place it is dubious whether they are compound *statements* at all. They are not compound statements unless their clauses express propositions, which are either true or false, and this does not seem to be the case. What proposition, for example, is expressed by a phrase such as 'I were you', or 'the general had been less cautious', or 'I would take poison'? Unlike their indicative counterparts 'I am you', 'the general was less cautious', and 'I will take poison', which have fairly straightforward truth-conditions, there seems to be no way to say what it would be like for 'I were you' to be true, *or* to be false.* But if, as this would indicate, the component clauses do not express propositions, then the subjunctive conditional is not a compound statement at all.

In the second place, when the truth or falsity of subjunctive conditionals is debated, the truth-value of the indicative counterparts of their clauses is not regarded as a relevant consideration. They are debated on quite different grounds than that, which is a further indication that they are not compound statements. For these reasons it is standard practice, in elementary logic at any rate, to treat subjunctive conditionals as *simple* statements and let matters go at that.

---

*Some logical theoreticians have suggested regarding the clauses of subjunctive conditionals as expressing the same propositions as their indicative counterparts, thereby equating 'If I were in Las Vegas, I would be having a good time' with 'If I am in Las Vegas, I am having a good time'. But this is unsatisfactory, for reasons that should be obvious. The latter is equivalent to 'If I'm not having a good time, then I'm not in Las Vegas', which someone could confirm, say, by ascertaining that I am not having a good time (in fact, I am in bed with a toothache), and then proceeding to discover that, sure enough, I am not in Las Vegas but in Grand Rapids. However, it is clear that these results (my *in fact* being in Grand Rapids and *in fact* being miserable) are wholly irrelevant to the question of what my state *would be* if I *were* somewhere else. Furthermore, since subjunctive conditionals are, as often as not, put forth with the full knowledge that the indicative counterparts of their clauses are false (so that they really *are* counterfactual conditionals), it would follow by the material interpretation that every such conditional is *true*, including such anomalies as 'If the moon were square, there would be no tides', which most of us would regard as false despite the fact that 'The moon *is* square ⊃ there *are* no tides' turns out to be true because of the mutual falsity of its components.

chapter 5

BICONDITIONALS; TRUTH-TABLES;
LOGICAL STATUS

§5.1 Biconditionals

One further type of compound statement is less common than those we have looked at so far. It is called the **biconditional**. A biconditional is a conditional which runs both ways. In ordinary discourse, biconditionals are frequently expressed as the conjunction of two conditionals, one of which is the reverse of the other. For example:

1. If that's poison, it will kill mice; and if it will kill mice, it's poison.
2. If it's raining, then the streets are wet; and if the streets are wet, it's raining.
3. Whenever I'm drinking beer, I'm having a good time; and whenever I'm having a good time, I'm drinking beer.

As often as not, one of the two conditionals will be replaced by its contrapositive. Thus, instead of (1), we might also say

4. If that's poison, it will kill mice; and if it's not poison, it won't.

Other examples of this are:

5. If litmus comes in contact with acid, it turns red; and if litmus doesn't come in contact with acid, it doesn't turn red.
6. The baby won't stop crying unless you feed him; but if you feed him, he'll stop.
7. If Jones is dead, then he isn't breathing; but if he isn't dead, then he is breathing.

When a biconditional is phrased in either of these two ways, it can easily be translated into the symbolic language with the operators already at our disposal. For example, (1) above might be translated as

1a. $(P \supset K) \cdot (K \supset P)$

Similarly, (5) might be translated as

5a. $(A \supset R) \cdot (\sim A \supset \sim R)$

For that matter, *all* biconditionals might be translated as the conjunction of two conditionals if we so desired. But this leads to fairly cumbersome formulae, and so for purposes of brevity we generally employ a biconditional operator.

In logic there is only one biconditional operator, the symbol '≡', called **triple bar**. When the triple bar is placed between two statements, abbreviated or otherwise, the resulting compound is a **material biconditional** whose components are the statements on either side of the triple bar. A material biconditional is a compound statement which is true if its components (they are called its **sides**.) both have the same truth-value, and is false if they have different truth-values.* The truth-table definition of the triple bar is

p	q	$p \equiv q$
T	T	T
T	F	F
F	T	F
F	F	T

Like the dot, wedge, tilde, and horseshoe, the triple bar is a pure truth-functional connective which has no exact synonym in English. When reading the symbolic language aloud, we customarily read the '≡', as "triple bar" or "if and only if."

When a biconditional is expressed as the conjunction of two conditionals, as in examples (1)–(7), the procedure for translating it by means of the triple bar is the following. Select *one* of the two conditionals (normally the first one, but it doesn't matter which) and use the components of that conditional as the sides of the biconditional. For example, (1) would be translated, using the triple bar, either as

    1b. That's poison ≡ it will kill mice

or as

    1c. That will kill mice ≡ it's poison

Similarly, (5) will translate in either of the following two ways:

    5b. Litmus comes into contact with acid ≡ it turns red
    5c. Litmus doesn't come in contact with acid ≡ it doesn't turn red

Exercises I

Translate the remaining examples (2, 3, 4, 6, and 7) first as the conjunction of two conditionals and then as a biconditional using the triple bar.

---

*Material biconditionals are sometimes called "statements of material equivalence," and practitioners of logic sometimes say that the sides of a material biconditional are "materially equivalent" to each other. "Materially equivalent" means "equivalent in truth-value" and nothing more.

TRANSLATION AID

The following English expressions are biconditional operators.

... if and only if ...
... is equivalent to ...
... is a necessary and sufficient condition for ...
... just in case ...*
... just if ...

Exercises II

Translate the following.

1. If Harvey is a bachelor if and only if he is not married, then he has a wife only if he is not a bachelor.
□ 2. If Harvey has a wife only if he is married, and he is a bachelor if and only if he is not married, then he is not a bachelor if he has a wife.
3. Either Billy didn't hit Jenny or they are over at the neighbor's house, inasmuch as Billy's hitting her is a necessary and sufficient condition for her screaming, and I didn't hear any screams.
4. I will swat Billy a good one, just in case Jenny is bruised if he hit her.

§5.2 Truth-Tables

So far, truth-tables have been used only for the purpose of defining the truth-functional operators of the symbolic language. But this is not their only use, nor even their most important one. The truth-table is also an instrument for logical evaluation.

Every statement which is built up out of simple statements and truth-functional operators, no matter how complex it may be, is a truth-function of the simple statements in it. The truth-values of its simple statements will ultimately determine its truth or falsity; hence, the truth-conditions for the entire compound are to be specified in terms of the (possible) truth-values of its simple statements. One of the most convenient ways of establishing the truth-conditions of a compound statement is by building a properly constructed truth-table for that statement. For no matter how complex a statement may be, a truth-table will show, clearly and unambiguously, the conditions which would make it true and those which would make it false. This is no small advantage, since unaided intelligence, no matter how great, will normally boggle if asked to specify the truth-conditions for something such as, say,

$$\sim(C \supset (D \equiv (C \lor \sim D))) \supset (\sim(C \cdot (E \lor (D \cdot C))) \equiv E)$$

*But see Appendix F.

To refresh our memory, a truth-table may be given the following precise definition:

> **Truth-Table.** A truth-table is a diagram which displays all possible combinations of truth-values of a given collection of statements, and which shows how each such combination affects the truth-value of some compound which is a truth-function of those statements.

Thus, a truth-table has two parts: the part which displays the possible combinations of truth-values, and the part which shows the effects of each. Learning how to use truth-tables involves learning how to construct both parts correctly.

Let us begin with an example. Consider the statement

1. If Clyde isn't invited to the party, then Harvey won't come.

translated as

1a. $\sim C \supset \sim H$

The complete truth-table for this statement is:

C	H	$\sim C$	$\sim H$	$\sim C \supset \sim H$
T	T	F	F	T
T	F	F	T	T
F	T	T	F	F
F	F	T	T	T

Briefly, what this truth-table tells us is that '$\sim C \supset \sim H$' is false when 'C' is false and 'H' is true, but is true otherwise. The columns to the left of the double vertical line—the **base columns**—display all possible combinations of truth-values of the simple statements occurring in '$\sim C \supset \sim H$' (namely, 'C' and 'H'). Reading the table across from left to right, and ignoring everything between the base columns and the final column to the right, the top row below the horizontal line tells us that when 'C' and 'H' are both true, then '$\sim C \supset \sim H$' is true; the second row down tells us that when 'C' is true and 'H' is false, then '$\sim C \supset \sim H$' is true; and so on.

Let us now look at how this truth-table was constructed. First, a horizontal line (sufficiently long to accommodate the truth-table) is drawn, and the compound under investigation is written above the line at the far right, thus:

$$\sim C \supset \sim H$$

Next, this formula is investigated to see if either of its components is itself compound. In fact, both of them are, so these two formulae are written above the line and to the left, with appropriate separators, thus:

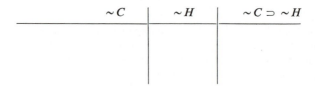

Next, these formulae are investigated to see if either of them has components which are themselves compound. Neither of them has, so the simple statements occurring in the original are written above the line and to the left, with a double separator, thus:

C	H	$\sim C$	$\sim H$	$\sim C \supset \sim H$

Next, base columns are constructed beneath the simple statements (the general rules for doing this are given later), thus:

C	H	$\sim C$	$\sim H$	$\sim C \supset \sim H$
T	T			
T	F			
F	T			
F	F			

At this point we are ready to begin constructing **derived columns**. We construct a derived column downward, one step at a time, by looking at the column(s) for the *component(s)* of the formula whose column we are deriving, and deciding at each row how *that* combination of truth-values affects the truth-value of the formula whose column we are deriving. This decision is made on the basis of the truth-table definitions of the various operators, which should be committed to memory. In deriving the column for '$\sim C$' we look at the column for its component—the column for 'C'. The formula '$\sim C$' is a negation; from the truth-table definition we know that a negation is true when its negate is false and false when its negate is true. Thus at the first row, where 'C' has the value T, we write the value F in the column for '$\sim C$'. We proceed on down in this fashion until the entire column is completed, thus:

C	H	$\sim C$	$\sim H$	$\sim C \supset \sim H$
T	T	F		
T	F	F		
F	T	T		
F	T	T		

Next, a column is derived for '$\sim H$':

C	H	$\sim C$	$\sim H$	$\sim C \supset \sim H$
T	T	F	F	
T	F	F	T	
F	T	T	F	
F	F	T	T	

And finally we are able to derive a column for '$\sim C \supset \sim H$'. Looking at the columns for its components (the columns for '$\sim C$' and '$\sim H$') and recalling the definition of the horseshoe, we write a T in the first row, a T in the second row, an F in the third row (since a conditional with a true antecedent and a false consequent is false), and a T in the fourth row:

C	H	$\sim C$	$\sim H$	$\sim C \supset \sim H$
T	T	F	F	T
T	F	F	T	T
F	T	T	F	F
F	F	T	T	T

With this account in mind, let us look at some general rules for constructing a truth-table. The proper array of formulae above the line is in order of increasing dominance from left to right. That is, at the far right comes the compound statement under consideration. To its left come (in no particular order) its components which are not simple statements (if any). To their left come their components which are not simple statements, if any; and so on. Finally, at the far left, come all of the simple statements in the original compound. It is customary to arrange them alphabetically from left to right, and this custom should be adhered to.

There is one cardinal rule in constructing derived columns, which should be obvious but which many beginners in logic nevertheless overlook: *never attempt to derive a column for a formula unless the table already contains columns for each of that formula's components.*

§5.3 Constructing Base Columns

The base columns for a set of *two* statements (such as those in the above example) can be seen intuitively to cover all possible combinations of truth-values of the two. But as the number of statements increases, this intuitive clarity tends to dim. Thus, it is helpful to have a rule to follow which will assure that no possibilities are left out of the base columns for larger collections.

The number of rows in a truth-table *doubles* every time another simple statement is added to the collection. A truth-table for one statement has two rows; for two statements it has four rows; for three statements, eight rows; for four statements, sixteen rows; and so on. This is sometimes expressed by saying: For a collection of n statements, the truth-table will contain 2^n (2 to the nth power) rows. This "doubling" feature is utilized in the rules for base-column building:

A. Under the letter furthest to the *right*, construct a column of alternating T's and F's (T F T F T F . . .). Base columns always begin with T's, never F's.
B. Working to the left, the clustering of T's and F's *doubles* for each succeeding letter. That is:
   i. Under the letter second from the right, construct a column of alternating *pairs* of T's and F's (T T F F T T F F . . .).
   ii. Under the letter third from the right, construct a column of alternating *quartets* of T's and F's (T T T T F F F F . . .).
   iii. And so on.
C. The base columns are completed when the column furthest to the *left* has one cluster of T's and one cluster of F's. At that point, the top row will be all T's, the bottom row will be all F's, and all other possibilities will occur in between.

As an illustration, here is a complete truth-table for the formula:

$$((A \supset B) \lor \sim(A \cdot C)) \supset B$$

A	B	C	$(A \supset B)$	$(A \cdot C)$	$\sim(A \cdot C)$	$(A \supset B) \lor \sim(A \cdot C)$	$((A \supset B) \lor \sim(A \cdot C)) \supset B$
T	T	T	T	T	F	T	T
T	T	F	T	F	T	T	T
T	F	T	F	T	F	F	T
T	F	F	F	F	T	T	F
F	T	T	T	F	T	T	T
F	T	F	T	F	T	T	T
F	F	T	T	F	T	T	F
F	F	F	T	F	T	T	F

§5.4 Tautologies, Contradictions, and Contingencies

Some compound statements are such that they are true for all possible combinations of truth-values of their components; they are "true no matter what the world is like." A statement of this type is called a **tautology** and is said to be **tautologous**. A simple example would be the statement "Either it is raining or it is not raining" ($R \lor \sim R$). It is shown to be a tautology by the following truth-table:

R	$\sim R$	$(R \lor \sim R)$
T	F	T
F	T	T

Notice that the statement $(R \lor \sim R)$ has only T's in the column beneath it. This is the defining mark of a tautology: its column in the truth-table contains all T's and no F's. Not all tautologies are as simple as this one; for example, the statement $(A \supset B) \supset \sim(A \cdot \sim B)$ is also a tautology. But no matter how complex a statement you are faced with, it is always an easy matter to discover whether or not it is a tautology. Simply construct a truth-table for it, then inspect its column to see whether it contains any F's. If there are no F's, then the statement is true under all possible conditions and is a tautology. But if the column contains one or more F's, then the statement could be false and is not a tautology.

Likewise, some compound statements are such that they are *false* for all possible combinations of truth-values of their components; they are *false* no matter what the world is like. A statement of this type is called a **contradiction** and is said to be **contradictory**. A simple example would be 'It is raining and it is not raining' $(R \cdot \sim R)$. As before, this can be shown to be a contradiction by a truth-table:

R	$\sim R$	$(R \cdot \sim R)$
T	F	F
F	T	F

The defining mark of a contradiction is that it has only F's in its truth-table column. Just as there are very complex tautologies, so there are very complex contradictions. But again, it is always possible to tell whether a statement is a contradiction by constructing a truth-table for it and inspecting its column for T's. If it contains only F's, then it is a contradiction. But if it contains one or more T's, it could be true, and it is not a contradiction.

A statement which is neither a tautology nor a contradiction is called a **contingency** and is said to be **contingent**. A contingency has at least one T *and* at least one F in its truth-table column, and so it is always possible to tell whether a statement is a contingency by constructing a truth-table for it and checking to see whether it has a T *and* an F in its truth-table column. If it has, it is a contingency; if not, it is either a tautology or a contingency.

§5.5 Logical Status

Every statement is either a tautology, a contradiction, or a contingency. To say *which* of these three a given statement is, is to give the statement's **logical status**. If you are given a statement and asked to determine its logical status, that means you are to determine whether it is a tautology or a contradiction or a contingency. The usual way of doing this is by a truth-table.

Exercises III

Construct a truth-table for each of the following statements in order to ascertain its logical status.

☐ 1. $A \supset \sim A$

2. $\sim A \supset A$

3. $(\sim A \supset A) \supset A$

☐ 4. $(A \supset \sim A) \supset \sim A$

5. $\sim A \supset (A \supset B)$

6. $\sim A \supset (A \supset \sim B)$

☐ 7. $A \supset (B \supset A)$

8. $A \supset (\sim B \supset A)$

9. $((A \supset B) \supset A) \supset A$

☐ 10. $((\sim A \supset \sim B) \supset A) \supset A$

11. $(A \supset B) \cdot \sim (B \lor \sim A)$

12. $(A \supset B) \supset ((A \supset B) \lor C)$

☐ 13. $\sim (A \lor \sim A)$

14. $(\sim (A \supset A) \lor (\sim B \cdot \sim \sim B)) \lor C$

15. $A \supset (A \supset A)$

☐ 16. $A \supset ((A \supset A) \supset A)$

17. $(A \cdot C) \supset (\sim D \lor (B \supset A))$

18. $(A \supset A) \supset \sim (B \supset B)$

☐ 19. $\sim (B \supset B) \supset (A \cdot \sim A)$

20. $(((((A \supset B) \supset A) \supset A) \supset A) \supset A) \supset A$

chapter 6

A LOGIC–ENGLISH TRANSLATION GUIDE

This chapter will bring together the previously given Translation Aids and also provide additional information on translating certain expressions.*

§6.1   Conjunctive Operators

and
but
although
however
... also ...
whereas
both ... and ...
but even so
after all
for
nevertheless
still (*except in the sense of* 'any more')
besides
even though (*but not* 'even if'; *see* §6.5)
not only ... but also ...
in spite of the fact that
plus the fact that
inasmuch as (*but not* 'insofar as'; *see* §6.3)
while (*in the sense of* 'although', *but not* 'during which time')
since (*in the sense of* 'whereas', *but not* 'after')
as (*in the sense of* 'whereas', *not* 'at the same time as')

Many of the words and expressions in English which serve as conjunctive

---

*An index of logical operators may be found at the back of the book.

operators sometimes play another role as temporal indicators—to indicate the time-relationship between the events mentioned in the conjuncts. This split personality belongs to the following connectives from the above list:

> still
> while
> since
> as
> and (*when used in the sense of* 'and then')

When 'still' is used in its temporal sense (as opposed to its straightforwardly conjunctive sense), it occurs as an auxiliary to the verb in one of the clauses rather than as a device to connect the clauses. For example:

> *Temporal:*   Harvey has been gone twenty years but she still remembers him.
> *Conjunctive:* Percy is a good boy; still, he sometimes gets into mischief.

Whenever 'still' is accompanied by another conjunctive operator in the same statement, the *other* operator is the one which connects the components; thus

>   1. Even though Clyde has been warned, he still drives recklessly.

will translate as

>   1a. Clyde has been warned · he still drives recklessly

rather than as

>   1b. Even though Clyde has been warned · he drives recklessly

which makes no sense at all.

Unfortunately, the other split-personality conjunctive operators give no such grammatical clues as to which of their personalities is showing; we must determine this, if at all, by understanding the particular statement in which the connective occurs. But here are some examples.

'while' 2. While Edna tended the campfire, Clyde went in search of water.
(*Temporal:* 'while' means 'at the same time as'.)

3. While New York is a nice place to visit, I wouldn't want to live there.
(*Conjunctive:* 'while' means 'although'.)

'since' 4. Since Clyde became famous, he has forgotten his old friends.
(*Temporal:* 'since' means 'after' or 'subsequently'.)

5. Since Harvey had the best qualifications, he got the job.
(*Conjunctive:* 'since' means 'whereas'.)

'as' 6. Clyde came down the stairs as Edna entered the house.
(*Temporal:* 'as' means 'at the same time'.)

7. They attend the theater daily as they do not care for television.
(*Conjunctive:* 'as' means 'inasmuch as'.)

'and' 8. Harvey got out of bed and took a shower.
(*Temporal:* 'and' means 'and afterwards'.)

9. Clyde hates Thelma and Thelma hates Clyde.
(*Conjunctive:* 'and' means 'and', period.)

When a split-personality conjunctive operator has its temporal sense, the resulting compound is not truth-functional and the operator cannot simply be translated as a dot. However, such compounds are truth-dependent. Their method of treatment is discussed in Appendix C.

It may be taken as a convention that, if there is no way to tell whether a split-personality operator has its temporal sense, it is to be treated as straight-forwardly conjunctive and translated as a dot.

§6.2   Disjunctive Operators

or
either . . . or . . .
or else
or, alternatively
otherwise
with the alternative that
unless

The word 'or', besides being a disjunctive operator, is often used as a synonym for 'that is to say'. For instance, the naturalist who says

1. This creature is a *bufo vulgaris* or common toad.

is not claiming that either it is the one or it is the other; rather, he is claiming that it is the one, *that is to say*, the other, since the two are different expressions for the same species of creature. Though not strictly proper to translate this 'or' as a wedge, it is harmless to do so since the resulting disjunction will always have the same truth-value as the original statement.

§6.3   Conditional Operators

Forms in which the antecedent comes first: (. . .) ⊃ (– – –)

if . . . then – – –
if . . . , – – –
given that . . . it follows that – – –
given that . . . , – – –
not . . . unless – – –
in case . . . , – – –*

———
*Cf. Appendix F.

insofar as . . . , – – –
so long as . . . , – – –
. . . implies – – –†
. . . leads to – – –†
. . . only if – – –
whenever . . . , – – –
. . . is a sufficient condition for – – –
. . . means that – – –
to the extent that . . . , – – –

Forms in which the consequent comes first: (. . .) ⊃ (– – –)

– – – if . . .
– – – in case . . .*
unless – – – , not . . .
– – – whenever . . .
– – – insofar as . . .
– – – so long as . . .
– – – follows from . . .†
– – – is implied by . . .†
– – – is a necessary condition for . . .
only if – – – , . . .
– – – provided that . . .
– – – to the extent that . . .

The inclusion of 'not . . . unless . . .' as a conditional operator may cause confusion, since 'not' has already been classified as a negative operator and 'unless' has already been classified as a disjunctive operator. By the latter,

1. not A unless B

should apparently be translated as

2. $\sim A \lor B$

whereas, if 'not . . . unless . . .' is a conditional operator, then the same statement should apparently be translated as

3. $A \supset B$

—and how is a student to know which translation to use? The answer is: use either one, since they are logically equivalent to each other. If the 'not' and the 'unless' in (1) are regarded as separate operators, the appropriate translation is (2). But if they are regarded as portions of the same operator (the operator 'not . . . unless . . .'), the appropriate translation is (3). From a logical point of view, either translation will be correct, since (2) and (3) have exactly the same truth-conditions and are therefore equivalent.

It is important that the 'not' be regarded *either* as a negative operator *or* as part of a conditional operator *but not both*. Forcing it to do double duty

---

*Cf. Appendix F.
†Cf. Appendix A and Appendix C.

invariably leads to mistranslations; for example, to the mistranslation of
(1) as

    4. $\sim A \supset B$

In colloquial English the expressions 'inasmuch as' and 'insofar as' are often used interchangeably. But apart from colloquialisms, the two expressions differ not only in their meaning, but in their logical force. 'Inasmuch as' is a *conjunctive* operator, whereas 'insofar as' is a *conditional* operator. The person who asserts a compound formed with the operator 'inasmuch as' is claiming that both components are true; the person who asserts a compound formed with the operator 'insofar as' is only claiming that, to the extent that the one component is true, so is the other—that is, if the one is true then the other is also. For example, if a detective says

    5. Smith had no motive for the robbery, inasmuch as he is wealthy.

his assistant might, quite properly, contradict him by saying "You're wrong about that; Smith doesn't have a dime to his name." And by recognizing that this reply *does* contradict (5), we see that part of what (5) asserts is that Smith is wealthy. However, the assistant might equally well have contradicted (5) by saying "You're wrong about that; Smith had an excellent motive." Clearly, in asserting (5), the detective is claiming both that Smith is wealthy and that he had no motive for the robbery. Contrast this with

    6. Smith had no motive for the robbery, insofar as he is wealthy.

Here, if the assistant replied "You're wrong; he had an excellent motive," the detective could properly reply, "That doesn't mean I'm wrong; it means Smith isn't really wealthy." For in asserting (6) the detective has not asserted flatly that Smith has no motive; rather he has asserted conditionally that Smith, *insofar as he is wealthy*, has no motive. Similar differences exist between the members of the following pairs of statements:

    7. Inasmuch as Jones is dead, his wife is entitled to the insurance.

    8. Insofar as Jones is dead, his wife is entitled to the insurance.

    9. Inasmuch as the plane was on time, Harvey will make it to the meeting.

    10. Insofar as the plane was on time, Harvey will make it to the meeting.

    11. Inasmuch as Lincoln was responsible for the Civil War, he was responsible for the excesses of the Reconstruction.

    12. Insofar as Lincoln was responsible for the Civil War, he was responsible for the excesses of the Reconstruction.

In each case the first member of the pair is a conjunction, and the second is a conditional.

It is important to remember that the operator 'if' always precedes the *antecedent*, while the operator 'only if' always precedes the *consequent*. For example,

    13. A if B

means the same as 'If B then A', and translates as $B \supset A$, whereas

    14. A only if B

means the same as 'Not A unless B', and translates as $A \supset B$.

A curiosity of the English language is that 'and' will function as a conditional operator, rather than a conjunctive one, when the clause preceding it is phrased in the Imperative mood and the clause following it is Declarative. For example,

    15. Touch me and I'll scream!

is an alternative way of expressing the straightforward conditional

    16. If you touch me, I'll scream!

Other examples of the same thing are:

    17. Do that once more and you will get a spanking.
    18. Ask her and she'll marry you.
    19. Drink from that glass and you will die.
    20. Bring me my slippers and I'll give you a nickel.

However, when the clause following it is also in the Imperative, 'and' once again becomes conjunctive. But the result will be a conjunction of imperatives rather than of propositions, and so will fall outside the scope of logic. For example,

    21. Bring me my slippers and give me a nickel.
    22. Touch me and scream.
    23. Drink from that glass and tell me how you like it.
    24. Love her and leave her.

are not conditionals, but conjunctive imperatives.

§6.4 Biconditional Operators

The biconditional operators likely to be encountered in English are:

    if and only if
    if but only if
    is equivalent to
    is a necessary and sufficient condition for
    just in case*
    just if
    just insofar as
    just to the extent that

---

*Cf. Appendix F.

§6.5 Miscellany

'even . . .'

In colloquial English the two expressions 'even though' and 'even if' are frequently used interchangeably. Nevertheless (just as with 'inasmuch' and 'insofar') the expressions differ not only in meaning but also in logical force. 'Even though' is a conjunctive operator, and compounds formed with its help are to be translated with the dot. But 'even if' is not a compounding operator at all. It functions rather as a disclaimer, and its force is that the truth or falsity of what follows it doesn't matter to what precedes it. Similar disclaimer-expressions are 'whether or not', 'regardless of (whether)', and 'irrespective of (whether)'.* Some examples of these are:

1. I won't tell the secrets, even if you have decided to torture me.
2. It rained yesterday, whether or not you noticed it
3. My client is innocent, regardless of what the police think.
4. I shall be there irrespective of whether it rains.

The logical force of such statements is simply to assert that their first component is true. The segment following the disclaimer-expression is, logically, a decoration added on for emphasis. Let us call the other portion of the statement the "main component." Then this point may be made by saying that the truth-conditions for the entire statement are the same as the truth-conditions for the main component. For example, if I don't tell the secrets, then (1) is true, and if I do tell the secrets, then (1) is false. The question of torture is irrelevant, for, decision to torture or not, if I tell the secrets then (1) is false. Similarly, (3) is true if the client is innocent and is false if the client is not innocent. The opinions of the police are irrelevant to the truth or falsity of (3). These may be contrasted with the genuine compounds (conjunctions):

5. I won't tell the secrets, even though you have decided to torture me.
6. It rained yesterday, even though you didn't notice it.
7. My client is innocent, even though the police think he's guilty.
8. I shall be there, even though it's going to rain.

The proper logical treatment for statements containing disclaimer-expressions is to *discard* the disclaimer-expression, together with what follows it, and to translate the statement as its main component. This is appropriate because the disclaimer-expression and what follows it do nothing more than provide emphasis to the main component, without in any way affecting the

---

*However, the two expressions 'regardless of the fact that' and 'irrespective of the fact that' are conjunctive operators. Here, the difference between 'whether' and 'the fact that' is the difference between merely supplying emphasis and supplying an additional conjunct.

truth-value of what is stated. Thus, the statement (1) above will abbreviate as

    1a. $\sim S$ even if T

and its proper translation will be

    1b. $\sim S$

'neither ... nor'

The expression 'neither ... nor ...' translates as the denial of a disjunction, not as the disjunction of two denials; an alternative is to translate it as the conjunction of two denials, but not as the denial of a conjunction. For example,

    9. Neither Harvey nor Clyde was invited to the party.

paraphrases to

    9a. Neither Harvey was invited to the party nor Clyde was invited to the party.

which abbreviates as

    9b. Neither H nor C

which may be translated, with equal correctness, either as

    9c. $\sim (H \lor C)$

or as

    9d. $(\sim H \cdot \sim C)$

'not both ... and ...'

The expression 'not both ... and ...' translates as the denial of a conjunction, not as the conjunction of two denials; an alternative is to translate it as the disjunction of two denials, but not as the denial of a disjunction. For example,

    10. Not both Edna and Thelma will be selected Queen of the May.

paraphrases to

    10a. It's false that both Edna will be selected Queen of the May and Thelma will be selected Queen of the May.

which abbreviates as

    10b. It's false that both E and T

which may be translated, with equal correctness, either as

    10c. $\sim (E \cdot T)$

or as

    10d. $(\sim E \lor \sim T)$

'instead of'; 'rather than'; 'without'

The operators 'instead of', 'rather than', and 'without' should always be paraphrased as 'but not'. For example, the statement

11. They went to the movies instead of the reception.

paraphrases as

11a. They went to the movies but not the reception.
11b. They went to the movies but they did not go to the reception.
11c. They went to the movies but it's not the case that they went to the reception.

which abbreviates to

11d. *M* but it's not the case that *R*

which translates as

11e. $M \cdot \sim R$

Similarly, the statement

12. Rather than to the reception, they went to the movies.

paraphrases as

12a. They went to the movies rather than to the reception.
12b. They went to the movies but not to the reception.

and

13. They entered without paying.

becomes

13a. They entered but they didn't pay.

and so on.

Exercises I

Some of the following can be translated into correctly punctuated formulae and some cannot. Translate those which can be, and explain what is the matter with each of the others.

    1. Either *P* or if *Q* then *R*

    2. If *P* then either *Q* or *R*

☐ **3.** Either if *P* or *Q* then *R*

    4. If *P* then both *Q* and *R*

    5. Either if *P* then *Q* or *R*

☐ **6.** If either *P* or *Q* then *R*

    7. Both *P* and if *Q* then *R*

    8. Neither both *P* nor *Q* and *R*

    9. If either *P* then *Q* or *R*

☐ **10.** If P then neither Q nor R

11. Neither P nor if Q then R

12. Both if P then Q and R

☐ **13.** Neither if P nor Q then R

14. If both P and Q then R

15. If neither P then Q nor R

☐ **16.** If neither P nor Q then R

Exercises II

Translate the following, paying special attention to punctuation.

1. Either P without Q or R $(P \cdot \sim Q) \vee R$

☐ **2.** P instead of either Q or R

3. Neither P instead of Q nor R $\sim [(P \cdot \sim Q) \vee R]$

4. Not both P and Q unless either R or S $\sim(P \cdot Q) \vee (R \vee S)$

☐ **5.** If P rather than both Q and R then S

6. If either P rather than Q or R then S $[(P \cdot \sim Q) \vee R] \supset S$

☐ **7.** If either P rather than either Q or R or S then either T or U

8. Either if P rather than either Q or R then T or U $\{[P \cdot \sim (Q \vee R)] \supset T\} \vee U$

9. Neither both either P or Q and R nor S $\sim [(P \vee Q) \cdot R] \cdot \sim S$

☐ **10.** Either both neither P nor Q and R or S

11. Both neither either P or Q nor R and S $[\sim (P \vee Q) \cdot \sim R] \cdot S$

12. Not both either P if Q or R and S $[(P \supset Q) \vee R] \vee S$

☐ **13.** If P then Q if R

14. If P if Q then R $P \supset (Q \supset R)$

15. If if P then Q then R $(P \supset Q) \supset R$

☐ **16.** Neither if both either neither P without Q nor R or S and T then U nor W

17. Both if both neither if either both P if Q and R or Z then neither S nor T nor W and X then either both P instead of Q and R but not S or W and Z

$\{[P \supset (Q \cdot R)] \vee Z\} \supset$

chapter 7

CONDENSED TRUTH-TABLES;
TRUTH-FUNCTIONAL EQUIVALENCE

§7.1 Condensed Truth-Tables

Chapter 5 explained how to construct a complete truth-table for any compound statement. Once one has mastered and understood the technique for constructing complete truth-tables, it is generally more convenient to employ what are called **condensed** truth-tables.

The major difference in a condensed truth-table is that nothing is written above the line except the compound statement under consideration and the simple statements occurring in it. A complete truth-table includes not only the statement under consideration, but its components, and the components of its components, and so on down to the simple statements; and the various columns are constructed beneath the appropriate formulae. A condensed truth-table has just as many columns as there would be in a complete truth-table, but they are constructed beneath the appropriate *operators*, within the formula under consideration. The *order* in which the columns are constructed is the same as in a complete truth-table: first for compounds of simple statements, then for compounds of those, and so on.

For example, suppose we wish to construct a condensed truth-table for the compound statement '$(\sim A \supset B) \lor (B \supset A)$'. We write all of the single letters, and the whole statement, above the line, and construct base columns:

A	B	$(\sim A \supset B) \lor (B \supset A)$
T	T	
T	F	
F	T	
F	F	

In a complete truth-table the subcomponent '$\sim A$' would be written out by itself above the line, and our next step would be to construct a column beneath it. In our condensed truth-table we do derive that column next, but

67

it is constructed directly beneath the tilde in '$\sim A$', thus:

A	B	$(\sim A \supset B) \vee (B \supset A)$
T	T	F
T	F	F
F	T	T
F	F	T

We then proceed as before, constructing columns for those formulae whose components already have columns in the table. Thus:

A	B	$(\sim A \supset B) \vee (B \supset A)$
T	T	F T
T	F	F T
F	T	T T
F	F	T F

Then:

A	B	$(\sim A \supset B) \vee (B \supset A)$	
T	T	F T	T
T	F	F T	T
F	T	T T	F
F	F	T F	T

And finally:

A	B	$(\sim A \supset B) \vee (B \supset A)$			
T	T	F	T	T	T
T	F	F	T	T	T
F	T	T	T	T	F
F	F	T	F	T	T

When a column has finally been derived beneath the dominant operator* in the original statement, the truth-table is finished. It is generally a good idea to draw a line around the column beneath the dominant operator to make it stand out as the column for the whole statement, so our completed truth-table looks like this:

A	B	$(\sim A \supset B) \vee (B \supset A)$			
T	T	F	T	T	T
T	F	F	T	T	T
F	T	T	T	T	F
F	F	T	F	T	T

*See §3.4

§7.2 Truth-Functional Equivalence

Two statements are said to be **logically equivalent** if they are both true under exactly the same conditions and are both false under exactly the same conditions—that is, if they have identical truth-conditions. Truth-functional compounds which are logically equivalent are **truth-functionally equivalent.*** Thus, truth-functional equivalence is a species of logical equivalence. Whether or not two statements are truth-functionally equivalent may easily be determined by a truth-table, since it displays the entire set of truth-conditions for a compound statement.

To determine whether two statements are truth-functionally equivalent, first take all the letters (simple statements) from *both* of them and write these above the line; then write the two compounds which are being compared above the line. Construct a set of base columns beneath the single letters and finish out the truth-table for both of the compounds being compared. Next compare, row by row, the columns under the dominant operators for the two compounds. If they are exactly alike all the way down, then the two statements are truth-functionally equivalent. But if they differ anywhere—that is, if there are any rows where one of the columns has T and the other has F—then the two statements are *not* truth-functionally equivalent.

In our notation there is no separate symbol for logical equivalence. Since the full English phrasing " 'P' is logically equivalent to 'Q' " is long and cumbersome, we shall employ the abbreviation '*equiv*' between formulae without quotation marks. Thus, instead of

    1. '$(A \cdot B)$' is logically equivalent to '$(B \cdot A)$'

we shall say

    1a. $(A \cdot B)$ *equiv* $(B \cdot A)$

as an abbreviated version of the same thing. For example, the first truth-table below shows that

    2. $(A \supset B)$ *equiv* $(\sim A \lor B)$

while the second one shows that

    3. $(A \supset A)$ *equiv* $(((A \supset B) \supset A) \supset A)$

and the third one shows that '$A \supset B$' is *not* logically equivalent to '$B \supset A$'—that is, that

    4. '$(A \supset B)$ *equiv* $(B \supset A)$' is false.

---

*There are complicated and logically trivial exceptions to this.

or, extending our abbreviation, that

4a. $(A \supset B)$ *not equiv* $(B \supset A)$

A	B	$(A \supset B)$	$(\sim A \lor B)$
T	T	T	F T
T	F	F	F F
F	T	T	T T
F	F	T	T T

The two circled columns are identical, row for row; hence the two statements are truth-functionally equivalent. Next,

A	B	$(A \supset A)$	$(((A \supset B) \supset A) \supset A)$
T	T	T	T T T
T	F	T	F T T
F	T	T	T F T
F	F	T	T F T

The two circled columns are identical, row for row; hence the two statements are truth-functionally equivalent. Finally,

A	B	$(A \supset B)$	$(B \supset A)$
T	T	T	T
T	F	F	T
F	T	T	F
F	F	T	T

The two circled columns differ at the second row (and again at the third row); hence the two statements are not truth-functionally equivalent.

Exercises I

Determine which of the following pairs of statements are truth-functionally equivalent.

☐ **1.** $\sim(A \cdot B)$, $(\sim A \cdot \sim B)$

 2. $\sim(A \supset B)$, $(A \cdot \sim B)$

 3. $(\sim A \lor A)$, $(\sim C \lor C)$

☐ **4.** $(A \cdot \sim A)$, $(C \cdot \sim C)$

 5. $(A \cdot (B \lor C))$, $((A \lor B) \cdot (A \lor C))$

 6. $(A \lor (B \cdot C))$, $((\sim A \supset B) \cdot (\sim A \supset C))$

☐ **7.** $\sim(A \lor B)$, $((A \supset B) \cdot \sim B)$

 8. $\sim(B \supset C)$, $(B \supset \sim C)$

 9. $(A \supset B)$, $(\sim B \supset \sim A)$

☐ **10.** $(\sim A \supset (A \supset B))$, $(B \supset (A \supset A))$

11. $((A \equiv B) \supset C), (\sim C \supset ((A \supset B) \supset B))$

12. $((A \supset A) \supset A), (A \equiv (A \supset A))$

Exercises II

Give logical translations of the following.

☐ **1.** If it's not the case that either it doesn't rain or Charlie stays home, then it rains only if Charlie stays home.

2. If Clyde hates Thelma insofar as Thelma loves Harvey, then Thelma loves Harvey provided that Clyde hates her.

3. If Percy didn't want to kick Julia unless he kicked her, then if he kicked her if he wanted to, then he didn't kick her just in case he didn't want to.

☐ **4.** Either both if Lucinda kicked Percy then Percy kicked Julia and Evangeline fainted if Julia kicked Percy or Percy kicked Evangeline, if Lucinda hates Percy.

5. Either if both either Harvey went to the mountains or to the beach and either both Edna went with him and Thelma is jealous or Clyde invited Thelma to the movies and she is happy then both either if Harvey hates Thelma then her heart will be broken or if Clyde loves Edna then Thelma's heart will be broken and Harvey didn't go to the mountains unless Edna went with him or else if if Harvey went to the beach then Thelma went with him then Clyde had to settle for Edna.

6. If today is Monday and tomorrow is Saturday, then I'm Julius Caesar.

☐ **7.** Either today is Monday and I have a test tomorrow or my calendar is wrong.

8. Either today is Monday or my calendar is wrong and I don't know what day it is.

9. Today is Friday, since yesterday was Wednesday.

☐ **10.** Provided that yesterday was Wednesday, today is Friday.

11. I have a test inasmuch as yesterday was Wednesday and today is Friday.

12. Abner wants someone to take him to town, but Bill's car isn't working and Charlie is sick in bed.

☐ **13.** If Charlie gets well or Bill fixes his car, then Abner will get to town after all.

14. If Bill's car is beyond repair, then Abner won't get to town unless Charlie gets well.

15. If Abner made it to town, that implies that either Charlie got well or Bill fixed his car.

☐ **16.** If it freezes tonight, then if you don't have antifreeze in your car, then if you haven't drained your radiator, then if no damage occurs, then you are the luckiest man in town.

17. If Charlie gets sick if he drinks too much, then given that he is healthy if and only if he is sober, he drinks too much if he gets sick.

18. If Charlie isn't sick unless he's drunk, then his being either both well and sober or sick rather than drunk implies that his being sick is a necessary condition for his being drunk.

☐ **19.** If either Charlie isn't in good health unless he's either sober or sleeping well or he has insomnia, then his being either both sick and drunk or in good health in case he's sober implies that his being sick is a sufficient condition for his either being drunk or not sleeping well.

20. If Bill spent the money on riotous living instead of for groceries, then if either the welfare check is late or his mother loses her job at the car-wash, then there won't be any groceries if Bill doesn't think of something pretty quick.

chapter 8

ARGUMENTS

§8.1 Validity

An argument is valid if there is no way for all of its premisses to be true and its conclusion false simultaneously. An argument may be valid either in virtue of its **form,*** or in virtue of the meanings of its premisses and conclusion. One which is valid in virtue of its form is said to be **formally valid.** One which is valid, but which is not valid in virtue of its form, is said to be **informally valid.**

Prior to the development of modern symbolic logic, many kinds of argument now recognized as formally valid were relegated to the other category. However, with the help of modern techniques and a more sophisticated conception of logical form, their formal validity can be, and has been, demonstrated. This does not mean that there is no such thing as an informally valid argument. There are many such, at any rate so far as we can tell at present, but their existence is a thorn in the side of formal logicians. An example of an informally valid argument would be

Harvey drank six glasses of water.
Thelma is Harvey's wife.
Therefore, Thelma's husband drank several glasses of liquid.

The reason why informally valid arguments are troublesome is that there is no rigorous procedure for *proving* their validity. We must rely upon intuition instead, with all its notorious fallibilities. Thus one of the major goals of theoreticians in applied formal logic is to reduce, as far as possible, the class of informally valid arguments by showing, with the help of increasingly complex and sophisticated techniques, that such arguments are really valid in virtue of some logical form which reveals itself under detailed analysis.

Formal logic, the subject of this book, is not concerned with informally

---

*The notion of "form" is discussed at some length in the next chapter.

valid arguments, but rather with arguments which are valid in virtue of their form. This being the case, we shall henceforth use the term "valid" to mean *formally valid*, and the term "invalid" to mean not formally valid. Within this terminology, arguments which are not valid at all and arguments which are informally valid will both be counted as "*invalid*."

To be completely precise, we should say that some arguments which are formally valid are valid because of certain *truth-functional* relationships between their premisses and conclusion. Such arguments are said to be **truth-functionally valid**, and an argument which is not truth-functionally valid is said to be **truth-functionally invalid**. However another sort of formally valid argument is studied in later chapters, whose validity comes from what are called "quantificational" relationships between premisses and conclusion. Such arguments are said to be "quantificationally valid," and an argument which is not quantificationally valid is "quantificationally invalid." For purposes of brevity we shall use the term "valid" to mean "either truth-functionally or quantificationally valid," and we shall use the term "invalid" to mean "either truth-functionally or quantificationally invalid." The term **absolutely invalid** will be reserved for those arguments which are *both* truth-functionally and quantificationally invalid. Thus informally valid arguments will still be regarded as absolutely invalid.*

§8.2   Assessing the Validity of Arguments

Let us now look at a procedure for evaluating the validity or invalidity of truth-functional arguments. This procedure, called the "Truth-Table Method," works because of two facts: (1) an argument is valid if there is no way for all of its premisses to be true and its conclusion false; and (2) a properly constructed truth-table shows all the "ways"—the ways in which all the premisses can be true—and how each such way must affect the truth-value of the conclusion.

It is conventional in logic to write out arguments as in the example above. First, the premisses are written, one below the other. Then the conclusion, prefaced by 'therefore', is written below the premisses and separated from them by a line. The argument "If Bill has a new car, then he must be very happy. Bill has a new car. Therefore, he must be very happy." would be written as

If Bill has a new car then he must be very happy.
Bill has a new car.
_____
Therefore, he must be very happy.

---

*The reasons for these complications are discussed in Appendix G.

The word 'therefore' is usually abbreviated as a pyramid of three dots
(∴). Thus the above argument, fully abbreviated and translated, would be
written out as

$$B \supset H$$
$$\underline{B}$$
$$\therefore H$$

The truth-table method consists in constructing a truth-table for the
argument and then inspecting it to see if it contains the possibility of all
premisses being true while the conclusion is false. If the table contains such
a possibility, the argument is invalid; if it does not, the argument is valid.
The specific procedure is this: First, pick out all of the single letters (simple
statements) in the argument—premisses *and* conclusion; write them above
the line, and construct base columns beneath them. Then write each of the
premisses and the conclusion above the line (the conclusion normally goes
to the far right) and, by the procedures already studied, derive columns for
each premiss and for the conclusion. Next inspect the table row by row to
see whether it contains any **invalidating rows**. An invalidating row is one
containing a T in the main column for each premiss, but an F in the main
column for the conclusion. The discovery of such a row will show that
it is *possible* for all the premisses to be true and the conclusion false simultaneously—if the combination of truth-values in the base columns at that
row were to obtain, then the premisses would be true and the conclusion
false—and hence will show that the argument is invalid.

The truth-table for an argument may contain several invalidating rows.
However, even a *single* invalidating row is sufficient to show the argument
invalid. If, on the other hand, the truth-table does not contain any invalidating rows, the argument is *valid*. Let us look at an example. The argument:

> If Harvey is going to the party then Clyde is going to the party.
> Clyde isn't going to the party.
> _____
> Therefore, neither Harvey nor Clyde is going to the party.

after suitable abbreviation and translation, becomes

$$H \supset C$$
$$\sim C$$
$$\overline{\therefore \sim(H \vee C)}$$

The truth-table for this argument is

C	H	$H \supset C$	$\sim C$	$\sim(H \vee C)$	
T	T	T	F	F	T
T	F	T	F	F	T
F	T	F	T	F	T
F	F	T	T	T	F

In the top row, the conclusion has the value F but one of the premises also has the value F, so it is not an invalidating row. In the second row, the conclusion has the value F but so has one of the premises, so it is not an invalidating row. In the third row, the conclusion has the value F but so has one of the premises, so it is not an invalidating row. In the fourth row, the conclusion has the value T, so it is not an invalidating row. Thus, there are no invalidating rows, which means that the argument is *valid*.

On the other hand, the similar-sounding argument

> If Harvey is going to the party then Clyde is going to the party.
> Harvey isn't going to the party.
> _____
> Therefore, neither Harvey nor Clyde is going to the party.

that is,

$$H \supset C$$
$$\sim H$$
$$\therefore \sim(H \lor C)$$

is shown to be *invalid* by the truth-table

C	H	$H \supset C$	$\sim H$	$\sim(H \lor C)$	
T	T	T	F	F	T
T	F	T	T	F	T ←
F	T	F	F	F	T
F	F	T	T	T	F

whose second row is an invalidating row (indicated by the arrow).

One final illustration emphasizes the fact that, when a truth-table is constructed for an argument, the base columns are contructed for the set of *all* letters in premises *and* conclusion. Consider the argument:

> If the automobile doesn't start, then something is wrong with the battery.
> Nothing is wrong with the battery.
> _____
> Therefore, if the automobile doesn't start, then something is wrong with the carburetor.

$$\sim A \supset B$$
$$\sim B$$
$$\therefore \sim A \supset C$$

A	B	C	$\sim A \supset B$	$\sim B$	$\sim A \supset C$
T	T	T	F T	F	F T
T	T	F	F T	F	F T
T	F	T	F T	T	F T
T	F	F	F T	T	F T
F	T	T	T T	F	T T
F	T	F	T T	F	T F
F	F	T	T F	T	T T
F	F	F	T F	T	T F

Is this argument valid or invalid?

Exercises I

Ascertain the validity or invalidity of each of the following arguments.

☐ 1. $A \supset B$
$\therefore \sim A \supset \sim B$

2. $A \supset B$
$\therefore A \supset (A \cdot B)$

3. $(A \lor B) \supset (A \cdot B)$
$\therefore A \equiv B$

☐ 4. $A \supset (B \cdot C)$
$\sim B$
$\therefore \sim A$

5. A
$\therefore (\sim B \lor B)$

6. $(A \cdot \sim A)$
$\therefore B$

☐ 7. $(A \cdot B)$
$\sim A$
$\therefore C$

8. $A \supset B$
$A \supset C$
$\therefore A \supset (B \cdot C)$

9. $A \supset B$
$A \supset \sim B$
$\therefore A$

☐ 10. $A \supset B$
$\sim A \supset B$
$\therefore B$

11. $A \supset (B \lor C)$
$B \equiv C$
$B \supset A$
$\therefore \sim C \equiv (\sim B \cdot \sim A)$

12. $A \supset (B \supset C)$
$C \supset (D \supset E)$
$\therefore A \supset E$

The truth-table method has two important features. First, it is absolutely *mechanical,* which means that it requires no human judgment and consequently leaves no room for human error, except insofar as humans, not being machines, may make mistakes in applying the mechanical procedure. The truth-table method is such that a machine can do it, and in fact it is a relatively simple procedure to program a computer to evaluate arguments by the truth-table method. Second, the truth-table method is what mathematicians call an **effective** procedure: it has a definite terminating point, and it is guaranteed to have produced an answer by the time that terminating point is reached. The procedure terminates when the last T or F is placed in the last derived column in the table; when that happens, the resulting truth-table is guaranteed to tell us whether the argument is valid or invalid.

However, from the human standpoint, the truth-table method has one drawback. As the arguments to be evaluated increase in complexity and more and more simple statements are involved, the truth-tables become unendurably long. For example, a complex argument involving twenty simple statements would have something in the neighborhood of a million rows in its truth-table and it is unlikely that even the most persistent logician would have enough patience, or enough pencils, to complete such a diagram. Thus it is desirable to have a less cumbersome method for evaluating complex arguments, even at the expense of mechanical effectiveness. Such a procedure is developed in the next and succeeding chapters.

§8.3   Two Oddities in Truth-Functional Logic

Within truth-functional logic are two rather queer-sounding facts which must be mentioned at some point.* The first is that any argument whose conclusion is a *tautology* is a valid argument, irrespective of the truth-value or logical status of its premises. This is just the reverse of what our intuitions might have led us to expect, since it is tantamount to saying that a statement which is necessarily true (like a tautology) follows from just any old statement you care to name, whereas our intuitions tell us that a necessarily true statement won't follow from anything but another necessarily true statement. This illustrates a point mentioned earlier, that it is unwise to rely too heavily upon intuition when it comes to matters of logic.

The reason why every argument with a tautologous conclusion is valid is this: if a statement is a tautology, then there is no way for it to be false. And if the conclusion to an argument is tautologous, then there is no way for the conclusion of that argument to be false. But clearly, if the conclusion cannot be false *at all*, then it cannot be false when all the premises are true. And this happens to be the defining characteristic of a valid argument: it is valid if its conclusion cannot be false when all of its premises are true. Thus, an argument with a tautologous conclusion is valid because its conclusion cannot be false.

This fact is not *simply* a logical curiosity. It is related, in a fairly complex fashion, to the fact that an argument can be valid even if it has excess premisses—that is, more premises than are needed to establish the conclusion.†

---

*Sometimes called the "Paradoxes of Entailment" (cf. §13.1), these are related in an obvious way to the so-called "Paradoxes of Material Implication," mentioned in §4.1 and in Appendix E.
†See Appendix H.

And *this* is surely a feature that logic could not do without. A "logic" which maintained that what follows from some information will not follow from that information plus more could not be taken seriously by anyone. Hence we can say that this feature, curious though it may sound, is a necessary ingredient in any satisfactory logical system.

The second logical stepchild is a mirror twin of the first. If one or more statements are such that they cannot all be true simultaneously, they are said to be **incompatible** or **inconsistent**. And any argument whose premises are inconsistent is a valid argument, irrespective of the truth-value or logical status of its conclusion. This too is the opposite of what our intuitions might have led us to expect; intuitively we would probably have said that *nothing at all* follows from inconsistent premises, whereas the fact is that anything and everything follows from inconsistent premises. Still, this principle is not *altogether* contrary to intuition: just as Archimedes said, "Give me a place to stand and I will move the world," so we might say, "Allow me inconsistent premises and I will prove whatever you like." For, starting out with inconsistent premises is only an extreme form of starting out with *false* premises (if they are inconsistent, then at least one of them *must* be false), and surely a person can "prove" anything at all if he is allowed to start out with false premises.

Of course, such an argument (one with inconsistent premises) does not *prove* anything, if by "prove" we mean "establish the truth of." The reason such arguments are valid is also a mirror-image of the reason arguments with tautologous conclusions are valid: if a set of premises is inconsistent (one way for a set of premises to be inconsistent is for one of them to be a contradiction), then they cannot all be true simultaneously. And if an argument is such that it cannot simultaneously have all true premises, then it cannot simultaneously have all true premises and a false conclusion, which is the defining characteristic of a valid argument: it is valid if all its premises cannot be true when its conclusion is false.

These two facts—the two logical "stepchildren"—are related to each other in much the same way that a conditional is related to its contrapositive, which means that they are, in effect, logically equivalent facts. Thus, insofar as we require the first as a necessary ingredient in an adequate logical system, we are forced to take the second along with it. They are not merely twins, they are Siamese twins. But the second fact, unlike the first, may be regarded simply as a logical curio, a conversation-piece of no real utility in its own right, except as it is related to its twin.

Although the intuitive beliefs that a tautology doesn't follow from anything but a tautology, and that nothing follows from a contradiction but another contradiction, are both incorrect, the reverse of each of them is true: nothing follows from a tautology but another tautology, and a contradiction doesn't follow from anything but another contradiction. (Or, to be strictly precise: nothing follows from a necessary truth except another necessary truth, and a necessary falsehood doesn't follow from anything but another necessary falsehood. This modification is required in order to allow for necessary truths other than tautologies, and necessary falsehoods other than (truth-functional) contradictions.)

§8.4   Showing Truth-Functional Consistency

Although an argument with inconsistent premisses is valid, such an argument *cannot* be sound. A "sound" argument, we may recall, is a valid argument with all true premisses, and if a set of premisses is inconsistent, they cannot all be true; hence an argument with an inconsistent set of premisses, though trivially valid, could not possibly be sound. This shows that validity, by itself, is not enough to make an argument a good one. An argument is not a good one unless there is at least a possibility that it does actually establish the truth of its conclusion—that is, unless there is a chance that it is sound. For present purposes, we may define "good argument" as follows:

> *Good Argument.*   An argument is a good argument if, and only if, it is a valid argument and has consistent premisses.

Thus, in order to find out whether an argument is a good one we must find out whether it is valid, and also whether its premisses are consistent. As we have already seen, the truth-table provides a way of testing for truth-functional validity. It also provides a way of checking the truth-functional consistency of a set of premisses: if there is any row in the truth-table giving a value of T to *every* premiss, then the set of premisses is **truth-functionally consistent**;* if there is no such row (that is, if each row assigns F to at least one premiss), then the set of premisses is inconsistent, and the argument, though trivially valid, is still a bad argument.

For example, consider the argument '$\sim(A \supset B)$, $\sim(B \supset A)$ / $\therefore \sim B$', and its truth-table:

A	B	$\sim(A \supset B)$		$\sim(B \supset A)$		$\sim B$
T	T	F	T	F	T	F
T	F	T	F	F	T	T
F	T	F	T	T	F	F
F	F	F	T	F	T	T

---

*There are other modes of inconsistency, though truth-functional inconsistency is the only kind revealed by a truth-table. (The two statements "All crows are black" and "Some crows are not black" are incompatible but not truth-functionally so; their incompatibility is *quantificational*.) Thus it is prudent to exercise some caution in characterizing arguments as good or bad on the basis of truth-tables. If an argument is shown valid by a truth-table, and has truth-functionally consistent premisses, then we can say that *truth-functionally* it is a good argument; but there is still the possibility that it may be a bad argument because of some unrevealed kind of incompatibility among its premisses.

Lines 1 and 3 are the ones where the conclusion is false; but at line 1 both premisses are also false, and at line 3 the first premiss is also false. Thus, there are no invalidating lines, and so the argument is valid. However, at each line at least one of the premisses is false. Therefore, the premisses are inconsistent, and so the argument, though valid, is no good. On the other hand, consider the argument '$A \supset B, C \supset \sim B \mid \therefore \sim(A \cdot C)$' and its truth-table:

	A	B	C	$A \supset B$	$C \supset \sim B$		$\sim(A \cdot C)$	
(1)	T	T	T	T	F	F	F	T
(2)	T	T	F	T	T	F	T	F
(3)	T	F	T	F	T	T	F	T
(4)	T	F	F	F	T	T	T	F
(5)	F	T	T	T	F	F	T	F
(6)	F	T	F	T	T	F	T	F
(7)	F	F	T	T	T	T	T	F
(8)	F	F	F	T	T	T	T	F

Lines 1 and 3 are the ones where the conclusion is false; but at line 1 the second premiss is false and at line 3 the first premiss is false. Thus this argument is also valid. But at line 2 (and also lines 6, 7, and 8) both premisses are true. This shows that it is possible for the premisses all (both) to be true—that they are consistent. Therefore, this argument is a good one.

Exercises II

Decide which of the arguments in Exercises I are good arguments and which are not.

chapter 9

STATEMENT FORMS
AND ARGUMENT FORMS

§9.1 Statement Forms

So far, the letters we have been using have been capital letters serving as abbreviations for particular simple statements. We now turn to a different use of letters of the alphabet, as **statement variables**. Statement variables are lower-case letters from the middle of the alphabet, generally 'p', 'q', 'r', or 's'. Their purpose is to represent *any statement whatever*, simple *or* compound. We use statement variables whenever we wish to talk about statements in general. For example, they were used in constructing the truth-table definitions of the dot, wedge, and other operators, since the import of those definitions is: "Where p and q are *any* statements, the conjunction $p \cdot q$ is true if both p and q are true and false otherwise," and so on.

In logic, any series of (one or more) parentheses, letters, and/or operators constitutes a formula. Each of the following is a formula.

1. $A \supset B$
2. $p \lor q$
3. $A \cdot (F \equiv ((\sim B \lor G) \cdot (K \supset B)))$
4. $ABABAB$
5. $\sim\sim \equiv A \cdot \lor B \supset \equiv p$
6. $A \cdot q$
7. p
8. $((p \supset q) \supset p) \supset p$
9. $\sim B$
10. $\sim \lor \sim \lor \sim \lor \sim \lor pq$
11. $(((((((((($
12. $\supset$

Obviously, not all formulae make sense. For example, 4, 5, and 10 above do not. A formula which does not make sense is said to be **not well-formed** (or **ill-formed**). Among formulae which *are* well-formed, some of them are statements (for example, 1, 3, and 9), and some of them are **statement forms**. The notion of a statement form may be defined as follows:

> *Statement Form.* A statement form is a formula which (1) contains at least one statement variable and which (2) does not contain any statements, abbreviated or otherwise, and which (3) can be transformed into a statement* by replacing each of its statement variables with a statement.

---

*That is, into a formula with a determinate (though perhaps unknown) truth-value.

For example, (2) above is a statement form, since it is a formula which contains statement variables but no statements, and if its variables '*p*', '*q*' were replaced by statements, the result would be a statement—namely, a disjunction. Likewise (7) and (8) above are statement forms. On the other hand, (6) is not a statement form because it contains the (abbreviated) statement '*A*', and a statement form contains no statements. [(6) is not a statement either, since every statement has a truth-value and '*A·q*' has none.] (10) is a formula which contains statement variables but no statements; however, it is not a statement form. If its variables were replaced by statements, the result would not be a statement; it would be ill-formed nonsense.

Exercises I

Which of the following formulae are statement forms? Which are statements? Which are neither?

☐ 1. $(A \cdot A) \cdot A$

2. $\sim \sim \sim \sim \sim \sim \sim \sim \sim (p \vee (p \vee p))$

☐ 3. $q \supset (A \supset A)$

4. $A \sim \supset B$

5. $((P \supset Q) \cdot (Q \supset R)) \supset (P \supset R)$

6. $((p \supset q) \supset P) \supset p$

☐ 7. $\sim (A \cdot \sim (\sim (A \sim) \equiv (B \cdot \sim (B))))$

8. $q \equiv s$

§9.2 Consistent Substitution

In logic, it is often important to compare a statement with a form to see whether or not the statement "has" that form. Such comparisons are made on the basis of whether or not the statement could be obtained from the form by consistent substitution of statements for variables. "Consistency" of substitution has two modes, which we shall call **strict consistency** and **strong consistency**, respectively. The difference between these may be explained as follows.

Suppose we are confronted with the statement form

1. $(p \cdot q) \supset (p \vee (r \cdot q))$

and we want to obtain a statement from this form by replacing its variables with statements. (Don't worry, for now, about *why* anyone would want to do this.) The first step is to construct a "Replacement Table," which we will then follow in performing our substitutions. The Replacement Table will tell us what to replace each variable with. First, we consult the form and then list its variables in a column:

Variables

p

q

r

Then, for each variable in the column, we decide (arbitrarily or otherwise) what statement we wish to replace it with. In making this decision, we are not restricted to *simple* statements. We can use any statements we like, no matter how complex they may be. Suppose, then, that we decide to replace 'p' with '$\sim A$', to replace 'q' with '$A \lor B$', and to replace 'r' with 'B'. We record this decision in another column on our Replacement Table:

Variables		Replacements
p	$\Rightarrow$	$\sim A$
q	$\Rightarrow$	$A \lor B$
r	$\Rightarrow$	B

The Replacement Table tells us that every time we come to 'p' in the form, we are to replace it with '$\sim A$'; every time we come to 'q' in the form, we are to replace it with '$A \lor B$'; and every time we come to 'r' in the form, we are to replace it with 'B'. By following the chart, we obtain

2. $(\sim A \cdot (A \lor B)) \supset (\sim A \lor (B \cdot (A \lor B)))$

as a **substitution instance** of (1). A statement is a **strictly consistent** substitution instance of a form if, and only if, it can be obtained from that form by following a Replacement Table that has *no repetitions in either column*. Thus, (2) is a strictly consistent substitution instance of (1), since no variable occurs more than once in the Variables column and no replacement occurs more than once in the Replacements column. (The fact that 'B' is a component of '$A \lor B$' is immaterial.)

The other mode of consistency is "strong" consistency. A statement is a **strongly consistent** substitution instance of a statement form if, and only if, it can be obtained from that form by following a Replacement Table which has *no repetitions in the Variables column*. Thus, for example, the statement

3. $(\sim A \cdot (A \lor B)) \supset (\sim A \lor (\sim A \cdot (A \lor B)))$

is a strongly consistent substitution instance of (1), since (3) can be obtained from (1) by following the Replacement Table

Variables		Replacements
p	$\Rightarrow$	$\sim A$
q	$\Rightarrow$	$A \lor B$
r	$\Rightarrow$	$\sim A$

which has no repetitions in the Variables column (though it does have one in the Replacements column).

The difference between the two modes of consistency may be summarized in this way: *Strict* consistency permits of no variation: each variable must have its own replacement, and no replacement may serve two different variables. *Strong* consistency still requires that each variable have just one replacement, but permits two (or more) different variables to have the same replacement. What it does *not* permit is one variable having two different replacements. For example,

4. $(\sim A \cdot (A \vee B)) \supset (A \vee (B \cdot (A \cdot B)))$

is neither a strictly nor a strongly consistent substitution instance of (1). To obtain (4) from (1), it would be necessary to follow the table

Variables		Replacements
p	$\Rightarrow$	$\sim A$
q	$\Rightarrow$	$A \vee B$
r	$\Rightarrow$	B
q	$\Rightarrow$	$A \cdot B$
p	$\Rightarrow$	A

which has repetitions in the Variables column—that is, which requires us to give 'p' (and also 'q') two different replacements.

In fact, it is seldom necessary actually to *construct* a Replacement Table. When faced with a statement form and a statement, it will usually be rather easy to tell just by visual inspection whether or not the statement could be obtained from the form by (strictly or strongly) consistent substitution. But in cases of doubt, the Replacement Table is a handy device to use.

§9.3 Alphabetic Variants

One statement form is an **alphabetic variant** of another if the one is obtainable from the other by strictly consistent replacement of variables with variables. Alphabetic variants are alike except for their lettering. For example,

1. $p \supset q$
2. $p \supset r$
3. $q \supset r$
4. $q \supset p$

are alphabetic variants of each other; any of them could be obtained from any of the others following a replacement table with no repetitions in either column. For example, (4) is obtained from (1) by following the table

Variables   *Replacements*

p $\Rightarrow$ q

q $\Rightarrow$ p

On the other hand,

    5. $p \supset p$

is not an alphabetic variant of any of (1)–(4).

For all logical purposes concerning single statement forms, alphabetic variants of each other all count as the same form. Thus, (1)–(4) are (merely alphabetic variants of) the same form—the form of a conditional; but (5) is a different form—the form of a conditional with identical antecedent and consequent. On the other hand, (5) is the same form as

    6. $q \supset q$

since the two are merely alphabetic variants of each other.

§9.4   Statements and their Forms

Any statement which is a (strictly or strongly consistent) substitution instance of a form is said to **have** that form. Thus, recalling the examples from §9.2, both (2) and (3) have the form (1), but (4) does not have that form. Of course, both (2) and (3) have other forms as well. (For that matter, every compound statement has more than one form, since *every* statement has the form 'p'.) For example, they both have the form '$(p \cdot q) \supset r$', and the form '$p \supset q$', and so on. As an exercise, you may wish to construct Replacement Tables showing that they have these last two forms.

A statement which *has* a certain form (that is, which is a strictly or strongly consistent substitution instance of that form) is also said to be **generated by** that form. In this terminology, (2) is generated by (1), by strictly consistent substitution, and (3) is generated by (1), by strongly consistent substitution.

Every statement has a form which generates it by *strictly* consistent replacement of variables with *simple* statements (or single capital letters). That form is called its **skeletal form** (or **skeleton**). Although (1) is a form belonging to both (2) and (3), it is not the skeleton of either of them. The skeleton of (2), for example, would be

    2a. $(\sim p \cdot (p \vee q)) \supset (\sim p \vee (q \cdot (p \vee q)))$

and the skeleton of (3) would be

    3a. $(\sim p \cdot (p \vee q)) \supset (\sim p \vee (\sim p \cdot (p \vee q)))$

A version of the method of describing statements given at the end of Chapter 3 is also applicable to statement forms. For example, the form '$\sim p$'

may be described as "the form of a negation"; the form '$p \supset q$' may be described as "the form of a conditional"; the form '$p \supset p$' may be described as "the form of a conditional whose antecedent and consequent are identical,"* the form '$\sim p \supset q$' may be described as "the form of a conditional whose antecedent is negative"; and so on. It is sometimes useful to think of forms in this descriptive way, when deciding whether a given statement does or does not have a given form, since any statement which has the form of a negation *is* a negation, and vice versa; any statement which has the form of a conditional *is* a conditional, and vice versa; and so on.

§9.5 Isomorphism

Two statements which have the same skeleton are said to be **isomorphic**. Isomorphic statements share exactly the same forms. For example, the two statements

1. $(A \supset B) \supset (B \supset A)$
2. $(K \supset T) \supset (T \supset K)$

are isomorphic. Thus, they both have the form 'p', they both have the form '$p \supset q$', and so on. And of course, they both have the skeletal form '$(p \supset q) \supset (q \supset p)$'. Any two statements which are isomorphic will have the same logical status.

Exercises II

Below are given a number of statement forms and a number of statements. For each statement, decide which of the forms it has, and which (if any) of them is its skeletal form.

(a) $p \supset q$	(e) p	(j) $(p \supset q) \vee (r \supset s)$
(b) $\sim p \vee q$	(f) $(p \cdot q) \supset r$	(k) $(p \cdot q) \vee (p \cdot r)$
(c) $\sim p \vee p$	(g) $p \cdot q$	(l) $p \vee q$
(d) $p \supset (q \cdot r)$	(h) $(p \vee q) \cdot r$	(m) $(p \vee q) \cdot (q \vee r)$

☐ 1. $A \cdot (B \vee C)$

2. $A \vee (B \cdot C)$

3. $(A \supset B) \supset C$

☐ 4. $A \supset (R \cdot (S \vee T))$

5. $\sim((A \equiv B) \cdot (\sim D \supset A)) \vee ((A \equiv B) \cdot (\sim D \supset A))$

6. $(\sim A \vee (B \cdot D)) \cdot ((B \cdot D) \vee \sim \sim J)$

☐ 7. $(A \supset C) \vee (B \supset D)$

---

*It is both unnecessary and incorrect to describe '$p \supset q$' as "the form of a conditional whose antecedent and consequent are different." Can you figure out why? [Think of what is permitted in strongly consistent substitution.]

8. $(A \supset B) \cdot ((A \supset (A \cdot B)) \cdot ((A \supset (A \cdot B)) \supset A))$

9. $((A \supset B) \cdot C) \lor ((A \supset B) \cdot (C \supset D))$

□ **10.** $(A \cdot B) \supset A$

11. $(A \cdot B) \supset (C \cdot D)$

12. $(\sim A \cdot \sim B) \lor C$

□ **13.** $(\sim A \lor \sim B) \cdot C$

14. $((K \supset L) \supset K) \supset K$

15. $(A \supset B) \lor (A \supset D)$

□ **16.** $\sim \sim \sim \sim A \lor \sim \sim \sim A$

17. $A \cdot \sim A$

18. $\sim ((A \cdot \sim B) \lor B) \lor B$

19. $(A \cdot \sim A) \supset \sim A$

20. $(A \cdot B) \supset K$

§9.6   Tautologous, Contradictory, and Contingent Statement Forms

Since a statement form has no truth-value, it cannot be a tautology. Nevertheless, a statement form will be **tautologous**, if it is the skeletal form of at least one tautology. In order to discover whether a given form is tautologous, it is necessary to discover a tautology having that form as its skeleton. But this is easier than it might sound. We already know that statements are isomorphic if and only if they have the same skeleton; and we already know that statements which are isomorphic have the same logical status. From this it follows that all statements having the same skeleton have the same logical status. Thus, in order to discover whether or not a given form is tautologous, it is only necessary to construct a statement having that form as its skeleton and then ascertain (for example, by a truth-table) whether or not that statement is a tautology. If it is, then the form is tautologous. If it is not, then *no* statement having that skeletal form is a tautology, and the form is *not* tautologous.

Tautologous statement forms are logically interesting because of the following two facts:

a. Every substitution instance of a tautologous form is a tautology.

b. Every tautology has (is a substitution instance of) a tautologous form.

The first of these is especially useful in deciding, on particular occasions, whether or not a given statement is a tautology. For example, if we are interested in the logical status of the statement

1. $\sim ((A \supset (B \lor (C \cdot D)))) \equiv (E \supset (F \lor \sim G))) \lor$
$((A \supset (B \lor (C \cdot D)))) \equiv (E \supset (F \lor \sim G)))$

we would require a truth-table of 128 rows to discover whether or not it is a tautology; but if we recognize that it has (is a substitution instance of) the tautologous form

$$\sim p \vee p$$

we can see that it is a tautology without the need for constructing a truth-table at all. (Can you see what substitution would be required to obtain (1) from the form '$\sim p \vee p$'?)

There are **contradictory** statement forms as well as tautologous ones. A statement form is contradictory if it is the skeletal form of at least one contradiction. To discover whether a given form is contradictory, it is only necessary to construct a statement having that skeleton and ascertain whether it is a contradiction. If it is, then the form is contradictory; if not, not. Just as with tautologous forms,

c. Every substitution instance of a contradictory form is a contradiction.
d. Every contradiction is a substitution instance of a contradictory form.

Along with tautologous and contradictory forms, there are also **contingent** statement forms. A statement form is contingent if it is the skeletal form of at least one contingency, and the method for discovering contingent forms is the same as that for discovering tautologous and contradictory forms. The important facts about contingent forms are these:

e. If the skeleton of a statement is contingent, then the statement is a contingency.
f. If a statement is a contingency, then every form which it has is contingent.

It is possible to discover that a statement is a tautology (or contradiction) by discovering that it has a tautologous (or contradictory) form. But it is not possible to discover that a statement is a contingency by discovering that it has a contingent form. This is because *every* statement, regardless of its logical status, has at least *one* contingent form (the form 'p'), and usually has more than one. To discover that a statement is a *contingency*, it is necessary to discover that its *skeletal* form is contingent—for example, by constructing a truth-table for the statement itself.

Exercises III

Ascertain which of the following statement forms are tautologous, which are contradictory, and which are contingent.

☐ 1. $p \supset p$
2. $(p \cdot q) \supset p$
3. $\sim p \vee (q \vee p)$
☐ 4. $p \supset (\sim p \supset q)$
5. $(p \cdot (\sim q \supset \sim p)) \supset q$
6. $(p \equiv q) \supset (p \supset q)$

☐ **7.** $(p \supset q) \supset (p \equiv q)$

    8. $\sim(p \vee \sim p)$

    9. $(p \vee \sim p) \supset (q \cdot \sim q)$

☐ **10.** $\sim(((p \supset q) \supset p) \supset p)$

   11. $\sim p \cdot p$

   12. $p \supset \sim p$

Exercises IV

On the basis of your answers to Exercises III, try to decide—without using truth-tables—which of the following are tautologies and which are contradictions.

☐ **1.** $(A \equiv (B \vee C)) \supset (A \equiv (B \vee C))$

    2. $\sim((K \vee \sim K) \vee \sim(K \vee \sim K))$

    3. $(A \supset (A \vee B)) \supset (A \equiv (A \vee B))$

☐ **4.** $\sim((((A \vee \sim A) \supset B) \supset (A \vee \sim A)) \supset (A \vee \sim A))$

    5. $(\sim C \vee D) \supset (\sim(\sim C \vee D) \supset (C \vee E))$

    6. $\sim K \vee (\sim K \vee K)$

☐ **7.** $((J \vee R) \cdot Z) \supset (J \vee R)$

    8. $\sim((A \cdot B) \cdot (C \cdot (D \cdot E))) \cdot ((A \cdot B) \cdot (C \cdot (D \cdot E)))$

    9. $(K \cdot \sim K) \supset \sim(K \cdot \sim K)$

☐ **10.** $(A \equiv \sim B) \supset (A \supset \sim B)$

   11. $((A \cdot B) \vee \sim(A \cdot B)) \supset (\sim C \cdot \sim \sim C)$

   12. $(\sim J \cdot (\sim K \supset \sim \sim J)) \supset K$

Exercises V

Decide which of the following statements are true, and which are false, and why.

☐ **1.** Every disjunction with one tautologous disjunct is a tautology.

    2. Every disjunction with one contradictory disjunct is a contradiction.

☐ **3.** Every conjunction with one tautologous conjunct is a tautology.

    4. Every conjunction with one contradictory conjunct is a contradiction.

☐ **5.** Every conditional whose antecedent is contradictory is a contradiction.

    6. Every conditional whose antecedent is contradictory is a tautology.

☐ **7.** Every conditional whose antecedent is tautologous is a contradiction.

    8. Every conditional whose antecedent is tautologous is a tautology.

☐ **9.** Every conditional whose consequent is tautologous is a tautology.

   10. Every conditional whose consequent is contradictory is a contradiction.

☐ **11.** Every conditional whose consequent is contingent is a contingency.

   12. Every conditional whose antecedent is contingent is a contingency.

☐ **13.** The negation of any tautology is a contradiction.

   14. The negation of any contradiction is a tautology.

   15. The negation of any contingency is a contingency.

§9.7   Argument Forms

Argument forms are related to arguments in the same way that statement forms are related to statements. An argument form may be defined as follows:

> **Argument Form.**   An argument form is a collection of (two or more) statement forms, which can be transformed into an argument by replacing each of its statement variables with a statement.

An argument form has a conclusion and premises, just as an argument has. But in the case of an argument *form*, these are statement *forms* rather than statements.

The definitions of strongly and strictly consistent substitution also apply to argument forms. We need only to understand that they refer to all variables in the *entire* argument form, not simply to those in its conclusion or one of its premises.

Whenever an argument can be obtained from a form by strictly or strongly consistent replacement of statement variables by statements, that argument is said to **have** that form, and is also said to be a **substitution-instance** of that form. Like statements, every argument has a skeletal form or skeleton: that form from which it can be obtained by strictly consistent substitution of simple statements for variables. Arguments which have the same skeleton are **isomorphic,** and isomorphic arguments are always alike with respect to truth-functional validity or invalidity.

As with statement forms, an argument form is an alphabetic variant of another if it is obtainable from the other by strictly consistent replacement of variables; they are just alike, except for their lettering. For all logical purposes, mere alphabetic variants of each other will count as the same argument form.

§9.8   Validating and Non-validating Argument Forms

Argument forms themselves are neither valid nor invalid. But an argument form will be **validating,** if it is the skeletal form of at least one truth-functionally valid argument. The procedure for discovering whether a given argument form is validating is similar to the procedure for discovering whether a given statement form is tautologous: construct an argument having that form as its skeleton, and then determine (for example, by a truth-table) whether the argument is truth-functionally valid. If it is, then the given form is a validating form; if it is not, then no argument having that skeleton is truth-functionally valid, and the form is *non-validating.*

Validating argument forms are of interest because of the following logical fact: *Any argument which has a validating form is valid.* This means that we can frequently recognize a valid argument without having to construct a truth-table for it, if we see that it has a form which we know to be validating. For example, it would require a lengthy truth-table to determine the validity or invalidity of the argument:

$$\sim (A \cdot B) \supset \sim ((C \equiv D) \equiv E)$$
$$\underline{\sim \sim ((C \equiv D) \equiv E)}$$
$$\therefore \; \sim \sim (A \cdot B)$$

But we do not need a truth-table at all if we recognize that it has the validating form:

$$p \supset q$$
$$\underline{\sim q}$$
$$\therefore \; \sim p$$

As an exercise, prove to yourself that the argument has this form by figuring out the substitutions necessary to obtain the argument from the form. You may also wish to prove to yourself that this form really is a validating form.

In logic, the *order* in which premisses occur is irrelevant. Premiss-order makes no difference to validity or invalidity. Consequently, the order of premisses is ignored for all logical purposes. This means that an argument may have a form even if the premisses of the form occur in a different order from the premisses of the argument. For example, the argument

$$A \cdot C$$
$$\underline{(A \lor B) \supset (C \equiv D)}$$
$$\therefore \; D$$

has the form

$$(p \lor q) \supset (r \equiv s)$$
$$\underline{p \cdot r}$$
$$\therefore \; s$$

even though their premisses occur in a different order.

Exercises VI

Determine which of the following argument forms are validating and which are not.

☐ 1. $p \supset q$
$\quad\quad \underline{p}$
$\quad\quad \therefore q$

2. $p \supset q$
$\quad\quad \underline{\sim p}$
$\quad\quad \therefore \sim q$

3. $p \supset q$
$\quad\quad \underline{q}$
$\quad\quad \therefore p$

☐ 4. $p \supset q$
$\quad\quad \underline{\sim q}$
$\quad\quad \therefore \sim p$

5. $p \lor q$
$\quad\quad \underline{\sim p}$
$\quad\quad \therefore q$

6. $p \lor q$
$\quad\quad \underline{p}$
$\quad\quad \therefore \sim q$

□ 7. $p \lor q$
$\underline{\sim q}$
$\therefore p$

8. $p \lor q$
$\underline{\sim q}$
$\therefore \sim p$

9. $p \supset q$
$\underline{p \supset r}$
$\therefore p \supset (q \cdot r)$

□ 10. $p \supset r$
$\underline{q \supset r}$
$\therefore (p \lor q) \supset r$

11. $p \supset q$
$\underline{q \supset r}$
$\therefore p \supset r$

12. $p \supset r$
$\underline{q \supset r}$
$\therefore p \supset q$

□ 13. $p \supset q$
$\underline{p \supset r}$
$\therefore q \supset r$

14. $p \supset q$
$\underline{p \supset \sim q}$
$\therefore \sim p$

15. $p \supset q$
$\underline{\sim p \supset q}$
$\therefore q$

□ 16. $(p \supset q) \cdot (r \supset s)$
$\underline{p \lor r}$
$\therefore q \lor s$

17. p
$\underline{q}$
$\therefore p \cdot q$

18. $p \cdot q$
$\therefore p \lor q$

□ 19. $\underline{p \lor q}$
$\therefore p \cdot q$

20. $\underline{p \cdot q}$
$\therefore p$

21. p
$\underline{\sim p}$
$\therefore q$

□ 22. p
$\therefore p \lor q$

23. $\underline{\sim (p \cdot q)}$
$\therefore \sim p \cdot \sim q$

24. $\underline{\sim p \lor \sim q}$
$\therefore \sim (p \lor q)$

RULES OF INFERENCE;
DERIVATIONS; PROOFS

As mentioned in Chapter 8, there is a way besides the truth-table method for showing a valid argument to be valid. It is called the "Derivation Method." This method consists in proving validity by literally *deducing* (or "deriving") the conclusion of an argument from its premisses, using rules of inference which have been proven to be logically satisfactory.

§10.1 Rules of Inference

A **rule of inference** is a rule to the effect that it is logically permissible to assert a certain conclusion when certain premisses are given. No rule of inference is satisfactory unless it is *valid*—that is, unless the inferences it permits are all valid. (An inference—the asserting of a conclusion on the basis of given premisses—is valid if and only if the argument consisting of those premisses and that conclusion is a valid argument.) To assure that our rules of inference are valid, they are constructed on the basis of certain relatively simple argument forms which can be proven, by truth-tables, to be validating forms. For example, one of the inference rules we shall use is based upon the argument form

$$p \supset q$$
$$\underline{p}$$
$$\therefore q$$

which may easily be proven validating by the methods discussed in the preceding chapter. The rule (called "Modus Ponens") based upon this argument form is phrased as follows:

> Given a conditional, and given the antecedent of that same conditional, it is permissible to infer the consequent of that same conditional.

The way this rule relates to its associated argument form is not hard to see. Since the argument form is validating, any argument which has the form is valid; that is, any argument one premiss of which is a conditional and the other premiss of which is the antecedent of that conditional, and the conclusion of which is the consequent of that conditional, is a valid argument. Thus, Modus Ponens does nothing more than specify a particular kind of valid inference—the one exemplified in the associated argument form.

We shall begin with ten rules of inference. Others will be added to the list after these become familiar. For ease of reference each rule has a name, which is more or less descriptive of what the inference involves.* These names are given, along with their abbreviation. Also, the associated (validating) argument form for each rule is given along with the rule, as an aid in visualizing the inference. In some cases there is more than one associated argument form. Can you figure out why?

RULES OF INFERENCE

1. CONJOINING (conj.):

$$p$$
$$q$$
$$\therefore p \cdot q$$

Given two statements, it is permissible to infer the conjunction having them as its conjuncts.

2. SEVERANCE OF CONJUNCTION (sev.):

$$\frac{p \cdot q}{\therefore p} \quad \frac{p \cdot q}{\therefore q}$$

Given a conjunction, it is permissible to infer either of its conjuncts separately.

3. DISJOINING (disj.):

$$\frac{p}{\therefore p \lor q} \quad \frac{p}{\therefore q \lor p}$$

Given a statement, it is permissible to infer *any* disjunction having that statement as one disjunct.

4. CANCELLATION OF A DISJUNCT (canc.):

$$\frac{p \lor q}{\sim p} \quad \frac{p \lor q}{\sim q}$$
$$\therefore q \qquad \therefore p$$

Given a disjunction, and given the denial of one of its disjuncts, it is permissible to infer the other disjunct.

5. MODUS PONENS (MP):

$$p \supset q$$
$$p$$
$$\therefore q$$

Given a conditional, and given the antecedent of that same conditional, it is permissible to infer the consequent of that same conditional.

6. MODUS TOLLENS (MT):

$$p \supset q$$
$$\sim q$$
$$\therefore \sim p$$

Given a conditional, and given the *negation* of its *consequent*, it is permissible to infer the *negation* of its antecedent.

---

*The exceptions are Modus Ponens and Modus Tollens. These are generally regarded as the most basic of all inference rules, and their Latin names are so thoroughly entrenched in the literature of logic that an attempt to change them would almost be an indictable offense. The *names* of the other rules are largely non-standard. Standard nomenclature is given in Appendix I.

7. OVERLAPPING CONDITIONALS (OC):

$$p \supset q$$
$$q \supset r$$
$$\therefore\ p \supset r$$

Given two conditionals such that the consequent of one matches the antecedent of the other, it is permissible to infer a conditional having the *unmatched* antecedent and the *unmatched* consequent.

8. DILEMMA (dilem.):

$$p \supset q$$
$$r \supset s \qquad (p \supset q) \cdot (r \supset s)*$$
$$p \lor r \qquad p \lor r$$
$$\therefore\ q \lor s \qquad \therefore\ q \lor s$$

Given two conditionals (or a conjunction of two conditionals), and given the disjunction of their antecedents, it is permissible to infer the disjunction of their consequents.

9. EQUIVALENCE (equiv.):

$$p \equiv q \quad p \equiv q$$
$$p \qquad q$$
$$\therefore\ q \qquad \therefore\ p$$

Given a biconditional, and given one side of that same biconditional, it is permissible to infer the other side of that biconditional.

10. REPETITION (rpt.):

$$p$$
$$\therefore\ p$$

Given a statement, it is permissible to infer that same statement.

§10.2 Premiss Conditions and Appropriate Conclusions

Each of the above rules of inference has two parts. First, it describes a set of (one or more) statements; second, it indicates what may be inferred from those statements. The first part, the descriptions prefaced by the word 'Given', specifies what are called the **premiss conditions** of the rule. Any set of statements fitting the given description is said to **satisfy** the premiss conditions of that rule. For example, in the rule Repetition, the description is simply: "a statement." Every statement fits this description, so every statement satisfies the premiss conditions for Repetition. In Severance, the description is: "a conjunction," so every conjunction satisfies the premiss conditions for Severance. In Modus Ponens, the description is: "a conditional and the antecedent of that same conditional"; hence, every pair of statements one of which is a conditional and the other of which is the antecedent of that conditional, satisfies the premiss conditions for Modus Ponens. And so on for the other rules.

This may be illustrated more specifically. The statements 'A ∨ D' and '(A ∨ D) ⊃ K' satisfy the premiss conditions for Modus Ponens, since one of them is a conditional and the other is the antecedent of that conditional. On the other hand, the pair of statements 'A' and '(A ∨ D) ⊃ K' does

---

*Actually, there are six argument forms associated with this rule. Can you figure out the other four?

not satisfy the premiss conditions for Modus Ponens because 'A' is not the antecedent of '$(A \lor D) \supset K$'. Likewise, the statement '$(\sim B \equiv J) \cdot (R \lor \sim Z)$' satisfies the premiss conditions for Severance, since it is a conjunction. On the other hand, the statement '$(A \cdot B) \lor C$' does not satisfy the premiss conditions for Severance because it is *not* a conjunction; it is a disjunction which happens to have a conjunctive component.

The second part of the inference rule gives what is called the **appropriate conclusion** for that rule; it describes the appropriate conclusion for a set of statements satisfying its premiss conditions. For example, the appropriate conclusion for the rule Modus Ponens plus the statements '$(A \lor D) \supset K$' and '$A \lor D$' will be the statement 'K', since 'K' is the consequent of the given conditional. Likewise, the appropriate conclusion for Cancellation plus the statements '$\sim(A \cdot B)$' and '$(A \cdot B) \lor (C \supset D)$' will be the statement '$C \supset D$', since that is the "other" disjunct—the one which remains after '$(A \cdot B)$' is cancelled by its negation.

Some of the inference rules allow for more than one appropriate conclusion. For example, Severance always has two appropriate conclusions: the appropriate conclusions for Severance plus the statement '$(A \supset B) \cdot C$' are the statements 'C' and '$A \supset B$'. And the rule of Disjoining allows for (literally) an *infinite* number of appropriate conclusions. For example, for Disjoining plus the statement 'A', one appropriate conclusion is '$A \lor B$'; another is '$C \lor A$'; another is '$A \lor \sim A$'; another is '$A \lor ((\sim K \equiv Q) \supset (Z \cdot \sim T))$'; and so on.

Exercises I

For each of the following, decide whether the given statements satisfy the premiss conditions for the indicated inference rule. If they do, give at least one appropriate conclusion for those statements and that rule.

☐ **1.** $A \supset (A \cdot B)$; $\sim(A \cdot B)$; Modus Tollens

   2. $A \supset (B \cdot C)$; $B \supset (C \supset D)$; Overlapping Conditionals

   3. $(A \equiv ((C \cdot D) \supset B)) \cdot G$; Severance

☐ **4.** $K \supset J$; K; Modus Ponens

   5. $K \supset J$; K; Conjoining

   6. $(G \cdot H) \lor (K \supset L)$; $G \cdot H$; Cancellation

☐ **7.** $((A \cdot B) \supset C)$; $D \supset A$; Dilemma

   8. $A \equiv Z$; $Z \cdot A$; Equivalence

   9. $A \equiv Z$; Disjoining

☐ **10.** $A \supset B$; Repetition

   11. $(L \equiv M) \lor (K \cdot T)$; $\sim(K \cdot T)$; Cancellation

   12. $A \supset (A \supset B)$; A; Modus Ponens

☐ **13.** $(A \cdot B) \supset (C \cdot D)$; Severance

   14. $K \supset (K \equiv L)$; K; Equivalence

   15. $(K \equiv L) \supset L$; $K \supset (K \equiv L)$; Overlapping Conditionals

□ **16.** $A \lor B$; $\sim A$; Conjoining

  17. $(A \supset (B \supset C)) \supset D$; $\sim D$; Modus Tollens

  18. $(A \lor B) \supset (A \cdot B)$; $B \supset A$; $(A \lor B) \lor B$; Dilemma

□ **19.** $K \cdot \sim K$; Disjoining

  20. $M \lor \sim M$; $\sim M$; Cancellation

§10.3 Derivations

The process of **constructing a derivation** consists in starting out with certain given formulae (premisses) and deriving other formulae from them by using the provided rules of inference. A derivation is written as a column of formulae, starting with the given formulae (premisses) written one below the other. As further formulae are derived, they are added to the column. The **derivation** is the entire column of formulae, and each of them is called a **line** in the derivation.

A line in a derivation is not a **valid line** unless it is either (1) a premiss, or (2) an assumption (these are discussed later on), or (3) follows validly from one or more previous lines in the derivation by an application of one of the rules. A derivation is not valid unless every line in it is valid. To make it easier to recheck the validity of a derivation, the lines in it are numbered consecutively, and we give each derived line a **justification** by citing the numbers of the lines from which it is derived and the name of the rule used to derive it.

A derivation is constructed in the following way. The initially given formulae (premisses) are inspected to see if any of them (or any set of them) satisfies the premiss conditions for any of the rules of inference. If some of them do satisfy such premiss-conditions, it is permissible to write the appropriate conclusion for those formulae and that rule as a further line in the derivation. For example, if two of the given formulae are 'B' and '$B \supset \sim A$', then these satisfy the premiss conditions for Modus Ponens and so it is permissible to write the appropriate conclusion '$\sim A$' as a further line in the derivation. After this derived line has been added, the derivation (including the new line) is inspected to see if any further premiss-conditions are satisfied. If they are, the appropriate conclusion may be added to the derivation. For example, suppose another of the given formulae is '$A \lor C$'. This, together with the newly derived line '$\sim A$', satisfies the premiss conditions for Cancellation. The appropriate conclusion for these formulae and that rule is 'C', so 'C' may be written as a further line in the derivation. This process of deriving new lines may be continued as long as one wishes.

Lines never get "used up" in the building of a derivation. Once a line is present in the derivation, it may be reused as often as one wishes or is able to do so, in order to derive further lines.

Here is a sample derivation. Suppose the following collection of statements is given to start with:

1. $\sim A \supset \sim B$
2. $B \lor (C \lor D)$
3. $\sim A \cdot K$
4. $(C \supset G) \cdot (D \supset F)$
5. $(\sim A \cdot K) \supset R$

These are the premisses of the derivation. Looking them over, we see that (3) satisfies the premiss conditions for Severance. One appropriate conclusion for (3) and Severance is '$\sim A$', so this may be added to the derivation.

6. $\sim A$ 3, sev.

(The *justification* for line (6) appears to the right.) Inspecting the list once more, we see that (1) and (6) satisfy the premiss conditions for Modus Ponens, which means we are permitted to add the appropriate conclusion to the derivation.

7. $\sim B$ 1, 6, MP

Looking again, we see that (2) and (7) satisfy the premiss conditions for Cancellation, and so we are permitted to write down the appropriate conclusion.

8. $C \lor D$ 2, 7, canc.

Looking again, we see that (8) and (4) satisfy the premiss conditions for Dilemma. We write down the appropriate conclusion.

9. $G \lor F$ 4, 8, dilem.

Looking again, we see that (3) and (5) satisfy the premiss conditions for Modus Ponens.

10. R 3, 5, MP

We also see that (9) and (10) satisfy the premiss conditions for Conjoining.

11. $R \cdot (G \lor F)$ 9, 10, conj.

And the derivation could be continued on indefinitely. A derivation is never *completed* in the sense of running out of possibilities for further derived lines (if nothing else, the rule of Disjoining assures us of this), though a derivation may be *finished*, in the sense that we decide to terminate it by refusing to add to it further. When a derivation is finished in this way, it is described as a derivation **from** the initially given formulae (premisses) **to** the last line in the derivation. Thus, the above is a derivation **from** statements (1) through (5) **to** the statement '$R \cdot (G \lor F)$'.

The premiss-conditions of the rules apply only to *whole lines* in the derivation, never to parts of lines. Thus, for example, it is illegitimate to try to apply the Severance rule to a conjunction which is only a part of a line; it is illegitimate, for example, to try to infer 'A' from '$(A \cdot B) \lor C$' by the Severance rule. The line '$(A \cdot B) \lor C$' does not satisfy the premiss conditions for Severance. Similarly, the lines '$(A \supset B) \cdot C$' and 'A' do not satisfy the premiss conditions for Modus Ponens, since the whole line '$(A \supset B) \cdot C$' is not a conditional.

Exercises II

Each of the following is a valid derivation. The premisses are separated from the derived lines by a series of dashes. Decide how each derived line was obtained, and give its justification.

1.

1. $(A \cdot B) \lor C$
2. $A \supset E$
3. $(E \lor F) \equiv (E \supset \sim G)$
4. $\sim D \cdot \sim C$
----
5. $\sim C$
6. $A \cdot B$
7. A
8. E
9. $E \lor F$
10. $E \supset \sim G$
11. $\sim G$
12. $\sim D$
13. $\sim G \cdot \sim D$
14. B
15. $(\sim G \cdot \sim D) \cdot B$

□ **2.**

1. $(A \supset B) \supset (C \supset D)$
2. $\sim E \lor (D \supset (E \cdot F))$
3. $\sim K \equiv (B \lor (E \cdot F))$
4. $\sim \sim E \cdot (A \lor C)$
5. $(A \supset B) \cdot (B \supset K)$
----
6. $A \supset B$
7. $C \supset D$
8. $\sim \sim E$
9. $D \supset (E \cdot F)$
10. $C \supset (E \cdot F)$
11. $A \lor C$
12. $(A \supset B) \cdot (C \supset (E \cdot F))$
13. $B \lor (E \cdot F)$

14. $\sim K$
15. $B \supset K$
16. $\sim B$
17. $\sim A$
18. C
19. $E \cdot F$
20. F
21. $F \lor A$

3.

1. $(A \lor B) \supset C$
2. $(C \lor D) \supset E$
3. $(E \lor F) \supset (G \lor H)$
4. $R \supset S$
5. $((C \lor D) \supset E) \supset A$
6. $\sim S \cdot \sim T$
7. $(G \supset \sim E) \cdot (H \supset \sim F)$
8. $(\sim E \lor \sim F) \equiv \sim R$
- -
9. A
10. $A \lor B$
11. C
12. $C \lor D$
13. E
14. $E \lor F$
15. $(E \lor F) \lor R$
16. $(G \lor H) \lor S$
17. $\sim S$
18. $G \lor H$
19. $\sim E \lor \sim F$
20. $\sim R$
21. $\sim T$

4.

1. $(A \supset C) \cdot (B \supset D)$
2. $(F \equiv G) \supset A$
3. $(C \lor D) \supset \sim F$
4. $(B \supset D) \supset (F \equiv G)$
5. $A \supset G$
- -
6. $B \supset D$
7. $F \equiv G$
8. A
9. G
10. F
11. $A \lor B$
12. $C \lor D$
13. $\sim F$
14. $F \lor \sim A$
15. $\sim A$
16. $\sim (F \equiv G)$

17. $\sim(B \supset D)$
18. $C \vee (B \supset D)$
19. C
20. $C \cdot \sim A$
21. $A \vee (Z \cdot \sim Z)$
22. $Z \cdot \sim Z$

§10.4 Proofs

People occasionally construct derivations simply for the purpose of exploration, to see what can be inferred from a given set of statements. But the most common reason for constructing a derivation is to prove that some given argument is valid. An argument is proven valid by constructing a derivation from its premises to its conclusion. When this is done, the resulting derivation is called an **extended proof of** (or more simply a "proof of") that argument. Thus, the example derivation given in the previous section constitutes a proof of the argument:

$\sim A \supset \sim B$
$B \vee (C \vee D)$
$\sim A \cdot K$
$(C \supset G) \cdot (D \supset F)$
$(\sim A \cdot K) \supset R$
$\therefore R \cdot (G \vee F)$

The derivation proves that the argument is valid by showing that its conclusion may validly be deduced from its premises.

Constructing a proof requires a more systematic approach than simply constructing an exploratory derivation, because we are attempting to derive a *particular* formula—the conclusion to the argument being proven—not simply making random deductions to see what happens. Thus, constructing a proof can be treated as a problem to be solved: the problem of getting from the given premises to the desired conclusion via the inference rules at our disposal. Unfortunately, there are no ironclad rules for constructing proofs; it is always a matter of *figuring out* how to solve the problem, and this is not always easy to do. The most that can be given are some helpful rules of thumb. But before starting them, let us look at a sample proof, to see the way someone might go about it. We shall construct a proof for the argument:*

---

*When an argument is written out to be proven, it is inconvenient to have the conclusion directly below the premises. Therefore, it is written to the right of the last premiss, separated from it by a slant line. This serves two purposes: it gets the conclusion out of the way of the rest of the derivation, and it serves to indicate, for someone reading the derivation later, which lines are premises and which are derived. The conclusion comes to the right of the *last* premiss, so every line below the one where the conclusion appears is a derived line.

1. $\sim A \lor (B \supset C)$
2. $\sim A \supset R$
3. $(\sim B \supset E) \cdot (\sim R \cdot \sim C)$ $/ \therefore E$

The problem is to derive 'E' from the given premisses. We might, if we wished, simply begin deriving lines in the hope of eventually getting 'E'. But there is a more rational way to go about it. Let us begin by inspecting the premisses to see which ones contain the letter 'E'. We see that 'E' appears in premiss (3). Is there any plausible way of "getting it out"? Well, 'E' is in the conditional '$\sim B \supset E$', which is a component of (3), and so we might say to ourselves:

a. If I could derive '$\sim B \supset E$' and I could also derive '$\sim B$', then I could get 'E' by Modus Ponens.

This gives us a direction to work in. First, is there a way to derive '$\sim B \supset E$'? It is a conjunct of line (3), which means we can derive it by Severance.

4. $\sim B \supset E$ 3, sev.

Now [remembering the strategy in (a)], is there a way to derive '$\sim B$'? Let us look to see which lines contain the letter 'B'. We see that 'B' appears in line (1); is there a plausible way of getting '$\sim B$' out of that line? Well, 'B' is in the conditional '$B \supset C$', which is a component of (1), and so we might think:

b. If I could derive '$B \supset C$' and I could also derive '$\sim C$', then I could get '$\sim B$' by Modus Tollens.

Is there a way to derive '$B \supset C$'? Perhaps not at present, but

c. If I could derive '$\sim \sim A$', then I could get '$B \supset C$' from (1) by Cancellation.

Now, how might we go about deriving '$\sim \sim A$'? Well,

d. If I could derive '$\sim R$', then I could get '$\sim \sim A$' from (2) by Modus Tollens.

So the problem is how to derive '$\sim R$'. Looking at the premisses, we can see that '$\sim R$' appears in premiss (3). Can it be gotten out? Well,

e. If I could derive '$\sim R \cdot \sim C$' then I could get '$\sim R$' by Severance.

And '$\sim R \cdot \sim C$' is a conjunct of (3), so

5. $\sim R \cdot \sim C$ 3, sev.

Remembering the strategy in (e), we then derive

6. $\sim R$ 5, sev.

Remembering the strategy in (d), we then derive

7. $\sim \sim A$ 6, 2, MT

Remembering the strategy in (c), we then derive

    8. $B \supset C$ 1, 7, canc.

which completes half the strategy in (b). Now, is there a way to derive '$\sim C$'? Inspecting what we have so far, we see that '$\sim C$' is a conjunct of line (5), so we derive:

    9. $\sim C$ 5, sev.

and then, recalling the strategy in (b),

    10. $\sim B$ 8, 9, MT

and finally, recalling the strategy in (a), we derive

    11. E 4, 10, MP

which completes the proof.

The strategies brought out in (a)–(e) illustrate one of the rules of thumb for constructing proofs: *"think in reverse" first.* Inspect the premises to see which might be likely sources of the conclusion you are after, then try to figure out what you would have to do to get the conclusion from those premisses. If it requires another formula to be derived, inspect the lines you already have to see which ones might be likely sources of *it*; and so on. Using this procedure, it frequently is possible to plot out the entire proof in reverse, before making any actual derivations at all.

As a further illustration, here is a proof of the argument

    1. $C \cdot (A \supset \sim B)$
    2. $A \cdot (\sim C \supset D)$
    3. $B \lor (A \lor \sim C)$ / $\therefore$ $\sim B \lor D$

The first thing to notice is that the conclusion to this argument is a disjunction. Two of the inference rules—Disjoining and Dilemma—yield nothing but disjunctions; therefore, chances are that the last step in the proof will involve one of those rules. So, "thinking in reverse," we look to see which of the premises might be used with one or the other of those rules to arrive at '$\sim B \lor D$'. In doing this we naturally focus our attention on the premises containing the letters in our conclusion. 'B' appears in the first premiss and 'D' appears in the second; in fact, each appears in the consequent of a conditional which is a component of those premisses. This seems promising, since

  a. If I could derive '$A \supset \sim B$' and also '$\sim C \supset D$', and also '$A \lor \sim C$', then I could get '$\sim B \lor D$' by Dilemma.

But deriving '$A \supset \sim B$' is easy, since it is a conjunct of (1).

    4. $A \supset \sim B$ 1, sev.

And deriving '$\sim C \supset D$' is equally easy.

5. $\sim C \supset D$ 2, sev.

Now [recall the strategy in (a)], how might we derive '$A \lor \sim C$'? Perhaps we notice that it is a disjunct of (3), and think

   b. If I could derive '$\sim B$', then I could get '$A \lor \sim C$' from (3) by Cancellation.

But is there a way to derive '$\sim B$'? Well, it is the consequent of (4), and so

   c. If I could derive 'A', then I could get '$\sim B$' from (4) by Modus Ponens.

And there is no trouble deriving 'A', since it is a conjunct of (2).

6. A 2, sev.

Then, following out our "reverse" strategy:

7. $\sim B$ 6, 4, MP
8. $A \lor \sim C$ 3, 7, canc.
9. $\sim B \lor D$ 4, 5, 8, dilem.

which completes the proof.

This illustrates a second rule of thumb for constructing proofs: *think of what the various rules can give you.* Certain rules always produce conclusions having certain forms: Dilemma always produces a disjunction, Overlapping Conditionals always produces a conditional, and so on. Thus, when "thinking in reverse" it is useful not only to attend to the letters in the conclusion and look for premises containing those letters, but also to attend to the *form* of the conclusion and think of rules which produce that form. Of course, this is *only* a rule of thumb. Some rules, such as Modus Ponens, can produce conclusions of every form, and there is no guarantee that your disjunctive conclusion will be produced by a rule which yields *only* disjunctions. Nevertheless, it is something to keep in mind.

There is no such thing as "*the* correct proof" of an argument. If an argument is valid, there will be indefinitely many proofs showing it to be valid, all of them equally correct. Any valid derivation from the premisses to the conclusion constitutes a proof of the argument. Logicians sometimes compare proofs as to their "elegance," the predominant criterion being shortness. But elegance is a matter of aesthetic appreciation and has nothing to do with logical correctness or incorrectness. So far as logic goes, a long proof is just as good as a short one, provided they are both valid. To illustrate the fact that an argument can have more than one proof, here is a different (and shorter) proof of the previous argument:

1. $C \cdot (A \supset \sim B)$
2. $A \cdot (\sim C \supset D)$
3. $B \lor (A \lor \sim C)$ $/ \therefore \sim B \lor D$

4. $A \supset \sim B$ 1, sev.
5. A 2, sev.
6. $\sim B$ 4, 5, MP
7. $\sim B \vee D$ 6, disj.

Exercises III

In each of the following examples, the statement enclosed in square brackets is the desired conclusion. It could be derived from the other statements by the indicated rule, with the help of one more statement which is not supplied. Supply the needed statement.

Example: $[A \vee B]$; $Y \supset A$; $Z \supset B$; Dilemma
       Needed: $Y \vee Z$

☐ **1.** $[P]$; $P \vee \sim(R \cdot S)$; Cancellation

    2. $[(A \vee B) \supset C]$; $N \supset C$; Overlapping Conditionals

    3. $[K \vee L]$; $R \supset L$; $Z \vee R$; Dilemma

☐ **4.** $[C \cdot (A \supset C)]$; C; Conjoining

    5. $[(Z \equiv R) \supset Z]$; $R \supset ((Z \equiv R) \supset Z)$; Modus Ponens

    6. $[A \cdot C]$; B; Equivalence

☐ **7.** $[\sim(P \supset Q)]$; $(P \supset Q) \supset (R \vee S)$; Modus Tollens

    8. $[\sim(A \vee B)]$; $\sim C$; Cancellation

    9. $[B]$; A; Modus Ponens

☐ **10.** $[A \supset B]$; $A \supset K$; Overlapping Conditionals

Exercises IV

Construct a proof for each of the following arguments. (Each of them can be done in two steps.)

☐ **1.**

    1. $\sim K$
    2. $C \supset (A \cdot B)$
    3. $K \vee C$ $/ \therefore A \cdot B$

  2.

    1. $A \equiv B$
    2. B $/ \therefore A \cdot B$

  3.

    1. $R \cdot (A \supset C)$
    2. $C \supset B$ $/ \therefore A \supset B$

☐ **4.**

    1. $A \supset (C \vee D)$
    2. $\sim(C \vee D)$ $/ \therefore B \vee \sim A$

  5.

    1. $H \supset (K \supset L)$
    2. $N \supset M$
    3. N $/ \therefore (K \supset L) \vee M$

6.

    1. $(H \supset B) \cdot (J \supset A)$
    2. $R \cdot (H \lor J)$ $/ \therefore B \lor A$

☐ **7.**

    1. $K \supset (A \cdot B)$
    2. $(A \cdot B) \supset L$
    3. $(K \supset L) \equiv \sim B$ $/ \therefore \sim B$

8.

    1. $A \lor \sim B$
    2. $\sim A$ $/ \therefore \sim A \cdot \sim B$

9.

    1. $K \supset L$
    2. $L \supset M$
    3. $(K \supset M) \supset M$ $/ \therefore M$

☐ **10.**

    1. $A \supset B$
    2. $A \lor \sim Z$
    3. $\sim B$ $/ \therefore \sim Z$

Exercises V

Complete the following proofs by filling in the missing lines and/or justifications.

1.

    1. $(A \cdot B) \supset \sim R$
    2. $B \cdot (C \lor S)$
    3. $S \supset R$
    4. $C \supset T$
    5. $A \equiv B$ $/ \therefore C$
    6.
    7. $R \lor T$ 3, 4, 6, dilem.
    8.
    9.
    10. $A \cdot B$ 8, 9, conj.
    11.
    12. $\sim S$ 3, 11, MT
    13. C 6, 12, canc.

☐ **2.**

    1. $(X \supset Y) \lor (Z \supset A)$
    2. $(X \supset Z) \supset A$
    3. $A \supset C$
    4. $(X \supset Y) \supset (X \supset Z)$
    5. $\sim C \cdot (Z \lor X)$
    6. $(X \supset B) \lor A$ $/ \therefore B$
    7.
    8.
    9. $\sim A$
    10. $\sim (X \supset Y)$ 8, 9, MT

11.
12.
13. $Z \lor X$
14. X 12, 13, canc.
15.
16. B 14, 15, MP

3.

1. $A \cdot (P \supset Q)$
2. $B \cdot (R \supset S)$
3. $C \cdot (P \lor R)$
4. $\sim Q \cdot (C \supset \sim R)$
5. $E \cdot (P \equiv D)$ $/ \therefore S \cdot (D \cdot E)$
6.
7.
8. $P \lor R$ 3, sev.
9.   6, 7, 8, dilem.
10.
11. S 9, 10, canc.
12.
13.
14. $\sim R$ 12, 13, MP
15.
16.
17. D 16, 15, equiv.
18.
19.
20. $S \cdot (D \cdot E)$ 11, 19, conj.

☐ **4.**

1. $P \supset Q$
2. $Q \supset R$
3. $(P \supset R) \supset (S \supset T)$
4. $(Q \cdot Q) \supset [\sim T \supset (S \lor U)]$
5. $(\sim S \lor \sim R) \supset P$
6. $(P \supset Q) \supset \sim T$ $/ \therefore U \cdot R$
7.
8.   7, 3, MP
9. $\sim T$
10.   8, 9, MT
11. $\sim S \lor \sim R$
12. P 11, 5, MP
13. Q
14.
15. $Q \cdot Q$
16.
17. $S \lor U$ 9, 16, MP
18. U
19.
20. $U \cdot R$ 18, 19, conj.

Exercises VI

Construct a proof for each of the following arguments.

1.
1. $(\sim A \vee B) \supset C$
2. $(D \cdot C) \supset E$
3. $B \cdot D$ $/ \therefore E \cdot B$

2.
1. $A \supset B$
2. $A \vee C$
3. $C \supset (C \supset D)$
4. $\sim B$ $/ \therefore B \vee D$

□ **3.**
1. $(A \supset B) \cdot (C \supset D)$
2. $E \vee (A \vee C)$
3. $\sim E \cdot ((B \vee D) \supset \sim C)$ $/ \therefore A$

□ **4.**
1. $(\sim B \supset C) \equiv \sim A$
2. $(C \supset D) \cdot (F \supset G)$
3. $(\sim B \supset D) \supset (A \vee F)$
4. $\sim A \cdot \sim D$ $/ \therefore B \vee G$

5.
1. $(A \supset B) \supset C$
2. $D \vee (E \supset (A \supset B))$
3. $(E \cdot \sim C) \cdot \sim D$ $/ \therefore B$

6.
1. $\sim A \supset (B \supset C)$
2. $(B \supset C) \supset (C \supset D)$
3. $(B \supset D) \supset (E \supset (D \supset F))$
4. $E \cdot \sim A$ $/ \therefore B \supset F$

chapter 11

TRANSFORMATION RULES

A set of logical rules is said to be **complete** if it is sufficient for proving the validity of all valid arguments within its domain. The set of inference rules given in the previous chapter does not constitute a complete set of rules for truth-functional logic; a great many arguments are truth-functionally valid but cannot be *proven* valid using just those rules. In this chapter the set of rules for truth-functional logic is completed by the addition of a set of *transformation rules*.

§11.1 Transformation Rules

A **transformation rule** is a rule for transforming an expression into a different, but logically equivalent, expression.* Transformation rules are valid only if the transformations they permit are valid. A transformation is valid if the result of the transformation is logically equivalent to the original expression. To insure that our transformation rules are valid, they are based upon certain pairs of statement forms whose equivalence may be shown by truth-table. (A pair of statement *forms* are logically equivalent if and only if every pair of statements s'multaneously generated by the pair of forms are logical equivalents.)

For example, one of the rules (called "Double Negation") is based upon the logical equivalence:

$$p \quad equiv \quad \sim \sim p$$

It is probably unnecessary to construct a truth-table to see that, no matter which statement we take, that statement will be logically equivalent to a

---

*Some writers use the label "transformation rule" to refer to *all* rules for deriving one statement from another, including those we have called "inference rules." When this happens, the sort of rules treated in the present chapter are generally called "equivalence rules" or "replacement rules."

statement which is just like the first except for having two more (or two fewer) tildes attached to its lefthand side. The transformation permitted by the rule of Double Negation is simply that of attaching (or removing) a contiguous pair of tildes. Thus, by the Double Negation rule 'A' can be transformed into '$\sim \sim A$', and '$\sim \sim A$' can be transformed into 'A'. Likewise, '$\sim \sim A \supset B$' can be transformed into '$\sim \sim \sim \sim A \supset B$', and so on. However, Double Negation does not permit '$\sim(\sim A \lor B)$' to be transformed into '$A \lor B$', since the two tildes are not *contiguous* (that is, right next to each other). There is something between them, namely a parenthesis, and so the Double Negation rule does not apply.

It is extremely cumbersome to state the transformation rules in English. Instead, we state them by means of the equivalent forms on which they are based. For example, the Double Negation rule is stated as:

DOUBLE NEGATION (DN): p transf $\sim \sim p$

Because of this, it may be helpful to explain, somewhat formally, exactly how these rules are to be applied. We begin by defining the following notion:

> ***Strong Counterparts.*** A pair of statements are strong counterparts with respect to a pair of statement forms if and only if they can be obtained from those forms by substitution which is strongly consistent with respect to the *pair* of forms.

Thus, for example, the two statements

$$\text{'}(A \supset B) \cdot C\text{'}\quad \text{and}\quad \text{'}(A \supset B) \lor C\text{'}$$

are strong counterparts with respect to the pair of forms

$$\text{'}p \cdot q\text{'}\quad \text{and}\quad \text{'}p \lor q\text{'}$$

since we may obtain the two statements from the forms by replacing all occurrences of 'p' (in both forms) with '$(A \supset B)$' and replacing all occurrences of 'q' (in both forms) with 'C'. On the other hand, the pair of statements

$$\text{'}A \cdot B\text{'}\quad \text{and}\quad \text{'}A \lor \sim B\text{'}$$

are *not* strong counterparts with respect to this pair of forms, since it is not possible to obtain these statements by replacing 'q' with the same thing throughout the pair of forms.

With this definition in mind, we may explain the application of the transformation rules as follows: Each transformation rule consists of a pair of (logically equivalent) forms, and the rule permits *any* formula having one of those forms to be transformed into its strong counterpart generated by the other form.

Thus two statements are strong counterparts with respect to the pair of forms

$$\text{'}p\text{'}\quad \text{and}\quad \text{'}\sim \sim p\text{'}$$

if and only if they are exactly alike except for a pair of contiguous tildes attached to one of them. For example,

$$'A \lor B' \quad \text{and} \quad '\sim \sim (A \lor B)'$$

are strong counterparts with respect to this pair of forms; and so are

$$'\sim \sim (A \lor B)' \quad \text{and} \quad '\sim \sim \sim \sim (A \lor B)'$$

Therefore, the rule of Double Negation permits '$A \lor B$' to be transformed into '$\sim \sim (A \lor B)$' and vice versa, and also permits '$\sim \sim \sim \sim (A \lor B)$' to be transformed into '$\sim \sim (A \lor B)$' and vice versa.

It is important to notice two things about the transformation rules. First, the transformations can go either way. Each of the rules permits *two* transformations: one from the form on the left to the form on the right, another from the form on the right to the form on the left. Double Negation permits attaching a pair of contiguous tildes, and it also permits removing a pair of contiguous tildes.

Second, the transformation rules (unlike the inference rules) apply to parts of lines, as well as to whole lines, within a derivation. It is permissible to *transform* a part of a line, though it is not permissible to *draw an inference from* a part of a line. Thus, for example, it is permissible to use Double Negation to transform '$A \cdot B$' into '$A \cdot \sim \sim B$', and so on. This may be stated more generally as: the transformation rules permit the transformation of any formula or any part of a formula into its strong counterpart.

From time to time throughout this book new rules will be introduced; some will be inference rules and some transformation rules. It is important to keep in mind which they are, since *transformation rules apply to parts of lines as well as whole lines, whereas inference rules apply to whole lines only.*

In the rules, the expression 'transf' reads as: "may be transformed from or into."

TRANSFORMATION RULES*

1. DOUBLE NEGATION (DN): p transf $\sim \sim p$

2. TRANSPOSITION (transp.): $p \cdot q$ transf $q \cdot p$
    $\qquad\qquad\qquad\qquad\quad\; p \lor q$ transf $q \lor p$
    $\qquad\qquad\qquad\qquad\quad\; p \equiv q$ transf $q \equiv p$

3. DUPLICATION (dup.): $p \cdot p$ transf p
    $\qquad\qquad\qquad\quad\; p \lor p$ transf p

4. REGROUPING OF CONJUNCTS (rgr.): $p \cdot (q \cdot r)$ transf $(p \cdot q) \cdot r$
    REGROUPING OF DISJUNCTS (rgr.): $p \lor (q \lor r)$ transf $(p \lor q) \lor r$

5. CONTRAPOSITION (contr.): $p \supset q$ transf $\sim q \supset \sim p$

---

*See Appendix I for alternative names for the rules.

6. DISTRIBUTION/EXTRACTION (dist./ext.):
  $p \cdot (q \lor r)$ transf $(p \cdot q) \lor (p \cdot r)$
  $p \lor (q \cdot r)$ transf $(p \lor q) \cdot (p \lor r)$

7. TILDE-DISTRIBUTION/TILDE-EXTRACTION (TD/TE):
  $\sim(p \lor q)$ transf $(\sim p \cdot \sim q)$
  $\sim(p \cdot q)$ transf $(\sim p \lor \sim q)$

8. CONDITIONAL EXCHANGE (CE): $p \supset q$ transf $\sim p \lor q$

9. BICONDITIONAL EXCHANGE (BE): $p \equiv q$ transf $(p \supset q) \cdot (q \supset p)$

10. DIVERGENCE (div.): $\sim(p \equiv q)$ transf $p \equiv \sim q$

11. EXPORTATION (exp.): $(p \cdot q) \supset r$ transf $p \supset (q \supset r)$

12. ABSORPTION (abs.): $p \supset q$ transf $p \supset (p \cdot q)$

Some of these transformations have fairly straightforward natural-language counterparts; others do not. **Double Negation**, as we have already seen, permits a pair of contiguous tildes to be attached to or removed from any statement or component of a statement. It is the formal counterpart of the familiar grammatical rule that two negatives are the same as an affirmative—that, for example, 'I don't want nothing' is the same as 'I want something'. The former translates successively as '$\sim$(I want nothing)' then '$\sim \sim$ I want something', which by Double Negation reduces to the latter.

Transposition permits the components of a conjunction (or of a disjunction, or of a biconditional) to "trade places" with each other—that is, to reverse their order. This rule gives formal recognition to the natural language fact that the order of conjuncts (in a "pure" conjunction, rather than a "temporal" one—see §6.1) or disjuncts is ordinarily immaterial: 'I like coffee and I like tea' is interchangeable with 'I like tea and I like coffee', and 'You can have soup or you can have salad' is interchangeable with 'You can have salad or you can have soup'. Biconditionals are fairly rare birds in natural discourse, but they are included in the Transposition rule because of the obvious validity of the transformation.

Regrouping permits a three-part conjunction or disjunction to be repunctuated, as in natural discourse we recognize that, of two '*and*'s in a compound, neither will really dominate the other, and likewise for two '*or*'s. Apart from the requirement of uniformity in a formal system (at least in its early stages of presentation), there would be no need to punctuate a many-part conjunction or disjunction at all.

Duplication has no obvious analogue in ordinary discourse. It permits any statement to be expanded into a conjunction (or disjunction) with repetitious components, and likewise permits a repeating conjunction (or disjunction) to be reduced to a single occurrence of the repeated element. Its most common use is the elimination of duplications which may occur in the course of a complex derivation.

Contraposition has already been discussed in §4.1. The formal rule permits us to transform any conditional into its contrapositive or vice versa by reversing the order of the components and either adding a tilde to both or removing a tilde from both.

Distribution is a transformation too complex to be reflected in natural grammar (although its validity is readily enough apparent). In fact, two distinct though clearly similar transformations go under this heading: Distribution of conjunction into disjunction, and Distribution of disjunction into conjunction. The first consists in distributing one conjunct "into" the other, when the other is disjunctive. The rule only permits a lefthand conjunct to distribute into a righthand one. Thus, the righthand one must be disjunctive before this type of Distribution can be done. For example, the formula

1. $(A \supset B) \cdot (C \lor D)$

may be transformed, by Distribution, into

1a. $((A \supset B) \cdot C) \lor ((A \supset B) \cdot D)$

But the formula

2. $(C \lor D) \cdot (A \supset B)$

cannot be transformed by Distribution until after its conjuncts have been transposed.

The other type of Distribution consists in distributing one disjunct of a disjunction into the other, when the other is conjunctive. Again, the rule only permits a lefthand disjunct to distribute into a righthand one, so the righthand one must be conjunctive before this type of Distribution can be done. For example, the formula

3. $(A \lor \sim B) \lor (C \cdot D)$

may be transformed, by Distribution, into

3a. $((A \lor \sim B) \lor C) \cdot ((A \lor \sim B) \lor D)$

As another example, (3a) is a conjunction whose righthand component is a disjunction, and so it may be transformed by Distribution into

3b. $[((A \lor \sim B) \lor C) \cdot (A \lor \sim B)] \lor [((A \lor \sim B) \lor C) \cdot D]$

And (3b) happens to be a disjunction whose righthand component is a conjunction. Therefore, if we were interested in doing so, we could transform (3b) into

3c. $([((A \lor \sim B) \lor C) \cdot (A \lor \sim B)] \lor ((A \lor \sim B) \lor C)) \cdot$
$([((A \lor \sim B) \lor C) \cdot (A \lor \sim B)] \lor D)$

And (as a point of illustration, not of practical logic), since (3c) is a conjunction whose righthand component is a disjunction, we could, if we wished, distribute its lefthand conjunct into its righthand one to obtain an ever more unmanageable formula.

Extraction is the other side of Distribution, and, like Distribution, has the two distinct but related forms. The first involves extracting a common left element from a pair of disjunctive conjuncts: for example, extracting 'A' from '$(A \lor B) \cdot (A \lor C)$'. The effect is to transform a conjunction of disjunctions into a disjunction with a conjunctive righthand component. For example, the formula '$(A \lor B) \cdot (A \lor C)$' is transformed into '$A \lor (B \cdot C)$'.

Similarly, the other type of Extraction involves extracting a common left element from a pair of conjunctive disjuncts: for example, extracting 'A' from '$(A \cdot B) \lor (A \cdot C)$', and its effect is to transform a disjunction of conjunctions into a conjunction with a disjunctive righthand side: for example, '$(A \cdot B) \lor (A \cdot C)$' is transformed into '$A \cdot (B \lor C)$'.

We may see examples of Extraction by reading the examples of Distribution in the opposite order. For example, (3c) may be transformed into (3b) by extracting '$[((A \lor \sim B) \lor C) \cdot (A \lor \sim B)]$'; (3b) may be transformed into (3a) by extracting '$((A \lor \sim B) \lor C)$'; and (3a) may be transformed into (3) by extracting '$(A \lor \sim B)$'.

Two things must be kept in mind in connection with Distribution. First, *two* operators are always involved, a dot and a wedge, one of them being dominant in the formula under transformation and the other being subordinate. In the course of the transformation the two operators always change roles: if, before distributing, the dot was dominant and the wedge subordinate, then after distributing the wedge will be dominant and the dot subordinate. For example, in

4. $A \cdot (B \lor C)$

the dot is dominant, the wedge subordinate. The result of Distribution is

4a. $(A \cdot B) \lor (A \cdot C)$

in which the wedge is dominant and the dot subordinate. Similarly, in the formula

5. $A \lor (B \cdot D)$

the wedge is dominant, the dot subordinate. The result of Distribution is

5a. $(A \lor B) \cdot (A \lor D)$

in which the two operators have traded roles. The same thing happens in Extraction, since Extraction is simply the reverse of Distribution.

The second thing to keep in mind is that the formula being distributed in will "become twins," with one of them attaching to each component in the side receiving the distribution. For example, in (4) above, the 'A' becomes double, with one 'A' attaching to 'B' and the other to 'C'.

Just the reverse happens in Extraction. The two identical elements being extracted coalesce into a single occurrence. For example, when we perform Extraction on (5a) the two occurrences of 'A' merge to become the single occurrence found in (5).

Tilde-Distribution and **Tilde-Extraction** are so called because of their close formal resemblance to Distribution and Extraction. Here again two distinct though similar transformations are involved. The first, "distributing negation into disjunction," formalizes the logic of the English 'neither . . . nor', which we recognize as a negative version of 'either . . . or'—$\sim(p \vee q)$—and which we also recognize as meaning "not the one, and not the other either"—$(\sim p \cdot \sim q)$, and vice versa. The formal transformation consists of turning a negated *dis*junction into a *con*junction of negatives—the tilde distributes to both elements of the disjunction, and the wedge turns to a dot. The second transformation, "distributing negation into conjunction," mirrors nothing as familiar as our 'neither . . . nor' but is nevertheless an obviously valid transformation. If a conjunction is false—that is, if $\sim(p \cdot q)$—then we know from the truth-table definition of the dot that one or the other or both of its conjuncts must be false—that is, that $(\sim p \vee \sim q)$. The formal transformation consists of turning a negated *con*junction into a *dis*junction of negatives. Tilde-Distribution applies only to a formula in which a tilde negates an entire disjunction or an entire conjunction. The thing to remember is that when a tilde is distributed into a compound, it "sticks" to each component and the dot is transformed into a wedge or the wedge into a dot.

Similarly for Tilde-Extraction, which is the reverse operation. "Extracting negation from conjunction" is just the other side of 'neither-nor': if not-each of two things, then neither of them. Formally, if both elements of a conjunction are negative, the negative can be pulled "outside" the compound, and the dot will become a wedge. "Extracting negation from disjunction" recognizes that if one or the other of two things is false—if $\sim p \vee \sim q$—then the conjunction of those two things must be false—$\sim(p \cdot q)$. Formally, if both elements of a disjunction are negative, the negative can be pulled outside the compound, and the wedge will become a dot.

As examples, the formula

6. $\sim((A \cdot B) \vee (C \cdot D))$

transforms, by Tilde-Distribution, into

6a. $\sim(A \cdot B) \cdot \sim(C \cdot D)$

and thence into

6b. $(\sim A \vee \sim B) \cdot \sim(C \cdot D)$

and thence into

6c. $(\sim A \vee \sim B) \cdot (\sim C \vee \sim D)$

The process, of course, may be reversed by applications of Tilde-Extraction.

If several tildes are involved, they must be distributed one at a time. For example, the formula

7. $\sim\sim(A \vee B)$

transforms, by Tilde-Distribution, into

    7a. $\sim(\sim A \cdot \sim B)$

and this transforms, by another application of Tilde-Distribution, into

    7b. $\sim\sim A \lor \sim\sim B$

Conditional Exchange is a procedure for transforming the horseshoe into a suitably placed tilde and wedge or, conversely, for transforming a suitably placed tilde and wedge into a horseshoe. It is the formal counterpart of the (harmless) ambiguity of 'not . . . unless' as both conditional and negative-disjunctive. 'It's not a mammal unless it's warm-blooded' may be paraphrased indifferently as 'Either it's not a mammal or it's warm-blooded' or as 'If it's a mammal then it's warm-blooded'. Conditional Exchange likewise has the effect of transforming conditionals into disjunctions and vice versa. A conditional is transformed into a disjunction by *attaching a tilde to the antecedent and replacing the horseshoe with a wedge*. For example,

    8. $A \supset (B \supset C)$

may be transformed, by Conditional Exchange, into

    8a. $A \supset (\sim B \lor C)$

and thence into

    8b. $\sim A \lor (\sim B \lor C)$

Contrariwise, a disjunction may be transformed into a conditional by *removing a tilde governing the lefthand disjunct and replacing the wedge with a horseshoe*. That is, (8b) may be transformed into (8a), and thence into (8).

    Clearly, a disjunction cannot be transformed into a conditional unless there is a tilde governing its lefthand disjunct, since part of the transformation is the removal of such a tilde. Nevertheless it is possible, with the help of Double Negation, to eliminate any wedge in favor of a horseshoe if we desire to do so. First, attach a pair of tildes to the lefthand disjunct by Double Negation; then remove one of them and replace the wedge with a horseshoe by Conditional Exchange. As an illustration:

    1. $A \lor (B \cdot C)$
    2. $\sim\sim A \lor (B \cdot C)$ 1, DN
    3. $\sim A \supset (B \cdot C)$ 2, CE

Biconditional Exchange has no ready analogue in ordinary discourse because of the rarity of full biconditionals outside technical disciplines. The operation consists in transforming a biconditional into the conjunction of two conditionals with opposite antecedent and consequent, or vice versa. If the nature of the transformation is not obvious, it may be helpful to reread §5.1.

Divergence is another rule more formal than familiar. It consists in transforming the negation of a biconditional into a biconditional whose righthand
side is negated. Its intuitive justification is that, if it is false that two propositions have the same truth-value—if $\sim(p \equiv q)$—then they have opposite
truth-values, so that each has the same truth-value as the *negation* of the
other, and in particular the first has the same truth-value as the negation of
the second—that is, $p \equiv \sim q$; and, of course, vice versa.

Exportation, a transformation cumbersome to describe in words but
easily seen in the rule, is simply a recognition of the equivalence of 'If p and
q then r' with 'If p, then if q then r'—for example, the logical equivalence
between

 9. If it rains and the busses aren't running, then Jones won't come.

and

 9a. If it rains, then if the busses aren't running, then Jones won't come.

Exportation is a superfluous rule, in the sense that the same transformations
can be effected using rules other than Exportation. For example, the transformation of '$(A \cdot B) \supset C$' into '$A \supset (B \supset C)$' may be brought about as
follows:

 1. $(A \cdot B) \supset C$
 2. $\sim(A \cdot B) \vee C$ 1, CE
 3. $(\sim A \vee \sim B) \vee C$ 2, TD
 4. $\sim A \vee (\sim B \vee C)$ 3, rgr.
 5. $A \supset (\sim B \vee C)$ 4, CE
 6. $A \supset (B \supset C)$ 5, CE

Nevertheless, Exportation is a handy rule to have around, since it is a very
common transformation.

Absorption is a transformation by which the consequent of a conditional
is permitted to "absorb" the antecedent, as a conjunct. It also works in
reverse; if one conjunct of the consequent is identical with the antecedent,
that conjunct may be dropped.

Exercises I

Each of the following is a valid proof. For each derived line, decide how it was obtained and give its justification. (These proofs involve inference rules as well as
transformation rules.)

 1.   1. $\sim A \vee B$
         2. $(A \cdot B) \supset \sim C$ $\mid \therefore \sim(A \cdot C)$
         3. $A \supset B$ 1   cE
         4. $A \supset (A \cdot B)$ 3   abs
         5. $A \supset \sim C$ 4, 2   O.C
         6. $\sim A \vee \sim C$ 5   cE
         7. $\sim(A \cdot C)$ 6   TD/E

2.   1. $A \supset B$
2. $\sim A \supset \sim C$
3. $\sim D \lor \sim\sim B$ / $\therefore \sim(\sim B \cdot (\sim D \supset C))$
4. $\sim B \supset \sim A$ 1   CONTRAPOSITION
5. $\sim B \supset \sim C$ 2,4   OVERLAPPING CONDITIONALS
6. $\sim\sim B \lor \sim C$ 5   CONDITIONAL EXCHANGE
7. $\sim\sim B \lor \sim D$ 3   TRANSPOSITION
8. $(\sim\sim B \lor \sim C) \cdot (\sim\sim B \lor \sim D)$ 6,7   CONJOINING
9. $\sim\sim B \lor (\sim C \cdot \sim D)$ 8   DIST/EXT
10. $\sim\sim B \lor \sim(C \lor D)$ 9   TILDE DIST/EXT
11. $\sim(\sim B \cdot (C \lor D))$ 10   TILDE DIST/EXT
12. $\sim(\sim B \cdot (D \lor C))$ 11   TRANSPOSITION
13. $\sim(\sim B \cdot (\sim\sim D \lor C))$ 12   DOUBLE NEGATIVE
14. $\sim(\sim B \cdot (\sim D \supset C))$ 13   CONDITIONAL EXCHANGE

☐ **3.**   1. $B \supset (G \cdot A)$
2. $H \supset K$
3. $G \supset \sim B$
4. $\sim H \supset B$
5. $\sim K \lor (L \lor (B \lor (N \cdot N)))$
6. $L \supset \sim K$ / $\therefore N$
7. $\sim B \lor (G \cdot A)$ 1   CONDITIONAL EXCHANGE
8. $(\sim B \lor G) \cdot (\sim B \lor A)$ 7   DIST/EXT
9. $\sim B \lor G$ 8   SEVERANCE
10. $B \supset G$ 9   CONDITIONAL EXCHANGE
11. $B \supset \sim B$ 10,3   OVERLAPPING CONDITIONALS
12. $\sim B \lor \sim B$ 11   CONDITIONAL EXCHANGE
13. $\sim B$ 12   DUPLICATION
14. $\sim\sim H$ 4,13   MT
15. H 14   DOUBLE NEGATION
16. K 2,15   MP
17. $\sim\sim K$ 16   DOUBLE NEGATION
18. $L \lor (B \lor (N \cdot N))$ 5,17   CANCELLATION
19. $(L \lor B) \lor (N \cdot N)$ 18   REGROUPING
20. $\sim L$ 6,17   MT
21. $\sim L \cdot \sim B$ 13,20   CONJOINING
22. $\sim(L \lor B)$ 21   TILDE DIST/EXT
23. $N \cdot N$ 19,22   CANCELLATION
24. N 23   DUPLICATION

4.   1. $\sim A \lor (B \supset C)$
2. $K \supset \sim C$
3. $\sim(K \cdot L) \equiv G$
4. $B \cdot A$
5. $\sim(F \cdot (H \lor Z)) \supset \sim G$
6. $F \supset \sim H$
7. $((K \cdot L) \equiv \sim G) \supset T$ / $\therefore Z \cdot T$
8. $A \supset (B \supset C)$ 1   CONDITIONAL EXCHANGE
9. $(A \cdot B) \supset C$ 8   EXPORTATION

10. $(B \cdot A) \supset C$ 9   TRANSPOSITION
11. C 4,10   MP
12. $\sim \sim C$ 11   DOUBLE NEGATION
13. $\sim K$ 2,12   MT
14. $\sim K \lor \sim L$ 13   Disjoining ?
15. $\sim (K \cdot L)$ 14   TILDE DIST/EXT
16. G 3,15   EQUIVALENCE
17. $G \supset (F \cdot (H \lor Z))$ 5   CONTRAPOSITION
18. $F \cdot (H \lor Z)$ 16,17   MP
19. $(F \cdot H) \lor (F \cdot Z)$ 18   DIST/EXT
20. $\sim F \lor \sim H$ 6   CONDITIONAL EXCHANGE
21. $\sim (F \cdot H)$ 20   TILDE DIST/EXT
22. $F \cdot Z$ 19,21   CANCELLATION
23. Z 22   SEVERANCE
24. $G \equiv \sim (K \cdot L)$ 3   TRANSPOSITION
25. $\sim (G \equiv (K \cdot L))$ 24   DIVERGENCE
26. $\sim ((K \cdot L) \equiv G)$ 25   TRANSPOSITION
27. $(K \cdot L) \equiv \sim G$ 26   DIVERGENCE
28. T 7,27   MP
29. $Z \cdot T$ 23,28   CONJOINING

Exercises II

Construct a proof for each of the following arguments.

(a)

   1.   1. A $/ \therefore B \supset A$

□ **2.**   1. $\sim A$ $/ \therefore A \supset B$

   3.   1. $A \supset (B \cdot C)$ $/ \therefore A \supset B$

   4.   1. $(A \lor B) \supset C$ $/ \therefore A \supset C$

□ **5.**   1. $A \supset B$
        2. $A \supset C$ $/ \therefore A \supset (B \cdot C)$

   6.   1. $A \supset C$
        2. $B \supset C$ $/ \therefore (A \lor B) \supset C$

   7.   1. B
        2. $\sim A$ $/ \therefore \sim (B \supset A)$

□ **8.**   1. $\sim (A \supset B)$ $/ \therefore A$

   9.   1. $\sim (A \supset B)$ $/ \therefore \sim B$

  10.   1. A
        2. $\sim A$ $/ \therefore B$

(b)

  11.   1. A $/ \therefore B \lor \sim B$

□ **12.**   1. $A \cdot B$ $/ \therefore \sim (A \supset \sim B)$

  13.   1. $B \lor C$ $/ \therefore A \supset (B \lor C)$

14. 1. $B \lor C$ /∴ $(A \supset B) \lor (A \supset C)$

□ **15.** 1. A
2. B /∴ $A \equiv B$

16. 1. $A \supset B$
2. $\sim B$ /∴ $A \equiv B$

17. 1. $\sim A$
2. $\sim B$ /∴ $A \equiv B$

□ **18.** 1. A
2. $\sim B$ /∴ $\sim(A \equiv B)$

19. 1. $(A \supset B) \lor (A \supset C)$ /∴ $A \supset (B \lor C)$

20. 1. $B \supset \sim B$ /∴ $\sim B$

□ **21.** 1. $A \supset B$ /∴ $A \supset (B \lor C)$

22. 1. $A \supset C$ /∴ $(A \cdot B) \supset C$

Exercises III

Construct a proof for each of the following arguments.

1. 1. $(A \supset B) \cdot (C \supset D)$ /∴ $(A \cdot C) \supset (B \cdot D)$

2. 1. $(A \lor B) \supset (C \lor D)$ /∴ $(A \supset C) \lor (B \supset D)$

□ **3.** 1. $(A \cdot B) \supset (C \supset D)$
2. $\sim D \lor \sim E$
3. $\sim(D \cdot E) \equiv E$ /∴ $B \supset (A \supset \sim C)$

4. 1. $\sim(\sim(A \supset B) \supset (C \supset A))$
2. $B \supset \sim D$ /∴ D

5. 1. $(A \supset B) \supset (C \cdot D)$
2. $\sim D$ /∴ $B \supset C$

6. 1. $(A \supset B) \supset (K \cdot L)$
2. $L \supset (G \supset \sim K)$
3. $A \supset \sim(G \supset A)$ /∴ $G \supset B$

□ **7.** 1. M /∴ $((K \supset R) \supset K) \supset K$

Exercises IV

Translate each of the following arguments, using the supplied abbreviations, and construct proofs for them.

1. You can have soup or salad, but not both. Therefore, you can have salad if and only if you don't have soup. (S : you can have soup; K : you can have salad.)*

---

*This notation for expressing abbreviations is employed throughout the book: the abbreviated version, followed by a colon, followed by the full text of the expression (proposition, or whatever) being abbreviated.

2. Either Percy didn't kick his sister or she didn't scream. If he didn't kick her then she fell accidentally, and if she didn't scream then she wasn't hurt. If she was hurt only if she fell accidentally then there is nothing to worry about. Therefore either Percy didn't kick her and there's nothing to worry about, or else she didn't scream and there's nothing to worry about. (*P* : Percy kicked his sister; *S* : she screamed; *F* : she fell accidentally; *H* : she was hurt; *W* : there is something to worry about.)

☐ **3.** Thelma went out with Harvey, and Clyde will be furious unless he didn't hear about it. If Edna knew about Thelma and Harvey, then Clyde heard about it. If Thelma went out with Harvey and Clyde didn't hear about it, his romance is on the rocks. Either his romance isn't on the rocks or Edna knew about Thelma and Harvey. Therefore, if Thelma went out with Harvey only if Clyde isn't furious, then Clyde's romance is on the rocks and Edna knew about Thelma and Harvey. (*T* : Thelma went out with Harvey; *F* : Clyde is furious; *H* : Clyde heard about it; *E* : Edna knew about Thelma and Harvey; *R* : Clyde's romance is on the rocks.)

4. If the government continues its present rate of defense spending then domestic programs will be cut back; and either the government will continue its present rate of defense spending or defense industry will suffer a decline in profits. If unemployment increases without welfare benefits increasing, then the crime rate will go up and the cities will collapse. If defense industry suffers a decline in profits, then unemployment will increase; however, if domestic programs are cut back, then it's false that if unemployment increases then welfare benefits will increase. Therefore, if the government continues its present rate of defense spending then the crime rate will go up and the cities will collapse. (*D* : the government continues its present rate of defense spending; *P* : domestic programs will be cut back; *I* : defense industry will suffer a decline in profits; *U* : unemployment will increase; *W* : welfare benefits will increase; *R* : the crime rate will go up; *C* : the cities will collapse.)

5. Abner won't get to town unless either Bill's car is working or Charlie has gotten over the flu. Bill's car is working if and only if someone fixed it, since it wasn't working last week. Someone fixed Bill's car if and only if Charlie fixed it, and if Charlie hasn't gotten over the flu then he didn't fix it. Therefore, if Charlie hasn't gotten over the flu then Abner won't get to town. (*A* : Abner will get to town; *B* : Bill's car is working; *C* : Charlie gets over the flu; *F* : someone fixed Bill's car; *W* : it was working last week; *K* : Charlie fixed Bill's car.)

☐ **6.** If either Bill's car isn't working or Charlie isn't over the flu, then Abner won't get to town. If the busses are running, then Abner will get to town without Charlie getting over the flu. Therefore, the busses aren't running. (*A* : Abner will get to town; *B* : Bill's car is working; *C* : Charlie gets over the flu; *R* : the busses are running.)

chapter 12

ASSUMPTIONS; CONDITIONAL PROOF; INDIRECT PROOF

§12.1 Assumptions

When constructing a derivation, we often wish to introduce a new statement which has not been derived from the original premisses, so that we can make further deductions that could not be made from the original premisses alone. A statement introduced into a derivation without being derived from previous lines is called an **assumption**; it is "assumed" as an additional premiss for the sake of the derivations we wish to perform. We identify an assumption introduced into a derivation by placing an arrow '→' to its *left*. The arrow means: "This is not a derived line."

It is important that assumptions be clearly identified, since their presence in a derivation has an effect upon what the derivation may be regarded as proving. If a regular derivation (one that doesn't contain any assumptions) is valid, we can be certain that its final line follows from the original premisses: it will be a proof from its premisses to its final line. However, once an assumption has been introduced into a derivation, all we can be certain of is that the final line follows from the premisses *plus the assumption.* It will no longer be a proof "from its premisses"; it will be a proof "from its premisses and assumptions." This means that if our goal in constructing a particular derivation is to prove the validity of a given argument, we can thwart our own purposes by introducing assumptions into the derivation. A proof of an argument must be a derivation from the premisses of *that* argument, not a derivation from some larger collection of statements.

However, so far as assumptions are concerned, there is a way of having our cake and eating it too. We do so by first introducing an assumption, and later, after it has served its purpose, nullifying or "discharging" it by means of certain inference rules. Once an assumption has been nullified, it is for all logical purposes "out" of the derivation; hence a derivation containing only nullified assumptions is the same as a derivation containing no assumptions at all, and it may be regarded as a proof from its original premisses to its

123

conclusion. The two rules for "discharging" assumptions are called, respectively, the Rule of Conditional Proof and the Rule of Indirect Proof.

An assumption may be introduced into a derivation at any time. The decision as to whether and when to introduce assumptions, and which assumptions to introduce, is normally guided by the strategy of the proof one is attempting to construct. But there are no *logical* restrictions on the introduction of assumptions. Logically, it is permissible to introduce *any* statement as an assumption, and it is permissible to introduce as many assumptions as one wishes. The only proviso is that each assumption be identified with an arrow.

§12.2 Conditional Proof

The Rule of Conditional Proof permits an assumption to be discharged (or "nullified" or "neutralized") through the inference of a particular *conditional* statement as a further line in the derivation. It is stated as follows:

> CONDITIONAL PROOF (CP): It is permissible to discharge an assumption after any subsequent line, and to infer the conditional whose *antecedent* is the assumption and whose *consequent* is the latest line in the derivation.

An assumption is **discharged** after a line (a formula) in a derivation by drawing a straight line (called a "discharge bar") beneath that formula, connected by a vertical line to the end of the arrow pointing to that assumption. A schematic representation of the Rule of Conditional Proof may be given as follows:

$$
\begin{array}{l}
\rightarrow p \\
\quad . \\
\quad . \\
\quad . \\
\underline{\quad q \quad} \\
p \supset q
\end{array}
$$

Here 'p' represents some assumption occurring in a derivation (it is identified as an assumption by the arrow pointing to it), and 'q' represents some line occurring after that assumption. When q has been arrived at, then q is the latest line in the derivation (so far). The Rule of Conditional Proof says that it is permissible to discharge p at this point, and to infer the conditional whose antecedent is the assumption (p) and whose consequent is the latest line in the derivation (q). The discharge is brought about by drawing the discharge bar beneath q, connecting it with the arrow at p, and writing the conditional $p \supset q$ as the next line in the derivation.

Here is an example of the way CP might be used in an actual proof.

1. $A \supset (\sim B \cdot C)$
2. $B \vee D$ $/ \therefore A \supset D$
→3. A
| 4. $\sim B \cdot C$ 1, 3, MP
| 5. $\sim B$ 4, sev.
| 6. D 5, 2, canc.
7. $A \supset D$ 3–6, CP

This proof was constructed in the following way. First, the assumption 'A' was introduced at line (3) and identified by an arrow. Line (4) was then derived by Modus Ponens, line (5) by Severance, and line (6) by Cancellation. At this point the latest line in the derivation was 'D'. We then discharged the assumption 'A' by drawing a discharge bar beneath line (6) and joining it to the arrow at line (3); and the conditional '$A \supset D$' was written as the next line in the derivation. Since the completed derivation contains only one assumption, and that one has been nullified, it constitutes a proof of the original argument.

This point is worth emphasizing. Our goal in proving this argument is to show that the given premises entail '**If A then D**'. In the present case, we show this by showing that *if* we assume A, *then* we can show D. This is what the Conditional Proof amounts to: a proof that if we assume one thing we can show another; and it proceeds by actually assuming the one and actually showing the other.

The Rule of Conditional Proof is the formal analogue of a very common procedure in ordinary (informal) reasoning. In discussing hypothetical (conditional) situations, we quite often assume something "for the sake of the argument" and then proceed to trace out the logical consequences of our assumption. When we do this, we do not show that those logical consequences are actually true; rather, we show that *if* our assumption were true, *then* the consequences would also be true. Such discussions normally do not proceed in a vacuum but rather start out with a substantial number of "premisses" or bits of information about the world. If properly conducted, they show that given our information about the world a certain "if-then" follows; that a certain conditional statement follows from our premises. And in the same way, the formal proof above shows that the conditional 'If A then D' follows from the premises 'If A then $\sim B$ and C' and 'B or D'.

Here is another example of the use of the Rule of Conditional Proof:

1. A $/ \therefore B \supset A$
→2. B
| 3. A 1, rpt.
4. $B \supset A$ 2–3, CP

The most obvious application of the Rule of Conditional Proof is in proving arguments with a conditional conclusion.* In such cases the strategy is

---

*For another strategy using CP, see Appendix L.

to introduce the antecedent of the conclusion as an assumption and derive the consequent of the conclusion, then discharge the assumption by CP. This is what was done in the two examples. But, of course, CP is appropriate any time you are after a conditional (whether it is the *conclusion* or not). It is also useful in deriving formulae which are *equivalent* to conditionals. For example, we know that the Conditional Exchange rule allows any disjunction to be transformed into a conditional and vice versa. And so, to prove an argument whose conclusion is a disjunction, the strategy would be to assume the *negation* of one of the disjuncts, derive the other disjunct, discharge the assumption by CP, and then transform the conditional into the desired disjunction by CE. Similarly, to prove an argument whose conclusion is a biconditional, the strategy would be to assume one side of the biconditional and derive the other, then discharge by the CP rule; then assume the *other* side, derive the first side, and discharge by CP again; then conjoin the two conditionals and transform the conjunction into the desired biconditional by BE. Here are some examples:

PROOF I

1. $A \supset B$
2. $\sim A \supset C$ $/ \therefore B \lor C$
3. $\sim B$
4. $\sim A$ 3, 1, MT
5. C 4, 2, MP
6. $\sim B \supset C$ 3–5, CP
7. $\sim \sim B \lor C$ 6, CE
8. $B \lor C$ 7, DN

PROOF II

1. $(A \cdot B) \lor (\sim A \cdot \sim B)$ $/ \therefore A \equiv B$
2. A
3. $\sim \sim A$ 2, DN
4. $\sim \sim A \lor \sim \sim B$ 3, disj.
5. $\sim (\sim A \cdot \sim B)$ 4, TE
6. $A \cdot B$ 5, 1, canc.
7. B 6, sev.
8. $A \supset B$ 2–7, CP
9. B
10. $\sim \sim B$ 9, DN
11. $\sim \sim A \lor \sim \sim B$ 10, disj.
12. $\sim (\sim A \cdot \sim B)$ 11, TE
13. $A \cdot B$ 12, 1, canc.
14. A 13, sev.
15. $B \supset A$ 9–14, CP
16. $(A \supset B) \cdot (B \supset A)$ 8, 15, conj.
17. $A \equiv B$ 16, BE

When giving the justification for a line inferred by CP, we cite the entire series of lines from the assumption down to its discharge bar.

You may have wondered why, in proof II above, the formulae derived at lines (4), (5), and (6) were derived a second time at lines (11), (12), and (13). Why repeat the process, rather than using the ones we already had? The reason is that, after an assumption has been discharged, it is not permissible to use lines derived with its help *before* it was discharged. Thus, after (2) was discharged at line (7), it was no longer permissible to use any of lines (2)–(7) for making further derivations in the proof. In nullifying the assumption at (2), we also nullified *all* the lines between (2) and its discharge bar.

This may be stated more generally. First, the "scope" of an assumption is defined as follows:

> ***Scope of an Assumption.*** The scope of an assumption within a derivation consists of the assumption itself, and all lines after the assumption down to the discharge bar for that assumption.

Thus, for example, in proof I above, the scope of the assumption '$\sim B$' is lines (3) through (5); in proof II the scope of the assumption 'A' is lines (2) through (7); and the scope of the assumption 'B' is lines (9) through (14). The restriction may now be stated as: *After an assumption has been discharged, no line within the scope of that assumption may be used for further inferences in the derivation.* Once an assumption has been discharged, everything within its scope is "dead."

As proof II illustrates, it is possible to have several assumptions within the same proof. It is likewise possible to introduce additional assumptions *without* first discharging the earlier ones. This happens commonly with arguments in which the conclusion is a conditional, and its consequent is also a conditional. For example:

1. $A \supset (B \supset D)$
2. $D \supset (B \supset E)$ $/ \therefore A \supset (B \supset E)$
3. A $/ \therefore B \supset E$
4. B $/ \therefore E$
5. $B \supset D$ 3, 1, MP
6. D 4, 5, MP
7. $B \supset E$ 6, 2, MP
8. E 4, 7, MP
9. $B \supset E$ 4–8, CP
10. $A \supset (B \supset E)$ 3–9, CP

The conclusion to this argument is a conditional, so its antecedent was assumed at line (3) for purposes of CP. Off to the right of that assumption, the consequent was written as a "subsidiary conclusion." Its purpose is to remind us of what is being sought in the derivation. It is standard practice, when introducing an assumption for purposes of CP, to indicate the subsidiary conclusion. In the above case, the subsidiary conclusion is also a conditional, so its antecedent was assumed at line (4) for purposes of CP and its consequent written off to the right as another subsidiary conclusion. The derivation then proceeded until the latest subsidiary conclusion had been obtained at line (8), at which point the assumption directed to that subsidiary conclusion was discharged by CP. This produced the next subsidiary conclusion, and so the assumption directed to *that* subsidiary conclusion was also discharged by CP. At that point, the proof was complete.

When constructing a proof into which assumptions have been introduced, there are three important regulations we *must* adhere to:

A. No assumption may be discharged until after all other assumptions within its scope have been discharged.
B. If one assumption lies within the scope of another, the entire *scope* of the one must lie within the scope of the other.
C. A proof is not completed until every assumption has been discharged.

The sense of regulations A and B is perhaps best explained pictorially. A "free arrow" is one which is not attached to a discharge bar (that is, an arrow pointing to an assumption which has not been discharged). Regulation A says that an assumption cannot be discharged if there are any free arrows (other than its own) within its scope. It rules out, for example, such things as

$$
\begin{array}{lll}
1. & A \supset B & / \therefore A \supset (B \cdot C) \\
\rightarrow 2. & A & \\
3. & B & 1, 2, \text{MP} \\
\rightarrow 4. & C & \\
5. & B \cdot C & 3, 4, \text{conj.} \\
6. & A \supset (B \cdot C) & 2\text{–}5, \text{CP (erroneous)}
\end{array}
$$

Here, the discharge at line (5) is illegitimate, since there is a free arrow within the scope of the assumption being discharged.

Regulation B actually follows from Regulation A, but it is important enough to state separately. Let us refer to an arrow, a discharge bar, and their connecting vertical line as a "discharge mechanism." Then we may explain the sense of Regulation B pictorially by saying that it is illegitimate for one discharge mechanism to intersect another. It rules out, for example, such things as

$$
\begin{array}{lll}
1. & A \supset (B \supset C) & \\
2. & B \supset D & / \therefore B \supset (A \supset (C \cdot D)) \\
\rightarrow 3. & A & \\
4. & B \supset C & 3, 1, \text{MP} \\
\rightarrow 5. & B & \\
6. & C & 1, 5, \text{MP} \\
7. & D & 2, 5, \text{MP} \\
8. & C \cdot D & 6, 7, \text{conj.} \\
9. & A \supset (C \cdot D) & 3, 8, \text{CP (erroneous)} \\
10. & B \supset (A \supset (C \cdot D)) & 5, 9, \text{CP (erroneous)}
\end{array}
$$

since, although the assumption at line (5) lies within the scope of the assumption at line (3), part of the *scope* of (5) lies outside the scope of (3).

Regulation C assures that when a derivation containing assumptions is offered as a proof, it is genuinely a proof from the original premises to the conclusion. Its sense is that a derivation containing free arrows cannot be regarded as a proof.

Exercises I

Construct a proof using CP for each of the following arguments.

1. 1. A / ∴ $B \supset B$

2. 1. $(A \supset C) \cdot (B \supset D)$ / ∴ $(A \cdot B) \supset (C \cdot D)$

□ 3. 1. $A \supset (B \supset C)$
   2. $B \supset (C \supset D)$ / ∴ $A \supset (B \supset D)$

4. 1. $A \supset B$
   2. $(A \cdot C) \supset D$
   3. $(B \cdot D) \supset E$ / ∴ $A \supset (C \supset E)$

5. 1. $(A \cdot B) \equiv C$
   2. $A \supset B$ / ∴ $A \equiv C$

□ 6. 1. $A \equiv (B \supset C)$
   2. $D \supset (E \cdot A)$
   3. B / ∴ $C \lor \sim D$

7. 1. $A \equiv \sim(C \cdot D)$
   2. $\sim B \supset (E \cdot F)$
   3. $G \cdot H$
   4. $\sim((E \supset D) \cdot (F \supset C)) \supset \sim(G \cdot H)$ / ∴ $A \supset B$

8. 1. A / ∴ $(B \supset C) \supset ((A \supset B) \supset C)$

9. 1. M / ∴ $((K \supset R) \supset K) \supset K$

□ 10. 1. $\sim((A \cdot B) \equiv G)$
    2. $\sim(G \lor E) \supset T$
    3. $C \supset (T \supset \sim D)$ / ∴ $A \supset (D \supset (C \supset (B \supset E)))$

§12.3 Indirect Proof* SKIP

The second rule for discharging assumptions is the Rule of Indirect Proof. In order to state it, we first need the following definition:

> ***Explicit Contradiction.*** An explicit contradiction is a statement which has either the form '$p \cdot \sim p$' or the form '$\sim p \cdot p$'—that is, which consists of a statement conjoined to its own negation.

---

*Indirect proof is also called *reductio ad absurdum* proof.

The Rule of Indirect Proof may then be stated as follows:

INDIRECT PROOF (IP): It is permissible to discharge an assumption after any subsequent line which is an explicit contradiction, and to infer the *negation* of that assumption.

A schematic representation of this rule is:

Here '*p*' represents some assumption occurring in a derivation and '$q \cdot \sim q$' represents some explicit contradiction occurring in the derivation subsequent to the assumption. The Rule of Indirect Proof says that when $q \cdot \sim q$ has been derived, then it is permissible to discharge *p* and to infer its negation—that is, to infer $\sim p$. Here is an example of the way IP might be used in an actual proof:

1. $A \lor (B \cdot C)$
2. $A \supset C$ $/ \therefore C$
→3. $\sim C$
    4. $\sim A$ 2, 3, MT
    5. $B \cdot C$ 4, 1, canc.
    6. C 5, sev.
    7. $C \cdot \sim C$ 3, 6, conj.
8. $\sim \sim C$ 3–7, IP
9. C 8, DN

The Rule of Indirect Proof is based upon the logical principle that whatever implies a falsehood must itself be false. More particularly, if, given a set of premisses, the introduction of an additional assumption can be made to lead to a contradiction, then it follows that, given those premisses, the assumption must be false.

This too follows a widely used pattern of informal reasoning: we show something to be false (in the light of our information) by showing that its consequences are false. "Suppose you were right. Then it would follow that such-and-such. But such-and-such is false. Therefore, you're wrong." This is precisely the pattern of the proof above: given the two premisses, we say, "Suppose *C* were false. Then it would follow (by the indicated steps) that *C* is both true and false, which is absurd. Therefore, the supposition leading to that conclusion is false."

It may be recalled from the Preliminaries that one definition of "deductive validity" is the following:

> An argument is deductively valid if, and only if, it would be self-contradictory to suppose that its conclusion is false and all of its premisses true.

The Indirect Proof above shows the argument to be valid by showing that, given its premisses, it would be self-contradictory to suppose that its conclusion is false.

The basic strategy for using Indirect Proof is quite simple: assume the *denial* of what you are after, and derive an explicit contradiction; then discharge by the IP rule. In following this strategy, *any* explicit contradiction will do. For example, the above IP might also have gone this way:

$$
\begin{array}{lll}
1. & A \lor (B \cdot C) & \\
2. & A \supset C \qquad /\therefore C & \\
\to 3. & \sim C & \\
4. & \sim A & 2, 3, \text{MT} \\
5. & B \cdot C & 4, 1, \text{canc.} \\
6. & \sim B \lor \sim C & 3, \text{disj.} \\
7. & \sim(B \cdot C) & 6, \text{TE} \\
8. & (B \cdot C) \cdot \sim(B \cdot C) & 5, 7, \text{conj.} \\
9. & \sim\sim C & 3\text{--}8, \text{IP} \\
10. & C & 9, \text{DN}
\end{array}
$$

Indirect Proof and Conditional Proof may be combined in the same proof. Here is an example:

$$
\begin{array}{lll}
1. & (A \lor B) \supset C & \\
2. & (C \lor D) \supset E \qquad /\therefore A \supset E & \\
\to 3. & A \qquad /\therefore E & \\
\to 4. & \sim E \qquad (\text{IP}) & \\
5. & \sim(C \lor D) & 2, 4, \text{MT} \\
6. & A \lor B & 3, \text{disj.} \\
7. & C & 1, 6, \text{MP} \\
8. & C \lor D & 7, \text{disj.} \\
9. & (C \lor D) \cdot \sim(C \lor D) & 5, 8, \text{conj.} \\
10. & E & 4\text{--}9, \text{IP, DN} \\
11. & A \supset E & 3\text{--}10, \text{CP}
\end{array}
$$

When an assumption is introduced for purposes of IP, our goal thereafter is simply to derive an explicit contradiction—any one. There is no *particular* contradiction we are after, so it is standard practice to write '(IP)' in place of a subsidiary conclusion, as a reminder that we are trying to derive a contradiction. This has the additional advantage of helping, in a complex proof involving many assumptions, to keep track of which ones are CP assumptions and which ones are IP assumptions. (We call them "CP assumptions" or "IP assumptions" in virtue of the strategy for which they were introduced—in virtue of the way we have in mind to discharge them later on—and not because of any inherent differences in the nature of the assumptions themselves.)

Indirect Proof is called "indirect" because it does not involve the actual derivation of the conclusion from the premises; rather, it shows—"indirectly"—that the conclusion *can* be derived directly from the premises. Strictly speaking, Conditional Proofs are also "indirect"; CP is a procedure for showing that a conditional *can* be derived from the preceding lines in the proof (by the "direct" rules of Inference and Transformation given in the two preceding chapters), not a procedure for deriving it directly.

The rule of IP is superfluous, in the sense that the same results could be obtained using CP and the other rules. It is included in the list of rules for two reasons: (1) it follows a commonly used pattern of informal reasoning, and (2) an inference using IP is six steps shorter than the same inference using CP. Nevertheless, it is interesting to know that we could get along without IP if we wanted to. For example, here is a proof in which IP is supplanted by CP. Notice that it parallels a normal Indirect Proof for the first eight steps.

$$
\begin{array}{lll}
& 1.\ A \lor (B \cdot C) & \\
& 2.\ A \supset C \qquad / \therefore C & \\
& 3.\ \sim C & \\
& 4.\ \sim A & \text{2, 3, MT} \\
& 5.\ \sim B \lor \sim C & \text{3, disj.} \\
& 6.\ \sim (B \cdot C) & \text{5, TE} \\
& 7.\ A & \text{1, 6, canc.} \\
& 8.\ A \cdot \sim A & \text{7, 4, conj.} \\
& 9.\ \sim C \supset (A \cdot \sim A) & \text{3–8, CP} \\
& 10.\ A & \\
& 11.\ \sim \sim A & \text{10, DN} \\
& 12.\ A \supset \sim \sim A & \text{10–11, CP} \\
& 13.\ \sim A \lor \sim \sim A & \text{12, CE} \\
& 14.\ \sim (A \cdot \sim A) & \text{13, TE} \\
& 15.\ \sim \sim C & \text{9, 14, MT} \\
& 16.\ C & \text{15, DN} \\
\end{array}
$$

The earlier proof, using IP, took only ten steps; line (9) was '$\sim \sim C$' by IP and line (10) was 'C' by DN.

Exercises II

For each of the following arguments, construct a proof which employs IP. (CP can be used along with IP, if you wish.)

(a)

1. 1. $A \supset (B \cdot C)$
   2. $(B \vee D) \supset E$
   3. $D \vee A$ / $\therefore E$

☐ **2.** 1. $(A \cdot B) \supset (C \cdot D)$
   2. $B \supset \sim D$ / $\therefore \sim A \vee \sim B$

3. 1. $(A \vee B) \supset (C \cdot D)$
   2. $(C \vee E) \supset (D \supset \sim A)$ / $\therefore \sim A$

4. 1. $W \supset (X \supset Y)$
   2. $W \supset X$
   3. $\sim Z \vee (Y \vee W)$ / $\therefore \sim Z \vee Y$

5. 1. $(B \supset A) \supset C$
   2. $(A \supset B) \supset C$ / $\therefore C$

☐ **6.** 1. $\sim E$ / $\therefore \sim (((A \supset B) \cdot (B \supset C)) \cdot ((A \supset C) \supset E))$

(b)

7. 1. $(\sim T \vee U) \supset (W \cdot X)$
   2. $(W \vee Y) \supset (X \supset T)$ / $\therefore T$

☐ **8.** 1. $(A \cdot B) \vee C$
   2. $\sim C \vee B$ / $\therefore A \supset B$

9. 1. $(A \cdot B) \supset (C \vee D)$
   2. $(A \supset C) \supset (B \supset D)$
   3. B / $\therefore D$

10. 1. $A \supset (\sim B \supset C)$
   2. $(A \supset B) \supset C$ / $\therefore C$

11. 1. $A \equiv (B \equiv C)$ / $\therefore (A \equiv B) \equiv C$

☐ **12.** 1. $(A \cdot B) \equiv \sim C$
   2. $A \supset B$ / $\therefore C \equiv \sim A$

chapter 13

PROVING TAUTOLOGIES;
PROVING LOGICAL EQUIVALENCE

As already noted, the truth-table method is a theoretically effective procedure for showing a statement to be a tautology, or for proving that a pair of statements are truth-functionally equivalent. But with these, as with arguments, it becomes unworkable in practice as the number of letters in the formulae increases. This chapter gives procedures for applying the method of derivation to proofs of tautologousness and logical equivalence.

§13.1 Entailment

As a preliminary, it will be helpful to understand the notion of "entailment." One statement is said to **entail** another if it is impossible for the first to be true without the second also being true. Or, stating it in the form of a definition:

> **Entailment.** A statement p **entails** a statement q if and only if it is impossible for $(p \cdot \sim q)$ to be true.

For example, the statement '$A \cdot B$' entails the statement 'A', since it is impossible for the former to be true without the latter also being true. Entailment is not confined to single statements; a collection of statements is also said to entail a further statement if it is impossible for every member of the collection to be true without the further statement also being true. For example, the premisses of a valid argument entail its conclusion.

A statement cannot validly be derived from another unless it is entailed by that other. Thus, every valid derivation may be regarded as a proof of entailment.

§13.2 Proving Tautologies

The first way of proving that a statement is a tautology involves the Rule of Indirect Proof and is based upon three facts:

1. The negation of any tautology is a contradiction, and the negation of any contradiction is a tautology.
2. Whatever entails a contradiction must also be a contradiction.
3. Whatever is entailed by a tautology will also be a tautology.

The first two facts have the following consequences: If we can prove that a statement entails a contradiction, we will have proved that the statement *is* a contradiction; and if we can prove that the negation of a statement is a contradiction, we will have proved that the statement itself is a tautology. That is, we can prove that a statement is a tautology by proving that its negation entails a contradiction.

A proof of a tautology (unlike a proof of an argument) *starts out* with an assumption. It is a proof without premises. To prove that a statement is a tautology by using IP, the procedure is to *assume the negation* of the statement. Then, using the various rules of inference and transformation, an explicit contradiction is derived, and the original assumption is discharged by the IP rule. When this is done, the last line in the derivation—the one after the discharge bar—will be a tautology. For example, here is a proof that '$A \supset (B \supset A)$' is a tautology.

→1.	$\sim(A \supset (B \supset A))$	(IP)
2.	$\sim(\sim A \lor (B \supset A))$	1, CE
3.	$\sim\sim A \cdot \sim(B \supset A)$	2, TD
4.	$\sim(B \supset A)$	3, sev.
5.	$\sim(\sim B \lor A)$	4, CE
6.	$\sim\sim B \cdot \sim A$	5, TD
7.	$\sim A$	6, sev.
8.	$\sim\sim A$	3, sev.
9.	$\sim A \cdot \sim\sim A$	7, 8, conj.
10.	$A \supset (B \supset A)$	1–9, IP, DN

A proof without premises, such as this one, always has the effect of showing that its conclusion is a necessary truth. This may be viewed as an extension of the general fact about proofs: a valid proof shows that its conclusion must be true, given its premises. When the premises are zero in number, it shows that its conclusion must be true, period: its conclusion is a necessary truth. The conclusion to a proof without premises is often referred to as a "zero-premiss conclusion." A zero-premiss conclusion is (in truth-functional logic*) always a tautology. And since whatever is entailed by a tautology will also be a tautology, in a derivation without premises *every* line that is not within the scope of an assumption is a tautology. If a line is not within the scope of an assumption, and there are no premises, then that line must have been derived from a tautology and so will be a tautology itself; hence, every line derived from it alone, or from it together with other tautologies, will be another tautology. As an illustration of this point, in the following proof every line below the discharge bar is a tautology, since none of them lies within the scope of an assumption and the proof is without premises.

$$\begin{array}{lll}
\rightarrow 1. & \sim(A \supset A) & \text{(IP)} \\
2. & \sim(\sim A \lor A) & 1, \text{CE} \\
3. & \sim\sim A \cdot \sim A & 2, \text{TD} \\
\hline
4. & A \supset A & 1\text{--}3, \text{IP, DN} \\
5. & A \supset (A \cdot A) & 4, \text{abs.} \\
6. & \sim A \lor (A \cdot A) & 5, \text{CE} \\
7. & (\sim A \lor A) \cdot (\sim A \lor A) & 6, \text{dist.} \\
8. & (A \supset A) \lor (B \cdot C) & 4, \text{disj.} \\
9. & ((A \supset A) \lor B) \cdot ((A \supset A) \lor C) & 8, \text{dist.} \\
10. & (A \supset A) \lor (D \cdot \sim D) & 4, \text{disj.}
\end{array}$$

Statements are presented for proof of tautologousness by setting them out as zero-premiss conclusions. This is exemplified in the exercises below.

Exercises I

Prove that each of the following is a tautology.

1. $/ \therefore \sim(A \cdot \sim((A \supset B) \supset B))$
2. $/ \therefore \sim B \supset \sim(A \cdot B)$
3. $/ \therefore (A \supset B) \lor (B \supset A)$
4. $/ \therefore (A \supset \sim A) \lor (\sim A \supset A)$
□ 5. $/ \therefore \sim(A \cdot B) \lor \sim(\sim A \cdot \sim B)$
6. $/ \therefore \sim A \supset (A \supset B)$

The second way of proving that a statement is a tautology involves the Rule of Conditional Proof and is based upon the fact that

A conditional is a tautology† if and only if its antecedent entails its consequent.

If a conditional is a tautology, then it is impossible for it to be false; that is, it is impossible for its antecedent to be true and its consequent false, which is precisely the definition of entailment. Thus, a *conditional* may be proven to be a tautology by showing that its antecedent entails its consequent. This

---

*A zero-premiss conclusion in quantifier logic is a "quantifier truth." See Chapters 19, 20.
†Or other necessary truth.

is done by assuming its antecedent, deriving its consequent, and then discharging the assumption by the CP rule, leaving the conditional as a zero-premiss conclusion. For example, here is a proof that '$(A \cdot \sim B) \supset \sim(A \supset B)$' is a tautology.

$$
\begin{array}{lll}
1.\ A \cdot \sim B & / \therefore \sim(A \supset B) \\
2.\ \sim\sim A \cdot \sim B & & 1,\ DN \\
3.\ \sim(\sim A \lor B) & & 2,\ TE \\
4.\ \sim(A \supset B) & & 3,\ CE \\
\hline
5.\ (A \cdot \sim B) \supset \sim(A \supset B) & & 1\text{-}4,\ CP
\end{array}
$$

A proof of a tautology may involve more than one assumption, and it may employ both CP and IP. The only thing to remember is that it is not a proof until every assumption has been discharged. Here, for example, is a proof of

$$/ \therefore (A \supset (B \lor C)) \supset (\sim B \supset (A \supset C))$$

$$
\begin{array}{lll}
1.\ A \supset (B \lor C) & / \therefore \sim B \supset (A \supset C) \\
2.\ \sim B & / \therefore A \supset C \\
3.\ A & / \therefore C \\
4.\ \sim C & (IP) \\
5.\ B \lor C & & 1,\ 3,\ MP \\
6.\ B & & 4,\ 5,\ canc. \\
7.\ B \cdot \sim B & & 2,\ 6,\ conj. \\
8.\ C & & 4\text{-}7,\ IP,\ DN \\
9.\ A \supset C & & 3\text{-}8,\ CP \\
10.\ \sim B \supset (A \supset C) & & 2\text{-}9,\ CP \\
11.\ (A \supset (B \lor C)) \supset (\sim B \supset (A \supset C)) & & 1\text{-}10,\ CP
\end{array}
$$

Exercises II

Prove that each of the following is a tautology.

  1. $/ \therefore A \supset (B \supset A)$
  2. $/ \therefore K \supset ((K \supset L) \supset L)$
  3. $/ \therefore (\sim(F \cdot \sim G) \cdot \sim G) \supset \sim F$
□ **4.** $/ \therefore X \supset (Y \equiv (X \supset Y))$
  5. $/ \therefore ((R \supset S) \supset R) \supset R$
  6. $/ \therefore \sim(((A \supset (B \supset C)) \cdot B) \cdot (A \cdot \sim C))$

§13.3 Proving Logical Equivalence

The procedure for proving that two statements are logically equivalent is merely an extension of the procedures discussed above. It is based upon two facts:

1. Two statements are truth-functionally equivalent if and only if the biconditional having them as its sides is a tautology.
2. A biconditional is a tautology* if and only if its sides entail each other.

A pair of statements are proven equivalent by proving that their biconditional is a tautology; and this is done by proving that each of them entails the other. Assume one of the statements and derive the other, then discharge the assumption by the CP rule. Assume the second statement, derive the first, and discharge the second assumption by the CP rule. Conjoin the two conditionals, and transform the conjunction into a biconditional by BE. This gives the biconditional as a zero-premiss conclusion and shows that its two sides are logically equivalent. For example, here is a proof that '$A \supset B$' is logically equivalent to '$\sim(A \cdot \sim B)$'.

```
  ┌─→1. A ⊃ B      / ∴ ~(A · ~B)
  │ ┌→2. A · ~B      (IP)
  │ │  3. A                               2, sev.
  │ │  4. B                               1, 3, MP
  │ │  5. ~B                              2, sev.
  │ │  6. B · ~B                          5, 6, conj.
  │ └─ 7. ~(A · ~B)                       2–6, IP
  └─── 8. (A ⊃ B) ⊃ ~(A · ~B)            1–7, CP
  ┌─→9. ~(A · ~B)    / ∴ A ⊃ B
  │   10. ~A ∨ ~ ~B                       9, TD
  │   11. ~A ∨ B                          10, DN
  └── 12. A ⊃ B                           11, CE
      13. ~(A · ~B) ⊃ (A ⊃ B)            9–12, CP
      14. ((A ⊃ B) ⊃ ~(A · ~B)) · (~(A · ~B) ⊃ (A ⊃ B))   8, 13, conj.
      15. (A ⊃ B) ≡ ~(A · ~B)            14, BE
```

Exercises III

Prove the following logical equivalences, in each case *without* using the indicated rule or rules.

1. / ∴ $(A \supset B) \equiv (\sim B \supset \sim A)$ without using Contraposition or Modus Tollens.
2. / ∴ $\sim(A \cdot B) \equiv (\sim A \vee \sim B)$ without using Tilde Distribution or Tilde Extraction.
☐ 3. / ∴ $\sim(A \vee B) \equiv (\sim A \cdot \sim B)$ without using Tilde Distribution or Tilde Extraction.
4. / ∴ $(A \supset (B \supset C)) \equiv ((A \cdot B) \supset C)$ without using Exportation.
5. / ∴ $(A \supset B) \equiv (A \supset (A \cdot B))$ without using Absorption.

---

*Or other necessary truth.

6. / ∴ $(A \cdot B) \equiv (B \cdot A)$ without using Transposition or Contraposition or Severance.

7. / ∴ $(A \lor B) \equiv (B \lor A)$ without using Transposition or Contraposition.

□ **8.** / ∴ $A \equiv \sim \sim A$ without using Double Negation.

9. / ∴ $(A \lor (B \cdot C)) \equiv ((A \lor B) \cdot (A \lor C))$ without using Distribution or Extraction.

10. / ∴ $(A \cdot (B \lor C)) \equiv ((A \cdot B) \lor (A \cdot C))$ without using Distribution or Extraction.

11. / ∴ $(A \equiv B) \equiv (\sim A \equiv \sim B)$

chapter 14

PROVING INVALIDITY BY THE
ABBREVIATED TRUTH-TABLE METHOD

§14.1   The Abbreviated Truth-Table Method

The method of derivation cannot be used to prove that an argument is invalid. However, invalidity can be proven by an application of the truth-table method which is generally quicker than constructing a full truth-table. It is called the "abbreviated truth-table" method.*

If an argument is truth-functionally invalid, then its truth-table contains at least one invalidating row; that is to say, if it is invalid, then there is at least one possible combination of truth-values of the *simple* statements in the argument which will make all of its premises true and its conclusion false. Such a combination of truth-values might be called an "invalidating combination," since it generates an invalidating row in the truth-table. If a row in a truth-table is an invalidating row, the base-column portion of that row will be an invalidating combination.

The abbreviated truth-table method is a trial-and-error procedure for arriving at an invalidating combination of truth-values. It serves to *prove* invalidity, since if there is an invalidating combination to be found by this method, it will also show up in the base columns of a full truth-table and will generate an invalidating row. The method consists in attempting, by trial and error, to assign truth-values to the simple statements (capital letters) in an argument in such a way as to make all the premises come out T while the conclusion comes out F. If that can be done, the resulting assignment will be an invalidating combination of truth-values. In order for the method to work, the assignment of truth-values must be *consistent*; that is, every occurrence of the same letter must be assigned the same truth-value.

It is usually, though not always, best to begin by assigning truth-values to the letters in the conclusion in such a way as to make the conclusion come

---

*It is also called the "Trial-and-Error Method" and the "Method of Truth-Functional Interpretation."

out F. Here is a simple illustration. The argument

$$A \supset B$$
$$\sim A \qquad / \therefore \sim B$$

is invalid. To prove it invalid, begin by assigning truth-values to each letter in the conclusion so as to make the conclusion come out F. In this case there is only one possible way to do so:

$$A \supset B$$
$$\sim A \qquad / \therefore \sim B$$
$$\qquad\qquad\qquad \mathbf{F(T)}$$

The only letter in the conclusion is '*B*', and if we assign it the value T, the whole conclusion comes out F. The next step is to assign the same truth-value to every occurrence of '*B*' in the entire argument, thus:

$$A \supset B$$
$$\qquad (\mathrm{T})$$
$$\sim A \qquad / \therefore \sim B$$
$$\qquad\qquad\qquad \mathbf{F(T)}$$

The next step is to try to find a way of assigning truth-values to the other letters in the argument so as to make all of the premisses come out T. One of the premisses is '$\sim A$', and in order for it to come out T the letter '*A*' must be assigned a value of F, thus:

$$A \supset B$$
$$\qquad (\mathrm{T})$$
$$\sim A \qquad / \therefore \sim B$$
$$\mathbf{T(F)} \qquad\quad \mathbf{F(T)}$$

The same value is then assigned to all other occurrences of '*A*', and both premisses come out T while the conclusion has come out F:

$$A \quad \supset \quad B$$
$$(\mathrm{F}) \ \ \mathbf{T} \ \ (\mathrm{T})$$
$$\sim A \qquad / \therefore \sim B$$
$$\mathbf{T(F)} \qquad\quad \mathbf{F(T)}$$

We complete the *proof* that the argument is invalid by writing out the words 'Shown invalid by' followed by the invalidating combination:

Shown invalid by $\dfrac{A \quad B}{\mathrm{F} \quad \mathrm{T}}$

You will not always come up with an invalidating combination on the first try. For example, if there are several different ways for a conclusion to

be false, some of them may not lead to an invalidating combination. If the
first assignment you try does not lead to an invalidating combination, the
only thing to do is try a different assignment. Here is an example:

$A \supset B$
$B \supset \sim C$ $/ \therefore \sim(A \supset C)$

The conclusion is a negation whose negate is '$A \supset C$'; to make the conclusion come out F, truth-values must be assigned so as to make '$A \supset C$' come
out T. However, there are three different assignments which will make
'$A \supset C$' come out T. We choose one of them at random and try it out:

$A \supset B$
$B \supset \sim C$ $/ \therefore \sim(A \supset C)$
                        F (T) T (T)

The same assignments are then given to the other occurrences of 'A' and 'C':

$A \supset B$
(T)
$B \supset \sim C$ $/ \therefore \sim(A \supset C)$
  F(T)   F (T) T (T)

But now there is no way of consistently assigning truth-values to the rest
of the letters (in this case 'B') so as to make all the premisses come out T.
If 'B' is assigned a value of T, that will make the *second* premiss False; but if
'B' is assigned a value of F, that will make the *first* premiss False. Thus, our
original assignment of truth-values to the letters in the conclusion does not
lead to an invalidating combination, and we must try again:

$A \supset B$
$B \supset \sim C$ $/ \therefore \sim(A \supset C)$
                        F (F) T (T)

This assignment is then given to the other occurrences of 'A' and 'C':

$A \supset B$
(F)
$B \supset \sim C$ $/ \therefore \sim(A \supset C)$
  F(T)   F (F) T (T)

Now it is possible to assign truth-values to the rest of the letters so as to make
all the premisses come out T:

$A \supset B$
(F) T (F)
$B \supset \sim C$ $/ \therefore \sim(A \supset C)$
(F) T F(T)   F (F) T (T)

This provides us with an invalidating combination of truth-values, and the argument is

Shown invalid by $\dfrac{A \quad B \quad C}{\text{F} \quad \text{F} \quad \text{T}}$

Exercises I

Prove the invalidity of each of the following arguments.

1. 1. $(A \supset B) \lor (C \supset D)$ $/ \therefore (A \lor C) \supset (B \lor D)$

2. 1. $(A \cdot B) \supset (C \cdot D)$ $/ \therefore (A \supset C) \cdot (B \supset D)$

□ **3.** 1. $(A \supset B) \lor (C \supset D)$
    2. $A \lor C$ $/ \therefore B \lor D$

4. 1. $A \equiv (B \equiv C)$
    2. $(A \equiv B) \equiv C$ $/ \therefore A \equiv C$

5. 1. $A \supset B$
    2. $C \supset \sim D$
    3. $D \supset A$ $/ \therefore \sim B \supset C$

6. 1. $A \supset (B \lor C)$
    2. $B \supset (D \lor E)$
    3. $A \supset \sim E$ $/ \therefore \sim(A \cdot \sim D)$

7. 1. $A \supset (B \equiv C)$
    2. $B \supset (C \equiv D)$
    3. $\sim A \equiv \sim C$ $/ \therefore \sim B \equiv \sim D$

□ **8.** 1. $(A \cdot C) \supset (B \lor D)$
    2. $A \equiv C$
    3. $\sim A \supset (D \supset E)$ $/ \therefore (C \supset D) \supset E$

9. 1. $(A \supset C) \lor (B \supset D)$
    2. $E \supset (A \supset B)$
    3. $\sim(E \supset \sim D)$ $/ \therefore \sim((E \supset A) \supset (E \supset C))$

10. 1. $(A \cdot B) \supset (C \cdot D)$
    2. $\sim E \supset (A \supset B)$
    3. $(E \supset A) \supset \sim C$ $/ \therefore \sim(A \supset D) \cdot E$

§14.2   Other Applications of the Abbreviated Truth-Table Method

The first stage of the abbreviated truth-table method—the trial-and-error assignment of truth-values—has other uses besides proving invalidity. It can also be used to decide *whether* a given argument is valid or invalid, when this is not known in advance. If an argument is valid, there is no invalidating combination of truth-values for its component statements; if it is invalid, then there is at least one invalidating combination. To decide whether or not an argument is (truth-functionally) valid, try *every* possible way of making its conclusion false, to see whether any of them can lead to an invalidating combination. If *none* of the ways of making its conclusion come out F allows all of its premisses to be T, then it is safe to conclude that the argument is valid. But if one of these ways allows all of its premisses to come out T, then of course the argument is invalid.

As an illustration, suppose we do not know whether the following argument is valid or invalid:

$(A \cdot B) \supset (C \cdot \sim D)$
$\sim (A \supset \sim B) \qquad / \therefore \sim (C \equiv D)$

There are two ways for the conclusion of this argument to be false: if '*C*' and '*D*' are both T, and if they are both F. Making the first of these assignments gives us

$(A \cdot B) \supset (C \cdot \sim D)$
$\qquad\qquad\quad (T)\ F\ F(T)$
$\sim (A \supset \sim B) \qquad / \therefore \sim (C \equiv D)$
$\qquad\qquad\qquad\qquad\quad F\ (T)\ T\ (T)$

The consequent of the first premiss has come out F; therefore, the antecedent must also come out F in order for the whole conditional to come out T. In order for the antecedent to come out F, at least one of the letters '*A*', '*B*' must be assigned a value of F. But if '*A*' is assigned a value of F, that will make the *second* premiss come out F; and if '*B*' is assigned a value of F, that will likewise make the second premiss come out F. Thus, our first way of making the conclusion '$\sim (C \equiv D)$' come out F does not permit all the premisses to come out T.

There is still one more way of making the conclusion come out F:

$(A \cdot B) \supset (C \cdot \sim D)$
$\qquad\qquad\quad (F)\ F\ T(F)$
$\sim (A \supset \sim B) \qquad / \therefore \sim (C \equiv D)$
$\qquad\qquad\qquad\qquad\quad F\ (F)\ T\ (F)$

But this leads to the same difficulty as before: there is no consistent way to assign truth-values to '*A*' and '*B*' so as to make both premisses come out T. Thus, neither of the ways of making the conclusion come out F permits all the premisses to come out T, and we may safely infer that the argument is valid.

Having discovered that the argument is valid, we know that its validity can be proven. But knowing that it can be proven is not the same thing as proving it. To give a *proof* that it is valid, it is necessary either to construct an extended proof (that is, a derivation) or to lay out the whole truth-table.

Exercises II

Decide which of the following arguments are valid and which are invalid. Then prove that the valid ones are valid, and prove that the invalid ones are invalid.

□ **1.** 1. $(A \supset B) \supset {\sim} C$
   2. $A \supset (B \supset {\sim} C)$
   3. $A \supset {\sim} B$ / $\therefore$ $B \supset ({\sim} A \supset C)$

2. 1. ${\sim}(A \supset {\sim} B) \cdot C$
   2. ${\sim} D \supset {\sim}(A \cdot B)$
   3. $C \supset {\sim}(E \equiv F)$ / $\therefore$ $[E \cdot (D \supset C)] \supset {\sim} F$

3. 1. ${\sim}(A \supset B) \cdot {\sim}(C \supset D)$
   2. $(B \supset C) \supset E$
   3. $((D \supset E) \supset {\sim} F) \cdot ({\sim}(E \supset F) \supset G)$
   4. ${\sim}(F \equiv (G \equiv {\sim} H))$ / $\therefore$ $H \supset D$

□ **4.** 1. ${\sim} A \lor {\sim}(B \supset C)$
   2. $(A \cdot C) \lor (D \cdot E)$
   3. $({\sim} D \supset {\sim} E) \supset {\sim} B$
   4. $A \cdot K$ / $\therefore$ $K \supset {\sim} B$

5. 1. $(A \lor B) \lor {\sim}(C \cdot D)$
   2. $(C \supset {\sim} E) \cdot (D \supset {\sim} F)$
   3. ${\sim}(E \lor F) \supset (A \lor B)$ / $\therefore$ ${\sim} A \supset (E \supset F)$

6. 1. $A \cdot (B \cdot (C \cdot (D \cdot E)))$
   2. $(A \supset F) \lor ((C \supset G) \lor (E \supset H))$
   3. $({\sim}({\sim} F \supset G) \supset H) \supset K$
   4. ${\sim}(D \supset K)$ / $\therefore$ $B \supset F$

The trial-and-error method may also be used to discover the *logical status* of a compound statement. First, attempt to assign truth-values to the letters in such a way as to make the statement come out F. If none turns up after trying every possible way, then the statement is a tautology. If one does turn up, then the statement is either a contingency or a contradiction. To decide which, attempt to assign truth-values in such a way as to make the statement come out T. If none turns up after trying every possible way, then the statement is a contradiction. If one does turn up, then you will have discovered that it is possible for the statement to be T as well as F, and thus that it is a contingency.

Exercises III

Decide the logical status of each of the following statements.

□ **1.** $E \supset ((A \supset B) \supset ((B \supset {\sim} E) \supset {\sim} B))$
   2. ${\sim}({\sim}(A \supset B) \supset (B \supset A))$
   3. $((A \cdot B) \supset {\sim}(A \lor B)) \cdot ({\sim}(A \lor B) \supset (A \cdot B))$
□ **4.** $(C \lor D) \supset (({\sim} C \cdot B) \lor ({\sim} D \cdot A))$

5. $\sim(A \cdot \sim B) \supset (\sim(A \supset B) \supset (A \cdot B))$

6. $\sim(((A \cdot B) \cdot C) \cdot \sim(\sim A \equiv \sim(B \cdot C)))$

☐ 7. $(A \vee (B \vee \sim C)) \supset (\sim A \supset (\sim C \supset B))$

8. $(((((A \supset B) \supset A) \supset B) \supset A) \supset B) \supset B$

The trial-and-error method can be used to check the truth-functional *consistency* of a set of statements. If a (consistent) assignment of truth-values to single letters can be given, so as to make all the statements come out T at the same time, the set is truth-functionally consistent; if not, not.

Exercises IV

For each valid argument in Exercises II, check to see whether it is a good argument.

Quantifier Logic

(a) *Monadic*
Predicate Logic

chapter 15

SINGULAR STATEMENTS; PROPOSITIONAL FUNCTIONS; QUANTIFIERS

In Part I we have been concerned exclusively with the logic of compound statements; the simple statements occurring in the compounds have been disregarded except for our subjecting them to drastic and heavy-handed abbreviation. We now turn our attention to the internal structure of (a certain class of) truth-functionally simple statements—namely, those capable of logical treatment by the techniques of what is called "quantifier logic."* As we shall see, this turns out to be quite a large class of statements.

§15.1 Singular Statements

Among simple statements (those which are not truth-functional compounds) the most basic type is the **singular statement**. Singular statements come in varying degrees of complexity, but the most elementary type is one in which an individual (person, thing, or whatever) is specified by name, and something is said about it. Some examples of elementary singular statements are:

1. Jones is fat.
2. DuBarry was a lady.
3. Nobody can whistle like Elmo.
4. Cincinnati has a rather large population.
5. The American Balloon-Eating Championship is held by Oscar Watkins.
6. Five is a prime number.
7. Excalibur remained caught in the stone.
8. Blarney Castle has a colorful history.
9. Africa is a continent.
10. Omicron Ceti varies greatly in magnitude.

---

*Quantifier logic is also called "predicate logic." The segment of quantifier logic covered in this book is called "first order predicate logic." Part II (a) treats *monadic*, or "single-object" predicates. *Polyadic*, or "many-object," predicates are examined in Part II (b).

These elementary singular statements have three characteristics in common:

(a) In each case an *individual* is specified. The individuals in the examples above are, respectively,

1a. Jones (a person)	6a. 5 (a number)
2a. DuBarry (a person)	7a. Excalibur (a sword)
3a. Elmo (a person)	8a. Blarney Castle (an edifice)
4a. Cincinnati (a city)	9a. Africa (a continent)
5a. Oscar Watkins (a person)	10a. Omicron Ceti (a star)

(b) In each case the individual is specified by *name*. In logic, "names" are the sorts of words (or expressions) that grammarians classify as *proper* names. Thus, 'cat' is not a name, although 'Cat Stevens' is.*

(c) In each case, something is asserted of the named individual; in (1) it is asserted of Jones that he is fat; in (5) it is asserted of Oscar Watkins that he holds the American Balloon-Eating Championship; in (6) it is asserted of Five that it is a prime number; and so on.

These three items—(a), (b), and (c)—are the defining characteristics of all singular statements; any statement which has all three is a singular statement, and any which does not have all three is not.

These defining characteristics of singular statements suggest a natural mode of analysis for purposes of logic. Any singular statement may be divided into two parts: the part which specifies the individual, and the part which says something about it. The first is called the **subject expression**; the second, the **predicate expression**. We have already listed the subject expressions of (1)–(10); the predicate expressions are:

1b. _____ is fat
2b. _____ was a lady
3b. Nobody can whistle like _____
4b. _____ has a rather large population
5b. The American Balloon-Eating Championship is held by _____
6b. _____ is a prime number
7b. _____ remained caught in the stone
8b. _____ has a colorful history
9b. _____ is a continent
10b. _____ varies greatly in magnitude

In each case, a "blank space" is included along with the rest of the predicate expression to indicate the place where the name goes. This is not an idle gesture; predicate expressions, together with their blank spaces where names may be inserted, form the whole groundwork for quantifier logic.

Whenever a subject expression and a predicate expression are appropriately put together, the result is a (singular) statement. And so, we might give

_____
*Expressions such as 'the third American president' or 'the tallest man in Kansas' are not names either. Rather, they are called "definite descriptions." Their full logical treatment is given later on, so for the time being we shall ignore them.

a preliminary formal definition of "predicate expression" as follows: A predicate expression is an expression which contains a blank space, such that when a proper name is inserted in the blank space the result is a statement.

In logic, it is standard practice to represent the blank spaces in predicate expressions not by a line (as in 1b–10b above), but by a lower-case letter called an **individual variable**. The letters most commonly used as individual variables are 'x', 'y', and 'z'—though, in a pinch, other letters may also be used. Thus, the logician's way of writing out the predicate expressions in the list above would be:

1c. x is fat
2c. y was a lady
3c. Nobody can whistle like z
4c. x has a rather large population
5c. The American Balloon-Eating Championship is held by y
6c. z is a prime number
7c. x remained caught in the stone
8c. y has a colorful history
9c. z is a continent
10c. x varies greatly in magnitude

The individual variables in these predicate expressions are simply *place-markers*; they indicate where names may be inserted to form statements. They are not themselves the names of anything; they are just a different way of indicating the blank spaces represented by blank lines in (1b)–(10b). Thus, none of (1c)–(10c) is a proposition; they are just predicate expressions. They don't assert anything of anything, and they are neither true nor false.

§15.2 Propositional Functions

A predicate expression written in this way (with individual variables indicating the blank spaces) is called a **propositional function.*** Thus each of (1c)–(10c) above is a propositional function. A formal definition of this notion is:

> *Propositional Function.* A propositional function is an expression which contains at least one individual variable, such that when all of its individual variables are replaced by names of individuals, the result is (expresses) a proposition (statement).

This definition hints at the fact that a propositional function may contain

---

*Other writers on the subject have used 'propositional function' to signify an abstract entity distinct from, but designated by, the predicate expression. Such is not our usage here.

more than one individual variable. We shall get to propositional functions of
that sort later on. For now, we need be aware only that there *are* propositional functions containing several variables.

Propositional functions are also called "open sentences," because they are
sentences (or rather, sentence-fragments) with an open space in them, which
become full-fledged sentences when the open space is filled with a name.
Propositional functions are also called "conditions," for reasons that will be
apparent later on. Since the phrase "propositional function" is long and
cumbersome, we shall generally refer to them simply as "functions." In the
remainder of this book the following four expressions will be taken to mean
exactly the same thing:

      propositional function   condition
      open sentence   function

A function containing only one individual variable is called a **single-place
function**. Thus, each of (1c)–(10c) is a single-place function. They are so
called because they have an opening for only one name to be inserted into
them. Single-place functions are also called "**monadic** functions" (from
mono, meaning *single*), or "functions of one variable."

When the variable in a single-place function is replaced with the name of
an individual, the resulting statement is called a **substitution instance** of the
function. More formally:

> *Substitution Instance* (of a monadic function).   If a statement can be obtained
> from a monadic function by replacing the variable in the function with the
> name of an individual, that statement is a substitution instance of that func-
> tion.

Every singular statement is a substitution instance of some propositional
function. For example, (1) above is a substitution instance of (1c). Similarly
for the others. A function is said to **generate** its substitution instances (it
generates them **by substitution**), and so (1c) would be said to generate (1),
along with any other proposition resulting from replacing the variable in
(1c) with a proper name.

An individual is said to **satisfy** a condition (function) if replacement of
the variable by that individual's name results in a *true* proposition. For
example, Baltimore satisfies the condition '*x* is a city', since the statement
'Baltimore is a city' happens to be true. On the other hand, Australia does
not satisfy the condition '*x* is a city', because the statement 'Australia is a
city' does not happen to be true. Australia is a continent, and a country.

Occasionally we wish to speak of the "properties" (or attributes, or
qualities) that an individual has. For logical purposes, this may be regarded
simply as an alternative way of speaking of the conditions that the individual
satisfies. A property (attribute, or whatever) is an abstract entity designated

by a propositional function. For instance, 'x is fat' designates the property of being fat; 'x has a colorful history' designates the property of having a colorful history; 'x varies greatly in magnitude' designates the property of varying greatly in magnitude; and so on. Saying that an individual has a certain property is the same as saying that it satisfies the function designating that property, and the two may be regarded as alternative ways of saying the same thing. Thus it doesn't matter whether we say that Nero has the property of being fat, or that Nero satisfies the function 'x is fat', since either claim will be true just in case Nero is fat.

Exercises I

Decide which of the following are singular statements and which are not. For the singular statements, give the propositional functions they are substitution instances of.

1. Socrates is human.
☐ 2. A policeman is human.
3. Grass is green.
4. Oregon is green.
☐ 5. Babe Ruth is the greatest baseball player of all time.
6. The greatest baseball player of all time played for the Yankees.
☐ 7. Babe Ruth played for the Yankees.
8. All the world loves a lover.
9. All the world loves Romeo.
10. Earth is thicker than water.
☐ 11. Earth is a satellite of the sun.
12. The sun is a star.
13. Independence is cherished by all men.
☐ 14. Independence is a city in Missouri.
15. Washington was America's first president.
16. Washington is where the White House is located.
17. Washington is on the west coast.
☐ 18. The love of money is the root of all evil.
19. The love of Edna is the root of all evil.
20. He is cruel to his sister.
21. Percy is cruel to his sister.
☐ 22. The bank has many depositors.
☐ 23. The Bank of America has many depositors.
24. A doctor will be here soon.
25. The doctor will be here soon.
26. Doctor Smith will be here soon.

§15.3 Abbreviating Monadic Functions
and Singular Statements

In truth-functional logic, simple statements were abbreviated as a single capital letter. In predicate logic, simple monadic functions are abbreviated as a capital letter followed by an individual variable (the variable in the function). The capital letter is normally the initial letter of some key word in the function, though this of course is not mandatory. For example, the function

    1. *x* is fat

may be abbreviated as

    1a. *Fx*

Similarly, the function

    2. The American Balloon-Eating Championship is held by *y*

may be abbreviated as

    2a. *Cy*

and the function

    3. *z* is a prime number

may be abbreviated as

    3a. *Pz*

Exercises II
Abbreviate each of the propositional functions discovered while doing Exercises I.

The procedure for abbreviating singular statements is quite similar. It results from the fact that every singular statement is a substitution instance of some propositional function.

When a singular statement is a substitution instance of a function, the name in the statement is called a **substituent for** the variable in the function. For example,

    4. Jones is fat.

is a substitution instance of

    4a. *x* is fat

hence, the name 'Jones' in (4) is a **substituent for** the variable '*x*' in (4a). A singular statement is abbreviated just like the function it is a substitution instance of, except that the variable is replaced by its substituent. Thus (ignoring for the moment what is said in the next paragraph), (4) above will be abbreviated as

    4b. *F jones*

Since the purpose of logical abbreviation is to produce formulae that are tidy and easy to work with, it is the practice to abbreviate not only functions, but proper names as well. A proper name is always abbreviated as a single *lower-case* letter, which is underlined. Thus, the name 'Jones' might be abbreviated as '$\underline{j}$' and so the complete abbreviation of (4) would be

   4c. *F$\underline{j}$*

The underline is not simply an ornament. It is possible, in practice, to use *any* lower-case letter (not merely '*x*', '*y*', or '*z*') as an individual variable. The purpose of the underline is to show that the lower-case letter is not being used as a variable, but as an abbreviated proper name. In logic, an abbreviated proper name is called an **individual constant**. An individual constant denotes a specific individual—the one whose name it abbreviates; whereas the variables in propositional functions do not stand for any individual at all—they simply indicate blank spaces where names may be inserted. As further illustrations,

   5. Nobody can whistle like Elmo.

would be completely abbreviated as

   5a. *W$\underline{e}$*

and

   6. The American Balloon-Eating Championship is held by Oscar Watkins.

would be completely abbreviated as

   6a. *C$\underline{w}$*

Exercises III

Abbreviate each of the singular statements in Exercises I.

§15.4   Quantifiers

A singular statement is an assertion to the effect that a specific, named individual satisfies a certain function. Another sort of statement, which superficially resembles a singular statement, is one which asserts not that a specific individual satisfies a certain function, but only that *some individual or other* satisfies that function. Such statements are called "quantified statements." An example would be the statement

   1. Something is fat.

This is not a *substitution instance* of the function '*x* is fat', and it would be a mistake to translate (1) as

   F$\underline{s}$

since the word 'something' is not the name of any particular individual. Rather, (1) is the sort of statement called, in logic, a **quantification** of the function '*x* is fat'. The proper translation of (1) requires the use of a unary operator called a **quantifier**. There are two types of quantifiers; the type required in this case is called an "existential quantifier."

An **existential quantifier** consists of a capital letter E written backwards, followed by an individual variable, with the whole enclosed in parentheses. For example, '($\exists x$)' is an existential quantifier, and '($\exists y$)' is another. Existential quantifiers are read as "Something *x* is such that . . . ," "Something *y* is such that . . . ," and so on. When an existential quantifier is attached to the lefthand side of a function containing the same variable, the result is a quantified statement to the effect that some individual or other satisfies that function, and such a statement is called the **existential quantification** of that function. Thus, using a quantifier, the proper translation of (1) would be

    1a. ($\exists x$)*x* is fat

or, with abbreviations,

    1b. ($\exists x$)*Fx*

which is the existential quantification of the function '*x* is fat'. The standard way of reading this aloud is "Something *x* is such that *x* is fat." (The purpose of the variable in the quantifier will become clear later on, when we study multiple quantification.) In logic, 'some' is always taken to mean 'at least one'—that is, 'one or more'. Therefore, an existentially quantified statement is understood to be true if there is* at least one thing (that is, one thing or more) which satisfies the quantified function. Statement (1a) will be true if there is one thing or more than one thing which is fat, and it will be false if there are no things which are fat.

English words and phrases which are translated by means of quantifiers are called "quantifier expressions." The word 'something' is an existential quantifier expression. Others are 'some', 'there is', 'there are', 'exist', 'at least one', and so on, and all of these are interpreted, in logic, as meaning *at least one*. For example, all of the following statements

    2. Something is a white elephant.
    3. White elephants exist.
    4. There are white elephants.
    5. There is at least one white elephant.
    6. At least one white elephant exists.
    7. There are some white elephants.

will be translated indifferently as

    8. ($\exists x$)*x* is a white elephant

---

*Or ever was, or ever will be. In logic, quantifier expressions are construed as "tenseless"— they apply to past and present and future all at once. Temporal restrictions, if any, must be expressed within the predicate expression.

This does not accord precisely with normal English usage. For example, we might normally regard (4) as saying that there are *several* white elephants—that is, more than one. Nevertheless, it is the standard convention in logic to interpret them all—in fact, to interpret any quantifier expression that concerns less than everything—on the model of "at least one," unless the quantifier expression explicitly mentions some number greater than one. (The treatment of such expressions will be covered later on.) Thus, even a statement such as "There are several white elephants" would be translated as (8).

Exercises IV

Translate the following, first without abbreviating the functions and then abbreviating fully.

1. There are living creatures on Mars.
2. Several things are larger than the solar system.
□ 3. Something is rotten in Denmark.
4. At least one unicorn exists.
5. There are lots of green Chevrolets.
□ 6. Many starving people exist.
7. There is a place called Shangri-La.
8. Carnivorous cows exist.
□ 9. All men have something in common.
10. Jones has come here to borrow at least one thing.

The second type of quantifier is called a **universal quantifier**. It is used to translate statements which assert that *everything* satisfies a certain propositional function, such as the statement

9. Everything has some value.

A universal quantifier consists of an individual variable enclosed in parentheses. For example, '(x)' is a universal quantifier, and '(y)' is another. When a universal quantifier is attached to a function containing the same variable, the result is a statement to the effect that each and every individual in the universe satisfies that function; such a statement is called the **universal quantification** of the function. A universally quantified statement is false if there is even one thing that does not satisfy the function in question. The translation of (9), using a universal quantifier, would be

9a. $(x)x$ has some value

or, with abbreviations,

9b. $(x)Vx$

Universal quantifiers are read as "Everything x is such that . . . ," "Everything y is such that . . . ," and so on. For example, (9a) would be read as "Every-

thing x is such that x has some value." Other common ways of reading the
universal quantifier are "Each thing x is such that . . . ," "For all individuals
x . . . ," "No matter which thing x you choose . . . ," "For any individual
x . . . ," and so on.

Exercises V

Translate the following, first without abbreviating the functions and then abbreviating fully.

☐ **1.** All things are interesting.
  2. Everything is a white elephant.
  3. Everything belongs to the government.
☐ **4.** The owner of the bank hates everything.
  5. Anything is better than starvation.

You should never try to translate a singular statement (or any other) by
putting a *constant* inside a quantifier: quantifiers with constants in them do
not make sense. For example, if Albert's name is abbreviated as 'a', the quantifier '($\exists a$)' would have to be read as "Something Albert is such that . . ."
and the quantifier '(a)' would have to be read as "Everything Albert is such
that . . ." or "For all individuals Albert . . . ," which are unintelligible gibberish. A properly written quantifier must contain an individual *variable*,
and the function it quantifies must contain the same variable.

§15.5 'Nothing', 'There are no . . . .'
and Related Matters

The word 'nothing' is not the opposite of 'everything'; it is the opposite
of 'something'. This is reflected in the fact that a pair of statements such as

  1. Nothing is older than the pyramids.
  2. Something is older than the pyramids.

have precisely opposite truth-conditions. The one is true if and only if the
other is false, and vice versa. Thus, statements involving the quantifier expression 'nothing' may be translated as the negations of statements involving the
quantifier expression 'something'. (1) may be treated as the negation of (2).
The proper translation of (2), using an existential quantifier, is

  2a. ($\exists x$)x is older than the pyramids

and so (1) may be translated as

  1a. $\sim$($\exists x$)x is older than the pyramids

In general, a statement involving the expression 'nothing' can always be
translated as the negation of an existentially quantified statement. Similarly

for the statements involving the quantifier expression 'there are no . . .', such as

    3. There are no unicorns.

This is the denial of the statement 'There are unicorns', and so its proper translation is

    3a. $\sim(\exists x)x$ is a unicorn

Statements such as (3), which assert that things of a certain kind do not exist, are called "negative existential statements." Negative existential statements may always be translated as the negation of existential statements; for instance,

    4. Dragons do not exist.

may be translated as

    4a. $\sim(\exists x)x$ is a dragon

Exercises VI

Translate the following, first without abbreviating the functions and then abbreviating fully.

☐ **1.** Nothing matters.
    2. There aren't any mermaids.
    3. Goblins are nonexistent.
☐ **4.** The watchman saw nothing.
    5. No true Christians exist.
    6. There is nothing that can live in a vacuum.
    7. There are no honest politicians.
☐ **8.** Different persons have nothing in common.
    9. There does not exist a five-sided triangle.
    10. Carnivorous cows do not exist.

chapter 16

COMPLEX FUNCTIONS;
CATEGORICAL STATEMENTS;
SOME TRANSFORMATION RULES

§16.1 Complex Functions

The singular statement

    1. Bessie is a brown cow.

ascribes to Bessie the attribute of being a brown cow; that is, it asserts that Bessie satisfies the function

    1a. x is a brown cow

This attribute, the property of being a brown cow, is called a "complex property." The notion of a complex property may be explained briefly as follows: if a singular statement (about some individual a) is equivalent to— says the same thing as—some *compound* statement whose components are about a, then the original singular statement ascribes a complex property to a. For example, (1) above says the same thing as the compound statement

    2. Bessie is brown · Bessie is a cow

whose components are about Bessie. Therefore the property ascribed to Bessie in (1) [and in (2)] is a complex property. In this case it is a conjunctive property, since (2) is a conjunction, and we can speak of its "conjuncts" as the properties of brownness and cowhood.

    Saying that Bessie has this conjunctive property is the same as saying that Bessie satisfies the propositional function

    2a. x is brown · x is a cow

which is an example of a **complex function** (in this case a *conjunctive* function). The complex function (2a) is equivalent to the simple function (1a), in the sense that whatever satisfies one of them will also satisfy the other. The difference between them is that (1a), being simple (non-compound), doesn't reveal on its face the nature of the complex property which it designates: it more or less conceals the fact that being a brown cow is a *conjunctive* property,

160

whereas (2a) makes this explicit by its very structure. Thus if 'Bessie is a brown cow' were translated and abbreviated as a substitution instance of (1a), the result would be

  1b. *Db̲*

which gives no indication that the property designated by the (abbreviated) function '*Dx*' is complex. On the other hand, if it were translated and abbreviated as a substitution instance of (2a), the result would be

  2b. *Bb̲ · Cb̲*

which clearly reveals the conjunctive nature of the property. Since one of the purposes of logical translation is to reveal the logical character of the statements in question, it is standard practice to translate every singular statement involving a complex property, and every function designating a complex property, as a (substitution instance of a) complex function. (2a) is a logical expansion of (1a); it does not say any more than (1a), it just makes the content of (1a) more explicit.

To keep the nomenclature straight, (2a) is not, as you might think, a "two-place function." It is a "complex single-place function." It is called "complex" because it contains a logical operator—in the present case, a dot for conjunction. It is still a "single-place" function, because its components are themselves single-place functions. (Genuine two-place functions will not appear until the chapter on "Relations.") *Anything that can be expressed by means of a complex function can also be expressed using a synonymous simple function.* [This means, for example, that whatever can be expressed by means of (2a) can also be expressed by means of (1a).] The reason for preferring the complex function is that it makes the logical structure more explicit and allows formal inferences which would not be possible otherwise.

There are as many different types of complex function as there are types of compound statement. For example, the statement

  3. Pierre is not an Irishman.

can be taken simply as an instance of the function

  4. *x* is not an Irishman

to be abbreviated as something like

  4a. *Np̲*

but it can also be seen as an instance of the *negative* function

  5. ~*x* is an Irishman

to be abbreviated as

  5a. ~*Ip̲*

Similarly, the statement

  6. Smith is either wounded or dead.

can be seen as an instance of the *disjunctive* function

    6a. x is wounded $\lor$ x is dead

to be abbreviated as

    6b. $W\underline{s} \lor D\underline{s}$

Similarly, the statement

    7. Andrew is mortal if he is human.

can be seen as an instance of the *conditional* function

    7a. x is human $\supset$ x is mortal

to be abbreviated as

    7b. $H\underline{a} \supset M\underline{a}$

and so on.

    Just as with compound statements, we can speak of the **components** of a complex function—for example, the conjuncts of a conjunctive function, the antecedent and consequent of a conditional function, and so on. An individual satisfies a complex function if and only if the result of replacing each occurrence of the variable with that individual's name is a true statement. Thus, for example, an individual satisfies a conjunctive function if and only if it satisfies both conjuncts; an individual satisfies a disjunctive function if and only if it satisfies at least one disjunct; an individual satisfies a conditional function if and only if it either satisfies the consequent or fails to satisfy the antecedent; and so on.

    Quantifiers may be applied to complex functions the same as to simple functions. For example, the statement 'Something is a brown cow' or 'Brown cows exist' may conveniently be translated as the existentially quantified complex function

    8. $(\exists x)(x$ is brown $\cdot$ x is a cow$)$

Similarly, the statement 'Everything is mortal if human' may be translated as the universally quantified complex function

    9. $(x)(x$ is human $\supset$ x is mortal$)$

When quantifying over a complex function (with more than one component) it is necessary to enclose the function in parentheses. This is to assure that the entire complex function falls "within the scope" of the quantifier. The notion of the "scope" of a quantifier will be given a formal definition later on. But informally, we can say that it is that portion of the formula which the quantifier asserts to be satisfied (or universally satisfied), and that the scope of a quantifier is always the smallest portion of the formula that the punctuation permits. For example, in the formula

    10. $(\exists x)x$ is brown $\cdot$ x is a cow

only the first conjunct is within the scope of the quantifier, and so (10) is not a quantified statement at all, but a peculiar sort of propositional function, since what it says is

10a. "Something is brown, and _____ is a cow."

Thus, it is necessary to insert punctuation in such a way that the entire function we wish to quantify over falls within the scope of the quantifier.

Exercises I

Translate each of the following either as an instance of a complex function or as a quantification over a complex function, first with the components unabbreviated and then with them abbreviated.

   1. Williams is a wealthy merchant.
   2. There are green lizards.
   3. Everything is either illegal or immoral.
☐ **4.** If Smith is alive he is very fortunate.
   5. Nothing is a five-sided triangle.
☐ **6.** Purple cows do not exist.
   7. If Smith is not alive he is unfortunate.
   8. At least one non-contagious disease exists.
☐ **9.** Everything is both illegal and immoral.
  10. Something is either brown or not a cow.

§16.2 Categorical Statements

A class of statements traditionally regarded as having great importance in logic are **categorical statements**. A standard definition is the following:

> *Categorical Statement.* A categorical statement is one asserting that all things of a specified kind, or some things of a specified kind, have a certain characteristic or attribute, or that they lack a certain characteristic or attribute.

From this definition, it follows that there are four different sorts of categorical statements: (1) the sort which asserts that *all* things of a given kind *have* a certain characteristic; (2) the sort which asserts that *all* things of a given kind *lack* a certain characteristic; (3) the sort which asserts that *some* things of a given kind *have* a certain characteristic; (4) the sort which asserts that *some* things of a given kind *lack* a certain characteristic. Certain grammatical forms commonly used to express categorical statements are called the **standard forms** for categorical statements. Where '*S*' and '*P*' represent grammatically appropriate general descriptive expressions (nouns or noun phrases),* the four standard forms for categorical statements may be given as follows:

1. Every *S* is a *P*.   (A)
2. No *S* is a *P*.   (E)
3. Some *S* is a *P*.   (I)
4. Some *S* is not a *P*.   (O)

Examples of categorical statements having each of these standard forms are:

1a. Every tiger is a maneater.
2a. No tiger is a maneater.
3a. Some tiger is a maneater.
4a. Some tiger is not a maneater.

Categorical statements which are about everything of a given kind are called **Universal** statements; thus, (1a) and (2a) are both Universal, and in fact any categorical statement having either form (1) or form (2) will be a Universal statement. Categorical statements which are about *some* things of a given kind are called **Particular** statements;† thus, (3a) and (4a) are both Particular, and any categorical statement having either form (3) or form (4) will be a Particular statement.

Categorical statements which assert that things *have* a certain property are called **Affirmative** statements; thus, (1a) and (3a) are both Affirmative statements, and any categorical statement having either form (1) or form (3) will be an Affirmative statement. Categorical statements which assert that things *lack* a certain property are called **Negative** statements; thus, (2a) and (4a) are both Negative statements, and any categorical statement having either form (2) or form (4) will be a Negative statement.

This means that the four types of categorical statement may be characterized as follows:

1. Universal Affirmative   (A)
2. Universal Negative   (E)
3. Particular Affirmative   (I)
4. Particular Negative   (O)

For reasons not historically important, each of the four standard forms has been tagged with one of the four vowels 'A', 'E', 'I', 'O', as indicated. Thus, traditionally, Universal Affirmative statements have been called "A" propositions; Universal Negative statements have been called "E" propositions; and so on. Since this is a convenient mode of reference, we shall continue to use it in this book.

---

*For purposes of phrasing things in "standard form," other types of general descriptive expression may easily be paraphrased into nouns or noun phrases by grammatical transformations or the use of neutral parameters such as 'thing which', as discussed in the next section.
†Following standard logical practice, 'some' is here understood to signify 'one or more'—that is, 'at least one'.

Exercises II

For each of the following categorical propositions, indicate whether it is an "A", "E", "I", or "O" proposition, and whether it is or is not in standard form.

☐ **1.** No cat is a reptile.

   2. Some crow is not honest.

   3. Some Eastern European is a Bulgarian.

   4. Every even number is expressible as the sum of two prime numbers.

☐ **5.** All cats are mammals.

   6. No crow is purple.

   7. Some crow is a tame bird.

   8. Some even numbers are smaller than 10.

   9. Every crow flies.

☐ **10.** Some Eastern European is not a vegetarian.

☐ **11.** No even number is an exact multiple of 3.

  12. Some cat is striped.

  13. Some cat is not an edible animal.

  14. Every Eastern European is a slave of the Soviet Union.

  15. No Eastern European is capable of learning logic.

☐ **16.** Some even number is not evenly divisible by 2.

§16.3 Paraphrasing into Standard Form

Our present interest in standard-form categorical statements is prompted by the fact that it is possible to give simple and *exceptionless* rules for translating them into the symbols of quantifier logic. Unfortunately, categorical statements are not always expressed in standard form. Therefore, in order to be able to take full advantage of the translation rules, it is worthwhile to understand something about how to paraphrase categorical statements to put them in standard form, before starting out to translate them.

The invariant features of standard-form categorical statements are these: In each case, the statement starts out with a quantifier word: 'Every', 'No', or 'Some'. This is followed by a word or phrase designating the kind of thing the statement is about (tiger, Eastern European, or whatever), which is called the **subject** of the statement. The subject is followed by the word 'is', which is called the **copula**.* The copula is followed by a word or phrase for the kind of thing (maneater, chess-player) that items of the subject-kind are said to be (or not be). This word or phrase is called the **predicate** of the statement. Grammatical requirements dictate that the subject and the predicate

---

*A copula, like a quantifier expression, is "tenseless": it refers indifferently to past, present, and future.

be phrased in the singular always. This standard structure can be schematized as:

Quantifier word—subject—copula—(not)—predicate.

Categorical statements in everyday English frequently deviate from this standard structure. Every categorical contains both a subject and a predicate, but the quantifier word is often either missing or different from the standard one, and the copula may be missing or represented by some form of the verb 'to be' other than the standard 'is'. For example, the statement

1. Lobsters are crustaceans.

is a categorical statement which is not in standard form, since it contains no quantifier word and its copula is plural. But even without a quantifier word, (1) would clearly be intended as a Universal statement about every lobster in general. And since it is an Affirmative statement, what is required to paraphrase it into standard form is to supply the quantifier word 'Every' and singularize the copula and the terms, so that we have the "A" proposition

1a. Every lobster is a crustacean.

If a categorical statement does not contain a quantifier word, it is uniform practice in logic to regard it as a Universal statement. This is not merely a stipulation; in ordinary discourse, when we utter a categorical statement without bothering to restrict it (by a word such as 'some', for instance), the normal way of understanding it would be as a Universal claim, and this is just the way such statements are treated in logic. As another example, consider the statement:

2. Lobsters are not molluscs.

This categorical statement contains no quantifier word, hence is to be treated as a Universal statement. Since it is also Negative, the appropriate paraphrase will be as a Universal Negative or "E" proposition—that is, as

2a. No lobster is a mollusc.

As another example, consider the statement

3. Every dog barks.

Here we have a categorical statement which is not in standard form, since it contains no copula. But it cannot be paraphrased into standard form simply by inserting the copula 'is', since the result would be 'Every dog is barks', which doesn't make sense. In addition to inserting the copula, we must also paraphrase the predicate in order to make the sentence grammatical. This is normally done either by using a verbal parameter, such as the phrase 'thing which', or by paraphrasing the verb into a noun form. For instance, (3) can be paraphrased into standard form either as

3a. Every dog is a thing which barks.

or as

3b. Every dog is a barker.

(3a) employs a parameter; (3b) involves paraphrasing the verb 'bark'; either is acceptable as a way of paraphrasing (3) into standard form.

Consider now the categorical statement

4. Fish breathe water.

which lacks both quantifier word and copula. Since it has no quantifier word, it is Universal, and since it is Affirmative, it is to be paraphrased into an "A" proposition. It must also be provided with a copula, and a parameter must be added to the predicate. The final result of all this will be

4a. Every fish is a thing that breathes water.

This may be contrasted with the statement

5. Fish don't fly.

Since (5) contains no quantifier word, it is to be treated as Universal. Since it is Negative, it is to be paraphrased into a Universal Negative or "E" proposition. A copula must also be supplied, and the predicate must be doctored up to make it grammatical. The result will be

5a. No fish is a thing that flies.

When a categorical statement contains the quantifier words 'any', 'all', or 'each', it is (except in special *negative* cases described later on) to be paraphrased as a Universal statement. In such cases, the copula may have to be changed from 'are' to 'is' and the subject and predicate may have to be doctored to make the final result grammatical. For example, the statement

6. All whales are mammals.

is a Universal statement; since it is Affirmative, it is to be paraphrased as an "A" proposition. The copula must be changed from 'are' to 'is', and the subject and predicate must be depluralized to make it grammatical. The result will then be

6a. Every whale is a mammal.

Statements containing 'everything that . . . ' or 'anything that . . . ' paraphrase as Universal statements, the former by an almost unnoticeable transformation. For example, the statement

7. Everything that is harmless is permitted by law.

will paraphrase as

7a. Every thing that is harmless is (a thing that is) permitted by law.

Similarly, the statement

8. Anything that is harmful is immoral.

will paraphrase as

    8a. Every thing that is harmful is (a thing that is) immoral.

or, if 'immoral' is interpreted as a negative property, (8) will paraphrase as

    8b. No thing that is harmful is (a thing that is) moral.

    Categorical statements containing the expression 'not any' paraphrase as Universal Negative propositions. For example,

    9. Not any cat is a reptile.

will paraphrase as the "E" proposition

    9a. No cat is a reptile.

On the other hand, categorical statements containing 'not every' or 'not all' are to be paraphrased as "O" propositions—that is, as *Particular* Negative statements. For example,

    10. Not every tiger is vicious.

will paraphrase as

    10a. Some tiger is not (a) vicious (creature).

Similarly, the statement

    11. Not all cats are black.

will paraphrase as the "O" statement

    11a. Some cat is not (a) black (one).

    Certain words in English, which might be called "semiquantifier words," call for a special parameter in the *subject*. For example, the word 'everyone' calls for the parameter 'persons' in the subject; the statement

    12. Everyone is basically honest.

is to be paraphrased as the Universal statement

    12a. Every person is (a thing that is) basically honest.

and similarly for the word 'anyone'; for example,

    13. Anyone can learn logic.

is to be paraphrased as

    13a. Any person can learn logic.

and thence as

    13b. Every person is a thing that can learn logic.

Another pair of semiquantifier words are 'anytime' and 'always', which normally call for a parameter of 'times' (meaning 'occasions'); for example,

    14. Jones is welcome anytime.

paraphrases as

    14a. Every time is one when Jones is welcome.

Similarly, the statement

15. Wars have always existed.

paraphrases as

15a. Every time is one when wars have existed.

A bit of common sense is sometimes required to paraphrase this sort of statement correctly. For example, the statement

16. The whistle always blows at eight o'clock.

would make very little sense if paraphrased mechanically as

16a. Every time is a time when the whistle blows at eight o'clock.

Rather, the import of (16) is that whenever it is eight o'clock, the whistle blows; and the appropriate standard form paraphrase of this would be

16b. Every time when it is eight o'clock is a time when the whistle blows.

Another reason why the semiquantifier 'always' cannot be treated mechanically is that it is frequently used simply to indicate *invariability* or *unchangingness* without making any direct reference to 'times' at all. For example, in

17. The sun always rises in the east.

the word 'always' refers not to location in time, but to location in *direction*, and the appropriate paraphrase would be

17a. Every place where the sun rises is (a place) in the east.

Semiquantifier words calling for a 'place' parameter are 'everywhere', 'anyplace', and the like. For example,

18. Insects are located everywhere.

will paraphrase as

18a. Every place is an insect-location.

There are also semiquantifier words which call for the statement to be paraphrased as Particular, rather than Universal. Examples are 'sometimes', 'somewhere', 'someplace', 'somebody', 'someone'. For example,

19. Somebody stole my book.

would be paraphrased into standard form as

19a. Some person is a thing which stole my book.

Similarly, the statement

20. I left my book someplace.

would be paraphrased into standard form as

20a. Some place is (a place) where I left my book.

The word 'sometimes', like the word 'always', requires caution. Normally it calls for a 'times' parameter; for example,

21. Sometimes I feel like a motherless child.

will paraphrase as

21a. Some time is (a time) when I feel like a motherless child.

However, there are cases when something else is required. For example,

22. Oysters are poisonous sometimes.

in most ordinary circumstances would not be regarded as being about 'times' at all, but simply as another way of saying

22a. Some oyster is (a) poisonous (thing).

However, if the sense of (22) is that there are seasons of the year when oysters should not be eaten, then the appropriate paraphrase would be

22b. Some time is a time when oysters are poisonous.

Semiquantifier words followed by a "function word" such as 'who', 'where', or 'that' will still normally require their special parameter. For example,

23. Anyone who drinks gasoline is going to be sick.

will paraphrase as

23a. Every *person* who drinks gasoline is (a thing which is) going to be sick.

Similarly,

24. Anywhere where there is smoke, there is fire.

will paraphrase as

24a. Every *place* where there is smoke is one where there is fire.

and so on.

Categorical statements that are not Universal are Particular and are always paraphrased into standard form with 'some', no matter what the original quantifier expression may be. Thus, 'many', 'most', 'lots of', 'nearly all', 'all but a few', 'a few', 'at least one', and so on will be paraphrased indifferently as 'some'. For example,

25. Nearly all tigers are vicious.

will paraphrase as the "I" proposition

25a. Some tiger is (a) vicious (creature).

Likewise, the statement

26. A few butterflies are vicious.

will paraphrase as the "I" proposition

26a. Some butterfly is (a) vicious (creature).

Categorical statements containing the quantifier word 'only' are Universal propositions, and the expression following 'only' is always the *predicate*. Thus, for example, the statement

27. Only *birds* have feathers.

will paraphrase into standard form as the "A" proposition

27a. Every thing that has feathers is a *bird*.

The quantifier expressions 'none except' and 'none but' function the same as 'only'. For instance,

28. None except citizens are eligible for the office.

will paraphrase into standard form as

28a. Every thing that is eligible for the office is a citizen.

and

29. None but the brave deserve the fair.

will paraphrase as

29a. Every thing that deserves the fair is (a) brave (thing).

A bit of thought is sometimes required to decide whether the whole expression following 'only' is the predicate, or whether only part of it is the predicate. For example, the statement

30. Only black leopards are valuable.

understood normally, would *not* mean

30a. Every thing that is valuable is a black leopard.

rather, it would normally mean

30b. Every leopard that is valuable is (a) black (one).

Similarly, the statement

31. Only clear diamonds are useful for jewelry.

would not normally mean

31a. Every thing that is useful for jewelry is a clear diamond.

rather, it would mean

31b. Every diamond that is useful for jewelry is (a) clear (one).

Or, to vary the example slightly,

32. Only thoroughbred horses are permitted to race.

would *not* correctly paraphrase as

32a. Every thoroughbred that is permitted to race is a horse.

but rather as

32b. Every horse that is permitted to race is a thoroughbred.

The word 'and' occurring in the subject of a nonstandard categorical is something to be wary of. When the quantifier word is 'all', or is missing (so that the proposition is Universal), the word 'and' usually becomes 'or' in the course of paraphrasing to standard form. For example, the statement

33. All employees and credit customers are required to show identification.

does not go into standard form as

33a. Every employee and credit customer is (a thing which is) required to show identification.

since the normal interpretation of (33a) is that it concerns employees *who are* credit customers—that its subject is things which are both employees and credit customers—whereas the normal interpretation of (33) would be that it concerns all employees (whether they are credit customers or not) *and* all credit customers (whether they are employees or not). To retain this interpretation when putting (33) into standard form, it is necessary to change the 'and' to an 'or'. The result will then be

33b. Every employee or credit customer is (a thing which is) required to show identification.

which effectively separates the two parts of the subject. Similarly, if the proposition

34. Quarter-horses and thoroughbreds are barred from the Amateur's Race.

were paraphrased as

34a. Every quarter-horse and thoroughbred is (a thing that is) barred from the Amateur's Race.

it would appear to be about thoroughbred quarter-horses, which is an impossible breed. To avoid this absurd appearance, (34) should be reduced to the standard form

34b. Every quarter-horse or thoroughbred is (a thing that is) barred from the Amateur's Race.

'And' also normally receives this treatment when it is the main operator directly following the quantifier word 'only', even though in the course of paraphrase this phrase will end up as the predicate. For example, the statement

35. Only freshmen and sophomores attended the meeting.

does not go into standard form as

35a. Every attender of the meeting is a freshman and sophomore.

for the sense of (35a) is that those attending the meeting each had dual class standing. Rather, the correct paraphrase of (35) will be

35b. Every attender of the meeting is a freshman or sophomore.

We say that 'and' behaves this way "normally," rather than "always," since there are exceptions: *sometimes* 'and' in the phrase following 'all' or 'only' will remain that way after paraphrasing to standard form. For example, the statement

36. Plays by Beaumont and Fletcher are outstanding examples of post-Shakespearean drama.

would usually be taken as a statement about their jointly written plays, rather than as one about their independent works. Thus, instead of paraphrasing (36) as

36a. Every play by Beaumont or Fletcher is an outstanding example of post-Shakespearean drama.

the correct rendition would be

36b. Every play by Beaumont and Fletcher is an outstanding example of post-Shakespearean drama.

in which the 'and' of (36) remains 'and'. This would be even more obvious in a statement such as

37. Plays by Beaumont and Fletcher are superior to their separately written works.

which cannot intelligibly be rendered as

37a. Every play by Beaumont or Fletcher is (one that is) superior to their separately written works.

but must be put into standard form as

37b. Every play by Beaumont and Fletcher is (one that is) superior to their separately written works.

There are no *grammatical* clues for when 'and' should become 'or' and when it should not; (34) has the same grammatical structure as (36) and (37), yet their treatment differs. Instead, it is necessary to rely upon the *meaning* of the proposition. If the proposition is meant to be about the things sharing both features at once (such as persons who are both employees and credit customers, or plays co-authored by Beaumont and Fletcher), then the 'and' should remain 'and'; if it is meant to be about all of the things having the one feature *and also* all of the things having the other, then the 'and' should become 'or' in the final version.

'And' in the subject of Particular propositions phrased in the *plural* can also cause problems, but slightly different ones. For example,

38. Some puffballs and bracket fungi are edible.

cannot be paraphrased into standard form as

38a. Some puffball and bracket fungus is (a thing that is) edible.

for the same reason that (34) cannot become (34a): the nonstandard one is about some puffballs and some bracket fungi, while the standard one, (38a), is about something which is *both* (and there is no such thing). However, this problem cannot be overcome by changing 'and' to 'or', for the result would be

38b. Some puffball or bracket fungus is (a thing that is) edible.

and this concerns something which is either the one or the other, whereas

(38) concerns something which is the one, and also something which is the other. The only correct way to treat (38) is to separate it into two distinct statements, predicating the same feature, and to paraphrase (38) as the conjunction of two standard-form categoricals:

> 38c. Some puffball is (a thing that is) edible, and
> some bracket fungus is (a thing that is) edible.

Just as with Universals, this only happens *sometimes*; for example, the statement

> 39. Some books by Russell and Whitehead contain more logic symbols than English words.

if it concerns *Principia Mathematica* (their only joint literary venture), goes into standard form as

> 39a. Some book by Russell and Whitehead is one that contains more logic symbols than English words.

and is true. On the other hand, if (39) is meant to be about one of Russell's books and one of Whitehead's books, then it goes into standard form as

> 39b. Some book by Russell is one that contains more logic symbols than English words, and some book by Whitehead is one that contains more logic symbols than English words.

and is false. As with Universal propositions, one must rely on the meaning of such propositions to determine their correct standard form.

Statements containing the quantifier expression 'there are no' are always Universal Negative.* For example,

> 40. There are no purple cows.

will paraphrase into standard form as the "E" proposition

> 40a. No cow is (a) purple (object).

Categorical statements are sometimes expressed by means of the "generic" use of the definite article 'the'. For example, it would not be unusual to come across a statement such as

> 41. The electron is a subatomic particle.

or

> 42. The echidna is an oviparous mammal.

Categorical statements of this form are usually Universal. For example, these two would be paraphrased into standard form, respectively, as

> 41a. Every electron is a subatomic particle.
> 42a. Every echidna is an oviparous mammal.

---

*This is an alternative to the procedure given in the preceding chapter for translating such sentences. The results of the two procedures are logically equivalent.

However, care must be exercised in cases of this sort, first to be sure that it is not a "specific" use of the article 'the',* and second to be sure that the statement *is* a categorical statement. As an illustration of the first, it would be a bizarre mistake to paraphrase

  43. The mayor had a heart attack.

as an "A" proposition:

  43a. Every mayor is a thing that had a heart attack.

because in (43) the article 'the' clearly is not being used generically. Statement (43) may be contrasted with

  44. The mayor is the municipal chief executive.

which, normally understood, would be perfectly correct to paraphrase as

  44a. Every mayor is a municipal chief executive.

As an illustration of the second point, there are "generic" uses of 'the' which do not occur in categorical statements at all. For example,

  45. The automobile changed the whole American way of life.

involves a generic use of 'the', yet (45) is not a categorical statement. This can be seen from the absurdity of paraphrasing it either as

  45a. Every automobile is a thing which changed the whole American way of life.

or as

  45b. Some automobile is a thing which changed the whole American way of life.

There is no easily statable formal criterion for distinguishing statements such as (45) from *bona fide* categorical statements. Fortunately, common sense will usually come to our aid if we are otherwise in doubt.

Sometimes, 'the' occurs generically in categorical statements which are Particular rather than Universal. Indicators of statements of this type are words such as 'usually', 'normally', and the like. For example,

  46. The pig is normally a filthy beast.

would, under its most likely interpretation, be taken to signify 'Most pigs are filthy beasts' and would be paraphrased as

  46a. Some pig is a filthy beast.

though of course there are contexts in which it would be appropriate to understand (46) as saying

  46b. Every pig is a normally filthy beast.

---

*It is "specific" when it introduces a phrase purporting to designate one specific individual.

The difference is whether we understand (46) as saying that most pigs are filthy all of the time, or as saying that all pigs are filthy most of the time.

Sentences beginning with the singular indefinite article 'A' or 'An' require some attention before being paraphrased into standard form, since their behavior can be erratic. Usually such sentences are Particular, and will paraphrase as "I" or "O" propositions. For example,

47. A bear ate Algy.

would paraphrase as the "I" proposition

47a. Some bear is an Algy-eater.

and the similar sentence

48. An important guest didn't show up.

will paraphrase as the "O" proposition

48a. Some important guest is not a thing which showed up.

However, *sometimes* such sentences are not Particular, and require paraphrase as "A" or "E" propositions. An example is the sentence

49. A whale is a mammal.

which would clearly be intended to express a fact about whales in general; it paraphrases into the "A" proposition

49a. Every whale is a mammal.

Similarly, the sentence

50. An aardvark isn't a marsupial.

paraphrases into the "E" proposition

50a. No aardvark is a marsupial.

There are no foolproof criteria for sorting out the sentences of this type which are Particular from those which are Universal. In general, if the sentence has the form 'An S is a P'—that is, with a copula 'is' and the predicate also governed by an indefinite article—and P isn't complicated by additional quantifier expressions such as 'sometimes' ('A bear is a harmless animal sometimes'), then the sentence is Universal: illustrations are (49) and (50). But the sentence may still be universal, even if the predicate begins in some other way, just as

51. A platypus is oviparous.

paraphrases into the "A" proposition

51a. Every platypus is (an) oviparous (creature).

This illustrates a final point to be made in this section: there can be no complete set of rules for paraphrasing categorical statements into standard form. What has been said so far is enough to give a pretty good idea, but there will always be cases not covered by any of the rules given. When in doubt, keep in mind the way in which the four types of categorical statements are defined (§16.2), and try to decide which of the four definitions the statement in question fits, if any; then paraphrase in accordance with your judgment.

Exercises III

Paraphrase each of the following into standard form.

1. All politicians are unregenerate thieves.
□ 2. There are no atheists in foxholes.
3. Most people are honest.
4. A great many tigers do not like the taste of oatmeal.
5. Dogs bark.
□ 6. A live coward is better than a dead hero.
7. Whoever steals my purse steals trash.
8. Rabbits don't usually eat hamburger.
9. The whale is not a fish.
10. Only seniors are admitted.
11. Sometimes the moon isn't visible.
□ 12. Not every congressman is a thief.
13. Where there is no freedom, the people perish.
14. Logic students don't study very hard.
□ 15. The North Star is always above the horizon.

Exercises IV

Paraphrase each of the following into standard form. (These are harder than the ones in Exercises III.)

□ 1. Months sometimes have thirty-one days.
2. The insect is found everywhere.
3. Not everyone inherits a million dollars on his eighteenth birthday.
4. The bell only tolls when someone dies.
□ 5. The aardvark abounds somewhere.
6. Nobody but a cad would steal from an old blind lady.
7. People over ten feet tall have trouble buying ready-made clothes.
8. Butterflies aren't usually vicious.
9. The atomic bomb is a dangerous weapon if a lunatic has control of it.
□ 10. People always die before their 200th birthday.
11. Chickens normally hatch from eggs.
12. Microbes can be found anyplace.
13. Almost no cows are purple.
14. A bachelor isn't married to anybody.
15. Everybody loves somebody sometime.
□ 16. The whistle only blows at eight o'clock.

§16.4   Translating Standard-Form Categorical Statements

The rules for translating standard-form categorical statements are invariant and without exception. This means that, after a statement is properly paraphrased into standard form, the following rules can always be used to assure a correct translation of the statement.

RULE 1: A Universal proposition is always translated as a universally quantified *conditional* function.

RULE 2: A Particular proposition is always translated as an existentially quantified *conjunctive* function.

RULE 3: The *subject* of the categorical statement is always translated as a propositional function which is the *lefthand* component of the complex function.

RULE 4: The *predicate* of the categorical statement is always translated as a propositional function which is the *righthand* component of the complex function.

RULE 5: In translating a Negative categorical statement, the righthand component of the complex function will always be a *negation*.

When translating standard-form categoricals into symbols, the *neutral* parameters ('thing', 'creature', 'one', and the like) inserted to obtain "standard form" will usually drop back out, so that instead of, for example, '*x* is (an) invisible (creature)', the translation will simply be '*x* is invisible'. Of course, the non-neutral parameters ('person', 'time') inserted when paraphrasing "semiquantifier words" do not drop out but remain as part of the translation.

The rules may be illustrated schematically by the following table:

A	Every *S* is a *P*	always translates as	$(x)(Sx \supset Px)$
E	No *S* is a *P*	always translates as	$(x)(Sx \supset \sim Px)$
I	Some *S* is a *P*	always translates as	$(\exists x)(Sx \cdot Px)$
O	Some *S* is not a *P*	always translates as	$(\exists x)(Sx \cdot \sim Px)$

These rules may be stated in yet another way, which will make the relationship between the standard form and the symbolic version more apparent.

RULE I: The quantifier-word of a Universal proposition always translates as a universal quantifier.

RULE II: The quantifier-word of a Particular proposition always translates as an existential quantifier.

RULE III: The copula of a Universal proposition always translates as a horseshoe; its subject translates as the antecedent and its predicate translates as the consequent.

RULE IV: The copula of a Particular proposition always translates as a dot; its subject translates as the left conjunct and its predicate translates as the right conjunct.

RULE V: The predicate of a Negative proposition always translates as a negation.

Here are some illustrations. The "A" proposition

1. Every cat is (a) lazy (creature).

will translate as the universally quantified conditional function

1a. $(x)(x$ is a cat $\supset x$ is lazy)

and the "E" proposition

2. No cat is (a) trustworthy (creature).

will translate as the universally quantified conditional with negative consequent

2a. $(x)(x$ is a cat $\supset \sim x$ is trustworthy)

Also, the "I" proposition

3. Some elephant is a circus performer.

will translate as the existentially quantified conjunctive function

3a. $(\exists x)(x$ is an elephant $\cdot x$ is a circus performer)

and the "O" proposition

4. Some person is not (a) friendly (thing).

will translate as the existentially quantified conjunction with negative right conjunct

4a. $(\exists x)(x$ is a person $\cdot \sim x$ is friendly)

Perhaps the easiest way of understanding this is that (1) 'Every cat is lazy' is interpreted, for purposes of logic, to mean 'If anything is a cat, then it is lazy'. Similarly, (2) 'No cat is trustworthy' is interpreted to mean 'If anything is a cat, then it is not trustworthy'. On the other hand, (3) and (4) are interpreted to mean, respectively, 'There is something which is both an elephant and a circus performer' (or 'Circus-performing elephants exist'), and 'There is something which is both a person and not friendly' (or 'Persons who aren't friendly exist').

Exercises V

Translate the standard-form categorical statements resulting from Exercises III without abbreviating the component functions.

Exercises VI

Translate the standard form categorical statements resulting from Exercises IV without abbreviating the component functions.

The interpretation of categorical statements underlying the translation rules above has some logical consequences that we might not expect, and which merit explanation. Under this interpretation, Universal categorical statements are understood to mean, not that *there are* items of the kind indicated in the subject, but only that *if* there are such items, then all of them have (or lack) the characteristic designated by the predicate. For example, neither (1a) nor (2a) asserts that there are cats; rather, (1a) asserts that *if* there are cats, then all of them are lazy, and (2a) asserts that *if* there are cats, then none of them is trustworthy. And since a conditional with a false antecedent is true, this means that both (1a) and (2a) would be true if there were no cats. Whenever the "subject class" of a Universal statement is an empty class— that is, whenever there are no things of the sort mentioned in the subject— then the statement will be true simply in virtue of that fact. This is called the "Boolean interpretation" of Universal categorical statements, after a nineteenth-century logician, George Boole. Thus, under a Boolean interpretation, the two statements

    5. Every unicorn is intelligent.

    6. No unicorn is intelligent.

are both true, in virtue of the fact that there are no unicorns. This rather strange-sounding result is, of course, related to the "paradoxes of material implication" mentioned in §4.1.

Another interesting result of the Boolean interpretation is that if an "A" and an "O" proposition have the same subject and predicate, then they necessarily have opposite truth-values. Categorical statements with the same subject and predicate are said to **correspond**, hence this fact is often expressed by saying that corresponding "A" and "O" propositions are **contradictories**: if one is true then the other must be false, and vice versa. For example, the corresponding "A" and "O" propositions

    7. $(x)(x$ is a cow $\supset x$ is carnivorous)

    8. $(\exists x)(x$ is a cow $\cdot \sim x$ is carnivorous)

are contradictories; and in fact it is easy to prove, using inference rules presented later in this chapter, that (7) is logically equivalent to the negation of (8), and vice versa. Similarly, corresponding "E" and "I" propositions are contradictories. For instance, the corresponding "E" and "I" propositions

    9. $(x)(x$ is a cow $\supset \sim x$ is sluggish)

    10. $(\exists x)(x$ is a cow $\cdot x$ is sluggish)

necessarily have opposite truth-values, and it can easily be proven that (9) is logically equivalent to the negation of (10), and vice versa.

§16.5 Complex Subjects and Predicates

It frequently happens that after a categorical statement has been translated according to the rules above, there will still remain further possible translation of the subject, or predicate, or both, as complex functions in their own right. For instance, the statement

    1. Every black leopard is (a) ferocious (creature).

translates as

    1a. $(x)(x$ is a black leopard $\supset x$ is ferocious)

Here the "subject" function is

    2. x is a black leopard

and it is not hard to see that this, like 'x is a brown cow' discussed earlier, will translate as the conjunctive function

    2a. x is black $\cdot$ x is a leopard

so that the full translation of (1) will be

    1b. $(x)((x$ is black $\cdot$ x is a leopard$) \supset x$ is ferocious)

to be abbreviated as

    1c. $(x)((Bx \cdot Lx) \supset Fx)$

Similarly, the statement 'Everything that is enjoyable is either illegal, immoral, or fattening', paraphrased as

    3. Every enjoyable thing is a thing that is either illegal, immoral, or fattening.

will translate as

    3a. $(x)(x$ is enjoyable $\supset x$ is either illegal, immoral, or fattening)

where the "predicate" function

    4. x is either illegal, immoral, or fattening

translates further as the disjunctive function

    4a. x is illegal $\vee$ (x is immoral $\vee$ x is fattening)

or, if 'immoral' is interpreted to mean 'not moral', and 'illegal' to mean 'not legal', as

    4b. $\sim x$ is legal $\vee$ ($\sim x$ is moral $\vee$ x is fattening)

so that the full translation of (3) will be

    3b. $(x)(x$ is enjoyable $\supset (\sim x$ is legal $\vee$ ($\sim x$ is moral $\vee$ x is fattening)))

to be abbreviated as

    3c. $(x)(Ex \supset (\sim Lx \vee (\sim Mx \vee Fx)))$

Expressions such as 'which is', 'that is', 'such that' occurring in the subject or predicate (except after the neutral noun 'things') indicate that it is to be translated as a conjunction. For example, the statement

    5. Every cake that is salty is (one that is) hard to digest.

translates first as

    5a. (x) (x is a cake that is salty $\supset x$ is hard to digest) and thence as

    5b. $(x)((x$ is a cake $\cdot$ x is salty) $\supset x$ is hard to digest)

Similarly, as a more complex example, the statement

    6. Every applicant who is either female or under 21 is required to have a special permit.

translates initially as

    6a. $(x)(x$ is an applicant who is either female or under 21 $\supset x$ is required to have a special permit)

thence as

    6b. $(x)((x$ is an applicant $\cdot$ x is either female or under 21) $\supset x$ is required to have a special permit)

thence as

    6c. $(x)((x$ is an applicant $\cdot$ (x is female $\lor$ x is under 21)) $\supset x$ is required to have a special permit)

which abbreviates as

    6d. $(x)((Ax \cdot (Fx \lor Ux)) \supset Px)$

Continuing on with the translation of complex predicates, the statement

    7. Some bulls become angry if they are teased.

paraphrases into standard form as

    7a. Some bull is a thing that becomes angry if it is teased.

and translates initially as

    7b. $(\exists x)(x$ is a bull $\cdot$ x becomes angry if it is teased)

thence as

    7c. $(\exists x)(x$ is a bull $\cdot$ (x is teased $\supset x$ becomes angry))

and abbreviates as

    7d. $(\exists x)(Bx \cdot (Tx \supset Ax))$

§16.6 'All and Only'

The quantifier expression 'all and only' is to quantifier logic what the operator 'if and only if' is to truth-functional logic. The best way to translate statements containing 'all and only' is first to paraphrase them as the conjunction of two "A" propositions: one with 'all' and one with 'only'. For example, the statement

    1. All and only students are eligible to participate.

would paraphrase as

    1a. All students are things that are eligible to participate, and only students are things that are eligible to participate.

and then as

    1b. All students are things that are eligible to participate, and all things that are eligible to participate are students.

and finally as

    1c. Every student is (a thing that is) eligible to participate, and every thing that is eligible to participate is a student.

which will translate as

    1d. $(x)(x$ is a student $\supset x$ is eligible to participate) $\cdot$
                              $(x)(x$ is eligible to participate $\supset x$ is a student)

and abbreviate as

    1e. $(x)(Sx \supset Ex) \cdot (x)(Ex \supset Sx)$

Alternatively, it may be translated as a universally quantified biconditional—that is, as

    1f. $(x)(x$ is a student $\equiv x$ is eligible to participate)

which abbreviates as

    1g. $(x)(Sx \equiv Ex)$

§16.7 Concerning 'All'

The sentence

    1. All the people in this room weigh more than a ton.

is ambiguous. It could mean either

    2. Each person in this room weighs over a ton.

(in which case it would almost certainly be false), or

    3. The combined weight of the persons in this room is more than a ton.

which has a good chance of being true if there are fifteen or twenty people in the room. These two possible interpretations of (1) illustrate the difference between the **distributive** and **collective** senses of the word 'all'. If the person uttering (1) meant what is expressed by (2), he would be using the word 'all' **distributively**; but if he meant what is expressed by (3), he would be using 'all' **collectively**.

A statement containing a distributive 'all' ascribes its predicate to each individual member of its subject class; for example, it ascribes the property of weighing more than a ton to each person in the room. A statement containing a collective 'all' ascribes its predicate to the *total collection* of members of its subject class; for example, it ascribes the property of weighing more than a ton to the crowd in the room. 'Every' is sometimes ambiguous in this same way: it has both a distributive and a collective sense.

Categorical statements are always *distributive*. That is to say, if (1) above is used to mean (3), then it is not expressing a categorical statement. Categorical statements ascribe their predicate to each individual member of their subject class.

A *collective* statement is not a statement about *many* things but a statement about *one* thing: a totality, which is composed of many things, but which itself is one, not many: "the totality of such-and-suches." The logical treatment of such statements requires the logic of definite descriptions, which is presented in the last chapter of this book.

Exercises VII

Complete the translations begun in Exercises V (some of them will require no further translation) and then abbreviate them.

Exercises VIII

Complete the translations begun in Exercises VI (some of them will require no further translation) and then abbreviate them.

Exercises IX

Give a complete translation of each of the following, first without abbreviations and then fully abbreviated. (These cannot be done mechanically; they require some thought.)

1. Clams and oysters are edible molluscs.
2. A cat or dog will chase a mouse.
3. No valuable diamonds are cracked or cloudy.
□ 4. All cats will purr if their ears are rubbed.
5. The bell only rings when someone dies or is married.
6. Only persons who are over 21 will be admitted.
7. All and only certified employees are permitted to enter the building.
8. Most lions and tigers will not eat turnips and carrots.
□ 9. Any healthy baby is pleased if people sing to him or show him bright objects.
10. There aren't any illegal acts that go unnoticed or unpunished.
11. Senators and congressmen from the southern states do not favor forced integration or higher taxes.
□ 12. Snails cannot be eaten if they are cooked too long.
13. Novels by Faulkner or Hemingway are depressing but worth reading.
14. Poems by Guest and Tennyson are neither depressing nor worth reading.

☐ **15.** Many jobs that pay well and require a great deal of skill if they are to be done properly are either boring and self-defeating or unrewarding and not worth the effort.

§16.8 Some Transformation Rules

In order to present the first set of transformation rules precisely, we need to define one new term, 'matrix'. A formal definition will be given later on; for now, we shall say that the **matrix** of a quantified statement is that portion of it coming after the quantifier. Thus, for the quantified statement

   1. $(x)(Fx \supset Gx)$

the matrix is the portion

   1a. $(Fx \supset Gx)$

Similarly, for the quantified statement

   2. $(\exists x) \sim (Fx \cdot (Gx \lor Hx))$

the matrix is the portion

   2a. $\sim (Fx \cdot (Gx \lor Hx))$

Only quantified statements have matrices. For example, the statement

   3. $(x)Fx \cdot G\underline{a}$

is not a quantified statement; it is a *conjunction*, whose first conjunct happens to be a quantified statement. Therefore (3) has no matrix. However, its first conjunct does have a matrix; namely, the portion 'Fx'.

The first set of transformation rules for quantifier logic is identical with the set of transformation rules for truth-functional logic. *Any of the transformation rules from Chapter 11 may be applied to the matrix of a quantified statement.* That is to say, those rules remain valid if we allow their propositional variables to stand for propositional functions as well as propositions. This means, for example, that the statement

   4. $(x)(Fx \supset Gx)$

may be transformed by Contraposition into

   4a. $(x)(\sim Gx \supset \sim Fx)$

which may then be transformed, by Conditional Exchange, into

   4b. $(x)(\sim \sim Gx \lor \sim Fx)$

which may then be transformed, by Tilde Extraction, into

   4c. $(x) \sim (\sim Gx \cdot Fx)$

and so on.

MATRIX TRANSFORMATION RULE: Any transformation permitted for truth-functions is permitted for the *matrices* of quantified statements.

A second set of transformation rules are called the rules for **quantifier negation**. To say that an individual has (or lacks) a certain property is the same as saying that it satisfies (or fails to satisfy) a certain propositional function. To say that an individual *fails* to satisfy a certain function is the same as saying that it satisfies the *negation* of that function. That is, the two statements

5. It is false that (g satisfies Fx)

5a. $\sim(g$ satisfies Fx).

6. g satisfies (it is false that Fx)

6a. g satisfies ($\sim Fx$).

both say the same thing and will be expressed indifferently in the notation of quantifier logic as

7. $\sim Fg$

If everything lacks a certain property, then it is false that something has that property. For example, since everything lacks the property of being taller than itself, it is true that

8. $(x)\sim x$ is taller than itself

Therefore, it is false that something has the property of being taller than itself; that is,

9. $\sim(\exists x)x$ is taller than itself

But the reverse is also true; that is, if it is false that something has a certain property, then it is true that everything lacks that property. And this holds regardless of the property in question. Thus, where the Greek letter 'Φ' (phi) stands for any matrix, and the Greek letter 'α' (alpha) stands for any individual variable,

$$(\alpha)\sim\Phi \quad equiv \quad \sim(\exists\alpha)\Phi$$

If something lacks a certain property, then it is false that everything has that property. For example, there are things which are not red; that is,

10. $(\exists x)\sim x$ is red

and therefore it is false that everything is red; that is,

11. $\sim(x)x$ is red

and of course the reverse is also true; and this holds regardless of the property in question. Therefore, we can also say

$$\sim(\alpha)\Phi \quad equiv \quad (\exists\alpha)\sim\Phi$$

These two logical equivalences form the basis for the rules of quantifier negation.

QUANTIFIER NEGATION (QN): Where α is any individual variable and Φ is any formula,

$$(\alpha) \sim \Phi \quad \text{transf} \quad \sim(\exists\alpha)\Phi$$
$$\sim(\alpha)\Phi \quad \text{transf} \quad (\exists\alpha)\sim\Phi$$

The simplest way to understand this transformation is to view it as an operation of "pushing a tilde through a quantifier" in one direction or the other. The effect is to change the quantifier from universal to existential, or from existential to universal. A tilde may be pushed through a quantifier from either direction, but only one may be pushed through at a time; and every time one is pushed through, the quantifier changes. For example, the statement

   12. $\sim \sim (x)(Fx \supset Gx)$

may be transformed, by one application of QN, into

   12a. $\sim(\exists x)\sim(Fx \supset Gx)$

and then, by another application of QN, into

   12b. $(x)\sim \sim(Fx \supset Gx)$

The rules of Matrix Transformation and QN belong specifically to quantifier logic; they have no application in propositional logic for the obvious reason that there are no matrices or quantifiers for them to apply to. On the other hand, a proposition is a proposition, whether it is abbreviated as a single letter (as in propositional logic) or expressed by means of quantifiers and functions. Thus, all of the rules of propositional logic apply to *statements* in quantifier logic in *exactly* the way they apply to the (abbreviated) statements in truth-functional logic, and all of them may be used in derivations in quantifier logic. But remember: the matrix of a quantified statement is not itself a statement, but only a part of one. For example, the argument

$(x)Fx \supset (y)Gy$
$\underline{(x)Fx}$
$\therefore (y)Gy$

may be proven valid by one step of Modus Ponens: its first premiss is a conditional, and its second premiss is the antecedent of that conditional. The fact that the components of the conditional are written in quantifier notation is irrelevant, so far as Modus Ponens goes. On the other hand, the argument

$(x)(Fx \supset Gx)$
$\underline{(x)Fx}$
$\therefore (x)Gx$

is *not* susceptible to Modus Ponens; neither of its premisses is a conditional, and so it does not satisfy the premiss conditions for that rule. Both of its premisses are truth-functionally simple and are susceptible to truth-functional rules only in the way that any simple statement would be.

To make inferences based upon the internal structure of quantified statements it is necessary to use rules specifically belonging to quantifier logic, such as Matrix Transformation, QN, and others presented throughout the remainder of the book.

Exercises X

Show that corresponding "A" and "O" propositions are contradictories, and that corresponding "E" and "I" propositions are contradictories, by proving the following logical equivalences.

□ 1. / ∴ $(x)(Fx \supset Gx) \equiv \sim(\exists x)(Fx \cdot \sim Gx)$
2. / ∴ $\sim(x)(Fx \supset Gx) \equiv (\exists x)(Fx \cdot \sim Gx)$
3. / ∴ $(x)(Fx \supset \sim Gx) \equiv \sim(\exists x)(Fx \cdot Gx)$
4. / ∴ $\sim(x)(Fx \supset \sim Gx) \equiv (\exists x)(Fx \cdot Gx)$

Exercises XI

Translate and prove each of the following arguments.

□ 1. No ducks are reptiles. Therefore, no reptiles are ducks.
2. Everything that's exciting is illegal. Therefore everything that's legal is unexciting.
3. Some fat policemen are Irish sergeants. Therefore some Irish policemen are fat sergeants.
4. All wealthy persons are either fortunate or industrious. Therefore, no unfortunates who are not industrious are wealthy persons.
□ 5. All white crows are albinos. Therefore, all crows are albinos if they are white.
6. All white crows are albinos. Therefore, all white things are albinos if they are crows.
7. No politicians are honest men. Therefore, no honest politicians are men.
8. No sophomores are brilliant students. Therefore, no students are brilliant sophomores.
□ 9. All cats that are hairless are ugly. Therefore, all hairless cats are ugly cats.
10. No cows are purple. Some cows are purple. Therefore, all cows are purple.

chapter 17

MULTIPLE QUANTIFIERS;
QUANTIFIER SHIFTING

§17.1 Multiple Quantifiers

Up to this point, attention has been concentrated upon statements containing only one quantifier. But, of course, many statements contain more than one. The easiest and most obvious examples are truth-functional compounds whose components are quantified statements, as for instance

1. $(x)(Fx \supset Gx) \lor (\exists x)(Fx \cdot \sim Gx)$
2. $(y)Fy \supset (\exists x)Gx$
3. $(\exists z)Fz \cdot (\exists y)Gy$
4. $(x)((Fx \cdot Gx) \supset \sim (Hx \lor Jx)) \lor \sim ((y)(Fy \supset Ky) \cdot (\exists z)\sim Tz)$

These complicated-looking formulae are in fact nothing but ordinary truth-functions, of the type studied in Part I. The complicated appearance results from the fact that here the components are translated, instead of merely being abbreviated. Statement (1), for example, is just a disjunction; its first disjunct is a universally quantified statement and its second is an existentially quantified one. Similarly, (2) is a conditional, (3) is a conjunction, and (4) is a disjunction whose second disjunct is the negation of a conjunction. Statement (1) has the form '$p \lor q$'; (2) has the form '$p \supset q$'; (3) has the form '$p \cdot q$'; and (4) has the form '$p \lor \sim(q \cdot r)$'.

These statements contain quantifiers, but they are not quantified statements. They are compounds of quantified statements. A quantified statement is truth-functionally simple. (More precisely, a quantified statement is a statement *all* of which falls within the scope of a single quantifier.) However, there are quantified statements which contain more than one quantifier. An example, in English, is the statement

5. If anything is red then something is colored.

translated as

5a. $(x)(Rx \supset (\exists y)Cy)$

Another, slightly more complex example, is

    6. There is a person such that if something was stolen then he is guilty.

translated as

    6a. $(\exists x)(Px \cdot ((\exists y)Sy \supset Gx))$

Other examples of quantified statements with more than one quantifier:

    7. $(x)((y)Fy \supset Fx)$
    8. $(\exists x)(y)(Fx \cdot \sim Gy)$
    9. $(z)\sim(\exists w)(Rw \supset Tz)$
    10. $(z)(\exists y)(x)(\exists w)(\exists t)((Fx \lor Gy) \supset \sim(Kt \lor (Rw \cdot Tx)))$

We shall worry about the English counterparts to these statements later on; the present point is simply that there are statements of this type—that is, quantified statements containing more than one quantifier. Notice that in the examples above no two quantifiers occurring in the same *quantified* statement contain the same variable. In statement (1), both quantifiers contain the variable 'x'; but statement (1) is not a quantified statement. Statement (7) is a quantified statement, but both of its quantifiers contain different variables. Similarly, each of the five quantifiers in (10) contains a different variable. To insure this practice, let us establish it as a formation rule:

> When one quantifier is within the scope of another, they must contain different variables.

A formula violating this rule is improperly written—ill-formed, and thus will not count as a genuine statement.

It will be helpful at this point to interject a brief comment on the relationship between the variable in the quantifier and the variable(s) in the function that it quantifies. Their relationship and purpose will become clearer as we proceed, but we can say now that they are related in much the same way that personal pronouns are related to their (grammatical) antecedents in natural languages, and that their purpose is to indicate exactly which function is governed by the particular quantifier in question. A quantifier governs (quantifies) that function whose "blank spaces" fall *exactly* where the variables matching the quantifier-variable fall. This means, for example, that

    11. $(x)(Fx \supset (y)(Gy \supset Hx))$

is a universal quantification over the function

    11a. $F\_\_ \supset (y)(Gy \supset H\_\_)$

(in which the "blank spaces" are indicated by a line). (11) asserts that (11a) is universally satisfied—that all substitution-instances of (11a) are true. This may be contrasted with

    12. $(x)(Fx \supset (y)(Gy \supset Hy))$

which is quite different and asserts that

    12a. $F\_\_ \supset (y)(Gy \supset Hy)$

is universally satisfied. It is easy to see that (11a) and (12a) are totally different functions; (11a) has "blank spaces" after the '*F*' and after the '*H*', whereas (12a) has only one blank space—the one after the '*F*'. Thus (11) and (12) are totally different statements, since they assert the universal satisfaction of these different functions. More will be said on this score later on.

§17.2 Quantifier Shifting

Quantifier shifting is a transformation whereby a quantifier expands or contracts its scope to take in or leave out a conjunct or disjunct that is irrelevant to the quantifier. (A formula is "irrelevant" to a quantifier if it does not contain any occurrences of the variable in the quantifier.) It has the effect of transforming compounds of quantified statements into quantified complex statements, and vice versa.

The statement

    1. Everything is valuable and everything is worth saving.

translated as

    1a. $(x)Vx \cdot (y)Wy$

is logically equivalent to the statement

    2. Everything is such that it is valuable and everything is worth saving.

translated as

    2a. $(x)(Vx \cdot (y)Wy)$

—that is to say, (1a) and (2a) have exactly the same truth-conditions; both will be true just in case each thing is valuable and each thing is worth saving. Furthermore, the fact that the second conjunct of (1a) is a universally quantified statement is irrelevant; (1a) and (2a) would be equivalent no matter what the second conjunct might have been. We can express this by saying that, where *p* is any statement at all,

    3. $(x)Vx \cdot p$

is logically equivalent to

    4. $(x)(Vx \cdot p)$

since their truth-conditions are the same: they will be true just in case each thing is valuable and *p* is true. And in general, where *p* is any statement, α is any variable, and Φ is any formula,

$$(\alpha)\Phi \cdot p \quad equiv \quad (\alpha)(\Phi \cdot p)$$

Similarly, we can see that (1a) is logically equivalent to

    5. $(y)((x)Vx \cdot Wy)$

since (5), like (1a), will be true just in case each thing is valuable and each thing is worth saving. And, in general,

$$p \cdot (\alpha)\Phi \quad equiv \quad (\alpha)(p \cdot \Phi)$$

Similar equivalences obtain with respect to disjunction. That is to say,

$$(\alpha)\Phi \vee p \quad equiv \quad (\alpha)(\Phi \vee p)$$

and

$$p \vee (\alpha)\Phi \quad equiv \quad (\alpha)(p \vee \Phi)$$

The same sorts of equivalences can be established for existential quantification. For instance,

6. Something is fat and something is greedy.

translated as

6a. $(\exists x)Fx \cdot (\exists y)Gy$

has the same truth-conditions as

7. There is something such that it is fat and something is greedy.

translated as

7a. $(\exists x)(Fx \cdot (\exists y)Gy)$

—that is to say, each of them will be true just in case at least one thing is fat and at least one thing is greedy. In general,

$$(\exists \alpha)\Phi \cdot p \quad equiv \quad (\exists \alpha)(\Phi \cdot p)$$

and

$$p \cdot (\exists \alpha)\Phi \quad equiv \quad (\exists \alpha)(p \cdot \Phi)$$
$$(\exists \alpha)\Phi \vee p \quad equiv \quad (\exists \alpha)(\Phi \vee p)$$
$$p \vee (\exists \alpha)\Phi \quad equiv \quad (\exists \alpha)(p \vee \Phi)$$

On the strength of these logical equivalences, we can state the following transformation rule:

QUANTIFIER SHIFTING (QS): Where Φ is any formula, α is any variable, and p is any formula in which α does not occur,*

(i)	$(\alpha)\Phi \cdot p$	transf	$(\alpha)(\Phi \cdot p)$
(ii)	$p \cdot (\alpha)\Phi$	transf	$(\alpha)(p \cdot \Phi)$
(iii)	$(\alpha)\Phi \vee p$	transf	$(\alpha)(\Phi \vee p)$
(iv)	$p \vee (\alpha)\Phi$	transf	$(\alpha)(p \vee \Phi)$
(v)	$(\exists \alpha)\Phi \cdot p$	transf	$(\exists \alpha)(\Phi \cdot p)$
(vi)	$p \cdot (\exists \alpha)\Phi$	transf	$(\exists \alpha)(p \cdot \Phi)$
(vii)	$(\exists \alpha)\Phi \vee p$	transf	$(\exists \alpha)(\Phi \vee p)$
(viii)	$p \vee (\exists \alpha)\Phi$	transf	$(\exists \alpha)(p \vee \Phi)$

*The restriction that α not occur in p is for the purpose of avoiding (i) "collision of variables"—the inadvertent capture of a place that ought to remain free (cf. Chapter 19)—and its converse, and (ii) ill-formation, which would result if two "overlapping" quantifiers contained the same letter.

Some examples of QS transformations are the following:

    8. $(x)(Fx \supset Gx) \vee (\exists y)(Fy \cdot \sim Gy)$

may be transformed [per line (iii) of the QS rule] into

    8a. $(x)[(Fx \supset Gx) \vee (\exists y)(Fy \cdot \sim Gy)]$

Furthermore, since the matrix of statement (8a) matches the form at line (viii), this may also be transformed by QS into

    8b. $(x)(\exists y)[(Fx \supset Gx) \vee (Fy \cdot \sim Gy)]$

and, of course, by reversing the transformations, (8b) can be transformed into (8a) and then into (8). It is also possible to transform (8), per line (viii) of the rule, into

    8c. $(\exists y)[(x)(Fx \supset Gx) \vee (Fy \cdot \sim Gy)]$

and to transform the matrix of (8c), per line (iii) of the rule, so as to produce

    8d. $(\exists y)(x)[(Fx \supset Gx) \vee (Fy \cdot \sim Gy)]$

and, by reversing the transformations, (8d) can be transformed into (8c) and thence into (8).

    Transformations such as that from (8) to (8a), or from (8a) to (8b), are referred to as transformations of "shifting to the left" or "shifting out" a quantifier; the reverse transformations are referred to as "shifting to the right" or "shifting in" a quantifier. The terminology of "shifting out" and "shifting in" can most easily be understood if each of the schemata in the lefthand column of the rule is viewed as having a set of invisible parentheses enclosing the whole (the same parentheses which are visible in the right-hand column). The transformation from left to right can then be seen as one of picking up the quantifier and carrying it outside these parentheses; and the transformation from right to left can be seen as one of picking up the quantifier and placing it inside the parentheses. As an illustration, consider the formula

    9. $(\exists x)Gx \vee A$

and imagine it to be enclosed in a set of "invisible" brackets, thus:

    9a. $\vdots [(\exists x)Gx \vee A \vdots$

When the existential quantifier is "shifted out," it moves outside the brackets and they become visible:

    9b. $(\exists x)[\ \ Gx \vee A]$

Under the reverse transformation, when the existential quantifier of (9b) is "shifted in," it moves inside the brackets and they become invisible as in (9a). Formulae such as (9) may look strange at first because of the presence of

'A', but there is nothing the matter with them. (9) is a perfectly good state-ment, which says, "There is something which is G, unless A," where 'A' is a statement abbreviated after the manner of Part I of the book.

When a quantifier is shifted out of a set of parentheses (or brackets, or whatever), it pushes aside anything else that happens to be there so that it sits *right next to* the parenthesis. For example, when the existential quantifier in (8a) shifted out, it pushed the universal quantifier aside and came to rest as in (8b). As another example, when the quantifier in

    10. $\sim [A \cdot (x)Fx]$

is shifted out, it pushes the tilde over and comes to rest right next to the bracket:

    10a. $\sim (x)[A \cdot Fx]$

Another point: if a quantifier has another quantifier or a tilde immediately next to it, it cannot be shifted in that direction. This means, for example, that in the statement

    11. $(x)\sim(G\underline{a} \lor Fx)$

the quantifier cannot be shifted in (that is, to the right) because there is a tilde immediately to its right. Before any shifting of the quantifier can take place, some other transformation must be performed; either the tilde must be pushed through the quantifier by QN, or it must be taken inside the paren-theses by TD. After that, the quantifier can be shifted in with no trouble. As another example, in the statement

    12. $(x)(\exists y)(Ry \cdot Tx)$

the universal quantifier cannot be shifted in, because there is another quan-tifier immediately to its right. The existential quantifier must be shifted in first. As another example, in the statement

    13. $A \cdot (\exists z)(w)(Kz \lor Mw)$

the universal quantifier cannot be shifted *out*, because there is another quantifier immediately to its left. The existential quantifier must be shifted out first. As a final example, in the statement

    14. $A \cdot \sim(\exists z)(w)\sim(Kz \lor Mw)$

no quantifiers can be shifted at all. The universal quantifier cannot be shifted in, because there is a tilde immediately to its right, and the existential quanti-fier cannot be shifted in, because there is a quantifier immediately to its right. Likewise, the existential quantifier cannot be shifted out, because there is a tilde immediately to its left, and the universal quantifier cannot be shifted out, because there is a quantifier immediately to its left. Thus, other trans-formations are necessary before any quantifier shift can take place.

Exercises I

Construct a proof for each of the following arguments.

    1. $A \cdot \sim(\exists z)(w) \sim (Kz \lor Mw)$ / $\therefore$ $(z)(\exists w)(A \cdot \sim(\sim Kz \cdot \sim Mw))$

□ **2.** $A \cdot \sim(\exists z)(w) \sim (Kz \lor Mw)$ / $\therefore$ $\sim(A \supset \sim((\exists w)Mw \lor (z)Kz))$

    3. $A \cdot \sim(\exists z)(w) \sim (Kz \lor Mw)$ / $\therefore$ $(z)(A \cdot (Kz \lor (\exists w)Mw))$

    4. $A \cdot \sim(\exists z)(w) \sim (Kz \lor Mw)$ / $\therefore$ $A \cdot \sim(w)(\exists z) \sim (Kz \lor Mw)$

> *Note:* When using QS, it is not necessary to cite a particular line [such as line (iv)] in the rule; simply cite QS.

§17.3 QS and Conditionals

The QS rule, as stated, permits shifting a quantifier with respect to an irrelevant *conjunct* or an irrelevant *disjunct*; it says nothing, directly, about irrelevant components to the other operators. But it is nevertheless adequate to handle other cases as well, since any conditional can be transformed into a disjunction by CE and any biconditional can be transformed into a conjunction of two conditionals by BE. However, certain oddities involved in shifting quantifiers with respect to a horseshoe or a triple bar are worth mentioning.

Suppose we wish to shift the quantifier out of the statement

    1. $A \supset (x)Fx$

QS says nothing about conditionals, so it is necessary to transform (1) into

    1a. $\sim A \lor (x)Fx$

by CE. It is then possible to transform (1a), by QS, into

    1b. $(x)(\sim A \lor Fx)$

and then to transform (1b), by another application of CE, into

    1c. $(x)(A \supset Fx)$

—and of course, these procedures are reversible. Thus we can see that shifting a quantifier with respect to the *consequent* of a conditional is no different from the shifts we have been making all along. But now, consider the statement

    2. $(x)Fx \supset A$

Since QS says nothing about conditionals, this must be transformed, by CE, into

    2a. $\sim(x)Fx \lor A$

but, having made this transformation, we still cannot shift the quantifier out. The tilde to its left prevents shifting it in that direction. To get around this, we must push the tilde through by QN. The result is

    2b. $(\exists x) \sim Fx \lor A$

The quantifier may now be shifted out, resulting in

    2c. $(\exists x)(\sim Fx \lor A)$

which by CE becomes

    2d. $(\exists x)(Fx \supset A)$

Now compare (2) and (2d). Instead of shifting out "normally," the universal quantifier has become existential in the course of the shift. And since the process is reversible, it would return from existential to universal if shifted back in. Furthermore, a little reflection will indicate that if it had started out in (2) as existential, it would have ended up in (2d) as universal, and vice versa. In general, whenever a quantifier is shifted with respect to the *antecedent* of a conditional, it will change from universal to existential, or from existential to universal, in the shift.

Since the QS rule is adequate as it stands to accommodate shifts with respect to the horseshoe, there is no real *need* to add anything further to it. Nevertheless, in the interests of simplicity, we shall make the following additions to eliminate tiresome applications of CE and QN.

    Q<small>UANTIFIER</small> S<small>HIFTING</small> (continued)

(ix)	$(\alpha)\Phi \supset p$	transf	$(\exists \alpha)(\Phi \supset p)$
(x)	$p \supset (\alpha)\Phi$	transf	$(\alpha)(p \supset \Phi)$
(xi)	$(\exists \alpha)\Phi \supset p$	transf	$(\alpha)(\Phi \supset p)$
(xii)	$p \supset (\exists \alpha)\Phi$	transf	$(\exists \alpha)(p \supset \Phi)$

As a final illustration of this fact about QS with respect to the antecedent of a conditional, consider the statement

    3. $((x)Fx \supset A) \supset B$

One step of QS transforms this into

    3a. $(\exists x)(Fx \supset A) \supset B$

in which the universal quantifier has become existential, since it was shifted with respect to the antecedent of a conditional. Another step of QS transforms (3a) into

    3b. $(x)[(Fx \supset A) \supset B]$

in which the existential quantifier has become universal, since it was shifted with respect to the antecedent of a conditional [(3a) is a conditional].

In summation, *every time* a quantifier shifts with respect to the antecedent of a conditional, it changes from universal to existential, or from existential to universal.

Exercises II

In each of the following, shift all of the quantifiers all the way *out*.

    1. $(x)Fx \supset ((y)Gy \supset (z)Hz)$

□ **2.** $((\exists x)Fx \supset (\exists y)Gy) \supset (\exists z)Hz$

    3. $((x)Fx \supset (\exists y)Gy) \cdot ((\exists z)Gz \supset (w)Fw)$

    4. $\sim (t)Mt \supset ([(z)Hz \supset ((x)Fx \supset (y)Gy)] \supset (w)Kw)$

There will be no separate QS rules for biconditionals. It is always necessary to transform a triple bar into something else in order to perform QS with respect to it. This, too, has some curious results. For example, the statement

    4. $A \equiv (x)Fx$

transforms, by BE, into

    4a. $(A \supset (x)Fx) \cdot ((x)Fx \supset A)$

which becomes, by two steps of QS,

    4b. $(x)(A \supset Fx) \cdot (\exists x)(Fx \supset A)$

Further shifting cannot be performed at this point, so we shall leave the subject of biconditionals temporarily, with the remark that whenever quantifiers are shifted *out* with respect to the triple bar, there will be twice as many of them at the end as there were at the beginning, half of them universal and half existential.

§17.4   Freedom, Bondage, and Scope

The restriction that α (that is, the variable in the quantifier) not occur in p (that is, in the formula being annexed to or expelled from the scope of the quantifier) is included in the QS Rule to assure that quantifiers are only shifted with respect to formulae that are irrelevant to them. For example, it would be invalid to proceed from

    1. $(\exists x)Fx \cdot Gx$

to

    2. $(\exists x)(Fx \cdot Gx)$

and this move is not permitted by the QS rule, since 'Gx' contains the variable in the quantifier. Similarly, the move from

    3. $(y)Ky \vee (\exists y)Ty$

to

    4. $(y)[Ky \vee (\exists y)Ty]$

results in a violation of the rule that quantifiers with overlapping scopes must contain different variables, and it is not permitted by QS, since '$(\exists y)Ty$'

contains the same variable as the one in the quantifier being shifted. Also, the restriction means that QS does not permit the move from

    5. $(x)(Fx \lor Gx)$

to

    6. $Fx \lor (x)Gx$

because 'Fx' contains the variable in the quantifier, and hence the quantifier cannot be shifted with respect to it in this way.

However, this appears on the surface to be unduly restrictive. Consider the statement

    7. $(x)Fx \cdot (x)Gx$

As the QS rule is stated, neither of the quantifiers in (7) can be shifted out, since both components contain the same variable. But (7) merely asserts "everything is F and everything is G," and this statement might just as well have been expressed as

    8. $(x)Fx \cdot (y)Gy$

in which QS is perfectly all right, since the components contain different variables exclusively. But it seems strange that a transformation could be correct for one formula, and incorrect for another, when both formulae say exactly the same thing. If QS is permitted with (8), why not permit it with (7), which says the same thing?

The way to resolve this complaint is by providing a procedure for transforming (7) into (8). With such a procedure the problem will disappear, and the advantages of the restrictions on QS can be retained without sacrificing anything. However, in order to state the procedure with precision, it is necessary to develop some preliminary definitions. As we shall see, these definitions are relevant not simply to the present question, but also to matters later on.

A **punctuation mark** is a parenthesis (bracket, brace, or whatever) which is not part of a quantifier.* A **mated pair** of punctuation marks consists of an opening punctuation mark and its corresponding closing punctuation mark (§2.5). A **well-punctuated formula** is one which contains no unmated punctuation marks, and which is either a formula enclosed by a mated pair of punctuation marks, preceded by zero or more tildes, or a formula containing no truth-functional operators except for zero or more tildes. For example: 'Fx' is a well-punctuated formula; '$(Fx$' is not; '$\sim \sim \sim \sim \sim \sim \sim Fx$' is a well-punctuated formula; '$\sim \sim (\sim \sim (\sim \sim Fx)$' is not; '$(Fx \supset A)$' is a well-punctuated formula; '$\sim ((Fx \supset A)$' is not; '$(Fx \supset (A \supset Gy))$' is a well-punctuated formula; '$((Fx \supset (A \supset Gy))$' is not.

---

*Or other variable-binding device, such as a descriptor (see Chapter 24).

The "scope of a quantifier" can now be defined:

> *Scope of a Quantifier.* The scope of a quantifier consists of (a) the quantifer itself, plus (b) the first well-punctuated formula to its right, plus (c) everything between (a) and (b).

A quantifier **binds** every occurrence of its variable within its scope and binds nothing else. If a quantifier binds an occurrence of a variable, that occurrence of that variable is **bound**. An occurrence of a variable which is not bound by any quantifier* is **free**.

The **range** of a quantifier consists of all and only those occurrences of variables bound by that quantifer. That is, the range of a quantifier consists of every occurrence of the variable of that quantifier within the scope of that quantifier, and nothing else. For example, in

9. $(x)(\exists y)(Fx \supset ((Gy \lor (z)Hz) \cdot Kx))$

the range of the universal quantifier '(x)' is in boldface type.

§17.5 Rewriting Bound Variables

The transformation rule we are after can now be stated as follows:

> REWRITING BOUND VARIABLES (RBV α/β): It is permissible to rewrite the variables in the range of a quantifier as some other letter, subject to the following restrictions: (a) *every* letter within the range of the quantifier must be rewritten as the same letter; (b) no letter that is not within the range of that quantifier may be rewritten as that letter; (c) the new letter must have no occurrences in the scope of that quantifier, except those produced by the rewriting.

This rule may be explained in another, slightly less formal, way. The letters constituting the range of a quantifier each occupy a place in the formula. For example, in (9) above the occurrences of 'x' which make up the range of the first quantifier occupy (i) the place between the first set of prens, (ii) the place after 'F', and (iii) the place after 'K'. This set of *places* constitutes the **domain** of the quantifier in question. The "domain" of a quantifier is a set of places, not of letters. (Think of the places as pockets, containing the letters. Each quantifier in a formula will have a set of "pockets" associated with it— the pockets containing *its* variables. That set of pockets constitutes its domain.) The RBV rule permits us to empty out the domain of a quantifier and refill it with occurrences of some "fresh" letter—a letter that doesn't occur anywhere else in the scope of that quantifier.

---

*Or other variable-binding device, such as a descriptor (see Chapter 24).

When this transformation rule is used in a derivation, its justification should indicate not only the rule, but the way in which the rewriting was done. This latter is indicated by giving the original variable, followed by a slash (the slash may be read as "to"), followed by the new variable, after the pattern shown in the abbreviated title of the rule. For example, two steps of RBV in a derivation might look like the following:

    1. $(x)Fx \supset (\exists x)Kx$
    2. $(x)Fx \supset (\exists y)Ky$ 1, RBV x/y
    3. $(z)Fz \supset (\exists y)Ky$ 2, RBV x/z

A **quantified formula** is one entirely within the scope of a quantifier. For example, '$(\exists x)(Fx \supset A)$' is a quantified formula; '$(\exists x)Fx \supset A$' is not a quantified formula; and '$\sim(\exists x)(Fx \supset A)$ is not a quantified formula. A quantifier is said to be **initially placed** if it is in a quantified formula and no part of the formula is to its left except for zero or more quantifiers or tildes.* For example, in the formula

    1. $(x)(\exists y)\sim(z)(Fx \supset (Gy \lor Hz))$

all of the quantifiers are initially placed; but in the formula

    2. $\sim(x)(\exists y)(z)(Fx \supset Gy \lor Hz))$

none of the quantifiers is initially placed, since (2) is not a quantified formula. (The tilde, which is part of the formula, does not fall within the scope of a quantifier; hence the formula is, by definition, not a quantified formula.) In the formula

    3. $(x)[(\exists y)Fy \cdot Gx]$

the universal quantifier is initially placed, but the existential quantifier is not, since a part of the formula (namely, an opening bracket) which is not a quantifier or a tilde lies to its left.

The **matrix** of a quantified formula is that part of the formula which is to the right of the initially placed quantifier furthest to the right. For example, in (1) above, the matrix is

    1a. $(Fx \supset (Gy \lor Hz))$

and in (3) above the matrix is

    3a. $[(\exists y)Fy \cdot Gx]$

A matrix is **quantifier-free** if it contains no quantifiers. For example, (1a)—the matrix of (1)—is quantifier-free; (3a)—the matrix of (3)—is not.

---

*In many logic texts, "initially placed" is defined in such a way that a quantifier is not initially placed if a tilde precedes it. Our definition is a deviation from this usage.

§17.5 Prenex Normal Form

A formula is said to be in **prenex normal form** if every quantifier in it is initially placed, and no quantifier is preceded by a tilde. A formula in prenex (PREE-nex) normal form consists of a string of zero or more quantifiers followed by a quantifier-free matrix. The string of initially placed quantifiers is called the **prefix** of the formula. None of the examples in the foregoing section were in prenex normal form. However, the formula

1. $(x)(\exists y) \sim (z)(Fx \supset (Gy \lor Hz))$

can be put in prenex normal form by one step of QN:

1a. $(x)(\exists y)(\exists z) \sim (Fx \supset (Gy \lor Hz))$

Similarly, the formula

2. $\sim (x)(\exists y)(z)(Fx \supset (Gy \lor Hz))$

may be put into prenex normal form by three steps of QN:

2a. $(\exists x)(y)(\exists z) \sim (Fx \supset (Gy \lor Hz))$

and the formula

3. $(x)[(\exists y)Fy \cdot Gx]$

can be put into prenex normal form by shifting the existential quantifier out:

3a. $(x)(\exists y)[Fy \cdot Gx]$

Any formula that contains a quantifier can be "prenexed" or reduced to prenex normal form by the transformation procedures explained so far: first, shift quantifiers to the left until they are all initially placed (rewriting bound variables as necessary), then use QN as needed to get tildes all to the right of the quantifiers. The formula will then be in prenex normal form. In prenexing, it is conventional to shift the quantifiers out *in order*, so that they have the same relative order from left to right as they had before shifting, and this convention should always be observed.

Let us now return to the subject of shifting quantifiers with respect to a triple bar. We have already seen that the triple bar must always be transformed into something else before a quantifier shift can be made; for example,

4. $(\exists x)Kx \equiv B$

transforms, by BE, into

4a. $((\exists x)Kx \supset B) \cdot (B \supset (\exists x)Kx)$

which, by QS, transforms into

4b. $(x)(Kx \supset B) \cdot (B \supset (\exists x)Kx)$

and thence into

4c. $(x)(Kx \supset B) \cdot (\exists x)(B \supset Kx)$

If we wish to go on and reduce (4c) to prenex normal form, we must first rewrite the range of one of the quantifiers—for example,

4d. $(x)(Kx \supset B) \cdot (\exists y)(B \supset Ky)$

and the reduction then proceeds by QS, first to

4e. $(x)[(Kx \supset B) \cdot (\exists y)(B \supset Ky)]$

and finally to

4f. $(x)(\exists y)[(Kx \supset B) \cdot (B \supset Ky)]$

It should be noticed that the matrix of (4f) can*not* be transformed back into a biconditional; 'Kx' and 'Ky' are different formulae, and so the matrix of (4f) does not have the proper form for applying BE.

As a final illustration of the complexity of QS with biconditionals, here is a derivation in which a biconditional with both sides quantified is reduced to prenex normal form.

1. $(x)Fx \equiv (x)Gx$	
2. $((x)Fx \supset (x)Gx) \cdot ((x)Gx \supset (x)Fx)$	1, BE
3. $((y)Fy \supset (x)Gx) \cdot ((x)Gx \supset (x)Fx)$	2, RBV x/y
4. $(\exists y)(Fy \supset (x)Gx) \cdot ((x)Gx \supset (x)Fx)$	3, QS
5. $(\exists y)[(Fy \supset (x)Gx) \cdot ((x)Gx \supset (x)Fx)]$	4, QS ['y' quantifier]
6. $(\exists y)[(x)(Fy \supset Gx) \cdot ((x)Gx \supset (x)Fx)]$	5, QS [first 'x' quantifier]
7. $(\exists y)[(z)(Fy \supset Gz) \cdot ((x)Gx \supset (x)Fx)]$	6, RBV x/z
8. $(\exists y)(z)[(Fy \supset Gz) \cdot ((x)Gx \supset (x)Fx)]$	7, QS ['z' quantifier]
9. $(\exists y)(z)[(Fy \supset Gz) \cdot ((w)Gw \supset (x)Fx)]$	8, RBV x/w
10. $(\exists y)(z)[(Fy \supset Gz) \cdot (\exists w)(Gw \supset (x)Fx)]$	9, QS
11. $(\exists y)(z)(\exists w)[(Fy \supset Gz) \cdot (Gw \supset (x)Fx)]$	10, QS
12. $(\exists y)(z)(\exists w)[(Fy \supset Gz) \cdot (x)(Gw \supset Fx)]$	11, QS ['x' quantifier]
13. $(\exists y)(z)(\exists w)(x)[(Fy \supset Gz) \cdot (Gw \supset Fx)]$	12, QS

Exercises III

Prenex each of the following.

□ **1.** $\sim((x)Fx \supset (x)Gx)$

2. $\sim(\exists x)\sim((\exists y)Fy \supset (Gx \cdot (z)Kz))$

3. $(x)\sim(\exists y)(z)(w)(Fx \supset ((t)Gt \supset (Hy \cdot (Kz \lor Mw))))$

□ **4.** $(x)(Fx \supset Gx) \lor (\exists x)(Fx \cdot \sim Gx)$

5. $(\exists x)Qx \equiv (x)Mx$

□ **6.** $((((x)Fx \supset (y)Gy) \supset (z)Hz) \supset (t)Kt) \supset (x)(Mx \supset Nx)$

7. $(x)Fx \lor ((x)\sim Fx \lor ((\exists x)Fx \lor (\exists x)\sim Fx))$

8. $(x)(\exists y)(Fx \supset ((Hy \lor Gx) \cdot ((\exists z)Kz \lor Kx))) \cdot (\exists y)(Ry \cdot \sim (G\underline{a} \lor (Ky \cdot Rx)))$

chapter 18

SOME TRANSLATION AIDS

§18.1 Flagging Pronouns

A personal pronoun ('he', 'him', 'she', 'her', 'it', 'they') is a pronoun which occurs in a piece of discourse for the purpose of making a cross-reference to something mentioned earlier. For example, in the sentence 'Percy kicked Evangeline and she screamed', the word 'she' is a personal pronoun which refers back to 'Evangeline'; and in the sentence 'Something was in the closet and it scared me', the word 'it' is a personal pronoun which refers back to 'something'.

In English grammar, the expression that a personal pronoun refers back to is called the "antecedent" of the pronoun. But since the word 'antecedent' is used in logic to designate one of the components of a conditional, it will be advantageous to use the word **base** for this other purpose. Thus, in the sentence

    1. Percy kicked Evangeline and she screamed.

the *base* of the pronoun 'she' is the proper name 'Evangeline'. Similarly, in the sentence

    2. Something was in the closet and it scared me.

the base of the pronoun 'it' is the quantifier word 'something'. The base of a personal pronoun may be either a proper name ('Clyde', 'Omaha') or a noun phrase ('a house', 'some cows', 'her brother'), or a basic quantifier word ('something', 'anything', and the like). Several pronouns within a sentence may have the same base. For example, in

    3. If something is in the closet and it roars, it will scare me.

both occurrences of the pronoun 'it' have the word 'something' as their base.

Any expression serving as the base for one or more pronouns has a **range**, consisting of all the pronouns for which it serves as a base. For example, in (1) above, the pronoun 'she' is in the range of the name 'Evangeline', and in

(3) both occurrences of the pronoun 'it' are in the range of the quantifier word 'something'.

Quite often, different pronouns in a sentence will have different bases. For example, in the sentence

4. Percy hit Willie, and he hit him back.

it is quite clear that the base of 'he' is 'Willie' and the base of 'him' is 'Percy'. However, personal pronouns sometimes occur in such a way that it is not easy to tell what their base is. In such a case the sentence will be ambiguous. For example,

5. Clyde put up his fists and Harvey shouted, but eventually he got tired and went home and he went back into the tavern.

might mean either that Clyde went home and Harvey went back into the tavern, or that Harvey went home and Clyde went back into the tavern. As in all cases of ambiguity, there is no way to translate (5) with the assurance that it is correct unless the ambiguity can be resolved (by reference to the speaker's intentions, the surrounding context, or something). But once the intended meaning of (5) is established, it can be rephrased in such a way that it is no longer ambiguous. If, for example, we discover it is intended to mean that Harvey went home and Clyde went back into the tavern, then we can eliminate the ambiguity of (5) by replacing each of the personal pronouns with its correct base:

5a. Clyde put up his fists and Harvey shouted, but eventually Harvey got tired and went home and Clyde went back into the tavern.

A more broadly useful procedure for accomplishing the same thing is called **flagging**. When the base of a personal pronoun has been established, we flag the pronoun by writing a lower-case letter (such as an individual variable) after it and then writing the same letter after its base. By flagging every pronoun in the range of a given base by the same letter, and using different flagging letters for each base and its range, we can render sentences containing personal pronouns completely unambiguous. For example, when (5) is flagged in this manner it becomes

5b. Clyde x put up his fists and Harvey z shouted, but eventually he z got tired and went home and he x went back into the tavern.

After pronouns have been flagged in this way, the pronouns themselves become superfluous. Their job of referring back to the base has been taken over by the flagging letters, and the pronouns themselves may be deleted.

5c. Clyde x put up his fists and Harvey z shouted, but eventually z got tired and went home and x went back into the tavern.

Whenever the base of a personal pronoun is a proper name (and only then), it is appropriate to use a constant (rather than a variable) as a flagging letter. For example, instead of the variables 'x' and 'z', the present example might have been flagged with the constants 'c' and 'h' to produce

> 5d. Clyde c put up his fists and Harvey h shouted, but eventually h got tired
> and went home and c went back into the tavern.

When this is done, the unabbreviated proper names can be eliminated along
with the pronouns, since there is no point in having both the abbreviated
and the unabbreviated version of the name. When (5) is treated in this way,
the final result is

> 5e. c put up his fists and h shouted, but eventually h got tired and went home
> and c went back into the tavern.

You will usually find it helpful, when translating into the language of
quantifier logic, to flag and eliminate all personal pronouns and proper names
as a preliminary step.

§18.2 'Any', 'Every', and 'Some'

The treatment of the quantifier words 'any', 'every', and 'some', as they
occur in categorical statements, has been discussed at length in an earlier
chapter. But more remains to be said about them as they occur in sentences
which are not (at least not obviously) categorical in nature.

First, the two words 'any' and 'every' (and their cognates 'anything',
'everything', and the like) are both universal quantifier words. But it doesn't
follow that they are logically interchangeable expressions. The difference in
their roles is important but subtle: it is a difference in the *relative scope* of
the quantifier expression, with respect to some other "scoping" expression
in the same context.* When 'any' occurs in a statement containing another
scoping expression, the scope of the quantification includes, or *dominates*,
that of the other expression; but when 'every' occurs in such a statement,
the scope of the quantification is *subordinate* to that of the other expression.
For example, consider the two statements:

> 1. Not every man is large enough to eat a horse.
> 2. Not any man is large enough to eat a horse.

In (1), what is asserted is the negation of 'Every man is large enough to eat
a horse', a proposition in which the quantifier expression 'every man' falls
within the scope of the negation operator. In (2), what is asserted is that *no*
man is large enough to eat a horse—that is, given any man, it is not the
case that he is large enough to eat a horse—a proposition in which the negation operator falls within the scope of the quantifier expression 'any man'.

---

*For "scopes," see Appendix D. See also W. V. Quine, "Logic as a Source of Syntactic
Insights," in his *The Ways of Paradox* (New York: Random House, 1965).

Formally, of course, the same distinction is reflected in the two statements

    1a. $\sim(x)(x$ is a man $\supset x$ is large enough to eat a horse)

    2a. $(x)(x$ is a man $\supset \sim(x$ is large enough to eat a horse))

which are the logical translations of (1) and (2). In (1a) the quantifier falls within the scope of the tilde—just as in (1) the quantifier expression is within the scope of the negation; and in (2a) the tilde falls within the scope of the quantifier—just as in (2) the negation is within the scope of the quantifier expression. Another illustration is in the two statements:

    3. Richard did not love everybody.

    4. Richard did not love anybody.

In (3) we have the simple denial of 'Richard loved everybody', to be rendered symbolically as

    3a. $\sim(x)(x$ is a person $\supset$ Richard loved $x)$

in which the subordinative character of 'every' is reflected in the subordination of the quantifier with respect to the tilde. In (4) however, what is asserted is that for each person, Richard did not love that person; in symbols

    4a. $(x)(x$ is a person $\supset \sim($Richard loved $x))$

in which the dominative character of 'any' is reflected in the dominance of the quantifier with respect to the tilde.

Since the purpose of the two expressions is to mark this sort of scope distinction, they are in fact interchangeable whenever the context contains no other scoping expression. There is no difference in meaning between the two statements

    5. Any man has his price.

    6. Every man has his price.

just because there is no difference of relative scope for the two expressions to demarcate. Thus either of them will translate indifferently as

    7. $(x)(x$ is a man $\supset x$ has his price)

The two are also interchangeable in the presence of a scoping expression whose scope is irrelevant to the truth or falsity of the proposition, such as a disjunctive (or conjunctive) operator or within the consequent of a conditional operator. The natural language equivalence of the two statements

    8. Every man has his price, or else some haven't.

    9. Any man has his price, or else some haven't.

which assert exactly the same thing, is reflected in the logical equivalence of the formulae

    8a. $(x)Fx \vee P$

    9a. $(x)(Fx \vee P)$

which are equivalent despite the different relative scopes of the wedge and the quantifier. Similarly for the pair of statements

10. Every man has his price, if you look hard enough.
11. Any man has his price, if you look hard enough.

and the corresponding formulae

10a. $H \supset (x)Px$
11a. $(x)(H \supset Px)$

which illustrate the irrelevance of the "righthand scope" (consequent) of a conditional operator relative to a quantifier.

Of course, occurrences within the *antecedent* of a conditional are not similarly interchangeable, precisely because the "lefthand scope" of a conditional can make a difference to the truth or falsity of the statement. The two statements

12. If everybody gets in the boat, it will sink.
13. If anybody gets in the boat, it will sink.

do not mean at all the same thing, just as the corresponding formulae

12a. $(x)x$ gets in the boat $\supset$ it will sink
13a. $(x)(x$ gets in the boat $\supset$ it will sink)

do not mean the same thing.

Within the context of the antecedent of a conditional, 'any' becomes interchangeable with '*some*', rather than with 'every'. This does not mean that, in such a context, 'any' ceases to be universal: rather, it means that in such a context 'some' *becomes* universal. The statement

14. If somebody gets into the boat, it will sink.

may be rendered, with certain restrictions on the variable,* as

14a. $(\exists x)x$ gets in the boat $\supset$ it will sink

which, as we know, is logically equivalent by QS to (13a). Thus, (14) could just as well have been translated as (13a) in the first place. In general, when 'some' occurs in the antecedent of a conditional statement, that statement may be translated as a universally quantified conditional matrix such as (13a), instead of as a conditional with an existentially quantified antecedent, such as (14a). This means that 'some' and 'any', occurring in the antecedent of a conditional, translate in exactly the same way and hence are interchangeable.

The equivalence of (13a) and (14a) *might* lead one to try a further generalization: when 'some' or 'any' occurs in the antecedent of a conditional statement, that statement may be translated as a conditional with an existentially quantified antecedent, such as (14a), rather than as a universally quanti-

---

*Cf. the final section of this chapter.

fied conditional matrix, such as (13a). But this generalization *is not true* without further qualification. Statements of the form of (13a) and (14a) are equivalent only when the variable of quantification does not occur in the consequent—recall the restriction on QS. In a statement such as (13a)—that is, one of the form

15. $(x)(Fx \supset \Phi)$

—the quantifier cannot be shifted in to produce a statement of the form

15a. $(\exists x)Fx \supset \Phi$

if the quantified variable occurs in Φ; for such a shift would free those occurrences, which is not permissible. There is a precise analogue of this in natural language. If 'some' or 'any' occurs in the antecedent of a conditional and *ranges into the consequent* of that conditional—that is, if it serves as the base for one or more pronouns in the consequent—then that statement cannot be translated after the manner of (15a), for to do so would be to eliminate the connection between those pronouns and their base: it would "free" them. For example, the statement

16. If somebody gets into the boat, he will get his feet wet.

in which 'somebody' ranges into the consequent, cannot be translated either as

16a. $(\exists x)x$ gets into the boat $\supset x$ will get his feet wet

or as

16b. $(\exists x)x$ gets into the boat $\supset$ he will get his feet wet

because both of these fail to capture the essential connection between the antecedent and consequent of (16)—namely, that they are about the same thing. Rather, (16) must be translated after the manner of (15),

16c. $(x)(x$ gets into the boat $\supset x$ will get his feet wet)

thereby preserving the connection.

The same is true for *any* quantifier expression which occurs in the antecedent of a conditional and ranges into the consequent: that statement will translate as a universally quantified conditional matrix, after the manner of (16c), and not in some other way. For example, the slightly ungrammatical-sounding statement

17. If everybody gets into the boat, they will get their feet wet.

must translate as (16c) in order to capture the cross-connection between the pronoun 'they' and its base 'everybody'. (If (17) is understood as a clumsy way of saying 'If everybody gets into the boat, everybody will get his feet wet', in which there is no pronoun overlap, then of course things will be different.)

These facts about quantifier expressions in the antecedents of conditionals may be summed up as follows:

1. 'Every' occurring in the antecedent and *not* ranging into the consequent *always* translates as a universal quantifier governing just the antecedent.
2. 'Any' or 'some' occurring in the antecedent and *not* ranging into the consequent *may* be translated as an existential quantifier governing just the antecedent; they may also be translated as a universal quantifier governing the whole conditional matrix.
3. 'Any', 'some', 'every', *or any expression to be translated by a quantifier* which occurs in the antecedent and ranges into the consequent will *always* translate as a universal quantifier governing the whole conditional matrix.

These rules obtain whether the conditional in question stands alone or is part of some larger statement.

Exercises I

Translate and abbreviate each of the following.

☐ **1.** If something is valuable then something is worth seeking.

2. If anything is valuable then something is worth seeking.

3. If everything is valuable then something is worth seeking.

☐ **4.** If something is valuable then it is worth seeking.

5. If anything is valuable then it is worth seeking.

6. Everything that is valuable is worth seeking.

7. If anyone starts a fight, then if someone calls the police, then someone will be arrested.

☐ **8.** If any man starts a fight, then if any woman calls the police, then he will be arrested.

9. If any man starts a fight, then if any woman calls the police, then she will be arrested.

10. Anyplace where nothing grows and which is more than a mile above sea level is a high desert.

11. Every juvenile who steals hubcaps is headed for the penitentiary.

12. If something will dissolve both gold and platinum then it is aqua regia.

☐ **13.** If every Assyrian is a man and if something is a man then it is not three-legged, then if anything is an Assyrian then something is not three-legged.

14. If Percy kicked Evangeline and she began to cry, then if everyone who makes his sister cry is a brat, then he is a brat.

§18.3 Matrices and Operators

In ordinary situations of discourse we are seldom inclined to make unconditional statements about *everything*, for the very good reason that most such statements are false. There are very few unconditional properties which are possessed by literally everything in the universe, and so we do not generally go out of our way to ascribe an unconditional property to *every-thing* (unless we are exaggerating for the sake of emphasis). Normally we are more circumspect, confining our generalizations to certain classes of things out of the total inventory of the universe. We often make statements about all cows, or all numbers, or all stars brighter than sixth magnitude, and ascribe to them some unconditional property (such as being a mammal, or having a successor, or being visible to the naked eye). But to do this is not to ascribe an unconditional property to each thing in the world (such as the property of being a mammal); it is rather to ascribe a *conditional* property to each thing in the world (such as the property of being a mammal *if* bovine).

To say that an individual has a certain conditional property is the same as saying that it satisfies a certain conditional function; for example, to say that Bessie has the property of being a mammal if bovine is the same as saying that Bessie satisfies the function 'x is bovine $\supset x$ is a mammal'.

Because in normal discourse (at least of the sort usually presented for logical evaluation) we are predisposed to say things which have at least a plausible chance of being true, it almost invariably turns out to be the case that, when a universally general statement from English is translated into the notation of formal logic, the universal quantifier will end up governing a *conditional* matrix rather than a matrix of some other form. This is not an absolute truth, but it is true for the vast majority of things we are inclined to assert.

Even more strongly, we seldom say anything in normal discourse which could correctly translate into logic as a universal quantification over a *conjunctive* matrix. For an individual satisfies a conjunctive function only if it has both of the properties designated by the two conjuncts, and if it is difficult to find a property possessed by everything, it is doubly difficult to find *two* properties simultaneously possessed by everything. It is extremely hard to think of a statement translatable into the form

$$(x)(Fx \cdot Gx)$$

which would be true, or which would even seem plausible. There are such statements, but they do not normally occur in discourse. Therefore, when translating from English into the notation of quantifier logic, if you should end up with a *universal* quantifier governing a *conjunctive* matrix, the odds are that you have mistranslated, and you would do well to recheck your work to be sure that you have done it correctly. In the normal course of things, the dominant operator within a matrix governed by a universal quantifier will be a horseshoe, rather than a dot. If the dominant operator is a dot, the statement is too strong to stand much of a chance of being true.

By the same token, we seldom say anything in general discourse which might accurately be translated as an *existential* quantification over a *conditional* matrix. There are such statements, but they occur infrequently. An

individual satisfies a conditional function if either it fails to satisfy the antecedent or it satisfies the consequent (recall the truth-table definition of the
horseshoe). But no matter what property is designated by the antecedent, the
odds are that at least one thing does not have that property (this is the same
as saying: the odds are that not everything has that property). And if this is
true, it is doubly true that given any pair of properties the odds are that there
is something, somewhere, which either lacks one or has the other. Thus, any
statement correctly translatable into the form

$$(\exists x)(Fx \supset Gx)$$

will be too weak to be of interest, and it will not be the sort of statement we
normally bother to make. As before, if in translating from English into logic
you should end up with an *existential* quantifier governing a *conditional*
matrix, chances are that you have mistranslated. In the vast majority of
cases the dominant operator within a matrix governed by an existential quantifier will be a dot, rather than a horseshoe. If you come up with something
other than this, it is a good idea to check carefully to be certain that you
have not made a mistake.

The above has to do with the results of *translation*, not the results of transformations or inferences made with logical formulae. Often it will be possible
to infer an unlikely statement from likely ones, and we should not be
bothered if, in the course of constructing a derivation, we come up with some
counterinstances to the above generalizations. But we should be hesitant if,
in the course of *translation*, we find ourselves with an existentially quantified
conditional matrix or a universally quantified conjunctive one.

These points have to do with normal translation; they apply with less
regularity to translations within restricted universes of discourse, as discussed
in the next section, for reasons that should become apparent.

§18.4   Restricted Universes of Discourse

A "universe of discourse" is the class of things which are mentioned or
are liable to be mentioned within a particular piece of discourse. Normally
when we are doing formal logic our universe of discourse is unrestricted and
consists simply of everything there is, including microbes, apartment houses,
human beings, numbers, places, quasars, and so on. However, for special
purposes it is sometimes advantageous to restrict our universe of discourse
in one way or another, since doing this usually leads to shorter formulae to
work with. For example, within many areas of mathematics the objects
discussed are numbers and nothing else, and in applying logic to those areas
of mathematics it is useful to restrict the universe of discourse to numbers.

Restricting one's universe of discourse to things of a single kind, such as
numbers, requires nothing more than a decision to talk about numbers and

nothing else. Nothing formal is required, except a memorandum of the decision in order to avoid possible confusion later on. Once this decision has been made, translation will proceed just as if everything in the universe were (say) a number. For example, the statement

    1. Every number has a successor.

which, in an unrestricted universe of discourse, translates as

    1a. $(x)(x$ is a number $\supset x$ has a successor)

will translate within a universe of discourse restricted to numbers simply as

    1b. $(x)x$ has a successor

Similarly, the statement

    2. Some numbers are prime.

which, in an unrestricted universe of discourse, translates as

    2a. $(\exists x)(x$ is a number $\cdot x$ is prime)

will translate within a universe of discourse restricted to numbers as

    2b. $(\exists x)x$ is prime

Within a universe of discourse restricted to numbers there is never any need to mention the property of being a number, since that is a property which everything (within the restricted universe of discourse) possesses, and thus it will not matter to any inferences. Therefore, we can eliminate the constant factor 'x is a number' from our formulae without affecting anything except their length. Statements translated for a restricted universe of discourse can be retranslated for the unrestricted universe simply by adding (say) 'x is a number' as the opening antecedent in the matrix of all universally quantified formulae, and as the opening conjunct in the matrix of all existentially quantified formulae; for example, (1b) can be retranslated as (1a), and (2b) can be retranslated as (2a).

A universe of discourse may be restricted to any kind of thing you choose. For example, it is often advantageous to restrict the universe of discourse to persons. When this is done, the statement

    3. Anyone who steals my purse steals trash.

which normally translates as

    3a. $(x)((x$ is a person $\cdot x$ steals my purse) $\supset x$ steals trash)

will instead translate simply as

    3b. $(x)(x$ steals my purse $\supset x$ steals trash)

And the statement

    4. At least one person is over a hundred years old.

will translate as

    4a. $(\exists x)x$ is over a hundred years old

Of course, when a universe of discourse has been restricted to persons, it will no longer be possible to talk about anything which is not a person; for example, it will not be possible to give an accurate translation of the statement

5. If a person dies then a dog howls.

It cannot be translated as

5a. $(\exists x)x$ dies $\supset (\exists y)(y$ is a dog $\cdot y$ howls)

for, within a universe restricted to persons, the consequent of this means "Some person is a dog and howls," which is surely no part of what is meant by (5).

Sometimes, instead of restricting our universe of discourse to things of a single kind, we wish to restrict it to two or more different kinds of things, such as points and lines, or men and women, or aardvarks and electrons. This cannot be done successfully by the method above, but requires a notational device called a "restricted-range variable" (or, sometimes, a restricted-range constant).

The role of individual variables in quantifier logic is largely identical with the role of personal pronouns in a natural language: both serve to facilitate cross-references between different parts of a sentence or statement. Certain pronouns in English have a *restricted range*, in the sense that they require their base to designate an object of a certain kind. For example, the pronouns 'she' and 'her' have a restricted range: they are restricted to objects which are female (or feminine). Similarly, the pronouns 'he', 'his', and 'him' have a range restricted to objects which are male (or masculine).* On the other hand, the pronoun 'it' has an unrestricted range.

The ordinary individual variables of quantification are like the pronoun 'it', in that their range is unrestricted. But it is possible to introduce a new type of variable, with a restricted range, and to restrict its range in any way we choose. Just as in English there can be two pronouns whose range is restricted in the same way (for example, to females), so in logic it is helpful—and sometimes necessary—to have at our disposal several variables with the same restricted range. This means that if we wish to restrict our universe of discourse to two different kinds of things—say, males and females—we will need an "alphabet" of variables whose range is restricted to males and a *different* alphabet of variables whose range is restricted to females. The members of these two "alphabets" must be sufficiently different that we can tell at a glance which alphabet they come from, and also different from the (standard lower-case English) alphabet of unrestricted variables normally used in logic. Thus, if we were sufficiently familiar with them, we might choose genuine foreign alphabets (Greek, Hebrew, Cyrillic, Old German) for our

---

*They also have a different use as pronouns restricted simply to persons or personified things, as in "Every student must show his ticket," or "Every dog has his day." This use is no longer encouraged.

restricted-range variables—for example, using the Greek alphabet for variables of one restricted range and using the Old German alphabet for variables of the other restricted range. But a handier way to develop distinctive alphabets is by adding diacritical marks to the letters of the standard alphabet. In this way we can develop

a diaeresis alphabet:	$\ddot{a}, \ddot{b}, \ddot{c}, \ddot{d}, \ddot{e} \ldots$
a prime alphabet:	$a', b', c', d', e', \ldots$
an overline alphabet:	$\bar{a}, \bar{b}, \bar{c}, \bar{d}, \bar{e}, \ldots$
a sub-one alphabet:	$a_1, b_1, c_1, d_1, e_1, \ldots$
a sub-two alphabet:	$a_2, b_2, c_2, d_2, e_2, \ldots$

and as many more alphabets as we may happen to need, just by attaching different distinguishing marks to the basic *abc*'s.

The range of an alphabet is restricted by stipulating (normally in writing, to avoid forgetfulness) exactly what sorts of things are permitted to fall under variables from that alphabet. This is done by setting down just the first letter in that alphabet, enclosed in braces and followed by the restriction; for example:

$$\{a'\} \quad \text{restricted to males}$$
$$\{\bar{a}\} \quad \text{restricted to females}$$

It should be recognized that 'a'' and '$\bar{a}$' are absolutely different *letters*; they come from different alphabets and are as different as 'g' and 'γ'. Using variables restricted in the way just indicated, we can translate the statement

6. All males are domineering.

as

6a. $(x')x'$ is domineering

Similarly, we can translate the statement

7. All females are demure.

as

7a. $(\bar{x})\bar{x}$ is demure

Also (unlike the case where our universe of discourse is restricted to a single kind of thing), we can translate

8. If all males are single then all females are happy.

as

8a. $(x')x'$ is single $\supset (\bar{y})\bar{y}$ is happy

Or, as a slightly more complex example, we can translate

9. If all males who are in the army are ineligible for marriage, then some single females are unfortunate.

as

9a. $(z')(z'$ is in the army $\supset \sim z'$ is eligible for marriage) $\supset$ ($\exists \bar{w})(\bar{w}$ is single $\cdot$ $\bar{w}$ is unfortunate)

which abbreviates as

9b. $(z')(Az' \supset \sim Ez') \supset$ ($\exists \bar{w})(S\bar{w} \cdot U\bar{w})$

It is also possible to develop restricted-range constants by underlining letters from the restricted alphabet. There is an analogue for this in English: proper names such as 'Martha' and 'Beatrice' are normally restricted to females, whereas proper names such as 'Kenneth' and 'Oscar' are normally restricted to males. In these cases the restriction is purely a matter of social convention; no doubt there are parents perverse enough to name their daughters 'Kenneth' and their sons 'Beatrice'. But in logic, a constant with a restricted range is *absolutely* restricted to things of the kind specified. For example, the statement

10. Edna is a female who drinks too much.

which would normally translate as

10a. $F\underline{e} \cdot D\underline{e}$

may instead be translated, with a restricted-range constant, simply as

10b. $D\underline{\bar{e}}$

which means exactly the same thing as (10a) but is shorter.

Formulae containing restricted-range letters can always be retranslated into formulae with unrestricted letters, by splicing in the appropriate formula as an antecedent (in the case of universally quantified formulae) or a conjunct (in the case of singular formulae or existentially quantified formulae) and rewriting the restricted letters as unrestricted ones. For example, (10b) can be retranslated as (10a). Similarly, (6a) can be retranslated as

6b. $(x)(x$ is a male $\supset x$ is domineering)

(7a) can be retranslated as

7b. $(x)(x$ is a female $\supset x$ is demure)

and (9b) can be retranslated as

9c. $(z)(Mz \supset (Az \supset \sim Ez)) \supset$ ($\exists w)(Fw \cdot (Sw \cdot Uw))$

It is *never* permissible to use a rule of inference or transformation in such a way as to replace letters from one alphabet with letters from a different one. The only way to change alphabets is by *retranslating* from restricted letters to unrestricted ones. For example, it is *not* permissible to use RBV to rewrite (7a) '$(\bar{x})\bar{x}$ is demure' either as

7c. $(x')x'$ is demure

or as

7d. $(x)x$ is demure

RBV must proceed from letters in a given alphabet to letters in that same alphabet. The same thing holds for the rules in the next chapter, which permit changes of letters under certain circumstances. The switching of letters must *always* take place within the same alphabet.

A final note on this matter. Instead of developing a full alphabet by means of diacritical marks, it is also possible to select a sub-"alphabet" from within the standard one and to use it with a restricted range. For example, we might say

$\{a, b, c, d\}$ restricted to human beings
$\{m, n, o, p\}$ restricted to tigers

With these restrictions, the statement

11. $(a)a$ is vicious

would mean "All humans are vicious," but the statement

12. $(m)m$ is vicious

would mean "All tigers are vicious." When things are done in this way, it is understood that the remaining letters (in this case, $e, f, g, h, i, j, k, l, q, r, s, t,$ u, v, w, x, y, z) are still unrestricted and constitute an "alphabet" separate from either of the restricted ones.

Exercises II

Translate and abbreviate each of the following, using the given restrictions.

$\{\bar{a}\}$ restricted to human beings $\{c, d, e\}$ restricted to males
$\{a'\}$ restricted to tigers $\{m, n, o\}$ restricted to females
$\{\ddot{a}\}$ restricted to domestic things $\{r, s, t\}$ restricted to young things

☐ 1. If somebody starts a fight then if anybody calls the police then somebody will be arrested.

2. If nobody starts a fight and nobody calls the police then nobody will be arrested.

3. If all tigers are vicious then some tigers are vicious.

4. If any milk-fed tigers are tame then some tigers are tame.

☐ 5. If any tiger starts a fight, then if somebody calls the zookeeper, then some tiger will be punished.

6. If all male tigers are vicious, then some tame male tigers are vicious. (There are two possible restricted translations of this one.)

7. If all men are domineering then some women are demure. (There are several ways to do this one.)

8. If all domestic tigers are female and some domestic tigers are tame then some female tigers are tame. (There are several ways to do this one.)

☐ 9. No domestic female tiger cubs are tame. (There are several ways to do this one.)

10. If all the boys come out to play, then all the girls will run away. (There are several ways to do this one.)

chapter 19

RULES OF INSTANTIATION
AND GENERALIZATION

§19.1 Quantifier Truths

A **logical truth** is a statement whose truth can be established by logic alone, without the need for extralogical procedures. All tautologies are logical truths. However, not all logical truths are tautologies.* A tautology is a statement whose truth can be demonstrated by the methods and procedures of truth-functional logic. But many logical truths require procedures of *quantifier* logic to demonstrate their truth. A statement which can be shown to be true by the methods and procedures of quantifier logic is called a **quantifier truth.** Quantifier truths are to quantifier logic what tautologies are to truth-functional logic. There are also **quantifier falsehoods**—statements whose falsity can be demonstrated by procedures of quantifier logic—which correspond to the contradictions of truth-functional logic. Both tautologies and quantifier truths are logical truths; both contradictions and quantifier falsehoods are logical falsehoods.

We have already had some limited encounters with quantifier truths. For instance, in an earlier chapter you were asked to prove, as an exercise, the zero-premiss conclusion

$$1.\ (x)(Fx \supset Gx) \equiv\ \sim (\exists x)(Fx \cdot \sim Gx).$$

This statement is a quantifier truth. It is a logical truth, but it cannot be shown to be true by the techniques of truth-functional logic alone; it requires techniques of quantifier logic as well. The fact that (1) is a biconditional, and that it is a logical truth, shows that its two sides are logically equivalent. They are not, of course, truth-functionally equivalent; rather, they are **quantificationally equivalent.** Quantificational equivalence is to quantifier logic what truth-functional equivalence is to truth-functional logic; they are two species of logical equivalence.

---

*Some writers use 'tautology' and 'logical truth' interchangeably.

The rules presently at our disposal for working with statements and arguments containing quantifiers are QN, QS, RBV, Matrix Transformation, and the inference rules and transformation rules of truth-functional logic. This set of rules is sufficient for demonstrating the validity of some fairly simple quantificational arguments and for demonstrating the truth of some fairly simple quantifier truths; the exercises in the previous chapters reveal this. But there remain a great many valid arguments and quantifier truths which cannot be proven valid or true without additional inference rules. For example, the two statements 'If everything is red then something is red' and 'All cats are cats', symbolized as

2. $(x)Rx \supset (\exists x)Rx$
3. $(x)(Cx \supset Cx)$

are both quantifier truths; but neither of them can be proven true with the rules given so far. Similarly, the venerable syllogism 'All humans are mortal; all Greeks are human; therefore, all Greeks are mortal', symbolized as

$(x)(Hx \supset Mx)$
$(x)(Gx \supset Hx)$ $/ \therefore (x)(Gx \supset Mx)$

is quantificationally valid, but it cannot be *proven* valid by the rules now at our disposal. The rules needed for these purposes are presented in this chapter.

§19.2 Variables and Places

The four rules presented in this chapter are, in an important sense, the fundamental rules of quantifier logic. They are not particularly difficult to apply, once they are understood. But it is quite easy to misunderstand them. For this reason, each of the four rules is explained in much greater detail than any of the inference rules encountered thus far. These detailed explanations may cause the four rules to appear more forbidding than they really are, since we are accustomed to explanations which are proportional in length to the difficulty of the matter being explained. In the present case, the disproportionately lengthy explanations are intended to serve two purposes: (1) to explain why the rules are stated in just the way they are, and (2) to explain the "logic" behind the rules—that is, to explain why the rules are valid.

In the remainder of this chapter and in subsequent ones we shall frequently encounter formulae containing free variables, such as '$(x)(Fx \supset Gy)$' or '$Kz \supset (\exists y)Ky$'. (In the first of these, 'y' occurs free; in the second of them, 'z' occurs free.) Heretofore, we have treated formulae with free variables as propositional functions—that is, as open sentences with the free variables indicating the blank spaces. But from now on we shall ordinarily treat such formulae not as open sentences, but as "indifferent" substitution instances of open sentences. That is to say, we shall ordinarily treat a formula such as

1. *x* is purple

not as a convenient way of writing the open sentence

2. ___ is purple

but as a statement which asserts of *x* that it is purple. And if the question is asked, "What exactly is *x*?" the appropriate reply will be, "I don't care." The difference is this: If (1) is regarded as an open sentence, then it is regarded as a linguistic fragment which has no truth-value (just as (2) has no truth-value); but if (1) is regarded as a substitution-instance of an open sentence, then it is regarded as a linguistic unit, which is either true or false, though we don't happen to know (or care) which.

This use of free variables as "indifferent" blank-fillers is a labor-saving device more than anything else; we use variables in this way to save ourselves the trouble of using constants. *We could use constants if we wished to take the trouble*; our proofs would remain valid, if we chose to do so. But it is the usual practice in logic not to use an individual constant unless there is a specific reason for doing so (for example, unless there is a proper name in the English version of the argument under consideration). Thus, in the remainder of the book, unless a formula with free variables is specifically labelled as a propositional function, it is to be regarded not as a propositional function, but as a substitution-instance of one, which we were too lazy to "fill out" with an individual constant.

Also, for purposes of exposition (especially in the present chapter) we shall revert to the practice of indicating blank spaces in propositional functions with a blank line; and we shall say, where it matters, that a propositional function is a formula containing one or more blank spaces, such that when all of the blanks are filled in with lower-case letters the result is a statement. (This may be regarded as an alternative definition to the one given earlier.)

The notion of "places" shows up quite often in the following pages. The "places" referred to are immediately to the right of the capital letters—the places for lower-case letters (or blank spaces). Each capital letter has a "place" after it; for example, in

3. *Fa* ⊃ *Gb*

there are two places: the one after '*F*' and the one after '*G*'; similarly, in

4. *Fa* ⊃ (*Fb* ∨ *Gb*)

there are three places: the one after '*F*' in the antecedent, the one after '*F*' in the consequent, and the one after '*G*' in the consequent. The first of these places is occupied by an occurrence of the letter '*a*'; the other two are occupied by occurrences of the letter '*b*'. Also,

   5. $(x)(Fy \supset (Fx \lor Gx))$

has the same array of places as (4): a place after '*F*' in the antecedent, a place after '*F*' in one disjunct of the consequent, and a place after '*G*' in the other disjunct of the consequent. In (5) the first of these is occupied by a free occurrence of '*y*', and the other two are occupied by bound occurrences of '*x*'. Of course, (4) and (5) are different in another important way: (4) is quantifier-free and (5) isn't. Finally, in

   6. $(y)(Fy \supset (Fy \lor Gy))$

all three of the places are occupied by bound occurrences of '*y*'. The point of these illustrations is to show that we can talk about the *places* independently of what may occupy them. Since the occupants of places sometimes change, it is important to be able to focus our attention on the places themselves and not be distracted by the fluctuating population.

    When reference is made to "letters" in the following pages, this will mean (unless otherwise specified) *lower-case* letters: individual variables and/or constants.

§19.3 Universal Instantiation

    A universally quantified statement, translated into the symbolic language, is a universal quantification over some function, and what it asserts is that everything in the universe satisfies that function—that every substitution-instance of that function is true. Thus, the universal quantification of a function *entails* every substitution-instance of that function (since it would be impossible for a substitution-instance to be false if the universal quantification were true). This is the essence of the principle of Universal Instantiation. For example, the universally quantified statement

   1. $(x)x$ is purple

asserts that *everything* satisfies the function

   2. ___ is purple

—that is, that all substitution-instances of (2) are true. Hence, from (1), it is legitimate to infer

     $\underline{a}$ is purple
     $\underline{b}$ is purple
     $\underline{c}$ is purple
     x is purple
     y is purple
     z is purple

and so on, since each of these is a substitution-instance of (2). Similarly, the universally quantified statement

   3. $(x)(x$ is human $\supset x$ is mortal)

asserts that everything satisfies the function

   4. __ is human $\supset$ __ is mortal

and hence, from (3), it is legitimate to infer any substitution-instance of (4) that we like, e.g.

   $\underline{s}$ is human $\supset \underline{s}$ is mortal
   x is human $\supset x$ is mortal
   p is human $\supset p$ is mortal

and so on. Again, the universally quantified statement

   5. $(x)(x$ is purple $\supset y$ is colored)

asserts that everything satisfies the function

   6. __ is purple $\supset y$ is colored

and so from (5) we may legitimately infer

   x is purple $\supset y$ is colored
   y is purple $\supset y$ is colored
   z is purple $\supset y$ is colored

and so on, since each of these is a substitution-instance of (6). The function whose (universal) satisfaction is asserted in a quantified statement is the one whose "blank spaces" exactly match the occurrences, in the matrix, of the variable in the quantifier. For example, in (1) the "variable of quantification" is the letter 'x'. In the matrix of (1), 'x' occurs in only one place: immediately before the word 'is'. The function whose blank space exactly matches this is (2). Thus, (1) asserts the universal satisfaction of (2). Similarly, in (3) the variable of quantification is 'x', which occurs in the matrix of (3) in exactly two places: before 'is' in the antecedent and before 'is' in the consequent. The function whose blank spaces exactly match this is (4). Thus, (3) asserts the universal satisfaction of (4).

   It is always a relatively easy matter, given a quantified statement, to isolate out the function involved. Simply delete the quantifier and then go through the matrix and eliminate each occurrence of its variable, leaving "blank spaces" in their place. The result will be a function whose gaps exactly match the range of the former quantifier—the function whose (universal) satisfaction was asserted by the original quantified statement. We shall refer to this as the **matric function** of the original quantified statement.

   It is important to bear in mind what a universally quantified statement does and does not assert of its matric function. For instance, the matric function of

   3. $(x)(x$ is human $\supset x$ is mortal)

is

4. ___ is human ⊃ ___ is mortal

but (3) does not assert that just any old way of filling in the blanks in (4) will result in a true statement. Rather, it asserts that every result of filling in the blanks *consistently* will be true. Here, "consistently" means filling in all the blanks with the same thing. Another way of saying this is that (3)—which happens to be true—does *not* entail

7. James Buchanan is human ⊃ Betelgeuse is mortal

(which happens to be false). For (7) is not a consistent substitution-instance of (4)—it requires that the two gaps be filled in with different names. And (3) only asserts that every *consistent* substitution-instance of its matric function is true.*

Recognizing these facts, we might attempt to state an inference rule in the following way: "From a universally quantified statement, it is permissible to infer any consistent substitution instance of its matric function." But this phrasing is unsatisfactory, because of a small but important complication that can and does arise. Consider the quantified statement

8. $(x)(Fx \supset (y)(Gy \supset Hx))$

whose matric function is

9. $F\_\_ \supset (y)(Gy \supset H\_\_)$

Since (8) asserts that everything satisfies (9), (8) entails every consistent substitution-instance of (9); but this does not mean that (8) entails every result of consistently filling in the blanks in (9). This is because *one* way of filling in the blanks in (9) does not produce a substitution-instance of (9). If the letter 'y' is chosen as the "variable of instantiation," the result is

10. $Fy \supset (y)(Gy \supset Hy)$

which is a substitution instance, not of (9), but of the quite different function

11. $F\_\_ \supset (y)(Gy \supset Hy)$

The nature of this case will be clearer if we look at (8) as a translation of some English statement, say

8a. If anyone tried to hide from the police, then if anything was stolen then he is guilty.

Now (8a), being a universally general statement, entails

9a. If Yokum tried to hide from the police, then if anything was stolen then Yokum is guilty.

---

*The requirement of consistency may be more easily understood if it is recalled (§16.1) that a complex function—such as (4)—is always logically equivalent to some *simple* function; that (4), for example, is logically equivalent to '__is mortal if human' [and (3) is logically equivalent to '$(x)x$ is mortal if human'], in which the consistency requirement is enforced by physical necessity, since there is only one gap to be filled.

But if we attempt to express this formally by filling in the blanks in (9) with '*y*' for 'Yokum', the result is (10); and what (10) says is

10a. If Yokum tried to hide from the police, then everything that was stolen is guilty.

This is because, when '*y*' is inserted into the blank following '*H*', it immediately becomes bound by the universal quantifier '(*y*)', within whose scope it lies. It no longer serves the purpose of designating Yokum but simply becomes another bound variable—a "pronoun" referring back to a quantifier. If we had chosen any other letter this would not have happened. It happened here because we carelessly chose '*y*' to fill a blank space within the scope of a quantifier containing '*y*'.

The situation thus illustrated is called a **collision of variables**. Collision of variables happens whenever, because of a careless choice of instantiating letters, one of our newly installed "blank-fillers" gets captured by a quantifier somewhere in the matric function. (Obviously, collision of variables is impossible when the matric function contains no quantifiers.) We can avoid it simply by being careful in the choice of instantiating letters. For example, if we had chosen '*k*' to abbreviate 'Yokum', none of the problems above would have arisen.

Since collision of variables leads to invalid inferences, it is important that we avoid it. One way of stating this point is as follows: When we infer, from a universally quantified statement, a substitution-instance of its matric function, it is essential that the letters installed in the blanks all remain *free*— that they not be gobbled up by some quantifier hiding elsewhere in the function. The effect of universal instantiation is to remove a quantifier, thereby freeing the places bound by it. A substitution-instance which keeps those places free (without allowing any of them to be captured by another quantifier in the formula) is called a **freedom-preserving** instance.

Strictly speaking, only freedom-preserving instances are real substitution-instances. For example, (10) is not really a substitution-instance of (9), even though (10) comes from (9) by consistent blank-filling. Nevertheless, avoidance of collision of variables is sufficiently important to warrant a special proviso when stating a Rule of Universal Instantiation.

In the official statement below, the Rule is formulated in two different (though logically equivalent) ways. The "conceptual formulation" is phrased to bring out the conceptual apparatus underlying the rule, given in the discussion preceding. The "operational formulation" is phrased for maximum ease of application and simply states the formal moves permitted by the rule.* For purposes of this phrasing, let us coin the term "ex-range" (on the model of "ex-husband" and "ex-president") to refer to the set of places which *were* the range of a quantifier eliminated by instantiation.

---

*For a more traditional formulation of the rules given in this chapter, see Appendix J.

UNIVERSAL INSTANTIATION (UI α/β)

Conceptual formulation: From a universally quantified line, it is permissible to infer any *consistent, freedom-preserving* substitution-instance of its matric function.

Operational formulation: It is permissible to eliminate a universal quantifier governing an entire line, thereby freeing its range,
(*"Free the range and*   and to rewrite its ex-range as any letter which will
keep it free.")   keep the entire ex-range free, or to leave it the same.

UI is also sometimes called "Universal Dequantification," since it is a rule for eliminating a universal quantifier. As the rule itself stresses, only *whole lines* within a derivation may be dequantified. It is not permissible to instantiate from a quantifier whose scope is less than the whole line.

When an inference is made by UI, the justification should indicate not only the rule, but also the letters involved in the instantiation. Give the rule, then the letter which was in the quantifier (the **variable of quantification**), then a slash—read as "to", then the letter in the ex-range (the **variable of instantiation**). Do this even if the two letters are the same. For example, here is the way a step of UI might appear within a derivation:

    1. $(x)(Fx \supset Gx)$
    2. $Fx \supset Gx$ 1, UI, x/x

Here, the variable of quantification and the variable of instantiation (or "instantiating letter") are both 'x', which is perfectly permissible. Another example of a correct application of UI is:

    1. $(x)(Fx \supset (Gx \lor Hx))$
    2. $Fy \supset (Gy \lor Hy)$ 1, UI, x/y

The rule of UI also allows inferences such as:

    1. $(x)((Fx \cdot Gy) \supset Hx)$
    2. $(Fy \cdot Gy) \supset Hy$ 1, UI, x/y

Here, the matric function of (1) is

    1a. $(F\_\_ \cdot Gy) \supset H\_\_$

Since (1a) contains no quantifiers, there can be no problem of collision of variables. Thus, any consistent substitution instance of (1a) may be inferred; and (2) is a consistent substitution instance of (1a), since it may be obtained from (1a) by filling in all the blanks with the same letter—'y'.

Let us now look at some invalid inferences of the sort *not* permitted by the rule of UI. First, consider

1. $(x)(Fx \supset Gy)$
2. $Fx \supset Gx$ 1, UI (erroneous)

The matric function of (1) is

1a. $F\_\_ \supset Gy$

But there is no way to obtain (2) from (1a) as a substitution-instance. To get from (1) to (2), it would also be necessary to change the 'y' to 'x' in the place after 'G', and there is nothing in the rule of UI to permit this.

Another type of invalid inference, which is not permitted by UI (or anything else), is exemplified in

1. $(x)(Fx \supset Gx)$
2. $Fx \supset Gy$ 1, UI (erroneous)

Here, the matric function of (1) is

1a. $F\_\_ \supset G\_\_$

but (2) is not a *consistent* substitution instance of (1a). To obtain (2) from (1a), it would be necessary to fill the first blank with 'x' and the second one with 'y', which is not consistent and which is not permitted by UI.

As another illustration, the following is not permitted by UI:

1. $(x)(\exists y)(Fx \supset (Gy \cdot Hx))$
2. $(\exists y)(Fy \supset (Gy \cdot Hy))$ 1, UI (erroneous)

Here, the matric function of (1) is

1a. $(\exists y)(F\_\_ \supset (Gy \cdot H\_\_))$

but while we might obtain (2) from this by consistently filling in the blanks with 'y', it is still invalid, since this substitution is not freedom-preserving. There is a collision of variables.

As a final example, the following is a type of inference which is not permitted by UI:

1. $(x)Mx \supset M\underline{e}$
2. $M\underline{c} \supset M\underline{e}$ 1, UI (erroneous)

The invalidity of this will be intuitively apparent when we recognize it as a translation of the patently absurd argument:

> If everyone has moved to Mexico then Edna has moved to Mexico.
> ∴ If Carlos has moved to Mexico then so has Edna.

This inference is disallowed, since it violates the stipulation that UI can only apply to a quantifier having the *entire line* within its scope. The scope of the quantifier in (1) is only a part of the line, so (1) cannot be universally instantiated.

Exercises I

Pick out the matric function of each of the following statements.

  1. $(x)(Fx \supset Gy)$

☐ **2.** $(y)(Fx \supset Gy)$

  3. $(x)(y)(Fx \supset Gy)$

  4. $(x)((Fx \cdot Gy) \supset (\exists y)(Fy \supset Kz))$

☐ **5.** $(z)((Fx \cdot Gy) \supset (\exists y)(Fy \supset Kz))$

  6. $(y)((Fy \cdot Gy) \supset (Fy \supset Ky))$

  7. $(z)((Fz \cdot Gy) \supset (Fy \supset Kz))$

☐ **8.** $(x)(\exists y)((Fx \supset Gx) \supset (Fy \supset Gx))$

  9. $(x)(y)(z)(Fx \supset (Gy \supset Hz))$

 10. $(y)(z)(x)(Fx \supset (Gy \supset Hz))$

☐ **11.** $(z)(x)(y)(Fx \supset (Gy \supset Hz))$

 12. $(z)(y)(x)(Fx \supset (Gy \supset Hz))$

§19.4   Existential Generalization

Any substitution instance of a propositional function entails the existential quantification of that function. From the statement

 1. Albert is fat.

it is permissible to infer the (less specific) statement that *something* is fat— that is,

 2. $(\exists x)x$ is fat

Similarly, the statement 'If Albert is fat then he is greedy,—that is,

 3. $F\underline{a} \supset G\underline{a}$

—is a substitution-instance of the function

 3a. $F\text{\_\_} \supset G\text{\_\_}$

and is also a substitution-instance of the function

 3b. $F\text{\_\_} \supset G\underline{a}$

and is also a substitution-instance of the function

 3c. $F\underline{a} \supset G\text{\_\_}$

Hence, from (3) it is valid to infer that 'There is *something* such that if it is fat then it is greedy'—that is, the existential quantification of (3a):

 4. $(\exists x)(Fx \supset Gx)$

and it is valid to infer that 'There is something such that if it is fat then Albert is greedy'—that is, the existential quantification of (3b):

5. $(\exists x)(Fx \supset G\underline{a})$

and it is valid to infer that 'There is something such that if Albert is fat then it is greedy'—that is, the existential quantification of (3c):

6. $(\exists x)(F\underline{a} \supset Gx)$

All of these inferences illustrate the principle of Existential Generalization. To "existentially generalize" from the case of a particular individual (say, Albert) is to go from a statement about that individual to an existentially quantified statement about "something-or-other": to go from a specific statement to an unspecific—that is, generalized—statement.

Let us say that a propositional function **underlies** a given statement if and only if that statement can be generated from that function by a *consistent* filling of the blanks with *free* letters. Within this terminology, (3a), (3b), and (3c) are all functions which underlie (3). By way of further illustration,

7. $F\underline{\quad} \lor G\underline{\quad}$

is *not* a function which underlies

8. $F\underline{a} \lor G\underline{b}$

since we could not obtain (8) from (7) by *consistently* filling in the blanks; it would be necessary to fill the blanks with different letters. However, both

9. $F\underline{\quad} \lor G\underline{b}$

and

10. $F\underline{a} \lor G\underline{\quad}$

are functions underlying (8). In a slightly different vein,

11. $F\underline{\quad} \lor (x)(Gx \supset H\underline{\quad})$

is a function which underlies

12. $Fy \lor (x)(Gx \supset Hy)$

whereas (11) does *not* underlie

13. $Fx \lor (x)(Gx \supset Hx)$

since we could not obtain (13) from (11) by consistently filling the blanks with *free* letters; once the place following 'H' is filled in with 'x', the 'x' is bound by the preceding (universal) quantifier.

Another way of getting at the same thing is this: any function which would result from blanking out one or more *free* occurrences of the same letter within a statement is a function underlying that statement, and nothing else is.

The **quantification of a function** is formed by (a) attaching a quantifier so that it has the entire function within its scope, and (b) inserting a fresh letter into the blank places and the quantifier, so that the quantifier binds *all* those places and no others. (A "fresh" letter is one that does not occur anywhere else in the function.) For example, to form the existential quantification of the function

3a. $F\_\_ \supset G\_\_$

we first select a fresh letter—easily done in this case, since (3a) contains no lower-case letters at all—say the letter 'y'; we attach an existential quantifier having the whole function in its scope, thus:

14. $(\exists \quad)(F\_\_ \supset G\_\_)$

and then fill in the quantifier and the blanks with our letter, to produce

15. $(\exists y)(Fy \supset Gy)$

which is the existential quantification of (3a). Similarly, to form the existential quantification of the function

11. $F\_\_ \vee (x)(Gx \supset H\_\_)$

we select a fresh letter (in this case, any letter but 'x'), attach an existential quantifier having the whole function in its scope,

16. $(\exists \quad)(F\_\_ \vee (x)(Gx \supset H\_\_))$

and fill in the quantifier and the blanks with our fresh letter,

17. $(\exists z)(Fz \vee (x)(Gx \supset Hz))$

forming the existential quantification of (11). As a final illustration, to form the existential quantification of the function

18. $(Fa \vee \sim G\_\_) \supset ((K\_\_ \cdot Rx) \vee (Gb \cdot Fy))$

we select a fresh letter (in this case, any letter but 'a', 'b', 'x', or 'y')—say 'w'. Then we attach an existential quantifier having the whole function in its scope:

19. $(\exists \quad)((Fa \vee \sim G\_\_) \supset ((K\_\_ \cdot Rx) \vee (Gb \cdot Fy)))$

and fill in the quantifier and the blanks with our letter to produce

20. $(\exists w)((Fa \vee \sim Gw) \supset ((Kw \cdot Rx) \vee (Gb \cdot Fy)))$

which is the existential quantification of (18).

The second rule of inference can now be stated as follows:

EXISTENTIAL GENERALIZATION (EG α/β)

Conceptual formulation:	It is permissible to infer the existential quantification of *any* function underlying an entire line.
Operational formulation: ("*Capture some free occurrences of a letter.*")	It is permissible to capture *some or all* free places occupied by some one letter by attaching an existential quantifier along with any punctuation needed to make it scope over the whole line. To capture just some of them, rewrite the letter in the places to be captured as a "fresh" letter (one not already in the line) and attach a quantifier containing that letter. In capturing *all* of them, it is also permissible to rewrite them as a fresh letter.

EG, like UI, is an *inference* rule and applies only to whole lines within a derivation. When justifying a step of EG, give the rule, then the variable which *was* free in the captured places, then the variable of quantification.

In becoming familiar with this rule, it is helpful to gain some skill in "seeing" the underlying functions hiding within a statement, without having to go to the trouble of actually blanking out letters and so on. Here are some typical applications of this rule.

1. $Fx \cdot Gx$
2. $(\exists y)(Fy \cdot Gy)$ 1, EG, x/y

In this case it is perhaps easy enough to see, without extraneous doodling on scratch-paper, that one of the functions underlying statement (1) is '$F\_\_ \cdot G\_\_$', and that the existential quantification of this function is line (2). Thus, the inference from (1) to (2) is permitted by EG. Looking at it operationally, (2) is obtained from (1) by rewriting all free occurrences of 'x' as the fresh letter 'y' and attaching the quantifier '$(\exists y)$' plus scoping punctuation. Therefore, the inference is permitted by EG.

1. $Fx \supset Gx$
2. $(\exists x)(Fx \supset Gx)$ 1, EG, x/x

This is almost as obvious as the last one. One of the functions underlying statement (1) is '$F\_\_ \supset G\_\_$'. This function contains no lower-case letters at all, hence any letter we choose as a variable of quantification will be "fresh". And line (2) is the existential quantification of this function, hence is permitted by EG.

1. $Fz \cdot Gy$
2. $(\exists x)(Fx \cdot Gy)$ 1, EG, z/x

In this case statement (1) has two functions underlying it, and one of them is '$F\_\_ \cdot Gy$'. Since this function contains 'y', some other letter must be used as the variable of quantification. The existential quantification of this function, using 'x', is line (2).

1. $Fz \cdot Gy$
2. $(\exists x)(Fz \cdot Gx)$ 1, EG, y/x
3. $(\exists w)(\exists x)(Fw \cdot Gx)$ 2, EG, z/w

Here once again statement (1) has two functions underlying it; one of them is '$Fz \cdot G\_\_$'. The existential quantification of this function, using 'x', is line (2). But line (2) is also a statement with an underlying function: the function '$(\exists x)(F\_\_ \cdot Gx)$'. And the existential quantification of this function, using 'w', is line (3).

1. $(x)Fx \supset Fy$
2. $(\exists y)((x)Fx \supset Fy)$ 1, EG, y/y

Here, the function underlying statement (1) is '$(x)Fx \supset F\_\_$'; its existential quantification, using 'y', is line (2).

    1. $Fy \cdot Gy$
    2. $(\exists x)(Fy \cdot Gx)$ 1, EG, y/x

In this case statement (1) has several underlying functions: "$F\_\_ \cdot G\_\_$', '$F\_\_ \cdot Gy$', and '$Fy \cdot G\_\_$'. Line (2) is the existential quantification of this last one, using 'x'.

It will be helpful to go back over these last five examples and trace through them on the basis of the operational formulation of the rule. This is left as an exercise.

Exercises II

Pick out all of the functions underlying each of the following statements. Some of them have only one underlying function, some have several, some have none.

    1. $Fx \supset A$
    2. $\sim(Ra \cdot \sim Sb)$
□   **3.** $Fa \supset (Gb \lor Hc)$
    4. $Fa \supset (Ga \supset (Fa \cdot Ga))$
    5. $Fa \supset (Gb \supset (Fa \cdot Gc))$
□   **6.** $(x)(Kx \supset Lx) \supset (Kx \supset Lx)$
    7. $(\exists y)(Gy \cdot (x)(Mx \supset Ny))$
    8. $(\exists y)(Gy \cdot (x)(Mx \supset Nz))$
□   **9.** $Fx \cdot ((y)(Fy \supset Gx) \cdot Hy)$
   10. $(x)((Fx \cdot Gy) \supset (\exists y)(Fx \cdot Gy))$

Exercises III

Construct the existential quantification of each function discovered in doing Exercise II.

An understanding of what is permitted by EG will be helped along by looking at some inferences it does *not* permit.

    1. $(Fx \cdot Gy)$
    2. $(\exists z)(Fz \cdot Gz)$ 1, EG (erroneous)

The invalidity of this sort of inference should be intuitively obvious. From the fact that x has the property F and y has the property G, it does not follow that there is something having both properties at once; from the fact that x is a Frenchman and y is a German, it does not follow that some Frenchmen are Germans. This sort of inference is not permitted by the Rule of EG;

line (2) is not the existential quantification of any function underlying (1). The functions underlying (1) are '*F___* · *Gy*' and '*Fx*· *G___*'; and there is no way, by attaching a quantifier and filling the blank with a *fresh* letter, to obtain (2) from either of these. Looked at operationally, the places following *F* and *G* cannot both be captured in a single step of EG, since they are not occupied by some *one* letter as the rule requires. Thus, EG does not permit this inference. Another sort of inference that is not permitted (and one so obvious it is almost silly) is exemplified in

      1. *Fx* · *Gy*
      2. (∃ *z*)(*Fz* · *Gw*)   1, EG (erroneous)

To get (2) from (1), it is necessary not only to bind the place after '*F*', but to change the letter in a place not bound by the quantifier (the place after '*G*'); and there is nothing in the EG rule to permit this latter move. Consequently, the inference is disallowed.

      1. *Fy* ∨ (*y*)(*Hy* ⊃ *Gy*)
      2. (∃ *x*)(*Fx* ∨ (*y*)(*Hy* ⊃ *Gx*))   1, EG (erroneous)

Here, once again, (2) is not the existential quantification of a function underlying (1). It is the existential quantification of '*F___* ∨ (*y*)(*Hy* ⊃ *G___*)'; but this function does not underlie (1), since we cannot obtain (1) from this function by filling the blanks with *free* letters; the occurrence of '*y*' in the place after '*G*' will be bound by the universal quantifier. In going from (1) to (2), the existential quantifier has stolen a place out of the range of another quantifier, and this is not permitted. It is ruled out operationally by the proviso that the captured places be free ones.

      1. *Ba* ⊃ *Le*
      2. (∃ *x*)*Bx* ⊃ *Le*   1, EG (erroneous)

This inference is disallowed, since it violates the stipulation that EG apply to whole lines only. Here, only the antecedent of (1) has been existentially quantified, which is not permitted. If it were permitted, it would sanction such obviously invalid arguments as

    If Albert is in Brazil, then Edna is lonesome.
    Therefore, if *anyone* is in Brazil then Edna is lonesome.

For EG to be valid, the new quantifier must take the entire line into its scope. Thus, the following *is* permitted:

      1. *Ba* ⊃ *Le*
      2. (∃ *x*)(*Bx* ⊃ *Le*)   1, EG, *a*/*x*

and the argument

> If Albert is in Brazil, then Edna is lonesome
> ∴. There is someone such that if he is in Brazil then Edna is lonesome

unlike the previous one, is valid.

Exercises IV

In each of the following exercises, statement (a) is the premiss and statement (b) is supposedly derived from it, either by UI or by EG. Some of these derivations are valid and some are not, since they are not permitted by the rule in question. Translate and abbreviate each exercise and decide whether or not the inference is permissible. If not, explain why.

1. (a) Whatever is fat is greedy.
   (b) If Yokum is fat then Yokum is greedy.
□ 2. (a) Whatever is fat is greedy.
   (b) If Yokum is fat then Zeke is greedy.
3. (a) Everything is such that if it is fat then Yokum is greedy.
   (b) If Zeke is fat then Zeke is greedy.
4. (a) Everything is such that if it breaks the law then Officer Yokum gets upset.
   (b) If Officer Yokum breaks the law then he gets upset.
□ 5. (a) Yokum is fat and greedy.
   (b) Something is fat and greedy.
6. (a) Yokum is fat and greedy.
   (b) There is something such that it is fat and Yokum is greedy.
7. (a) Yokum is fat but Zeke is not fat.
   (b) Something is both fat and not fat.
□ 8. (a) If Yokum is fat then Yokum is greedy.
   (b) If something is fat then Yokum is greedy.

Exercises V

Translate and prove each of the following arguments.

1. All humans are mortal. Socrates is human. Therefore, Socrates is mortal.
2. Cats and dogs are mammals. Fido is not a mammal. Therefore, Fido is neither a cat nor a dog.
□ 3. Cats and dogs are mammals. Either Fido is a dog or Jemima is a cat. Therefore, mammals exist.*
4. All cats are mammals. All mammals are warm-blooded. Therefore, if Fido is not warm-blooded then Fido is not a cat.
5. If cats exist then all cats are mammals. Mammals and birds are warm-blooded. All warm-blooded things are vertebrates. If vertebrates exist, then if some

---

*For a different way of proving this, see Appendix L.

vertebrates are cats, then all vertebrates are intelligent. Jemima is a cat. Therefore, some intelligent vertebrates are warm-blooded.

☐ **6.** All unicorns are friendly. Therefore, if no unicorns are friendly, then not everything is a unicorn.

§19.5 Existential Instantiation

The rule of existential instantiation is slightly more complicated, both in its statement and in the explanation of why it is valid, than either of the two rules discussed so far in this chapter. Unlike UI, it does not involve straight-forwardly *inferring* a substitution-instance from an existentially quantified function, because *inferences* of that sort are invalid. '$(\exists x)Fx$' never entails 'Fy', since no matter which entity 'y' stands for, if more than one thing exists then it is always *possible* for '$(\exists x)Fx$' to be true and 'Fy' to be false.

The principle of existential instantiation is a formalized version of a practice common in ordinary informal reasoning: the practice of bestowing names upon "unknowns," for the purpose of reasoning about them. When-ever we know that there is an object satisfying a certain description, but don't know which object it is, we say that it is an "unknown." Unknowns enter into our reasoning quite often; and when they do, since we are ignorant of their real identity, we *give* them a kind of pseudo-"identity" by *stipulating* a name for them, to facilitate our reasoning. For example, we can imagine a detective engaged in a burglary investigation saying something like the following:

> We know that a burglar has been here, but we don't know who he was. Let's call him X. Now, from the footprints we know that X came in the back door. Since the back door is not damaged in any way, we can see that X did not have to force it open. Therefore, the back door was left unlocked.

Here, the detective is using 'X' as the name of an unknown. He could just as well have used 'Y', or 'Smith', or 'Jimmy Valentine' for the purpose. It is immaterial which name he picked, since in saying "Let's call him X" the detective was not trying to *guess* the actual identity of the burglar; he was merely stipulating a name, to make it easier to refer to the unknown. His conclusion ("The back door was left unlocked") is independent of any partic-ular choice of names for the unknown; it was inferred simply from the general facts that a burglar came in through the back door and the door was not damaged. Of course, certain intermediate steps in his reasoning are *not* independent of the choice of names, since they involve mention of the name which the detective did in fact choose. The intermediate step "We can see that X did not have to force it open" is legitimate precisely *because* the detective selected the letter 'X' to name the unknown; if he had selected the letter 'Y' instead, then this intermediate step would have had to be: "We can see that Y did not have to force it open." The choice of names is (in this minimal sense) relevant to the intermediate steps, but not to the final conclusion, since the final conclusion involves no mention of the name chosen for the unknown.

The above is not an example of purely deductive reasoning. Let us now look at an example of purely deductive reasoning which involves the same process of naming an unknown. Consider the argument:

1. All people over eight feet tall are pituitary cases.
2. There is at least one person over eight feet tall.
   / ∴ There exists at least one pituitary case.

An unformalized proof of the validity of this argument might go as follows: Premiss (2) tells us that there is at least one person over eight feet tall; we don't know who he is, but let's call him Jones (here 'Jones' is operating as the name of an unknown). So, Jones is a person over eight feet tall. Now, from premiss (1), we know that if Jones is a person over eight feet tall, then Jones is a pituitary case. Therefore, it follows that Jones is a pituitary case, from which it follows that there exists at least one pituitary case.

As in the case of the burglar, the final conclusion here is completely independent of the choice of the name 'Jones' as a name for the unknown giant, though the intermediate steps are not independent of that choice. If we had chosen a different name, say 'Smith', then the intermediate steps would have been slightly different (they would have contained the name 'Smith' instead of the name 'Jones'), but the final conclusion would have been the same. Furthermore, in saying "Let's call him Jones," we are not attempting to guess, or figure out, or otherwise discover the real identity of the unknown giant whose existence is asserted in premiss (2); we are making a *stipulation*. Now, from a logical point of view, making a stipulation is the same thing as making an assumption. The two expressions "Let us assume that . . ." and "Let us stipulate that . . ." may differ in meaning, but they have the same logical force. Both are used in putting forth assertions that were not part of the originally given information. Therefore, the way to introduce a stipulation into a derivation is by means of the assumption-arrow. Knowing this, we can see that the above proof might be formalized step by step as follows:

$$
\begin{array}{lll}
1. & (x)(Tx \supset Px) & \\
2. & (\exists x)Tx & / \therefore (\exists x)Px \\
\rightarrow 3. & Tj & \text{(stipulation)} \\
4. & Tj \supset Pj & 1,\ \text{UI},\ x/j \\
5. & Pj & 3,\ 4,\ \text{MP} \\
6. & (\exists x)Px & 5,\ \text{EG},\ j/x \\
7. & (\exists x)Px & \\
\end{array}
$$

Here, the assumption at line 3 corresponds to the stipulation "Let's call him Jones," and the remaining steps are strictly parallel to the steps in the unformalized proof. At line 6 we arrive at a conclusion which is independent of our choice of 'Jones' (rather than 'Smith' or '*X*' or 'Rosenkrantz') as a name for the unknown; its independence is shown by the fact that the name 'Jones' doesn't appear in it. And since this conclusion *is* independent of our choice of names, we do away with the name 'Jones' altogether by discharging the stipulation in which the name was introduced, and we assert the independent conclusion directly.

This formalized proof is a straightforward illustration of the principle of Existential Instantiation. But some preliminaries are required before the rule can be stated with precision.

> *Clean Letters.* A letter (variable or constant) in a derivation is *clean* if, and only if, it does not occur free in any (i) premiss or (ii) undischarged assumption anywhere *earlier* in the derivation.

From this definition it follows that the same letter may be "clean" at one point in a derivation and "contaminated" at some other point in the same derivation. For example, suppose the first ten lines in a derivation contain no occurrences of the letter '*a*' at all. Then up through line 10 of that derivation the letter '*a*' is clean (if it doesn't occur at all, then it doesn't occur free at all, and *a fortiori* it doesn't occur free in any premiss or undischarged assumption). Suppose that at line 11 '*Fa*' is assumed. Then we will have introduced an assumption containing a clean letter. But in doing this we shall have "contaminated" the letter '*a*'. From line 12 onward '*a*' will no longer be a clean letter, since from line 12 onward '*a*' occurs free in an undischarged assumption earlier in the derivation—the assumption made at line 11. Suppose this assumption is discharged after line 15. This discharge will "decontaminate" the letter '*a*', and from line 16 onward it will once again be clean, since it does not occur free in an *undischarged* assumption earlier in the derivation.

Of course, if a letter occurs free in a *premiss*, there is no way to decontaminate it; it will remain contaminated throughout the derivation.

To ascertain, at any given point in a derivation, whether a certain letter is or is not clean at that point, it is only necessary to inspect the premisses and undischarged assumptions in the derivation up to that point to see whether or not the letter occurs *free* in any of them. Bound occurrences do not matter. Occurrences in assumptions already discharged do not matter. And mere occurrences in the *scope* of assumptions do not matter; what matters is whether the letter occurs free in the undischarged assumption itself, or in a premiss. If it does so occur, it is contaminated; if not, it is clean.

> *Clean Instance.* A clean instance of a *function* is an instance generated by filling the "blank spaces" with occurrences of a single *clean* letter. A clean instance of a *quantified statement* is a clean instance of its matric function.

As before, the same formula may be a clean instance at one point in a derivation but not at a different point, depending upon whether the instantiating letter is or is not clean at that point.

An inferred line may be called **independent** of an earlier assumption just in case the line contains no free occurrences of any letter which *became* contaminated by that assumption. In the proof above, line (6) is independent of the assumption at (3), since (6) contains no free occurrence of the instantiating letter 'j'—the only letter to *become* contaminated by (3).

A **fresh instance** of a *function* is one generated by filling the "blank spaces" with occurrences of a single *fresh* letter. A **fresh letter** is one that does not already appear anywhere in the function. For example, the letter 'y' is fresh with respect to the function '$F\_\_ \supset Gx$', since 'y' does not appear in that function, and so '$Fy \supset Gx$' will be a fresh instance of that function. On the other hand, '$Fx \supset Gx$' is *not* a fresh instance of that function, since the function itself already contains the (instantiating) letter 'x'. As with "clean" instances, a fresh instance of a *quantified statement* is a fresh instance of its matric function.

The Rule of Existential Instantiation can now be stated precisely. It provides a new way, in addition to CP and IP, of discharging assumptions.

EXISTENTIAL INSTANTIATION (EI α/β)

Conceptual formulation:	If an assumption is a (1) *fresh* and (2) *clean* instance of (3) an existentially quantified *line* earlier in the derivation,
	then,
	after any subsequent *independent* line, the assumption may be discharged and the independent line inferred outside its scope.
Operational formulation:	Eliminate an existential quantifier governing an entire line, thereby freeing its range, and rewrite
(*"Assume a fresh clean instance and discharge after an independent line."*)	the ex-range if necessary, to assure that it contains a *fresh, clean* letter; then introduce the resulting formula as an *assumption*.
	After any subsequent line in which the clean letter does not occur free, it is permissible to discharge the assumption and infer that same line below the bar.

To illustrate the workings of this rule, let us refer it back to the earlier formalized argument about tall people and pituitary cases. The assumption at line (3) is a fresh clean instance of line (2)—which is an existentially quantified statement. The instantiating letter in this case is 'j'. Line (6) is a line in which 'j' does not occur free. Thus, the assumption is discharged after line (6), and the same formula is inferred immediately below the discharge bar (lines (6) and (7) are exactly the same).

EI is a "discharge rule" which sets conditions both upon the assumption and upon the line preceding the discharge. In order for EI to apply, the assumption must be a fresh clean instance of some existentially quantified line earlier in the derivation; also, the line preceding the discharge must be "independent" of the choice of instantiating letters—that is, the instantiating letter must not occur free in it. When all of these conditions are met, then the rule of EI may be applied. But if any of them is not met, then the rule does not apply.

EI, like UI and EG, is an inference rule and thus applies only to whole lines within a derivation. That is, the existentially quantified statement must constitute an entire line within the derivation; the existential quantifier must have the whole line in its scope. Otherwise, EI does not apply.

The "clean letter" and "clean instance" requirement is necessary to avoid what is called a **confusion of unknowns**. Confusion of unknowns occurs whenever the same "name" is bestowed upon two (possibly different) unknowns, so that they appear to be the same one, or when a name belonging to something else is bestowed upon an unknown so that they appear to be identical. In the case of the burglary, the detective said, "We don't know who this burglar was; let's call him X." But suppose he had gone on to say, "Another burglary was committed last night on the other side of town. We don't know who that burglar was either, so let's call him X too." This would be a confusion of unknowns. The mere fact that two burglaries were committed does not by itself warrant the conclusion that they were committed by the same person. Yet this is just the sort of invalid inference that is encouraged by stipulating the *same* name for two *different* (or possibly different) unknowns. It confuses one unknown with a different (or possibly different) one by giving them both the same name. The proper procedure would be for the detective to say, "Let's call the other burglar Y." He might then go on to speculate as to whether or not X and Y are the same person. After collecting further evidence, he might eventually conclude that they *are* the same person and so conclude that one person committed both burglaries. But if this conclusion is to be valid, it must be arrived at by reasoning, not by conflating the two unknowns from the start.

An even more bizarre example of the same error would be the following. Suppose the detective said, "We don't know who this burglar was; let's call him Jesse James. Jesse James has been dead for a long time, so he can't be arrested. Therefore, the case is closed." In this case, the confusion of unknowns consists in labelling the unknown with a name also belonging to a known individual and then concluding that the unknown *is* that known individual.

Confusion of unknowns arises whenever we take a name that has already been assigned to something and reassign it as a name for an unknown. Thus, EI requires that the letter (in the assumption) which is chosen to "name" the unknown must be a *clean* letter; it cannot occur free—"used"—anywhere earlier in the proof, except (a) within the scopes of *discharged* assumptions and (b) in places where it happened to be introduced by UI or disj., since lines within the scope of a discharge assumption are "dead" and can have no effect on the rest of the proof, and since (virtually) any letter may validly be introduced by UI or disj., including those which "name" unknowns.

The "fresh letter" requirement has a basis similar to that of the "clean letter" requirement. From the premiss that everybody has had a mother, we can infer by UI that some person is (or was) the mother of X, and 'X' will be a clean letter. If there were no fresh letter requirement, we could then stipulate "Let's call that person X," and so infer that someone is his own mother. To avoid this type of confusion of unknowns, it is required that the stipulated "name" be one that is fresh to that context.

An additional result of the fresh letter requirement is to rule out collision of variables, which can only occur when the instantiating letter already appears in (a quantifier within) the context—that is, when it isn't fresh.

When using the rule of EI, it is usual to annotate both the assumption and the line below the discharge-bar. The assumption is annotated by citing the line it is an instance of, together with the variable of quantification and the instantiating letter. The line below the discharge-bar is justified by citing all lines within the scope of the assumption, and the rule of EI. As an illustration, here is a fully annotated proof involving EI.

1. $(x)((Fx \lor Gx) \supset Hx)$
2. $(\exists x)Fx$ / $\therefore$ $(\exists x)(Fx \cdot Hx)$
    3. Fy 2, x/y
    4. $(Fy \lor Gy) \supset Hy$ 1, UI, x/y
    5. $Fy \lor Gy$ 3, disj.
    6. Hy 4, 5, MP
    7. $Fy \cdot Hy$ 3, 6, conj.
    8. $(\exists x)(Fx \cdot Hx)$ 7, EG, y/x
    9. $(\exists x)(Fx \cdot Hx)$ 3–8, EI

Exercises VI

Each of the following "proofs" contains at least one error. Find the errors and decide which part of the rules is violated.

1.   1. $(\exists x)(Fx \cdot (\exists y)(Gy \cdot \sim Gx))$ / $\therefore$ $(\exists y)(Gy \cdot \sim Gy)$
           2. $Fy \cdot (\exists y)(Gy \cdot \sim Gy)$ 1, x/y
           3. $(\exists y)(Gy \cdot \sim Gy)$ 2, sev.
           4. $(\exists y)(Gy \cdot \sim Gy)$ 2–3, EI

□ **2.**   1. $(\exists x)(Fx \cdot (\exists y)(Gy \cdot Hx))$ / $\therefore$ $(\exists x)(Fx \cdot (Gx \cdot Hx))$

$\quad\quad \longrightarrow$ 2. $Fa \cdot (\exists y)(Gy \cdot Ha)$ 1, x/a

$\quad\quad\quad$ 3. $(\exists y)(Gy \cdot Ha)$ 2, sev.

$\quad\quad \rightarrow$ 4. $Ga \cdot Ha$ 3, y/a

$\quad\quad\quad$ 5. Fa 2, sev.

$\quad\quad\quad$ 6. $Fa \cdot (Ga \cdot Ha)$ 4, 5, conj.

$\quad\quad\quad$ 7. $(\exists x)(Fx \cdot (Gx \cdot Hx))$ 6, EG, a/x

$\quad\quad$ 8. $(\exists x)(Fx \cdot (Gx \cdot Hx))$ 4–7, EI

$\quad\quad\quad$ 9. $(\exists x)(Fx \cdot (Gx \cdot Hx))$ 2–8, EI

3.   1. $(\exists x)(Fx \cdot Gx)$

$\quad\quad\quad$ 2. $(x)(Gx \supset Hx)$ / $\therefore$ $(\exists x)Fx \cdot Hy$

$\quad\quad\quad$ 3. $Gy \supset Hy$ 2, UI, x/y

$\quad\quad \rightarrow$ 4. $Fy \cdot Gy$ 1, x/y

$\quad\quad\quad$ 5. Gy 4, sev.

$\quad\quad\quad$ 6. Hy 3, 5, MP

$\quad\quad\quad$ 7. Fy 4, sev.

$\quad\quad\quad$ 8. $(\exists x)Fx$ 7, EG, y/x

$\quad\quad\quad$ 9. $(\exists x)Fx \cdot Hy$ 6, 8, conj.

$\quad\quad$ 10. $(\exists x)Fx \cdot Hy$ 4–9, EI

Exercises VII

Translate and prove each of the following arguments.

   1. All men are mortal. Some men are Greeks. Therefore, some Greeks are mortal.

☐ **2.** All cats are mammals. Some cats are females. If some mammals are females then some cats are striped. Therefore, some mammals are striped.

   3. Cats and dogs are mammals. Either some cats exist or some dogs exist. Therefore, there are mammals.

☐ **4.** All Greeks are men. All men are mortal. Therefore, if Greeks exist then mortals exist.

   5. If some cats are warm-blooded then all cats are friendly. Cats and dogs are fur-bearing mammals. Every mammal is warm-blooded. If some cats are friendly then some dogs are friendly. Therefore, if cats exist then fur-bearing dogs exist.

§19.6 Universal Generalization

The principle of universal generalization is basically the formalization of the following three valid principles of reasoning:

   a. If an individual has a certain property, and *from that fact alone* it can be deduced that he (or it) also has another property, then it follows that having the first property *entails* having the second, so that *everything* with the first property also has the second.

b. If it can be deduced from completely universal facts that an individual has a certain property, then it follows that *everything* has that property.
c. Whatever is *necessarily* true of some individual, is true of everything. (Necessary properties are universal properties.)

These principles enable us, in certain restricted circumstances, to infer a universal statement about *everything* from a singular statement about a single individual. But since this sort of inference is not always valid, it is important to understand the circumstances required for it to be a valid inference. Obviously, from the fact that Jones happens to have a certain property, it doesn't follow that everything has it; if Jones happens to be a politician, it doesn't follow that everything is a politician, and so it would be invalid to universally generalize over the statement "Jones is a politician."

But consider instead the statement "If Jones is a wealthy politician then Jones is a politician." This is a statement about Jones; but it isn't something that just happens to be true of him; it is a *logical* truth about Jones, a statement which is necessarily true, and which can be proven by methods already studied. Moreover, its being a logical truth does not depend upon its being about Jones; it would still be a logical truth no matter whose name we substituted for 'Jones'. Thus in this case it is valid to universally generalize and to infer that *everything* is such that if it is a wealthy politician then it is a politician. In general, whenever a statement about an individual is a logical truth, it is valid to universally generalize from that individual's case.

But this is not the only circumstance in which universal generalization is legitimate. It is legitimate to universally generalize over the facts about an individual whenever those facts have themselves been inferred from *universal* statements, and only universal statements. It is not valid to universally generalize about those facts which serve (or may serve) to differentiate Jones from other individuals. But if our facts about Jones have been inferred from *universal* statements, then they do *not* serve to differentiate Jones from any other individual, since those same facts could have been inferred about any other individual you care to mention.

For example, given only the piece of information that Jones is not both a professional quarterback and a lingerie model, it would not be valid to universally generalize and infer that *no* professional quarterbacks are lingerie models; it would not be valid since the isolated statement 'If Jones is a professional quarterback then Jones is not a lingerie model' might, for all we know, simply be an idiosyncratic fact about Jones (for example, it might be true because Jones is too lazy to hold two jobs).

On the other hand, suppose we are given the two pieces of information 'All professional quarterbacks are men' and 'No men are lingerie models'. From these two universal statements we may validly infer (by UI and OC) that if Jones is a professional quarterback then Jones is not a lingerie model; but in this case there is no chance of its being an idiosyncratic fact, because the same thing could have been inferred about any individual. Thus, in this case, it *is* valid to universally generalize from Jones's case, and to infer that 'No professional quarterbacks are lingerie models'. This argument, when formalized, appears as follows:

1. $(x)(Qx \supset Mx)$
2. $(x)(Mx \supset \sim Lx)$ $/ \therefore (x)(Qx \supset \sim Lx)$
3. $Qj \supset Mj$ 1, UI, x/j
4. $Mj \supset \sim Lj$ 2, UI, x/j
5. $Qj \supset \sim Lj$ 3, 4, OC
6. $(x)(Qx \supset \sim Lx)$

—line (6) being a universal generalization over line (5).

There are many formal similarities between universal generalization and EG. Both start with an instance of a function, and proceed to a quantification of that function. In the above illustration, (5) is an instance of the function '$Q\_\_ \supset \sim L\_\_$' and (6) is the universal quantification of that function. But because universal generalization is a much more touchy business than EG, it is necessary to lay some groundwork before attempting to state a Rule of Universal Generalization.

First, universal generalization over an instance of a function is only valid when the instance is a *clean* one. If the instance is not a clean one, this means that its instantiating letter occurs free in a premiss, or an undischarged assumption, or both. But a statement in which a letter occurs free is a particular statement about the individual whom that letter "names." And if the statement is a premiss, then it is a given datum, rather than an inference from universal facts; it is, for all we know, an idiosyncratic statement about that individual, telling us something which *differentiates* that individual from others. But it is never valid to universally generalize over the idiosyncratic features of an individual. So if a letter occurs free in a premiss, it is thereby "contaminated by particularity"; and it remains contaminated throughout the entire derivation, since later lines will have been derived from the contaminated premiss, inheriting the contamination.

The same thing is true if the letter occurs free in an undischarged assumption: the assumption is not an inference from universal facts, but an assumed datum, and consequently it is contaminated with particularity. However, when the assumption is discharged, then *that* source of contamination is nullified.

There are two ways for a *clean* letter to show up free in a derivation: either through Universal Instantiation or through assumptions which have since been discharged. If the former, then the line in which it occurs was inferred from universal facts, and so there is no taint of particularity: that line is a valid target for universal generalization. If the clean letter was not introduced by UI but by assumptions which have since been discharged, then the line in which it occurs is either a zero-premiss conclusion or is inferred from premisses and assumptions in which the clean letter does not occur (free). If the line containing the clean letter is a zero-premiss conclusion, then it is a necessary truth and consequently holds true not only for the "named" individual but for everything in the universe, and the line is a valid target for universal generalization. If the line containing the clean letter is not a zero-premiss conclusion but is inferred from premisses or assumptions in which it does not occur free, then those premisses and assumptions could in no way have dictated our use of *that* letter, rather than some other. We could construct a similar proof using any letter (that is, the name of any individual) we care to choose. Consequently, the line is a valid target for universal generalization.*

From these considerations, it follows that clean instances of functions, and *only* clean instances of functions, are legitimate to universally generalize over.

But it doesn't follow that we can universally generalize over every clean instance of a function that may occur in a derivation. Further refinements are needed to avoid invalidity.

There is a big difference between asserting that everything satisfies a given compound function and asserting that everything satisfies one of its components. A premiss which entails the one assertion may not entail the other. For example, the statement 'If Albert is fat then Albert is fat'—that is,

    1. $Fa \supset Fa$

is a necessary truth about Albert and is also true of everything else in the universe: if Bobby Fischer is fat then Bobby Fischer is fat; if California is fat then California is fat; and so on. Consequently, it is legitimate to universally generalize over Albert's case and assert

    2. $(x)(Fx \supset Fx)$

On the other hand, it is *not* legitimate to infer from (1) that if Albert is fat then everything is:

    3. $Fa \supset (x)Fx$

The invalidity of such an inference is conveniently attested to by the fact that (1) is true (because tautologous), whereas (3) is false: Albert is fat but some things aren't. And so we can say that although it is permissible to generalize over the entire statement about Albert, it is not permissible to generalize over a part of it.

The formal way to avoid inferences such as the one from (1) to (3) is to require that, when universally generalizing over a (clean instance of a) function, the quantifier must take the entire function into its scope. Since the quantifier in (3) only scopes over part of the formula, this requirement would disallow the inference from (1) to (3).

---

*A clean letter can also sneak into a derivation via Disjoining. A letter introduced in that way is a legitimate target for universal generalizing, since we could just as well have disjoined on the Universally General formula in the first place.

But even this requirement is not strong enough to avoid invalidity. For, supposing 'a' to be a clean letter, (1) is a clean instance of the function

4. $Fa \supset F\_\_$

which we may quantify over in accordance with the latest restriction to obtain

5. $(x)(Fa \supset Fx)$

in which the quantifier does scope over the whole formula. But now, *by shifting the quantifier in*, we can still obtain (3). The restrictions so far given to regulate the use of universal generalization are not strong enough to prevent this invalid inference; something more is needed.

The trouble with the inference from (1) to (5) is that (5) is not really a generalization over the *whole* fact about Albert: the *scope* of the quantifier is right, but its *range* is wrong. Despite the scope of the quantifier, (5) is still a generalization over only one component of the (conditional) fact about Albert. The formal manifestation of this is that the quantifier in (5) only binds one of the two places where 'a' occurs in (1). To universally generalize over Albert's case, it is necessary for the quantifier to bind *every* place where Albert's name occurs, not just some of them.

These difficulties arose when we recognized (1) as a clean instance of the function '$Fa \supset F\_\_$' and then inferred the universal quantification of *that* function. But not only is (1) a clean instance of this function, it is also a clean instance of '$F\_\_ \supset Fa$' and of '$F\_\_ \supset F\_\_$'; and the *last* of these is the one whose quantification should have been inferred: the one whose blank spaces *exactly match* the occurrences of 'a' in (1).

Let us say that a statement is an **isomorphic instance** of a function if, and only if, one could get that statement from that function by filling in the blanks with a *fresh* letter (one not already in the function). (1) is an instance of several different functions, but it is an *isomorphic* instance of only one of them: '$F\_\_ \supset F\_\_$'. Functions and their isomorphic instances are such that the blanks in the function *exactly match* the (free) occurrences of *one* of the letters in the instance. When a statement is an isomorphic instance of a function, we can call that function an **isomorphic underlying function** of the statement; and what was said above can be phrased alternatively as: statements and their isomorphic underlying functions are such that the *free* occurrences of *one* of the letters in the statement exactly match the blanks in the function. The result of blanking out all free occurrences of some one letter in a statement will be an isomorphic underlying function.

As we have seen, universal generalization is not valid unless it is an inference from a statement to the universal quantification of one of its *isomorphic* underlying functions. The new quantifier must capture *all and only* places occupied by occurrences of some one clean letter. And so, the rule may be stated officially as follows:

UNIVERSAL GENERALIZATION (UG α/β)

Conceptual formulation: If a line is a *clean, isomorphic* instance of a function, it is permissible to infer the universal quantification of that function.

Operational formulation:
("*Capture all free occurrences of a clean letter.*")

It is permissible to capture *all* free places occupied by some one *clean* letter, by attaching a universal quantifier containing that letter, along with any punctuation needed to make it scope over the whole line. In making the capture, the range of the new quantifier may be rewritten as any fresh letter.

UG, like UI, EG, and EI, is an inference rule and applies only to whole lines in a derivation; the universal quantifier attached in a step of UG must scope over an entire line. Also, like the other rules, UG is annotated by indicating not only the rule but the letters involved: first the clean letter generating the instance, then the variable of quantification. Here is an illustration of the correct use of UG.

1. $(x)(Fx \supset Gx)$
2. $(x)Fx$ / $\therefore (x)Gx$
3. $Fy \supset Gy$ 1, UI, x/y
4. Fy 2, UI, x/y
5. Gy 3, 4, MP
6. $(x)Gx$ 5, UG, y/x

This is a perfectly valid proof, and a paradigm of the correct use of UG. Similarly,

/ $\therefore (x)((Fx \cdot Gx) \supset Fx)$
→ 1. $Fy \cdot Gy$
   2. Fy 1, sev.
   3. $(Fy \cdot Gy) \supset Fy$ 1–2, CP
   4. $(x)((Fx \cdot Gx) \supset Fx)$ 3, UG, y/x

contains a correct application of UG. The inference from (3) to (4) is permissible, since (a) the universal quantifier scopes over the whole line, (b) the range of the quantifier exactly matches the free occurrences of 'y', and (c) the letter generalized over, 'y', does not occur free in any undischarged assumptions in the derivation prior to line (3). However, the following derivation is *not* valid:

1. $(x)(Fx \supset Gx)$
2. $(\exists x)Fx$ / $\therefore (x)Gx$
→ 3. Fy 2, x/y
   4. $Fy \supset Gy$ 1, UI, x/y
   5. Gy 3, 4, MP
   6. $(x)Gx$ 5, UG, y/x (erroneous)
   7. $(x)Gx$ 3–6, EI

The step from (5) to (6) is invalid since, at the time it was made, 'y' was free in an undischarged assumption. Another illegitimate application of UG occurs in the following derivation:

1. $(\exists x)Fx \supset Gy$
2. $(x)(Fx \supset Gy)$ 1, QS
3. $Fy \supset Gy$ 2, UI, x/y
4. $(x)(Fx \supset Gx)$ 3, UG, y/x (erroneous)

The step from (3) to (4) is invalid, since 'y' occurs free in premiss (1). As a final illustration, the following derivation is invalid:

1. $(x)(Fx \supset (y)(Gy \supset Hy))$
2. $Fy \supset (y)(Gy \supset Hy)$ 1, UI, x/y
3. $(x)(Fx \supset (y)(Gy \supset Hx))$ 2, UG, y/x (erroneous)

The step from (2) to (3) is invalid since the new quantifier in (3) has "stolen" a place which was not free in (2)—namely, the place after 'H'.

Exercises VIII

Translate and prove each of the following arguments.

1. All men are mortal. All Greeks are men. Therefore all Greeks are mortal.
□ 2. Clams and oysters are edible molluscs. Therefore, clams are edible.
3. All cats are mammals. Some cats are not striped. Therefore, some mammals are not striped.
4. Some dragons are green. Dragons don't exist. Therefore, everything is green.
5. Cats and dogs are fur-bearing mammals. If all cats are mammals then some cats are striped. Therefore, some mammals have stripes.
□ 6. Cats and dogs are fur-bearing mammals. If all cats are mammals then all dogs are carnivorous. All carnivorous mammals are predatory. Therefore, all dogs are predatory.
7. Snails and insects are edible only if properly cooked. Insects are never properly cooked. Therefore, insects are not edible.
8. All cats are mammals. All dogs are mammals. All mammals are warm-blooded. Therefore cats and dogs are warm-blooded mammals.
9. If vampires exist then all vampires are dreadful. Things that are bloodthirsty and dreadful are not trustworthy. Dracula is a bloodthirsty vampire. If some bats are friendly then Dracula is trustworthy. Therefore, if all vampires are bats then some dreadful things are unfriendly.
□ 10. Either everything is interesting or everything is trivial. Therefore, everything is either interesting or trivial.

chapter 20

CP AND IP WITH QUANTIFIERS;
PROVING QUANTIFIER TRUTHS

§20.1 IP with Quantified Formulae

The Rule of Indirect Proof is employed in derivations involving quantifiers exactly as in derivations involving only truth-functions. The principle is the same in both cases: assume the negation of what you wish to derive and work for an explicit contradiction. When the contradiction is arrived at, discharge the assumption by IP in the usual fashion. As an illustration, here is a simple proof using IP.

$$1.\ (x)(Fx \supset Gx)$$
$$2.\ (\exists x)Fx \quad / \therefore (\exists x)Gx$$

3.	$\sim(\exists x)Gx$	(IP)
4.	$(x)\sim Gx$	3, QN
5.	$Fy \supset Gy$	1, UI, x/y
6.	$\sim Gy$	4, UI, x/y
7.	$\sim Fy$	5, 6, MT
8.	$(x)\sim Fx$	7, UG, y/x
9.	$\sim(\exists x)Fx$	8, QN
10.	$(\exists x)Fx \cdot \sim(\exists x)Fx$	2, 9, conj.
11.	$(\exists x)Gx$	3–10, IP, DN

As an example of a slightly more sophisticated use of IP, here is a derivation involving both IP and EI:

$$1.\ (x)(Fx \supset Gx)$$
$$2.\ (x)Fx \quad / \therefore (x)Gx$$

3.	$\sim(x)Gx$	(IP)
4.	$(\exists x)\sim Gx$	3, QN
5.	$\sim Gy$	4, x/y
6.	$Fy \supset Gy$	1, UI, x/y
7.	$\sim Fy$	5, 6, MT
8.	Fy	2, UI, x/y
9.	$Fy \lor (A \cdot \sim A)$	8, disj.
10.	$A \cdot \sim A$	7, 9, canc.
11.	$A \cdot \sim A$	5–10, EI
12.	$(x)Gx$	3–11, IP, DN

The strategy of this proof may require some explanation. At line (3) an assumption was made for purposes of IP, and at line (5) an assumption was made for purposes of EI. After arriving at line (8), we could have obtained the contradiction '$Fy \cdot \sim Fy$' simply by conjoining lines (7) and (8). But what would we have done then? It was necessary to discharge line (5) before discharging line (3); but we could not have discharged line (5) by EI after a line '$Fy \cdot \sim Fy$', because that line would contain free 'y', thereby violating one of the restrictions to EI ("the instantiating letter does not occur free"). To circumvent this problem, the two lines (7) and (8) were used, in a familiar maneuver, to derive the contradiction '$A \cdot \sim A$' which does *not* contain free 'y', enabling the discharge of line (5) by EI. This left a contradiction, and no undischarged assumptions except (3), and so it was possible to discharge (3) by IP.

§20.2 CP with Quantified Formulae*

When Conditional Proof is used in derivations involving quantifiers, certain subtleties of application are legitimate but may not be immediately apparent. These involve no change in the principles involved, but merely changes in the tactics of the proof.

If the conclusion being sought is a genuine conditional (that is, a formula in which the dominant operator is a horseshoe which is not within the scope of any quantifier), then of course the old strategy still applies: assume the antecedent, derive the consequent, and then discharge the assumption by CP. As a simple illustration:

1. $(x)(Fx \supset Gx)$ / ∴ $(x)Fx \supset (\exists y)Gy$
→2. $(x)Fx$ / ∴ $(\exists y)Gy$
   3. $Fx \supset Gx$ 1, UI, x/x
   4. Fx 2, UI, x/x
   5. Gx 3, 4, MP
   6. $(\exists y)Gy$ 5, EG, x/y
   7. $(x)Fx \supset (\exists y)Gy$ 2-6, CP

However, if the conclusion being sought is a quantified formula with a conditional matrix (that is, a formula falling entirely within the scope of a quantifier, and having a horseshoe as the dominant operator in the matrix), the appropriate strategy is to assume the antecedent of the *matrix*, derive the consequent of the matrix, discharge the assumption by CP, and then attach the needed quantifier or quantifiers by UG and EG. As a simple illustration:

1. $(x)(Fx \supset Gx)$ / ∴ $(x)(Fx \supset (\exists y)Gy)$

---

*Also see Appendix L.

$\rightarrow$2. Fx $/ \therefore (\exists y)Gy$
    3. $Fx \supset Gx$ 1, UI, x/x
    4. Gx 2, 3, MP
    5. $(\exists y)Gy$ 4, EG, x/y
    6. $Fx \supset (\exists y)Gy$ 2–5, CP
    7. $(x)(Fx \supset (\exists y)Gy)$ 6, UG, x/x

However, there are situations in which this simple procedure will not be successful, and the following section is intended to help in coping with them.

§20.3   Proof Strategies

As you have learned by now, a proof often goes more easily if, instead of attempting simply to derive the conclusion as it is given, one first transforms it into something else easier to derive—a "surrogate conclusion." Once derived, this can then be turned into the *given* conclusion by a reversal of the original transformations. With this as the basic strategy, the following "rules" will in most cases help to arrive at a completed proof.

Rule 1. Attempt to transform the conclusion into a truth-functional compound by shifting as many quantifiers as far *in* as possible. Sometimes this cannot be done; initially placed quantifiers may remain which cannot be shifted in. However, *if* the attempt is successful, then

   a. If the resulting compound is a *conditional* (or a *disjunction*), use CP in the normal fashion: assume the antecedent (or the negation of one disjunct), derive the consequent (or the other disjunct), and discharge the assumption by CP.

   b. If the resulting compound is a *conjunction*, treat each conjunct as a separate "surrogate conclusion" and derive each separately using the appropriate strategy.

   c. If the resulting compound is a *negation*, distribute the tilde in and proceed by either (*a*) or (*b*).

Rule 2. If, after as many quantifiers have been shifted as far in as possible, there still remain initially placed quantifiers that cannot be shifted in, then

   a. Apply QN as needed, to assure that no initially placed quantifier is preceded by a tilde; then

   b. If possible, transform the matrix into a conditional matrix (one whose dominant operator is a horseshoe); then

   c. If all of the remaining initially placed quantifiers are *universal*, use CP as follows:

      i. If the letter in *any* of the remaining initially placed quantifiers occurs *free* in the *premisses*, rewrite the range of that quantifier to some other letter; then

      ii. Assume the antecedent of the matrix as the first step in the proof. Derive the consequent of the matrix and discharge the assumption by CP. The needed quantifiers can then be attached by UG, since after the rewriting [per (*i*) above] none of the variables to be captured will appear free in a premiss, nor in an undischarged assumption, since the now-discharged antecedent was the *first* assumption.

d. If one or more of the initially placed quantifiers in the surrogate conclusion is *existential*, and there are no existential quantifiers *anywhere* in the premisses, proceed as in (*c*). The needed quantifiers can then be attached by EG or UG.

e. If one or more of the initially placed quantifiers in the surrogate conclusion are existential and there is an existential quantifier or free letter in the premises, *or*, regardless of the quantifiers, if the matrix of your surrogate conclusion cannot be transformed into a conditional matrix, then *forget about CP*. Either work the derivation direct, or use IP.

Rule 3. *Do not* get involved in elaborate matrix transformations for the sake of the preceding rules. If the way to do what you want to do to the matrix isn't fairly obvious to you at the start, forget about it and follow Rule 4.

Rule 4. When in doubt, try a straightforward Indirect Proof; assume the negation of the conclusion as the first step in the derivation and work for an explicit contradiction, then discharge the assumption by IP.

By way of illustrating some of these strategies, first consider the argument

1. $(\exists x)Fx$ $/ \therefore (\exists x)(\exists y)[(Fx \supset Gx) \supset Gy]$

Following strategy (*1*) above, we first try to transform the conclusion into a truth-functional compound by using QS. One step of QS transforms the conclusion into

$(\exists x)[(Fx \supset Gx) \supset (\exists y)Gy]$

and a second step transforms it into

$(x)(Fx \supset Gx) \supset (\exists y)Gy$

which is a truth-functional compound. Since it is a conditional, the strategy to employ is that of (*1a*) above; that is, assume the antecedent of this conditional and do a conditional proof:

1. $(\exists x)Fx$ $/ \therefore (\exists x)(\exists y)[(Fx \supset Gx) \supset Gy]$	
2. $(x)(Fx \supset Gx)$ $/ \therefore (\exists y)Gy$	
3. Fx	1, x/x
4. $Fx \supset Gx$	2, UI, x/x
5. Gx	3, 4, MP
6. $(\exists y)Gy$	5, EG, x/y
7. $(\exists y)Gy$	3–6, EI
8. $(x)(Fx \supset Gx) \supset (\exists y)Gy$	2–7, CP

and then, having derived the surrogate conclusion, transform it back into the original conclusion:

    9. $(\exists x)[(Fx \supset Gx) \supset (\exists y)Gy]$ 8, QS
10. $(\exists x)(\exists y)[(Fx \supset Gx) \supset Gy]$ 9, QS

which completes the proof.

As another illustration, consider the argument

    1. $(x)(Fx \supset Hx)$
    2. $(x)(Gx \supset {\sim}Hx)$
    3. $(\exists x)Hx$ $/ \therefore$ ${\sim}(\exists x)(y)[(Fx \cdot Gx) \lor Gy]$

Following the strategy of (1), we try to transform the conclusion into a truth-functional compound using QS; the result is

    ${\sim}[(\exists x)(Fx \cdot Gx) \lor (y)Gy]$

This is a negation, so, following (1c), the tilde is distributed in, to produce

    ${\sim}(\exists x)(Fx \cdot Gx) \cdot {\sim}(y)Gy$

This is a conjunction, and the strategy at (1b) says to treat each conjunct separately, then conjoin them after they have both been derived. Start with the first conjunct:

    ${\sim}(\exists x)(Fx \cdot Gx)$

This has an initially placed quantifier which cannot be shifted further in, so it falls under the strategy of (2). Following (2a), we apply QN to get the tilde inside the quantifier:

    $(x){\sim}(Fx \cdot Gx)$

Then, following (2b), we apply TD and CE to produce a conditional matrix:

    $(x)(Fx \supset {\sim}Gx)$

The remaining initially placed quantifier is universal—cf. (2c). The letter in that quantifier—'x'—does not occur free in the premises—cf. 2c(i). The strategy at 2c(ii) is to assume the antecedent of the matrix, for purposes of CP, which we do at line (4):

    1. $(x)(Fx \supset Hx)$
    2. $(x)(Gx \supset {\sim}Hx)$
    3. $(\exists x)Hx$ $/ \therefore$ ${\sim}(\exists x)(y)[(Fx \cdot Gx) \lor Gy]$
→ 4. Fx $/ \therefore$ ${\sim}Gx$
    5. $Fx \supset Hx$ 1, UI, x/x
    6. Hx 4, 5, MP
    7. $Gx \supset {\sim}Hx$ 2, UI, x/x
    8. ${\sim}{\sim}Hx$ 6, DN
    9. ${\sim}Gx$ 7, 8, MT
10. $Fx \supset {\sim}Gx$ 4–9, CP
11. $(x)(Fx \supset {\sim}Gx)$ 10, UG, x/x

and the earlier transformations are reversed, thus:

> 12. $(x)(\sim Fx \lor \sim Gx)$ 11, CE
> 13. $(x) \sim (Fx \cdot Gx)$ 12, TE
> 14. $\sim (\exists x)(Fx \cdot Gx)$ 13, QN

which is one conjunct of the surrogate conclusion. The other conjunct is

> $\sim (y)Gy$

Since this cannot be transformed into a formula with a conditional matrix—cf. (*2e*), CP strategies are out, and IP or direct proof is in order. A direct proof is easy:

> 15. $Gx \supset \sim Hx$ 2, UI, x/x
> →16. Hx 3, x/x
> ⎡ 17. $\sim \sim Hx$ 16, DN
> ⎢ 18. $\sim Gx$ 15, 17, MT
> ⎣ 19. $(\exists y) \sim Gy$ 18, EG, x/y
> 20. $(\exists y) \sim Gy$ 16–19, EI
> 21. $\sim (y)Gy$ 20, QN

which is the other conjunct of the surrogate conclusion. Now the two are conjoined and the early transformations reversed to produce the original conclusion:

> 22. $\sim (\exists x)(Fx \cdot Gx) \cdot \sim (y)Gy$ 14, 21, conj.
> 23. $\sim [(\exists x)(Fx \cdot Gx) \lor (y)Gy]$ 22, TE
> 24. $\sim (\exists x)[(Fx \cdot Gx) \lor (y)Gy]$ 23, QS
> 25. $\sim (\exists x)(y)[(Fx \cdot Gx) \lor Gy]$ 24, QS

which completes the proof.

As an illustration of the reason for strategy *2c(i)*, consider the simple argument:

> 1. $(x)(Fx \supset Gy)$
> 2. $(x)(Gy \supset Hx)$ $/ \therefore (y)(Fy \supset Hy)$

This argument is valid; but if we attempt to prove it valid using CP, by assuming the antecedent of the matrix, deriving the consequent, and then generalizing, without first rewriting the bound variable in the conclusion, we will get into the following predicament:

> ⎡→3. Fy $/ \therefore Hy$
> ⎢ 4. $Fy \supset Gy$ 1, UI, x/y
> ⎢ 5. $Gy \supset Hy$ 2, UI, x/y
> ⎢ 6. Gy 3, 4, MP
> ⎣ 7. Hy 5, 6, MP
> 8. $Fy \supset Hy$ 3–7, CP

Having arrived at the desired formula, we *cannot* universally generalize over it, because the variable '*y*' occurs free in the premisses. We could have avoided this problem by rewriting '*y*' in the conclusion as some other letter, say '*z*', so that the proof would go:

> 3. *Fz* | ∴ *Hz*
> 4. *Fz* ⊃ *Gy*   1, UI, *x/z*
> 5. *Gy* ⊃ *Hz*   2, UI, *x/z*
> 6. *Gy*   3, 4, MP
> 7. *Hz*   5, 6, MP
> ———
> 8. *Fz* ⊃ *Hz*   3–7, CP
> 9. (*z*)(*Fz* ⊃ *Hz*)   8, UG, *z/z*
> 10. (*y*)(*Fy* ⊃ *Hy*) 9, RBV, *z/y*

Of course (10) could have been derived from (8) in one step, by UG, *z/y*; it is done in two steps here merely for the sake of the illustration.

By way of illustrating proof-strategy (*4*), here is a proof of an argument which looks quite simple but which *refuses* to be proven by any of the CP strategies outlined in (*1a*) and (*2a–d*) above.

> 1. (*x*)(*Fx* ⊃ (*Gx* · (∃ *y*)*Hy*)) | ∴ (∃ *y*)(*x*)(*Fx* ⊃ (*Gx* · *Hy*))
> 2. ~(∃ *y*)(*x*)(*Fx* ⊃ (*Gx* · *Hy*))   (IP)
> 3. (*y*)(∃ *x*)~(*Fx* ⊃ (*Gx* · *Hy*))   2, QN twice
> 4. (*y*)(∃ *x*)~(~*Fx* ∨ (*Gx* · *Hy*))   3, CE
> 5. (*y*)(∃ *x*)(*Fx* · ~(*Gx* · *Hy*))   4, TD, DN
> 6. (∃ *x*)(*Fx* · ~(*Gx* · *Hy*))   5, UI, *y/y*
> 7. *Fx* · ~(*Gx* · *Hy*)   6, *x/x*
> 8. *Fx* ⊃ (*Gx* · (∃ *y*)*Hy*)   1, UI, *x/x*
> 9. *Gx* · (∃ *y*)*Hy*   7, 8, sev., MP
> 10. (∃ *y*)*Hy*   9, sev.
> 11. *Hz*   10, *y/z*
> 12. (∃ *x*)(*Fx* · ~(*Gx* · *Hz*))   5, UI, *y/z*
> 13. *Fw* · ~(*Gw* · *Hz*)   12, *x/w*
> 14. ~(*Gw* · *Hz*)   13, sev.
> 15. ~*Gw* ∨ ~*Hz*   14, TD
> 16. ~*Gw*   11, 15, DN, canc.
> 17. *Fw* ⊃ (*Gw* · (∃ *y*)*Hy*)   1, UI, *x/w*
> 18. *Gw* · (∃ *y*)*Hy*   13, 17, sev., MP
> 19. *Gw*   18, sev.
> 20. *Gw* ∨ (*A* · ~*A*)   19, disj.
> 21. *A* · ~*A*   16, 20, canc.
> 22. *A* · ~*A*   13–21, EI
> 23. *A* · ~*A*   11–22, EI
> 24. *A* · ~*A*   7–23, EI
> 25. (∃ *y*)(*x*)(*Fx* ⊃ (*Gx* · *Hy*))   2–24, IP, DN

Exercises I

Construct a proof for each of the following, using the proof strategies outlined in
§20.3.

1. 1. $(x)(Ax \supset \sim Bx)$
   2. Cy $/ \therefore (\exists y)(\exists x)((Cy \supset By) \supset \sim Ax)$

2. 1. $(x)(Ax \supset Bx)$
   2. $(x)(Cx \supset Dx)$ $/ \therefore \sim (x)(\exists y)((Bx \supset Cx) \cdot (Ay \cdot \sim Dy))$

☐ **3.** 1. $(\exists x)Px \supset (y)(Qy \supset Py)$
   2. $(\exists x)(Rx \cdot Tx) \supset (y)(Py \supset Ty)$
   $/ \therefore (x)(y)((Px \cdot (Rx \cdot Tx)) \supset (Qy \supset Ty))$

4. 1. $(x)(Fx \supset (Gx \cdot (y)Hy))$ $/ \therefore (\exists y)(x)(Fx \supset (Gx \cdot Hy))$

5. 1. $(x)((Ax \cdot Bx) \supset (Cx \cdot Dx))$
   $/ \therefore (x)(\exists y)((Ax \cdot Ex) \supset (((Ay \cdot Ey) \supset By) \supset Cx))$

☐ **6.** 1. $(x)((Mx \cdot Nx) \supset Ox)$
   2. $(x)(Ox \supset Px)$
   3. $(\exists x)(Px \cdot \sim Sx) \supset (y)(Ny \supset \sim Py)$
   $/ \therefore (x)\sim(\exists y)((My \cdot \sim (Ox \supset Sx)) \cdot Ny)$

7. 1. $(x)(Fx \supset (\exists y)Gy)$
   2. $(x)(Gx \supset Hx)$
   3. $(\exists x)Fx$ $/ \therefore (\exists x)(\exists y)((Gx \cdot Fy) \cdot Hx)$

8. 1. $(x)((Fx \cdot Gx) \supset ((Hx \supset Ix) \supset \sim Hx))$
   $/ \therefore (\exists x)(\exists y)((Gx \cdot Ix) \supset ((Gy \supset Fy) \supset \sim Hx))$

9. 1. $(x)((Px \cdot Qx) \supset ((y)(Sy \supset Ty) \supset Rx))$
   2. $(\exists z)(Sz \cdot Tz) \supset (y)(Sy \supset Ty)$
   $/ \therefore (x)((Px \cdot Qx) \supset (z)((Sz \cdot Tz) \supset Rx))$

10. 1. $(x)((Fx \lor Gx) \supset \sim (Mx \supset Nx))$
   2. $(x)Nx \lor (y)(My \supset Py)$
   $/ \therefore (\exists z)(\exists y)(\exists x)((Fz \supset (Gz \cdot Gy)) \supset ((Py \supset Hy) \supset (Fx \supset Hy)))$

☐ **11.** 1. $(x)(Fx \supset ((\exists y)Hy \supset Gz))$
   2. $(x)(Gz \supset ((y)(Gy \supset Ky) \lor Hx))$
   $/ \therefore (z)(y)(x)(Hx \supset ((Gy \cdot \sim Ky) \supset ((Fz \supset Hz) \cdot Gy)))$

12. 1. $(x)(Px \supset Qx) \supset (y)((Ry \cdot Sy) \supset Ty)$
   2. $(x)(Wx \supset Px)$
   3. $(\exists x)(Px \cdot (\sim Qx \lor \sim Ux)) \supset (y)(Py \supset \sim Qy)$
   4. $(x)(Yx \supset Rx)$ $/ \therefore (x)((Sx \cdot Yx) \supset ((\exists y)(Wy \cdot Qy) \supset Tx))$

§20.4 Proving Quantifier Truths

The procedures for proving quantifier truths are, in principle, no different
from those for proving tautologies. The proof must start out with an assumption for either CP or IP, with the object of eventually discharging that

assumption and deriving the desired formula as a zero-premiss conclusion. For example:

PROOF I

$\quad$ / ∴ $(x)Fx \supset (\exists y)Fy$
$\quad\;\;$ → 1. $(x)Fx$
$\qquad\;\;$ 2. Fy $\qquad\qquad\qquad\qquad$ 1, UI, x/y
$\qquad\;\;$ 3. $(\exists y)Fy$ $\qquad\qquad\qquad\;$ 2, EG, y/y
$\qquad\;\;$ 4. $(x)Fx \supset (\exists y)Fy$ $\qquad\;$ 1–3, CP

PROOF II

$\quad$ / ∴ $(x)((Fx \cdot Gx) \supset Fx)$
$\quad\;\;$ → 1. $\sim(x)((Fx \cdot Gx) \supset Fx)$ $\qquad$ (IP)
$\qquad\;\;$ 2. $(\exists x)\sim((Fx \cdot Gx) \supset Fx)$ $\quad$ 1, QN
$\qquad\;\;$ → 3. $\sim((Fx \cdot Gx) \supset Fx)$ $\qquad\;$ 2, x/x
$\qquad\;\;$ 4. $\sim(\sim(Fx \cdot Gx) \vee Fx)$ $\qquad$ 3, CE
$\qquad\;\;$ 5. $(Fx \cdot Gx) \cdot \sim Fx$ $\qquad\qquad$ 4, TD, DN
$\qquad\;\;$ 6. $Fx \cdot Gx$ $\qquad\qquad\qquad\;\;$ 5, sev.
$\qquad\;\;$ 7. Fx $\qquad\qquad\qquad\qquad\;$ 6, sev.
$\qquad\;\;$ 8. $\sim Fx$ $\qquad\qquad\qquad\qquad$ 5, sev.
$\qquad\;\;$ 9. $Fx \vee (B \cdot \sim B)$ $\qquad\qquad$ 7, disj.
$\qquad\;\;$ 10. $B \cdot \sim B$ $\qquad\qquad\qquad\;\;$ 8, 9, canc.
$\qquad\;\;$ 11. $B \cdot \sim B$ $\qquad\qquad\qquad\;\;$ 3–10, EI
$\qquad\;\;$ 12. $(x)((Fx \cdot Gx) \supset Fx)$ $\qquad$ 1–11, IP, DN

or, as a shorter proof of the same thing:

$\quad$ / ∴ $(x)((Fx \cdot Gx) \supset Fx)$
$\quad\;\;$ →1. $Fx \cdot Gx$
$\qquad\;\;$ 2. Fx $\qquad\qquad\qquad\qquad\;$ 1, sev.
$\qquad\;\;$ 3. $(Fx \cdot Gx) \supset Fx$ $\qquad\;\;$ 1–2, CP
$\qquad\;\;$ 4. $(x)((Fx \cdot Gx) \supset Fx)$ $\quad$ 3, UG, x/x

The proof strategies discussed earlier are, of course, applicable to proofs of quantifier truths as well as to proofs of quantified arguments.

§20.5 Combining Steps

In the sample proofs given in this chapter, many of the steps are "combination steps"—steps derived by using more than one rule. Proofs in quantifier logic tend to be rather long, and combining steps in this way is an accepted method for shortening them, provided that it is not overdone (to the point where the proofs become difficult to follow). If you are inclined to combine steps in your proofs, always try to adhere to the guidelines given below.

1. When combining steps, be sure to cite *all* lines and *all* rules involved in the step.
2. Try to avoid combination steps involving more than two different rules.
3. When the same rule is combined with itself several times (such as two or three applications of "sev." to a complex conjunction), don't complicate things by combining in another rule.
4. Avoid combinations that are difficult to follow, such as "dist., dist."
5. Avoid using the following rules as part of a compound step (the opportunities for error are too great): QN, QS, RBV, UI, EG, EI, UG, CP, IP; except that several steps of QN may be combined together, and IP may be combined with DN.
6. Remember, it is more important that a proof be easy to follow than that it be short.

Exercises II

Construct a proof for each of the following.

☐ **1.** / ∴ $(\exists x)(Fx \supset (y)Fy)$

2. / ∴ $(\exists x)(Gx \supset Gx)$

3. / ∴ $(\exists x)(\exists y)(z)((Fx \supset Gx) \supset (Fy \supset Gz))$

4. If anything is a fish, then if all fish are vertebrates, then it is a vertebrate.

5. If everything is perishable, then if all perishable things are worthless, then something is worthless.

☐ **6.** / ∴ $[(x)Fx \cdot (\exists y)Gy] \supset (\exists z)(Fz \cdot Gz)$

7. / ∴ $[(x)(Fx \supset Gx) \cdot (\exists y)(Fy \lor Hy)] \supset (\exists z)(Gz \lor Hz)$

8. / ∴ $\sim(\exists x)Fx \equiv [(y)(Fy \supset Gy) \cdot (z)(Fz \supset \sim Gz)]$

9. / ∴ $(x)(\exists y)(\exists z)(Fx \supset (Fy \cdot Fz))$

☐ **10.** / ∴ $[(\exists x)Fx \cdot (\exists y)Gy] \supset [((z)(Fz \supset Hz) \cdot (w)(Gw \supset Kw)) \equiv$
$(t)(u)((Ft \cdot Gu) \supset (Ht \cdot Ku))]$

chapter 21

PROVING INVALIDITY
IN QUANTIFIER LOGIC

To prove that an argument containing quantifiers is invalid, it is necessary to produce what is called an "invalidating interpretation" of that argument. Two sorts of invalidating interpretations are **natural interpretations** and **interpretations for a model universe**.

§21.1 Natural Interpretation

As a preface, it will be helpful to review some facts from Part I about validity and invalidity with respect to *truth-functional arguments*. When an argument is truth-functionally valid, it is valid irrespective of the *actual* truth-values of the simple statements in it; for example, both of the following arguments are (truth-functionally) valid, in spite of the fact that one of them contains only true simple statements and the other contains only false simple statements:

Aardvarks are mammals ⊃ Birds are oviparous
Aardvarks are mammals
──────────────────────────────
∴ Birds are oviparous

Apples are citrus fruits ⊃ Bananas grow underground
Apples are citrus fruits
──────────────────────────────
∴ Bananas grow underground

We can make this point another way by saying that the argument

$A \supset B$
A
─────
$\therefore B$

is valid regardless of whether 'A' is an abbreviation of the true statement 'Aardvarks are mammals' or of the false statement 'Apples are citrus fruits', and regardless of whether 'B' is an abbreviation of the true statement 'Birds are oviparous' or of the false statement 'Bananas grow underground'. The fully abbreviated argument is valid regardless of the actual truth-values of '*A*' and '*B*', hence it is valid regardless of what statements '*A*' and '*B*' may be abbreviations of. It is valid in virtue of its *form*, and this remains the case no matter how we understand '*A*' and '*B*'. Likewise, the invalid argument

$$A \supset B$$
$$\underline{B}$$
$$\therefore A$$

remains (truth-functionally) *invalid* no matter how we understand '*A*' and '*B*'; it is invalid because it does not have a validating form, and its actual components are irrelevant to this fact.

The case is quite similar for arguments in quantifier logic. An argument is (quantificationally) valid only if it has a validating "quantificational form." Quantificational forms can be defined in something like the way that truth-functional forms were defined in Chapter 9.* A **truth-functional form** is a framework into which specific statements may be inserted to produce a statement "having that form." Similarly, a **quantificational form** is a framework into which specific predicate expressions, individual constants, and individual variables may be inserted to produce a statement or argument "having that form." We can see, without formal definitions, that the following two statements both have the same quantificational form:

1. $(x)(Fx \supset \sim Gx) \supset F\underline{a}$
2. $(y)(Ky \supset \sim My) \supset K\underline{b}$

That is, they have the same essential framework though the specific occupants of that framework are different in the two cases; (2) has '*y*' instead of '*x*', '*K*' instead of '*F*', '*M*' instead of '*G*', and '*b̲*' instead of '*a̲*'; but its *structure* is the same as that of (1).

An argument which is quantificationally valid is valid because of its form. If it is valid because of its form, then every argument with that form is also valid. This means that, if an argument is valid, then it is valid no matter which predicates are actually abbreviated by its predicate letters. (Just as with truth-functional validity: a valid argument is valid no matter which statements are actually abbreviated by its capital letters.) For example, both of the following arguments are quantificationally valid:

All satyrs are unicorns
All unicorns are leprechauns
∴ All satyrs are leprechauns

All seniors are upperclassmen
All upperclassmen are lazy
∴ All seniors are lazy

---

*See Appendix K, for the actual formal definition.

which is to say, the argument

$(x)(Sx \supset Ux)$
$(x)(Ux \supset Lx)$
$\therefore (x)(Sx \supset Lx)$

is valid, regardless of whether 'Sx' abbreviates 'x is a satyr' or 'x is a senior' (or 'x is made of polyethylene' or 'x is not in the Andromeda galaxy'); it is valid no matter *how* we understand 'S' and 'U' and 'L'. And, conversely, the argument

$(x)(Sx \supset Ux)$
$(x)(Sx \supset Lx)$
$\therefore (x)(Ux \supset Lx)$

is *invalid* no matter how we understand 'S' and 'U' and 'L'. We can prove it to be invalid by giving a "natural interpretation" of it. A **natural interpretation** of a quantificational formula is *any arbitrary (but consistent) assignment of meanings to the **predicate letters** and **free individual letters** in the formula.* We "assign meaning" to a predicate letter by regarding it as an abbreviation of some predicate expression; we assign meaning to an individual letter by regarding it as an individual constant—that is, as the abbreviation of a name of some individual. "Natural interpretation" doesn't mean "plausible interpretation"; it is called "natural" because the meanings we assign are usually taken from our natural language. For example, we could give one natural interpretation of the argument above by assigning 'Sx' to mean 'x is a winged horse', assigning 'Ux' to mean 'x loves parsnips', and assigning 'Lx' to mean 'x drives a Cadillac'. Thus interpreted, the above argument would say:

All winged horses love parsnips
All winged horses drive Cadillacs
$\therefore$ Anything that loves parsnips drives a Cadillac

As another example, the argument

All thieves are politicians
Senator Claghorn is a politician
$\therefore$ Senator Claghorn is a thief

translates and abbreviates as

$(x)(Tx \supset Px)$
$P\underline{c}$
$\therefore T\underline{c}$

By assigning 'Tx' to mean 'x is an operatic tenor', 'Px' to mean 'x has a pleasing voice', and '$\underline{c}$' to mean 'Smokey (the Bear)', we arrive at the natural interpretation

All operatic tenors have pleasing voices
Smokey the Bear has a pleasing voice
$\therefore$ Smokey the Bear is an operatic tenor

The way to prove an argument quantificationally invalid by this method is to discover (think up) a natural interpretation of that argument such that all of its premises are *as a matter of fact* true and its conclusion is *as a matter of fact* false. This will suffice to show that the argument, so interpreted, is invalid (if it *does* have true premises and a false conclusion, then obviously it *can* have true premises and a false conclusion, and so it is invalid). In showing that the argument, so interpreted, is invalid, you will have shown that the argument does not have a validating quantificational form. That is, you will have shown that having *that* form is not sufficient for quantificational validity, and hence you will have shown that the original argument (the one prior to interpretation) was not quantificationally valid either. Such an interpretation is called an **invalidating natural interpretation**.

The examples above are probably invalidating natural interpretations. But if, say, we are not altogether certain that the conclusion of the first example is false (the premises are vacuously true, because there are no winged horses), it is easy enough to give another interpretation which is unmistakably invalidating: assign '*Sx*' to mean '*x* is a snake', assign '*Ux*' to mean '*x* is a vertebrate', and assign '*Lx*' to mean '*x* is a reptile'. The result will be

> All snakes are vertebrates
> All snakes are reptiles
> ∴ All vertebrates are reptiles

which, as a glance at any biology book will show, has premises which are definitely true and a conclusion which is definitely false. Similarly, if we are not altogether certain of the truth of the premises of the second example, we can remedy it with a different interpretation: assign '*Tx*' to mean '*x* is a king', assign '*Px*' to mean '*x* is a monarch', and assign '*c*' to mean 'Elizabeth II'. The resulting interpreted argument is

> All kings are monarchs
> Elizabeth II is a monarch
> ∴ Elizabeth II is a king

which definitely has true premises and a false conclusion. This way of showing an argument to be invalid is sometimes called "Refutation by Analogy." The proof of invalidity consists simply in listing, alongside the argument, the assignments of meaning which lead to the invalidating interpretation, prefaced by the words "Shown invalid by"; thus:

$(x)(Sx \supset Ux)$ Shown invalid by Sx : x is a snake
$(x)(Sx \supset Lx)$ Ux : x is a vertebrate
∴ $(x)(Ux \supset Lx)$ Lx : x is a reptile

or,

$(x)(Tx \supset Px)$ Shown invalid by Tx : x is a king
$P\underline{c}$ Px : x is a monarch
∴ $T\underline{c}$ $\underline{c}$: Elizabeth II

The primary disadvantage to this method is that there are no rules to follow for coming up with an invalidating interpretation. It requires ingenuity, and that's all. Sometimes you will be able to think of an invalidating interpretation quite easily, but sometimes none will occur to you no matter how hard you try. However, the primary *advantage* to this method is that, when it works for you, it is easier than the other method (described in the next section) for proving the invalidity of quantified arguments.

Exercise I

All of the arguments below are quantificationally invalid. Translate and abbreviate each of them, and prove their invalidity by giving an invalidating natural interpretation of each.

1. All crows are birds. All crows are warm-blooded. Therefore, all birds are warm-blooded.

□ 2. If everything is destructible then something is perishable. Everything is perishable. Therefore, something is destructible.

3. No senators are Democrats. No Democrats are governors. Therefore, no senators are governors.

4. Some senators are Republicans. Some Republicans are smart politicians. Therefore, some senators are smart politicians.

5. If anything is waterproof then it is washable. Some shoes are not waterproof. Therefore, some shoes are not washable.

6. If any cats are striped then some cats are tabbies. Therefore, if any cats are striped then they are tabbies.

□ 7. Apples and oranges are edible fruits. Whatever is edible is nourishing. If all fruits are edible then bananas are edible. Therefore apples and bananas are nourishing fruits.

8. No senators or representatives are both Republicans and Democrats. Some senators are Republicans and some representatives are Democrats. Therefore, some senators are Democrats and some representatives are Republicans.

9. Only men are eligible for Selective Service. Edna is a woman. Therefore, Edna is not eligible for Selective Service.

□ 10. Anytime it snows, it also freezes. Whenever it freezes the streets are slippery. If the streets are ever slippery then there are accidents. Sometimes it doesn't snow. Therefore, sometimes there are no accidents.

11. All politicians are liars. If Harvey is a politician, he will soon be wealthy. Therefore, if Harvey is a liar, he will soon be wealthy.

12. All Communists are atheists. Some atheists are Republicans. No Presbyterians are Republicans. Bishop Sheen is an atheist. Therefore, if Bishop Sheen is a Presbyterian, he's a Communist.

The method of natural interpretation may also be used to show that a set of statements is **quantificationally consistent**—that the quantificational relationships among the statements allow the possibility of their all being true at once. After the set of statements has been translated and abbreviated, simply assign meanings to each predicate letter and each free individual letter in such a way that all of the statements are *in fact* true; such an assignment will show that the original set of statements is quantificationally consistent. By showing that an argument is valid, and that its premises are quantificationally consistent, we show that it is, quantificationally, a good argument.

But as before (§8.1), there are modes of inconsistency which cannot be revealed by any formal procedures of quantifier logic. For example, the statements 'Harvey is unmarried' and 'Harvey's wife is a blonde' are incompatible, not in virtue of their quantificational structure but in virtue of the meanings of the nouns and adjectives in them. Thus, if we wish to be cautious, we will not claim to prove that an argument is (absolutely) a "good argument" by these procedures, but only that quantificationally it is a good argument.

§21.2 Interpretation for a Model Universe

A universally quantified statement asserts that everything in the universe satisfies the function quantified over. For example,

1. $(x)Fx$

asserts that everything in the universe satisfies the propositional function 'Fx'. If it were possible to construct a list of every object in the universe

$$\underline{a}$$
$$\underline{b}$$
$$\underline{c}$$
$$\underline{d}$$
.
.
.

we could then construct a substitution instance of the function 'Fx' for each object on the list

$$F\underline{a}$$
$$F\underline{b}$$
$$F\underline{c}$$
$$F\underline{d}$$
.
.
.

If all of these substitution-instances were then compounded together into one long conjunction

2. $F\underline{a} \cdot F\underline{b} \cdot F\underline{c} \cdot F\underline{d} \cdot \ldots$

the result would be a conjunction with as many conjuncts as there are objects in the universe (a rather lengthy formula). This conjunction would assert, of each thing in the universe, that it satisfies the function '*Fx*'. It would be true if all of its conjuncts were true, and false if one or more of them were false. We can see that the truth-conditions for this long conjunction are the same as those for the universally quantified statement (1): the two of them will be true if every object in the universe has the property designated by '*F*' and false if one or more objects do not have that property. Since they have the same truth-conditions, the universally quantified statement (1) and the long conjunction (2) would be logically equivalent. In general, a universally quantified formula is logically equivalent to a conjunction with one conjunct for each object in the universe.

In the same vein, an existentially quantified statement has the same truth-conditions as a *dis*junction with one disjunct for each object in the universe. For example,

3. $(\exists x)Gx$

asserts that at least one thing in the universe satisfies the propositional function '*Gx*'. And the disjunction

4. $Ga \lor Gb \lor Gc \lor Gd \lor \ldots$

continued out until it contains a disjunct for each object in the universe says the same thing. The long disjunction (4) will be true if one or more of its disjuncts is true—that is, if one or more things in the universe have the property designated by '*G*'—and false if all of its disjuncts are false—that is, if nothing in the universe has the property designated by '*G*'. But these are likewise the truth-conditions for the existentially quantified statement (3). Thus (3) is logically equivalent to a disjunction with one disjunct for every object in the universe. In general, any existentially quantified formula is logically equivalent to a disjunction with one disjunct for each object in the universe.

The conjunction or disjunction to which a quantified formula is logically equivalent is called the **interpretation** of that quantified formula.

A **model universe** is an imaginary universe containing a restricted number of things, which we specify by enumerating or listing the objects it contains. The actual, physical universe that we live in contains a vast number of things. It contains not only the things within our solar system, but things elsewhere in the galaxy and things in galaxies beyond. But however many things our actual universe contains, it is a contingent matter of fact that it contains that many and not fewer. It is consistently imaginable that the universe might have contained nothing except our own galaxy, or, for that matter, nothing except our own solar system. Or, for that matter, it is consistently imaginable that the universe might have contained nothing except a pair of electrons, named Adam and Bertha. Such a "two-member universe" would be quite easy to specify by enumeration, since there are only two names to list. The accepted way of specifying a model universe is by writing down the (abbreviated) names of its members, separated by commas, and enclosing the whole in braces. Thus, the two-member universe just indicated would be specified as

$$\{a, b\}$$

Similarly, a model universe containing only one object—say, a neutrino named Clarence—would be specified as the one-member universe

$$\{c\}$$

and a three-member universe containing Adam and Bertha and Clarence and nothing else would be specified as

$$\{a, b, c\}$$

and so on.

If an argument is valid, then it is valid irrespective of empirical matters of fact. The *validity* of an argument will not be affected by what the world happens to be like. For example, if an argument is truth-functionally valid, then it is valid regardless of which of its components happen to be true and which happen to be false. By the same token, if an argument is valid, then it is valid regardless of how many things there happen to be in the world.* The actual inventory of the universe is completely irrelevant to the validity of a genuinely valid argument. This is sometimes expressed by saying: an argument is valid if and only if it is valid in every possible universe, imaginary or actual. Thus, if it can be shown that there is a model universe in which a particular argument would be invalid (a model universe in which it *could* have all true premises and a false conclusion), that will be the same as showing that the argument is invalid, period.

The procedure for showing this is based upon the method presented in Chapter 14 for demonstrating truth-functional invalidity. It has two stages. The first consists in *constructing an interpretation* of the argument in question *for a model universe*. The second consists in applying the abbreviated truth-table method to that interpretation. The interpretation of a quantified formula for a model universe is like the interpretation of that formula for the actual universe, except for containing fewer conjuncts or disjuncts. For the model universe

$$\{a, b, c\}$$

the interpretation of the universally quantified formula

  5. $(x)Kx$

would be the conjunction

  5a. $Ka \cdot Kb \cdot Kc$

---

*So long as there is something. There are certain otherwise valid arguments which would be invalid if the universe were totally empty, if there were not even one object in the universe. An example is the argument: $(x)Fx, / \therefore (\exists x)Fx$. This is a technical point which we can safely ignore for purposes of applied logic.

Similarly, the interpretation, for the same universe, of the statement

   6. $(x)(Fx \supset Gx)$

would be the conjunction

   6a. $(Fa \supset Ga) \cdot (Fb \supset Gb) \cdot (Fc \supset Gc)$

and the interpretation, for the same universe, of the existentially quantified statement

   7. $(\exists x)(Rx \cdot \sim Mx)$

would be the disjunction

   7a. $(Ra \cdot \sim Ma) \lor (Rb \cdot \sim Mb) \lor (Rc \cdot \sim Mc)$

The process of giving an interpretation of a quantified statement is a process of "interpreting away" a quantifier by constructing an equivalent statement in which it does not appear. It is possible to set down formal directions for properly constructing an interpretation. To understand these directions, it is necessary to know that the **suffix** of a quantifier is everything within the scope of the quantifier except the quantifier itself. For example, in the formula '$(x)(y)(Fx \supset Gy)$' the suffix of '(x)' is '$(y)(Fx \supset Gy)$', and the suffix of '(y)' is '$(Fx \supset Gy)$'. With this in mind, we can state the directions as follows:

1. If the formula to be interpreted begins with a universal quantifier, the interpretation will be a conjunction with the same number of conjuncts as there are members in the model universe.
2. If the formula to be interpreted begins with an existential quantifer, the interpretation will be a disjunction with the same number of disjuncts as there are members in the model universe.
3. Each conjunct (or disjunct) will be a substitution-instance of the *suffix* of the quantifier to be "interpreted away." The substituent for the variable of quantification will be one (and only one) of the letters from the specification of the model universe. For example, if the model universe is $\{a, b\}$, then the first conjunct (or disjunct) in the interpretation will be *just like* the *suffix* of the quantifier that is being interpreted away, except that each place in the domain of that quantifier will contain an occurrence of 'a'; and the second conjunct (or disjunct) will be just like the suffix of that quantifier except that each place in the domain of that quantifier will contain an occurrence of 'b'.

Giving an interpretation is not a process of *inference*. It is a process of *construction*. And it is a process which can be applied to any quantified formula, whether it is a part of a larger formula or not. This means that no matter how many quantifiers a formula may contain, we can eventually interpret them all away, leaving an equivalent formula which contains no quantifiers but is simply a truth-functional compound. This is the ultimate goal of the process of giving interpretations for model universes, since its purpose is to allow us to apply the procedures learned in truth-functional logic (for example, the abbreviated truth-table method) to demonstrate invalidity in quantifier logic. In the following illustrations, all interpretations are for the two-member universe {a, b}.

The formula

8. $(x)Fx \supset (\exists y)Gy$

is not a quantified formula; it is a conditional whose antecedent and consequent are both quantified formulae. A complete interpretation of (8)—that is, an interpretation which contains no quantifiers—will require an interpretation of each of the two components of (8). The antecedent of (8) is the universally quantified statement '$(x)Fx$', and its interpretation for our two-member universe will, by Rule 1, be a conjunction with two conjuncts. Its suffix is 'Fx', and by Rule 3 each conjunct will be a substitution-instance of this: one where 'x' is replaced by 'a' and the other where 'x' is replaced by 'b'. Thus, a partial interpretation of (8) will be

8a. $(Fa \cdot Fb) \supset (\exists y)Gy$

However (8a) still contains a quantifier in its consequent. The consequent is the existentially quantified statement '$(\exists y)Gy$', and its interpretation for our two-member universe will, by Rule 2, be a disjunction with two disjuncts. Its suffix is 'Gy', and by Rule 3 each disjunct will be a substitution instance of this: one where 'y' is replaced by 'a' and the other where 'y' is replaced by 'b'. And so, the complete interpretation of (8) will be

8b. $(Fa \cdot Fb) \supset (Ga \lor Gb)$

Matters become slightly more complicated when the formula to be interpreted contains quantifiers with overlapping scopes, as in

9. $(x)(y)(Fx \supset Gy)$

This is a universally quantified statement, and by Rule 1 its interpretation will contain two conjuncts. Its suffix is '$(y)(Fx \supset Gy)$', and by Rule 3 each conjunct will be a substitution-instance of this: one where 'x' is replaced by 'a' and the other where 'x' is replaced by 'b'. Thus, when the quantifier '(x)' is interpreted away, the result is the conjunction

9a. $(y)(Fa \supset Gy) \cdot (y)(Fb \supset Gy)$

But (9a) still contains two quantifiers; to arrive at a full interpretation both of these must be interpreted away. The first conjunct is a universally quantified statement; by Rule 1 its interpretation will contain two conjuncts. Its suffix is '$(Fa \supset Gy)$', and by Rule 3 each conjunct will be a substitution-instance of this: one where 'y' is replaced by 'a' and the other where 'y' is replaced by 'b'. Thus, when the quantifier in the first conjunct of (9a) is interpreted away, the result is

9b. $[(Fa \supset Ga) \cdot (Fa \supset Gb)] \cdot (y)(Fb \supset Gy)$

This leaves one quantifier to go. The second conjunct of (9b) is a universally quantified statement, so its interpretation will contain two conjuncts. Its suffix is '(*Fb* ⊃ *Gy*)', so each conjunct will be a substitution-instance of this: one where '*y*' is replaced by '*a*' and the other where '*y*' is replaced by '*b*'. Thus, the complete interpretation of (9) for our two-member universe will be

9c. [(*Fa* ⊃ *Ga*) · (*Fa* ⊃ *Gb*)] · [(*Fb* ⊃ *Ga*) · (*Fb* ⊃ *Gb*)]

When a quantified statement is only a part of a formula, its interpretation replaces *just* that part of the formula. We have already seen examples of this in the interpretation of (8). Another example is

10. ~(∃*x*)(*Fx* · *Gx*)

which is a negation whose negate is a quantified statement. The interpretation of (10) will be a negation whose negate is the interpretation of that quantified statement. Since it is an existentially quantified statement, its interpretation will, by Rule 2, contain two disjuncts. Its suffix is '(*Fx* · *Gx*)', so by Rule 3 each disjunct will be a substitution-instance of this. The interpretation of the quantified statement is thus '(*Fa* · *Ga*) ∨ (*Fb* · *Gb*)', and the interpretation of the negation of the quantified statement is

10a. ~[(*Fa* · *Ga*) ∨ (*Fb* · *Gb*)]

This may be contrasted with

11. (∃*x*)~(*Fx* · *Gx*)

which is an existentially quantified statement with a negative suffix, and whose interpretation is

11a. ~(*Fa* · *Ga*) ∨ ~(*Fb* · *Gb*)

As another illustration, here are the successive steps in constructing a complete interpretation of a fairly complex formula.

12.   (*x*)~(∃*y*)(*Fx* ⊃ (*Gy* ⊃ *Hx*))
12a.   ~(∃*y*)(*Fa* ⊃ (*Gy* ⊃ *Ha*)) · ~(∃*y*)(*Fb* ⊃ (*Gy* ⊃ *Hb*))
12b. ~[(*Fa* ⊃ (*Ga* ⊃ *Ha*)) ∨ (*Fa* ⊃ (*Gb* ⊃ *Ha*))] · ~(∃*y*)(*Fb* ⊃ (*Gy* ⊃ *Hb*))
12c. ~[(*Fa* ⊃ (*Ga* ⊃ *Ha*)) ∨ (*Fa* ⊃ (*Gb* ⊃ *Ha*))] ·
                          ~[(*Fb* ⊃ (*Ga* ⊃ *Hb*)) ∨ (*Fb* ⊃ (*Gb* ⊃ *Hb*))]

As we see from this example, complete interpretations naturally lead to rather lengthy formulae. This cannot be avoided altogether; it is the nature of the process to generate long formulae. Nevertheless, it can be ameliorated to some extent by shifting as many quantifiers as far *in* as possible, before starting to construct the interpretation. The resulting formulae will still be long, but not as long as if the quantifiers had been left outside. For example, if the '*y*' quantifier in (12) above is shifted all the way in, the result is

13. (*x*)~(*Fx* ⊃ ((*y*)*Gy* ⊃ *Hx*))

a complete interpretation of which will be, successively,

13a.   ~(*Fa* ⊃ ((*y*)*Gy* ⊃ *Ha*)) · ~(*Fb* ⊃ ((*y*)*Gy* ⊃ *Hb*))
13b. ~(*Fa* ⊃ ((*Ga* · *Gb*) ⊃ *Ha*)) · ~(*Fb* ⊃ ((*y*)*Gy* ⊃ *Hb*))
13c. ~(*Fa* ⊃ ((*Ga* · *Gb*) ⊃ *Ha*)) · ~(*Fb* ⊃ ((*Ga* · *Gb*) ⊃ *Hb*))

which is considerably shorter than the other interpretation. You may wish to prove, as an exercise, that the two interpretations are logically equivalent.

In general, the smaller the scope of a quantifier is, the shorter the interpretation will be. Another legitimate measure which leads to shorter formulae is to employ *transformation* rules in addition to QS, to shorten up the scopes of the quantifiers as much as possible. (This is legitimate, since the result of transformation is always logically equivalent to the original.) For example, (13) above can be transformed, successively, into

14. $(x)\sim(\sim Fx \lor (\sim(y)Gy \lor Hx))$ 13, CE twice
15. $(x)(Fx \cdot \sim(\sim(y)Gy \lor Hx))$ 14, TD, DN
16. $(x)(Fx \cdot ((y)Gy \cdot \sim Hx))$ 15, TD, DN
17. $(x)((Fx \cdot \sim Hx) \cdot (y)Gy)$ 16, transp., rgr.
18. $(x)(Fx \cdot \sim Hx) \cdot (y)Gy$ 17, QS

in which the two quantifiers have their smallest possible scope. The complete interpretation of (18) is, successively,

18a. $[(Fa \cdot \sim Ha) \cdot (Fb \cdot \sim Hb)] \cdot (y)Gy$
18b. $[(Fa \cdot \sim Ha) \cdot (Fb \cdot \sim Hb)] \cdot (Ga \cdot Gb)$

which is shorter than either of the earlier interpretations. You may wish to prove, as an exercise, that this is logically equivalent to the other two interpretations. The interpretations are logically equivalent, because the formulae they interpret are equivalent. (12), (13), and (18) are all logically equivalent, since only transformation rules were used in their derivation from each other.

A final point: If the original formula contains *free letters* (variables or constants), the specification of the model universe used to interpret that formula *must* contain those same letters (perhaps along with others). For example, any model universe used in constructing an interpretation of '$(x)(Fx \supset Fy)$' must contain 'y' as one of the letters in its specification.

Exercises II

Give an interpretation of each of the following for the model universe $\{c, d\}$.

1. $(x)(Fx \supset \sim Fx)$
2. $(\exists x)(Kx \lor Mx)$
□ 3. $(x)(Fx \supset (\exists y)Gy)$
4. $\sim(x)\sim(Fx \cdot \sim Gx)$
5. $(x)(y)((Fx \cdot Gy) \supset (Fy \cdot Gx))$
□ 6. $(\exists x)(\exists y)((Fx \cdot Gy) \lor (Fy \cdot Gx))$
7. $(x)(y)(z)(Fx \supset (Fy \supset Fz))$
8. $(x)(Fx \supset Gd)$
□ 9. $(x)Fx \supset Gd$
10. $(x)(\exists y)(z)((Fx \cdot Gy) \supset (\exists w)(Hz \cdot Gw))$

§21.3   Model Universes and Invalidity

The procedures for showing an argument invalid for a given model universe are the same as those for showing an argument to be truth-functionally invalid. First we construct an interpretation of the argument for that model universe by constructing an interpretation of each premiss and the conclusion for that model universe. Then we apply the abbreviated truth-table method to the interpretation, by giving trial-and-error assignments of truth-values to the simple statements within the interpretation, in order to arrive at an invalidating assignment. For example, the argument

> Some Republicans are Senators
> Some Republicans are Conservatives
> ∴ Some Senators are Conservatives

translates as

> $(\exists x)(Rx \cdot Sx)$
> $(\exists x)(Rx \cdot Cx)$
> ∴ $(\exists x)(Sx \cdot Cx)$

The interpretation of this argument for the two-member universe $\{a, b\}$ is

> $(Ra \cdot Sa) \vee (Rb \cdot Sb)$
> $(Ra \cdot Ca) \vee (Rb \cdot Cb)$
> $/ \therefore (Sa \cdot Ca) \vee (Sb \cdot Cb)$

which can be shown to be invalid by the assignment:

Ca	Cb	Ra	Rb	Sa	Sb
F	T	T	T	T	F

Since the interpretation for $\{a, b\}$ of the original quantified argument is shown invalid by this assignment, we can say that the original quantified argument is

Shown invalid for $\{a, b\}$ by	Ca	Cb	Ra	Rb	Sa	Sb
	F	T	T	T	T	F

This illustrates the standard pattern for writing out the "proof of invalidity"; it specifies the model universe used in constructing the interpretation and gives the invalidating assignment of truth-values within that interpretation.

A quantified argument which is invalid cannot always be *proven* invalid for the model universe you may happen to choose. Many invalid arguments are valid for universes below a certain size, in the sense that within those universes it would be impossible for the premisses to be true and the conclusion false. For example, the argument just considered is valid for a one-member universe, so it could not be proven invalid for the model universe $\{a\}$.*

This has important consequences for the method under discussion. Within the realm of truth-functional arguments, if all possible assignments of truth-values are tried and none of them is invalidating, it is safe to conclude that the argument is valid. But within the realm of quantified arguments, if all possible assignments of truth values *within a given interpretation* are tried and none of them is invalidating, this might mean only that the interpretation does not involve a large enough model universe. There is a chance that an interpretation for a *larger* universe might turn out to be invalid. Thus, if the interpretation of an argument for a given model universe fails to produce an invalidating assignment of truth-values, we may *not* conclude that the argument is valid; we must choose a larger model universe and try again.

This has a rather discouraging sound to it, since it appears to leave no stopping-place, except for the extralogical ones imposed by fatigue, impatience, or death. Is there *no* upper limit to the size of the model universes we must consider, before concluding that the argument must, after all, be valid for every model universe? In *general*, the answer is: No, there is none. However, there is an exception in the case of arguments containing only *monadic* predicates. For any such argument there is a "largest relevant model universe"—a model universe such that, if the argument is valid within that universe, then it is valid for every larger universe and so is valid. Where n is the number of different *predicate* letters in the argument (it doesn't matter how many occurrences of each letter there are), and where all predicates in the argument are monadic, the largest relevant model universe for that argument will be one of 2^n members.† This means that, for most of the monadic arguments encountered in real life, their largest relevant model universe will be quite large and their interpretation for that universe will be correspondingly lengthy. In practice it is usual to try smaller model universes first,

---

*An argument which is valid within a given universe is valid within all smaller ones (except the empty one); an argument which is invalid within a given universe is invalid within all larger ones.

†If polyadic predicates (treated in subsequent chapters) are available, it is easy to construct arguments in which *no finite* universe can reveal their invalidity, since an *infinite* universe would be required to make all their premises true. An example of such an argument is:

> Every person is younger than somebody or other. There are persons, but no person is younger than himself. If one person is younger than another, and that one is younger than another, then the first is younger than the last. Therefore, some person is younger than everybody else.

Because of this, the method of Natural Interpretation given in the first part of this chapter is especially useful when one is working with complicated arguments containing polyadic predicates.

rather than proceeding to the decisive case. The practical value of knowing the largest relevant universe is not that it gives a place to start, but that it gives a place to stop, in the event that no satisfactory result is achieved with smaller models.

A useful rule of thumb to follow in employing the method under discussion is this: start out with a universe having the same number of members as there are existentially quantified premisses in the argument (that is, premissess which begin with an initially placed existential quantifier); or if the argument contains less than two existentially quantified premissess, start out with a two-member universe. This rule does not guarantee results on the first try; but it is the author's opinion that by following it more time will be saved than wasted.

Exercises III

Prove the invalidity of each of the following arguments. (None of them requires anything larger than a four-member universe, and most of them do not require even that.)

  1. $(x)(Fx \supset Gx)$
     Gy $/ \therefore Fy$

  2. $(x)(Fx \supset Gx)$
     $(\exists x)(Hx \cdot \sim Gx)$ $/ \therefore (\exists x)(Gx \cdot \sim Fx)$

  3. $(x)(Fx \supset \sim Gx)$
     $(\exists x)(Hx \cdot Gx)$ $/ \therefore (x)(Fx \supset \sim Hx)$

□ **4.** $(x)(Fx \supset Gx)$
     $(\exists x)(Hx \cdot Gx)$
     $(\exists x)(Hx \cdot \sim Gx)$ $/ \therefore (x)(Fx \supset \sim Hx)$

  5. $(x)(Fx \supset Mx)$
     $(\exists x)((Fx \cdot Gx) \cdot \sim Hx)$
     $(\exists x)(Hx \cdot \sim Mx)$
     $(\exists x)(Fx \cdot \sim Gx)$
     $(x)(\sim Gx \supset \sim Hx)$
     $(\exists x)((Hx \cdot Mx) \cdot \sim Fx)$ $/ \therefore (x)(y)(\sim Hy \supset (\sim Fx \lor \sim Fy))$

  6. $(x)(Fx \supset (Gx \lor Hx))$
     $(\exists x)(Fx \cdot \sim Hx)$
     $(\exists x)Gx \supset Hx$
     $\sim(x)(\sim Hx \supset Gx)$ $/ \therefore (x)(Fx \supset Gx) \supset (\exists y)(Hy \cdot Gy)$

Exercises IV

Translate each of the following and prove its invalidity. (None of them requires anything larger than a four-member universe.)

  1. If cats exist then mammals exist. All cats are mammals. Therefore, mammals exist.

  2. If all Rhodesians are Africans then some Africans are Englishmen. Most Englishmen are born in England. All who are born in England are loyal to the Queen. Some Rhodesians are Africans. Therefore, some Rhodesians are loyal to the Queen.

3. Some Texans own both oil wells and much cattle. On the other hand, some Texans don't own much cattle, and some Texans don't own oil wells. Therefore, some Texans don't own either oil wells or much cattle.

☐ 4. Everyone who attended was either a freshman or a sophomore. Therefore, either everyone who attended was a freshman or everyone who attended was a sophomore.

5. Not all senators or representatives are dishonest. Therefore, some senators are honest.

6. All snakes are reptiles. Some vertebrates are reptiles, but some aren't. Therefore, all snakes are vertebrates.

☐ 7. All freshmen are students. Some freshmen work hard without getting good grades, and some freshmen get good grades without working hard. However, not all students are freshmen. Therefore, some students work hard and get good grades.

8. All students are ambitious. Some students are happy but unsuccessful, and some students are successful but unhappy. Not all who are ambitious are students. Therefore, those who are neither ambitious nor students are either happy or successful.

§21.4 Additional Uses of the Methods

The method of interpretation for a model universe, and the method of natural interpretation, may also be used for showing that a given formula is not a quantifier truth. For example, consider the statement

1. If all registered voters are citizens, then some citizens are registered voters.

which translates as

1a. $(x)(Rx \supset Cx) \supset (\exists x)(Cx \cdot Rx)$

To show that this is not a quantifier truth by the method of natural interpretation, we give interpretations of 'R' and 'C' which render (1a) false. One such would be to assign 'Rx' to mean 'x is a unicorn' and 'Cx' to mean 'x is a quadruped'. Under this interpretation, (1a) says

2. If all unicorns are quadrupeds, then some quadrupeds are unicorns.

which is false; the antecedent is true because there are no unicorns, and the consequent is false for the same reason. This shows that (1) is *not* true merely in virtue of its quantificational form, and so shows that it is not a quantifier truth. Alternatively, (1) can be shown not to be a quantifier truth by interpreting it for the model universe $\{a\}$, as

1b. $(Ra \supset Ca) \supset (Ca \cdot Ra)$

and assigning the value F to 'Ra'.

When the latter method is used with single statements, as in the last example, the same limitations (and lack of them) apply as when it is used with arguments. That is, provided that the statement contains n predicates, all of them monadic, the largest relevant universe is one of 2^n members. If a falsifying assignment of truth-values cannot be found within the interpretation for that universe, then the statement is, after all, a quantifier truth.

The method of interpretation for a model universe may also be used to reveal the **quantificational consistency** of a set of statements. Construct an interpretation of the set of statements for some chosen model universe, and then use the abbreviated truth-table method to assign truth-values in such a way as to make (the interpretation of) each statement T at the same time. This will show the set to be quantificationally consistent.

The same limitations apply here as when we are trying to show invalidity. That is, a failure to come up with a desired assignment of truth-values within a given interpretation will not show the set to be inconsistent; it may only mean that the chosen model universe was too small. If the set of statements contains only monadic predicates, then for n separate predicates, the largest relevant model universe will be one with 2^n members; and so on.

Exercises V

For each of the following, show by the method of Natural Interpretation that it is not a quantifier truth.

1. Either everyone over 18 deserves to be drafted, or no one over 18 deserves to be drafted.

☐ 2. If some wealthy professors are intelligent, then any professor who is not wealthy is not intelligent.

3. Some politicians are honest, or some are dishonest.

4. If all subatomic particles are too small to see, then if anything is too small to see then it is subatomic.

5. If anyone commits a crime, then if nobody calls the police then he will get away without being arrested.

☐ 6. If some tigers are friendly animals and all friendly animals can be tamed, then all friendly tigers can be tamed.

7. Nobody can bite his own elbow.

Exercises VI

For each of the above, show that it is not a quantifier truth by the method of interpretation for a model universe.

Quantifier Logic

(b) Polyadic Predicates, Identity, and Definite Descriptions

chapter 22

RELATIONS

§22.1 Polyadic Predicates

The two statements

1. Albert is fat.
2. Albert is taller than Bertha.

are both singular statements. But whereas (1) mentions a single individual and ascribes a property to him, (2) mentions two individuals and ascribes a relationship to the pair of them. Singular statements such as (2) are called **singular relational statements**. Statement (2) also differs from the singular statements discussed previously (Chaper 15) in that the predicate expression which it contains, namely

2a. ___ is taller than ___

has two "blank spaces" in it rather than just one; or, using the familiar notation in which blank spaces are indicated by individual variables,

2b. x is taller than y

contains two variables rather than just one. Propositional functions such as (2b), which are non-compound and contain two variables, are called **two-place functions** or **dyadic functions**. Statement (2) is a substitution-instance of the dyadic function (2b). Substitution-instances were previously defined only for monadic functions, but we can now give a general definition.

> *Substitution-Instance of a Function.* A statement is a substitution-instance of a propositional function if and only if we can obtain it from that function by substituting occurrences of names for free occurrences of variables in the function.

A singular statement which is a substitution-instance of a dyadic function is called a **dyadic singular statement**. (2) is a dyadic singular statement. Other examples of dyadic singular statements are:

   3. Percy kicked Evangeline.
   4. Clyde and Edna are man and wife.
   5. Thelma has an abiding hatred for Harvey.
   6. 2 is the square root of 4.
   7. Evangeline is Percy's sister.
   8. Thelma tried to call Edna.
   9. Harvey works for Clyde.
  10. Albert and Bertha live twenty miles apart.
  11. Quebec is north of Patagonia.
  12. Excalibur belonged to King Arthur.
  13. Edna is preparing to divorce Clyde.
  14. Lake Erie flows into the Colorado River.
  15. Betelgeuse is hotter than Arizona.
  16. Evangeline has waited for years to avenge herself against Percy.
  17. Tulsa is surrounded by Oklahoma.
  18. Shakespeare wrote *Hamlet*.

As a simple exercise you may wish to pick out the functions that these are substitution-instances of.

Not all singular relational statements are dyadic. For example, the statement

  19. Cleveland is between Chicago and Baltimore.

is a **triadic** singular statement and is a substitution-instance of the triadic (three-place) function

  19a. x is between y and z

Triadic functions are, of course, non-compound functions containing three variables. Some other examples of triadic functions are:

  20. x introduced y to z
  21. x extends from y to z
  22. x gave y to z
  23. x stole y from z
  24. x hates y because of z
  25. x is the sum of y and z
  26. x never got over the sight of y kicking z

As a simple exercise you may wish to construct some substitution-instances of these functions.

Just as there are dyadic and triadic statements and functions, so there are **tetradic** (four-place) statements and functions, such as

  27. Los Angeles is further from Sacramento than New York is from Boston.
  27a. x is further from y than z is from w
  28. Clyde entertained Thelma while Harvey was entertaining Edna.

28a. *x* entertained *y* while *z* was entertaining *w*

29. Bertha introduced Albert to Edna at Harvey's request.

29a. *x* introduced *y* to *z* at *w*'s request

30. When two times three is subtracted from six the result is zero.

30a. When *x* times *y* is subtracted from *z* the result is *w*

and **pentadic** (five-place) statements and functions, such as

31. Edna hates Harvey because Thelma reported that Clyde was being transferred to Indianapolis.

31a. *x* hates *y* because *z* reported that *w* was being transferred to *k*

32. Albert drove Bertha through Utah to Denver in order to visit Percy.

32a. *x* drove *y* through *z* to *w* in order to visit *k*

33. When 2 + 3 is multiplied by 4 + 5 the result is 58.

33a. When *x* + *y* is multiplied by *z* + *w* the result is *k*

and so on. Statements and functions greater than monadic are referred to generically as **polyadic** (many-place) statements and functions, and it is possible in theory to encounter a polyadic statement or function of any size you care to mention. However, it would be unusual to run across anything like a million-place function, and in ordinary discourse the standard thing is for them to run to the lower numbers. In the present text the discussion and examples will normally be confined to dyadic and triadic statements and functions. But the principles given will be applicable to any polyadic statement or function, regardless of the number of places involved.

Just as monadic functions are said to designate "properties," so polyadic functions designate **relations**. For example, the function '*x* is taller than *y*' designates the relation of being taller than; the function '*x* is between *y* and *z*' designates the relation of being between; and so on.

§22.2 Abbreviating Polyadic Functions

The method of abbreviating polyadic functions is a simple extension of the method for abbreviating monadic functions. A monadic function is abbreviated as a predicate letter (a capital letter) followed by the variable in the function being abbreviated. A polyadic function is abbreviated as a predicate letter followed by all of the variables in the function.* For example, the function

1. *x* is taller than *y*

---

*Another popular notation for dyadic relations consists in putting the two variables on either side of the predicate letter. In this notation, '*x* is taller than *y*' would be abbreviated as '*xTy*'.

abbreviates as

   1a. *Txy*

and the function

   2. *x* is between *y* and *z*

abbreviates as

   2a. *Bxyz*

and so on. We can describe this by saying: a single-place function abbreviates as a predicate letter followed by a single place, a two-place function as a predicate letter followed by two places, a three-place function as a predicate letter followed by three places, and so on. Each place following the predicate letter represents one of the places ("blank spaces" indicated by variables) in the unabbreviated function.

For example, when (1) is abbreviated as (1a), the first place following '*T*' represents the place before 'is' in 'is taller than' and the second place following '*T*' represents the place after 'than' in 'is taller than'. This correspondence is depicted in the way the variables are located in the abbreviated and unabbreviated versions of the function. Thus, the place occupied by '*x*' in the abbreviated version represents the place occupied by '*x*' in the unabbreviated version, and similarly for '*y*'.

Since (1a) is merely an abbreviation of (1), the result of inserting constants into the places occupied by variables in (1a) will be the same as the result of inserting those same constants into the corresponding places in (1). For example,

   3. *Tab*

says the same thing as

   3a. *a* is taller than *b*

and

   4. *Tba*

says the same thing as

   4a. *b* is taller than *a*

Despite the fact that (3) and (4) contain the same predicate letter and the same constants, they do not assert the same thing. They differ in precisely the way that (3a) differs from (4a). (3a) says, for example, that Albert is taller than Bertha, whereas (4a) says that Bertha is taller than Albert. In the same way, (3) and (4) are totally different (abbreviated) statements.

Thus, after a polyadic function has been abbreviated, it is important to remember not only what the predicate letter stands for, but also what each of the places represents. For example, when (2) has been abbreviated as (2a), we cannot later abbreviate the statement

   5. Akron is between Baltimore and Chicago.

as

    5a. *Bbac*

for, given the previous abbreviation, what (5a) says is 'Baltimore is between Akron and Chicago'. In the light of the previous abbreviation, (5) must be abbreviated as

    5b. *Babc*

which means

    5c. *a* is between *b* and *c*

That is, the result of putting '*a*' for '*x*', '*b*' for '*y*', and '*c*' for '*z*' in (2a) is the same as the result of those substitutions in (2).

In summation, the places following the predicate letter in an abbreviated polyadic function are not mere undifferentiated locations. Each of them represents a definite place in the unabbreviated version, and the correspondence between the places must be kept in mind.

§22.3 Quantification and Relational Statements

Not all relational statements are singular; that is, not all of them are of the type in which two or more individuals are specified and a relationship is ascribed to them. Another type involves specifying an individual, or two individuals, or more, and asserting that that individual, or those individuals, stand in a certain relationship to *something* or to *everything*. Statements of this type are partly singular and partly general. An example is the statement

    1. Something is taller than Bertha.

This statement obviously is based upon the function '*x* is taller than *y*', but not in any way we have encountered thus far. It is not a *substitution-instance* of that function, since it cannot be obtained by substituting names for variables in the function. But neither is it a *quantification* of that function, since it cannot be obtained simply by quantifying over the places in the function. Rather, it is a **partially general** relational statement, which can be obtained from the function '*x* is taller than *y*' by substituting into *one* of its places and quantifying over the *other* one. The appropriate translation of (1) is

    1a. $(\exists x)x$ is taller than *b*

'There is something such that it is taller than Bertha'—which, fully abbreviated, becomes

    1b. $(\exists x)Txb$

Another example of a partially general relational statement based upon the same function is

    2. Albert is taller than everything.

which translates as

    2a. $(x)a$ is taller than x

'Everything is such that Albert is taller than it'—which, fully abbreviated, is

    2b. $(x)Tax$

Some examples of partially general statements involving the triadic function 'x is between y and z' are

    3. Something is between Baltimore and Chicago.

    4. Akron is between something and Chicago.

    5. Akron is between Baltimore and something.

which translate, respectively, as

    3a. $(\exists x)x$ is between b and c

'There is something such that it is between Baltimore and Chicago';

    4a. $(\exists x)a$ is between x and c

'There is something such that Akron is between it and Chicago'; and

    5a. $(\exists x)a$ is between b and x

'There is something such that Akron is between Baltimore and it.' When fully abbreviated, these become, respectively,

    3b. $(\exists x)Bxbc$

    4b. $(\exists x)Baxc$

    5b. $(\exists x)Babx$

In each of these examples, only one quantifier word occurs. However, there are also partially general relational statements which contain more than one quantifier word, such as

    6. Akron is between something and something.

In such cases (in fact, whenever more than one quantifier word is involved), it is best to carry out the translation by stages. Thus, as a first step, (6) will translate as

    6a. $(\exists x)a$ is between x and something

The matrix of (6a), 'a is between x and something', may then be translated as

    6b. $(\exists y)a$ is between x and y

so that the final translation becomes

    6c. $(\exists x)(\exists y)a$ is between x and y

or, fully abbreviated,

    6d. $(\exists x)(\exists y)Baxy$

In addition to partially general relational statements such as these, there are completely general relational statements in which no names appear at all. An example would be

7. Everything is taller than something.

Since this contains two quantifier words, it is best translated by stages. The first step gives

7a. $(x)x$ is taller than something

then, translating the matrix 'x is taller than something' as '$(\exists y)x$ is taller than y', we obtain

7b. $(x)(\exists y)x$ is taller than y

which, fully abbreviated, becomes

7c. $(x)(\exists y)Txy$

Another example is the statement

8. Something is taller than everything.

which translates, by stages, as

8a. $(\exists x)x$ is taller than everything
8b. $(\exists x)(y)x$ is taller than y

and abbreviates as

8c. $(\exists x)(y)Txy$

As a final example,

9. Everything is between something and something.

translates, by stages, as

9a. $(x)x$ is between something and something
9b. $(x)(\exists y)x$ is between y and something
9c. $(x)(\exists y)(\exists z)x$ is between y and z

and abbreviates as

9d. $(x)(\exists y)(\exists z)Bxyz$

§22.4 Reflexive Pronouns

Reflexive pronouns such as 'itself', 'himself', and so on occur only in relational statements. When the base* of the pronoun is a name (as in 'Clyde hates himself'), the appropriate treatment is to replace the reflexive pronoun by another occurrence of the name, as a first step in translation. For example, the (false) statement

1. Albert is taller than himself.

---

*That is, grammatical antecedent, see §18.1.

will be translated first as

    1a. Albert is taller than Albert.

and then as

    1b. $T\underline{aa}$

However, when the base of the pronoun is a quantifier word, the effect in translation will be that one quantifier binds several places in the function. For example, the (false) statement

    2. Something is taller than itself.

will translate as

    2a. $(\exists x)x$ is taller than x

and abbreviate as

    2b. $(\exists x)Txx$

Similarly, the (true) statement

    3. Something multiplied by itself equals 9.

translates as

    3a. $(\exists x)x$ multiplied by x equals 9

and abbreviates as

    3b. $(\exists x)Mxx\underline{n}$

As a final example, the (false) statement

    4. Everything is between itself and itself.

will translate as

    4a. $(x)x$ is between x and x

and abbreviate as

    4b. $(x)Bxxx$

§22.5 Some Advice on Translation

Relational generalizations about "everything" or "something," without qualification, are as uncommon as monadic generalizations of that sort (cf. §18.3). In the vast majority of cases, the generalizations we make in ordinary discourse have to do with everything or something *of a certain kind*, such as persons or cats or prime numbers or brown cows. The translation procedures learned, in this connection, for use with monadic functions may also be used with polyadic functions. For example, the statement

    1. Every elephant is taller than something.

will translate, successively, as

    1a. $(x)(x$ is an elephant $\supset x$ is taller than something$)$
    1b. $(x)(x$ is an elephant $\supset (\exists y)x$ is taller than $y)$
    1c. $(x)(Ex \supset (\exists y)Txy)$

Similarly, the statement

    2. Someone is taller than Bertha.

will paraphrase as

    2a. Some person is taller than Bertha.

and will translate successively as

    2b. $(\exists x)(x$ is a person $\cdot x$ is taller than $\underline{b})$
    2c. $(\exists x)(Px \cdot Tx\underline{b})$

Similarly, the statement

    3. Everyone is younger than someone.

will paraphrase as

    3a. Every person is younger than some person.

and will translate as

    3b. $(x)(x$ is a person $\supset x$ is younger than some person$)$
    3c. $(x)(x$ is a person $\supset (\exists y)(y$ is a person $\cdot x$ is younger than $y))$
    3d. $(x)(Px \supset (\exists y)(Py \cdot Yxy))$

Just as with translations involving only monadic functions, remember: Do not bite off too big a piece of translation at once. Translations that are difficult when done all at once become easy when done in stages.

Exercises I

Translate and abbreviate the following, using the supplied abbreviations.

☐ **1.** Everybody loves somebody. $(Px : x$ is a person; $Lxy : x$ loves $y.)$
    2. Somebody loves everybody.
    3. Everybody is loved by somebody.
☐ **4.** Somebody is loved by everybody.
    5. Some trees are taller than some elephants. $(Ax : x$ is a tree; $Ex : x$ is an elephant; $Txy : x$ is taller than $y.)$
    6. Some trees are taller than every elephant.
    7. Every tree is taller than some elephant.
☐ **8.** Anybody who loves everybody loves himself.

9. Anybody who loves himself loves somebody.
10. Some elephants love any person which is taller than they are.

Exercises II

Translate and abbreviate the following, using the supplied abbreviations.

1. Somebody gave something to Edna. (*Gxyz* : *x* gave *y* to *z*.)
☐ 2. Somebody gave an elephant to Edna.
3. Edna gave an elephant to somebody.
4. An elephant gave Edna to somebody.
5. Somebody gave Edna an elephant which is taller than she is.
☐ 6. Anybody who gave Edna an elephant gave Clyde a wombat. (*Wx* : *x* is a wombat.)
7. Everybody who loves Edna gave her something.
8. Everybody who loves somebody gave them something.
☐ 9. If anybody gave something to everybody then somebody gave something to himself.
10. If anybody gave an elephant to everybody who doesn't own one, then everybody owns an elephant. (*Oxy* : *x* owns *y*.)

Exercises III

Translate and abbreviate the following, using the supplied abbreviations.

1. Nobody who loves somebody is a complete failure. (*Fx* : *x* is a complete failure.)
☐ 2. Anybody who loves nobody is a complete failure.
3. Nobody loves himself.
4. Nobody who loves nobody loves himself.
5. If nobody gave Edna anything, then she is a complete failure.
☐ 6. Anybody to whom Edna gave something is not a complete failure.
7. If Edna did not give anything to somebody, then she does not love him.
8. If Edna gave something to somebody, then if she did not own it, then whoever owns it will have her arrested. (*Hxy* : *x* will have *y* arrested.)
9. If anyone gives something she owns to someone and he has her arrested, he is a complete failure.
☐ 10. Anyone who gives everything he owns to someone he loves is not a complete failure and nobody will have him arrested.

§22.6 Mixed Quantifiers and Quantifier Order

A quantified formula which contains quantifiers of both types (universal and existential) is said to contain **mixed quantifiers**. A formula which contains only quantifiers of one type contains **unmixed quantifiers**. In a formula containing unmixed quantifiers, the *order* in which the quantifiers occur is logically immaterial. It doesn't matter which comes before which. We can also express this by saying: Every contiguous arrangement of universal quantifiers in a formula is logically equivalent to every other contiguous arrangement of those quantifiers in that formula; and similarly every contiguous arrangement of existential quantifiers in a formula is logically equivalent to every other contiguous arrangement of those quantifiers in that formula. For example, the two formulae

  1. $(x)(y)Rxy$
  2. $(y)(x)Rxy$

are logically equivalent, even though the order of the quantifiers is reversed. Similarly, the two formulae

  3. $(\exists x)(\exists y)Rxy$
  4. $(\exists y)(\exists x)Rxy$

are logically equivalent even though the order of the quantifiers is reversed.

However, the order of *mixed* quantifiers, relative to each other, can make a radical difference in the meaning of the formula. Consider, for example, the two statements:

  5. Everything is caused by something.
  6. There is something which everything is caused by.

These two statements are quite different in meaning; but when they are translated into quantifier notation, the two formulae will be identical *except for the order of the quantifiers*. The first of them translates, by stages, as

  5a. $(x)x$ is caused by something
  5b. $(x)(\exists y)x$ is caused by y
  5c. $(x)(\exists y)Cxy$

while the second of them translates, by stages, as

  6a. $(\exists y)$ everything is caused by y
  6b. $(\exists y)(x)x$ is caused by y
  6c. $(\exists y)(x)Cxy$

Both of these assert that everything has a cause. But (6) asserts that everything has *the same* cause, while (5) does not. (5) only asserts of each thing that it is caused by something, and this something might be different in each case. On the other hand, (6) asserts that there is some object y of which it is true that everything is caused by y—that is, that some one object is the cause of everything.

Both translations consist of mixed quantifications over the function '__ is caused by __'—universal quantification with respect to the place before 'is' and existential quantification with respect to the place after 'by.' Both quantifiers have exactly the same *range* in both formulae; they differ only as to their *scope*—that is, as to their order relative to each other. In (5b) the existential quantifier lies within the scope of the universal; in (6b) the universal quantifier lies within the scope of the existential. This is what accounts for their difference in meaning. As a further illustration, consider the first-stage translation of (5):

5a. $(x)x$ is caused by something

When this universal quantifier is "interpreted away" (§21.2), the result is

5d. a is caused by something $\cdot$ b is caused by something $\cdot$ c is caused by something $\cdot$ ...

illustrating that (5) only asserts that each thing has its cause, and leaves open the possibility that different things may have different causes. This contrasts with

6b. $(\exists y)(x)x$ is caused by y

When this universal quantifier is interpreted away, the result is

6d. $(\exists y)(a$ is caused by $y \cdot b$ is caused by $y \cdot c$ is caused by $y \cdot$ ...$)$

which asserts that the same object y is the cause of a and is also the cause of b, and so on.

When an existential quantifier is within the scope of a universal quantifier, as in (5b), it is **distributed** with respect to that universal quantifier; it says that there is something-or-other standing in the given relation to *each* object in the domain of the relation. In effect, each object gets its own existential quantifier, as reflected in (5d)—hence, "distributed."

On the other hand, when an existential quantifier has a universal quantifier within its scope, as in (6b), it is **specific** with respect to that universal quantifier; it says that there is one thing which stands in the given relation to all objects in the domain, just as in (6d) a single existential quantifier serves for all objects.

Exercises IV

In the light of the discussion above, decide which of the following statements are true and which are false. In all cases the values of 'y' are restricted to persons.

☐ **1.** $(\exists x)(y)x$ gave birth to y
☐ **2.** $(y)(\exists x)x$ gave birth to y
☐ **3.** $(x)(\exists y)x$ gave birth to y
☐ **4.** $(\exists y)(x)x$ gave birth to y
☐ **5.** $(\exists x)(\exists y)x$ gave birth to y
☐ **6.** $(\exists y)(\exists x)x$ gave birth to y

☐ **7.** $(y) \sim (\exists x) \sim x$ gave birth to y
☐ **8.** $\sim (y) \sim (\exists x)x$ gave birth to y

The number of different statements we can express by manipulating quantifier order increases with the number of mixed quantifiers. In the previous example there are only two quantifiers and consequently only two ways to permute them. Let us look now at some examples containing three quantifiers (in these first examples, the values of the variables are restricted to rational numbers):

7.   Every number is the quotient of two numbers.

7a. $(x)(\exists y)(\exists z)x = y/z$

Both (7) and (7a) are obviously true. In (7a) both existential quantifiers lie within the scope of the universal quantifier, and so both are distributed with respect to it. Thus (7a) asserts that for each rational number x there is some fraction (proper or improper) which is equal to it, and this is certainly true (each rational number which is a fraction is equal to itself, and each whole number is equal to the fraction whose denominator is 1 and whose numerator is the number itself).

8.   There is a number such that every number is the quotient of it and some number.

8a. $(\exists y)(x)(\exists z)x = y/z$

(8) and (8a) are also true, however suspicious they may look. In (8a) the first existential quantifier is specific with respect to the universal, while the second existential quantifier is distributed with respect to the universal. Thus (8a) says that there is a specific number y such that every number is equal to some fraction having y as the *numerator*, and this is true: for example, 1 is such a number. $1 = 1/1$; $2 = 1/(1/2)$; $3 = 1/(1/3)$; $2/3 = 1/(3/2)$; $2/5 = 1/(5/2)$; and so on. (It should be obvious that 1 is not the only such number.)

9.   There is a number such that every number is the quotient of some number and it.

9a. $(\exists z)(x)(\exists y)x = y/z$

Again, these are true. Again, the first existential quantifier is specific with respect to the universal while the second existential is distributed with respect to the universal. Thus (9a) says that there is a specific number z such that every number is equal to some fraction having z as the *denominator*; and this is true: 1 is such a number, since every number is equal to the fraction with 1 as denominator and the number itself as numerator.

10.   There are numbers such that every number is equal to their quotient.

10a. $(\exists y)(\exists z)(x)x = y/z$

Both (10) and (10a) are false. In (10a) both existential quantifiers are specific with respect to the universal quantifier. Thus (10a) in effect asserts that there is a specific fraction y/z which is equal to every number, and so (10a) is false. (If there were such a fraction, all numbers would be equal to each other.)

The next set of examples will require a bit more explanation of the situations to be described in quantifier notation. In these examples, the values of 'x' and 'z' are restricted to members of a mythical organization, the Bide-a-wee Bridge Club, and each example involves people giving things to each other in one way or another.

The first situation to be described is that of a mutual exchange of presents, as at Christmas time: the club has sixteen members, and each member buys sixteen presents—one for each member of the club. We can express this sort of present-exchange by saying

11. Each person gave each person something or other.

11a. $(x)(z)(\exists y)x$ gave y to z

Here, the existential quantifier is distributed with respect to both universal quantifiers. It asserts that between each member x and each member z some gift changed hands, without any indication that the same present was given or received by more than one person.

This is to be contrasted with another sort of case. Suppose that Thelma, a typical member of the club, has an unusually ugly Chinese vase, inherited from a wealthy uncle, which she has been trying to give away. Each year, on some member's birthday, she gives him the vase; but each year on *her* birthday she receives it back. She does not seem to be able to give it away for keeps. In the course of sixteen years she gives the vase to everybody. And suppose further that Thelma is not alone in having such a problem; every member has a "white elephant" of one sort or other which he is unable to get rid of, though he has given it to everybody. This is a situation where

12. Each member has a specific thing which he gave to everybody.

12a. $(x)(\exists y)(z)x$ gave y to z

In (12a) the existential quantifier is distributed with respect to the first universal—the one concerning givers—and is specific with respect to the second universal—the one concerning receivers. Thus, it asserts that each giver had his own gift (distributed), but that for each such gift everyone received *it* (specific). 'For each x there is a y which everyone received.'

Since the club members aren't very good at bridge, they spend a lot of time playing "Hearts," a game in which points are lost for taking a trick containing a heart or a Queen of Spades, and in which the strategy is to give these penalty cards to others. Charlie, one of the members, *always* gets the Queen of Spades. Everybody gives Charlie the Spade Queen whenever possible, which is quite often. Charlie doesn't like that. He tries to get even by giving the Ace of Hearts to Bertha every chance he gets. The fad catches on, and pretty soon everybody is giving Bertha the Ace of Hearts whenever possible. Eventually, each member has his own personal jinx card, which everyone gives him; that is,

    13.   Every member has a specific thing which everyone gives him.

    13a. $(z)(\exists y)(x)x$ gives y to z

In (13a) the existential quantifier is distributed with respect to the universal quantifier concerning receivers, but is specific with respect to the universal quantifier concerning givers. Thus it asserts that each receiver has his own thing, but that everyone gives that thing to him. 'For each z there is a y which everyone gives.'

After a few years of the business described in the previous case, Charlie finally rebels, declaring he will resign from the club if somebody else doesn't start getting the Queen of Spades once in a while. He proposes a by-law to the effect that every member has to take a turn at being the Spade Queen Receiver for a month, with the order of turns to be established by drawing lots. Since Charlie owns the deck, the by-law is quickly adopted. For the first month everyone gives the Spade Queen to Bertha; for the second month everyone gives it to Harvey; and so on. At the end of sixteen months everyone has taken his turn at receiving the Spade Queen from everyone. And so,

    14.   There is something which everyone gave to everyone.

    14a. $(\exists y)(x)(z)x$ gave y to z

In (14a) the existential quantifier is specific with respect to both universal quantifiers: the one concerning givers and the one concerning receivers. Thus it asserts that there is some *one* thing which everyone gave to everyone (namely, the Queen of Spades).

A final point: the rule about contiguous quantifiers of the same type, given at the beginning of this section, holds even if there is a quantifier of the other type somewhere in the formula. Thus, in (7a) and (10a) the existential quantifiers are contiguous (next to each other), and so their order is immaterial: they could be reversed without changing anything. Similarly, in (11a) and (14a) the universal quantifiers are contiguous, and so nothing would be changed by reversal of their order.

Exercises V

Translate and abbreviate each of the following.

    1. All men admire something.
    2. There is something which all men admire.
□ **3.** There is something such that all men who admire anything admire it.
    4. There is something such that if there is anything which all men admire, then they admire it.
    5. All men desire something from somebody.
□ **6.** There is something which all men desire from somebody.
    7. There is something which all men desire from everybody.

8. All men desire something from everybody.

☐ **9.** Some men desire something from everybody.

10. There is something which some men desire from everybody.

Exercises VI

Describe the different sorts of situations depicted by the following statements ($\{x, z\}$ restricted to members of the bridge club).

☐ **1.** $(\exists x)(\exists y)(z)x$ gave y to z

2. $(\exists x)(z)(\exists y)x$ gave y to z

3. $(z)(\exists x)(\exists y)x$ gave y to z

4. $(\exists y)(z)(\exists x)x$ gave y to z

☐ **5.** $(x)(\exists y)(\exists z)x$ gave y to z

6. $(\exists y)(x)(\exists z)x$ gave y to z

7. $(\exists y)(\exists z)(x)x$ gave y to z

☐ **8.** $(\exists z)(x)(\exists y)x$ gave y to z

§22.7 Genitives and Possessives

The Genitive Case is a grammatical category covering certain pronouns and noun structures. It is commonly referred to as the "Possessive Case— misleadingly, since, although all possessives are genitive, not all genitives have to do with possession. The most common genitives involve pronouns such as 'his', 'hers', 'its', 'their', and 'whose' and nouns with apostrophe plus 's' such as 'Jones's' and 'policeman's'. The genitive case is employed to indicate a relationship between one thing and another—hence its relevance to the area of logic under discussion. When phrases in the genitive case are translated into logic, their translation always involves a relational expression—that is, a polyadic (usually dyadic) function.

Some of the relations most frequently expressed in the genitive case are those of *possessing* or *owning* or *having* or *belonging to*. This no doubt accounts for the nickname "Possessive Case." For example, in the phrase 'Clyde's dog' the relationship expressed by the genitive is that of possessing or owning; Clyde's dog is a dog which Clyde owns or possesses. But in the phrase 'Clyde's brother' the relationship expressed is not that of possession or ownership; it is the relationship of brotherhood. Clyde's brother is not a brother which Clyde owns; he is simply a brother of Clyde, and *ownership* does not enter into the picture at all. Similarly, in the phrase 'Clyde's birthplace' the relationship is not that of possession; it is the relationship of having been born at. Clyde's birthplace is not a birthplace which belongs to Clyde; it is, simply, where Clyde was born. Again, in the phrase 'Clyde's mortal enemy' the relationship indicated by the genitive is not that of possession;

it is the relationship of mortal enmity. In these last three examples the genitive tells us *that* a relationship exists; the rest of the phrase indicates *which* relationship.

The equation of genitive with possessive is helped along by the fact that in English (and many other languages) the verb 'have' (or its counterpart) serves a dual role in the language: to indicate possession, and also as an adjunct to non-possessive genitive structures. We say "Clyde has a dog" and we also say "Clyde has a brother"; however, if we were listing Clyde's possessions, we might list the dog, but we would certainly not list the brother. 'Clyde has a dog' means that there is a dog which belongs to Clyde, but 'Clyde has a brother' does not mean that there is a brother which belongs to Clyde; it means, straightforwardly, that someone is a brother to Clyde. In the same vein we might say, "Clyde has a birthplace," recognizing that what this means is that Clyde was born somewhere.

The point of this brief exposition is that sentences which are grammatically indistinguishable, such as 'Clyde has a dog' and 'Clyde has a brother', may require different treatment when translated into logic. For a translation to be appropriate, it should indicate the actual relationship involved and not some other one. By way of illustration, the first of these sentences,

    1. Clyde has a dog.

means that there is a dog which belongs to Clyde, so we shall translate it as

    1a. $(\exists x)(x$ is a dog $\cdot$ x belongs to Clyde)

whereas the second sentence,

    2. Clyde has a brother.

means that someone has the relationship of brotherhood to Clyde, so we shall translate it as

    2a. $(\exists x)x$ is brother to Clyde

There are no formal criteria for distinguishing possessive from non-possessive genitives. One must, ultimately, rely on common sense.

Genitives normally call for the existential quantifier. (1a) and (2a) above are simple examples. As a pair of slightly more complex examples, consider

    3. Clyde's dog is vicious.
    4. Clyde's brother is wealthy.

The first of these, understood straightforwardly, means "There is a dog which belongs to Clyde and which is vicious"—that is,

    3a. $(\exists x)(x$ is a dog $\cdot$ x belongs to c $\cdot$ x is vicious)

The second, understood straightforwardly, means "There is something which is brother to Clyde and which is wealthy":

    4a. $(\exists x)(x$ is brother to c $\cdot$ x is wealthy)

Genitives often combine with other sorts of quantified relational expressions. In such cases, translation will follow the normal pattern. For example,

  5. Clyde's dog bit a postman.

will translate, successively, as

  5a. (∃ x)(x is a dog · x belongs to c · x bit a postman)

  5b. (∃ x)(x is a dog · x belongs to c · (∃ y)(y is a postman · x bit y))

which, using the obvious abbreviations plus '*Kxy* : x belongs to y', abbreviates as

  5c. (∃ x)(Dx · Kxc · (∃ y)(Py · Bxy))

Similarly,

  6. Clyde's dog bit Harvey's brother.

will translate, successively, as

  6a. (∃ x)(x is a dog · x belongs to c · x bit Harvey's brother)

  6b. (∃ x)(Dx · Kxc · (∃ y)(y is brother to h · x bit y))

and, using '*Fxy* : x is brother to y'

  6c. (∃ x)(Dx · Kxc · (∃ y)(Fyh · Bxy))

  Genitives which are *universal* call, of course, for the universal quantifier. For example,

  7. All of Harvey's brothers were valiant.

will translate as

  7a. (x)(x is a brother of Harvey ⊃ x was valiant)

It is conventional to treat plural genitives which are not restricted or qualified in some way as *universal* (cf. §16.3) Thus, for example, a statement such as

  8. Clyde's dogs are hungry.

is to be treated as if it said

  8a. All of Clyde's dogs are hungry.

and is to be translated as

  8b. (x)((x is a dog · x belongs to Clyde) ⊃ x is hungry)

Exercises VII

Translate and abbreviate each of the following, using the supplied abbreviations.

  ☐ **1.** Clyde's dog bit somebody. (*Dx* : x is a dog; *Px* : x is a person; *Kxy* : x belongs to y; *Bxy* : x bit y.)

  ☐ **2.** Somebody bit Clyde's dog.

  3. Somebody's dog bit Clyde.

  4. Clyde's dog bit somebody's dog.

  ☐ **5.** Nobody's dog bit Clyde.

6. Somebody's dog bit everybody.

7. Everybody who was bitten by Clyde's dog bit somebody.

8. Anybody who has a brother that was bitten by Clyde's dog has an unhappy brother. (*Fxy* : *x* is brother to *y*; *Ux* : *x* is unhappy.)

☐ 9. Clyde's dog bit somebody's brother.

10. Clyde's dog's brother bit somebody.

11. Clyde's dogs bit somebody's brother.

☐ 12. Clyde's dogs bit somebody's brothers.

Exercises VIII

Translate and abbreviate each of the following, using the supplied abbreviations.

1. Arthur brought a present to Galahad. (*Gx* : *x* is a present; *Bxyz* : *x* brought *y* to *z*.)

2. Arthur brought a present to his father. (*Pxy* : *x* is father to *y*.)

☐ 3. Arthur's father brought him a present.

4. Arthur's father brought a present to Galahad.

5. Arthur's father brought a present to Galahad's father.

☐ 6. Arthur's father brought a present to himself.

7. Arthur's father brought a present to his father.

8. Arthur's father brought a present to his father's father.

☐ 9. Arthur brought Galahad's father a dog that belongs to Arthur's father's brother.

10. Arthur's father was Uther.

§22.8 Prepositional Phrases

In English it is quite common to attach a preposition, such as 'with', to a noun phrase in order to express relationships. Expressions of this sort usually translate with the existential quantifier. For example, the statement

1. Albert bought a dog with a collar from a man with a hat.

translates, by stages, as

1a. $(\exists x)(x$ is a dog with a collar $\cdot$ a bought x from a man with a hat$)$

1b. $(\exists x)(Dx \cdot (\exists y)(y$ is a collar $\cdot$ x has $y) \cdot a$ bought x from a man with a hat$)$

1c. $(\exists x)(Dx \cdot (\exists y)(Cy \cdot Hxy) \cdot (\exists z)(z$ is a man with a hat $\cdot$ a bought x from $z))$

1d. $(\exists x)(Dx \cdot (\exists y)(Cy \cdot Hxy) \cdot (\exists z)(Mz \cdot (\exists w)(w$ is a hat $\cdot$ z has $w) \cdot Baxz))$

1e. $(\exists x)(Dx \cdot (\exists y)(Cy \cdot Hxy) \cdot (\exists z)(Mz \cdot (\exists w)(Hw \cdot Hzw) \cdot Baxz))$

The existential quantifier is called for in such cases by the indefinite article 'a' or 'an'. Phrases containing the indefinite article are called "indefinite descriptions." Indefinite descriptions, like phrases containing the definite article 'the', have a "generic" use (cf. §16.3), which requires them to be translated by means of the universal quantifier. For example, the statement 'A platypus is an oviparous mammal' would translate as '$(x)(x$ is a platypus $\supset x$ is an oviparous mammal)'. Apart from such uses, indefinite descriptions almost invariably translate as saying 'there is a . . .'. When a preposition attaches to an indefinite description, the resulting prepositional phrase will translate, as illustrated above, as an existentially quantified formula containing a polyadic (usually dyadic) predicate. Of course one must exercise common sense. For example, the statement

    2. Lulu had a baby.

can be translated as

    2a. $(\exists x)(x$ is a baby $\cdot$ Lulu had $x)$

but the statement

    3. Lulu had a relapse.

could not plausibly be treated as saying

    3a. $(\exists x)(x$ is a relapse $\cdot$ Lulu had $x)$

This would be as anomalous as translating

    4. Albert went for a swim.

as

    4a. $(\exists x)(x$ is a swim $\cdot$ Albert went for $x)$

The world does not contain such objects as relapses and swims, waiting for people to take possession of them. To have a relapse is to do something on one's own; it is not the undertaking of a relationship with a queer object called a "relapse." The proper translation of (3) and (4) would be as monadic singular statements about Lulu and Albert.

Exercises IX

Translate and abbreviate each of the following.

☐ **1.** Under a spreading chestnut tree a village smithy stands.

   2. Clyde bought a skinny horse from Harvey.

   3. Clyde bought a skinny horse from someone and sold it to Harvey.

   4. A man with a gun on his hip rode into town.

   5. A man in a raincoat stood there.

   6. Edna threw a glance at a passing policeman.

   7. Albert saw a man who was driving away in a Cadillac with a broken taillight.

   8. Someone died from a bullet from a gun in the hand of a madman.

   9. A flower in a crannied wall attracted Al's attention.

☐ **10.** In a cavern in a canyon, excavating for a mine, dwelt a miner, forty-niner, and his daughter Clementine.

Exercises X

Translate and prove each of the following arguments.

1. Something is attracted by everything. Therefore, everything attracts something.

□ 2. There is a person who is loved by all persons. Therefore, everybody loves somebody.

3. There is a person who is loved by all persons at all times. There is a time when someone is loved by someone. Therefore, everybody loves somebody sometime.

4. All horses are animals. Therefore, all heads of horses are heads of animals.

□ 5. If anybody stole something from everybody, then he stole something from Gertrude. Nobody stole anything from Gertrude. Therefore, nobody stole something from everybody.

6. There is somebody who is loved by everybody who loves anybody at all. Everybody loves somebody. Therefore, somebody is loved by everybody.

7. Some nails are made of brass. Some magnets attract brass nails. Anything which will attract something made of brass will attract anything. Therefore, something attracts itself.

8. Any student who receives good recommendations from every advisor will find a decent job. Every advisor is also a professor. Therefore, if any student receives good recommendations from every professor, then he will find a decent job.

□ 9. Any politician who accepts money from someone who desires a favor of him will soon become wealthy. Any wheeler-dealer is a person who desires favors from every politician. No honest politicians will become wealthy. Therefore, any politician who accepts money from a wheeler-dealer is dishonest.

10. A broker will be successful only if he has the confidence of all of his clients. Every broker has at least one of his in-laws for a client. One's in-laws are one's wife's relatives. Therefore, every successful broker has the confidence of at least one of his wife's relatives.

§22.9 Invalidity Proofs Involving Relations

The methods of Natural Interpretation and Interpretation for Model Universes presented in Chapter 21 may be applied without modification to arguments containing polyadic predicates. The instructions and procedures remain exactly the same. When using the method of Natural Interpretation, the only requirement is that the polyadic predicate letters be interpreted as relations of the appropriate number of places (dyadic, triadic, and so on). For example, the argument

> Every citizen pays taxes to some Federal agency.
> Therefore, there is a Federal agency such that every citizen pays taxes to it.

translates as

$$\frac{(x)(Cx \supset (\exists y)(Fy \cdot Pxy))}{\therefore (\exists y)(Fy \cdot (x)(Cx \supset Pxy))}$$

and is shown invalid by

$Cx : x$ is a person
$Fx : x$ is a person
$Pxy : y$ is x's mother

since under this interpretation the premiss says "Every person has a mother," which is true, and the conclusion says "Some person is mother to everybody," which is false.

The same argument may also be shown invalid for the model universe $\{a, b\}$. The interpretation of the premiss proceeds by stages as

1. $(Ca \supset (\exists y)(Fy \cdot Pay)) \cdot (Cb \supset (\exists y)(Fy \cdot Pby))$
1a. $(Ca \supset ((Fa \cdot Paa) \lor (Fb \cdot Pab))) \cdot (Cb \supset (\exists y)(Fy \cdot Pby))$
1b. $(Ca \supset ((Fa \cdot Paa) \lor (Fb \cdot Pab))) \cdot (Cb \supset ((Fa \cdot Pba) \lor (Fb \cdot Pbb)))$

while the interpretation of the conclusion proceeds as

2. $(Fa \cdot (x)(Cx \supset Pxa)) \lor (Fb \cdot (x)(Cx \supset Pxb))$
2a. $(Fa \cdot ((Ca \supset Paa) \cdot (Cb \supset Pba))) \lor (Fb \cdot (x)(Cx \supset Pxb))$
2b. $(Fa \cdot ((Ca \supset Paa) \cdot (Cb \supset Pba))) \lor (Fb \cdot ((Ca \supset Pab) \cdot (Cb \supset Pbb)))$

and the argument is shown invalid for $\{a, b\}$ by

Ca	Cb	Fa	Fb	Paa	Pab	Pba	Pbb
T	T	T	T	T	F	F	T

and many other assignments.

As a more complex illustration of the way interpretations are constructed for relational arguments, consider

$$\frac{(x)(\exists y)(z)Rxyz}{\therefore (\exists y)(x)(z)Rxyz}$$

The interpretation of the premiss for $\{a, b\}$ proceeds by stages as

3. $(\exists y)(z)Rayz \cdot (\exists y)(z)Rbyz$
3a. $((z)Raaz \lor (z)Rabz) \cdot (\exists y)(z)Rbyz$
3b. $((Raaa \cdot Raab) \lor (z)Rabz) \cdot (\exists y)(z)Rbyz$
3c. $((Raaa \cdot Raab) \lor (Raba \cdot Rabb)) \cdot (\exists y)(z)Rbyz$
3d. $((Raaa \cdot Raab) \lor (Raba \cdot Rabb)) \cdot ((z)Rbaz \lor (z)Rbbz)$
3e. $((Raaa \cdot Raab) \lor (Raba \cdot Rabb)) \cdot ((Rbaa \cdot Rbab) \lor (z)Rbbz)$
3f. $((Raaa \cdot Raab) \lor (Raba \cdot Rabb)) \cdot ((Rbaa \cdot Rbab) \lor (Rbba \cdot Rbbb))$

and the interpretation of the conclusion will develop similarly to

4. $((Raaa \cdot Raab) \cdot (Rbaa \cdot Rbbb)) \lor ((Raba \cdot Rabb) \cdot (Rbba \cdot Rbbb))$

The argument is shown invalid for $\{a, b\}$ by

Raaa	Raab	Raba	Rabb	Rbaa	Rbab	Rbba	Rbbb
F	F	T	T	T	T	F	F

Notice that the interpreted argument contains as simple components *every* permutation of the two elements *a*, *b* through the three places following *R*, for 2^3 or eight distinct simple components. This is a general feature of model interpretations with polyadic predicates. For a universe of *n* members and a predicate of *m* places, the final interpretation will contain n^m simple elements containing *that* predicate letter, and similarly for its other predicate letters. Thus, in practice the method of interpretation for model universes will complicate itself to death with predicates of more than three places and universes of more than three or four members. After that, the method of Natural Interpretation is the only practical course to invalidity proofs, unless one has access to a computer.

Exercises XI

Prove the invalidity of each of the following, first by the method of natural interpretation and then by the method of interpretation for a model universe.

1. Everybody loves somebody. Therefore, there is a person who is loved by all persons.
☐ 2. All heads of horses are heads of animals. Therefore, all horses are animals.
3. Any student who receives good recommendations from every advisor will find a decent job. Some advisors are also professors. Therefore, any student who does not receive good recommendations from every professor will not find a decent job.
4. Everyone received a present from someone. Someone received a present from everyone. Every present was received by someone from someone. Therefore, there is a present which everyone received from someone.

§22.10 Properties of Relations

If one thing is taller than a second, and the second thing is taller than a third, then the first thing is taller than the third, no matter what the three things are. This fact about the relationship 'taller than' is expressed by saying that it is a **transitive relation**. Transitivity is a property of many relations, but it is taken so thoroughly for granted that it is seldom mentioned outside formal logic, even though it often plays a strong role in our reasoning about things. For example, the relationship 'older than' is another transitive relation, and it would not be at all unusual to hear someone argue informally as follows:

> I know that Fred must be older than Charlie, because Bill is older than Charlie and I know that Fred is older than Bill.

We recognize intuitively that this argument is valid; and yet, when it is formalized in the way we have learned, the result is

$$\frac{\begin{array}{l} Obc \\ Ofb \end{array}}{\therefore\ Ofc}$$

which is demonstrably invalid. The validity of the informal argument depends upon the additional *unspoken* premiss, so obvious that we don't even mention it but take it for granted, that 'older than' is a transitive relation. However, in formal logic nothing is taken for granted, and so, because this unspoken premiss does not appear in the formalized version, the formalized version is invalid. To render it valid, we must explicitly include the unspoken premiss that 'older than' is a transitive relation. This can be expressed in symbols as

$(x)(y)(z)((x$ is older than $y \cdot y$ is older than $z) \supset x$ is older than $z)$

for, in general, for any relation K,

K is Transitive   if and only if $(x)(y)(z)((Kxy \cdot Kyz) \supset Kxz)$.

When this unspoken premiss is included, the formalized argument becomes

$$\frac{\begin{array}{l} Obc \\ Ofb \\ (x)(y)(z)((Oxy \cdot Oyz) \supset Oxz) \end{array}}{\therefore\ Ofc}$$

which may easily be proven valid. In doing formal logic we often find ourselves faced with arguments whose validity depends upon some property of the relations involved. When that happens, we must supply additional premisses stating what the relevant properties of those relations are, in order to be able to prove the validity of the argument.

Some other examples of transitive relations are 'is the same age as', 'is at least as old as', 'is an ancestor of', 'is a kinsman of', 'is a descendant of', 'is a factor of', 'is higher in rank than', 'has more money than'.

On the other side of the coin is **intransitivity**. A relation is intransitive if it is never the case that, when one thing has that relation to a second and the second has it to a third, then the first also has it to the third; or, stated formally:

K is Intransitive   if and only if $(x)(y)(z)((Kxy \cdot Kyz) \supset \sim Kxz)$.

An example of an intransitive relation is 'fatherhood', since if x is the father of y and y is the father of z, then it is never the case that x is the father of z. Other examples of intransitive relations are 'is exactly two years older than', 'is the father of', 'is the immediate successor of', 'is a square root of' (except in the cases of 0 and 1), 'is one grade ahead of'.

Clearly, no relation can be both transitive and intransitive. But some relations are neither; they are **non-transitive**. Some examples of non-transitive relations are 'is acquainted with' (from the fact that x is acquainted with y and y is acquainted with z, it neither follows that x is acquainted with z nor that x is not acquainted with z), 'loves', 'hates', 'loaned money to', 'voted for'.

A different sort of property possessed by some relations is **symmetry**. A relation is symmetrical if, whenever one thing has that relation to another, then the second has that same relation to the first; or, formally:

K is Symmetrical if and only if $(x)(y)(Kxy \supset Kyx)$.

An example of a symmetrical relation is 'is a next-door neighbor of'; if x is a next-door neighbor of y, then it follows that y is a next-door neighbor of x. Other examples are 'is married to' (which is also intransitive), 'is a kinsman of' (which is also transitive), 'is a cousin of' (which is also non-transitive), 'is the same age as', 'is a sibling of', 'smokes the same brand as'.

The other side of this coin is **asymmetry**. A relation is asymmetrical if, whenever one thing has it to another, it is never the case that the second has that same relation to the first. Its formal definition is:

K is Asymmetrical if and only if $(x)(y)(Kxy \supset \sim Kyx)$.

An example of an asymmetrical relation (which also happens to be intransitive) is 'is mother to'; if x is mother to y, then it follows that y is not mother to x. Some other examples are 'is older than' (which is transitive), 'begat', 'raises better horses than', 'is an ancestor of', 'is underneath', 'is north of', 'is a husband of'.

As before, no relation is both symmetrical and asymmetrical,* but some relations are neither; they are **non-symmetrical**. Some examples of non-symmetrical relations are 'is a brother of' (if x is a brother of y it doesn't follow that y is a brother of x—y might be a sister of x—nor does it follow that y is not a brother of x), 'killed' (Hamlet and Claudius killed each other, but this doesn't always happen), 'loves', 'borrowed money from', 'shouted at', 'remembers', 'voted for'.

Yet another sort of property possessed by relations is **reflexivity**. A relation is reflexive if, whenever a thing has that relation to something (or something has that relation to it), then it also has that relation to itself; or formally:

K is Reflexive if and only if $(x)((\exists y)(Kxy \lor Kyx) \supset Kxx)$.

*There are logically trivial exceptions to this.

We cannot adequately discuss reflexivity without understanding the related property of **total reflexivity**. A relation is totally reflexive if everything has that relation to itself; or, formally:

> *K is Totally Reflexive*   if and only if $(x)Kxx$.

Many relations that we might initially regard as totally reflexive are not. For example, 'weighs the same as' is a relation which most things that immediately come to mind have to themselves: Jones weighs the same as Jones, the earth weighs the same as the earth, the solar system weighs the same as the solar system. Nevertheless 'weighs the same as' is not a totally reflexive relation, since there are many things we wish to talk about that do not weigh the same as anything (including themselves) because the notion of "weight" does not apply to them. Some examples would be Beethoven's Ninth Symphony, the square root of -1, the class of points on a sphere, the International Date Line, sounds, numbers, and abstract entities in general. A similar example is the relation 'less than or equal to', as expressed by the algebraic symbol '$\leq$'. Every number bears this relation to itself; but nothing which is not a number bears this relation to anything, for it is an algebraic relation and simply does not apply to things which are not numbers. Both of these relations are reflexive (though not totally reflexive). If an object weighs the same as something (that is, if it is the sort of object for which the notion of "weight" makes sense), then it weighs the same as itself. If an object is less than or equal to something (or something is less than or equal to it), then it is less than or equal to itself.

It is not easy to think of examples of totally reflexive relations. The most obvious one (and one of the few outside technical disciplines) is 'identity': everything is identical with itself, regardless of what sort of thing it is. But many relations are *reflexive*. Some examples are 'has the same parents as' (which is also transitive and symmetrical), 'went somewhere with' (which is non-transitive and symmetrical), 'eats as much as', 'does not weigh less than'.

The counterpart of reflexivity is **irreflexivity**. A relation is irreflexive if nothing has that relation to itself; that is,

> *K is Irreflexive*   if and only if $(x) \sim Kxx$.

'Taller than' is an irreflexive relation, since nothing is taller than itself. It is also transitive and asymmetric (in fact, every asymmetric relation is irreflexive). Some other examples of irreflexive relations are 'is a sibling of', 'is underneath', 'is a cousin of'.

As with the other cases, 'reflexive' and 'irreflexive' are mutually exclusive but do not exhaust the possibilities. A relation is **non-reflexive** if it is neither reflexive nor irreflexive. Some examples of non-reflexive relations are 'loves', 'voted for', 'wrote to', 'bit', 'killed'.

Generally speaking, the "non" properties of relations (non-transitivity, non-symmetry, non-reflexivity) have little relevance to applied logic, since there are few interesting inferences to be based upon them. The others enter into our reasoning quite frequently, and so it is often necessary to include one or more "unspoken" premisses, specifying the properties of the relevant relations, in order to make an argument provable.

In addition to these properties of relations, one *relation* between relations is worth mentioning. A relation is the **converse** of another if, whenever something has the first relation to something, that thing has the second relation to it, and vice versa. The formal definition is

> *K is the Converse of M*   if and only if $(x)(y)(Kxy \equiv Myx)$.

For example, 'taller than' is the converse of 'shorter than'. If x is shorter than y, then y is taller than x, and vice versa. (The relation 'is a converse of' is symmetric; if K is the converse of M, then M is the converse of K. It is also non-reflexive and non-transitive.) Similarly, the converse of 'father of' is 'was begotten by', the converse of 'ancestor' is 'descendant', the converse of 'successor' is 'predecessor', the converse of 'bit' is 'was bitten by', and so on.

'Son of' is not the converse of 'parent of'; from the fact that x is a parent of y it doesn't follow that y is a son of x, for y might be a daughter of x. However, 'son of' might be called the **partial converse** of 'parent of', since $(x)(y)(x$ is a son of $y \supset y$ is a parent of $x)$. Similarly, 'mother of' isn't the converse of 'child of', since it is possible for x to be a child of y without y being x's mother (y might be x's father), though it is a *partial* converse, since it is true that $(x)(y)(x$ is mother to $y \supset y$ is a child of $x)$. However, 'parent' and 'child' are full converses. Every relation has a converse, though not always one easily stated in English. Every symmetric relation is its own converse.

The converse of a relation is *not* the same as its negation. 'Taller than' is not the same as 'not shorter than', since 'not shorter than' also covers cases where the two are exactly the same height, in which case neither is taller than the other, as well as cases where one or both of the parties has no height at all—for example, if one is a symphony and the other is a negative square root. It is a truth of logic that, for any x and y, either x is taller than y or it is false that x is taller than y; that is,

$$(x)(y)(Txy \lor \sim Txy)$$

(symphonies and square roots fall under the second disjunct). But it is not a truth of logic that, given any x and y, either x is taller than y or x is shorter than y, for the reasons just indicated.

Just as it is sometimes necessary to supply "unspoken" premisses about the properties of relations, in order for an argument to be susceptible of formal proof, it is also sometimes necessary to supply unspoken premisses to the effect that one relation is the converse of another. For example, the argument

> Albert is taller than Bill; Charlie is shorter than Bill; therefore, Albert is taller than Charlie

is intuitively valid; but if translated just as it stands, the result is

$$\frac{\begin{array}{l} T\underline{ab} \\ S\underline{cb} \end{array}}{\therefore\ T\underline{ac}}$$

which is demonstrably invalid. If this argument is to be proven formally, it requires the additional premissess that 'shorter than' is the converse of 'taller than', and that 'shorter than' (or 'taller than') is transitive. When these premisses are added, the argument is easily proven as follows:

	1.	$T\underline{ab}$	
	2.	$S\underline{cb}$	
(Supplied premiss)	3.	$(x)(y)(Sxy \equiv Tyx)$	
(Supplied premiss)	4.	$(x)(y)(z)((Txy \cdot Tyz) \supset Txz)$	$/ \therefore\ T\underline{ac}$
	5.	$(y)(Sc\underline{y} \equiv Ty\underline{c})$	3, UI, $x/\underline{c}$
	6.	$S\underline{cb} \equiv T\underline{bc}$	5, UI, $y/\underline{b}$
	7.	$T\underline{bc}$	2, 6, Eq.
	8.	$(y)(z)((T\underline{a}y \cdot Tyz) \supset T\underline{a}z)$	4, UI, $x/\underline{a}$
	9.	$(z)((T\underline{ab} \cdot T\underline{b}z) \supset T\underline{a}z)$	8, UI, $y/\underline{b}$
	10.	$(T\underline{ab} \cdot T\underline{bc}) \supset T\underline{ac}$	9, UI, $z/\underline{c}$
	11.	$T\underline{ab} \cdot T\underline{bc}$	1, 7, conj.
	12.	$T\underline{ac}$	10, 11, MP

Exercises XII

Translate and prove each of the following, supplying the needed premisses that are missing.

1. Albert is older than Clyde. Clyde is older than Harvey. Therefore, Albert is older than Harvey.

□ 2. Albert is older than Clyde. Clyde is older than Harvey. Therefore, Harvey is younger than Albert.

3. Albert is the same age as Fred. Bill is not the same age as Albert. Therefore, Fred is not the same age as Bill.

□ 4. Caleb is Zeke's father. Zeke is Maude's father. One's father's father is one's grandfather. An individual's grandfather is one of his ancestors. Therefore Maude is one of Caleb's descendants.

5. Caleb is an ancestor of Ezra. Ezra is an ancestor of Bert. All of Caleb's descendants are stupid. Therefore, Bert is stupid.

6. Bert eats more than Emma. Anyone who eats more than Lucille is fatter than she. Lucille eats less than Emma. Anyone who is thinner than Bert has some-

thing to be thankful for. Bert and Lucille are lucky people. Therefore, Lucille has something to be thankful for.

☐ **7.** Emma studies less than Bert. Lucille studies less than Emma, but more than Bert. Therefore, Bert is the smartest one in the class.

8. Bert is older than Emma. Emma is the same age as Lucille. Two things are the same age if and only if neither of them is older than the other. Therefore Lucille is younger than Bert.

§22.11   More on Supplying Missing Premisses

In the previous section, arguments which were valid but not provable were rendered provable when we supplemented them with premisses, not explicitly given in the original, stating properties of the relations occurring in the original. This procedure, of supplying "missing premisses" to render an argument provable, has obvious application in other sorts of cases. For example, the argument

> Jones is a bachelor
> Only married people are happy
> ∴ Jones is not happy

is quite obviously valid. But as it stands it cannot be proven valid with the procedures of quantifier logic, since its translation

$$Bj$$
$$(x)(Hx \supset Mx) \quad / \therefore \sim Hj$$

may be "proven invalid" for a universe of one or more individuals. What is needed to render the original argument provable is the supplementary premiss 'No bachelors are married.' There is no problem about whether this premiss is true, since 'bachelor' *means* 'unmarried man'. Since we know this missing premiss to be true, it is permissible to splice it into the original argument. When this is done, the result is

$$Bj$$
$$(x)(Hx \supset Mx)$$
$$(x)(Bx \supset \sim Mx) \quad / \therefore \sim Hj$$

which is easily proven valid.

An argument with a "missing premiss" may be supplemented in this way provided that the missing premiss is known *with certainty* to be true. Normally, this degree of certainty is achieved only when the missing premiss is true by definition (as in the case of 'bachelor' and 'unmarried') or when it is an established truth of science, such as 'all snakes are reptiles', 'molten iron is incandescent', 'the planets orbit around the sun', or is true in virtue of some standard and accepted system of classification, such as 'Sculpture is an

art form', 'Chemists are scientists', 'Cats are house pets'. If the missing premiss is not absolutely certain in this way, it may still be added to the original
argument but it must be treated as an *assumption*—indicated by the arrow
and so on.

Exercises XIII

Translate and prove each of the following, supplying the needed premisses that are
missing.

1. Percy failed his algebra class. Therefore, Percy failed a math class.
□ 2. Percy failed his algebra class. Therefore, Percy didn't pass all of his math classes.
3. Some doctors are psychiatrists. Therefore, some doctors are physicians.
4. Frankie is Johnny's sister. Therefore, Frankie is a female.
5. Frankie is Johnny's sister. All of Johnny's female relatives went to prison. Therefore, Frankie was a convict.
□ 6. Clyde is a bachelor. Clyde hates his sister-in-law. Therefore, Clyde has a brother.
7. Clyde is an only child. Clyde hates his sister-in-law. Therefore, Clyde is married.
8. Frankie is either a bachelor or a spinster and is an only child. Therefore, Frankie has no sisters-in-law.

chapter 23

IDENTITY

§23.1 Identity in Logic

The relations so far mentioned, such as 'being taller than' or 'being between', have no *special* place in logic; they appear in logical formulae in the same way that such properties as 'being red' or 'being human' or 'being eleven feet tall' appear—that is, in the course of applying logic to particular situations. However, one relation does have a special place in logic itself as an integral part of what is applied rather than as a result of particular application. This is the relationship of identity, as expressed in the dyadic function 'x is identical with y'.

Identity, as it occurs in logic, is not to be confused with similarity. In logic, when two things are said to be identical, this does not mean merely that they are similar in some respects; it means that they are literally not two, but one and the same object. In ordinary speech we sometimes say, for example, that two new Chevrolets, or two newly minted coins, are "identical," meaning that they are exactly similar, have the same properties, and so on. This is not the logical conception of identity; the fact that there are *two* automobiles or *two* coins is sufficient to show that they are not identical in the logical sense. The logical concept is that of literal numerical identity. A statement of numerical identity is true only if it contains two specifications of *the same* object. For example, Mark Twain is numerically identical with Samuel Clemens; the names 'Mark Twain' and 'Samuel Clemens' are two specifications of one and the same individual.

Because of the special place of identity in logic, its symbolic treatment is different from that of other relations. Instead of abbreviating the function 'x is identical with y' in the standard fashion as 'Ixy', we use the familiar symbol '$=$', called **double bar**, and place the two variables on either side of it rather than both to its right. Thus, the logical abbreviation of 'x is identical with y' is

1. $x = y$

so that the statement 'Mark Twain is identical with Samuel Clemens' would be translated as

2. $t = c$

Also, it is standard practice to express the *negation* of an identity-statement in a slightly different fashion. Instead of prefixing a tilde to the statement, we place a slash through the double-bar. Thus, the statement 'Mark Twain is not identical with O. Henry' would not be written as

3. $\sim t = h$

but as

3a. $t \neq h$

(3) and (3a) mean exactly the same thing; (3a) is just a different way of writing (3). If it is helpful to do so, we may regard the slash in (3a) as the tilde in (3) which has been straightened out and laid across the double-bar. In all logical operations involving negation—such as TD and the like, (3a) may be treated exactly as if it were (3).

§23.2 Exceptives

The relation of identity, and its negation, enable us to say many things not otherwise expressible in the language of symbolic logic. For example, we can express **exceptive** propositions, such as

1. Clyde is taller than everyone but Harvey.

Here, the word 'but' functions not as a conjunctive operator but as an "exceptor," setting Harvey aside as an exception to the general case. The general case covers everyone else—that is, everyone who is not Harvey. And so (1) may be translated as

1a. $(x)((x$ is a person $\cdot x \neq$ Harvey$) \supset$ Clyde is taller than $x)$

which says that Clyde is taller than every person who is not Harvey. Two things must be noted about (1) and (1a). First, despite appearances, neither of them says (or entails) that Clyde is *not* taller than Harvey. Clyde's being taller than everyone other than Harvey is compatible with his also being taller than Harvey, just as Edna's hating everyone in the room is compatible with her hating some people who are not in the room as well. (1) specifies a certain class of persons (the class of persons other than Harvey) and asserts that Clyde is taller than any member of that class; it does not rule out the possibility that Clyde may also be taller than someone who is not a member of that class (namely, Harvey). Second, if Clyde happens to be a person other than Harvey, then both (1) and (1a) are necessarily false, since if taken literally they would entail that Clyde is taller than himself. However, there is a proposition very much like (1) that does not suffer from this defect and thus has a chance of being true—namely,

  2. Clyde is taller than everyone else but Harvey.

This is a doubly exceptive proposition; 'everyone else' means everyone except Clyde, with another exception being made for Harvey in the final clause. Thus, (2) says that Clyde is taller than everyone who is neither Clyde nor Harvey, translating as

  2a. $(x)((x$ is a person $\cdot$ $x \neq$ Clyde $\cdot$ $x \neq$ Harvey$) \supset$ Clyde is taller than $x)$*

Exceptive propositions are recognizable by the occurrence of such "exceptors" as 'else', 'except', 'besides', 'but', and so on. It is standard practice in formal logic to give them a "minimal interpretation" of the sort indicated above, even though in ordinary discourse we sometimes regard them as asserting, or implying, something stronger. For example, if we encountered (1) in normal discourse we might very well take it to imply (in some sense) that Clyde is *not* taller than Harvey. Similarly, a statement such as

  3. Everyone is eligible except Clyde.

might be taken, in ordinary discourse, as saying that Clyde is not eligible but everybody else is. But in the absence of some specific reason to the contrary it is standard in formal logic to give the "minimal interpretation" to (3), treating it as a bare assertion that everyone other than Clyde is eligible, which translates as

  3a. $(x)((x$ is a person $\cdot$ $x \neq$ Clyde$) \supset x$ is eligible)

and makes no commitment as to whether Clyde is or is not eligible as well. The reason for this practice is the general rule of applied logic: In case of doubt, it is better to leave something legitimate out than to smuggle something illegitimate in. If a sentence may be construed as making one or the other of two assertions (that is, it is ambiguous or equivocal), then in the absence of reasons to the contrary, interpret it as making the weaker of the two.

Another type of exceptive proposition involves the word 'only' as in

  4. Albert is the only one who loves Bertha.

or

  4a. Only Albert loves Bertha.

(4) and (4a) are, for all purposes, the same statement, expressed two different ways. They both assert two things: that Albert loves Bertha, and that nobody else does. (We would regard them as false if Albert didn't love Bertha; and we

---

*In the interest of shorter formulae, we will hereafter regard it as legitimate to drop the extra punctuation out of a multiple conjunction (or multiple disjunction). The lack of a dominant operator in these formulae is logically harmless, since every grouping of conjuncts (or of disjuncts) is logically equivalent to every other.

would also regard them as false if somebody else did love Bertha.) Consequently, these 'only' statements translate as the conjunction of two propositions:

4b. Albert loves Bertha · $(x)(x \neq$ Albert $\supset\ \sim(x$ loves Bertha$))$

—'Albert loves Bertha and nobody other than Albert loves Bertha'—or, fully abbreviated,

4c. $L\underline{ab} \cdot (x)(x \neq \underline{a} \supset\ \sim Lx\underline{b})$

As an extension of this, the negation of an 'only' statement of this sort will translate as the negation of a conjunction. For example,

5. Albert is not the only one who loves Bertha.

or

5a. Not only Albert loves Bertha.

might be true because Albert doesn't love Bertha, or because somebody else does, or both. Thus, the proper translation is

5b. $\sim[L\underline{ab} \cdot (x)(x \neq \underline{a} \supset\ \sim Lx\underline{b})]$

or its logical equivalent

5c. $\sim L\underline{ab} \lor\ \sim(x)(x \neq \underline{a} \supset\ \sim Lx\underline{b})$

—'Either Albert doesn't love Bertha, or somebody else does, or both.'

§23.3 Superlatives

Another sort of 'exceptive' proposition involves **superlatives**, such as 'tallest', 'oldest', 'richest'. For example,

1. Bill is the oldest member of the team.

This statement asserts two things: that Bill is a member of the team and that he is older than any other member; thus, it translates as the conjunction

1a. Bill is a member of the team ·
    $(x)((x$ is a member of the team · $x \neq$ Bill$) \supset$ Bill is older than $x)$

or, fully abbreviated,

1b. $T\underline{b} \cdot (x)((Tx \cdot x \neq \underline{b}) \supset O\underline{b}x)$

Just as with 'only' statements, the negation of a superlative statement will translate as the negation of a conjunction. For example,

2. Bill is not the oldest member of the team.

might be true because Bill isn't on the team, or because some other team member is at least as old as he is, or both. Its proper translation is

2a. $\sim(T\underline{b} \cdot (x)((Tx \cdot x \neq \underline{b}) \supset O\underline{b}x))$

or its logical equivalent

    2b. $\sim T\underline{b} \lor \sim(x)((Tx \cdot x \neq \underline{b}) \supset O\underline{b}x)$

—'Either Bill isn't on the team, or there is another team member whom Bill is not older than, or both.'

Yet another sort of exceptive proposition involves what might be called a **qualified superlative**, such as 'one of the tallest', 'one of the oldest'. For example,

    3. Charlie is one of the tallest members of the team.

Qualified superlatives are sometimes used in a loose way, merely to indicate, say, that Charlie is taller than most members of the team. When the qualified superlative is intended in this loose fashion, then of course the proper way to treat it will be as we have already learned to translate 'most':

    3a. Charlie is a member of the team·
                   ($\exists x)(x$ is a member of the team · Charlie is taller than x)

However, when a qualified superlative is used *strictly*, it means more; it means that *no* member of the team is taller than Charlie (but leaves open the possibility that someone may be just as tall as he is). In the strict sense, (3) would be false if even one team member were taller than Charlie; but (3) would be true if, say, Charlie and a couple of other team members were tied for first place in the height contest. Understood strictly, then, (3) says that Charlie is a member of the team and no team member is taller than he; that is,

    3b. $M\underline{c} \cdot (x)(Mx \supset \sim Tx\underline{c})$

And, of course, the denial of a qualified superlative statement, such as

    4. Abner isn't one of the tallest members of the team.

will translate as the negation of a conjunction:

    4a. $\sim(M\underline{a} \cdot (x)(Mx \supset \sim Tx\underline{a}))$

Exercises I

Translate and abbreviate each of the following.

    1. Harvey is the richest man in town.
□ **2.** Edna is not the richest man in town.
    3. Everyone loves Edna except Harvey.
    4. Only Thelma loves Harvey.
    5. Not only Harvey loves Thelma.
□ **6.** Everyone hates someone else.
    7. Someone hates everyone else.
    8. Abner is the only person who hates everyone other than himself.
    9. Anyone who hates everyone else also hates himself.
    10. Nobody else in Podunk drinks as much as Clyde.

☐ **11.** Nobody else except Harvey drinks as much as Clyde.

12. Clyde is not the only one who drinks as much as Harvey.

13. Nobody besides Harvey drinks more than Bertha.

14. Clyde gave a present to somebody other than Edna.

15. Everyone except Thelma received a present from somebody.

☐ **16.** Everyone except Thelma received a present from somebody else.

17. Only Edna received a present from everybody else.

18. Thelma did not receive a present from everybody else.

☐ **19.** Harvey is the only one who received no presents.

20. Harvey is not the only one who received presents.

21. Clyde is the ugliest man in town.

☐ **22.** Clyde is the ugliest man in town, and one of the dumbest.

23. Clyde is the ugliest man in town, but not the smartest.

24. Clyde is one of the wealthiest men in town, and one of the most popular.

☐ **25.** Clyde is not one of the handsomest men in town.

§23.4 Numerical Statements

A numerical statement is one that contains a number-word, which asserts that there are at least so many, or at most so many, or exactly so many, things of a certain kind, or having a certain property. Some examples are:

1. There is at least one good hotel in Chicago.
2. There are at least two horses in the race.
3. At least three people have applied for the job.
4. There is at most one counter-example to Fermat's Last Theorem.
5. There are at most two good hotels in Chicago.
6. At most three people will be hired.
7. Thirty-five senators will vote for the tax bill, at most.
8. One person survived the crash.
9. Two persons who survived the crash intend to sue the company.
10. Twelve states have ratified the new Prohibition Amendment.
11. There is exactly one even prime number.
12. There are three months between July and November.

The numerical expression 'at least one' can be translated into logic without difficulty, since the existential quantifier means 'at least one'. Statement (1) above translates simply as

1a. $(\exists x)(x$ is a good hotel $\cdot$ x is in Chicago)

However, other numerical expressions are not so simple. For example,

2. There are at least two horses in the race.

cannot adequately be translated as

$(\exists x)(x$ is a horse in the race$) \cdot (\exists y)(y$ is a horse in the race$)$

for all this says is 'There is at least one horse in the race and there is at least one horse in the race', which, by the rule of Duplication, is equivalent simply to 'There is at least one horse in the race'. Mere repetitions of the existential quantifier will not express 'at least two', for it remains possible that the quantifier is about the same one each time it is repeated. So long as this possibility remains, 'at least one' and 'at least one' add up to only 'at least one', not to 'at least two'. To express 'at least two' it is necessary to assert that the two quantifiers are *not* about the same one:

2a. $(\exists x)(x$ is a horse in the race $\cdot (\exists y)(y$ is a horse in the race $\cdot y \neq x))$

—'There is at least one horse in the race, and there is at least one other horse in the race'—which abbreviates as

2b. $(\exists x)(Hx \cdot (\exists y)(Hy \cdot y \neq x))$

To say 'at least two' we say 'at least one, and at least one *more*'. Similarly, to say 'at least three' we say 'at least one, and at least one more, and at least one more'. For example, using the abbreviation $Px : x$ is a person who has applied for the job, the statement

3. At least three people have applied for the job.

may be translated as

3a. $(\exists x)(Px \cdot (\exists y)(Py \cdot y \neq x \cdot (\exists z)(Pz \cdot z \neq x \cdot z \neq y)))$

which says: 'At least one person applied for the job, and at least one person besides the first one applied for the job, and at least one person besides them applied for the job,' adding up to at least three applicants. The same general pattern applies for all numbers: 'at least n' is expressed as 'at least one and at least one more and at least one more . . .' and so on up to n. At each stage we express 'one *more*' by saying that this one is different from (not identical with) those previously mentioned. For example,

13. Jupiter has at least five moons.

will be expressed, using $Jx : x$ is a moon of Jupiter, as

13a. $(\exists x)(Jx \cdot$
$(\exists y)(Jy \cdot y \neq x \cdot$
$(\exists z)(Jz \cdot z \neq x \cdot z \neq y \cdot$
$(\exists w)(Jw \cdot w \neq x \cdot w \neq y \cdot w \neq z \cdot$
$(\exists t)(Jt \cdot t \neq x \cdot t \neq y \cdot t \neq z \cdot t \neq w)))))$

'More than one' means 'at least two'; 'more than two' means 'at least three'; and so on.

'At most one' means 'not more than one' and may be so translated. That is,

14. At most one person applied for the job.

may be translated as the negation of 'More than one person applied for the job'—that is, as the negation of 'At least two persons applied for the job:

14a. $\sim(\exists x)(Ax \cdot (\exists y)(Ay \cdot y \neq x))$

Similarly for higher numbers: 'At most two persons applied for the job' may be translated as the negation of 'At least three persons applied for the job', and so on. However, it is standard practice to treat 'at most' statements in another (but logically equivalent) fashion. (14), for example, translates as

14b. $(x)(y)((Ax \cdot Ay) \supset y = x)$

which says, in effect, 'Any "two" persons who applied for the job turn out to be the same person'—that is, there is no second person who applied for the job. (You may wish to prove, as an exercise, that (14a) and (14b) are logically equivalent.) In a similar vein,

5. There are at most two good hotels in Chicago.

may be translated as saying 'Given any "three" good hotels in Chicago, two or more of them will be the same'; or, using $Gx : x$ is a good hotel in Chicago,

5a. $(x)(y)(z)((Gx \cdot Gy \cdot Gz) \supset (x = y \lor x = z \lor y = z))$

—'If x and y and z are all good hotels in Chicago, then either x is the same hotel as y or x is the same hotel as z or y is the same hotel as z'—that is, there is no third good hotel in Chicago.

It should be noted that the translation of 'at most one' requires two quantifiers; the translation of 'at most two' requires three quantifiers; and so on. In general, 'at most n' requires $n + 1$ quantifiers for its translation. This is because we say 'There are at most n things' of a certain kind by saying 'Given any $n + 1$ things of that kind, at least two of them will be the same one.' This final clause is one whose construction requires a bit of care. It must be an exhaustive disjunction of the identity possibilities among the variables of quantification; each of the variables in the $n + 1$ quantifiers must be paired with each of the others. The easiest way to make sure that no possibilities are left out is to pair the variable in the first quantifier with the variable in each quantifier after it, then to pair the variable in the second quantifier with the variable in each quantifier after it, and so on. For example, in the final clause of (5a), 'x' is paired first with 'y' and then with 'z', and then 'y' is paired with 'z'.

As a final illustration, using $Hx : x$ is a person who will be hired,

6. At most three people will be hired.

translates as

6a. $(x)(y)(z)(w)[(Hx \cdot Hy \cdot Hz \cdot Hw) \supset$
$(x = y \lor x = z \lor x = w \lor y = z \lor y = w \lor z = w)]$

—'Of any "four" persons who are hired, at least two will be the same person'.

In the final clause of (6a), 'x' is paired with 'y' and with 'z' and with 'w', then 'y' is paired with 'z' and with 'w', then 'z' is paired with 'w', so that all possibilities are covered.

'Exactly one' means the same as 'at least one and at most one' and may be so translated. For example, using $Ex : x$ is an even prime number, we may translate the statement

11. There is exactly one even prime number.

as the conjunction of the two statements 'There is at least one even prime number' and 'There is at most one even prime number'—that is, as

11a. $(\exists x)Ex \cdot (y)(z)((Ey \cdot Ez) \supset y = z)$

However, there is an easier (and logically equivalent) way of combining these statements so as to say the same thing. We can also assert (11) by saying 'There is at least one even prime number, and no others.'

11b. $(\exists x)(Ex \cdot (y)(Ey \supset y = x))$

The existential quantifier tells us that there is an even prime number; the second clause within the matrix says that there is no second one, by saying that all even prime numbers are identical with that one—that it is the *only* even prime. This same pattern may be followed for larger "exact" numbers. For example, we may translate

15. There are exactly two major political parties.

by saying 'There are at least two major political parties, and no third one.' Using $Mx : x$ is a major political party,

15a. $(\exists x)(Mx \cdot (\exists y)(My \cdot y \neq x \cdot (z)(Mz \supset (z = x \lor z = y))))$

The first half of (15a) tells us that there are at least two major parties; the second half says that there is no third one, by saying that every major party is identical with one or the other of the two already mentioned. As a final illustration,

12. There are three months between July and November.

translates, using $Kx : x$ is a month between July and November, as

12a. $(\exists x)(Kx \cdot (\exists y)(Ky \cdot y \neq x \cdot (\exists z)(Kz \cdot z \neq x \cdot z \neq y \cdot$
$(w)(Kw \supset (w = x \lor w = y \lor w = z)))))$

We can see from the examples above that when numbers much greater than 3 are involved, the formulae in question will become unendurably long and hence useless for practical purposes. However, numerical inferences involving larger numbers are usually carried out by the procedures of arithmetic rather than those of predicate logic, so we need not feel too worried about this practical problem.

Exercises II

Translate and abbreviate each of the following.

1. Abner has at least two brothers.
2. There is at most one President.
3. If there are more than two persons on the committee, one of them is chairman.
☐ 4. If there are less than two persons on the committee, none of them is chairman.
5. There is at least one liger.
6. Every person has at least one father.
☐ 7. Every person has at most one father.
8. Every state has at most two senators.
9. Clyde has one sister at least, and two at most.
10. Utah has more than one senator.
11. If Nebraska has exactly two senators, they are both conservative.
12. There are at least two states which have more than one senator.
☐ 13. There is exactly one carnivorous liger.
☐ 14. There is exactly one liger, and it is carnivorous.
15. Abner has exactly two girl friends.
16. Abner has exactly two friends, and they are girls.
17. Three wise men of Gotham went to sea in a bowl.
18. There are exactly four months whose names do not contain 'r'.
☐ 19. There are two axolotls in the tank and one of them is dead.
20. There are two axolotls in the tank and one of them is longer than the other.
☐ 21. If there are two axolotls in the tank then one of them is invisible.
22. There are two axolotls in the tank, a brown one and a gray one, and the gray one is longer than the brown one.
☐ 23. There are two axolotls in the tank, and one of them is longer than the other but the short one is smarter than the long one.
24. There are three axolotls in the tank, and two of them hate the other one.
25. If there are three axolotls in the tank, then two of them hate the other one.
26. Two of the axolotls in the tank hate all of the others.

§23.5 Laws of Identity and Rules of Inference

Because of the special place of the relation of identity, it is necessary to have some special rules to permit inferences concerning identity. The rules we shall adopt are based upon two principles, commonly referred to as Laws of Identity since they are fundamental and universal truths concerning identity.

FIRST LAW OF IDENTITY: Everything is identical with itself.

SECOND LAW OF IDENTITY: If A and B are identical, then whatever is true of A is also true of B and vice versa.*

The rules based upon these laws are given below in English, alongside the associated argument form,† as an illustration of what the rule allows. The one based upon the First Law is

SELF-IDENTITY (SI):

| $/ \therefore \alpha = \alpha$ | It is permissible at any point in any derivation to infer any statement of self-identity. Operationally, |
| | At any point in any derivation it is permissible to insert a line consisting of a double bar flanked by occurrences of the same lower-case letter. |

The one based upon the Second Law is here tagged with the name given it by Quine:

INDISCERNIBILITY OF IDENTICALS [Id. $(\alpha/\beta$ IN $N)$]:

$$\alpha = \beta$$
$$\Phi\alpha$$
$$\therefore \Phi\beta$$

Given an identity statement, and an assertion about one member to the identity, it is permissible to infer a corresponding assertion about the other member to the identity. Operationally,

$$\beta = \alpha$$
$$\Phi\alpha$$
$$\therefore \Phi\beta$$

Given an identity statement (a formula consisting just of a double bar flanked by lower-case letters) as a line in a derivation, and given a line in the derivation containing one or more free occurrences of one of the letters in the identity statement, it is permissible to infer the result of replacing, in that line, some or all free occurrences of that letter with free occurrences of the other letter in the identity statement.

The rule may be stated even less formally as: Given an identity statement as a line, either letter may replace the other in any context, provided that the replaced occurrence is free and freedom is preserved. When using Id., the justification should describe the substitution fully, citing both of the lines involved and indicating which letter was changed to which, and saying which line the substitution was performed on.

---

*The converse of this principle—'If everything which is true of A is also true of B and vice versa, then A and B are identical'—is also commonly regarded as a law of identity. This is substantially the principle which Leibniz enunciated as the "Law of Identity of Indiscernibles." It lies beyond the scope of first-order predicate logic.
†Appendix K.

Here are some illustrations of the use of the identity rules.

Proof I

    1. $(x)(Gx \supset x = a)$
    2. $(x)(Fx \supset Gx)$
    3. Fb / $\therefore$ $Fa \cdot Ga$
    4. $Fb \supset Gb$ 2, UI, x/b
    5. Gb 3, 4, MP
    6. $Gb \supset b = a$ 1, UI, x/b
    7. $b = a$ 5, 6, MP
    8. Fa 3, 7, Id. (b/a in 3)
    9. Ga 5, 7, Id. (b/a in 5)
    10. $Fa \cdot Ga$ 8, 9, conj.

The identity statement at line (7), along with Id., permits any free occurrence of 'b' to be replaced by a free occurrence of 'a'. Lines (3) and (5) each contain a free occurrence of 'b'; when this is replaced by 'a', the result is lines (8) and (9).

Proof II

    1. $(x)(Gx \supset x = \underline{b})$
    2. $G\underline{a}$ / $\therefore$ $\underline{b} = \underline{a}$
    3. $G\underline{a} \supset \underline{a} = \underline{b}$ 1, UI, $x/\underline{a}$
    4. $\underline{a} = \underline{b}$ 2, 3, MP
    5. $\underline{a} = \underline{a}$ SI
    6. $\underline{b} = \underline{a}$ 4, 5, Id. ($\underline{a}/\underline{b}$ in 5)

The identity statement at line (4), along with Id, permits any free occurrence of '$\underline{a}$' to be replaced by a free occurrence of '$\underline{b}$'. Line (5) contains two free occurrences of '$\underline{a}$'. Replacing the lefthand one with '$\underline{b}$' results in line (6). The last three steps in this proof show that identity is a *symmetrical* relation (cf. §22.10): from $\alpha = \beta$ it is always legitimate to infer $\beta = \alpha$. To avoid needless complications in constructing proofs, we shall admit this as an additional rule:

Symmetry of Identity (*sym.*):

    $\alpha = \beta$ transf $\beta = \alpha$ It is permissible to reverse the order of the letters in any identity formula occurring either as a line or as a part of a line.

As a final illustration of the way in which identity rules can enter into a derivation, here is a proof of the argument: 'There is exactly one Pope. Every bishop of Rome is Pope. Bishops of Rome exist. Therefore, there is exactly one bishop of Rome.' ($Fx : x$ is Pope; $Gx : x$ is bishop of Rome.)

PROOF III

1. $(\exists x)(Fx \cdot (y)(Fy \supset y = x))$
2. $(x)(Gx \supset Fx)$
3. $(\exists x)Gx$ $/ \therefore (\exists x)(Gx \cdot (y)(Gy \supset y = x))$
4. $Fx \cdot (y)(Fy \supset y = x)$ 1, x/x
5. $(y)(Fy \supset y = x)$ 4, sev.
6. Ga 3, x/a
7. $Ga \supset Fa$ 2, UI, x/a
8. Fa 6, 7, MP
9. $Fa \supset a = x$ 5, UI, y/a
10. $a = x$ 8, 9, MP
11. Gx 6, 10, Id. (a/x in 6)
12. $(\exists y)(Gy \cdot y \neq x)$ (IP)
13. $Gz \cdot z \neq x$ 12, y/z
14. $Gz \supset Fz$ 2, UI, x/z
15. Fz 13, 14, sev., MP
16. $Fz \supset z = x$ 5, UI, y/z
17. $z = x$ 15, 17, MP
18. $A \cdot \sim A$ 17, 13, disj., sev., canc.
19. $A \cdot \sim A$ 13–18, EI
20. $\sim (\exists y)(Gy \cdot y \neq x)$ 12–19, IP
21. $(y)(Gy \supset y = x)$ 20, QN, TD, DN, CE
22. $Gx \cdot (y)(Gy \supset y = x)$ 11, 21, conj.
23. $(\exists x)(Gx \cdot (y)(Gy \supset y = x))$ 22, EG, x/x
24. $(\exists x)(Gx \cdot (y)(Gy \supset y = x))$ 6–23, EI
25. $(\exists x)(Gx \cdot (y)(Gy \supset y = x))$ 4–24, EI

Exercises III

Prove each of the following.

□ 1. $/ \therefore (x)(x = x)$
2. $/ \therefore (x)(y)(z)((x = y \cdot y = z) \supset x = z)$
3. $/ \therefore (x)(y)((Fx \cdot \sim Fy) \supset x \neq y)$
□ 4. $/ \therefore (x)(\exists y)(x = y)$
5. $/ \therefore (x)(Fx \supset (y)(y = x \supset Fy))$
6. $/ \therefore (y)((x)(x = y \supset Fx) \supset Fy)$
□ 7. $/ \therefore (x)(Fx \supset (\exists y)(y = x \cdot Fy))$
8. $/ \therefore (x)(\exists y)(x = y \cdot (z)(x = z \supset z = y))$

Exercises IV

Translate and prove each of the following.

1. Bill is the oldest member of the team. Bill is not older than Mr. Smith. Mr. Smith is a member of the team. Therefore, Mr. Smith is Bill.
□ 2. Everyone detests Martha. Martha is Mrs. Jones. Mrs. Jones is a fat lady. Therefore, there is a fat lady whom everyone detests.

3. Clyde is the only one who drinks more than Harvey. Abner loves pretzels. Clyde does not love pretzels. Therefore, Abner does not drink more than Harvey.

4. Albert is the only blacksmith in the county. O'Bease is the only farrier in the county. Some blacksmiths in the county are farriers. Therefore, Albert is O'Bease.

☐ 5. At least two city councilmen are Republicans. Brown is a member of the city council, and he's a Democrat. No Republicans are Democrats. Andrews and Carlyle are the only ones on the city council besides Brown. Therefore, exactly two Republicans are on the city council.

6. There are exactly two magistrates in town, and exactly one lawyer. Smith is the only honest individual in town, and he is a lawyer. No lawyers are city councilmen. At least one of the town magistrates is also a lawyer. Oscar is a town magistrate and city councilman. Therefore, the only dishonest magistrate in town is Oscar.

Exercises V

Prove each of the following.

1. 1. $(x)(y)((Fx \cdot x \neq y) \supset Rxy)$
   2. $Fa \cdot \sim Fb$ / $\therefore$ Rab

☐ 2. 1. $(\exists x)(Fx \cdot (y)(Fy \supset y = x) \cdot x = a)$
   2. Fb / $\therefore$ $a = b$

3. 1. $(\exists x)(Fx \cdot (y)(Fy \supset y = x) \cdot x = a)$
   2. Gb
   3. $b = a$ / $\therefore$ $(\exists x)(Fx \cdot (y)(Fy \supset y = x) \cdot Gx)$

☐ 4. 1. $(\exists x)(Fx \cdot (y)(Fy \supset y = x) \cdot (\exists z)(Gz \cdot (w)(Gw \supset w = z) \cdot z = x))$
   2. Ga / $\therefore$ $(x)(Fx \supset x = a)$

5. 1. $(\exists x)(\exists y)(Fx \cdot Fy \cdot x \neq y \cdot Mxy)$
   2. $(x)((\exists y)(Mxy \lor Myx) \supset Gx)$
   3. $(x)(y)((Gx \cdot \sim Qy) \supset (Syx \supset x = y))$
   4. $(z)(w)(Fz \supset Swz)$ / $\therefore$ $(\exists x)(\exists y)(Qx \cdot Qy \cdot x \neq y)$

6. 1. $(\exists x)((\exists y)Kxy \cdot (z)((\exists y)Kzy \supset z = x))$
   2. $(x)(y)(Kxy \equiv Ty)$
   3. $(z)(w)(Kzw \supset Kwz)$ / $\therefore$ $(\exists x)(Tx \cdot (y)(Ty \supset y = x))$

☐ 7. 1. $(\exists x)(\exists y)(Fx \cdot Fy \cdot x \neq y \cdot (z)(Fz \supset (z = x \lor z = y)))$
   2. $(\exists x)((Fx \cdot Gx) \cdot (y)((Fy \cdot Gy) \supset y = x))$
   / $\therefore$ $(\exists x)((Fx \cdot \sim Gx) \cdot (y)((Fy \cdot \sim Gy) \supset y = x))$

8. 1. $(\exists x)(\exists y)(\exists z)(Fx \cdot Fy \cdot Fz \cdot x \neq y \cdot x \neq z \cdot y \neq z \cdot$
                              $(w)(Fw \supset (w = x \lor w = y \lor w = z)))$
   2. $(\exists x)(\exists y)(Fx \cdot Fy \cdot x \neq y \cdot Gx \cdot Gy)$
   3. $(\exists x)(Fx \cdot Hx)$
   4. $(x)(Hx \supset \sim Gx)$ / $\therefore$ $(\exists x)((Fx \cdot Hx) \cdot (y)((Fy \cdot Hy) \supset y = x))$

Exercises VI

Translate and prove each of the following, supplying the needed premisses that are missing.

   1. Albert is fat. Mr. Jones is skinny. Therefore, Albert is not Mr. Jones.
☐ **2.** Albert is either fat or smart. Jones is either skinny or dumb. Therefore, if Albert is Jones, then if he's fat he's dumb.
   3. Bert is older than his sister. Caleb's only children are twins. Therefore, Bert isn't Caleb's son.
☐ **4.** Bert is older than his only sister. Billy is Maude's father, and Maude is older than J.B. Therefore, if Bert is Frankie's son, then if Bert is J.B. and Bert's mother is also Maude's, then Frankie isn't Billy.

§23.6 Invalidity

Proofs of invalidity for arguments involving identity proceed along the same lines as other invalidity proofs in quantifier logic. However, when using the method of interpretation for a model universe, we need to keep in mind that *everything* is identical with itself and that consequently, when assigning truth-values to the simple elements in the interpretation, we must assign every element of the form '$\alpha = \alpha$' (that is, every element consisting of a double bar flanked by two occurrences of the same letter) the value 'T', never 'F'. If a "proof" of invalidity requires the stipulation that something is not self-identical, then the "proof" is logically absurd; and if an argument can only be "proven invalid" with the help of such a stipulation (that is, by assigning 'F' to a self-identity element), then the argument cannot be proven invalid. For example, the argument

$$P \supset Fa$$
$$(x)(Fx \supset x = b)$$
$$\therefore P \supset b = b$$

has, as its interpretation for $\{a, b\}$,

$$P \supset Fa$$
$$(Fa \supset a = b)\cdot(Fb \supset b = b)$$
$$\therefore P \supset b = b$$

and may be "shown invalid for $\{a, b\}$" by

P	Fa	Fb	$a = b$	$b = b$
T	T	F	T	F

But this is an impossible assignment, since it requires '$b = b$' to be false. And since it is the *only* assignment which will make the conclusion come out F and the premisses come out T, it follows that there is no "possible" invalidating assignment; that is, the argument is valid.

To repeat: the rule to follow in constructing invalidity proofs is *always* to assign the value 'T' to self-identity elements, never 'F'.

Exercises VII

Prove the invalidity of each of the following arguments, using first the method of natural interpretation and then the method of interpretation for a model universe.

1. Harvey isn't the only one who likes garlic ice cream. Therefore, somebody besides Harvey likes garlic ice cream.

2. Clyde is the tallest member of the team. Harvey is the oldest member of the team. Therefore, Clyde is either taller or younger than Harvey. (*Note:* This has a suppressed premiss which should be supplied before giving the proof.)

☐ 3. Everybody loves his mother. Everybody has exactly one mother. Therefore, everybody loves exactly one individual.

4. There are exactly two Dakotas. There are exactly two capital cities of Dakotas. Therefore, each Dakota has exactly one capital city.

5. Three people read the report. At least one person who read the report leaked it to the press. Anyone who read the report but didn't leak it to the press knows how to keep a secret. Therefore, at least two people know how to keep a secret.

chapter 24

DEFINITE DESCRIPTIONS

§24.1 Definite Descriptions

Definite descriptions have been traditionally defined as "any expression of the form 'the so-and-so'." A more precise definition is that a **definite description** is an expression consisting of the singular definite article 'the' followed by a singular (non-plural) descriptive expression. Some examples of definite descriptions are:

the lungfish	the author of *Hamlet*
the man	the tallest of men
the old man	the infield fly rule
the archbishop of Canterbury	the center of mass of the solar system
the last of the Mohicans	at 12:00 noon GMT, July 1, 1900

Since the expression 'definite description' is cumbersome, we shall hereafter refer to them generally as 'descriptions', bearing in mind that we mean **definite** descriptions.

Descriptions enter into our discourse in several different ways. One of them, involving the "generic" use of the article 'the', has already been discussed in Chapter 16. Two others, discussed in the present chapter, involve the use of descriptions as singular expressions.

§24.2 Specifying and Non-Specifying Descriptions

Sometimes in our discourse we use a description when (apart from considerations of clarity or ambiguity) a personal pronoun would do just as well. An example is the sentence

1. A man walked up to a bear and the bear ate the man.

Here there are two descriptions, 'the bear' and 'the man'. Either or both could be replaced by an appropriate personal pronoun without altering the sense of (1). The proposition expressed by (1) could just as well be expressed by

1a. A man walked up to a bear and it ate him.

in which there are no descriptions. In giving a grammatical characterization of (1a), we would say that the base of the pronoun 'it' is the phrase 'a bear', and the base of the pronoun 'him' is the phrase 'a man'. This being the case, we can also speak of the *descriptions* in (1) as having grammatical antecedents or bases: the base of the description 'the bear' is the phrase 'a bear', and the base of the description 'the man' is the phrase 'a man'.

In these examples no specific man (or bear) is picked out as the subject of discourse. That is, in (1) the description 'the man' does not specify any particular individual man; rather, both (1) and (1a) make indefinite assertions about some man or other whose identity is left unstated. In (1) the description 'the man' is no more specific than its antecedent 'a man' is, and the phrase 'a man' is not specific at all.

Sometimes, however, we use a definite description in such a way that a pronoun would not do just as well. We do this whenever the description is used to specify a definite individual, as when we say

2. The author of *Hamlet* was English.

Here the description 'the author of *Hamlet*' appeals to no antecedent in the conversation; it is not used merely to make a cross reference to an author of *Hamlet* mentioned earlier in the discourse; rather, it is used to specify a particular individual, in order to assert of that individual that he was English. Descriptions occurring in this way may be called **specifying** descriptions. Descriptions occurring in the other way (in such a way that a pronoun would serve just as well) may be called **non-specifying** descriptions.

As usual, there are no ironclad exceptionless criteria for separating the two kinds of descriptions. Of course, if a description *has* a grammatical antecedent in the discourse, then it is a non-specifying description. But the fact that no antecedent is actually presented does not automatically indicate that a description is specifying. For example, just by looking at the isolated sentence

3. The man shook hands with the author of *Brave New World*.

it seems clear that the description 'the man' is non-specifying, even though no antecedent is given. We recognize that, for a sentence such as (3) to occur intelligibly in discourse, it would normally need an antecedent for the description 'the man' to make sense.

Furthermore, a given description may be specifying in one context and non-specifying in another. For example, in

4. The former vice-president has been disbarred in Maryland.

the description 'the former vice-president' obviously has a specifying use, whereas in

5. The defense attorney was accompanied by a former vice-president, but after a few minutes the former vice-president left.

it obviously has a non-specifying use. As a rule of thumb, we can say that a description cannot serve as a specifying description unless it could be used to open a conversation with the expectation that the hearer would understand who was being talked about. Thus, such things as 'the man', 'the fat man', 'the plant' occur primarily as non-specifying descriptions. But, as we shall see below, there are many exceptions to this rule.

It occasionally happens that there is simply no way to tell, from the portion of the context available, whether a description is specifying or non-specifying. In such cases the convention to follow is to treat the description as *non-specifying*.

§24.3   Translating Non-Specifying Descriptions

The procedures for translating non-specifying descriptions involve nothing new. They may be stated as two rules, which cover all cases.

a. If the antecedent of the description is actually given, replace the description with an appropriate personal pronoun and translate in accordance with the procedures given in preceding chapters.

b. If the antecedent of the description is not given, paraphrase the description to an indefinite description by replacing the definite article 'the' with the indefinite article 'a' or 'an', and translate in accordance with the procedures given in preceding chapters.

Nothing more needs to be said on the subject of non-specifying descriptions. In the remainder of this chapter we shall be concerned only with specifying descriptions.

§24.4   Translating Specifying Descriptions

There are two basic ways of treating specifying descriptions, one of which is much simpler than the other. We shall refer to them as "the simple treatment" and "the complete treatment." The simple treatment has the disadvantage of concealing (or failing to reveal) certain logical characteristics of the description, thereby ruling out many formal inferences made possible by the complete treatment.

The simple treatment consists in treating descriptions as if they were ordinary proper names and "translating" them by abbreviating them as constants. Following this simple method, the statement

    1. The author of *Hamlet* is English.

will translate, using *Ex* : *x* is English, as

    1a. *E$\underline{a}$*

where '$\underline{a}$' abbreviates the description 'the author of *Hamlet*'. Similarly, the statement

    2. The author of *Hamlet* is the husband of Anne Hathaway.

will translate simply as

    2a. $\underline{a} = \underline{h}$

where '$\underline{a}$' abbreviates the description 'the author of *Hamlet*' and '$\underline{h}$' abbreviates the description 'the husband of Anne Hathaway'.

    Certain kinds of descriptions *require* this method of treatment, rather than the more complex method given later on. Among these are descriptions which have "grown capital letters" and have actually become proper names, such as 'the Bank of America', 'the Holy Roman Empire', 'the King of the Cowboys', and descriptions employed as nicknames for well-known individuals such as 'the father of the H-bomb', 'the great emancipator', 'the cradle of democracy'. Also, there are descriptions which, though not associated with a particular individual, are nevertheless used in particular contexts as quasi-nicknames for some individual, as for example 'the old man' (meaning the boss, or daddy, or the teacher), 'the chariot' (meaning one's own automobile), and so on. Other descriptions susceptible to this sort of treatment are those presupposing a suppressed demonstrative clause such as 'this' or 'the present'. Examples are 'the President' (meaning the present president), as in the statement

    3. The President has just held a news conference.

or 'the planet' (meaning the planet we inhabit, Earth), as in the statement

    4. The planet will be unable to sustain life in another fifty years.

or 'the war' (meaning the war currently going on, or the last major war), as in

    5. Many people are enthusiastic about the war.

However, descriptions of this sort may also be given the complete treatment if they are first "filled in" with the suppressed clause.

    Apart from cases where the simple treatment is *required*, it is *permitted* whenever the inferences we are interested in do not themselves involve the content of the description. For example, the statement

    The author of *Hamlet* is an Englishman. All Englishmen are British. Therefore, the author of *Hamlet* is British.

requires no translation more complex than

$$Ea$$
$$(x)(Ex \supset Bx)$$
$$\therefore Ba$$

for its formal proof. However, if the inferences we are interested in *do* involve the content of the description, then the simple method will be inadequate. For example, the argument

> The author of *Hamlet* is the husband of Anne Hathaway. Therefore, the husband of Anne Hathaway authored something.

cannot be proven valid if it is translated, by the simple method, as

$$a = h$$
$$\therefore (\exists x)Ahx$$

A more explicit, and therefore more complicated, treatment is required.

We are already familiar with the method for treating statements containing descriptions that are superlative, descriptions that are exceptive, and so on (cf. Chapter 22). For example, the argument

> Bill is the oldest person in Cleveland. Bill is not the only person in Cleveland. Therefore, Bill is older than some person in Cleveland.

will translate, by those procedures, as

$$Cb \cdot (x)((Cx \cdot x \neq b) \supset Obx)$$
$$\sim(Cb \cdot (x)(Cx \supset x = b))$$
$$\therefore (\exists x)(Cx \cdot Obx)$$

Similarly, the argument

> The tallest member of the team plays center. Smith alone plays center. Smith and Jones are different individuals. Therefore, either Smith is taller than Jones or Jones is not a member of the team.

will translate as

$$(\exists x)(Mx \cdot (y)((My \cdot y \neq x) \supset Txy) \cdot Cx)$$
$$Cs \cdot (x)(Cx \supset x = s)$$
$$s \neq j$$
$$\therefore Tsj \supset \sim Mj$$

which can be proven valid by the rules already learned. But descriptions which are not of this type require a different approach.*

§24.5 Descriptors

A description consists of the article 'the' followed by a descriptive phrase, and descriptions in general may be schematized as having the form 'the Φ',

---

*The "complete treatment" given here is based upon that developed by Russell, "On Denoting." It is not suitable for superlative or exceptive descriptions. These should be given the treatment outlined in Chapter 22.

where Φ represents the descriptive phrase. For purposes of logic, expressions having the form

    1. the Φ

are understood as equivalent to expressions having the form

    2. the thing which is Φ

or

    3. the thing which satisfies the condition Φ

Thus, for example, the description

    4. the author of *Hamlet*

may be paraphrased for purposes of logic as

    4a. the thing which authored *Hamlet*

or as

    4b. the thing which satisfies the condition: ___ authored *Hamlet*

or, using individual variables, as

    4c. the x such that x authored *Hamlet*

The reason for this paraphrase is that it enables us to see clearly the way in which descriptions are based upon propositional functions. For example, (4c) divides logically into two parts: the expression 'the x such that' (called a **descriptive operator**) and the function 'x authored *Hamlet*, (called the **descriptive condition**). A description specifies a particular individual by referring to it as the individual which satisfies a certain condition, and descriptions are translated as a descriptive operator followed by the condition in question.

The descriptive operator 'the x such that' is symbolized in logic as

$$(\imath x)$$

which is also called an **iota operator**, since it consists of an upside-down Greek letter iota followed by a variable, with the whole enclosed in parentheses. Using the iota operator, we may translate (4c) as

    4d. $(\imath x)x$ authored *Hamlet*

which, using the abbreviation $Axy : x$ authored y, may then be abbreviated as

    4e. $(\imath x)Ax\underline{h}$

Whenever a description is translated in this way, by means of the iota operator, it will be standard practice to enclose the whole in square brackets, thus:

    4f. $[(\imath x)Ax\underline{h}]$

A formula such as (4f) is called a **descriptor**. A descriptor is the logical translation of a description and consists of an iota operator followed by a condition, at least one of whose (free) variables is the same as that in the iota operator, with the whole enclosed in square brackets. The iota operator serves to bind all occurrences of its variable within the condition which follows it. Thus, in (4f), all occurrences of 'x' are bound.

A descriptor is somewhat similar to a quantifier, in that it may be attached to a propositional function to form a statement. Like a quantifier, a descriptor binds variables in the function to which it is attached; and, like a quantifier, a descriptor has a scope and a range, defined exactly as for quantifiers. Descriptors are *unlike* quantifiers in that a descriptor may also contain free occurrences of letters, or occurrences of letters bound by earlier quantifiers or descriptors. This complication, however, need not concern us at the moment.

When a descriptor is attached to the lefthand side of a function containing the same variable as the one in the iota operator, the result is a **descriptor formula**—a formula which says that the thing satisfying the condition in the descriptor is such that it satisfies the attached function. For example, the statement

5. The author of *Hamlet* is English.

may be translated, by means of (4f), as

5a. $[(\iota x)Ax\underline{h}]x$ is English

which can be read as 'The individual which authored *Hamlet* is such that it is English.' And of course, (5a) abbreviates fully as

5b. $[(\iota x)Ax\underline{h}]Ex$

In a descriptor formula, such as (5b), the condition within the descriptor is the **descriptive condition**, and the portion following the descriptor is called the **predicate** of the formula.

When translating statements containing descriptions, it is usually helpful to begin by paraphrasing after the manner of (4c). For example, the statement

6. Shakespeare is the author of *Hamlet*.

will paraphrase as

6a. The author of *Hamlet* is such that Shakespeare is he.

and then will translate, successively, as

6b. $[(\iota x)x$ authored *Hamlet*] Shakespeare is x
6c. $[(\iota x)Ax\underline{h}]$ Shakespeare is x
6d. $[(\iota x)Ax\underline{h}]$ Shakespeare $= x$
6e. $[(\iota x)Ax\underline{h}]\underline{s} = x$

Similarly, the statement

7. Nobody is wealthier than the shah of Kuwait.

will paraphrase as

7a. The shah of Kuwait is such that nobody is wealthier than he.

and then will translate, using $Sx : x$ is shah of Kuwait, as

7b. $[(\imath x)Sx]$Nobody is wealthier than x

7c. $[(\imath x)Sx](y)(y$ is a person $\supset \sim y$ is wealthier than $x)$

7d. $[(\imath x)Sx](y)(Py \supset \sim Wyx)$

Exercises I

Translate and abbreviate each of the following.

1. A man met a bear and the bear ate the man.

☐ **2.** The man shook hands with the author of *Brave New World*.

3. The tallest man in Podunk is a bartender.

4. The tallest bartender in Podunk is a man.

☐ **5.** The Holy Roman Empire was neither holy nor Roman nor an empire.

6. There is no intelligent life on the planet.

7. The even prime number is greater than zero.

☐ **8.** Oberon is the king of the fairies.

9. If Oberon is the king of the fairies than Titania is the queen of the fairies.

§24.6 Multiple Descriptors

If a sentence contains more than one description, it will usually translate as a formula containing more than one descriptor. For example, the statement

1. The queen of Sheba antedated the king of Siam.

translates, by stages, as

1a. The queen of Sheba is such that she antedated the king of Siam.

1b. $[(\imath x)Qx]x$ antedated the king of Siam

1c. $[(\imath x)Qx]$the king of Siam is such that x antedated him

1d. $[(\imath x)Qx][(\imath y)Ky]x$ antedated y

1e. $[(\imath x)Qx][(\imath y)Ky]Axy$

Similarly, the statement

2. The wife of the king of Siam dresses elegantly.

translates, by stages, as

2a. The wife of the king of Siam is such that she dresses elegantly.

2b. $[(\imath x)x$ is wife of the king of Siam$]x$ dresses elegantly

2c. $[(\imath x)$the king of Siam is such that x is his wife$]x$ dresses elegantly

2d. $[(\imath x)[(\imath y)Ky]x$ is wife to $y]x$ dresses elegantly

2e. $[(\imath x)[(\imath y)Ky]Wxy]x$ dresses elegantly

2f. $[(\imath x)[(\imath y)Ky]Wxy]Dx$

in which one descriptor is nested inside another. However, formulae containing nested descriptors are rather awkward, and it is better to avoid them. In this case the nesting of descriptors could have been avoided via the alternative

2g. The king of Siam is such that his wife dresses elegantly.

2h. $[(\imath x)Kx]$the wife of x dresses elegantly

2i. $[(\imath x)Kx]$the wife of x is such that she dresses elegantly

2j. $[(\imath x)Kx][(\imath y)y$ is wife to $x]y$ dresses elegantly

2k. $[(\imath x)Kx][(\imath y)Wyx]Dy$

in which the descriptors are separated. In this case, the two translations are logically equivalent; the latter is preferable only because it is easier to work with when doing proofs. However, if the predicate of the statement asserts a *relationship* between the two individuals specified by the descriptions (rather than ascribing a property to one of them, as in (2)), the translation *must* proceed so that the two descriptors are *separated*, rather than nested. This is because, if the predicate asserts a relationship between the two, then in the translation each of the descriptors must bind a place in the predicate; and if one is nested inside the other the internal one cannot bind anything in the predicate, since its scope is confined within the other descriptor. For example, the statement

3. The wife of the king of Siam is smarter than he is.

cannot be translated as

3a. $[(\imath x)[(\imath y)Ky]Wxy]Sxy$

for what (3a) says is 'The wife of the king of Siam is smarter than y', where 'y' is a free letter having no logical connection with the descriptor 'the king of Siam'. Rather, it must be translated as

3b. $[(\imath y)Ky][(\imath x)Wxy]Sxy$

in which the two descriptors are separate.

If a statement contains two descriptions, and one of them is superlative or exceptive, then it will not translate as a descriptor but in the way indicated in Chapter 22. For example, the statement

4. The richest man in Podunk is the mayor of Podunk.

translates by stages (using the abbreviation $Px : x$ is a man in Podunk) as

4a. $(\exists x)(Px \cdot (y)((Py \cdot y \neq x) \supset x$ is richer than $y) \cdot x$ is the mayor of Podunk)

4b. $(\exists x)(Px \cdot (y)((Py \cdot y \neq x) \supset Rxy) \cdot [(\imath z)z$ is mayor of Podunk]x is z)

4c. $(\exists x)(Px \cdot (y)((Py \cdot y \neq x) \supset Rxy) \cdot [(\imath z)Mzp]x = z)$

Exercises II

Translate and abbreviate each of the following.

☐ 1. The author of *Hamlet* is the husband of Anne Hathaway.

2. The butler at Carfax has a sister.

3. The sister of the butler at Carfax is lovely.

4. The sister of the butler at Carfax is taller than he.

☐ 5. The king of the Boohoos is the tallest member of the tribe.

6. The sister of the wife of the valet of the owner of Carfax is bald.

7. The ruler of the universe defeated the prince of darkness.

8. The archbishop of Canterbury married the king of Sheba to the queen of Siam.

9. The butler at Carfax has two sisters.

☐ 10. The butler at Carfax has two sisters and one of them is married to the owner of Carfax.

§24.7 Inferences Involving Descriptors

Consider any simple description statement, such as

1. The ruler of the universe is wise. $[(\imath x)Rx]Wx$

Anyone seriously uttering (1) would be committing himself to the truth of three propositions, in the sense that the truth of (1) entails the truth of all three of them:

2 a. There is a ruler of the universe.
$(\exists x)Rx$

b. There isn't more than one ruler of the universe.
$(y)(z)((Ry \cdot Rz) \supset y = z)$

c. Whoever rules the universe is wise.
$(t)(Rt \supset Wt)$

If any of these three should be false, then the person asserting (1) would be mistaken: if the universe is unruled, then there is no ruler of the universe to be wise, and so (1) is false; if the universe is ruled by a Committee, then it is a mistake to speak of *the* ruler (one should either speak of 'the rulers' or else of 'one of the rulers'), and so (1) is false; and of course, if the universe is ruled by something which is not wise, then (1) is also false.* Furthermore, if all of (a), (b), and (c) are true, then (1) is also true. The three propositions (a), (b), and (c) provide the **standard analysis** of (1). Under the standard analysis, (1) is regarded as saying the same thing as the conjunction of (a), (b), and (c). That is,

1a. $[(\imath x)Rx]Wx$

---

*Some logical theoreticians have argued that (a) and (b) are not *entailed* by (1), but are *presupposed* by it, so that if either of them should be false, (1) would be a semantic misfire—on a par with telling someone "Shut the door" when the door is already shut—rather than being straightforwardly false. According to this theory, the only way for (1) to be false is for (a) and (b) both to be true while (c) is false; if either (a) or (b) is false, then (1) is not a genuine *statement*. Nevertheless, the standard analysis as presented herein is accepted by the majority of formal logicians.

says the same thing as

2a. $(\exists x)Rx \cdot (y)(z)((Ry \cdot Rz) \supset y = z) \cdot (t)(Rt \supset Wt)$

which is a formula in ordinary quantifier notation, containing no descriptors or other innovations. This means that, if there were a rule for transforming descriptor formulae such as (1a) into straightforward quantifier formulae such as (2a), description sentences could then be taken care of without the need for special inference rules; the regular rules of quantifier logic already available to us would be sufficient.

(2a) is a rather cumbersome formula. A slightly less cumbersome one, which is logically equivalent, is the translation of

3. There is exactly one ruler of the universe, and it is wise.

that is,

3a. $(\exists x)(Rx \cdot (y)(Ry \supset y = x) \cdot Wx)$

Since (3a) is logically equivalent to (2a)—their equivalence may be proven, as an exercise—(3a) may be seen as just another way of expressing the standard analysis of (1a).

(1a) and (3a) say the same thing. The difference between them is that (1a) is a descriptor formula, which asserts that the thing which satisfies its descriptive condition '$R\_\_$' also satisfies its predicate '$W\_\_$', whereas (3a) is a straightforward quantifier formula, which asserts that there is exactly one thing which satisfies the condition '$R\_\_$' and it also satisfies the condition '$W\_\_$'.

In general, the standard analysis of a description statement (or descriptor formula) will be a statement to the effect that exactly one thing satisfies the descriptive condition and it also satisfies the predicate condition. We may thus bring descriptor formulae within the realm of quantifier logic by providing a rule for transforming them into their standard analysis.

In the following transformation rule, the lower-case Greek letters α and β represent any individual variable. The capital Greek letters Φ and Ψ represent any predicate expressions, $\Phi\alpha$ represents any formula containing the variable represented by α, and so on. (For a more detailed account of this symbolism, see Appendix K.)

Descriptor Transformation (DT):

$[(\imath\alpha)\Phi\alpha]\Psi\alpha$ transf $(\exists \alpha)(\Phi\alpha \cdot$

$$(\beta)(\Phi\beta \supset \beta = \alpha) \cdot$$
$$\Psi\alpha)$$

where $\Phi\alpha$ and $\Phi\beta$ are just alike except that the one contains occurrences of α in all and only those places where the other contains occurrences of β.

It will be helpful, in understanding this rule, to note that $\Phi\_\_$ is the descriptive condition—the condition governed by the iota-operator in the descriptor—and $\Psi\_\_$ is the predicate—the condition governed by the *entire* descriptor. As an illustration of the use of this rule, the formula

4. $[(\imath x)Fx](\exists y)Rxy$

may be transformed, by DT, into

4a. $(\exists x)(Fx \cdot (z)(Fz \supset z = x) \cdot (\exists y)Rxy)$

Here, the descriptive condition ('Φ__') is 'F__', and the predicate condition ('Ψ__') is '$(\exists y)R$__y'. (4a) asserts that exactly one thing satisfies the descriptive condition, and it also satisfies the predicate. Similarly, the descriptor formula

5. $[(\imath x)Fx][(\imath y)Rxy]Syx$

may be transformed by DT into

5a. $(\exists x)(Fx \cdot (z)(Fz \supset z = x) \cdot [(\imath y)Rxy]Syx)$

Here the descriptive condition ('Φ__') is 'F__', and the predicate ('Ψ__') is '$[(\imath y)R$__$y]Sy$__'. The final clause in the matrix of (5a) is a descriptor formula, and so DT may also be applied to (5a), to produce

5b. $(\exists x)(Fx \cdot (z)(Fz \supset z = x) \cdot (\exists y)(Rxy \cdot (w)(Rxw \supset w = y) \cdot Syx))$

Here the descriptive condition ('Φ__') is 'Rx__', and the predicate ('Ψ__') is 'S__x'. As a final example, the formula

6. $[(\imath x)[(\imath y)Fy]Rxy]Sx$

(which contains nested descriptors) may be transformed by DT into

6a. $(\exists x)([(\imath y)Fy]Rxy \cdot (z)([(\imath y)Fy]Rzy \supset z = x) \cdot Sx)$

Here the descriptive condition ('Φ__') is '$[(\imath y)Fy]R$__y', and the predicate ('Ψ__') is 'S__'. The first clause within the matrix of (6a) is a descriptor expression, and so (6a) may be transformed by DT into

6b. $(\exists x)((\exists y)(Fy \cdot (t)(Ft \supset t = y) \cdot Rxy) \cdot (z)([(\imath y)Fy]Rzy \supset z = x) \cdot Sx)$

The second clause within the matrix of (6b) also contains a descriptor formula, which may be eliminated by DT to produce

6c. $(\exists x)((\exists y)(Fy \cdot (t)(Ft \supset t = y) \cdot Rxy) \cdot$
$(z)((\exists y)(Fy \cdot (t)(Ft \supset t = y) \cdot Rzy) \supset z = x) \cdot Sx)$

Exercises III

Translate each of the following into descriptor formulae, and then transform them into quantifier formulae containing no descriptors.

1. The present king of Sweden is tall.

☐ 2. Scott is the author of *Ivanhoe*.

3. The author of *Hamlet* is the husband of Anne Hathaway.

4. The butler at Carfax has a sister.

☐ 5. The sister of the butler at Carfax is lovely.

6. If the queen of Sheba is alive, she is older than the king of Siam.

7. If Oberon is the king of the fairies, then Titania is the queen of the fairies.

☐ 8. The man who loves everybody loves somebody.

Exercises IV

Translate and prove each of the following arguments.

1. Mark Twain is the author of *Tom Sawyer*. Samuel Clemens was born in Missouri. Samuel Clemens is Mark Twain. Therefore, the author of *Tom Sawyer* was born in Missouri.

☐ 2. Scott is the author of *Ivanhoe*. The author of *Ivanhoe* is British. Therefore, Scott is British.

3. Charlie took the mother of his children to the beach. Charlie took only Edna to the beach. Therefore, Edna is the mother of Charlie's children.

☐ 4. Voltaire is the author of *Candide*. Arouet authored *Candide*. Therefore, Voltaire is Arouet.

5. George was the king of England. George was the emperor of India. Therefore the king of England was the emperor of India.

6. Edna is a woman. Charlie married Edna. Charlie married only one woman. Edna burned the house down. Not more than one woman burned the house down. Therefore, the woman who burned the house down is the woman Charlie married.

☐ 7. Every king of Belsnavia has had at least one son. No king of Belsnavia has had more than one son. All sons of Belsnavian kings are wealthy. No wealthy sons of Belsnavian kings are industrious. Belsnavia has had only one king. Therefore, the son of the king of Belsnavia is not industrious.

8. The sister of the butler at Carfax is a person who does not remember the owner of Carfax's birthday. Anyone who loves something remembers its birthday. If none of the sisters of the butler loves the owner, then the owner is a person who will never get married, and the butler will inherit his money. Therefore, the butler at Carfax stands to inherit the owner's money.

§24.8 Descriptor Extraction

Strictly speaking, DT is the only rule needed for working with descriptor-formulae. But when DT is the only rule available, proofs often tend to be quite complicated. Thus, while it is not necessary, it is useful to have some additional rules.

First, some definitions: the scope of a descriptor consists of the descriptor itself, plus the first well-punctuated formula to its right, plus everything in between. The descriptor **binds** occurrences of the letter which is in its first (leftmost) iota operator; every occurrence of that letter, within its scope, is bound by the descriptor. The **range** of a descriptor consists of all and only those occurrences of letters bound by it.

The RBV rule may be used to rewrite the range of a descriptor to some other letter. The same restrictions apply as when rewriting the range of a quantifier.

Transformation rules may be applied within descriptors, just as within the matrices of quantificational formulae.

Nested descriptors can be a strong source of complication, and it is best to avoid them as much as possible. As an illustration of this point, the formula

  1. $[(\imath y)Fy][(\imath x)Rxy]Sx$

is logically equivalent to formula (6) from the previous section:

  6. $[(\imath x)[(\imath y)Fy]Rxy]Sx$

the only difference between them is that in (6) the descriptors are nested, while in (1) they are not. However, when DT was used to eliminate the descriptors from (6), the result was a formula—(6c)—sixty-eight symbols long, whereas when the descriptors are eliminated from (1) by DT, the result is

  1a. $(\exists y)(Fy \cdot (z)(Fz \supset z = y) \cdot (\exists x)(Rxy \cdot (t)(Rty \supset t = x) \cdot Sx))$

which is only forty-five symbols long, or about two-thirds as long as (6c). Here, the difference between nested and unnested descriptors turns out to be twenty-three symbols. (You may wish to prove the equivalence of (6c) and (1a) as an exercise.)

The following rule is useful in eliminating nested descriptors.

DESCRIPTOR EXTRACTION (DX):

  $[(\imath\alpha)\ [(\imath\beta)\Phi\beta]\ \Psi\alpha]\Theta\alpha$ transf $[(\imath\beta)\Phi\beta]\ [(\imath\alpha)\Psi\alpha]\Theta\alpha$

  provided that there are no occurrences of α in $\Phi\beta$, and no occurrences of β in $\Theta\alpha$.

This rule provides a means for "pulling out" a nested descriptor, provided that no changes in freedom or bondage result from the extraction. The following illustration shows a descriptor being extracted and settled outside its original nest.

$\overbrace{[(\imath x)[(\imath y)Gy]Rxy]Fx}$ After DX: $[(\imath y)Gy][(\imath x)Rxy]Fx$

When DX is performed, the internal descriptor (the 'y' descriptor in the above illustration) is lifted out and placed immediately to the left of the descriptor which contained it (the 'x' descriptor in the illustration), pushing aside anything else that might happen to be there. Since DX is a transformation rule, the reverse operation is also permitted; but the need for it will occur very infrequently.

Note that a descriptor cannot be extracted unless there is an iota-operator *immediately* to its left (with nothing between them). Similarly, one descriptor cannot be inserted into another unless they are contiguous (there is nothing between them).

The restrictions given in the DX rule are to assure that no changes in freedom or bondage result from the transformation. If α occurred in $\Phi\beta$, then extracting $[(\imath\beta)\Phi\beta]$ would free those occurrences of α; thus DX is permissible only when α does not occur in $\Phi\beta$. Likewise, if β occurred in $\Theta\alpha$, then extracting $[(\imath\beta)\Phi\beta]$ would put $\Theta\alpha$ within its scope, binding those occurrences of β. Thus DX is permissible only when β does not occur in $\Theta\alpha$. By way of illustration, in

2. $[(\imath x)[(\imath y)Ryx]Sxy]Gx$

the descriptor '$[(\imath y)Ryx]$' cannot be extracted, since it contains an occurrence of 'x' (an occurrence which is bound in (2)), and that occurrence would be freed by the extraction, since it would no longer be within the scope of the descriptor which begins with '$(\imath x)$'. Similarly, in

3. $[(\imath x)[(\imath y)Fy]Sxy]Ryx$

the descriptor '$[(\imath y)Fy]$' cannot be extracted, for the predicate 'Ryx' contains an occurrence of 'y' which is free; but if '$[(\imath y)Fy]$' were extracted, then 'Ryx' would fall within its scope and that occurrence of 'y' would be bound. (In this case, the problem could be overcome by rewriting the range of '$[(\imath y)Fy]$' as some other letter.)

As a further illustration, here are some correct applications of the DX rule. Arrow diagrams are included to show what is being extracted from where.

1. $[(\imath x)[(\imath y)[(\imath z)Fz]Ryz]Sxy]Gx$

2. $[(\imath x)[(\imath z)Fz][(\imath y)\quad Ryz]Sxy]Gx$ 1, DX

3. $[(\imath z)Fz][(\imath x)\quad [(\imath y)Ryz]Sxy]Gx$ 2, DX

4. $[(\imath z)Fz][(\imath y)Ryz][(\imath x)\quad Sxy]Gx$ 3, DX

It should be noted that the DX rule permits only the descriptor immediately to the right of the first iota operator to be extracted. Thus, it was necessary after step (2) to extract the 'z' descriptor before extracting the 'y' descriptor. Alternatively, the derivation might have gone

1. $[(\imath x)[(\imath y)[(\imath z)Fz]Ryz]Sxy]Gx$

2. $[(\imath y)[(\imath z)Fz]Ryz][(\imath x)\quad Sxy]Gx$ 1, DX

3. $[(\imath z)Fz][(\imath y)\quad Ryz][(\imath x)Sxy]Gx$ 2, DX

but the result would have been exactly the same. In general, the more deeply buried a descriptor is, the further to the left it will be after extraction. (If this were not the case, scopes and ranges would get hopelessly botched up.)

Exercises V

Using DT, eliminate all descriptors from (1) in the first derivation above. Then eliminate all descriptors from (4). Compare the two formulae. How much longer is the first one?

Exercises VI

Translate and prove numbers 7 and 8 from Exercises IV, this time using DX to eliminate nested descriptors whenever possible. Compare these proofs with the earlier ones as to length and complexity.

Exercises VII

Translate and prove each of the following.

1. The even prime number is smaller than 3. Whatever is smaller than 3 is smaller than 4. Therefore, there is an even number smaller than 4.
2. The king of France is bald. Any king of France is a nobleman. Therefore, some nobleman is bald.
3. The king of France is bald. Therefore, France has a bald king.
4. Every natural satellite of Earth is made of cheese. Earth has just one natural satellite. Therefore, the natural satellite of Earth is made of cheese.
5. Scott is the author of *Ivanhoe*. Whoever authored *Ivanhoe* authored *Waverley*. *Waverley* does not have more than one author. Therefore Scott is the author of *Waverley*.
6. The even prime number is less than 3. 3 is less than 4. Whatever is less than 3 is less than 4. 3 is a prime number, but is not even. Therefore, there are at least two prime numbers less than 4.
7. The king of Belsnavia is a rather stupid person. Anyone who is rather stupid is incompetent. Any king of a country is a monarch of that country. Belsnavia is a country with at most one monarch. Therefore, the monarch of Belsnavia is incompetent.
8. Belsnavia is a small Balkan country. Balkan countries always have their oldest man for prime minister. No country has more than one prime minister. Therefore, there is a small country whose oldest man is the prime minister of Belsnavia.
9. The successor of 1 is prime. Any number which is prime has itself as its only factor. Every odd number is succeeded by an even number. 1 is an odd number. Therefore there is an even number whose only factor is the successor of 1.
10. The king of England is the emperor of India. The king of England is British. If any king of a European country is emperor of an Asiatic country, then at most one Asiatic country has an emperor who is king of a European country. Every emperor of a country is king of a country. England is a European country and India is an Asiatic country. No country that has an emperor has

a democratic government. Only England has a British king. Therefore, the Asiatic country that has a British emperor does not have a democratic government.

§24.9 More on Translation

In an earlier chapter, procedures were given for translating sentences containing genitive phrases, such as 'Clyde's brother', as existentially quantified relational statements. Quite often it is possible (and even more correct) to translate genitive phrases as definite descriptions. For example, the expression

1. Harvey's wife

would, in most instances, mean the same as '*the* wife of Harvey', rather than simply '*a* wife of Harvey'. And so, the most appropriate translation of the statement

2. Harvey's wife is bald.

would ordinarily be

2a. $[(\imath x)Wx\underline{h}]Bx$

rather than merely

2b. $(\exists x)(Wx\underline{h} \cdot Bx)$

It is usually possible to tell, from the context, which mode of translation is the more appropriate. As a rule of thumb it is sometimes helpful to ask: Would the statement mean the same thing if the genitive phrase were paraphrased as an indefinite description by means of the expressions 'a' or 'an' or 'one of'? If it would mean the same when so paraphrased, then the appropriate translation will be as an indefinite description, after the manner of (2b), rather than as a definite description after the manner of (2a). For example, the statement

3. Clyde's brother is wealthy.

would, in most contexts, mean the same as

4. One of Clyde's brothers is wealthy.

and so would translate as

3a. $(\exists x)(Bx\underline{c} \cdot Wx)$

(4) carries a psychological implication that Clyde has more than one brother, but this is irrelevant for purposes of logic. What is relevant is that it does not *rule out* the possibility that he has more than one brother, and so it must be translated by the simple existential quantifier. On the other hand, the statement

5. Clyde's mother bit a postman.

would not normally mean 'One of Clyde's mothers bit a postman', and so, normally, it would translate as

    5a. $[(\imath x)Mx\underline{c}]x$ bit a postman

—that is, as

    5b. $[(\imath x)Mx\underline{c}](\exists y)(Py \cdot Bxy)$

Thus, when translating a sentence containing a genitive phrase, it is worthwhile to hesitate for a moment in order to decide whether it requires a descriptor or merely a quantifier.

It cannot be overemphasized that the translation of complex statements goes much easier, and is much more likely to be correct, if we carry it out *by stages* rather than attempting to get it into symbols all at once. For example, the statement

    6. The singer whose business manager is one of his brothers is quite wealthy.

contains a very complex definite description. But it can be translated correctly and without undue difficulty provided the translation is done a step at a time:

    6a. $[(\imath x)x$ is a singer whose business manager is one of his brothers]x is quite wealthy

    6b. $[(\imath x)(x$ is a singer $\cdot$ the business manager of x is one of x's brothers)]Wx

    6c. $[(\imath x)(Sx \cdot [(\imath y)y$ is business manager to $x]y$ is one of x's brothers)]Wx

    6d. $[(\imath x)(Sx \cdot [(\imath y)Myx]y$ is brother of $x)]Wx$

    6e. $[(\imath x)(Sx \cdot [(\imath y)Myx]Byx)]Wx$

Similarly, the complex statement

    7. The king whose father was his wife's former husband blinded himself.

may be translated, by stages, as

    7a. $[(\imath x)x$ is a king whose father was his wife's former husband]x blinded himself

    7b. $[(\imath x)(x$ is a king $\cdot$ the father of x was x's wife's former husband)]Bxx

    7c. $[(\imath x)(Kx \cdot [(\imath y)y$ fathered $x]y$ was x's wife's former husband)]Bxx

    7d. $[(\imath x)(Kx \cdot [(\imath y)Fyx]$the wife of x is such that y was her former husband)]Bxx

    7e. $[(\imath x)(Kx \cdot [(\imath y)Fyx][(\imath z)z$ is wife to $x]y$ was z's former husband)]Bxx

    7f. $[(\imath x)(Kx \cdot [(\imath y)Fyx][(\imath z)Wzx]$the former husband of z was $y)]Bxx$

    7g. $[(\imath x)(Kx \cdot [(\imath y)Fyx][(\imath z)Wzx][(\imath w)w$ is former husband to $z]z = y)]Bxx$

    7h. $[(\imath x)(Kx \cdot [(\imath y)Fyx][(\imath z)Wzx][(\imath w)Hwz]z = y)]Bxx$

§24.10 Ambiguities of Scope

An expression with a **scope** is one which is capable of modifying or attaching to another expression in some way that matters. Among other sorts of expressions, such things as quantifiers and descriptors have scopes. The **scope** of an expression can be explained generally as the amount of the other expression it "applies to." Thus, in addition to quantifiers and descriptors, such things as adjectives, adverbs, and truth-functional operators all have scopes.

A statement or expression contains an **ambiguity of scope** whenever the scopes of two or more expressions within it are capable of being interpreted in more than one way. Ambiguity of scope does not occur in the language of formal logic,* but it occurs with great frequency in a natural language such as English. As a simple example, the statement

    1. It is false that Clyde loves Edna or Clyde is a fool.

contains an ambiguity of scope: if the scope of the operator 'It is false that' falls within the scope of the operator 'or', then (1) says

    1a. ($\sim$ Clyde loves Edna $\lor$ Clyde is a fool)

But if the scope of 'or' falls within the scope of 'it is false that', then (1) says

    1b. $\sim$ (Clyde loves Edna $\lor$ Clyde is a fool)

Both (1a) and (1b) are unambiguous as to how the scopes of the two operators are related; but (1) is ambiguous, since it is capable of being interpreted, with equal plausibility, as either (1a) or (1b). Scope ambiguities with truth-functional operators are avoided in logic by means of punctuation.

Other opportunities for scope ambiguity arise when quantifier expressions get into the picture. For example, the statement

    2. Everything is not destructible.

is ambiguous as to the scopes of the operator 'not' and the quantifier expression 'everything'. If 'not' is interpreted as falling within the scope of 'everything', then (2) says

    2a. $(x) \sim x$ is destructible

but if 'everything' is interpreted as falling within the scope of 'not', then (2) says

    2b. $\sim (x)x$ is destructible

The difference between (2a) and (2b) appears, not as a difference in punctuation, but as a difference in the *order* of the two expressions '$\sim$' and '(x)', since it is a convention of the language of logic that the scope of a unary operator (quantifier, descriptor, tilde) extends to the right of the operator but not to its left. Thus, in (2a) the tilde is within the scope of the quantifier, hence is part of what is modified by the quantifier, whereas in (2b) the quantifier is within the scope of the tilde, thus is part of what is modified by the tilde.

---

*We permit the ambiguity of multiple conjunctions, such as '$A \cdot B \cdot C$' or multiple disjunctions such as '$K \lor L \lor M$', since it makes no difference to their truth-value.

Similar ambiguities can arise in statements containing "mixed quantification" and relations: relational statements involving both universal and existential quantification. For example, the statement

    3. Somebody is loved by everybody.

might be interpreted to mean either

    3a. $(\exists x)(x$ is a person $\cdot$ $(y)(y$ is a person $\supset x$ is loved by $y))$

or

    3b. $(y)(y$ is a person $\supset (\exists x)(x$ is a person $\cdot$ x is loved by $y))$

(3a) says that there is a person such that everyone loves him; (3b) says that every person is such that he loves somebody (or other). In the first case, the universal quantifier expression 'everybody' is interpreted as falling within the scope of the existential quantifier expression 'somebody'; in the second, the existential quantifier expression is interpreted as falling within the scope of the universal quantifier expression. These two possible interpretations of (3) are represented unambiguously in the two formula (3a) and (3b).

Another example of the same sort of ambiguity is in

    4. Something repels everything.

which may be interpreted either as

    4a. $(\exists x)(y)x$ repels y

or as

    4b. $(y)(\exists x)x$ repels y

(4a) says that there is an individual such that it repels everything; (4b) says that everything is such that there is something (or other) which repels it. These are different statements, and have quite different truth-conditions; (4a) says that everything is repelled by the same individual, while (4b) does not.

Of course, there are also opportunities for scope ambiguity when quantification is *not* "mixed"; but these are not troublesome, since the ambiguity makes no difference to the truth-conditions of the statement. For instance, the statement

    5. Everything attracts everything.

might mean either

    5a. $(x)(y)x$ attracts y

or

    5b. $(y)(x)x$ attracts y

but, since both quantifiers are universal, the difference is trivial: (5a) and (5b) have identical truth-conditions and hence are logically equivalent.

Scope ambiguity can also arise in connection with phrases containing certain psychological verbs such as 'believes that', 'thinks that', 'wishes to know whether'. For example, the statement

    6. Officer Pup believes that every lawbreaker is a communist.

could mean either

    6a. Officer Pup believes that $(x)(x$ is a lawbreaker $\supset x$ is a communist)

or

    6b. $(x)(x$ is a lawbreaker $\supset$ Officer Pup believes that x is a communist)

These do not say the same thing. (6a) simply affirms Officer Pup's belief in the truth of the statement 'All lawbreakers are communists', and could be true whether Officer Pup is acquainted with any lawbreakers or not; it does not ascribe to him a belief about any particular individuals, but a belief about a *proposition*. On the other hand, (6b) says that it is true of each lawbreaker that Officer Pup believes *him* to be a communist, and this could be true whether Officer Pup knows he is a lawbreaker or not. If there were just two lawbreakers, a and b, and Officer Pup were ignorant that they were lawbreakers but believed a to be a communist because of the length of a's beard, and believed b to be a communist because b spoke out in favor of Stalin, then (6b) would be true. It would be true that, for each lawbreaker, Officer Pup believes him to be a communist. The difference between (6a) and (6b) is of interest from the point of view of applied logic, since the logical treatment of (6a) can proceed no further than single-letter abbreviation, for purposes of truth-functional logic, whereas (6b) is a quantified statement from which we can derive inferences by the methods of quantifier logic. The case is similar with

    7. Officer Pup is hoping to surprise a burglar.

which could mean either

    7a. Officer Pup is hoping that $(\exists x)(x$ burgles $\cdot$ Officer Pup surprises $x)$

or

    7b. $(\exists x)(x$ burgles $\cdot$ Officer Pup is hoping to surprise $x)$

The first would be true, for example, if Officer Pup needed to surprise only one more burglar to win an award, and set out in his rounds hoping he would discover a burglar to surprise; the second would be true if Jones (perhaps unknown to Pup) were a burglar, and Pup had bought Jones a birthday present hoping to surprise Jones with it.

    The scope ambiguities which arise in connection with descriptions and descriptors are similar to those illustrated above. For example, the statement

    8. It's false that the author of *Principia Mathematica* is English.

may be interpreted either as

    8a. $[(\imath x)x$ authored *Principia Mathematica*] $\sim x$ is English

—'The author of *Principia Mathematica* is such that it is false that he is English', or as

8b. $\sim[(\imath x)x$ authored *Principia Mathematica*]x is English

—'It's false that the author of *Principia Mathematica* is such that he is English'. In (8a) the negation operator falls within the scope of the descriptor; in (8b) the descriptor falls within the scope of the negation operator. Since *Principia Mathematica* had two authors, Whitehead and Russell, (8a) is false and (8b) is true.

Whenever a descriptor falls within the scope of another expression, it is said to have a **secondary occurrence** in the statement with respect to the other expression; when the other expression falls within the scope of the descriptor, the descriptor is said to have a **primary occurrence** with respect to the other expression. In (8a) the descriptor has a primary occurrence with respect to the tilde; in (8b) it has a secondary occurrence with respect to the tilde. Ambiguity as to primary and secondary occurrences of descriptions can occur in English even where we least expect it. For example, the statement

9. If the sea god becomes angry, there will be a tidal wave tomorrow.

may not appear to be ambiguous, but it is nevertheless susceptible to two quite different interpretations:

9a. $[(\imath x)x$ is a sea god] (x becomes angry $\supset$ there will be a tidal wave tomorrow)

and

9b. $[(\imath x)x$ is a sea god]x becomes angry $\supset$ there will be a tidal wave tomorrow

In (9a), the descriptor has a primary occurrence with respect to the conditional operator, and says 'There is exactly one sea god, and if he becomes angry there will be a tidal wave tomorrow', which is false since there is no sea god. But in (9b) the descriptor has a secondary occurrence with respect to the conditional operator, and says 'If there is exactly one sea god and he becomes angry then there will be a tidal wave tomorrow', which is vacuously true because there is no sea god and so its antecedent is false. Similarly, the statement

10. All mermaids are ruled by the sea god.

is susceptible to two interpretations, in one of which the description 'the sea god' has a primary occurrence with respect to the phrase 'all mermaids', and in the other of which it has a secondary occurrence with respect to that phrase. Under the first interpretation, (10) will translate as

10a. $[(\imath x)x$ is a sea god] $(y)(y$ is a mermaid $\supset x$ rules $y)$

and under the second interpretation it will translate as

10b. $(y)(y$ is a mermaid $\supset [(\imath x)x$ is a sea god]x rules $y)$

The difference between these interpretations is that (10a) entails that there is a sea god, and so is false, whereas (10b) only entails that *if* there are mermaids, then there is a sea god who rules them, and so is true because there are no mermaids.

This type of ambiguity is very deeply buried, so that often we require a great deal of insight into the intentions of the speaker to determine the intended meaning of the ambiguous statement. Sometimes we cannot tell whether a statement should be translated with a primary occurrence or a secondary occurrence of a descriptor. In cases of this sort (when there is no way to tell which interpretation is correct) the appropriate thing to do is to translate the statement with a *secondary* occurrence of the descriptor. This follows from the principle we have mentioned earlier: it is better to leave something out in the course of translation than to smuggle something in. Statements containing secondary occurrences are weaker claims than statements containing primary occurrences, and in the absence of contrary reasons, translation should always proceed in accordance with the weaker interpretation.

However, in one class of statements the primary-secondary behavior of descriptions is sufficiently regular to warrant discussion. These are *negative* identity statements containing descriptions, such as

11. Homer is not the author of the *Iliad*.

From what has already been said, we know that (11) is capable of being interpreted either as

11a. $[(\imath x)x$ authored the *Iliad*]Homer $\neq x$

or as

11b. $\sim[(\imath x)x$ authored the *Iliad*]Homer $= x$

But of these two interpretations the more plausible is (11b), in which the descriptor has a secondary occurrence. If someone were to assert (11), he would not normally be regarded as commiting himself to there being a unique individual who authored the *Iliad*; rather, (11) is the phrasing one would use if one believed that Homer was only one among several persons who participated in authoring the *Iliad*, or if one believed that the *Iliad* was not authored at all but simply developed as a verbal legend. Similarly, if someone were to say

12. Richard Burton is not the king of England.

we would not normally regard him as asserting that the king of England is someone *other* than Burton—that is, that there is a king of England but it isn't Burton:

12a. $[(\imath x)x$ is king of England]Richard Burton $\neq x$

Rather, we would take him simply to be saying, 'It's false that Burton is the king':

12b. $\sim[(\imath x)x$ is king of England]Richard Burton $= x$

On the other hand, if someone were to assert the statement

13. The author of the *Iliad* is not Homer.

we normally *would* regard him as claiming that some unique individual authored the *Iliad* but it wasn't Homer:

13a. $[(\imath x)x$ authored the *Iliad*$]x \neq$ Homer

rather than the weaker claim:

13b. $\sim[(\imath x)x$ authored the *Iliad*$]x =$ Homer

And similarly, if someone were to say

14. The king of England is not Richard Burton.

we normally would take him to be claiming that the king of England is someone other than Richard Burton:

14a. $[(\imath x)x$ is king of England$]x \neq$ Richard Burton

and not merely denying Burton's kinghood:

14b. $\sim[(\imath x)x$ is king of England$]x =$ Richard Burton

These points can be generalized as follows: in a negative identity statement, if the description occurs *first* in the sentence, it will translate as a descriptor with a *primary* occurrence relative to the negation operator; if the description does not occur first, it will translate as a descriptor with a secondary occurrence. Thus,

15. Cleopatra was not the wife of Caesar.

will translate as

15a. $\sim[(\imath x)x$ is wife to Caesar]Cleopatra $= x$

but

16. The wife of Caesar was not Cleopatra.

will translate as

16a. $[(\imath x)x$ is wife to Caesar$]x \neq$ Cleopatra

The case is similar when a negative identity statement contains two descriptions, rather than one description and one proper name. The description given first will have a primary occurrence relative to the negation operator; the other will have a secondary occurrence relative to the negation operator. For example,

17. The husband of Queen Elizabeth is not the king of England.

will translate as

17a. $[(\imath x)x$ is husband to Queen Elizabeth$]\sim[(\imath y)y$ is king of England$]x = y$

but

18. The king of England is not the husband of Queen Elizabeth.

will translate as

18a. $[(\imath y)y$ is king of England$] \sim [(\imath x)x$ is husband to Queen Elizabeth$]y = x$

Exercises VIII

Translate and abbreviate each of the following. Where there is ambiguity, give all plausible translations.

1. The even prime number is the number whose square is its own double.
□ 2. The oldest man in Albuquerque is shorter than the second-tallest player for the Celtics.
3. The philosopher whose first book was a disappointment to him is the author of *Dialogues Concerning Natural Religion.*
4. Everyone is familiar with the story about the princess whose stepmother tried to poison her with an apple.
□ 5. Hamlet is a Danish prince whose mother's second husband was his father's brother.
6. Professor Snark believes that all freshmen are stupid.
7. Uncle Sam is not the prime minister of the United States.
8. The Shah of Iran is not wealthier than the Queen of Sheba.
□ 9. Nobody is acquainted with the composer of "Yankee Doodle Dandy."
10. Every number is smaller than its successor.
11. If the spirit of creation is not the form of the good, then Plato was mistaken.
12. Every animal species was represented on Noah's ark.
13. The nation whose capital was founded by Romulus is south of the country whose national hero is William Tell.
14. The country whose third president drafted its declaration of independence is not the native land of the author of *Common Sense.*
15. If all mermaids are ruled by the sea god then all wood nymphs are ruled by the forest god.
16. The author of *Tristram Shandy* is not the author of "Slawkenbergius on noses."
17. Not all wood nymphs are ruled by the forest god.
18. Professor Snark thinks that the author of "Slawkenbergius on noses" was Tristram Shandy.
19. George IV wished to know whether the author of *Waverley* was the author of *Waverley.*
20. If Junius Booth is the father of Edwin Booth and Edwin Booth is the brother of John Wilkes Booth, then Junius Booth is the father of the assassin of Lincoln.

appendix A

STATEMENTS AND SENTENCES

Both the definition of 'statement' in §1.1 and the characterization of 'compound statement' in §1.3 are oversimplified, in view of what can actually be done by way of logical analysis and evaluation within Propositional Logic. The primary sort of statement is that expressed by a declarative sentence, and the primary sort of compound statement is that expressed by a compound sentence as explained in Chapter 1. But from a logical point of view, it is advantageous to recognize statements or propositions which are expressed by grammatical forms other than full-blown declarative sentences (for example, propositions expressed by noun phrases) and so to recognize *compound* statements expressed by sentences which are not "compound" in the way explained.

Strictly speaking, if a statement concerns two distinct states of affairs, it is usually possible to regard the statement as a compound, even though the two states of affairs may not be presented by distinct independent clauses within the sentence. For example,

1. Stopping by the woods, Robert had a vision of his future.

is not a compound sentence, as explained in the text. However, it does concern two distinct states of affairs: stopping by the woods, and having a vision of the future. Consequently, it may be regarded as expressing a compound statement. In fact, (1) is roughly equivalent to the statement

2. Robert stopped by the woods and (he) had a vision of his future.

which is a compound even by the criteria given in the text. The reason for saying that (1) expresses a compound statement is that (1) is synonymous with a statement which is compound in the primary sense explained in the text. Both (1) and (2) say the same thing, and since (2) is compound it follows that (1) is also compound. By paraphrasing (1) as the explicit compound sentence (2), we may apply to it the standard translation procedures given in the text, in order to subject it to formal logical evaluation.

As another example,

3. Bert's having a diploma implies his being a graduate.

is not a compound sentence as defined in the text; nevertheless, it may be regarded as the expression of a compound statement, since it means roughly the same thing as

4. If Bert has a diploma then Bert is a graduate.

which *is* a compound sentence (its components are 'Bert has a diploma' and 'Bert is a graduate'). In (3) the two separate components are expressed by the (gerundial) noun phrases 'Bert's having a diploma' and 'Bert's being a graduate'; in (4) they are expressed by regular independent clauses. The proper treatment of statements such as (3) is to paraphrase them along the lines of (4), so that the components are expressed in the primary fashion, and then to apply the translation rules given in the text.

In both of the examples above, the vehicle of the component statement is a gerundial noun phrase (a noun phrase containing a main verb ending in "-ing"). But other sorts of phrases may also express component statements. For example,

5. That Bert has a diploma implies that he has graduated.

can be seen to mean the same thing as (4), even though (5) does not contain any gerundial expressions. Similarly, in

6. On her way through the forest, Evangeline met a bear.

the opening phrase 'on her way through the forest' may be seen as expressing the statement that Evangeline went through the forest, so that (6) might be paraphrased as

7. Evangeline went through the forest, and she met a bear.

When we are translating out of English into the notation of formal logic, cases like these will be rather common. They should always be approached with some care and caution, however. If one is in doubt as to how to paraphrase a sentence, the safest course from the point of view of logic will be to abstain from paraphrase altogether and to treat it as a simple statement. This conservative approach may sometimes rule out certain formal inferences that would otherwise be possible, but that is logically preferable to the risk of unwarranted inferences based upon faulty paraphrases.

appendix B

ON SIMPLE SENTENCES EXPRESSING
TRUTH-FUNCTIONAL COMPOUNDS

Once paraphrasing has been admitted as a permissible procedure, it becomes apparent that the question of whether a given sentence is "compound" or "simple," and whether the proposition it expresses is compound or simple, will not always have a single straightforward answer. It often happens that a sentence which is *simple* by the given criteria may be paraphrased into one which is *compound* by the given criteria, without any relevant change of meaning. This is illustrated by the examples in Appendix A. Another illustration can be given in the two statements

1. Percy and Evangeline are children.
2. Percy is a child and Evangeline is a child.

Sentence (1) is, by the given criteria, a simple sentence, while sentence (2) is a compound sentence. Nevertheless, the two sentences mean the same thing and it is proper to regard (2) as an accurate paraphrase of (1). They both express the same proposition. Is it a compound proposition or a simple one? Sentence (2) certainly expresses a compound proposition (in fact, a truth-functional compound). Since we recognize intuitively that (2) and (1) express the same proposition, it is logically appropriate to say that the proposition expressed by (1) is also compound: the proposition in question is compound, regardless of how it is expressed. Thus, compound statements can sometimes be expressed by simple sentences.

This can be a minor problem when we are attempting to decide what logical treatment should be given to a particular statement. If a given simple sentence may accurately be paraphrased into a compound one, then of course the proper thing to do is to so paraphrase it—that is, to treat it as expressing a compound statement. The problem consists in the lack of any objective, easily statable criteria for what will constitute an "accurate" paraphrase, if accuracy requires sameness of *meaning*. Whether or not two sentences "mean the same thing" can seldom be decided with any uniformity of agreement.

348

However, for purposes of logic "sameness of meaning" is not a requirement. All that is required is sameness of *truth-conditions*, and this usually
can be uniformly agreed upon. A paraphrase is accurate, for purposes of
logic, if it preserves the truth-conditions of the original, whether or not it
preserves the entire *meaning* of the original. And so, we can say that a simple
sentence expresses a compound statement if, and only if, it can accurately
be paraphrased as a compound sentence. That is to say, a simple sentence
expresses a compound statement if and only if the proposition it expresses
has the same truth-conditions as the proposition expressed by some compound sentence. For example, statement (1) above is compound, since it has
the same truth-conditions as statement (2)—even though *sentence* (1) is
simple.

TREATING CERTAIN
NON-TRUTH-FUNCTIONAL COMPOUNDS

The procedures given here provide a general method for treating truth-dependent compounds which are not truth-functional, and even certain statements which would not normally be regarded as truth-dependent compounds. Essentially, it is a method of partial analysis whereby a statement which is truth-functionally simple yields up a fragment of itself so as to permit inferences which would be impossible if the statement were simply taken as an unanalyzed unit. The original statement is then treated as the conjunction of itself with all of the statements that may be squeezed out of it.

Stripping Off Modifiers

The process of logical "distillation" is most easily seen in connection with statements that contain modifying adverbs or adjectives. When such modifiers are stripped away, the result will be a statement which was "contained within" (entailed by) the original. For ease of reference, we will call this statement a *product* of the original. For example,

    1. Harvey owns a striped elephant.

contains the modifying adjective 'striped'. When this is removed, the result is

    1a. Harvey owns an elephant.

Now it is clear that (1) cannot be true unless (1a) is also true; hence, (1a) is a product of (1). For purposes of logic we cannot treat (1) as if it were equivalent to its product, because it isn't. But we *can* treat it as the conjunction of itself with its product, because that conjunction is equivalent to the original: the conjunction of (1) with (1a) is logically equivalent to (1) alone. Let us refer to the conjunction of (1) with (1a) as a *conjoint product* of (1). Thus a conjoint product of (1) is

    1b. Harvey owns an elephant · Harvey owns a striped elephant

(1) and (1b) are logically equivalent, in the sense that they have identical truth-conditions. Therefore, it is permissible to treat (1b) as a logical translation of (1). The reason for preferring the more cumbersome (1b) to the shorter (1) is that (1b) permits certain inferences that (1) does not. An example will be given in a moment. But first, consider

    2. Harvey is extremely odd.

This contains the modifying adverb 'extremely'. When this is stripped away, the result is

    2a. Harvey is odd.

and so, a conjoint product of (2) is

    2b. Harvey is odd · Harvey is extremely odd

and (2) may be translated, for logical purposes, as (2b). By way of illustrating the point of this, the argument

> Harvey owns a striped elephant.
> If Harvey owns an elephant then Harvey is extremely odd.
> If Harvey is odd then Thelma will adore him.
> ∴ Thelma will adore him.

though valid, cannot be proven valid if the truth-functionally simple statements in it are merely abbreviated without analysis. Treated in this way, the argument will be

$$S$$
$$E \supset X$$
$$O \supset A$$
$$\therefore A$$

which is truth-functionally invalid. However, if the first premiss and the consequent of the second premiss are treated as their conjoint products, the result will be

$$E \cdot S$$
$$E \supset (O \cdot X)$$
$$O \supset A$$
$$\therefore A$$

whose validity is easily demonstrated.

Depending upon how many modifiers a statement contains, it may be possible to distill out various different products from the same statement. For example,

    3. Harvey owns a striped three-legged elephant.

has the following three products:

    3a. Harvey owns a striped elephant.
    3b. Harvey owns a three-legged elephant.
    3c. Harvey owns an elephant.

and a conjoint product of (3) will be the conjunction of (3), (3a), (3b), and (3c):

3d. Harvey owns an elephant · (Harvey owns a striped elephant · (Harvey owns a three-legged elephant · (Harvey owns a striped three-legged elephant)))

which will abbreviate as

3e. $E \cdot (S \cdot (T \cdot O))$

Extreme care must be exercised when treating *comparative* modifiers, such as 'tall', 'large', and so on. For example,

4. Irving is a tall midget wrestler.

does not contain

4a. Irving is a tall wrestler.

as a product; a tall midget wrestler is not someone who is tall, and is a midget, and is a wrestler, it is someone who is tall *for a midget*, and is a wrestler. Because of complications of this sort, it is best *never* to take comparative modifiers alone when considering the products of a given statement. With this in mind, the only two products of (4) will be

4b. Irving is a midget wrestler.

4c. Irving is a wrestler.

and its conjoint product will be

4d. $W \cdot (M \cdot T)$

Modifiers such as 'nearly' and 'almost' should, obviously, never be stripped, since to do so would be to destroy the sense of the statement. For example, 'Jones is almost dead' does not have, as a product, 'Jones is dead'.

Not only single words, but entire phrases may be stripped away in appropriate circumstances, to produce a product of the original statement. For example, one product of 'Clyde was bitten by a vicious dog' is 'Clyde was bitten' (another is 'Clyde was bitten by a dog'). Similarly, 'Harvey is ill with influenza' has, as a product, 'Harvey is ill'; and so on.

Statements of Motive

Statements such as

5. Clyde pinched Edna for laughing too loud.

are compounds but not truth-functional compounds. They are called "statements of motive," since they assert not only what someone did but what his motive was for doing it. In (5) what Clyde did was to pinch Edna; his motive for doing it was her laughing too loud. Statements of motive such as (5) consist of both an "action clause" ('Clyde pinched Edna') and a "motive clause" ('for laughing too loud'). It should be obvious that the proposition expressed by the action clause is a product of the statement; (5) cannot be true unless

   5a. Clyde pinched Edna.

is also true; consequently (5a) is a product of (5). This does *not* hold for the proposition expressed by the motive clause. The statement

   6. Edna laughed too loud.

is not a product of (5), since (5) could be true even though (6) is false. This is even clearer in a case such as

   7. Clyde spanked Percy for breaking the lamp.

As anyone who recalls his childhood can testify, it is possible to be spanked for something you didn't do. Thus, although

   7a. Clyde spanked Percy.

is a product of (7),

   8. Percy broke the lamp.

is not. We can express this generally by saying that while it is permissible to strip away the motive clause to arrive at a product of the original, it is not legitimate to strip away the action clause: that is, it is not in general legitimate to regard the motive clause (or any part of it) as expressing a product of the original.

   Some other examples of motive statements are:

   Percy kicked Evangeline in order to make her shut up.
   James was rewarded for bravery.
   The window was broken out of spite.
   They flooded the fields to make their crops grow better.
   Harvey was fired for incompetence.
   Caryl Chessman was executed for rape.

'Because'

   Although motivation and causation are totally different things, the word 'because' is used to indicate both relationships. For example, the word 'because' is used correctly in both of the following statements:

   9. I ran over him because I didn't like his looks.
   10. I ran over him because my brakes failed.

But it does not signify the same thing in both cases, since (9) is a motive statement and (10) is a causal statement. The first gives the motive for my running over him; the second gives the cause of my running over him. The difference between the two is significant, since there are important logical differences between motive statements and causal ones. Both motives and causes are "reasons for" a person's doing something: in (9) the *reason why* I ran over him is that I didn't like his looks; in (10) the reason why I ran over him is that the brakes failed; but they are totally different kinds of reasons.

When we give the *cause* of an event (such as a human action), we are giving an explanation which involves a (tacit or explicit) appeal to general mechanical or scientific principles. When we give the *motive* for a human action, we explain it in terms of the agent's *personal* reasons for doing it. This is reflected in the fact that, while it makes sense to ask for the *causes* of an event which is not a human action, it doesn't make sense to ask for the *motives* for such an event. For example, we can give a causal answer to the question "Why is the window broken?" ("Charlie threw a brick through it"), but it wouldn't make sense to cite the window's *motive* for being broken ("It was despondent and decided to commit suicide"). For this reason, whenever 'because' is used in connection with events that are not actions, we can be certain that a cause is being cited, rather than a motive. But when the event is an action, no simple formal criterion can be given for deciding whether an explanation concerns cause or concerns motive. All we can say is that an explanation concerns *cause* if it is a mechanical or scientific explanation, and that it concerns *motive* if it involves the agent's own reason for performing the action in question.

A statement containing the word 'because' as indicating a *motive* is to be treated like any other statement of motive.

Translating Causal Statements

A statement to the effect that one event caused, or causes, or will cause, another event is called a *causal statement*. While causal statements are not truth-functional compounds, many of them can be treated in truth-functional logic by the process of "distillation" presented in this appendix.

First, it is necessary to distinguish between *general* and *particular* causal statements. Some causal statements are to the effect that events (in general) of a certain kind cause events (in general) of a certain kind. Examples are such statements as:

11. Speeding causes accidents.
12. Vitamin deficiency causes rickets.
13. Cooling distilled water below 32°F. causes it to freeze.
14. Smoking causes lung cancer.

These are general causal statements. However, some causal statements are to the effect that a *particular* event is (or was, or will be) the cause of some other particular event. Examples of such statements are:

15. Jones got cancer from smoking.
16. I ran over him because my brakes failed.
17. Percy's hitting Evangeline caused the bruise on her arm.
18. The freeze last night caused the pipes to burst.
19. Overeating is ruining Clyde's health.
20. Drinking this glass of water will make your hiccups go away.

These are particular causal statements. At the level of truth-functional logic, nothing can be done with *general* causal statements except to treat them as simple statements. (Any further treatment requires techniques of quantifier logic.) But particular causal statements are truth-dependent compounds and allow of something more satisfactory.

A particular causal statement contains a part which describes the cause and a part which describes the effect. We may call these the "cause clause" and the "effect clause," respectively. As the examples above illustrate, these clauses are not always expressed *as* clauses; sometimes they are phrased as gerunds, and so on (cf. Appendix A). But in any case, each of the two clauses can be regarded as expressing a proposition. Referring back to the previous examples, these propositions can be presented as:

CAUSE CLAUSE	EFFECT CLAUSE
15. Jones smoked.	Jones got cancer.
16. My brakes failed.	I ran over him.
17. Percy hit Evangeline.	Evangeline has a bruised arm.
18. It froze last night.	The pipes burst.
19. Clyde overeats.	Clyde's health is suffering.
20. You will drink this glass of water.	Your hiccups will go away.

A particular causal statement in either the *past* tense or the *present* tense has, as products, the propositions expressed by both of its clauses. This is because the causal statement cannot be true unless both of those propositions are also true; for example, it cannot be true that I ran over him *because* my brakes failed unless it is true both that I ran over him *and* that my brakes failed. Similarly, it can't be true that overeating is ruining Clyde's health unless it is true that both Clyde overeats and Clyde's health is suffering. Hence, we can say that when a particular causal statement is in the past or present tense, a product of the statement is the conjunction of the propositions expressed by its two clauses. And since it is always permissible to treat a statement as its own conjoint product, the examples above can be translated as:

15a. (Jones smoked · Jones got cancer) · Jones got cancer from smoking

16a. (My brakes failed · I ran over him) ·
     I ran over him because my brakes failed

17a. (Percy hit Evangeline · Evangeline has a bruise on her arm) ·
Percy's hitting Evangeline caused the bruise on her arm

18a. (It froze last night · the pipes burst) ·
the freeze last night caused the pipes to burst

19a. (Clyde overeats · Clyde's health is suffering) ·
overeating is ruining Clyde's health

Particular causal statements in the *future* tense are different from these,
in that they do not assert that the states of affairs mentioned in the two
clauses actually are occurring or have occurred, nor even that they actually
will occur in the future. Future-tense causal statements are quite strongly
hypothetical in nature, and part of what they assert is that *if* the state of affairs
described in the cause clause comes to pass *then* the state of affairs described
in the effect clause will also come to pass. The conjunction of the propositions expressed by the two clauses is not a product of the causal statement;
rather, the *conditional* whose antecedent is expressed by the cause clause
and whose consequent is expressed by the effect clause is a product of the
causal statement; the conditional

20a. You will drink this glass of water $\supset$ your hiccups will go away

is a product of (20). It is not *equivalent* to (20), since (20) asserts a causal
relationship between the two states of affairs, and causal relationships are
not truth-functional. Nevertheless, it is a part of what the causal statement
asserts. And so, a conjoint product of (20) is

20b. (You will drink this glass of water $\supset$ your hiccups will go away) ·
drinking this glass of water will make your hiccups go away

In general, when p is a particular causal proposition in the future tense, and
c and e are its clauses, a conjoint product of p will be

$$(c \supset e) \cdot p$$

and every such causal statement can be translated as its own conjoint product—that is, as a conditional (distilled out as indicated) conjoined with the
original causal statement.

Exercises

Translate and abbreviate each of the following.

1. Percy drives recklessly.
2. Willie was run over by a Porsche.
3. Harvey lives in a yellow brick house in Los Angeles.
4. The zoo owns a large pygmy hippopotamus.
5. He was awarded a medal for heroism in battle.
6. The Aztecs offered human sacrifices to placate the serpent god.
7. Leroy was fired from his job as a high-school janitor for incompetence.
8. I ran over him because I didn't like his looks.

9. I ran over him because my brakes failed.
10. The window is broken because Charlie threw a brick through it.
11. Drinking all that beer caused your hiccups.
12. Smoking two packs a day is ruining your lungs.
13. Your being vaccinated will prevent your catching smallpox.
14. His stupidity makes them insult him.
15. A sugar-free diet and good hygiene will result in fewer dental cavities for you.
16. Frequent applications of this tonic will cure your dandruff.
17. Fertilizer made my roses grow better.
18. Shooting or stabbing a person causes severe injuries.

The cases discussed above exemplify some of the more common sorts of non-truth-functional statements capable of being treated by this method. But the method itself is quite general. A statement which, by itself, is truth-functionally simple, may have certain products (that is, may entail certain propositions) which it is important to bring out for some logical purpose or other. In such a case it is proper to treat (and translate) the statement as the conjunction of itself with those of its products that are relevant to the particular purpose. Another application of this same principle is found in Appendix E.

appendix D

PUNCTUATION

Although the system of punctuation employed in this book is the one most widely used by practitioners of formal logic, a number of other systems exist. Their purpose is, for the most part, to reduce (sometimes to zero) the number of parentheses occurring in logical formulae, on the grounds that a thicket of parentheses makes a formula difficult to read.

To understand the general principles underlying these systems of punctuation, it is necessary to have some grasp of the notion of "scope" as it occurs in formal logic. Stated briefly, the **scope** of an operator in a formula is the amount of the formula it operates upon. For example, when a tilde '∼' occurs in a formula, its scope is the amount of the formula which it negates; when a dot '·' occurs in a formula, its scope is the amount of the formula which it conjoins; and so on.

Our truth-functional operators '∼', '∨', '·', '⊃', '≡' consist of one **unary** operator (the tilde) and four **binary** operators (the wedge, dot, horseshoe, and triple bar). The difference is that a unary operator operates upon a *single* formula (for example, to negate it), while a binary operator operates upon a *pair* of formulae (for example, to conjoin them). In our notation, the unary operator is placed before (to the left of) the formula it is to operate upon, and the binary operators are placed between the formulae they are to operate upon. Thus, the unary operator has a scope going away from it in only one direction, while a binary operator has scopes going away from it in both directions: the tilde negates something to its right, never anything to its left; the dot conjoins something on its left with something on its right.* We can therefore speak of the "left scope" and the "right scope" of a binary operator: the left scope of a dot (for instance) is the amount of the formula to its left which it conjoins to something on its right; the right scope of the dot is the amount of the formula to its right which it conjoins to something on its left;

---

*Quantifiers and descriptors are also unary operators.

the dot conjoins its left scope to its right scope. For example, in

    1. $A \lor (B \cdot (C \lor D))$

the left scope of the dot is 'B' and the right scope of the dot is '$(C \lor D)$'.

Whenever one operator lies within the scope of another, the second is said to **scope over** the first. Thus, in (1), the first wedge scopes over the dot, and the dot scopes over the second wedge. Similarly, in

    2. $(\sim A \lor B)$

the wedge scopes over the tilde; while in

    3. $\sim(A \lor B)$

the tilde scopes over the wedge. The purpose of logical punctuation is to show, in the case of formulae with more than one operator, which of them scope over which of the others.

When parenthesis punctuation is used absolutely rigorously, every formula that contains an operator (that is, any formula other than a single letter) will also contain a set of parentheses enclosing its scope, so that we can say: every mated pair of parentheses encloses a scope, and every scope (except for single letters) is enclosed by a mated pair of parentheses. With rigorous parenthesis punctuation, the negation of the proposition 'A' is written as

    4. $(\sim A)$

and the negation of '$(\sim A)$' is written as

    5. $(\sim(\sim A))$

and so on. Similarly, the conjunction of the two propositions 'A' and 'B' will be written as

    6. $(A \cdot B)$

and so on. If we then define a "scope" generally as "either a single letter or a formula enclosed by a mated pair of parentheses," it is easy to define the scope of an operator: The scope of a unary operator is the first scope to its right plus the operator itself;* the left scope of a binary operator is the first scope to its left and the right scope of a binary operator is the first scope to its right; and the total scope of a binary operator will consist of its left scope, plus the operator itself, plus its right scope. However, as the examples above show, absolute rigor of this sort leads to a multiplication of parentheses beyond necessity. Consequently, it is standard practice to accept (as we have done in this book) two deviations from absolute rigor which do not lead to ambiguity:

    a. The outer parentheses enclosing an *entire* formula may be eliminated.
    b. Parentheses between unary operators (and also the mates of those parentheses) may be eliminated.

---

*It is standard practice to regard an operator as part of its own scope. This is a mere formalism and does *not* mean that the operator is regarded as operating upon itself.

Convention (a) says, for example, that (6) above may be written as

    6a. $A \cdot B$

and convention (b) says, for example, that (5) may be written as

    5a. $(\sim \sim A)$

which, by convention (a), may also be written as

    5b. $\sim \sim A$

Parenthesis punctuation, even as modified by (a) and (b), has the advantage of making it easy to say, and relatively easy to see, what the scopes of the various operators in a formula are. But it still leaves a great many parentheses to contend with; thus logicians often find it convenient to introduce certain further modifications. Some of the more common ones are given below.

Grouping Conventions

One of the simplest modifications of parenthesis punctuation involves the introduction of a "grouping convention" to eliminate some of the parentheses from certain (not all) formulae. Since grouping is also called "Association," these are also called "Associative conventions." One of the most widely used is the following:

    c. If a formula contains several occurrences of a single binary operator, and no other operators, then unless parentheses indicate otherwise the formula is to be read as *grouping to the left* (Rule of Association to the Left).

Perhaps an easier, though slightly less formal, formulation of this convention is:

    c'. If a formula contains several occurrences of a single binary operator, and no other operators, then unless parentheses indicate otherwise the left scope of each operator is all of the formula to the left of the operator.

This means, for example, that the formula

    7. $(((A \cdot B) \cdot C) \cdot D) \cdot E$

may be written simply as

    7a. $A \cdot B \cdot C \cdot D \cdot E$

Since, by convention (c), the left scope of the first dot in (7a) is 'A'; the left scope of the second dot is '$A \cdot B$'; and so on, precisely as set out in (7). Similarly,

    8. $((P \supset Q) \supset R) \supset S$

can be written simply as

    8a. $P \supset Q \supset R \supset S$

at a considerable saving in parentheses. As should be obvious from these examples, when we know the left scope of every operator, we can easily determine the total scope of every operator, since when one operator is dominated (scoped over) by another, the scope of the subordinate one ends at the dominant one. (For example, in (8) the first horseshoe is dominated by the second horseshoe; and the (right) scope of the first horseshoe extends up to, but not beyond, the second horseshoe.) An important part of (c) is that grouping indicated by parentheses has precedence over grouping indicated by the convention. Thus,

9. $(P \supset (Q \supset R)) \supset S$

can still be written, in terms of convention (c), as

9a. $P \supset (Q \supset R) \supset S$

since, in (9a), the left scope of the first horseshoe is—by (c)—all of the formula to its left; the scope of the second horseshoe is established by the parentheses; and the left scope of the third horseshoe is—again by (c)—all of the formula to its left.

Convention (c) may also be applied to formulae which are parts of larger formulae; for example,

10. $((P \supset Q) \supset R) \cdot \sim S$

may, by (c), be written simply as

10a. $(P \supset Q \supset R) \cdot \sim S$

An even simpler grouping convention, not very widely used, is the following:

d. A formula is to be read as grouping to the left, except as parentheses indicate otherwise.

Using this convention, for example, we can write the formula

11. $((A \cdot B) \vee C) \supset D$

simply as

11a. $A \cdot B \vee C \supset D$

and the formula

12. $(A \cdot (B \vee C)) \supset D$

simply as

12a. $A \cdot (B \vee C) \supset D$

and so on. A similar and widely used convention governing unary operators is

e. Unless parentheses indicate otherwise, the scope of a unary operator is the first letter to its right and nothing more.

If we used (d) and (e) together, for example, the formula

   13. $((\sim A \cdot B) \lor \sim C) \supset D$

could be written without parentheses as

   13a. $\sim A \cdot B \lor \sim C \supset D$

but the formula

   14. $(\sim (A \cdot B) \lor \sim C) \supset D$

would be written as

   14a. $\sim (A \cdot B) \lor \sim C \supset D$

and the formula

   15. $\sim ((A \cdot B) \lor \sim C) \supset D$

would be written as

   15a. $\sim (A \cdot B \lor \sim C) \supset D$

Dominance Conventions

A different type of modification of parenthesis punctuation involves assigning a "pecking order" of dominance to the various operators so that, unless parentheses indicate otherwise, one kind of operator will automatically scope over another kind. One of the simplest of these is

   f. Unless parentheses indicate otherwise, conjunction is subordinate to the other binary operations.*

Under this convention, for example,

   16. $A \lor B \cdot C$

is a way of writing

   16a. $A \lor (B \cdot C)$

without using parentheses. But one still needs parentheses to write

   17. $(A \lor B) \cdot C$

or the like.†

Various conventions of this type are used. The most complex, and the most complete, involves a total ordering of the operators as to dominance; a typical example is

---

*Cf. Quine, *Methods of Logic*, pp. 23-28. Quine's notation differs slightly from ours.
†Similar conventions are often used in mathematics, for example the convention in algebra that addition dominates multiplication, so that $x \cdot y + z$ means $(x \cdot y) + z$ rather than $x \cdot (y + z)$.

*g. Unless parentheses indicate otherwise:

(i) '≡' scopes over all other operators;

(ii) '⊃' scopes over all other operators except '≡';

(iii) '∨' scopes over all other operators except '≡' and '⊃';

(iv) '·' scopes over '~'.

Using this convention, for example, the formula

18. $\sim A \supset B \cdot C \equiv B \vee \sim D \cdot A$

will mean

18a. $(\sim A \supset (B \cdot C)) \equiv (B \vee (\sim D \cdot A))$

Complete dominance conventions of this sort are not as widely used as some others, since they are less perspicuous and harder to read.

Dot Punctuation

The foregoing are all modifications of basic parenthesis punctuation. But not all systems of punctuation are this way. As we have already said, the purpose of a system of logical punctuation is to indicate which operators in a formula scope over which of the others. And it is not a matter of necessity that we use parentheses for this. For example, we might very well decide to indicate the dominant operator in a formula simply by underlining it. Using this system of punctuation, the underlined operator in a formula would scope over all the others, so that the formula

19. $(A \cdot B) \supset (C \vee D)$

which is written with parenthesis punctuation, could be written with underline punctuation as

19a. $A \cdot B \supseteq C \vee D$

In (19a) the underline beneath the horseshoe indicates that the horseshoe scopes over both the dot and the wedge—that is, that the left scope of the horseshoe is the whole conjunction '$A \cdot B$' and the right scope of the horseshoe is the whole disjunction '$C \vee D$'. We could explain our system of punctuation quite clearly by saying: an underlined operator scopes over any operator that is not underlined.

However, this simple system of underline punctuation is of limited usefulness. For example, it gives us no way of writing

20. $A \supset (B \vee (C \cdot D))$

without using parentheses. If we write it as

20a. $A \supseteq B \vee C \cdot D$

---

*Cf. Elliott Mendelson, *Introduction to Mathematical Logic*, pp. 19-20. Mendelson also uses the Rule of Association to the Left.

it is ambiguous as to whether the wedge dominates the dot or vice versa. And if we write it as

   20b. $A \supseteq B \underline{\vee} C \cdot D$

so as to avoid that ambiguity, it becomes ambiguous as to whether the horseshoe dominates the wedge or vice versa. The obvious way to overcome this is by increasing the number of underlines beneath the operator of greatest scope, stating our rule as: An operator scopes over all operators with fewer underlines.* (20) can then be written unambiguously, with underline punctuation, as

   20c. $A \underline{\underline{\supseteq}} B \underline{\vee} C \cdot D$

Though underline punctuation would be cumbersome, it would be perfectly workable. For example,

   21. $(((A \supset B) \vee \sim(C \vee D)) \cdot \sim B) \supset (A \vee D)$

could be written, without parentheses, as

   21a. $A \supset B \underline{\vee} \sim C \vee D \cdot \underline{\underline{\;}} \sim B \underline{\underline{\supseteq}} A \vee D$

This illustrates an important fact: It is possible to have an adequate system of punctuation which consists simply in attaching recognizable marks to the operators in a formula to signal their relative order of dominance. The same job could be done by attaching subscript numerals to the operators, with the understanding that an operator with a higher number scopes over those with lower ones. By this method, (21) would be written as

   21b. $A \supset_0 B \vee_2 \sim_1 \quad C \vee_0 D \cdot_3 \sim_0 \quad B \supset_4 A \vee_0 \quad D$

Neither of these systems of punctuation has actually been used; but one quite similar to them has. Instead of numerals or underlines, it employs various numbers of dots, inserted alongside the operator, to indicate its scope on that side.† The general principle behind dot punctuation is that if an operator has a certain number of punctuation dots on its left side, it scopes over all operators to its left having fewer dots; and similarly for dots and operators on its right side. Thus, if an operator has a certain number of punctuation dots by its left side, its left scope does not stop until it comes either to a greater number of dots, or to the end of the formula; and similarly for the right side. For example, the difference between

   22. $(A \vee B) \supset C$

and

   23. $A \vee (B \supset C)$

shows up, using dot punctuation, as the difference between

   22a. $A \vee B . \supset C$

---

*To be precise, the rule should be: The scope of an operator extends up to, but not beyond, an operator with a greater number of underlines.
†The punctuation system explained here is that of Whitehead and Russell, *Principia Mathematica*, Vol. I, pp. 9–11. It continues to be a widely-used system.

and

23a. $A \lor . B \supset C$

In (22a) the dot to the left of the horseshoe indicates that its left scope includes all operators with less than one dot—that is, the whole disjunction; in (23a) the dot to the right of the wedge indicates that its right scope includes all operators with less than one dot—that is, the whole conditional. Similarly,

24. $(A \lor B) \supset (C \lor D)$

is written, using dot punctuation, as

24a. $A \lor B . \supset . C \lor D$

while

25. $((A \lor B) \supset C) \lor D$

will be written, using dot punctuation, as

25a. $A \lor B . \supset C : \lor D$

and

26. $(A \lor (B \supset C)) \lor D$

will be written as

26a. $A . \lor . B \supset C : \lor : D$

or, even more simply, as

26b. $A \lor . B \supset C : \lor D$

The only difference between (26a) and (26b) is that the former has more punctuation than it really needs. It should be obvious that (26b) is fully punctuated and completely unambiguous. The left scope of the first wedge is simply 'A'; and since there is one dot to its right, its right scope includes the (dotless) horseshoe but stops at the two dots at the left of the second wedge. The scope of the dotless horseshoe is confined by the single dot on one side and the double dot on the other. The left scope of the second wedge extends over both the dotless horseshoe and the single-dotted wedge; and its right scope is simply 'D'. The number of dots may be increased as needed; for example,

27. $(((A \lor B) \supset C) \lor D) \equiv E$

will be written as

27a. $A \lor B . \supset C : \lor D . : \equiv E$

and

28. $((((A \lor B) \supset C) \lor D) \equiv E) \supset F$

will be written as

28a. $A \lor B . \supset C : \lor D . : \equiv E : : \supset F$

and so on.

A minor complication in dot punctuation results from the fact that the dot is also used as a conjunctive operator. Thus, when a punctuation dot is placed alongside an operator dot, there is no way to tell which is which, and so no way to tell whether the right scope or the left scope is being indicated. This problem is solved by stipulating that punctuation dots added to operator dots set the scope in *both* directions. Thus, for example,

29. $(A \lor B) \cdot (C \lor D)$

will be written as

29a. $A \lor B : C \lor D$

It is perhaps needless to mention that the double dot in (29a) does not have the force of two punctuation dots but the force of one punctuation dot attached to an operator (the conjunctive operator). To illustrate this further,

30. $A \lor (B \cdot C)$

will be written as

30a. $A \lor . B \cdot C$

The punctuation dot to the right of the wedge indicates that its right scope extends over the dotless conjunctive operator. (The dot between the propositions '*B*' and '*C*' is clearly an operator, rather than a punctuation mark, since it is the only symbol between the two propositions.) Similarly,

31. $(A \cdot (B \lor C)) \cdot D$

will be written as

31a. $A : B \lor C :. D$

The classic system of dot punctuation does not avoid parentheses entirely; it uses them to indicate the scope of a negation-operator when this is more than a single letter. When dots and parentheses are mixed in this way, it is understood that an operator enclosed in a mated pair of parentheses does not scope beyond them, regardless of the number of dots it has. Thus, even using dot punctuation,

32. $\sim(A \lor (B \supset C))$

will still be written as

32a. $\sim(A \lor . B \supset C)$

But the use of parentheses in this way is an unnecessary frill; the same thing could be accomplished using only dots. For example, (32) can be written with no parentheses as

32b. $\sim : A \lor . B \supset C$

Similarly,

33. $\sim(A \cdot B) \supset \sim(C \lor D)$

can be written as

33a. $\sim : A \cdot B .: \supset : \sim . C \lor D$

and the negation of (33)—that is,

34. $\sim(\sim(A \cdot B) \supset \sim(C \vee D))$

can be written as

34a. $\sim :: \sim : A \cdot B .: \supset .: \sim . C \vee D$

and so on.

Dot Punctuation with Quantifiers

Since quantifiers are nothing more than unary operators, dot punctuation works for them the same way it does for negation. For example, the difference between

35. $(\exists x)Fx \cdot Gx$

and

36. $(\exists x)(Fx \cdot Gx)$

may be rendered with dot punctuation as the difference between (35) and

36a. $(\exists x). Fx \cdot Gx$

Similarly,

37. $(x)(Fx \supset Gx)$

will be rendered using dot punctuation as

37a. $(x). Fx \supset Gx$

and so on.

Polish Notation

We may entirely eliminate the need for punctuation marks by using a different symbolic system of notation. This notation, invented by the Polish logician Jan Łukasiewicz, is commonly referred to as "Polish Notation." In Polish notation certain capital letters are used as operator symbols, as follows:

Principia	Polish
$\sim$	N ("negation," "not")
$\vee$	A ("alternation")
$\supset$	C ("conditional")
$\cdot$	K ("konjunction")
$\equiv$	E ("equivalence")

Instead of writing binary compounds with the operator between the two components, in Polish notation we write the operator *first*, followed by the components in their proper order. Thus,

    1. $p \lor q$

will be written in Polish notation as

    1a. *Apq*

while

    2. $q \lor p$

will be written as

    2a. *Aqp*

and so on. The components to a binary operator are always the first two statements which follow it. Thus, there is never any need to use punctuation marks at all. For example, the difference between

    3. $p \cdot (q \lor r)$

and

    4. $(p \cdot q) \lor r$

is sustained in Polish notation as the difference between

    3a. *KpAqr*

and

    4a. *AKpqr*

Similarly,

    5. $(p \cdot q) \supset (r \lor \sim s)$

will be

    5a. *CKpqArNs*

and

    6. $p \cdot (q \supset \sim (r \lor s))$

will be

    6a. *KpCqNArs*

and so on.

In spite of its formal elegance, Polish notation has not gained wide acceptance by practitioners of applied logic because its formulae are rather difficult to read. Perhaps the easiest way to read them, at least at first, is after the manner of the exercises at the end of Chapter 3. For example, (3a) may be read as

    3b. The conjunction of p with the alternation of q and r

while (4a) can be read as

    4b. The alternation of the conjunction of p and q with r

(5a) can be read as

    5b. The conditional of the conjunction of p and q with the alternation of r and the negation of s

(6a) can be read as

    6b. The conjunction of p with the conditional of q and the negation of the alternation of r and s

and so on. In Polish notation, the dominant operator is always the first one in the formula.

In Polish notation, the universal quantifier is written as a capital letter pi followed by a variable, without parentheses, and the existential quantifier is written as a capital letter sigma followed by a variable, also without parentheses. Thus, what is expressed in standard Principia notation by

    7. $(x)Fx$

would be expressed in Polish notation as

    7a. ΠxFx

and what is expressed in Principia notation as

    8. $(\exists x)Gx$

would be expressed in Polish notation as

    8a. ΣxGx

Even with quantifiers, Polish notation requires no parentheses. For example, the difference between

    9. $(x)Fx \supset Gx$

and

    10. $(x)(Fx \supset Gx)$

is sustained in Polish notation as the difference between

    9a. $C\Pi xFxGx$

and

    10a. $\Pi xCFxGx$

Similarly, the difference between

    11. $(\exists x)Fx \cdot Gx$

and

    12. $(\exists x)(Fx \cdot Gx)$

is preserved as the difference between

    11a. $K\Sigma xFxGx$

and

    12a. $\Sigma xKFxGx$

Exercises

1. Rewrite the arguments in Exercises III, Ch. 11, using dot punctuation.
2. Rewrite the arguments in Exercises II, Ch. 12, using dot punctuation.
3. Rewrite the arguments in Exercises III, Ch. 11, using Polish notation.
4. Rewrite the arguments in Exercises II, Ch. 12, using Polish notation.
5. Rewrite the formulae in Exercises II, Ch. 20, using dot punctuation.
6. Rewrite the formulae in Exercises II, Ch. 20, using Polish notation.
7. Translate the arguments in Exercises X, Ch. 22, using dot punctuation.
8. Translate the arguments in Exercises X, Ch. 22, using Polish notation.

appendix E

CONDITIONALS AND MATERIAL
CONDITIONALS: AN ALTERNATIVE
APPROACH

The practice of translating natural-language conditionals ("if-thens") as material conditionals ("MCs") for purposes of formal logic has frequently been criticized, but nearly always for the wrong reasons. The reasons usually cited are the "Paradoxes of Material Implication": that an MC with a true consequent is true irrespective of its antecedent, and one with a false antecedent is true irrespective of its consequent. It is argued, for instance, that this interpretation requires us to give the value "true" to anomalous conditionals whose antecedent and consequent have absolutely no connection with each other, such as

    1. If the moon is a planet then Junior wrecked the car.

or

    2. If there is extraterrestrial life then $2 + 2 = 4$.

whereas there at least ought to be *some* connection between the elements of a conditional before it is counted as true.

But this line of criticism, if it were valid, would cut against all of truth-functional logic and not merely against MCs. For if it were required that there be some connection between the elements of a conditional, some connection likewise ought to be required between the elements of a conjunction or a disjunction; yet truth-functional logic recognizes both the following anomalous cases as true:

    3. The moon is not a planet and Chicago is in Illinois.
    4. Either there is extraterrestrial life or $2 + 2 = 4$.

If the MC interpretation of if-thens is to be rejected on grounds of potential anomaly, the whole of propositional logic should be rejected for the same reason. But, of course, anomaly isn't logical grounds for rejecting anything, since anomaly is logically harmless and hence logically irrelevant.

A second, but related, line of objection is that the MC interpretation assigns the value "true" to certain *misleading* conditionals, thereby *implying* (in some sense of the word) things that are false. For example, under the MC interpretation,

 5. If the earth is flat then Columbus was right.

counts as true, since its consequent is true (Columbus believed the earth to be round, and it is). Yet anyone hearing (5) would take it to imply that Columbus believed the earth to be flat, which is false. But it may be replied that this sort of "implication" is a matter of psychology, wholly irrelevant to pure logic, and furthermore that it too would cut against the whole of truthfunctional logic. For a precisely similar psychological implication is carried by the conjunction

 6. Lincoln died and Booth cried.

—namely, that the crying was in response to the dying, which is no doubt false.

An objection which is closer to the mark is that, whereas MCs have only one way of being false (by having a true antecedent and a false consequent), if-thens have that way and other ways as well (intuitively, 'If he falls off the cliff, he will plunge upwards' is false irrespective of the actual truth-values of its elements). Thus, MCs do not duplicate the truth-conditions for if-thens, and so the practice of interpreting the one as the other is faulty.

A standard line of response is that the accusation is true but logically unimportant for the following reasons. Let us call a statement p **logically stronger** than a statement q just in case p entails q but not vice versa. Then the accusation is that if-thens are logically stronger than their counterpart MCs, and the defense is that it is always logically permissible to proceed from a stronger statement to a weaker one. Even though MCs do not have *the same* truth-conditions as if-thens, it is permissible to proceed from the latter to the former via the standard canon of translation, since this is just a case of going from stronger statements to weaker ones, which is fully admitted by the principles of logic.

But there is an important misstep in this defense. It is certainly true that an MC is weaker, in our sense, than its corresponding if-then, just because *the* falsity condition for MCs is *a* falsity condition for if-thens. But it is not true that every case of going from if-then to MC is a case of going from a stronger statement to a weaker one. This is because not all the modes of statement composition are "transparent" with respect to logical strength and weakness. In certain contexts, and specifically in certain truth-functional contexts, replacing a stronger statement with a weaker one will effectively convert the larger statement into one stronger than the original, in violation of the principles of logic. The "positions" in which this occurs are those of **negate** and of **antecedent**. Within a negation, replacing the negate by a weaker statement produces a *stronger* negation than the original (since if p entails q, then $\sim q$ entails $\sim p$). Similarly, within a conditional,* replacing the antecedent by a weaker statement produces a stronger conditional than the original (since if p entails q then, for example, $(q \supset r)$ entails $(p \supset r)$). The standard canon of translation makes no distinction between primary if-thens and if-thens which are components of some larger statement; therefore it sanctions this logical misstep.

The results show up in the following two sorts of cases. In an election year we might very well expect to hear someone say, in the course of a political discussion:

7. It's false that if a Conservative wins there will be an increase in welfare programs.

without supposing the speaker to be either expecting or predicting a Conservative victory. But if, following the standard canon, we translate (7) as

8. $\sim$ (A Conservative will win the election $\supset$ there will be an increase in welfare programs)

we get something logically equivalent to

9. A Conservative will win the election and there won't be an increase in welfare programs.

which is *not* what was asserted in (7). Similarly, we can imagine someone asserting, in an appropriate context,

10. If Smith was convicted only if he was guilty, then justice was served.

without his either believing or meaning

11. If Smith was acquitted then justice was served.

But if (10) is translated in accordance with the standard canon, the result is

12. (Smith was convicted $\supset$ he was guilty) $\supset$ justice was served

which, assuming non-conviction to be the same as acquittal, is demonstrably equivalent to

13. (Smith was acquitted $\supset$ justice was served) $\cdot$ (Smith was guilty $\supset$ justice was served)

whose English counterpart is

14. If Smith was acquitted then justice was served, and if Smith was guilty then justice was served.

Since (10) can be asserted without any commitment to (11) or (14), it follows that the standard canon is faulty.

The question then is how best to correct it. We may begin with the following set of facts. If a statement p entails a statement q, then p is logically equivalent to the conjunction of itself with q—that is, to $(p \cdot q)$. Since an if-then entails

---

*More precisely, a conditional with contingent antecedent and consequent.

its corresponding MC, an if-then is equivalent to the conjunction of itself with its corresponding MC: 'If A then B' is logically equivalent to '(If A then B) · $(A \supset B)$'. Let us call this formula the **conjunctive product** of the if-then.

Since if-thens are logically equivalent to their conjunctive products, no changes in strength or weakness can result from replacing the one with the other, regardless of the context. And so, a possible modification in the standard canon is the following:

> MODIFICATION A. Translate each natural-language conditional statement as its own conjunctive product.

If we *abbreviate* (not translate) natural-language conditional operators as the new symbol '$\rightarrow$', so that 'If A then B' is abbreviated as '$A \rightarrow B$', then Modification A can be represented symbolically as:

> Translate 'if p then q' as '$(p \rightarrow q) \cdot (p \supset q)$'.

This modification will effectively rule out the earlier sorts of missteps, since the arrow formula is truth-functionally simple ("atomic") and so can't be manipulated by any of the rules governing MCs in standard logic. For example, the invalid inference from (7) to (9) will be avoided because Modification A no longer renders that argument as

$$\sim(C \supset W) \qquad / \therefore \ C \cdot \sim W$$

but rather as

$$\sim((C \rightarrow W) \cdot (C \supset W)) \qquad / \therefore \ C \cdot \sim W$$

whose truth-functional invalidity is revealed by the following assignment of truth-values to its elements:

C	W	$C \rightarrow W$
F	T	F

Similarly, Modification A renders the argument from (10) to (14) not as

$$(C \supset G) \supset J \qquad / \therefore \ (\sim C \supset J) \cdot (G \supset J)$$

but rather as

$$([(C \rightarrow G) \cdot (C \supset G)] \rightarrow J) \cdot ([(C \rightarrow G) \cdot (C \supset G)] \supset J)$$
$$/ \therefore \ [(\sim C \rightarrow J) \cdot (\sim C \supset J)] \cdot [(G \rightarrow J) \cdot (G \supset J)]$$

whose truth-functional invalidity is shown by the assignment:

J	$\sim C \rightarrow J$	$[(C \rightarrow G) \cdot (C \supset G)] \rightarrow J$
T	F	T

(Keep in mind that every formula with the arrow as "dominant operator" is truth-functionally *simple*.)

However, as plausible as Modification A may sound, it is unacceptable in practice. It is far too stringent. If we adopt Modification A, most arguments with conditional conclusions will turn out to be unprovable within standard logic, including those with such well-established forms as OC. For example,

> If A then B
> If B then C
> $\therefore$ If A then C

will abbreviate and translate by Modification A as

> $(A \longrightarrow B) \cdot (A \supset B)$
> $(B \longrightarrow C) \cdot (B \supset C)$
> $\therefore (A \longrightarrow C) \cdot (A \supset C)$

But the first conjunct of the conclusion cannot be derived from the premises by standard logic, and the argument is shown truth-functionally invalid by the assignment:

A	B	C	$A \rightarrow B$	$A \rightarrow C$	$B \rightarrow C$
F	F	F	T	F	T

For the same reason, most other inferences to if-then conclusions will be formally impossible under Modification A.

Let us refer to the fallacy involved in going from (7) to (9) as **Misnegation**, and to that involved in going from (10) to (14) as **Misdistribution**. Since all positions in truth-functional logic except those of negate and antecedent are "transparent" with respect to logical strength and weakness, the practice of rendering if-thens as MCs can cause logical trouble only in these two positions—that is, only through misnegation or misdistribution. Therefore, the standard canon can be applied wherever it will not lead to either of these fallacies.

A position within the scope of a single negation-operator is a "reversal" position, since when that position is taken over by a weaker proposition the resulting compound becomes stronger, and vice versa. On the other hand, a position within the scope of a pair of negation operators, being the reversal of a reversal position, is a "non-reversal" position. Similarly, a position within the left (antecedent) scope of a single conditional operator is a reversal position, while a position within the left scope of two conditional operators is a non-reversal position. In general, a position lying within an even number of negation scopes or antecedent scopes or both is a non-reversal position, while one within an odd number of such scopes is a reversal position. The inferences permissible under Modification A may therefore be increased, without logical hazard, by altering it to

> Modification B. Translate each natural-language conditional within a reversal position as its own conjunctive product; translate all others as the corresponding MC.

The canon thus modified will diminish the number of provable natural-language arguments, but not as drastically as Modification A. It will block the provability of arguments requiring a step of misnegation or misdistribution; but as far as I can tell, it will block only those arguments. I have no formal proof of this latter point at present. If Modification **B** is followed, '**P** unless **O**' must be translated as "$\sim$ **Q** $\supset$ **P**", rather than as '**P** V **O**'.

appendix F

SOME AMBIGUOUS OPERATORS

Several phrases called "conditional operators" in the early chapters of this book are not completely regular in their behavior. Sometimes they are conditional operators and sometimes not. Examples are 'in case', 'just in case', and 'if' (as distinct from 'if . . . then'). All of these have normal occurrences in sentences which are not plausibly to be translated as conditionals, or which are ambiguous as to whether they are conditionals or not.

Consider, for instance, the sentence

1. I'll take the umbrella with me, in case it rains.

If 'in case' is regarded as a conditional operator here, (1) will mean roughly the same thing as

1a. If it rains, I'll take the umbrella with me.

and it certainly is possible to express the same statement with these two sentences. However, (1) is capable of expressing another statement, in which 'in case' does not function as a conditional operator, but as an auxiliary introducing a subordinate clause which specifies some eventuality toward which, or against which, the action or state of affairs in the main clause is relevant. Construed in this way, (1) means the same as

1b. I'll take the umbrella with me, in case it should rain.

or perhaps

1c. I'll take the umbrella with me, to provide for the possibility of its raining.

Under this interpretation, we can say that 'in case' has its *auxiliary* sense rather than its *conditional* sense.

Not all sentences are ambiguous in the way (1) is. For example,

2. I'll take the umbrella with me, in case I want to poke something.

would unhesitatingly be understood to contain an auxiliary 'in case' rather than a conditional one.

The phrase 'just in case' can be ambiguous in the same way. Consider the following sentence, uttered to someone who is preparing to go for more refreshments:

3. I'll put in another couple of dollars, just in case you don't have enough.

This could be understood as a biconditional, as an offer to donate another couple of dollars if, but only if, there isn't enough already. But it could also be understood as an unconditional offer of a couple more dollars, to provide for the possibility that there may not be enough already. Understood in the first way, 'just in case' is working as a biconditional operator; understood in the second way, it is working as an auxiliary. (3) is ambiguous as to which way 'just in case' is working; but

4. I had better take along an extra pair of shoes, just in case I ruin these.

is unmistakably an example of the "auxiliary" sense of 'just in case'; and

5. Smith will get his promotion just in case he manages to secure the Johnson contract.

is an unmistakable example of its "biconditional" sense.

The little word 'if' also has its "auxiliary" use as well as its "conditional" use. An example of the former occurs in

6. There is beer in the refrigerator, if you want some.

which is hardly to be construed as meaning

6a. You want some ⊃ There is beer in the refrigerator

but rather means something more along the lines of

6b. There is beer in the refrigerator (and so the eventuality of your wanting some is provided for).

Other examples of this auxiliary use of 'if' are

7. If you need razor blades, the drugstore is open until 10 o'clock.
8. The car keys are on the table, if you're going out.
9. My old umbrella is still good, if yours has a hole in it.

None of these can plausibly be construed as a conditional. Rather, in each case the main clause is asserted unconditionally with the auxiliary "if" clause providing additional commentary (for example, to indicate the reason for asserting the main clause in the first place). A related auxiliary use of 'if' occurs in statements such as

10. He likes his whiskey a lot, if you know what I mean.
11. I went to Cincinnati last week, if you remember.
12. If you recall, he said the key would be under the mat.

There can be no formal or grammatical criterion for distinguishing "conditional" uses of these phrases from "auxiliary" uses. They may be distinguished semantically on the basis of whether the main clause is or is not being asserted categorically (unconditionally), with the auxiliary clause being an added flourish. For example, when (1) contains an auxiliary use of the operator, it asserts

1d. I'll take the umbrella with me.

unconditionally, the 'in case it rains' providing additional commentary rather than setting a condition on (1d). Similarly, (4) asserts unconditionally that

4a. I had better take along an extra pair of shoes.

with the 'just in case' clause providing an explanation. Again, (6) asserts that

6c. There is beer in the refrigerator.

whether anybody happens to want beer or not. The 'if you want some' clause does not give a condition for there being beer in the refrigerator; it merely indicates why you might be interested in the fact of beer in the refrigerator. And so on for the other cases.

Since in the "auxiliary" cases what is really asserted is the main clause of the sentence, it is appropriate to treat such sentences logically as if there were nothing to them but the main clause; that is, for purposes of logic, drop the auxiliary clause and proceed in the appropriate way from there.

Since auxiliary-containing sentences of the present sort virtually never occur as components of larger sentences, it is also permissible to treat them as conditionals if you wish to do so. It is logically harmless to treat 'Q' as '$P \supset Q$', since the latter is weaker than the former, and it is nearly always permissible (though not necessarily desirable) to treat a stronger statement as a weaker one.*

---

*For exceptions to this principle, see Appendix E.

appendix G

VALIDITY AND INVALIDITY

The standard definition of validity—"An argument is valid if and only if it is impossible for its premisses to be true and its conclusion false"—is completely general and says nothing about logical form. It does not say that the impossibility must be the result of formal considerations, or that it must be demonstrable by this or that set of formal rules. It recognizes, as we must, that there are valid arguments whose validity cannot be demonstrated by any formal logical system so far developed, the one in §8.1 being a prime example.

An argument is "formally valid" if it can be proven valid by some system of formal rules, such as those of truth-functional logic. If an argument can be proven formally valid by the rules of truth-functional logic, that shows it to be "valid" in the unrestricted sense: if its premisses are true, its conclusion cannot be false. When this happens, we can say that it is valid *because* of its truth-functional form: its truth-functional form guarantees its validity. The procedures of truth-functional logic allow us to assess whether or not a given argument has a truth-functional form which guarantees validity. If it has such a form, that proves it to be valid. But if it does not have such a form, that does not prove it to be *in*valid. An argument might very well lack a validating truth-functional form but still be valid for some other reason—for example, because it has some type of validating form other than a truth-functional one, or simply because of the semantic relationships between its premisses and conclusion.

The most that truth-functional logic can do toward proving *in*validity is to show that an argument has no validating truth-functional form. Thus, we call this "truth-functional invalidity," since it is the closest that truth-functional logic can come to proving invalidity. But for the reasons already mentioned, a proof that an argument is "truth-functionally invalid" is perfectly compatible with its being valid. For example, the argument

All humans are mortal
Smith is a human
∴ Smith is mortal

translates truth-functionally as

$$H$$
$$\underline{S}$$
$$\therefore M$$

and is shown "invalid" (truth-functionally invalid) by the assignment

H	S	M
T	T	F

but at the same time, the argument translates quantificationally as

$$(x)(Hx \supset Mx)$$
$$\underline{H\underline{s}}$$
$$\therefore M\underline{s}$$

which is valid, and may be proven valid by the procedures of quantifier logic.

But again, the most that quantifier logic can do toward proving *in*validity is to show that an argument has no validating quantificational form. Such a proof shows that the argument is "quantificationally invalid," since it is the closest that quantifier logic can come to proving invalidity. And, as before, a proof that an argument is quantificationally invalid is compatible with its being valid. For example, the argument

Some bachelors are wealthy
$$\overline{\therefore \text{ Some unmarried persons are wealthy}}$$

has the quantificational translation

$$(\exists x)(Bx \cdot Wx)$$
$$\overline{\therefore (\exists x)(\sim Mx \cdot Px \cdot Wx)}$$

and is shown quantificationally invalid by the assignment, for {a},

Ba	Ma	Pa	Wa
T	T	F	T

But the argument, though quantificationally invalid, is nevertheless valid because 'bachelor' *means* 'unmarried adult male person'.

In general, it is possible to demonstrate validity absolutely, but it is not possible to demonstrate invalidity absolutely—the most one can do is to prove invalidity relative to the formal system in which one is working, such as truth-functional invalidity or quantificational invalidity. Quite often this will be sufficient for all practical purposes. But if one wishes to be logically rigorous, one must recognize that a proof which is good enough for all practical purposes is still not absolute. So long as there is informal validity, there can be no formal proofs of absolute invalidity.

appendix H

TAUTOLOGOUS CONCLUSIONS, EXCESS PREMISSES, AND VALID ARGUMENTS

The equivalence of the two apparently disparate facts:

(a) An argument with a tautologous conclusion is valid, irrespective of the truth-value or logical status of its premisses.

(b) A valid argument remains valid if more premisses are added to it.

may be shown briefly as follows. Given any argument, it is possible to construct a material conditional, based upon that argument, as follows: its *antecedent* is the conjunction of all the argument's premisses, and its *consequent* is the argument's conclusion. This is called the argument's **corresponding conditional**. For example, the argument

(1) $P \supset \sim Q$
  P
  —————
  $\therefore \sim Q$

has as its corresponding conditional

(2) $((P \supset \sim Q) \cdot P) \supset \sim Q$

and the argument

(3) $\sim A \supset (B \lor C)$
  $C \supset D$
  $\sim D$
  —————
  $\therefore A \lor B$

has as its corresponding conditional

(4) $((\sim A \supset (B \lor C)) \cdot (C \supset D) \cdot \sim D) \supset (A \lor B)$

Similarly, given any material conditional it is possible to construct a corresponding argument, whose premiss is the antecedent of the conditional and whose conclusion is the consequent. The relationship between arguments and their corresponding conditionals is: the argument is valid if and only if the conditional is a tautology.* Now, every tautology can be expressed (in a sense that we shall not go into here) as a conditional. Thus, every valid argument corresponds to a tautology and every tautology corresponds to a valid argument.

By the Deduction Theorem (or "Principle of Exportation"), a set of n premisses $P_1, P_2, \ldots, P_n$ entails a conclusion C if and only if $P_1, P_n, \ldots, P_{n-1}$ entails $P_n \supset C$. That is, if a set of premisses entails a conclusion, then the set consisting of all but one of the original premisses entails the material conditional whose antecedent is the missing premiss and whose consequent is the original conclusion; and if a set of premisses entails a conditional, then the set consisting of all the original premisses plus the antecedent of the conditional will entail the consequent of the conditional. It follows from this that an argument with a tautology for a conclusion is equivalent to an argument whose premisses are those of the original argument *plus* the antecedent of the tautology, and whose conclusion is the consequent of the tautology. This latter argument will remain valid even when the original premisses are eliminated; thus they may be regarded as "excess premisses" in this argument. Insofar as the two arguments are equivalent, the one is valid if and only if the other is; that is, the one with the "excess premisses" is valid if and only if the one with the tautologous conclusion is valid. Hence, any logical system in which (a) is false will be a system in which either (b) is also false or the Deduction Theorem fails to hold.

However, the Deduction Theorem is the property of no particular logical system but embodies quite basic and fundamental logical principles. And the same is true for (b) above. Thus, any system in which (a) is false will be a system which diverges so radically from the basic and intuitive norms of reasoning that it could scarcely be accepted as a formal medium for the evaluation of arguments. Hence, no system in which (a) is false can be a satisfactory logical system.

---

*More precisely, a logical truth: tautology, quantifier-truth, or the like.

appendix I

NAMES OF THE INFERENCE
AND TRANSFORMATION RULES

Although the inference and transformation rules presented in this text are fairly standard ones, the *names* given many of them are new, adopted in the hope of making them more descriptive of the actual operations, and thus easier to remember than the names in standard usage. The purpose of this appendix is to help the reader to follow the terminology of other writers, by providing a list of the various names that have been used for these same rules.

In the listing below, the alternate name most widely used is given in parentheses, followed by other common names in no special order. Where nothing is given in parentheses, the name used in this book is the only one in common usage.

Absorption: $p \supset q$ transf $p \supset (p \cdot q)$

Biconditional Exchange: $p \equiv q$ transf $(p \supset q) \cdot (q \supset p)$ (material equivalence, $\equiv$-introduction/elimination, biconditional, law of biconditionals)

Cancellation: $p \lor q$, $\sim p \mid \therefore q$ (disjunctive syllogism, modus tollendo ponens, $\lor$-elimination, elimination of alternate, denying one alternant)

Conditional Exchange: $p \supset q$ transf $\sim p \lor q$ (material implication, law of conditional, implication)

Conjoining: $p, q \mid \therefore p \cdot q$ (conjunction, adjunction, $\cdot$-introduction)

Contraposition: $p \supset q$ transf $\sim q \supset \sim p$ (contraposition, transposition)

Dilemma: $(p \supset q), (r \supset s), p \lor r \mid \therefore q \lor s$ (constructive dilemma)

Disjoining: $p \mid \therefore p \lor q$ (addition, development, supplementation, $\lor$-introduction, dilution)

Distribution/Extraction: $p \cdot (q \lor r)$ transf $(p \cdot q) \lor (p \cdot r)$
$\qquad\qquad\qquad\qquad p \lor (q \cdot r)$ transf $(p \lor q) \cdot (p \lor r)$ (distribution)

Divergence: $\sim (p \equiv q)$ transf $p \equiv \sim q$ Not a standard rule.

Double Negation: p transf $\sim \sim p$

Duplication: $p \cdot p$ transf p
$p \lor q$ transf p (idempotence, tautology)

Equivalence: $p \equiv q, p \mid \therefore q$ ($\equiv$-elimination)

Existential Generalization: (existential generalization, existential quantification, EQ-introduction)

Existential Instantiation: (existential instantiation, existential dequantification, EQ-elimination)

Modus Ponens: $p \supset q, p \mid \therefore q$ (modus ponens, modus ponendo ponens, detachment, $\supset$-elimination)

Modus Tollens: $p \supset q, \sim q \mid \therefore \sim p$ (modus tollens, modus tollendo tollens)

Overlapping Conditionals: $p \supset q, q \supset r \mid \therefore p \supset r$ (hypothetical syllogism, transitivity, principle of the syllogism, syllogism, transitivity of implication)

Quantifier Negation: (quantifier negation, quantificational equivalence, change-of-quantifier rule, quantificational denial)

Quantifier Shift: (laws of confinement) Infrequently given as an explicit rule.

Regrouping: $p \cdot (q \cdot r)$ transf $(p \cdot q) \cdot r$
$p \lor (q \lor r)$ transf $(p \lor q) \lor r$ (association)

Repetition: $p \mid \therefore p$ (repeat, repetition, law of identity, reiteration)

Severance of Conjunction: $p \cdot q \mid \therefore p$ (simplification, separation, $\cdot$-elimination)

Tilde Distribution/Extraction: $\sim(p \cdot q)$ transf $\sim p \lor \sim q$
$\sim(p \lor q)$ transf $\sim p \cdot \sim q$ (DeMorgan's laws, DeMorgan's theorems)

Transposition: $p \cdot q$ transf $q \cdot p$
$p \lor q$ transf $q \lor p$ (commutation)

Universal Generalization: (universal generalization, universal quantification, UQ-introduction)

Universal Instantiation: (universal instantiation, universal dequantification, UQ-elimination)

appendix J

INSTANTIATION
AND GENERALIZATION RULES

It is usual in logic books to present the instantiation and generalization rules much more abruptly than we have done here. The standard approach is to give each rule by way of a validating quantificational argument-form,* together with a paragraph of "restrictions" to assure that the rule is applied only when conditions are suitable. This is called a *formal* presentation of the rules. The four rules of instantiation and generalization are thus formally presented below. The rules formulated in this fashion permit exactly the same inferences as those given in the body of the text.

UNIVERSAL INSTANTIATION (UI α/β):

$(\alpha)\Phi\alpha$

$\therefore \Phi\beta$

where $\Phi\beta$ is just like $\Phi\alpha$ except that $\Phi\beta$ contains a free occurrence of β in every place within the domain† of (α) in $(\alpha)\Phi\alpha$.

EXISTENTIAL GENERALIZATION (EG β/α):

$\Phi\beta$

$\therefore (\exists \alpha)\Phi\alpha$

where $\Phi\beta$ is just like $\Phi\alpha$ except that $\Phi\beta$ contains a free occurrence of β in every place within the domain of $(\exists \alpha)$ in $(\exists \alpha)\Phi\alpha$.

EXISTENTIAL INSTANTIATION (EI α/β):

$(\exists \alpha)\Phi\alpha$

$\rightarrow\Phi\beta$
.
.
.
p

$\therefore p$

where $\Phi\beta$ is just like $\Phi\alpha$ except that $\Phi\beta$ contains a free occurrence of β in every place within the domain of $(\exists \alpha)$ in $(\exists \alpha)\Phi\alpha$, and *only* in those places:

and

β does not occur free in any premiss or undischarged assumption earlier than $\Phi\beta$, and does not occur free in p.

---

*Cf. Appendix K.

†Here, the *domain* of a quantifier is the set of places occupied by its *range*, except the place within the quantifier itself. A domain is a set of *places*, not letters.

UNIVERSAL GENERALIZATION (UG β/α):

$$\frac{\Phi\beta}{\therefore (\alpha)\Phi\alpha}$$

where $\Phi\beta$ is just like $\Phi\alpha$ except that $\Phi\beta$ contains a free occurrence of β in every place within the domain of (α) in $(\alpha)\Phi\alpha$, and *only* in those places;

and

β does not occur free in any premiss or undischarged assumption.

appendix K

QUANTIFICATIONAL FORM

Chapter 9 introduced, explained, and discussed the notion of "form" as it applies within truth-functional logic. The analogous notion of "form" as it applies within quantifier logic—that is, the notion of "quantificational form" —is much more difficult to characterize adequately, and the characterization is necessarily much more complex.

Truth-functional forms involve "propositional variables"—dummy letters which stand in for propositions. A truth-functional form is a scaffolding of operators and punctuators, with dummy letters indicating the pockets where propositions go. The discussion of truth-functional forms manages with only one sort of variable, since in truth-functional logic there is only one basic kind of item: the proposition.

In quantifier logic, however, there are two basic kinds of items: predicates and individuals; and whereas in truth-functional logic the basic kind of formula consists of just a single symbol (a capital letter, abbreviating a statement), in quantifier logic the basic kind of formula consists of at least two symbols of different kinds: a capital letter, abbreviating a predicate expression, and one or more lower-case letters signifying the individual or individuals to which the predicate attaches. Thus in discussing quantificational form we shall need *two* sorts of variables or dummy letters: one to represent predicate expressions and one to represent individual expressions (individual constants or variables). Variables of the first sort may be called "predicate variables." For predicate variables we shall use the three capital Greek letters: Φ (phi), Ψ (psi), and Θ (theta). We shall not need more than three, though obviously we could have more if we wanted. Variables of the second sort may be called "individual metavariables" or simply "metavariables" (meta-variables). For metavariables we shall use the three lower-case Greek letters: α (alpha), β (beta), and γ (gamma). Again, though we shall not need more than three, we could have more if we wanted. Quantificational forms, as we might have expected, will eventually turn out to be scaffoldings of operators and punctuators, with predicate variables and metavariables holding the places for predicates and individual letters.

A singular statement, whether monadic or polyadic, simple or compound, consists of two fundamental logical ingredients: (1) the expressions (such as proper names) which designate individuals, and (2) the rest. This second ingredient, "the rest," contains the individual letters like raisins in a cake —a metaphor which we shall exploit to the fullest in the next few paragraphs.

It is important that singular statements be thought of in the fashion just indicated—as a lump of predicate with names of individuals lodged in it here and there, in places reserved for them. (Just so, a raisin cake is a lump of dough with raisin pockets in it, each of them filled with a raisin.) The predicate part may have a discernible structure (as a marble cake has a discernible pattern of colors); but if it does, we have the option of ignoring that structure and simply regarding it *as a predicate*—a thing with pockets for names of individuals. For example, the predicate part of the statement

    1. $\sim(Fa \cdot Gb)$

is the part

    2. $\sim(F\underline{\quad} \cdot G\underline{\quad})$

which has a discernible structure (for example, the structure of the denial of a conjunction); but we may, if we like, ignore this feature and simply attend to the fact that it is a predicate with pockets for two individual letters.

Moreover, in considering a singular statement containing the names of several individuals, we may focus our attention on one of them as "the one the statement is about" and simply regard the other names as part of "the rest" of the statement. Depending upon our interests of the moment, we may focus now on one name, now on another. Metaphorically, when confronted with the raisin cake we may single out a particular raisin for special attention and simply regard the others as "part of the cake", though on different occasions we might choose different raisins in the same cake for this special attention. As a simple illustration, the statement

    3. Albert loves Bertha.

may be considered as saying something about the two individuals Albert and Bertha—that is, as involving a predicate '_____ loves _____' with pockets for two individual letters. However, Albert's parents might very well view it merely as a statement about their only son, to the effect that he loves Bertha; that is, they might see it as involving a predicate '_____ loves Bertha' with one pocket, Bertha being shrugged off as part of what is said about their boy. And similarly, Bertha's parents might see it simply as a dismaying statement about their youngest daughter, to the effect that Albert loves her; that is, they might see it as involving the predicate 'Albert loves _____', where Albert is relegated to the status of a piece of furniture in a fact about

their darling girl. And however socially undesirable these prejudiced out-
looks might be, they are quite permissible from a logical point of view. That
is to say: when examining a singular statement, there is nothing wrong with
allowing some of the names in it to be absorbed into the predicate part, as
Albert's parents did with 'Bertha' and Bertha's parents did with 'Albert'.
If, for logical purposes, we map out the logical structure of an assertion by
setting down the predicate part, followed by the names in the order of their
occurrence (which in fact is almost exactly what we do in predicate logic),
then we see that there are three possible ways to map statement (3):

    3a. '_____ loves _____' (Albert) (Bertha)
    3b. '_____ loves Bertha' (Albert)
    3c. 'Albert loves _____' (Bertha)

Similarly, the statement

    4. Irving bit himself in Wichita.

can be mapped in the following variety of ways:

    4a. '_____ bit _____ in _____ ' (Irving) (Irving) (Wichita)
    4b. '_____ bit _____ in Wichita' (Irving) (Irving)
    4c. '_____ bit Irving in _____' (Irving) (Wichita)
    4d. 'Irving bit _____ in _____' (Irving) (Wichita)

    4e. '_____ bit Irving in Wichita' (Irving)
    4f. 'Irving bit _____ in Wichita' (Irving)
    4g. 'Irving bit Irving in _____ ' (Wichita)

and similarly, the (compound singular) statement

    5. ~(Albert is fat · Bertha is greedy)

can be mapped in a number of different ways, including

    5a. '~(_____ is fat · _____ is greedy)' (Albert) (Bertha)
    5b. '~(Albert is fat · _____ is greedy)' (Bertha)
    5c. '~(_____ is fat · Bertha is greedy)' (Albert)

This means that, when we are faced with the task of translating a statement such as (3), (4), or (5) into the notation of quantifier logic, there is no
single correct translation (though there will be a single "most thorough"
translation); rather, there will be a variety of "correct" translations, and
the one we decide to use will depend upon the scope of our interests. But
this is not the end of the story. What has just been said, about natural-language singular statements *is also true of formulae which are already in quantifier notation.* For example, the logical structure of statement (1) can be
mapped in three ways:

    1a. '~(F__ · G__)' ($\underline{a}$) ($\underline{b}$)
    1b. '~(F$\underline{a}$ · G__)' ($\underline{b}$)
    1c. '~(F__ · G$\underline{b}$)' ($\underline{a}$)

Let us define a **raw predicate expression** as one which contains at least one gap or blank space, such that when all of its gaps are filled with names of individuals the result is a statement. And let us say that a singular statement (or a formula with at least one free occurrence of an individual letter) *contains* a given raw predicate expression just in case that expression can be generated by eliminating one or more names of individuals (or by eliminating one or more free occurrences of individual letters) from that statement. We can then formally define the "structure maps" we have been talking about in the earlier examples: An **elementary map** of a singular statement (or formula) consists of a raw predicate expression contained in that statement (or formula), followed by the names (or individual letters) whose elimination produced the raw predicate expression, in the original order of their occurrence. It is easy to see that the earlier examples fit this definition: each of (1a)–(1c) is an elementary map of (1); each of (4a)–(4g) is an elementary map of (4); and so on.

Returning now to our primary topic, we shall say that an **elementary quantificational form** (EQF) is any formula consisting of a predicate variable followed by one or more metavariables. For example, each of the following is a (different) EQF:

$$\Phi\alpha \quad \Psi\alpha\beta \quad \Theta\alpha\beta\gamma \quad \Phi\alpha\beta\alpha \quad \Psi\beta\beta \quad \Theta\alpha\alpha\beta\alpha\gamma\beta$$

And we can now say that a statement (or formula) *has* a given EQF if an elementary map of that statement (or formula) can be generated from that EQF by (strictly or strongly) consistent replacement of predicate variables with raw predicate expressions and of metavariables with individual names (or individual letters). For example, statement (4) has the form

6. $\Phi\alpha$

(and in fact, every singular statement or formula with a free occurrence of an individual letter has this form), since, for example, (4e), which is an elementary map of (4), can be obtained from (6) by replacing the predicate variable Φ with the raw predicate expression '____ bit Irving in Wichita' and the metavariable α with the individual name 'Irving'. Of course, other elementary maps of (4) can also be generated from (6); but one is enough to show that statement (4) has form (6). Likewise, statement (4) also has the form

7. $\Psi\alpha\beta$

(as does every singular statement or formula with at least two free occurrences of individual letters). As one example, (4b)—which is an elementary map of (4)—can be generated from (7) by replacing Ψ with the raw predicate expression '____ bit ____ in Wichita' and replacing all occurrences of α with 'Irving' and all occurrences of β with 'Irving' (which is strongly consistent replacement). As another example, (4c)—which is another elementary map of (4)—can be generated from (7) by replacing Ψ with the raw predicate expression '____ bit Irving in ____' and replacing all occurrences of α with

'Irving' and all occurrences of β with 'Wichita' (which is strictly consistent replacement).

Statement (4) also has the form

    8. $\Psi\beta\beta$

since it is possible to obtain (4b) from (8) by strictly consistent substitution of '___ bit ___ in Wichita' for Ψ and 'Irving' for β.

As a final illustration, statement (1) has form (7) but not form (8). It has form (7) since it is possible to obtain (1a)—an elementary map of (1)—from (7) by replacing Ψ with the raw predicate expression '$\sim(F\_\_ \cdot G\_\_)$', and replacing all occurrences of α with '$\underline{a}$' and all occurrences of β with '$\underline{b}$' (which is strictly consistent replacement). However, statement (1) does not have form (8) since there is no consistent way of replacing metavariables in (8) with individual letters to produce a map of (1).

The next step beyond elementary maps is what we may call "contour maps." A **contour map** of a singular statement is designed to reveal something of the internal logical structure of the statement. (Thus, contour maps are interesting only when the statement in question is a compound statement—that is, when it has an internal logical structure to reveal.) A contour map *of* a given statement is a formula which is just like that statement except that, in at least one place where the statement has a component, the contour map has an elementary map of that component. For example, the formula

    1. $\sim(F\underline{a} \cdot G\underline{b})$

has, as one contour map,

    1d. $\sim('F\_\_ \cdot G\_\_' (\underline{a})(\underline{b}))$

(1) is a negation, and (1d) is just like (1) except that, in the place where (1) has its negate, (1d) has an elementary map of (1)'s negate. Another contour map of (1) is

    1e. $\sim('F\_\_'(\underline{a}) \cdot G\underline{b})$

(1) is the negation of a conjunction, and (1e) is just like (1) except that, in the place where (1) has the first conjunct of its negate, (1e) has an elementary map of the first conjunct of (1)'s negate. Another contour map of (1) is

    1f. $\sim('F\_\_'(\underline{a}) \cdot 'G\_\_'(\underline{b}))$

since (1f) is just like (1) except that in the place where (1) has the first conjunct of its negate, (1f) has an elementary map of the first conjunct of (1)'s negate, and in the place where (1) has the second conjunct of its negate, (1f) has an elementary map of the second conjunct of (1)'s negate. Finally, and trivially,

    1g. '$\sim(F\_\_ \cdot G\_\_)'(\underline{a})(\underline{b})$

is a contour map of (1), since (1g) is just like (1) except that, where (1) has itself, (1g) has an elementary map of (1). In general, an elementary map of *any* statement is (trivially) also a contour map of that statement.

Let us now define a **secondary quantificational form** (SQF) as any well-formed* array of EQF's, propositional variables, truth-functional operators, identity-signs, metavariables, and/or punctuation marks. For example, each of the following is a secondary quantificational form:

$$\sim\!\Phi\alpha \qquad \Phi\beta\beta \supset p \qquad \sim\!(\Psi\gamma\beta \lor (q \cdot \Theta\alpha))$$
$$\alpha = \beta \qquad \sim\!\sim\!\sim\!\Theta\beta \qquad \Phi\alpha \equiv \Psi\beta$$

Also, any statement form (Chapter 9) is trivially an SQF, and an EQF standing alone is trivially an SQF.

We can now say that a statement or formula *has* a given SQF if a contour map of that statement or formula can be produced from that SQF by (strictly or strongly) consistent replacement of propositional variables with propositions, predicate variables with raw predicate expressions, and metavariables with individual names (or individual letters). For example, statement

1. $\sim\!(F\underline{a} \cdot G\underline{b})$

has the form

9. $\sim\!\Phi\alpha$

(as does every negative singular statement) since, when Φ is replaced by the raw predicate expression '$F\_\_ \cdot G\underline{b}$' and α is replaced by the individual letter '$\underline{a}$,' the result is

1h. $\sim\!('F\_\_ \cdot G\underline{b}'(\underline{a}))$

which is a contour map of (1). Of course, (1) also has a number of other secondary quantificational forms, including

10. $\sim\!\Psi\alpha\beta$
11. $\sim\!(\Phi\alpha \cdot p)$
12. $\sim\!(p \cdot \Phi\alpha)$
13. $\sim\!(\Phi\alpha \cdot \Psi\beta)$

You may wish to prove to yourself that (1) has all these forms by working out the substitutions involved. As another example, the statement

14. $Fa \supset ((\exists x)Gx \lor Ha)$

has, among its various secondary quantificational forms, the following:

15. $\Phi\alpha \supset (p \lor q)$
16. $\Phi\alpha \supset (p \lor \Psi\beta)$
17. $\Phi\alpha \supset \Psi\alpha$

You may wish to prove to yourself that (14) has all these forms by working out the substitutions involved.

---

*Where "well-formed" may be explained, as before, in the following way: the formula is well-formed if the result of replacing all statement variables with statements, predicate variables with predicates, and metavariables with individual letters, is a statement.

Yet a third sort of map is what may be called a **quantifier map**. Just as a contour map is designed to bring out "logical contours" of the statement mapped, a quantifier map is designed to map the operations of the quantifiers in the statement mapped. A quantifier map of a given statement is a formula which is just like that statement except that, in at least one place where the statement has a matrix, the quantifier map has a contour map of that matrix. For example, the statement

18. $(\exists x)(x$ is a girl $\cdot$ (Albert is alive $\supset$ Albert loves $x))$

has, as one quantifier map, the formula

18a. $(\exists x)$ '___ is a girl $\cdot$ (___ is alive $\supset$ ___ loves ___)' $(x)(\underline{a})(\underline{a})(x)$

since (18a) is just like (18) except that where (18) has the matrix

$(x$ is a girl $\cdot$ (Albert is alive $\supset$ Albert loves $x))$

(18a) has the formula

'___ is a girl $\cdot$ (___ is alive $\supset$ ___ loves ___)' $(x)(\underline{a})(\underline{a})(x)$

which is a contour map (and also an elementary map) of that matrix. Another quantifier map of (18) would be

18b. $(\exists x)($ '___ is a girl' $(x) \cdot ($ '___ is alive' $(\underline{a}) \supset$ '___ loves ___' $(\underline{a})(x)))$

since (18b) is just like (18) except that its matrix

('___ is a girl' $(x) \cdot ($ '___ is alive' $(\underline{a}) \supset$ '___ loves ___' $(\underline{a})(x)))$

is a contour map of the matrix of (18). As another example, the statement

19. $(x)(Fx \supset Gx) \supset (\exists y)(Fy \cdot Gy)$

has, among its various quantifier maps, the following three:

19a. $(x)($ 'F___'$(x) \supset$ 'G___'$(x)) \supset (\exists y)(Fy \cdot Gy)$
19b. $(x)(Fx \supset Gx) \supset (\exists y)($ 'F___'$(y) \cdot$ 'G___'$(y))$
19c. $(x)($ 'F___ $\supset G$___'$(x)(x)) \supset (\exists y)($ 'F___ $\cdot G$___'$(y)(y))$

since each of these is just like (19) except for having at least one contour map of a matrix in (19) in place of the matrix itself. If a statement contains no matrices (that is, contains no quantifiers), then every contour map of it is, trivially, also a quantifier map of it.

A **regular quantificational form** may be defined as any well-formed array of SQF's, backward E's, metavariables, and/or parentheses. For example, each of the following is a regular quantificational form:

$(\alpha)\sim\Phi\alpha$ $(\exists \beta)(\Psi\beta \supset \Theta\gamma)$ $(\alpha)\Phi\alpha \equiv (\exists \beta)\Psi\beta$ $(\exists \alpha)(\beta)\Theta\beta\alpha$

Of course, by definition, every EQF and every SQF is also a regular quantificational form.

One regular quantificational form is an *alphabetic variant* of another if the one is obtainable from the other by strictly consistent replacement of variables with variables: alphabetic variants are just alike except for their lettering. For all logical purposes involving single quantificational forms, alphabetic variants will count as the same form. Thus, for instance, '$(\exists \alpha)\Phi\alpha$' and '$(\exists \beta)\Psi\beta$' are the same form, since they are mere alphabetic variants of each other.

A statement *has* a given regular quantificational form if a quantifier map of that statement may be obtained from that form by (strictly or strongly) consistent substitution of statements for statement variables, raw predicate expressions for predicate variables, and individual letters for metavariables. For example, statement (18) has, among its regular quantificational forms, the form

 20. $(\exists \alpha)\Phi\alpha$

since when Φ is replaced by the raw predicate expression

 '_____ is a girl · (Albert is alive $\supset$ Albert loves _____)'

and α is replaced by 'x', the result is a quantifier map of (18). Likewise, every existentially quantified formula has form (20). Some other regular quantificational forms which (18) has are

 21. $(\exists \alpha)(\Phi\alpha \cdot \Psi\alpha)$
 22. $(\exists \alpha)\Phi\alpha\alpha$
 23. $(\exists \alpha)\Phi\alpha\beta\alpha$
 24. $(\exists \alpha)(\Phi\alpha \cdot (p \supset \Psi\alpha))$
 25. $(\exists \alpha)(\Phi\alpha \cdot (\Psi\beta \supset \Theta\beta\alpha))$

A formula has a regular quantificational form as its **skeletal form** (or **skeleton**) if and only if that formula can be obtained from that form by strictly consistent replacement of propositional variables with simple statements, predicate variables with predicate letters, and metavariables with individual letters. Formulae with the same skeleton are said to be **isomorphic**.

A regular quantificational form is said to be **formally true** if it is the skeleton of at least one quantifier truth (a statement which can be proven true by the procedures of quantifier logic). It is said to be **formally false** if it is the skeleton of at least one quantifier falsehood (a statement which can be proven false by the procedures of quantifier logic). A form which is neither formally true nor formally false is **formally contingent**.

Any formula with at least one formally true quantificational form is a quantifier truth. Any formula with at least one formally false quantificational form is a quantifier falsehood. The skeletal form of every quantifier truth is formally true. The skeletal form of every quantifier falsehood is formally false. A formula is a quantifier contingency if and only if every quantificational form which it has is formally contingent.

A **quantificational argument form** is any set of regular quantificational forms which will become an argument if all propositional variables are replaced by statements, all predicate variables are replaced by predicates, and all metavariables are replaced by individual letters. "Having" a given quantificational form and "skeletal" form are defined for arguments in the same way as for formulae.

A quantificational argument form is **validating** if it is the skeleton of at least one quantificationally valid argument. Every quantificationally valid argument has at least one validating quantificational argument form. The skeleton of every quantificationally valid argument is a validating form. An argument which has no validating quantificational argument form is quantificationally invalid.

One quantificational argument form is an alphabetic variant of another if the one is obtainable from the other by strictly consistent replacement of variables with variables—that is, if they are just alike except for their lettering. For all logical purposes, mere alphabetic variants of each other will count as the same quantificational argument form.

appendix L

"PROOF BY CASES"

One proof strategy which utilizes CP, and which has shown itself to be enormously valuable, is called the strategy of **proof by cases**. Since it is, initially, more easily seen than described, we may begin with an illustration.

$$
\begin{array}{lll}
1. & A \supset B & \\
2. & A \lor C & \\
3. & C \supset (C \supset D) & / \therefore B \lor D \\
\hookrightarrow 4. & A & \\
\quad 5. & B & 4, 1, \text{MP} \\
\quad 6. & B \lor D & 5, \text{disj.} \\
\hline
7. & A \supset (B \lor D) & 4\text{–}6, \text{CP} \\
\hookrightarrow 8. & C & \\
\quad 9. & C \supset D & 3, 8, \text{MP} \\
\quad 10. & D & 8, 9, \text{MP} \\
\quad 11. & B \lor D & 10, \text{disj.} \\
\hline
12. & C \supset (B \lor D) & 8\text{–}11, \text{CP} \\
13. & (B \lor D) \lor (B \lor D) & 2, 7, 12, \text{dilem.} \\
14. & B \lor D & 13, \text{dup.}
\end{array}
$$

A "proof by cases" is always based on a disjunctive line (often, but not always, a premiss) in the derivation. It proceeds by showing that each disjunct implies the same desired formula, then inferring that since at least one of the disjuncts is true, the desired formula must be true. This is done by taking each "case" in turn and showing, by CP, that that case implies the desired formula. Once this is done, the desired formula may be inferred from the conditionals and the disjunction by Dilemma and Duplication. In the illustration above, the disjunction upon which the proof is based is premiss 2 (thus it is a "proof by cases on line 2").

In constructing this proof, one of the disjuncts was assumed and the desired formula (in this case, the conclusion) was derived, then the assumption was discharged by CP. Next, the other disjunct was assumed and the desired formula was derived, then that assumption was discharged by CP. This gave the conditionals at lines 7 and 12; these two conditionals plus the disjunction at line 2 yield line 13 by Dilemma, which reduces to the desired conclusion by Duplication.

Because "proof by cases" is a standard strategy, it is commonly abbreviated and annotated slightly differently from the pattern above. Abbreviated and reannotated, the proof above would look like this:

```
 1. A ⊃ B
 2. A ∨ C
 3. C ⊃ (C ⊃ D)      / ∴ B ∨ D
 4. A                (proof by cases on 2)
 5. B                1, 4, MP
 6. B ∨ D            5, disj.
 7. C                (proof by cases on 2)
 8. C ⊃ D            3, 7, MP
 9. D                7, 8, MP
10. B ∨ D            9, disj.
11. B ∨ D            4-6, 7-10, Proof by Cases on 2
```

The chief feature of this abbreviation is that it doesn't bother to include the obvious and standard steps. Because they *are* obvious and standard, they can always be provided on demand if the need arises.

Proof by cases is always based on a disjunction which provides the "cases". Thus, if a derivation contains no disjunctions, but contains something which can be transformed into a disjunction, a proof by cases is still possible. Or, if a derivation contains more than one disjunction, a proof by cases may be based on either of them. To illustrate both of these points, the proof above might have gone as follows:

```
 1. A ⊃ B
 2. A ∨ C
 3. C ⊃ (C ⊃ D)      / ∴ B ∨ D
 4. ~A ∨ B           1, CE
 5. ~A               (proof by cases on 4)
 6. C                2, 5, canc.
 7. C ⊃ D            6, 3, MP
 8. D                6, 7, MP
 9. B ∨ D            8, disj.
10. B                (proof by cases on 4)
11. B ∨ D            10, disj.
12. B ∨ D            5-9, 10-11, Proof by Cases on 4
```

In this example, the conditional at line (1) was converted into a disjunction and the proof by cases was then based upon that disjunction. Similarly, the conditional at line (3) could have been transformed into a disjunction, and a proof by cases could then have been based upon that disjunction. Yet another application of the strategy is shown in the following proof of the same argument:

1. $A \supset B$
2. $A \lor C$
3. $C \supset (C \supset D)$ $/ \therefore B \lor D$
4. $\sim(\sim A \lor A)$ (IP)
5. $\sim \sim A \cdot \sim A$ 4, TD
6. $\sim A \lor A$ 4–5, IP, DN
7. $\sim A$ (proof by cases on 6)
8. C 7, 2, canc.
9. $C \supset D$ 8, 3, MP
10. D 8, 9, MP
11. $B \lor D$ 10, disj.
12. A (proof by cases on 6)
13. B 12, 1, MP
14. $B \lor D$ 13, disj.
15. $B \lor D$ 7–11, 12–14, Proof by Cases on 6

The relevant feature of this proof is that the **exhaustive disjunction** '$\sim A \lor A$' (so called because it "exhausts the possibilities"—there are no possibilities besides $\sim A$ and A) was first derived, and the proof by cases was then based upon it. Every exhaustive disjunction (disjunction of the form '$\sim p \lor p$' or '$p \lor \sim p$') is a tautology and hence can always be worked into any derivation in three steps, as was done in steps 4–6 above. Because these three steps are obvious and standard, it is usual to abbreviate proofs such as the one above—proofs based upon some exhaustive disjunction—by leaving them out altogether. So abbreviated, the proof above would have gone:

1. $A \supset B$
2. $A \lor C$
3. $C \supset (C \supset D)$ $/ \therefore B \lor D$
4. $\sim A$ (proof by cases)
5. C 4, 2, canc.
6. $C \supset D$ 5, 3, MP
7. D 5, 6, MP
8. $B \lor D$ 7, disj.
9. A (proof by cases)
10. B 9, 1, MP
11. $B \lor D$ 10, disj.
12. $B \lor D$ 4–8, 9–11, Proof by Cases

The justification for the last line simply cites "Proof by Cases" without mentioning any particular line in the proof. This is the sign that the proof is not based upon any disjunctive line in the derivation, but upon an exhaustive

400
Appendix L

disjunction which could have been introduced into the derivation had we
chosen to do so. Such a proof is called a "Pure Proof by Cases"—one based
not upon any contingent truth within the derivation [such as line (2)] but
upon a pure truth of logic (such as '$\sim A \lor A$').

The illustrations above all come from truth-functional logic. But the real
value of proof by cases comes out in quantifier logic. As a simple illustration:

1.	$(x)(Fx \supset Gx)$	
2.	$Fa \lor Fb$	$/ \therefore (\exists x)Gx$
3.	Fa	(proof by cases on 2)
4.	$Fa \supset Ga$	1, UI, x/a
5.	Ga	3, 4, MP
6.	$(\exists x)Gx$	5, EG, a/x
7.	Fb	(proof by cases on 2)
8.	$Fb \supset Gb$	1, UI, x/b
9.	Gb	7, 8, MP
10.	$(\exists x)Gx$	9, EG, b/x
11.	$(\exists x)Gx$	3–6, 7–10, Proof by Cases on 2

And, as a slightly more complicated example:

1.	$(x)[(Fx \lor Gx) \supset Hx]$	
2.	$(\exists x)Fx \lor (\exists x)Gx$	$/ \therefore (\exists x)Hx$
3.	$(\exists x)Fx$	(proof by cases on 2)
4.	Fa	3, x/a
5.	$(Fa \lor Ga) \supset Ha$	1, UI, x/a
6.	$Fa \lor Ga$	4, disj.
7.	Ha	5, 6, MP
8.	$(\exists x)Hx$	7, EG, a/x
9.	$(\exists x)Hx$	4–8, EI
10.	$(\exists x)Gx$	(proof by cases on 2)
11.	Ga	10, x/a
12.	$(Fa \lor Ga) \supset Ha$	1, UI, x/a
13.	$Fa \lor Ga$	11, disj.
14.	Ha	12, 13, MP
15.	$(\exists x)Hx$	14, EG, a/x
16.	$(\exists x)Hx$	11–15, EI
17.	$(\exists x)Hx$	3–9, 10–16, Proof by Cases on 2

appendix M

SYLLOGISTIC: THE LOGIC OF CATEGORICAL PROPOSITIONS

Basics

From ancient times until relatively recently (within the last thirty or forty years) the formal logic most widely taught in colleges and universities consisted of syllogistic logic. Syllogistic, now generally recognized as simply an elementary part of symbolic logic, is a formal system which treats of inferences involving only categorical propositions (cf. Chapter 16), and especially of a particular type of argument called a **categorical syllogism**, consisting of two premisses and a conclusion all of which are categorical propositions. For purposes of the formal system, only categorical propositions in **standard form** will be considered.

The four standard forms* of categorical propositions are:

Universal Affirmative:	Every S is a P	(A proposition)
Universal Negative:	No S is a P	(E proposition)
Particular Affirmative:	Some S is a P	(I proposition)
Particular Negative:	Some S is not a P	(O proposition)

The affirmative or negative character of a proposition is traditionally called its **quality**; the universal or particular character is traditionally called its **quantity**. In the forms above, 'S' and 'P' represent expressions for *kinds of things*, which for formal purposes must be given as nouns or noun phrases, rather than as adjectives or adjectival phrases. These expressions are called **terms**. Each standard-form categorical proposition (which we shall hereafter

---

*In times not far past, the usual practice in logic books was to take the forms

All S are P	(A)
No S are P	(E)
Some S are P	(I)
Some S are not P	(O)

as standard. This long-standing practice had, as one consequence, a substantial complicating of the procedures for putting categoricals into standard form, and as another, a substantial obscuring of the **distributive** (§16.7) nature of categoricals. The forms used as standard in the present work are now becoming accepted over the older forms.

abbreviate as 'SFCP') contains just two terms: the one occurring first in the proposition is called the **subject** term of the proposition, and the one occurring second is called the **predicate** term of the proposition. An item of the kind designated by a term is said to "fall under" that term. For example, all and only cows fall under the term 'cow'.

A term under which nothing falls, such as 'unicorn' and 'round triangle', is called an **empty** term, and one under which everything falls, such as 'thing which either is or is not a cow', is called a **universal** (*or* **exhaustive**) term. In traditional syllogistic, empty terms and exhaustive terms are both regarded as illegitimate, and an SFCP containing such a term is not admissible for logical treatment.

For every term there is an associated term called its **complement**: the term under which fall all and only those things which do *not* fall under the original term. The usual way to form the complement of a term is by prefixing 'non-' to it, or deleting a prefixed 'non-' from it. Thus, 'non-cow' is the complement of 'cow', and 'cow' is the complement of 'non-cow'. The illegitimacy of empty and universal terms is usually stated by way of the phrase "existential import": every *term* occurring in a legitimate SFCP is said to have **existential import**—its occurrence implies that *there are* things of the kind designated by that term. And since, if a term is legitimate its complement is also legitimate, it follows that if a term has existential import so will its complement, meaning that the term can be neither empty nor exhaustive.

Two SFCP's having the same subject term and the same predicate term are called **corresponding** SFCP's. For example, for the A proposition 'Every raven is a bird' the corresponding O proposition will be 'Some raven is not a bird'—the O proposition whose subject and predicate correspond to the subject and predicate of the A proposition. The logical relationships among the four different corresponding SFCP's is traditionally displayed by means of the accompanying diagram, called the **square of opposition**.

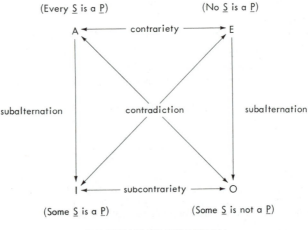

THE SQUARE OF OPPOSITION

To say that two propositions are **contraries**, or that they stand in the relationship of **contrariety** to each other, is to say that they cannot both be true (though they might both be false). For example, the corresponding A and E propositions

Every crustacean is an aquatic creature.

No crustacean is an aquatic creature.

cannot *both* be true (given that 'crustacean' is not an empty term); however, they can both be false, and in fact are, since some crustaceans are aquatic and some aren't.

To say that two propositions are **contradictories**, or that they stand in the relationship of **contradiction** to each other, is to say that each is equivalent to the denial of the other—that is, that they necessarily have opposite truth-values. Thus, the corresponding A and O propositions

Every resident of Estonia is a Presbyterian.

Some resident of Estonia is not a Presbyterian.

are contradictories, since if either of them is true it follows that the other one is false, and conversely if either of them is false it follows that the other one is true. Similarly, the corresponding E and I propositions

No porpoise is a better mathematician than Einstein.

Some porpoise is a better mathematician than Einstein.

are contradictories, since they necessarily have opposite truth-values.

To say that two propositions are **subcontraries**, or that they stand in the relation of **subcontrariety** to each other, is to say that they cannot both be false (though they might both be true). For example, the corresponding I and O propositions

Some typewriter is a steam-powered machine.

Some typewriter is not a steam-powered machine.

are subcontraries. Given that there are typewriters, it follows that either some of them are steam-powered or some of them are *not* steam-powered (or both)—that is, that the two propositions cannot *both* be false. This may become clearer if we reflect that, were they both false, their respective contradictories would both be true. But their respective contradictories are corresponding A and E propositions, which *cannot* both be true because they are contraries. Thus, corresponding I and O propositions cannot both be false.

One SFCP is related to another by **subalternation** just in case the one is entailed by the other, but not vice versa. Thus an I proposition is the **subalternate** of its corresponding A proposition. (This can also be expressed by saying that an A proposition is the **superalternate** of its corresponding I proposition.) For example, given that no empty terms are involved, the A proposition

Every Doberman pinscher is a watchdog.

entails the corresponding I proposition

>Some Doberman pinscher is a watchdog.

since it is impossible for the first to be true without the second also being true. But the reverse entailment does not hold: from the fact that some Dobermans are watchdogs it does not follow that they all are. The same is true for corresponding E and O propositions. Given that no empty terms are involved, the E proposition

>No Poland China is a watchpig.

entails the corresponding O proposition

>Some Poland China is not a watchpig.

though the reverse entailment does not hold: from the fact that some Poland Chinas are not watchpigs, it scarcely follows that none are.

   In addition to inferences based upon the square of opposition, traditional syllogistic also recognizes certain inferences based upon *transformations* of SFCP's. The simplest operation, called **conversion**, consists of interchanging the subject and predicate terms of an SFCP to obtain a new SFCP whose subject is the same as the predicate of the original and whose predicate is the same as the subject of the original. The proposition thus obtained is called the **converse** of the original. Conversion is a valid transformation for E and I propositions, but not for A and O propositions. For example, from the E proposition

>No German is a Frenchman.

it follows immediately that

>No Frenchman is a German.

Also, from the I proposition

>Some bachelor is a millionaire.

it follows immediately that

>Some millionaire is a bachelor.

On the other hand, from the A proposition

>Every Holstein is a cow.

it certainly does not follow that

>Every cow is a Holstein.

and similarly, from the O proposition

>Some dog is not a beagle.

it doesn't follow that

>Some beagle is not a dog.

Thus rules for conversion may be stated in a familiar format as

CONVERSION (conv.): No S is a P *transf* No P is an S

Some S is a P *transf* Some P is an S

A second transformation traditionally recognized is called **obversion**. To obvert an SFCP, reverse its *quality* (its "polarity") from positive to negative or from negative to positive and replace the predicate term with its complement. The result is called the **obverse** of the original. For example, when the (universal *affirmative*) A proposition

> Every beagle is a dog.

is obverted, it becomes the (universal *negative*) E proposition

> No beagle is a non-dog.

Similarly, when the (particular *negative*) O proposition

> Some bachelor is not a millionaire.

is obverted, it becomes the (particular *affirmative*) I proposition

> Some bachelor is a non-millionaire.

Obversion is a valid transformation for every SFCP. The rule may be given as

OBVERSION (obv.):   Every S is a P *transf*   No S is a non-P
                  No S is a P *transf*   Every S is a non-P
                  Some S is a P *transf*   Some S is not a non-P
                  Some S is not a P *transf*   Some S is a non-P

A third transformation traditionally recognized is called **contraposition**. But since it is equivalent to a series of applications of the above two rules (specifically, to obversion-then-conversion-then-obversion) we shall not give it separate treatment here.

The Syllogism

An argument that consists of two premises and a conclusion all of which are categorical propositions is called a **categorical syllogism**. Just as it is advantageous to have "standard" forms for categorical propositions, it is advantageous to define standard forms for categorical syllogisms. A syllogism thus defined will be a **standard form categorical syllogism**, which we shall abbreviate as "SFCS." For purposes of the formal system, only syllogisms in standard form will be considered.

A syllogism is in standard form (is an SFCS) if and only if it satisfies all three of the following conditions (a), (b), and (c):

(a) Each of the three propositions which make up the syllogism must be an SFCP.
(b) The three SFCP's must contain, collectively, exactly three terms, each SFCP must contain two different terms, and no two SFCP's may contain the *same* two terms.

Condition (b) assures that there is exactly one term which occurs in both premisses but not in the conclusion. This term is called the **middle term**. The term serving as the subject of the conclusion is called the **minor term**. The term serving as the predicate of the conclusion is called the **major term**. The premiss containing the minor term is called the **minor premiss**; the premiss containing the major term is called the **major premiss**.

(c) The *first* premiss must be the *major* premiss, and the second one the minor premiss.

The **mood** of an SFCS is a specification of the *type* of each of its SFCP's. For example, we can specify the mood of the SFCS

> No mammal is a reptile
> Some quadruped is a mammal
> ∴ Some quadruped is not a reptile

by saying that its major premiss is an E proposition, its minor premiss is an I proposition, and its conclusion is an O proposition; or, more succinctly, that it is of **mood EIO**. When we give the mood in this way, the first letter is the type of the major premiss, the second is the type of the minor premiss, and the third is the type of the conclusion.

The logical form of an SFCS is not completely determined by its mood; there is one further relevant factor: the positioning of the *middle term* within the two premisses. There are four different possibilities. It may occur as the subject of the major premiss and the predicate of the minor premiss, or as the predicate of both, or as the subject of both, or as the predicate of the major premiss and as the subject of the minor premiss. Each of these possibilities is called a **figure**, and every SFCS has one of the four figures. If we let S stand for any minor term, P for any major term, and M for any middle term, the four figures may be represented graphically as follows:

first figure	*second figure*	*third figure*	*fourth figure*
M–P	P–M	M–P	P–M
S–M	S–M	M–S	M–S
∴ S–P	∴ S–P	∴ S–P	∴ S–P

Thus, we may fully characterize the logical form of the syllogism above by saying that it is an SFCS of **mood EIO in the first figure**, or, more succinctly, that it is **EIO-1**. The mood and figure "fully characterize the logical form" because, if a syllogism is valid, then any other syllogism of the same mood and figure is likewise valid, and similarly for invalidity. Thus, to assess the validity or invalidity of an SFCS we need only know its "type"—its mood and figure. The actual terms in it make no difference.

Before giving rules for assessing the validity or invalidity of an SFCS, we must define the concept of "distribution" of a term, since this is a central concept in the rules.

The traditional definitions of "distribution" are totally semantical (rather than syntactical) and consequently are not easy to apply in any rigorous fashion. Briefly, a term is **distributed** in an occurrence just in case it is about *all* of the things which fall under it (that is, if in that occurrence it concerns the whole totality of things falling under it), and a term is **undistributed** just in case it is about *only some* of the things which fall under it (that is, if in that occurrence it concerns less than the whole totality of things falling under it). Fortunately, this difficult semantical definition has been reduced by syllogistic theoreticians to a quite simple *syntactical* definition, which is the one we shall use:

> ***Distribution.*** A term is **distributed** just in case it is either the *subject* term of a *universal* SFCP or the *predicate* term of a *negative* SFCP. Otherwise, it is **undistributed**.

This may be set out visually as in the accompanying diagram.

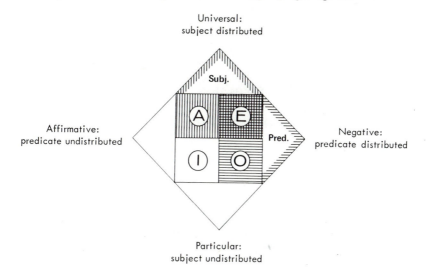

DISTRIBUTION OF TERMS

From the diagram it is easy to see that an E proposition distributes both its terms, an I distributes neither of its terms, an A distributes its subject only, and an O distributes its predicate only.

The test for validity of an SFCS may be given in terms of two "validity conditions," *both* of which a syllogism must satisfy in order to be valid. Any SFCS satisfying both of them is valid; any which fails one or both is (syllogistically) invalid.*

---

*Though perhaps not *absolutely* invalid. Cf. Appendix G.

POLARITY CONDITION: A valid SFCS must contain exactly the same number of negative premisses as negative conclusions (that is, one of each or else none of each).

DISTRIBUTION CONDITION: Each term must be distributed at least as many times in the premisses as in the conclusion, and the middle term at least once.

By these rules, it may be determined that of the 256 different types or forms of SFCS, just 24 are valid. The remaining 232 violate one or both of the two validity conditions. For example, any SFCS with two negative premisses, or with a negative conclusion and two affirmative premisses, will violate the polarity condition. Also, any SFCS with two I premisses will fail to distribute the middle term and so will violate the distribution condition. Apart from these broad cases, it can be seen, for example, that AOO-3 is invalid, since the major term is distributed more times (namely once) in the conclusion than in the premisses (namely none). For AOO-3 is the form

Every *M* is a P
Some *M* is not an *S*
∴ Some *S* is not a *P*

in which the negative conclusion distributes its predicate—the major term, but the affirmative major premiss does *not* distribute its predicate—the major term.

On the other hand, AOO-2 is perfectly valid. For AOO-2 is the form

Every *P* is an *M*
Some *S* is not an *M*
∴ Some *S* is not a *P*

which has the same number of negative premisses and conclusions (one of each), and which distributes the middle term at least once (in its minor premiss), and whose conclusion distributes *S* not at all, but does distribute *P*—and whose major premiss also distributes *P*. Thus AOO-2 satisfies both validity conditions and so is valid.

The two rules give us a procedure for evaluating each SFCS as to its validity or invalidity. And it is a simple matter to extend this procedure to other syllogisms. First of all, any argument which can be transformed into a valid SFCS by conversion and/or obversion and/or reversing the order of premisses is also valid, since the two transformations generate propositions that are logically equivalent to the originals, and the order of premisses is irrelevant to the validity of an argument. For example, the syllogism

No non-*M* is an *S*
No *P* is an *M*
∴ Every *S* is a non-*P*

is pretty obviously not an SFCS, since it contains five terms (M, non-M, P, non-P, and S), and its minor premiss comes first; furthermore, it looks suspiciously invalid, since it has two negative premisses and zero negative conclusions, and thus is doubly in violation of the Polarity Condition. However, by obverting the minor premiss and the conclusion, and transposing the two premisses, we arrive at the EAE-2 SFCS

> No P is a M
> Every S is an M
> ∴ No S is a P

which is easily proven valid; therefore, we can say that the original non-standard syllogism was valid, also.

Similarly, if an argument with a universal conclusion is valid, the result of replacing its conclusion with the subalternate of that conclusion (called "subalternating the conclusion") will also be valid; and if an argument with a particular premiss is valid, the result of replacing that premiss with its super-alternate (called "superalternating a premiss") will also be valid. This is because superalternates entail their subalternates, and entailment is transitive.

Similarly, if the elements of a categorical syllogism are not SFCP's but can be turned into SFCP's by paraphrase, and if the resulting syllogism can be shown to be valid either with or without the use of further transformations, then we can say that the original preparaphrase argument was also valid.

Syllogistic with Empty Terms

One of the more unsatisfactory features of traditional syllogistic is its rejection of empty terms—that is to say, its underlying presupposition that every legitimate term must be non-empty. For quite often we do not *know* whether a term is empty or not (cf. the term 'prime number between 1,000,000,000,000 and 1,000,000,000,173'), and it seems quite arbitrary to require us always to suppose or assume that a term is non-empty before we are allowed to evaluate reasoning involving that term. On these grounds, it is desirable to eliminate the non-emptiness restriction and to admit any SFCP whose terms are intelligible.

However, the admission of empty (or possibly empty) terms is not a casual step: it has quite far-reaching consequences. First of all, it requires us to say something about the truth conditions of propositions whose terms are or may be empty. What, for example, are we to say about propositions such as

Some unicorns are vegetarians.

or

Every mermaid is a beautiful creature.

or

No five-sided triangle is a circle.

or

Some unicorns are not vegetarians.

Are we to count them as true, or as false, or what? No matter what we do, the traditional square of opposition will need to be modified. If we elect, for example, to call every proposition *false* whose subject term is empty, we effectively give up the notion that corresponding A and O propositions, and corresponding E and I propositions, are contradictories. For an A and its corresponding O (or an E and its corresponding I) will have the same truth-value (namely, False) whenever their subject term is empty.

For this reason, the historically preferred alternative has been to regard a universal proposition with an empty subject term as *true* and to regard a particular proposition with an empty subject term as *false*, thereby retaining the relation of contradictoriness between the corresponding A and O, and between the corresponding E and I. That is, when empty terms are admitted, the preferred course is to accept a **Boolean interpretation** (§16.4) of categorical propositions. This interpretation is said to accord *existential import* to particular propositions but not to universal ones (a *proposition* has existential import if its truth requires a non-empty subject term—that is, if it entails that there exist things—at least one thing—falling under its subject term).

However, the result of this interpretation, which sustains the traditional contradictoriness relationships, is to eradicate the *other* relations shown in the square of opposition. For example, corresponding A and E propositions are no longer contraries, since they can both be true—and will be if their subject term is empty. Similarly, corresponding I and O propositions are no longer subcontraries, since they can both be false when their subject term is empty. Finally, the relation of subalternation no longer obtains, since it will be possible for an A (or E) proposition to be true while its corresponding I (or O) proposition is false.

The Boolean interpretation also has effects in the area of the syllogism. By giving up the existential import of universal propositions, we give up the validity of those syllogisms with two universal premises and a particular conclusion; for the particular conclusion will entail the existence of things falling under its subject term, while the universal major premiss will not; thus, it will be possible for the premises to be true while the conclusion is false, and so the argument will be invalid. Thus, when empty terms are admitted, some amendment must be made to the validity conditions so as to rule out as invalid those arguments with two universal premises and a particular conclusion. The desired restriction can be obtained simply by changing 'at least' to 'exactly' in the distribution condition, thus:

MODIFIED DISTRIBUTION CONDITION: Each term must be distributed exactly as many times in the premisses as in the conclusion, and the middle term exactly once.

Under this condition, the SFCS AAI-1, which was valid under the old rule, becomes invalid, since its minor term is distributed more times in the premisses than in the conclusion. AAI-1 is

Every *M* is a *P*
Every *S* is an *M*
∴ Some *S* is a *P*

and while *S* is undistributed in the conclusion, it is distributed in the second premiss, which violates the modified distribution condition. Likewise, the SFCS EAO-4, valid under the old rule, becomes invalid, since in

No *P* is an *M*
Every *M* is an *S*
∴ Some *S* is not a *P*

the middle term is distributed twice, which is a violation of the modified distribution condition. In a similar fashion, the modified condition rules out every SFCS with two universal premisses and a particular conclusion. There are nine such forms satisfying the original validity conditions:

AAI-1	AEO-2	AAI-3	AAI-4	AEO-4
EAO-1	EAO-2	EAO-3	EAO-4	

When these are eliminated, of the 256 possible syllogistic forms there remain just fifteen which satisfy both the Polarity Condition and the Modified Distribution Condition. These are:

AAA-1	AEE-2	AII-3	AEE-4
AII-1	AOO-2	EIO-3	EIO-4
EAE-1	EAE-2	IAI-3	IAI-4
EIO-1	EIO-2	OAO-3	

Syllogistic and Symbolic Logic

To see that syllogistic covers the same territory as a portion of quantifier logic, we need first to bring the notion of the *complement* of a term into the realm of quantification. A usual notation for complements is an overline: when we put a line over a term, we produce the complement of that term.

Thus, for the complement of T we write '$\bar{T}$' instead of 'non-T'. If we then construe terms as predicates, so that 'x is a T' is translated as 'Tx', we can introduce the notion of a complement via the following transformation rule:

COMPLEMENTARITY: $\bar{\Phi}\alpha$ *transf* $\sim\Phi\alpha$

(The effect is to make the overline an alternative notation for the tilde.)

For traditional syllogistic, in which it is presupposed that no legitimate term is empty and that the complement of any legitimate term is also a legitimate term, we add the special inference rule

COMPREHENSION: $/ \therefore (\exists \alpha)\Phi\alpha$

where it is understood that Φ can represent any term, and therefore also the complement of any term (since complements are also terms).

This rule also bestows existential import upon universal propositions (inter-preted as in Chapter 16) by allowing us to infer that each such proposition has a non-empty subject term. Within this framework it is easy to prove the validity of Conversion for E and I propositions, and the validity of Obversion for all four categorical forms, using the regular techniques of quantifier logic plus the two special rules. It can also be proven that corresponding A and O propositions, and corresponding E and I propositions, are con-tradictories, that is, that the one is equivalent to the denial of the other. It can also be proven that corresponding E and A propositions cannot both be true (by assuming that they are both true and deriving a contradiction) but that they can both be false (by the method of natural interpretation), and similarly, that corresponding I and O propositions cannot both be false but can both be true. It can also be shown that an A entails its corresponding I, and an E entails its corresponding O. Thus, all of the inferences based upon the traditional square of opposition will follow as a matter of quantifier logic.

It can also be shown, on a case-by-case basis, that of the 256 types of SFCS, only those twenty-four which are valid by the rules of traditional syllogistic are valid by the rules of quantifier logic.

Modified Syllogistic and Symbolic Logic

For the modified syllogistic which includes empty terms, we discard the rule of Comprehension. It can then be shown, by the procedures of quanti-fier logic, that the only part of the square of opposition which remains valid is the contradictoriness of diagonal opposites, and that of the 256 types of SFCS, only those fifteen which are valid by the rules of modified syllogistic are valid by the rules of quantifier logic.

These proofs amount to a proof that syllogistic is not needed as a separate discipline, since whatever can be done with it can be done with quantifier logic instead.*

Exercises I

For each of the following, construct its three *corresponding* SFCP's.

1. Every student is an honors student.
□ 2. Some marsupial is an opossum.
3. No opossum is a reptile.
4. Some interest-bearing note is not a fully negotiable security.
□ 5. Every counterclockwise ocean current is a phenomenon of the Northern Hemisphere.
6. Some set of hangover symptoms is a result of the residual alcohols in distilled beverages.

Exercises II

1. Give three pairs of corresponding E and A propositions which are both false
2. Give three pairs of corresponding O and I propositions which are both true.

Exercises III

Construct the converse of each of the convertible (E or I) propositions given in Exercises I.

Exercises IV

Construct the obverse of each of the following.

1. Some philosophy student is a student of logic.
2. Every student of logic is a philosophy student.
□ 3. No Born-Again Baptist is a disbeliever in total immersion.
4. Some resident of the Soviet Union is not a Russian.
□ 5. Every combat soldier is a believer.
6. Some porpoise is an intelligent creature.
7. No chicken is an intelligent creature.
8. Every chicken is a retard.
9. Some Nebraska senator is not a Democrat.
□ 10. Every hangover symptom is a result of dehydration of the brain lining.

Exercises V

For each result of Exercises IV which is convertible, give its converse.

---

*For a comprehensive exposition of syllogistic, see Otto Bird, *Syllogistic and Its Extensions* (Englewood Cliffs, N.J.: Prentice-Hall, Inc., 1964).

Exercises VI

For each result of Exercises V, give its obverse.

Exercises VII

Determine which of the following are standard-form categorical syllogisms and which are not. For those which aren't, say why not.

☐ **1.**   Every honors student is a sophomore.
        Some philosophy student is an honors student.
        ∴ Some philosophy honors student is a sophomore.

2.   Some doggie is a cockapoo.
        Some doggie is a pekipoo.
        ∴ Every pekipoo is a cockapoo.

3.   Every kind of communist is a kind of communist.
        Every filthy hippie is a socialist.
        ∴ Every filthy hippie is a kind of communist.

☐ **4.**   Every Greek is a human.
        Every human is a mortal.
        ∴ Every Greek is a mortal.

5.   No Republican is a longhaired freak.
        No Republican is a traitor.
        ∴ No Republican is a Democrat.

6.   No chicken is an intelligent creature.
        Some intelligent creature is a philosopher.
        ∴ Every philosopher is a chicken.

☐ **7.**   Some cats are black.
        Every cat is a mammal.
        ∴ Some mammal is black.

8.   Every Latin American is an ardent lover.
        Some ardent lover is not a Latin American.
        ∴ Some gringo is an ardent lover.

9.   No serious Christian is a believer in astrology.
        Some Senator is a believer in astrology.
        ∴ Some Senator is not a serious Christian.

10.   Every black cat is a cat.
        Every coal black cat is a cat.
        ∴ Every coal black cat is a black cat.

Exercises VIII

Give the mood and figure of each of the following.

1.   Some student is not a resident.
No student is a native of Pasadena.
∴ Some native of Pasadena is not a resident.

□ 2.   Every white horse is a horse.
Every snow white horse is a horse.
∴ Every snow white horse is a white horse.

3.   Every important world record is an entry in the *Guinness Book of Records*.
No distance-spitting record is an important world record.
∴ No distance-spitting record is an entry in the *Guinness Book of Records*.

4.   Some syllogism is an invalid argument.
Every invalid argument is an absurdity.
∴ Some absurdity is not a syllogism.

□ 5.   Every smoker is a nicotine addict.
Every nicotine addict is a tobacco user.
∴ Every tobacco user is a smoker.

6.   Every mink is a prime source of fur.
No prime source of fur is a mangy skunk.
∴ Some mangy skunk is not a mink.

7.   Some college student is a logic student.
Some student is not a college student.
∴ Some student is not a logic student.

□ 8.   Every computer is a perfect mathematician.
Every computer is an intelligent machine.
∴ Some intelligent machine is a perfect mathematician.

9.   Every bear is a furry beast.
Some mammal is a furry beast.
∴ Some mammal is a bear.

10.   No person to be trusted is a politician.
Every politician is a lawyer.
∴ Some lawyer is not a person to be trusted.

□ 11.   No Persian is a Medean.
Some Medean is a Syrian.
∴ Some Syrian is not a Persian.

12.   Some Republican is not an Independent.
            Some Democrat is not a Republican.
            ∴ Some Democrat is not an Independent.

13.   Some racehorse is a quarter-horse.
            No thoroughbred is a quarter-horse.
            ∴ Some thoroughbred is not a racehorse.

14.   Every precious metal is a non-magnetic substance.
            Every platinum alloy is a precious metal.
            ∴ Every platinum alloy is a non-magnetic substance.

☐ **15.**   No chess master is an intellectual cripple.
            Every logician is an intellectual cripple.
            ∴ Some logician is not a chess master.

16.   No yellow ticket is a winning ticket.
            Every yellow ticket is a losing ticket.
            ∴ No losing ticket is a winning ticket.

17.   Some play by Shakespeare is not a tragedy.
            Every play by Shakespeare is a superb drama.
            ∴ Some superb drama is not a tragedy.

18.   Some specimen of gibberish is an item of important information.
            Some piece of pure nonsense is a specimen of gibberish.
            ∴ No piece of pure nonsense is an item of important information.

Exercises IX

Using the two rules of traditional syllogistic, decide which of the syllogisms in Exercises VIII are valid and which are not. For each invalid one, indicate what rule is violated and how.

Exercises X

Of the traditionally valid syllogisms turned up in Exercises IX, decide which of them remain valid under the modified rules for syllogistic with empty terms. For each invalid one, specify how it violates the rule.

appendix N

CONSISTENCY AND COMPLETENESS

Preliminaries

A system of logic is said to be **complete** if it is capable of proving the validity of *every* valid argument within its domain, including zero-premiss arguments (such as tautologies and quantifier-truths). By construing premisses as assumptions, susceptible to discharge, we can reduce any argument to a zero-premiss argument, so that a *proof* of completeness need concern itself only with zero-premiss arguments. We can then say that a system of logic is complete if it is capable of generating every valid zero-premiss conclusion within its domain (for example, the domain of tautologies, or of quantifier-truths, or of quantifier-truths with identity-theorems)—that is, if it is capable of generating every **valid formula** within its domain as a zero-premiss conclusion. (A *formula* is "valid" if there is no way for it to be false—that is, if it has no falsifying interpretations—that is, if it is a logical truth.)

A system of logic is said to be **consistent** if its proof-capabilities are limited to genuinely *valid* arguments (including zero-premiss arguments) within its domain—that is, if it is incapable of "proving" an invalid argument, or of generating a non-valid formula as a zero-premiss conclusion. Again, when *proving* consistency it is useful to eliminate the artificial distinction between premisses and assumptions, so that there is only one notion to contend with instead of two.

With most systems of logic that are rich enough to be easily applied, proofs of their completeness and consistency tend to be unmanageably long and complicated. Therefore, it is the usual practice with such systems to prove

---

I am indebted to my colleague David Bennett for the underlying structure of the completeness and consistency proofs of OI contained in this appendix. I assume full responsibility, however, for their present formulations. For original versions of the completeness proof, see D.W. Bennett, "An Elementary Completeness Proof for a System of Natural Deduction," *Notre Dame Journal of Formal Logic*, July 1973; and "A Note on the Completeness Proof for Natural Deduction," *NDJFL*, forthcoming in 1975.

417

them complete and consistent by showing them to be equivalent to some other, simpler, system whose completeness and consistency may be proven more concisely and easily. This procedure will be followed here.

We shall begin by laying out a system of logic much simpler in its formal structure than the one in the body of the book. It has fewer symbols and far fewer rules and thus is easier to deal with *as a system*. Nevertheless, as we shall show at the end, it is logically equivalent to the fuller system in the book. We shall refer to this simpler logical system as "System O."

The System O

1. *The Symbols:*
   a. A set of capital letters with or without diacritical marks (cf. Chapter 18), to serve as propositional and predicate letters.
   b. A set of lower-case letters with or without diacritical marks, but not underlined, to serve as bound variables.
   c. A set of underlined lower-case letters with or without diacritical marks, to serve as free variables. (The purpose of the underline is to make them typographically distinct from the bound variables, which will help facilitate the completeness proof. This use of the underline is somewhat different from that in the body of the text, since it does away with the artificial distinction between free letters as constants and variables.)
   d. Three operators: negation '$\sim$', conjunction '$\cdot$', and universal quantification '( )'.
   e. Parentheses for punctuation.

2. *The Formation Rules.* These rules provide a formal account of the notion of a "well-formed formula," abbreviated "wff." Nothing is a wff unless its being such follows from these rules:
   a. A capital letter standing alone is a wff (an atomic propositional wff).
   b. A capital letter followed by one or more "free" (underlined) lower-case letters is a wff (an atomic predicate wff).
   c. If Φ is a wff then $\sim\Phi$ is a wff.
   d. If Φ and Ψ are wffs, then $(\Phi \cdot \Psi)$ is a wff.
   e. If Φ is like a wff except for containing one or more occurrences of a single "bound" (non-underlined) lower-case letter α where a wff would contain a "free" letter, and if the quantifier (α) does not occur *within* Φ, then $(\alpha)\Phi$ is a wff.

3. *The Rules of Derivation.* These specify the permissible inferences in System O.
   a. INDIRECT PROOF: From an explicit contradiction (a formula of the form $(\Phi \cdot \sim\Phi)$, *discharge* the most recent assumption and *infer* its negation.
   b. SEVERANCE: From a conjunction, *infer* either conjunct (or both of them).

c. CONJOINING: From two lines, *infer* their conjunction.
d. DOUBLE NEGATION: From Φ *infer* $\sim\sim\Phi$; from $\sim\sim\Phi$ *infer* Φ.
e. UNIVERSAL INSTANTIATION: From $(\beta)\Phi\beta$ *infer* $\Phi\underline{\alpha}$ ($\Phi\beta$ and $\Phi\underline{\alpha}$ just alike, except that every occurrence of β becomes one of $\underline{\alpha}$).
f. UNIVERSAL GENERALIZATION: From $\Phi\underline{\alpha}$, where $\underline{\alpha}$ doesn't occur in any undischarged assumption, *infer* $(\beta)\Phi\beta$ ($\Phi\underline{\alpha}$ and $\Phi\beta$ just alike except that every occurrence of $\underline{\alpha}$ changes to an occurrence of β and every occurrence of β comes from such a change).

4. *Miscellany:*
   a. A **derivation** is any sequence of formulae obtainable by the procedure of taking on assumptions, plus the above rules. (This means that derivations never contain un-arrowed premisses; premisses must be taken on as assumptions.)
   b. A formula is **proved** (is a zero-premiss conclusion or "theorem") of the system just in case it is the final step in a derivation containing no undischarged assumptions.

This completes the specification of System O.

Completeness of System O

To prove that System O is complete, we need only show that any of its formulas which are not provable in it are not valid formulas—that is, that any valid formula of O is provable within O.

Let Λ be some arbitrary formula which cannot be proved in O. It can be shown (via a *Reductio ad absurdum* proof) that Λ is not valid.

We define a **D-deduction** as a derivation each of whose assumptions is undischarged and remains so in every extension of the derivation—that is, a derivation each of whose assumptions is undischargeable.

We define the **B-extension** of a D-deduction as the result of treating each step in the D-deduction, in order, by the appropriate Extension Rule (given below) and adding the result to the deduction, omitting repetitions of earlier lines as they occur.

Extension Rules:
1. From a step of the form $(\Phi \cdot \Psi)$, introduce inferences of the form Φ and then of the form Ψ by Severance.
2. From a step of the form $\sim\sim\Phi$, introduce an inference of the form Φ by Double Negation.
3. From a step of the form $(\beta)\Phi\beta$, introduce inferences of the form $\Phi\underline{\alpha}$ by Universal Instantiation, using each free variable already in the derivation, in their given order, and then the first free variable *not* already in the derivation.
4. From a step of the form $\sim(\Phi \cdot \Psi)$, introduce an *assumption* of the form $\sim\Phi$, or, if that would be dischargeable, introduce an assumption of the form $\sim\Psi$.

5. From a step of the form $\sim(\beta)\Phi\beta$, introduce an *assumption* of the form $\sim\Phi\alpha$, where the free variable is the first in order that does not already occur in the derivation.

It is easy to show that the B-extension of a D-deduction will also be a D-deduction (that is, that all of *its* assumptions will be undischargeable). Extension rules 4 and 5 are the ones by which new assumptions get into a B-extension. If such an assumption were dischargeable, it would mean that an earlier assumption would also be dischargeable, which is impossible in a D-deduction.

Proof: First, suppose $\sim(\Phi \cdot \Psi)$ is a step in some D-deduction. Rule 4 says assume $\sim\Phi$, or if it were dischargeable assume $\sim\Psi$. If it were also possible to discharge $\sim\Psi$, it would be possible to obtain Φ (by discharging $\sim\Phi$) and also to obtain Ψ (by discharging $\sim\Psi$), and so to obtain $(\Phi \cdot \Psi)$ by Conjoining, and so to obtain $(\Phi \cdot \Psi) \cdot \sim(\Phi \cdot \Psi)$, which is an explicit contradiction; thus it would be possible to discharge some earlier assumption in the D-deduction. But that is impossible. Therefore, an assumption introduced into a D-deduction by Rule 4 cannot be discharged.

Next, suppose $\sim(\beta)\Phi\beta$ is a step in some D-deduction. Rule 5 says to assume $\sim\Phi\alpha$, where α is a fresh letter. If this assumption were discharged, the result would be $\Phi\alpha$, with α not occurring in any undischarged assumption (since it was a fresh letter in $\sim\Phi\alpha$, and that has been discharged). Hence, by Universal Generalization we could infer $(\beta)\Phi\beta$, and thus infer $(\beta)\Phi\beta \cdot \sim(\beta)\Phi\beta$, which is an explicit contradiction. Therefore, we could discharge some earlier assumption in the D-deduction. But that isn't possible. Therefore, an assumption introduced into a D-deduction by Rule 5 cannot be discharged.

Thus, the B-extension of a D-deduction is also a D-deduction. And therefore, the B-extension of the B-extension of a D-deduction will also be a D-deduction, and the B-extension of the B-extension of the B-extension of a D-deduction will also be a D-deduction; and so on. Call every such B-extension (including the first one) a **recursively developed B-extension** of the original D-deduction, since they are obtained by recursive (repeated and successive) applications of the B-extension procedure. The matter can then be stated succinctly as: every recursively developed B-extension of a D-deduction is also a D-deduction.

Now let us return to Λ, the arbitrary formula which cannot be proved within System O, and to our proof that Λ is not a valid formula.

First, $\sim\Lambda$ is undischargeable in the derivation (call it **D**) whose only assumption is $\sim\Lambda$. (If it were dischargeable, Λ would be provable.) Since $\sim\Lambda$ is the only assumption in **D**, and is undischargeable, **D** is a D-deduction.

Call a formula **attainable** (relative to $\sim\Lambda$) just in case it occurs as a line in some recursively developed B-extension of **D**.

Now give the system O the following interpretation **W** (which is relative to **D**): let the quantifiers range over the natural numbers, and let free variables (in their given order) designate distinct natural numbers.

Let an *atomic* formula be assigned the value True if and only if it is *attainable*—that is, if and only if it occurs as a line in some recursively developed B-extension of **D**. This interprets the propositional and predicate letters "in extension." If something further is wanted, interpret each of them as any intension (proposition, or property, or relation) conforming to this truth-value assignment.

Let non-atomic formulae have their truth-values determined by those of the atomic formulae under the customary (truth-functional and quantificational) interpretation of the logical operators.

It can be shown that every formula *attainable* relative to $\sim\Lambda$ has the value True under the interpretation **W**. To show it, assume its negation—that there are *False, attainable* formulae relative to $\sim\Lambda$: let λ be a shortest such. Then λ is False and is attainable relative to $\sim\Lambda$, and no False formula attainable relative to $\sim\Lambda$ is shorter than λ.

First, λ cannot be atomic, for under **W** all attainable atomic formulae are True.

Also, λ cannot be the negation of an atomic formula μ; for since λ is False, μ would be True, and because atomic, attainable. Hence, both μ and its negation λ would be attainable, permitting the discharge of an assumption. But this is not possible in a D-deduction, such as the one to which λ belongs.

Therefore, λ must have one of the five forms treated in Extension Rules 1–5. But from a False formula, the appropriate Extension Rule will generate a *shorter* False formula, so that there would be a False formula shorter than λ, which contradicts the hypothesis that λ was shortest.

Therefore, λ does not exist. There are no shortest attainable False formulae, and hence *no* attainable False formulae.

Therefore, every formula attainable relative to $\sim\Lambda$ is True under **W**, and this includes $\sim\Lambda$ itself.

Therefore, if Λ cannot be proved, there is an interpretation (namely **W**) under which $\sim\Lambda$ is True—that is, an interpretation under which Λ is False.

But Λ is valid if and only if it is *True* under *every* interpretation.

Therefore, if Λ cannot be proved, Λ is not a valid formula.

Therefore (by contraposition), if Λ is a valid formula, Λ can be proved.

Therefore, every valid formula of O can be proven within O.

System O contains only the operators of negation, conjunction, and universal quantification. However the remaining truth-functions can be *defined* in terms of negation and conjunction, via the following "abbreviative definitions":

Let $\Phi \supset \Psi$ mean $\sim(\Phi \cdot \sim\Psi)$

Let $\Phi \vee \Psi$ mean $\sim(\sim\Phi \cdot \sim\Psi)$

Let $\Phi \equiv \Psi$ mean $\sim(\Phi \cdot \sim\Psi) \cdot \sim(\Psi \cdot \sim\Phi)$

and existential quantification can be defined in terms of universal quantification and negation, via the abbreviative definition:

Let $(\exists\,\alpha)\Phi$ mean $\sim(\alpha)\sim\Phi$

"Abbreviative definitions" such as these are employed in derivations by way of the Principle of Definitional Substitution: "A definiendum (defined expression) may be substituted for its definiens (defining expression) in any context, and vice versa." When definitions are added to a system, this principle automatically goes along with them.

When System O is supplemented by the above four definitions (call the resulting system O+), any valid formula expressible within the full symbolism of regular predicate logic will be demonstrably equivalent, via these definitions, to a valid (hence provable) formula of O, containing only negation, conjunction, and universal quantification. Thus, every valid formula of predicate logic is provable within O+.

Completeness with Identity

We can expand System O to a system of predicate logic with identity by making the following additions to it.

Symbols:
f. A predicate constant '$=$', called **double bar**.

Formation Rules:
f. A double bar flanked by free variables is a wff (an atomic identity wff).

Rules of Derivation:
g. SELF-IDENTITY: At any point in a derivation, *infer* $\alpha = \alpha$.
h. INDISCERNIBILITY: From $\Phi\alpha$ and $\alpha = \beta$ or $\beta = \alpha$, *infer* $\Phi\beta$ ($\Phi\alpha$ and $\Phi\beta$ just alike except that one or more occurrences of α change to β).

Call this System OI.

An **identity formula** is any formula containing a double bar. A **valid identity formula** (or "identity theorem") is any identity formula which, when the double bar is interpreted as identity (defined below), remains true under every interpretation.

The double bar is "interpreted as identity" just in case: an atomic identity-formula is to be assigned the value True if and only if its two terms denote exactly the same object, entity, or thing.

A system of predicate logic with identity is **complete** just in case it generates not only every theorem of predicate logic, but every identity theorem as well.

We may expand the proof of O's completeness into a proof of the completeness of OI, using essentially the same strategy. To avoid complications later, we introduce one now.

A **substitution series** is a series (that is, an ordered set) of formulae obtained from an identity statement $\alpha = \beta$ and a formula $\Phi\alpha$ (containing one or more occurrences of α) by the following recipe. Suppose the occurrences of α (in $\Phi\alpha$) numbered sequentially 1 through n from left to right. Then the first member of the series is the formula which results from replacing occurrence 1 of α with β; the second member is the formula which results from replacing occurrence 2 of α with β, and so on across until each single occurrence of α has been replaced by β to generate a formula in the series. The next member of the series is the formula which results from replacing occurrences 1 and 2 of α with β, then occurrences 1 and 3, and so on up to occurrences 1 and n; then occurrences 2 and 3, 2 and 4, . . . , 2 and n, and so on, until each *pair* of occurrences of α has been replaced by β to generate formulae in the series. The next member of the series will be the result of replacing occurrences 1, 2, and 3 with β, then 1, 2, 4, . . . , 1, 2, n, then 1, 3, 4, . . . , 1, 3, n, . . . , 2, 3, 4, . . . , 2, 3, n, and so on, until each *trio* of occurrences has generated its replacement-member in the series . . . and so on. A **full substitution series** generated by $\alpha = \beta$ and $\Phi\alpha$ is the series which results from following this process all the way to its conclusion, at which point the last member of the series will be the result of replacing all n occurrences of α with β.

The proof of OI's completeness requires two additional Extension Rules:

6. If a step is of the form $\alpha = \beta$, then for each step in the derivation of the form $\Phi\alpha$, in the order of their occurrence, infer the full substitution series generated by the two formulae, by Indiscernibility.

7. After each step in the derivation has been treated by the appropriate rule 1–6, introduce new inferences of the form $\alpha = \alpha$ for each free variable already in the derivation, in the order of their occurrence, and then for the first free variable *not* already in the derivation.

If a formula $\alpha = \beta$ constitutes a line in the derivation, call α an **equate** of β and β an **equate** of α in that line. Modify the earlier interpretation **W** to a new interpretation **WI**, as follows: let each free variable designate the class of its own equates within attainable formulae, and let the quantifiers range over the classes so designated.

Let an atomic formula be assigned the value True if and only if it is attainable. (Let it be assigned the value False otherwise.) Note that if an atomic formula $\alpha = \beta$ is attainable, α and β will have the same class of equates, and so $\alpha = \beta$ will be true. Note also that if $\alpha = \beta$ is not attainable, then α and β will have distinct classes of equates, so that $\alpha = \beta$ will be false. Thus the present interpretation of atomic formulae is fully compatible with the underlying interpretation of the double bar as "identity." The interpretation of the free variables and quantifiers was designed to achieve this.

A potential type of ambiguity in this interpretation—which would occur if $\Phi\underline{\alpha}$ and $\underline{\alpha} = \underline{\beta}$ were attainable but $\Phi\underline{\beta}$ were not attainable, thus making the same proposition (but not the same formula) both True and False—is ruled out by Extension Rule 6, which makes $\Phi\underline{\beta}$ attainable whenever $\Phi\underline{\alpha}$ and $\underline{\alpha} = \underline{\beta}$ are.

Let non-atomic formulae have their truth-values determined by those of the atomic formulae under the customary interpretation of the logical operators.

The proof then proceeds as before, and constitutes a proof that every valid formula of OI (that is, every valid formula expressible by negation, conjunction, universal quantification, and the double bar) can be proven within OI.When the four abbreviative definitions are added to OI, the resulting system OI+ will be able to express every formula within the full symbolism of regular predicate logic with identity. Thus, every valid formula of predicate logic with identity is provable within OI+.

Consistency of System O

A system of logic would be **inconsistent** if it were possible to start with a set of true assumptions (premisses) and, using just the rules of that system, to derive a false conclusion—or, as a special case of this, if it were possible, using just the rules of that system, to derive a false proposition (either a contingent falsehood or a contradiction) as a zero-premiss conclusion.

Thus, we may prove a system of logic **consistent** by proving that it does not admit of this possibility: by proving that the rules of the system lead from truth only to truth, that within a derivation in the system each derived line is genuinely *entailed* by the assumptions it is derived from, and that no zero-premiss conclusion derivable in the system is a contradiction or a contingency (clearly, if even a *true* contingency were derivable, there would be a false contingency of the same form derivable).

Let entailment be defined as follows: P **entails** Q just in case Q has the value True under every interpretation which gives P the value True—that is, if and only if there is no interpretation which simultaneously makes P True and Q False.

In the proof below, the following symbolism is presupposed: 'A_1' to represent the first undischarged assumption in a derivation, 'A_2' to represent the second, and, in general, 'A_n' to represent the nth undischarged assumption in the derivation. A three-dot ellipsis will be used to represent the steps intervening between two given steps: thus '$A_k \ldots A_z$' will represent all steps from the kth assumption through the zth assumption, inclusive, '$A_n \ldots P$' will represent all steps from the nth assumption through some line P inclusive, and so on. Nothing in the symbolism should be taken to imply than n must be greater than zero. If $z = 0$, for example, then $A_k \ldots A_z$ will be all steps through the zeroth undischarged assumption—that is, an empty collection of steps. The proof thus will apply to derivations having only *discharged* assumptions, as well as to derivations having undischarged ones.

To Prove: In any derivation using only the six rules of System O, each derived line will be entailed by its assumptions (those assumptions within whose scope it lies). Underived lines will fall into place automatically, for each of them is an assumption, lying within its own scope, and entailed by its assumptions because it entails itself.

Proof (by *Reductio ad absurdum*): Assume that there is a derivation **G** generated by the six rules, but such that at least one derived line in **G** is *not* entailed by its assumptions; call the *earliest* unentailed line **S**. It will be shown that there must be an earlier one, which is a contradiction, thus refuting the assumption that there is a derivation such as **G**. There are six different cases to consider, one for each of the rules of System O.

Case 1: *Suppose* **S** *was derived by IP*. Then **G** has the structure

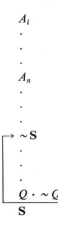

$$A_i$$
.
.
.
$$A_n$$
.
.
.

→ $\sim$**S**
.
.
.
$$Q \cdot \sim Q$$
S

Since **S** is not entailed by $A_i \ldots A_n$, there is (by the definition of entailment) an interpretation **I** under which all of the assumptions in $A_i \ldots A_n$ are True and **S** is False. Therefore, **I** is an interpretation under which the assumptions in $A_i \ldots A_n$ *and* $\sim$**S** (the assumption leading to $Q \cdot \sim Q$) are all True while $Q \cdot \sim Q$ is, of course, False. Thus, the existence of **I** shows that $A_i \ldots A_n$ and $\sim$**S** do not entail $Q \cdot \sim Q$, making it an unentailed line earlier than the earliest one, **S**, which is a contradiction. Therefore, the supposition is false and **S** was not derived by IP.

Case 2: Suppose S *was derived by UG.* Then S has the form $(\beta)\Phi\beta$, and G has the structure

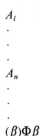

A_i

.

.

.

A_n

.

.

.

$(\beta)\Phi\beta$

where $(\beta)\Phi\beta$ comes from some earlier line $\Phi\alpha$ whose assumptions are included in $A_i \ldots A_n$, such that α does not occur in any assumption in $A_i \ldots A_n$, by the restriction on UG. Since $(\beta)\Phi\beta$ is not entailed by its assumptions, there is an interpretation I under which each assumption in $A_i \ldots A_n$ is True but $(\beta)\Phi\beta$ is False. However, since the assumptions leading to $\Phi\alpha$ are devoid of α, no interpretation of *them* can force an interpretation of the free variable α: its interpretation remains open after the assumptions in $A_i \ldots A_n$ have been fully interpreted. Since $(\beta)\Phi\beta$ is False under I, there are (under I) things which are not Φ. Interpret α as the name of one of them, and call I thus supplemented I+. Under I+, all the assumptions for $\Phi\alpha$ are True (since they are included in $A_i \ldots A_n$) but $\Phi\alpha$ is False, making it an unentailed line earlier than the earliest one, which is a contradiction. Therefore, the supposition is false and S was not derived by UG.

Case 3: Suppose S *was derived by UI.* Then S has the form $\Phi\alpha$ and comes from an earlier line $(\beta)\Phi\beta$ whose assumptions are included in $A_i \ldots A_n$. Since $\Phi\alpha$ is not entailed by its assumptions, there is an interpretation I under which each assumption in $A_i \ldots A_n$ has the value True but $\Phi\alpha$ has the value False. However, I is also an interpretation under which each assumption for $(\beta)\Phi\beta$ is True (because they are included in $A_i \ldots A_n$) while $(\beta)\Phi\beta$ is False (because $\Phi\alpha$ is False). Thus, $(\beta)\Phi\beta$ is an unentailed line earlier than the earliest one, which is a contradiction. Therefore, the supposition is false and S was not derived by UI.

Case 4: Suppose S *was derived by Conj.* Then S has the form $(\Phi \cdot \Psi)$ and comes from earlier lines Φ and Ψ whose assumptions are included in $A_i \ldots A_n$. Since $(\Phi \cdot \Psi)$ is not entailed by its assumptions, there is an interpretation I under which each assumption in $A_i \ldots A_n$ is True but $(\Phi \cdot \Psi)$ is False. However, I is also an interpretation under which the assumptions for Φ and Ψ are True and under which (because of the definition of the dot) at least one of Φ, Ψ is False, so that at least one of Φ, Ψ is an unentailed line earlier than the earliest one, which is a contradiction. Therefore, the supposition is false and S was not derived by Conj.

Case 5: Suppose **S** *was derived by Sev.* Then there is an earlier line **P** which is a conjunction, of which **S** is one conjunct, whose assumptions are included in $A_i \ldots A_n$. Since **S** is not entailed by its assumptions, there is an interpretation **I** under which each assumption in $A_i \ldots A_n$ is True while **S** is False. But since one of its conjuncts is False, **P** is (by the definition of conjunction) also False under **I**, so **P** is an unentailed line earlier than the earliest one, which is a contradiction. Therefore the supposition is false, and **S** was not derived by Sev.

Case 6: Suppose **S** *was derived by DN.* Then there is an earlier line **P** from which **S** is derived, whose assumptions are included in $A_i \ldots A_n$, and which is just like **S** except that it is prefixed by two more, or two fewer, tildes than **S**. Since **S** is not entailed by its assumptions, there is an interpretation **I** under which each assumption in $A_i \ldots A_n$ is True but **S** is False. But then, by the definition of the tilde, **P** is also False, making it an unentailed line earlier than the earliest one, which is a contradiction. Therefore, the supposition is false and **S** was not derived by DN.

Therefore, **S** was not derived by any of the six derivation rules. Therefore, there is no such line as **S**—that is, no earliest unentailed line—and so there are no unentailed lines in **G**. Therefore, there is no such derivation as **G**, which was supposed to be a derivation containing an unentailed derived line. In every derivation generated by the six rules, every line will be entailed by its assumptions. In the special case where a line has zero assumptions, there will be no interpretation under which that line is False: it will be a valid formula. Therefore, System O is consistent.

Consistency with Identity

We may easily extend the above to a proof of the consistency of OI by considering two more cases.

Case 7: Suppose **S** *was derived by Indiscernibility.* Then **S** has the form $\Phi\beta$ and is derived from line $\Phi\alpha$ and $\alpha = \beta$, whose assumptions are included in $A_i \ldots A_n$. Since $\Phi\beta$ is not entailed by its assumptions, there is an interpretation **I** under which each assumption in $A_i \ldots A_n$ is True but $\Phi\beta$ is False. But if $\alpha = \beta$ is True under **I**, then (since the double bar is interpreted as identity) $\Phi\alpha$ must also be False under **I**; and if $\Phi\alpha$ is True under **I**, then $\alpha = \beta$ must be False under **I**. So if either of $\Phi\alpha$, $\alpha = \beta$ is True under **I** the other must be False under **I**, so at least one of them must be False under **I**, making it an unentailed line earlier than the earliest one, which is a contradiction. Therefore, the supposition is false and **S** was not derived by Indiscernibility.

Case 8: Suppose **S** *was derived by Self-Identity.* Then **S** has the form $\alpha = \alpha$. When the double bar is interpreted as identity (as it is in OI), there is no consistent interpretation of α under which $\alpha = \alpha$ is False—that is, $\alpha = \alpha$ is True under every interpretation. Therefore, there is no interpretation **I** under which the assumptions in $A_i \ldots A_n$ are all True and $\alpha = \alpha$ is False, so the earliest unentailed line is entailed by its assumptions, which is a contradiction. Therefore, the supposition is false and **S** was not derived by Self-Identity.

Consistency of O+ and OI+

So long as the new symbols introduced into a consistent system by "abbreviative definitions" remain uninterpreted, no set of abbreviative definitions can be inconsistent. However, when an interpretation is imposed upon the new symbols, it might turn out that that interpretation is incompatible with the sense injected into the symbols by the definitions. Thus, it is necessary to show that the four abbreviative definitions used to transform O (and OI) into O+ (and OI+) are consistent and compatible with O (and OI) whenever the new symbols ($\vee$, $\supset$, $\equiv$, and $\exists$) are given their standard interpretation as truth-functors and existential quantification. To do this we need only show that under this interpretation the definiendum and definiens of each definition will be logical equivalents—that there is no (further) interpretation under which they differ in truth-value.

For the first three definitions this is easily shown by truth-tables. Giving the wedge, horseshoe, and triple bar (and of course the dot and tilde) their standard interpretation, definiens and definiendum will be tautologous equivalents in each case.

For the fourth definition, we may employ a *Reductio ad absurdum*. Suppose, under the interpretation of $\exists$ as existential quantification, $(\exists \beta)\Phi$ and $\sim(\beta) \sim \Phi$ are not logically equivalent. Then there will be an interpretation **I** under which they differ in truth-value. There are two possibilities.

Case 1: Suppose that under **I**, $(\exists \beta)\Phi$ *is True and* $\sim(\beta) \sim \Phi$ *is False.* Then Φ is satisfied under **I**. Call one of the things which satisfies it α. Since $\sim(\beta) \sim \Phi$ is False, $(\beta) \sim \Phi$ is True—that is, under **I**, everything satisfies $\sim \Phi$; and this includes α. Thus α satisfies both Φ and $\sim \Phi$, which is a contradiction. Therefore, the supposition is false.

Case 2: Suppose that under **I**, $(\exists \beta)\Phi$ *is False and* $\sim(\beta) \sim \Phi$ *is True.* Then $(\beta) \sim \Phi$ is False, and so it follows that, under **I**, at least one thing fails to satisfy $\sim \Phi$. Call one such thing α. By the definition of 'satisfy' and of the tilde, α satisfies Φ since it fails to satisfy $\sim\Phi$. But then at least one thing satisfies Φ, so $(\exists\,\beta)\Phi$ is True. Thus $(\exists\,\beta)\Phi$ is both False and True, which is a contradiction. Therefore, the supposition is false.

Thus, the abbreviative definitions are consistent with the standard interpretation of the "new" symbols. Therefore, under the standard interpretation of operators, both O+ and OI+ are consistent.

A final point may also be made about the *completeness* proof. Since the four definitions generate logical equivalents, it follows that definiens and definiendum will always have the same logical status. Thus, from a valid formula in the full symbolism of regular predicate logic, the four definitions will generate a valid, hence provable, formula in the symbolism of O. Thus, every valid formula of regular predicate logic (or predicate logic with identity) may be proven in O+ (or OI+).

Completeness and Consistency of the Main System of the Book

Whatever entails a complete system is itself complete. Whatever is entailed by a consistent system is itself consistent. Therefore, whatever entails and is entailed by—that is, whatever is logically equivalent to—a complete and consistent system is itself complete and consistent.

Two logical systems are logically equivalent just in case every inference validated by the one is likewise validated by the other, and vice versa. Thus, to prove two systems equivalent, we need only show that every inference rule of the one is obtainable, either as a primitive rule or as a "derived rule," within the other, and vice versa. Let us refer to the system of logic presented in the body of this book as "the Main System." In what follows we shall show that it is logically equivalent to System OI+, and hence that it is both complete and consistent.

1. *Proof that the Main System entails* OI+

Each of the derivation rules of OI is a derivation rule of the Main System, except DN. Since DN is a transformation rule of the Main System, the (weaker) DN inference rule may easily be obtained as a derived rule.

The four abbreviative definitions which convert OI into OI+ may be construed as transformation rules. The standard way of justifying a transformation rule within a system is by showing that the two forms involved in the translation are logically equivalent to each other. Thus, we may show the four transformation rules to be "part of" the Main System by showing that the following four equivalences are provable within the Main System.

/ ∴ (Φ ⊃ Ψ) ≡ ~(Φ · ~Ψ)
/ ∴ (Φ ∨ Ψ) ≡ ~(~Φ · ~Ψ)
/ ∴ (Φ ≡ Ψ) ≡ (~(Φ · ~Ψ) · ~(Ψ · ~Φ))
/ ∴ (∃ β)Φ ≡ ~(β)~Φ

Their actual proofs are easy and are left as exercises.

2. *Proof that* OI+ *entails the Main System*

The Main System contains 42 rules: CP, IP, 10 inference rules for truth-functions, 12 transformation rules for truth-functions, 4 inference rules for quantifiers, 11 transformation rules for quantifiers, 2 inference rules for identity, and one transformation rule for identity. Not all of them will be derived here. Instead, proofs of a few of the main ones will be given and the rest left as exercises. When attempting these exercises, bear in mind that after (and only after) a rule belonging to the Main System has been established within OI+, it may be used in deriving further rules belonging to the Main System. A rule is derived by showing that the inference (or transformation) permitted by that rule can also be obtained through some combination of other rules.

A. *A derivation of CP*

This is one of the more complicated and difficult rules to derive within OI+; it also provides one of the most useful tools for generating further derived rules and so will be presented first.

We will begin by restating the CP rule in a slightly different phrasing, which has exactly the same results as the original.

> CONDITIONAL PROOF REPHRASED: If, following an assumption Φ, a line Ψ is inferred, then *infer* Φ ⊃ Ψ without leaving Φ as an undischarged assumption.

Within the Main System the last part of this rule would simply mean: discharge Φ and infer Φ ⊃ Ψ. But within OI+ a discharge of the most recent assumption requires a contradiction, since IP is the only discharge rule, and Φ will not yield a contradiction in all cases. Therefore, it is necessary to let the last part of the rule mean something more complicated.

Suppose then that for some formula Φ, when Φ is assumed at line *i* in the proof (*i* can be any positive number), it is possible to obtain a formula Ψ at a later line *n*, thus:

```
        ·
        ·
        ·
→i   Φ
        ·
        ·
        ·
 n   Ψ
```

Then it would also have been possible to have assumed ($\Phi \cdot \sim\Psi$) at line h (that is, immediately before the assumption Φ) and still to have conducted the derivation from i through n, thus:

$$\longrightarrow h \quad (\Phi \cdot \sim\Psi)$$
$$\rightarrow i. \quad \Phi$$

as in the original derivation

$$n. \quad \Psi$$

(if it was possible to proceed from Φ to Ψ *without* assumption h, it will still be possible *with* it). The derivation could then be continued as follows:

$\longrightarrow h.$	$(\Phi \cdot \sim\Psi)$	
$\rightarrow i.$	Φ	
$n.$	Ψ	
$o.$	$\sim\Psi$	h, sev.
$p.$	$(\Psi \cdot \sim\Psi)$	n, o, conj.
$q.$	$\sim\Phi$	i–p, IP
$r.$	Φ	h, sev.
$s.$	$(\Phi \cdot \sim\Phi)$	q, r, conj.
$t.$	$\sim(\Phi \cdot \sim\Psi)$	h–s, IP
$u.$	$\Phi \supset \Psi$	t, def. of $\supset$

in which $\Phi \supset \Psi$ has been inferred without leaving Φ as an undischarged assumption.

Thus, we may regard the rephrased version of Conditional Proof as shorthand for the following explicit instructions:

> CONDITIONAL PROOF REPHRASED AGAIN: If, following an assumption Φ, a line Ψ is inferred, then insert an assumption ($\Phi \cdot \sim\Psi$) immediately before the assumption Φ and derive $\sim(\Phi \cdot \sim\Psi)$ by IP; then infer $\Phi \supset \Psi$ by the definition of the horseshoe.

Since each such proof will follow the invariant pattern given above, we may introduce a shorthand notation for the sequence of steps h through u—namely, the following structure:

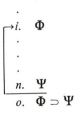

$i.$ Φ

.
.
.

$n.$ Ψ

$o.$ $\Phi \supset \Psi$

It is to be understood that, on demand, this shorthand version can be unpacked into the full sequence of steps depicted earlier; thus it is simply an abbreviation for a proof technique from OI+, using only the rules of OI+.

B. *The Rules for Truth-Functions*

With CP, IP, and the rules and definitions of OI+, it is an elementary exercise to derive the truth-functional inference and transformation rules of the Main System. As an illustration, a derivation is given of Modus Ponens. The remaining proofs are left as exercises.

1. $\Phi \supset \Psi$	
2. Φ $/ \therefore \Psi$	
3. $\sim\!\Psi$	
4. $\sim(\Phi \cdot \sim\!\Psi)$	1, def. of $\supset$
5. $(\Phi \cdot \sim\!\Psi)$	2, 3, conj.
6. $((\Phi \cdot \sim\!\Psi) \cdot \sim(\Phi \cdot \sim\!\Psi))$	4, 5, conj.
7. $\sim\!\sim\!\Psi$	3–6, IP
8. Ψ	7, DN

C. *Quantifier Negation*

With CP, IP, the Main System truth-functional rules, and the rules and definitions of OI+, it is an elementary exercise to derive the rules of Quantifier Negation by deriving the equivalences

$$/ \therefore \sim(\alpha)\Phi\alpha \equiv (\exists \alpha)\sim\!\Phi\alpha$$
$$/ \therefore \sim(\exists \alpha)\Phi\alpha \equiv (\alpha)\sim\!\Phi\alpha$$

As an illustration, one half of the first one is proven below. The rest are left as exercises.

1. $(\exists \alpha)\sim\!\Phi\alpha$ $/ \therefore \sim(\alpha)\Phi\alpha$	
2. $(\alpha)\Phi\alpha$	
3. $\sim(\alpha)\sim\!\sim\!\Phi\alpha$	1, def. of $\exists$
4. $\Phi\beta$	2, UI α/β
5. $\sim\!\sim\!\Phi\beta$	4, DN
6. $(\alpha)\sim\!\sim\!\Phi\alpha$	5, UG β/α
7. $((\alpha)\sim\!\sim\!\Phi\alpha \cdot \sim(\alpha)\sim\!\sim\!\Phi\alpha)$	6, 3, conj.
8. $\sim(\alpha)\Phi\alpha$	2–7, IP
9. $(\exists \alpha)\sim\!\Phi\alpha \supset \sim(\alpha)\Phi\alpha$	1–8, CP

D. *QS for Conditionals, part 1*

To facilitate the derivation of EI (below), we give a derivation of one of the logical equivalences generating the Quantifier Shift rules of the Main System.

1. $(\alpha)(\Phi\alpha \supset \Psi)$	
2. $(\exists\alpha)\Phi\alpha$ /∴ Ψ	
3. $\sim\Psi$	
4. $\Phi\beta \supset \Psi$	1, UI α/β
5. $\sim\Phi\beta$	3, 4, MT
6. $(\alpha)\sim\Phi\alpha$	5, UG β/α
7. $\sim(\exists\alpha)\Phi\alpha$	6, QN
8. $(\exists\alpha)\Phi\alpha \cdot \sim(\exists\alpha)\Phi\alpha$	2, 7, conj.
9. Ψ	3–8, IP
10. $(\exists\alpha)\Phi\alpha \supset \Psi$	2–9, CP
11. $(\alpha)(\Phi\alpha \supset \Psi) \supset ((\exists\alpha)\Phi\alpha \supset \Psi)$	1–10, CP
12. $(\exists\alpha)\Phi\alpha \supset \Psi$	
13. $\Phi\beta$	
14. $\sim\Psi$	
15. $\sim(\exists\alpha)\Phi\alpha$	12, 14, MT
16. $(\alpha)\sim\Phi\alpha$	15, QN
17. $\sim\Phi\beta$	16, UI α/β
18. $\Phi\beta \cdot \sim\Phi\beta$	13, 17, conj.
19. Ψ	14–18, IP, DN
20. $\Phi\beta \supset \Psi$	13–19, CP
21. $(\alpha)(\Phi\alpha \supset \Psi)$	20, UG β/α
22. $((\exists\alpha)\Phi\alpha \supset \Psi) \supset (\alpha)(\Phi\alpha \supset \Psi)$	12–21, CP
23. $(\alpha)(\Phi\alpha \supset \Psi) \equiv ((\exists\alpha)\Phi\alpha \supset \Psi)$	11, 22, conj. BE

E. *Existential Instantiation*

To facilitate the proof, we shall restate EI in a slightly different phrasing.

EXISTENTIAL INSTANTIATION REPHRASED: If $(\exists\beta)\Phi\beta$ is a line in a derivation, and after introducing an assumption $\Phi\alpha$ (α occurring neither in $\Phi\beta$ nor in any earlier assumption, and $\Phi\beta$ and $\Phi\alpha$ just alike except that every occurrence of β becomes one of α) it is possible to derive a line Ψ not containing α, then *infer* Ψ without leaving $\Phi\alpha$ as an undischarged assumption.

The first part of the rephrased rule describes a derivation of the following structure:

.
.
.

i. $(\exists\beta)\Phi\beta$

.
.
.

$\rightarrow k.$ $\Phi\underline{\alpha}$ (suppose $\underline{\alpha}$ not free in earlier assumptions)
.
.

.

$n.$ Ψ

Using only the rules of OI+ and rules derived from them, we can obtain Ψ without leaving $\Phi\underline{\alpha}$ undischarged, by extending the derivation as follows:

.
.

.

$i.$ $(\exists\,\beta)\Phi\beta$
.

.

$\rightarrow k.$ $\Phi\underline{\alpha}$
.
.
.

$n.$ Ψ

$o.$	$\Phi\underline{\alpha} \supset \Psi$	$k{-}n$, CP
$p.$	$(\beta)(\Phi\beta \supset \Psi)$	o, UG $\underline{\alpha}/\beta$
$q.$	$(\exists\,\beta)\Phi\beta \supset \Psi$	p, QS for Conditionals, part 1
$r.$	Ψ	i, q, MP

Note that step (p), UG, is valid precisely because $\underline{\alpha}$ is a clean letter, and that step (q), QS, is valid precisely because $\underline{\alpha}$ doesn't occur in Ψ, and that step (r), MP, is possible precisely because $\underline{\alpha}$ in (k) occupied *just* the places bound by the quantifier in (i)—that is, it was a fresh letter; and that these are the conditions in the original phrasing of EI.

As with CP, the above invariant sequence may be given a shorthand abbreviation as follows:

.
.

.

$i.$ $(\exists\,\beta)\Phi\beta$
.

.

$\rightarrow k.$ $\Phi\alpha$
.
.
.

$m.$ Ψ

$n.$ Ψ

F. *Existential Generalization*

1. $\Phi\beta$ / $\therefore$ ($\exists\,\alpha$)$\Phi\alpha$
2. $\sim$($\exists\,\alpha$)$\Phi\alpha$
3. $(\alpha)\sim\Phi\alpha$ 2, QN
4. $\sim\Phi\beta$ 3, UI α/β
5. $\Phi\beta \cdot \sim\Phi\beta$ 1, 4, conj.
6. ($\exists\,\alpha$)$\Phi\alpha$ 2–5, IP, DN

G. *Matrix Transformation*

With UI, UG, EI, EG, and the truth-functional rules available, the Matrix Transformation Rule may be derived as an abbreviation of the following rephrased version:

> MATRIX TRANSFORMATION REPHRASED: To perform a transformation (of the sort permitted by the truth-functional transformation rules) upon a matrix, remove all quantifiers by UI and/or EI, perform the desired transformation using the appropriate truth-functional rule, and reattach the quantifiers using UG and/or EG.

H. *Quantifier Shifting Rules, part 2*

With the derived rules now available, it is an elementary exercise to derive the equivalences which generate the remaining portions of the QS rule. The proofs are left as exercises.

I. *Identity Rules*

Self-Identity and Indiscernibility are already primitive rules in OI+. The proof of the Symmetry of Identity is left as an exercise.

The derivation of the full complement of Main System rules from the rules in OI+, together with the earlier derivation of the OI+ rules from those of the Main System, shows that the two systems are logically equivalent: they validate exactly the same arguments and generate exactly the same theorems. Since OI+ is both complete and consistent, it follows that the Main System is likewise both complete and consistent.

ANSWERS TO SELECTED EXERCISES

Ch. 1, Ex. I

(1) components: They invited me to the party.
   I didn't go. Component: I went.
(3) simple
(5) simple
(7) component: The earth is flat.
(9) simple

Ch. 1, Ex. II

(1) It's not the case that P, even though I.
(3) C or S
(5) If W, then D whether or not K.
(7) If R or S it's not the case that G unless W

Ch. 2, Ex. I

(2) $\sim K \cdot S$
(4) If $\sim K \cdot \sim S$ then either $\sim G$ or L
(6) $\sim S \cdot K$

Ch. 2, Ex. II

(1) false	(10) false
(4) true	(13) false
(7) true	(16) true
	(19) false

Ch. 3, Ex. I

(1) $(C \cdot \sim T) \vee (S \cdot I)$
(3) $T \vee (L \cdot (\sim S \vee E))$
(5) If $\sim (R \vee S) \cdot F$ then $M \vee (B \cdot D)$

Ch. 3, Ex. II

(1) false

(4) false

(7) false

(10) true

(13) true

Ch. 3, Ex. III

(2) $((M \cdot P) \vee (B \cdot S)) \cdot \sim ((M \cdot P) \cdot (B \cdot S))$

(4) $(\sim R \vee \sim C) \cdot \sim (\sim R \cdot \sim C)$

Ch. 3, Ex. IV

(2) wedge

(5) wedge

(8) wedge after X

(11) first tilde

(14) wedge before B

Ch. 3, Ex. V

(4) A conjunction whose first conjunct is
  a disjunction whose disjuncts are simple, and
  whose second conjunct is simple.

(7) A conjunction whose first conjunct is simple, and
  whose second conjunct is a disjunction
    whose first disjunct is simple, and
    whose second disjunct is
      a conjunction whose conjuncts are simple

Ch. 3, Ex. VI

(14) A disjunction
  whose first disjunct is
    a disjunction
      whose first disjunct is simple, and
      whose second disjunct is a disjunction
        whose first disjunct is simple, and
        whose second disjunct is
          a negation, whose negate is
            a disjunction whose disjuncts
            are simple; and
  whose second disjunct is simple.

Ch. 4, Ex. I

(1) $\sim S \vee P$ or $S \supset P$

(4) $L \supset (M \cdot R)$

(7) $E \supset (\sim G \supset B)$

(11) $(((F \supset S) \cdot (F \supset C)) \cdot (C \supset \sim S)) \supset (\sim L \supset K)$

Ch. 4, Ex. II

(1) true

(4) true

(7) true

(10) false

(13) false

Ch. 5, Ex. I

(3) $(D \supset H) \cdot (H \supset D)$ $D \equiv H$
(6) $(\sim F \supset \sim S) \cdot (F \supset S)$ $\sim F \equiv \sim S$ or $F \equiv S$

Ch. 5, Ex. II

(2) $((W \supset M) \cdot (B \equiv \sim M)) \supset (W \supset \sim B)$

Ch. 5, Ex. III

(1) contingency
(4) tautology
(7) tautology
(10) contingency

(13) contradiction
(16) tautology
(19) tautology

Ch. 6, Ex. I

(3) Can't be done. 'If' within the scope of 'either' means the disjunction dominates the conditional, but 'or' within the scope of 'if' means the conditional dominates the disjunction; impossible to have it both ways.
(6) $(P \lor Q) \supset R$
(10) $P \supset \sim(Q \lor R)$
(13) Can't be done for reasons similar to (3): 'Neither' governs 'if' but 'if' governs 'nor'; impossible to have it both ways.
(16) $\sim(P \lor Q) \supset R$

Ch. 6, Ex. II

(2) $P \cdot \sim(Q \lor R)$
(5) $(P \cdot \sim(Q \cdot R)) \supset S$
(7) $((P \cdot \sim(Q \lor R)) \lor S) \supset (T \lor U)$
(10) $(\sim(P \lor Q) \cdot R) \lor S$
(13) $(P \supset Q)$ if R *or* $P \supset (Q$ if $R)$
Since there is no way to tell which 'if' dominates, either of the following is correct:
(i) $R \supset (P \supset Q)$
(ii) $P \supset (R \supset Q)$
(16) $\sim((((\sim((P \cdot \sim Q) \lor R) \lor S) \cdot T) \supset U) \lor W)$

Ch. 7, Ex. I

(1) not equiv.
(4) equiv.

(7) equiv.
(10) equiv.

Ch. 7, Ex. II

(1) $\sim(\sim R \lor S) \supset (R \supset S)$
(4) Either both if L then P and E if J or K, if H
                              becomes
$H \supset (((L \supset P) \cdot E$ if $J) \lor K)$
Since there is no indication whether the 'if' dominates the dot or vice versa,

there are two possible translations, of equal plausibility:
(i) $H \supset (((L \supset P) \cdot (J \supset E)) \lor K)$
(ii) $H \supset ((J \supset ((L \supset P) \cdot E)) \lor K)$

(7) $(M \cdot T) \lor W$

(10) $W \supset F$

(13) $(C \lor B) \supset A$

(16) $F \supset (\sim A \supset (\sim R \supset (\sim D \supset L)))$

(19) If either $\sim H$ unless either S or W or I, then (either both K and D or H in case S) implies K is sufficient for either D or $\sim W$
becomes
$((\sim H \lor (S \lor W)) \lor I) \supset (((K \cdot D) \lor H \text{ in case } S) \supset (K \supset (D \lor \sim W)))$
Since there is no indication whether the 'or' dominates the 'in case' or vice versa, there are two possible translations of equal plausibility:
(i) $((\sim H \lor (S \lor W)) \lor I) \supset (((K \cdot D) \lor (S \supset H)) \supset (K \supset (D \lor \sim W)))$
(ii) $((\sim H \lor (S \lor W)) \lor I) \supset ((S \supset ((K \cdot D) \lor H)) \supset (K \supset (D \lor \sim W)))$
Also, if 'sick' is taken to mean 'not in good health', 'having insomnia' is taken to mean 'not sleeping well', and 'drunk' is taken to mean 'not sober', then 'K' may be replaced with '$\sim H$', 'I' may be replaced with '$\sim W$', and 'D' may be replaced with '$\sim S$'; and so on.

Ch. 8, Ex. I

(1) invalid
(4) valid

(7) valid
(10) valid

Ch. 8, Ex. II

(1) no good (invalid)
(4) good
(7) no good (inconsistent premisses)
(10) good

Ch. 9, Ex. I

(1) statement
(3) neither
(7) neither

Ch. 9, Ex. II

(1) e, g
(4) a, d, e
(7) e, j, l

(10) a, e, f
(13) e, g, h
(16) b, c, e, l

Ch. 9, Ex. III

(1) tautologous
(4) tautologous

(7) contingent
(10) contradictory

Ch. 9, Ex. IV

(1) tautology
(4) contradiction

(7) tautology
(10) tautology

Ch. 9, Ex. V

(1) true   (7) false   (11) false
(3) false   (9) true   (13) true
(5) false

Ch. 9, Ex. VI

(1) validating   (13) not validating
(4) validating   (16) validating
(7) validating   (19) not validating
(10) validating   (22) validating

Ch. 10, Ex. I

(1) $\sim A$
(4) J
(7) don't satisfy
(10) $A \supset B$
(13) doesn't satisfy
(16) $(A \lor B) \cdot \sim A$ or $\sim A \cdot (A \lor B)$
(19) $(K \cdot \sim K) \lor A$

Ch. 10, Ex. II

(2) 6. 5, sev.   14. 13, 3, equiv.
     7. 6, 1, MP   15. 5, sev.
     8. 4, sev.   16. 14, 15, MT
     9. 8, 2, canc.   17. 16, 6, MT
    10. 7, 9, OC   18. 11, 17, canc.
    11. 4, sev.   19. 18, 10, MP or 16, 13, c·
    12. 6, 10, conj.   20. 19, sev.
    13. 11, 12, dilem.   21. 20, disj.

Ch. 10, Ex. III

(1) $\sim \sim (R \cdot S)$
(4) $A \supset C$
(7) $\sim (R \lor S)$
(10) $K \supset B$

Ch. 10, Ex. IV

(1) 4. C 1, 3, canc.
    5. $A \cdot B$ 2, 4, MP

(4) 3. $\sim A$ 1, 2, MT
    4. $B \lor \sim A$ 3, disj.

(7) 4. $K \supset L$ 1, 2, OC
    5. $\sim B$ 3, 4, equiv.

(10) 4. $\sim A$ 1, 3, MT
     5. $\sim Z$ 2, 4, canc.

Ch. 10, Ex. V

(2)	7. $\sim C$	5, sev.
	8. $(X \supset Y) \supset A$	4, 2, OC
	9. $\sim A$	7, 3, MT
	10. $\sim (X \supset Y)$	8, 9, MT
	11. $Z \supset A$	1, 10, canc.
	12. $\sim Z$	9, 11, MT
	13. $Z \vee X$	5, sev.
	14. X	12, 13, canc.
	15. $X \supset B$	9, 6, canc.
	16. B	14, 15, MP
(4)	7. $P \supset R$	1, 2, OC
	8. $S \supset T$	7, 3, MP
	9. $\sim T$	1, 6, MP
	10. $\sim S$	8, 9, MT
	11. $\sim S \vee \sim R$	10, disj.
	12. P	11, 5, MP
	13. Q	1, 12, MP
	14. Q	13, rpt.
	15. $Q \cdot Q$	13, 14, conj.
	16. $\sim T \supset (S \vee U)$	4, 15, MP
	17. $S \vee U$	9, 16, MP
	18. U	10, 17, canc.
	19. R	13, 2, MP
	20. $U \cdot R$	18, 19, conj.

Ch. 10, Ex. VI

(3)	1. $(A \supset B) \cdot (C \supset D)$	
	2. $E \vee (A \vee C)$	
	3. $\sim E \cdot ((B \vee D) \supset \sim C)$	$/ \therefore A$
	4. $\sim E$	3, sev.
	5. $A \vee C$	4, 2, canc.
	6. $B \vee D$	5, 1, dilem.
	7. $(B \vee D) \supset \sim C$	3, sev.
	8. $\sim C$	6, 7, MP
	9. A	5, 8, canc.
(4)	1. $(\sim B \supset C) \equiv \sim A$	
	2. $(C \supset D) \cdot (F \supset G)$	
	3. $(\sim B \supset D) \supset (A \vee F)$	
	4. $\sim A \cdot \sim D \quad / \therefore B \vee G$	
	5. $\sim A$	4, sev.
	6. $\sim B \supset C$	5, 1, equiv.
	7. $C \supset D$	2, sev.
	8. $\sim B \supset D$	6, 7, OC
	9. $A \vee F$	3, 8, MP
	10. F	5, 9, canc.
	11. $F \supset G$	2, sev.

12. G 10, 11, MP
13. $B \lor G$ 12, disj.

Ch. 11, Ex. I

(3)   1. $B \supset (G \cdot A)$
        2. $H \supset K$
        3. $G \supset \sim B$
        4. $\sim H \supset B$
        5. $\sim K \lor (L \lor (B \lor (N \cdot N)))$
        6. $L \supset \sim K$ / $\therefore N$
        7. $\sim B \lor (G \cdot A)$ 1, CE
        8. $(\sim B \lor G) \cdot (\sim B \lor A)$ 7, dist.
        9. $\sim B \lor G$ 8, sev.
     10. $B \supset G$ 9, CE
     11. $B \supset \sim B$ 10, 3, OC
     12. $\sim B \lor \sim B$ 11, CE
     13. $\sim B$ 12, dup.
     14. $\sim \sim H$ 13, 4, MT
     15. H 14, DN
     16. K 15, 2, MP
     17. $\sim \sim K$ 16, DN
     18. $L \lor (B \lor (N \cdot N))$ 17, 5, canc.
     19. $(L \lor B) \lor (N \cdot N)$ 18, rgr.
     20. $\sim L$ 17, 6, MT
     21. $\sim L \cdot \sim B$ 20, 13, conj.
     22. $\sim (L \lor B)$ 21, TE
     23. $N \cdot N$ 19, 22, canc.
     24. N 23, sev. (or dup.)

Ch. 11, Ex. II

(2) 1. $\sim A$ / $\therefore A \supset B$
     2. $\sim A \lor B$ 1, disj.
     3. $A \supset B$ 2, CE

(5) 1. $A \supset B$
     2. $A \supset C$ / $\therefore A \supset (B \cdot C)$
     3. $\sim A \lor B$ 1, CE
     4. $\sim A \lor C$ 2, CE
     5. $(\sim A \lor B) \cdot (\sim A \lor C)$ 3, 4, conj.
     6. $\sim A \lor (B \cdot C)$ 5, ext.
     7. $A \supset (B \cdot C)$ 6, CE

(8) 1. $\sim (A \supset B)$ / $\therefore A$
     2. $\sim (\sim A \lor B)$ 1, CE
     3. $\sim \sim A \cdot \sim B$ 2, TD
     4. $\sim \sim A$ 3, sev.
     5. A 4, DN

(12) 1. $A \cdot B$ $/ \therefore \sim(A \supset \sim B)$
2. $\sim\sim(A \cdot B)$ 1, DN
3. $\sim(\sim A \vee \sim B)$ 2, TD
4. $\sim(A \supset \sim B)$ 3, CE

(15) 1. A
2. B $/ \therefore A \equiv B$
3. $\sim B \vee A$ 1, disj.
4. $B \supset A$ 3, CE
5. $\sim A \vee B$ 2, disj.
6. $A \supset B$ 5, CE
7. $(A \supset B) \cdot (B \supset A)$ 4, 6, conj.
8. $A \equiv B$ 7, BE

(18) 1. A
2. $\sim B$ $/ \therefore \sim(A \equiv B)$
3. $\sim\sim B \vee A$ 1, disj.
4. $\sim B \supset A$ 3, CE
5. $\sim A \vee \sim B$ 2, disj.
6. $A \supset \sim B$ 5, CE
7. $(A \supset \sim B) \cdot (\sim B \supset A)$ 4, 6, conj.
8. $A \equiv \sim B$ 7, BE
9. $\sim(A \equiv B)$ 8, div.

(21) 1. $A \supset B$ $/ \therefore A \supset (B \vee C)$
2. $\sim A \vee B$ 1, CE
3. $(\sim A \vee B) \vee C$ 2, disj.
4. $\sim A \vee (B \vee C)$ 3, rgr.
5. $A \supset (B \vee C)$ 4, CE

Ch. 11, Ex. III

(3)   1. $(A \cdot B) \supset (C \supset D)$
2. $\sim D \vee \sim E$
3. $\sim(D \cdot E) \equiv E$ $/ \therefore B \supset (A \supset \sim C)$
4. $\sim(D \cdot E)$ 2, TE
5. E 3, 4, equiv.
6. $\sim\sim E$ 5, DN
7. $\sim D$ 2, 6, canc.
8. $((A \cdot B) \cdot C) \supset D$ 1, exp.
9. $\sim((A \cdot B) \cdot C)$ 7, 8, MT
10. $\sim(A \cdot B) \vee \sim C$ 9, TD
11. $(A \cdot B) \supset \sim C$ 10, CE
12. $(B \cdot A) \supset \sim C$ 11, transp.
13. $B \supset (A \supset \sim C)$ 12, exp.

(7)   1. M $/ \therefore ((K \supset R) \supset K) \supset K$
2. $\sim K \vee M$ 1, disj.
3. $K \supset M$ 2, CE
4. $K \supset (K \cdot M)$ 3, abs.
5. $\sim K \vee (K \cdot M)$ 4, CE

6. $(\sim K \vee K) \cdot (\sim K \vee M)$ 5, dist.
7. $\sim K \vee K$ 6, sev.
8. $K \vee \sim K$ 7, transp.
9. $(K \vee \sim K) \vee R$ 8, disj.
10. $K \vee (\sim K \vee R)$ 9, rgr.
11. $(K \vee (\sim K \vee R)) \cdot (K \vee \sim K)$ 10, 8, conj.
12. $K \vee ((\sim K \vee R) \cdot \sim K)$ 11, ext.
13. $((\sim K \vee R) \cdot \sim K) \vee K$ 12, transp.
14. $(\sim \sim (\sim K \vee R) \cdot \sim K) \vee K$ 13, DN
15. $\sim (\sim (\sim K \vee R) \vee K) \vee K$ 14, TE
16. $(\sim (\sim K \vee R) \vee K) \supset K$ 15, CE
17. $((\sim K \vee R) \supset K) \supset K$ 16, CE
18. $((K \supset R) \supset K) \supset K$ 17, CE

Ch. 11, Ex. IV

(3) 1. $T \cdot (F \vee \sim H)$
2. $E \supset H$
3. $(T \cdot \sim H) \supset R$
4. $\sim R \vee E$ $/ \therefore (T \supset \sim F) \supset (R \cdot E)$
5. T 1, sev.
6. $T \supset (\sim H \supset R)$ 3, exp.
7. $\sim H \supset R$ 5, 6, MP
8. $R \supset E$ 4, CE
9. $\sim H \supset E$ 7, 8, OC
10. $\sim H \supset H$ 9, 2, OC
11. $\sim \sim H \vee H$ 10, CE
12. $\sim \sim H \vee \sim \sim H$ 11, DN
13. $\sim \sim H$ 12, dup.
14. $F \vee \sim H$ 1, sev.
15. F 14, 13, canc.
16. $T \cdot F$ 5, 15, conj.
17. $\sim \sim (T \cdot F)$ 16, DN
18. $\sim (\sim T \vee \sim F)$ 17, TD
19. $\sim (T \supset \sim F)$ 18, CE
20. $\sim (T \supset \sim F) \vee (R \cdot E)$ 19, disj.
21. $(T \supset \sim F) \supset (R \cdot E)$ 20, CE

(6) 1. $(\sim B \vee \sim C) \supset \sim A$
2. $R \supset (A \cdot \sim C)$ $/ \therefore \sim R$
3. $\sim (B \cdot C) \supset \sim A$ 1, TE
4. $A \supset (B \cdot C)$ 3, contr.
5. $\sim A \vee (B \cdot C)$ 4, CE
6. $(\sim A \vee B) \cdot (\sim A \vee C)$ 5, dist.
7. $\sim A \vee C$ 6, sev.
8. $\sim A \vee \sim \sim C$ 7, DN
9. $\sim (A \cdot \sim C)$ 8, TE
10. $\sim R$ 9, 2, MT

Ch. 12, Ex. I

(3) 1. $A \supset (B \supset C)$
2. $B \supset (C \supset D)$ $/ \therefore A \supset (B \supset D)$
→ 3. A $/ \therefore B \supset D$
→ 4. B $/ \therefore D$
  5. $B \supset C$ 1, 3, MP
  6. C 4, 5, MP
  7. $C \supset D$ 4, 2, MP
  8. D 6, 7, MP
  9. $B \supset D$ 4–8, CP
10. $A \supset (B \supset D)$ 3–9, CP

(6) 1. $A \equiv (B \supset C)$
2. $D \supset (E \cdot A)$
3. B $/ \therefore C \vee \sim D$
→ 4. D $/ \therefore C$
  5. $E \cdot A$ 2, 4, MP
  6. A 5, sev.
  7. $B \supset C$ 1, 6, equiv.
  8. C 3, 7, MP
9. $D \supset C$ 4–8, CP
10. $\sim D \vee C$ 9, CE
11. $C \vee \sim D$ 10, transp.

(10) 1. $\sim((A \cdot B) \equiv G)$
2. $\sim(G \vee E) \supset T$
3. $C \supset (T \supset \sim D)$ $/ \therefore A \supset (D \supset (C \supset (B \supset E)))$
→ 4. A $/ \therefore D \supset (C \supset (B \supset E))$
→ 5. D $/ \therefore C \supset (B \supset E)$
→ 6. C $/ \therefore B \supset E$
→ 7. B $/ \therefore E$
  8. $(C \cdot T) \supset \sim D$ 3, exp.
  9. $\sim \sim D$ 5, DN
  10. $\sim(C \cdot T)$ 8, 9, MT
  11. $\sim C \vee \sim T$ 10, TD
  12. $C \supset \sim T$ 11, CE
  13. $\sim T$ 6, 12, MP
  14. $\sim \sim (G \vee E)$ 2, 13, MT
  15. $G \vee E$ 14, DN
  16. $(A \cdot B) \equiv \sim G$ 1, div.
  17. $A \cdot B$ 4, 7, conj.
  18. $\sim G$ 16, 17, equiv.
  19. E 18, 15, canc.
  20. $B \supset E$ 7–19, CP
21. $C \supset (B \supset E)$ 6–20, CP
22. $D \supset (C \supset (B \supset E))$ 5–21, CP
23. $A \supset (D \supset (C \supset (B \supset E)))$ 4–22, CP

Ch. 12, Ex. II

(2)   1. $(A \cdot B) \supset (C \cdot D)$
      2. $B \supset \sim D$ / ∴ $\sim A \lor \sim B$
      → 3. A / ∴ $\sim B$
      → 4. B (IP)
        5. $A \cdot B$ 3, 4, conj.
        6. $C \cdot D$ 1, 5, MP
        7. D 6, sev.
        8. $\sim D$ 2, 4, MP
        9. $D \cdot \sim D$ 7, 8, conj.
       10. $\sim B$ 4–9, IP
       11. $A \supset \sim B$ 3–10, CP
       12. $\sim A \lor \sim B$ 11, CE

(6)   1. $\sim E$ / ∴ $\sim(((A \supset B) \cdot (B \supset C)) \cdot ((A \supset C) \supset E))$
      → 2. $((A \supset B) \cdot (B \supset C)) \cdot ((A \supset C) \supset E)$ (IP)
        3. $(A \supset B) \cdot (B \supset C)$ 2, sev.
        4. $A \supset B$ 3, sev.
        5. $B \supset C$ 3, sev.
        6. $A \supset C$ 4, 5, OC
        7. $(A \supset C) \supset E$ 2, sev.
        8. E 6, 7, MP
        9. $E \cdot \sim E$ 1, 8, conj.
       10. $\sim(((A \supset B) \cdot (B \supset C)) \cdot ((A \supset C) \supset E))$ 2–9, IP

(8)   1. $(A \cdot B) \lor C$
      2. $\sim C \lor B$ / ∴ $A \supset B$
      → 3. A / ∴ B
      → 4. $\sim B$
        5. $\sim C$ 4, 2, canc.
        6. $A \cdot B$ 1, 5, canc.
        7. B 6, sev.
        8. $B \cdot \sim B$ 7, 4, conj.
        9. $\sim \sim B$ 4–8, IP
       10. B 9, DN
       11. $A \supset B$ 3–10, CP

(12) 1. $(A \cdot B) \equiv \sim C$
      2. $A \supset B$ / ∴ $C \equiv \sim A$
      → 3. C / ∴ $\sim A$
      → 4. A (IP)
        5. B 4, 2, MP
        6. $A \cdot B$ 4, 5, conj.
        7. $\sim C$ 6, 1, equiv.
        8. $C \cdot \sim C$ 3, 7, conj.
        9. $\sim A$ 4–8, IP

10. $C \supset \sim A$ 3–9, CP
11. $\sim A$ $/ \therefore C$
12. $\sim C$ (IP)
13. $A \cdot B$ 12, 1, equiv.
14. A 13, sev.
15. $A \cdot \sim A$ 11, 14, conj.
16. $\sim \sim C$ 12–15, IP
17. C 16, DN
18. $\sim A \supset C$ 11–17, CP
19. $(C \supset \sim A) \cdot (\sim A \supset C)$ 10, 18, conj.
20. $C \equiv \sim A$ 19, BE

Ch. 13, Ex. I

(5)

1. $\sim(\sim(A \cdot B) \vee \sim(\sim A \cdot \sim B))$ (IP)
2. $\sim\sim((A \cdot B) \cdot (\sim A \cdot \sim B))$ 1, TE
3. $(A \cdot B) \cdot (\sim A \cdot \sim B)$ 2, DN
4. $A \cdot B$ 3, sev.
5. $\sim A \cdot \sim B$ 3, sev.
6. A 4, sev.
7. $\sim A$ 5, sev.
8. $A \cdot \sim A$ 6, 7, conj.
9. $\sim\sim(\sim(A \cdot B) \vee \sim(\sim A \cdot \sim B))$ 1–8, IP
10. $\sim(A \cdot B) \vee \sim(\sim A \cdot \sim B)$ 9, DN

Ch. 13, Ex. II

(4)

1. X $/ \therefore Y \equiv (X \supset Y)$
2. Y $/ \therefore X \supset Y$
3. X $/ \therefore Y$
4. Y 2, rpt.
5. $X \supset Y$ 3–4, CP
6. $Y \supset (X \supset Y)$ 2–5, CP
7. $X \supset Y$ $/ \therefore Y$
8. Y 1, 7, MP
9. $(X \supset Y) \supset Y$ 7–8, CP
10. $(Y \supset (X \supset Y)) \cdot ((X \supset Y) \supset Y)$ 6, 9, conj.
11. $Y \equiv (X \supset Y)$ 10, BE
12. $X \supset (Y \equiv (X \supset Y))$ 1–11, CP

Ch. 13, Ex. III

(3)

```
┌──→ 1. ~(A ∨ B)      / ∴ ~A · ~B
│  ┌→ 2. A                                              (IP)
│  │  3. A ∨ B                                          2, disj.
│  │  4. (A ∨ B) · ~(A ∨ B)                             1, 3, conj.
│  └─ 5. ~A                                             2–4, IP
│   ┌→ 6. B                                             (IP)
│   │  7. A ∨ B                                         6, disj.
│   │  8. (A ∨ B) · ~(A ∨ B)                            7, 1, conj.
│   └─ 9. ~B                                            6–8, IP
│     10. ~A · ~B                                       5, 9, conj.
└──── 11. ~(A ∨ B) ⊃ (~A · ~B)                          1–10, CP
   ┌→12. ~A · ~B      / ∴ ~(A ∨ B)
   │┌→13. A ∨ B                                         (IP)
   ││ 14. ~A                                            12, sev.
   ││ 15. B                                             13, 14, canc.
   ││ 16. ~B                                            12, sev.
   ││ 17. B · ~B                                        15, 16, conj.
   │└─18. ~(A ∨ B)                                      13–17, IP
   └─ 19. (~A · ~B) ⊃ ~(A ∨ B)                          12–18, CP
      20. (~(A ∨ B) ⊃ (~A · ~B)) · ((~A · ~B) ⊃ ~(A ∨ B))   11, 19, conj.
      21. ~(A ∨ B) ≡ (~A · ~B)                          20, BE
```

(8)

```
┌→ 1. A        / ∴ ~~A
│┌→ 2. ~A                                               (IP)
││ 3. A · ~A                                            1, 2, conj.
│└─ 4. ~~A                                              2–3, IP
└─ 5. A ⊃ ~~A                                           1–4, CP
┌→ 6. ~~A       / ∴ A
│┌→ 7. A        / ∴ A                                   (IP)
│└─ 8. A                                                7, rpt.
│  9. A ⊃ A                                             7–8, CP
│ 10. ~A ∨ A                                            9, CE
└─11. A                                                 6, 10, canc.
  12. ~~A ⊃ A                                           6–11, CP
  13. (A ⊃ ~~A) · (~~A ⊃ A)                             5, 12, conj.
  14. A ≡ ~~A                                           13, BE
```

Ch. 14, Ex. I

(3) Shown invalid by either of

A	B	C	D
T	F	F	F
F	F	T	F

(8) Shown invalid by any of

A	B	C	D	E
T	T	T	T	F
T	F	T	T	F
F	T	F	F	F
F	F	F	F	F

Ch. 14, Ex. II

(1) Shown invalid by

A	B	C
F	T	F

(4)   1. $\sim A \lor \sim(B \supset C)$
      2. $(A \cdot C) \lor (D \cdot E)$
      3. $(\sim D \supset \sim E) \supset \sim B$
      4. $A \cdot K$ $/ \therefore K \supset \sim B$

5. A	4, sev.
6. $\sim \sim A$	5, DN
7. $\sim(B \supset C)$	6, 1, canc.
8. $\sim(\sim B \lor C)$	7, CE
9. $\sim \sim B \cdot \sim C$	8, TD
10. $\sim \sim B$	9, sev.
11. $\sim(\sim D \supset \sim E)$	3, 10, MT
12. $\sim(E \supset D)$	11, contr.
13. $\sim(\sim E \lor D)$	12, CE
14. $\sim \sim E \cdot \sim D$	13, TD
15. $\sim D$	14, sev.
16. $\sim D \lor \sim E$	15, disj.
17. $\sim(D \cdot E)$	16, TE
18. $A \cdot C$	17, 2, canc.
19. C	18, sev.
20. $\sim C$	9, sev.
21. $C \lor (K \supset \sim B)$	19, disj.
22. $K \supset \sim B$	20, 21, canc.

Ch. 14, Ex. III

(1) tautology
(4) contingency: true when A B C D; false otherwise.

T	T	F	T
T	T	F	F
T	F	F	F
F	T	F	T
F	T	F	F
F	F	F	T
F	F	F	F

(7) contingency: False when A B C; true otherwise.

F	F	F

Ch. 14, Ex. IV

(4) No good (inconsistent premises).

Ch. 15, Ex. I

(2) not singular
(5) x is the greatest baseball player of all time
(7) x played for the Yankees
        or   (either answer is correct)
    Babe Ruth played for x
(11) x is a satellite of the sun
(14) x is a city in Missouri
        or   (either answer is correct)
    Independence is a city in x
(18) not singular
(22) not singular
(23) x has many depositors

Ch. 15, Ex. II

(5) Gx
(7) Yx or Bx
(11) Sx
(14) Mx or Ix
(23) Dx

Ch. 15, Ex. III

(5) $G\underline{r}$
(7) $Y\underline{r}$ or $B\underline{y}$
(11) $S\underline{e}$
(14) $M\underline{i}$ or $I\underline{m}$
(23) $D\underline{a}$

Ch. 15, Ex. IV

(3) $(\exists x)x$ is rotten in Denmark
    $(\exists x)Rx$
(6) $(\exists y)y$ is a starving person
    $(\exists y)Sy$
(9) $(\exists z)$ all men have z in common
    $(\exists z)Hz$

Ch. 15, Ex. V

(1) $(x)x$ is interesting
    $(x)Ix$
(4) $(y)$the owner of the bank hates y
    $(y)Oy$

Ch. 15, Ex. VI

(1) $\sim(\exists x)x$ matters
   $\sim(\exists x)Mx$
(4) $\sim(\exists y)$the watchman saw y
   $\sim(\exists y)Wy$
(8) $\sim(\exists z)$different persons have z in common
   $\sim(\exists z)Dz$

Ch. 16, Ex. I

(4) $\underline{s}$ is alive $\supset$ $\underline{s}$ is very fortunate
   $A\underline{s} \supset F\underline{s}$
(6) $\sim(\exists x)(x$ is purple $\cdot$ x is a cow)
   $\sim(\exists x)(Px \cdot Cx)$
(9) $(y)(y$ is illegal $\cdot$ y is immoral)
   $(y)(Iy \cdot Jy)$
   or
   $(y)(\sim y$ is legal $\cdot$ $\sim y$ is moral)
   $(y)(\sim Ly \cdot \sim My)$

Ch. 16, Ex. II

(1) E—standard   (11) E—standard
(5) A—not standard   (16) O—not standard
(10) O—standard

Ch. 16, Ex. III

Some of these have an indefinite number of correct answers; the answers given here are not necessarily the only right ones.

(2) No atheist is a foxhole-inhabitant.
(6) Every live coward is (a thing that is) better than a dead hero.
(12) Some congressman is not a thief.
(15) Every time is a time when the North Star is above the horizon.
   Every time is one at which the North Star is above the horizon.

Ch. 16, Ex. IV

(1) Some month is one with thirty-one days.
   (the following "alternative" is not acceptable:)
   Some time is a time when months have thirty-one days.
(5) Some place is one with an abundance of aardvarks.
   Some place is a place where the aardvark abounds.
   (the following "alternative" is not acceptable:)
   Every aardvark is a thing that abounds somewhere.
(10) Every person is one who dies before its 200th birthday.
   (the following "alternative" is not acceptable:)
   Every time is one at which people die before their 200th birthday.

(16) The whistle doesn't blow unless it is eight o'clock—that is,
      If the whistle blows, then it is eight o'clock—that is,
      Every occasion when the whistle blows is an occasion when it is eight o'clock.

Ch. 16, Ex. V

 (2) $(x)(x$ is an atheist $\supset \sim x$ is a foxhole inhabitant)
 (6) $(y)(y$ is a live coward $\supset y$ is better than a dead hero)
(12) $(\exists z)(z$ is a congressman $\cdot \sim z$ is a thief)
(15) $(x)(x$ is a time $\supset x$ is a time when the North Star is above the horizon)
      or
      $(x)(x$ is a time $\supset$ the North Star is above the horizon at $x)$

Ch. 16, Ex. VI

 (1) $(\exists x)(x$ is a month $\cdot x$ has thirty-one days)
 (5) $(\exists y)(y$ is a place $\cdot$ aardvarks abound at $y)$
(10) $(x)(x$ is a person $\supset x$ dies before its 200th birthday)
(16) $(z)(z$ is an occasion when the whistle blows $\supset z$ is an occasion when it is eight o'clock)

Ch. 16, Ex. VII

 (2) $(x)(Ax \supset \sim Fx)$
 (6) $(y)((Ly \cdot Cy) \supset By)$
(12) $(\exists z)(Cz \cdot \sim Tz)$
(15) $(x)(Tx \supset Wx)$

Ch. 16, Ex. VIII

 (1) $(\exists x)(Mx \cdot Hx)$
 (5) $(\exists y)(Py \cdot Ay)$
(10) $(x)(Px \supset Dx)$
(16) $(z)(Wz \supset Ez)$

Ch. 16, Ex. IX

Proceeding by stages:

 (4) Every cat is one that will purr if its ears are rubbed.
      $(x)(x$ is a cat $\supset x$ will purr if its ears are rubbed)
      $(x)(x$ is a cat $\supset (x$'s ears are rubbed $\supset x$ will purr))
      $(x)(Cx \supset (Rx \supset Px))$

 (9) Every healthy baby is (one that is) pleased if people sing to him or show him bright objects.
      $(x)(x$ is a healthy baby $\supset x$ is pleased if people sing to x or show x bright objects)
      $(x)((x$ is healthy $\cdot x$ is a baby) $\supset x$ is pleased if people sing to x or show x bright objects)
      $(x)((Hx \cdot Bx) \supset$ (people sing to x or show x bright objects $\supset x$ is pleased))
      $(x)((Hx \cdot Bx) \supset$ ((people sing to x $\lor$ people show x bright objects) $\supset x$ is pleased))
      $(x)((Hx \cdot Bx) \supset ((Sx \lor Ox) \supset Px))$

(12) Every snail is a thing which cannot be eaten if it is cooked too long.
$(x)(x$ is a snail $\supset x$ cannot be eaten if x is cooked too long)
$(x)(x$ is a snail $\supset (x$ is cooked too long $\supset x$ cannot be eaten$))$
$(x)(x$ is a snail $\supset (x$ is cooked too long $\supset \sim(x$ can be eaten$)))$
$(x)(Sx \supset (Cx \supset \sim Ex))$

(15) Some job that pays well and requires a great deal of skill if it is to be done properly is (one that is) either boring and self-defeating or unrewarding and not worth the effort.
$(\exists x)(x$ is a job that pays well and requires a great deal of skill if it is to be done properly $\cdot x$ is either boring and self-defeating or unrewarding and not worth the effort)
$(\exists x)((x$ is a job that pays well $\cdot x$ requires a great deal of skill if x is to be done properly$) \cdot (x$ is boring and self-defeating $\vee x$ is unrewarding and not worth the effort$))$
$(\exists x)(((x$ is a job $\cdot x$ pays well$) \cdot (x$ is to be done properly $\supset x$ requires a great deal of skill$)) \cdot ((x$ is boring $\cdot x$ is self-defeating$) \vee (x$ is unrewarding $\cdot x$ is not worth the effort$)))$
$(\exists x)(((Jx \cdot Wx) \cdot (Px \supset Sx)) \cdot ((Bx \cdot Dx) \vee (\sim(x$ is rewarding$) \cdot \sim(x$ is worth the effort$))))$
$(\exists x)(((Jx \cdot Wx) \cdot (Px \supset Sx)) \cdot ((Bx \cdot Dx) \vee (\sim Rx \cdot \sim Ex)))$

Ch. 16, Ex. X

(1)
1. $(x)(Fx \supset Gx)$ $/ \therefore \sim(\exists x)(Fx \cdot \sim Gx)$
2. $\sim\sim(x)(Fx \supset Gx)$ 1, DN
3. $\sim(\exists x)\sim(Fx \supset Gx)$ 2, QN
4. $\sim(\exists x)\sim(\sim Fx \vee Gx)$ 3, CE
5. $\sim(\exists x)(\sim\sim Fx \cdot \sim Gx)$ 4, TD
6. $\sim(\exists x)(Fx \cdot \sim Gx)$ 5, DN
7. $(x)(Fx \supset Gx) \supset \sim(\exists x)(Fx \cdot \sim Gx)$ 1–6, CP
8. $\sim(\exists x)(Fx \cdot \sim Gx)$ $/ \therefore (x)(Fx \supset Gx)$
9. $(x)\sim(Fx \cdot \sim Gx)$ 8, QN
10. $(x)(\sim Fx \vee \sim\sim Gx)$ 9, TD
11. $(x)(\sim Fx \vee Gx)$ 10, DN
12. $(x)(Fx \supset Gx)$ 11, CE
13. $\sim(\exists x)(Fx \cdot \sim Gx) \supset (x)(Fx \supset Gx)$ 8–12, CP
14. $((x)(Fx \supset Gx) \supset \sim(\exists x)(Fx \cdot \sim Gx)) \cdot$
    $(\sim(\exists x)(Fx \cdot \sim Gx) \supset (x)(Fx \supset Gx))$ 7, 13, conj.
15. $(x)(Fx \supset Gx) \equiv \sim(\exists x)(Fx \cdot \sim Gx)$ 14, BE

Ch. 16, Ex. XI

(1) 1. $(x)(Dx \supset \sim Rx)$ $/ \therefore (x)(Rx \supset \sim Dx)$
2. $(x)(\sim\sim Rx \supset \sim Dx)$ 1, contr.
3. $(x)(Rx \supset \sim Dx)$ 2, DN

(5) 1. $(x)((Wx \cdot Cx) \supset Ax)$ $/ \therefore (x)(Cx \supset (Wx \supset Ax))$
2. $(x)((Cx \cdot Wx) \supset Ax)$ 1, transp.
3. $(x)(Cx \supset (Wx \supset Ax))$ 2, exp.

(9) 1. $(x)((Cx \cdot Hx) \supset Ux)$ $/ \therefore (x)((Cx \cdot Hx) \supset (Ux \cdot Cx))$
     2. $(x)((Hx \cdot Cx) \supset Ux)$ 1, transp.
     3. $(x)(Hx \supset (Cx \supset Ux))$ 2, exp.
     4. $(x)(Hx \supset (Cx \supset (Cx \cdot Ux)))$ 3, abs.
     5. $(x)((Hx \cdot Cx) \supset (Cx \cdot Ux))$ 4, exp.
     6. $(x)((Cx \cdot Hx) \supset (Cx \cdot Ux))$ 5, transp.
     7. $(x)((Cx \cdot Hx) \supset (Ux \cdot Cx))$ 6, transp.

Ch. 17, Ex. I

(2) 1. $A \cdot \sim(\exists z)(w)\sim(Kz \vee Mw)$ $/ \therefore \sim(A \supset \sim((\exists w)Mw \vee (z)Kz))$
     2. $A \cdot \sim(\exists z)\sim(\exists w)(Kz \vee Mw)$ 1, QN
     3. $A \cdot \sim\sim(z)(\exists w)(Kz \vee Mw)$ 2, QN
     4. $A \cdot \sim\sim(z)(Kz \vee (\exists w)Mw)$ 3, QS
     5. $A \cdot \sim\sim((z)Kz \vee (\exists w)Mw)$ 4, QS
     6. $A \cdot \sim\sim((\exists w)Mw \vee (z)Kz)$ 5, transp.
     7. $\sim\sim A \cdot \sim\sim\sim((\exists w)Mw \vee (z)Kz)$ 6, DN
     8. $\sim(\sim A \vee \sim((\exists w)Mw \vee (z)Kz))$ 7, TE
     9. $\sim(A \supset \sim((\exists w)Mw \vee (z)Kz))$ 8, CE

Ch. 17, Ex. II

(2) $(\exists x)(y)(\exists z)((Fx \supset Gy) \supset Hz)$

Ch. 17, Ex. III

(1) $(x)(\exists y)\sim(Fx \supset Gy)$
(4) $(x)(\exists y)((Fx \supset Gx) \vee (Fy \cdot \sim Gy))$
(6) $(x)(\exists y)(z)(\exists t)(w)((((Fx \supset Gy) \supset Hz) \supset Kt) \supset (Mw \supset Nw))$

Ch. 18, Ex. I

(1) $(\exists x)x$ is valuable $\supset (\exists y)y$ is worth seeking
    $(\exists x)Vx \supset (\exists y)Wy$
(4) $(x)(x$ is valuable $\supset x$ is worth seeking$)$
    $(x)(Vx \supset Wx)$
(8) $(x)((x$ is a man $\cdot x$ starts a fight$) \supset$
    $((\exists y)(y$ is a woman $\cdot y$ calls the police$) \supset x$ will be arrested$))$
    $(x)((Mx \cdot Sx) \supset ((\exists y)(Wy \cdot Cy) \supset Ax))$
(13) $((x)(x$ is an Assyrian $\supset x$ is a man$) \cdot (y)(y$ is a man $\supset \sim y$ is 3-legged$)) \supset$
    $((\exists z)z$ is an Assyrian $\supset (\exists w)\sim w$ is 3-legged$)$
    $((x)(Ax \supset Mx) \cdot (y)(My \supset \sim Ty)) \supset ((\exists z)Az \supset (\exists w)\sim Tw)$

Ch. 18, Ex. II

(1) $(\exists \bar{x})\bar{x}$ starts a fight $\supset ((\exists \bar{y})\bar{y}$ calls the police $\supset (\exists \bar{z})\bar{z}$ will be arrested$)$
    $(\exists \bar{x})S\bar{x} \supset ((\exists \bar{y})C\bar{y} \supset (\exists \bar{z})A\bar{z})$
(5) $(\exists x')x'$ starts a fight $\supset ((\exists \bar{y})\bar{y}$ calls the zookeeper $\supset$
    $(\exists z')z'$ will be punished$)$
    $(\exists x')Sx' \supset ((\exists \bar{y})C\bar{y} \supset (\exists z')Wz')$

(9) $(\ddot{x})((\ddot{x}$ is female $\cdot$ $(\ddot{x}$ is a tiger $\cdot$ $\ddot{x}$ is young)$)$ $\supset$ $\sim\!\ddot{x}$ is tame)
$(\ddot{x})((F\ddot{x} \cdot (T\ddot{x} \cdot Y\ddot{x})) \supset \sim\!K\ddot{x})$

or

$(m)((m$ is domestic $\cdot$ $(m$ is a tiger $\cdot$ m is young)$)$ $\supset$ $\sim\!m$ is tame)
$(m)((Dm \cdot (Tm \cdot Ym)) \supset \sim\!Km)$

or

$(x')((x'$ is domestic $\cdot$ $(x'$ is female $\cdot$ x' is young)$)$ $\supset$ $\sim\!x'$ is tame)
$(x')((Dx' \cdot (Fx' \cdot Yx')) \supset \sim\!Kx')$

or

$(r)((r$ is domestic $\cdot$ $(r$ is a female $\cdot$ r is a tiger)$)$ $\supset$ $\sim\!r$ is tame)
$(r)((Dr \cdot (Fr \cdot Tr)) \supset \sim\!Kr)$

or

$(\bar{m})((\bar{m}$ is a tiger $\cdot$ $\bar{m}$ is young$)$ $\supset$ $\sim\!\bar{m}$ is tame)
$(\bar{m})((T\bar{m} \cdot Y\bar{m}) \supset \sim\!K\bar{m})$

or

$(m')((m'$ is domestic $\cdot$ m' is young$)$ $\supset$ $\sim\!m'$ is tame)
$(m')((Dm' \cdot Ym') \supset \sim\!Km')$

or

$(r')((r'$ is domestic $\cdot$ r' is female$)$ $\supset$ $\sim\!r'$ is tame)
$(r')((Dr' \cdot Fr') \supset \sim\!Kr')$

or

$(\ddot{r})((\ddot{r}$ is female $\cdot$ $\ddot{r}$ is a tiger$)$ $\supset$ $\sim\!\ddot{r}$ is tame)
$(\ddot{r})((F\ddot{r} \cdot T\ddot{r}) \supset \sim\!K\ddot{r})$

Ch. 19, Ex. I

(2) $Fx \supset G\_\_$
(5) $(Fx \cdot Gy) \supset (\exists y)(Fy \supset K\_\_)$
(8) $(\exists y)[(F\_\_ \supset G\_\_) \supset (Fy \supset G\_\_)]$
(11) $(x)(y)(Fx \supset (Gy \supset H\_\_))$

Ch. 19, Ex. II

(3) $F\_\_ \supset (Gb \lor Hc)$
$Fa \supset (G\_\_ \lor Hc)$
$Fa \supset (Gb \lor H\_\_)$
(6) $(x)(Kx \supset Lx) \supset (Kx \supset L\_\_)$
$(x)(Kx \supset Lx) \supset (K\_\_ \supset Lx)$
$(x)(Kx \supset Lx) \supset (K\_\_ \supset L\_\_)$
(9) $F\_\_ \cdot ((y)(Fy \supset Gx) \cdot Hy)$
$Fx \cdot ((y)(Fy \supset G\_\_) \cdot Hy)$
$Fx \cdot ((y)(Fy \supset Gx) \cdot H\_\_)$
$F\_\_ \cdot ((y)(Fy \supset G\_\_) \cdot Hy)$

Ch. 19, Ex. III

(3) $(\exists x)(Fx \supset (Gb \lor Hc))$
$(\exists x)(Fa \supset (Gx \lor Hc))$
$(\exists x)(Fa \supset (Gb \lor Hx))$

(6) $(\exists y)[(x)(Kx \supset Lx) \supset (Kx \supset Ly)]$
$(\exists y)[(x)(Kx \supset Lx) \supset (Ky \supset Lx)]$
$(\exists y)[(x)(Kx \supset Lx) \supset (Ky \supset Ly)]$

(9) $(\exists z)[Fz \cdot ((y)(Fy \supset Gx) \cdot Hy)]$
$(\exists z)[Fx \cdot ((y)(Fy \supset Gz) \cdot Hy)]$
$(\exists z)[Fx \cdot ((y)(Fy \supset Gx) \cdot Hz)]$
$(\exists z)[Fz \cdot ((y)(Fy \supset Gz) \cdot Hy)]$

Ch. 19, Ex. IV

(2) a. $(x)(Fx \supset Gx)$ — invalid—not all places in the domain of the quantifier
   b. $Fy \supset Gz$ — end up with the same letter

(5) a. $Fy \cdot Gy$ — valid
   b. $(\exists x)(Fx \cdot Gx)$

(8) a. $Fy \supset Gy$ — invalid—quantifier does not scope over the entire
   b. $(\exists x)Fx \supset Gy$ — line

Ch. 19, Ex. V

(3) 1. $(x)((Cx \lor Dx) \supset Mx)$
  2. $Df \lor Cj$ $/ \therefore (\exists x)Mx$
  3. $(Cf \lor Df) \supset Mf$ — 1, UI, x/f
  4. $\sim(Cf \lor Df) \lor Mf$ — 3, CE
  5. $(\sim Cf \cdot \sim Df) \lor Mf$ — 4, TD
  6. $Mf \lor (\sim Cf \cdot \sim Df)$ — 5, transp.
  7. $(Mf \lor \sim Cf) \cdot (Mf \lor \sim Df)$ — 6, dist.
  8. $Mf \lor \sim Df$ — 7, sev.
  9. $\sim Df \lor Mf$ — 8, transp.
  10. $Df \supset Mf$ — 9, CE
  11. $(Cj \lor Dj) \supset Mj$ — 1, UI, x/j
  12. $\sim(Cj \lor Dj) \lor Mj$ — 11, CE
  13. $(\sim Cj \cdot \sim Dj) \lor Mj$ — 12, TD
  14. $Mj \lor (\sim Cj \cdot \sim Dj)$ — 13, transp.
  15. $(Mj \lor \sim Cj) \cdot (Mj \lor \sim Dj)$ — 14, dist.
  16. $Mj \lor \sim Cj$ — 15, sev.
  17. $\sim Cj \lor Mj$ — 16, transp.
  18. $Cj \supset Mj$ — 17, CE
  19. $Mf \lor Mj$ — 2, 10, 18, dilem.
  20. $(\exists x)(Mf \lor Mx)$ — 19, EG, j/x
  21. $(\exists y)(\exists x)(My \lor Mx)$ — 20, EG, f/y
  22. $(\exists y)(My \lor (\exists x)Mx)$ — 21, QS
  23. $(\exists y)My \lor (\exists x)Mx$ — 22, QS
  24. $(\exists x)Mx \lor (\exists x)Mx$ — 23, RBV, y/x
  25. $(\exists x)Mx$ — 24, dup.

(6) 1. $(x)(Ux \supset Fx)$ $/ \therefore (x)(Ux \supset \sim Fx) \supset \sim(y)Uy$
  2. $Ux \supset Fx$ — 1, UI, x/x
  3. $Ux \supset (Ux \cdot Fx)$ — 2, abs.
  4. $\sim(Ux \cdot Fx) \supset \sim Ux$ — 3, contr.
  5. $(\sim Ux \lor \sim Fx) \supset \sim Ux$ — 4, TD
  6. $(Ux \supset \sim Fx) \supset \sim Ux$ — 5, CE
  7. $(\exists y)((Ux \supset \sim Fx) \supset \sim Uy)$ — 6, EG, x/y
  8. $(Ux \supset \sim Fx) \supset (\exists y)\sim Uy$ — 7, QS

9. $(Ux \supset \sim Fx) \supset \sim(y)Uy$ 8, QN
10. $(\exists x)((Ux \supset \sim Fx) \supset \sim(y)Uy)$ 9, EG, x/x
11. $(x)(Ux \supset \sim Fx) \supset \sim(y)Uy$ 10, QS

Ch. 19, Ex. VI

(2) Confusion of unknowns at line (4).

Ch. 19, Ex. VII

(2)
1. $(x)(Cx \supset Mx)$
2. $(\exists x)(Cx \cdot Fx)$
3. $(\exists x)(Mx \cdot Fx) \supset (\exists y)(Cy \cdot Sy)$ $/ \therefore (\exists x)(Mx \cdot Sx)$
4. $Cx \supset Mx$ 1, UI, x/x
5. $Cx \cdot Fx$ 2, x/x
6. Cx 5, sev.
7. Mx 4, 6, MP
8. Fx 5, sev.
9. $Mx \cdot Fx$ 7, 8, conj.
10. $(\exists x)(Mx \cdot Fx)$ 9, EG, x/x
11. $(\exists y)(Cy \cdot Sy)$ 10, 3, MP
12. $Cy \cdot Sy$ 11, y/y
13. $Cy \supset My$ 1, UI, x/y
14. Cy 12, sev.
15. My 13, 14, MP
16. Sy 12, sev.
17. $My \cdot Sy$ 15, 16, conj.
18. $(\exists x)(Mx \cdot Sx)$ 17, EG, y/x
19. $(\exists x)(Mx \cdot Sx)$ 12–18, EI
20. $(\exists x)(Mx \cdot Sx)$ 5–19, EI

(4)
1. $(x)(Gx \supset Hx)$
2. $(x)(Hx \supset Mx)$ $/ \therefore (\exists x)Gx \supset (\exists y)My$
3. $(\exists x)Gx$ $/ \therefore (\exists y)My$
4. Gx 3, x/x
5. $Gx \supset Hx$ 1, UI, x/x
6. $Hx \supset Mx$ 2, UI, x/x
7. $Gx \supset Mx$ 5, 6, OC
8. Mx 4, 7, MP
9. $(\exists y)My$ 8, EG, x/y
10. $(\exists y)My$ 4–9, EI
11. $(\exists x)Gx \supset (\exists y)My$ 3–10, CP

Ch. 19, Ex. VIII

(2)
1. $(x)((Cx \lor Ox) \supset (Ex \cdot Mx))$ $/ \therefore (x)(Cx \supset Ex)$
2. $(Cx \lor Ox) \supset (Ex \cdot Mx)$ 1, UI, x/x
3. Cx $/ \therefore Ex$
4. $Cx \lor Ox$ 3, disj.
5. $Ex \cdot Mx$ 2, 4, MP
6. Ex 5, sev.
7. $Cx \supset Ex$ 3–6, CP
8. $(x)(Cx \supset Ex)$ 7, UG, x/x

(6) 1. $(x)((Cx \lor Dx) \supset (Bx \cdot Mx))$
         2. $(x)(Cx \supset Mx) \supset (y)(Dy \supset Vy)$
         3. $(x)((Mx \cdot Vx) \supset Px)$ $/ \therefore (x)(Dx \supset Px)$
         4. $(Cx \lor Dx) \supset (Bx \cdot Mx)$ 1, UI, x/x
         5. Cx
         6. $Cx \lor Dx$ 5, disj.
         7. $Bx \cdot Mx$ 6, 4, MP
         8. Mx 7, sev.
         9. $Cx \supset Mx$ 5–8, CP
        10. $(x)(Cx \supset Mx)$ 9, UG, x/x
        11. $(y)(Dy \supset Vy)$ 2, 10, MP
        12. $Dx \supset Vx$ 11, UI, y/x
        13. Dx
        14. $Cx \lor Dx$ 13, disj.
        15. $Bx \cdot Mx$ 4, 14, MP
        16. Mx 15, sev.
        17. Vx 12, 13, MP
        18. $Mx \cdot Vx$ 16, 17, conj.
        19. $(Mx \cdot Vx) \supset Px$ 3, UI, x/x
        20. Px 18, 19, MP
        21. $Dx \supset Px$ 13–20, CP
        22. $(x)(Dx \supset Px)$ 21, UG, x/x

(10) 1. $(x)Ix \lor (y)Ty$ $/ \therefore (z)(Iz \lor Tz)$
          2. $(x)(Ix \lor (y)Ty)$ 1, QS
          3. $(x)(y)(Ix \lor Ty)$ 2, QS
          4. $(y)(Iz \lor Ty)$ 3, UI, x/z
          5. $Iz \lor Tz$ 4, UI, y/z
          6. $(z)(Iz \lor Tz)$ 5, UG, z/z

Ch. 20, Ex. I

(3) 1. $(\exists x)Px \supset (y)(Qy \supset Py)$
         2. $(\exists x)(Rx \cdot Tx) \supset (y)(Py \supset Ty)$
                $/ \therefore (x)(y)((Px \cdot (Rx \cdot Tx)) \supset (Qy \supset Ty))$
         3. $(\exists x)(Px \cdot (Rx \cdot Tx))$ $/ \therefore (y)(Qy \supset Ty)$
         4. Qy $/ \therefore Ty$
         5. $Px \cdot (Rx \cdot Tx)$ 3, x/x
         6. Px 5, sev.
         7. $(\exists x)Px$ 6, EG, x/x
         8. $(y)(Qy \supset Py)$ 1, 7, MP
         9. $Qy \supset Py$ 8, UI, y/y
        10. Py 4, 9, MP
        11. $Rx \cdot Tx$ 5, sev.
        12. $(\exists x)(Rx \cdot Tx)$ 11, EG, x/x
        13. $(y)(Py \supset Ty)$ 12, 2, MP
        14. $Py \supset Ty$ 13, UI, y/y
        15. Ty 10, 14, MP
        16. Ty 5–15, EI
        17. $Qy \supset Ty$ 4–16, CP
        18. $(y)(Qy \supset Ty)$ 17, UG, y/y

19. $(\exists x)(Px \cdot (Rx \cdot Tx)) \supset (y)(Qy \supset Ty)$ 3–18, CP
20. $(x)((Px \cdot (Rx \cdot Tx)) \supset (y)(Qy \supset Ty))$ 19, QS
21. $(x)(y)((Px \cdot (Rx \cdot Tx)) \supset (Qy \supset Ty))$ 20, QS

(6)   1. $(x)((Mx \cdot Nx) \supset Ox)$
     2. $(x)(Ox \supset Px)$
     3. $(\exists x)(Px \cdot \sim Sx) \supset (y)(Ny \supset \sim Py)$
        $/ \therefore (x) \sim (\exists y)((My \cdot \sim (Ox \supset Sx)) \cdot Ny)$
     4. $(\exists y)(My \cdot Ny)$ $/ \therefore (x)(Ox \supset Sx)$
     5. Ox $/ \therefore Sx$
     6. $My \cdot Ny$ 4, y/y
     7. $(My \cdot Ny) \supset Oy$ 1, UI, x/y
     8. Oy 6, 7, MP
     9. $Oy \supset Py$ 2, UI, x/y
    10. Py 8, 9, MP
    11. Ny 6, sev.
    12. $Ny \cdot Py$ 10, 11, conj.
    13. $(\exists y)(Ny \cdot Py)$ 12, EG, y/y
    14. $\sim \sim (\exists y)(Ny \cdot Py)$ 13, DN
    15. $\sim (y) \sim (Ny \cdot Py)$ 14, QN
    16. $\sim (y)(\sim Ny \lor \sim Py)$ 15, TD
    17. $\sim (y)(Ny \supset \sim Py)$ 16, CE
    18. $\sim (\exists x)(Px \cdot \sim Sx)$ 3, 17, MT
    19. $(x) \sim (Px \cdot \sim Sx)$ 18, QN
    20. $(x)(\sim Px \lor \sim \sim Sx)$ 19, TD
    21. $(x)(Px \supset Sx)$ 20, CE, DN
    22. $Ox \supset Px$ 2, UI, x/x
    23. $Px \supset Sx$ 21, UI, x/x
    24. Px 5, 22, MP
    25. Sx 23, 24, MP
    26. Sx 6–25, EI
    27. $Ox \supset Sx$ 5–26, CP
    28. $(x)(Ox \supset Sx)$ 27, UG, x/x
    29. $(\exists y)(My \cdot Ny) \supset (x)(Ox \supset Sx)$ 4–28, CP
    30. $\sim (\exists y)(My \cdot Ny) \lor (x)(Ox \supset Sx)$ 29, CE
    31. $(x)(Ox \supset Sx) \lor \sim (\exists y)(My \cdot Ny)$ 30, transp.
    32. $\sim \sim [(x)(Ox \supset Sx) \lor \sim (\exists y)(My \cdot Ny)]$ 31, DN
    33. $\sim [\sim (x)(Ox \supset Sx) \cdot \sim \sim (\exists y)(My \cdot Ny)]$ 32, TD
    34. $\sim [\sim (x)(Ox \supset Sx) \cdot (\exists y)(My \cdot Ny)]$ 33, DN
    35. $\sim [(\exists x) \sim (Ox \supset Sx) \cdot (\exists y)(My \cdot Ny)]$ 34, QN
    36. $\sim (\exists x)[\sim (Ox \supset Sx) \cdot (\exists y)(My \cdot Ny)]$ 35, QS
    37. $\sim (\exists x)(\exists y)[\sim (Ox \supset Sx) \cdot (My \cdot Ny)]$ 36, QS
    38. $(x) \sim (\exists y)[\sim (Ox \supset Sx) \cdot (My \cdot Ny)]$ 37, QN
    39. $(x) \sim (\exists y)[(\sim (Ox \supset Sx) \cdot My) \cdot Ny]$ 38, rgr.
    40. $(x) \sim (\exists y)[(My \cdot \sim (Ox \supset Sx)) \cdot Ny]$ 39, transp.

(11)   1. $(x)[Fx \supset ((\exists y)Hy \supset Gz)]$
     2. $(x)[Gz \supset ((y)(Gy \supset Ky) \lor Hx)]$
        $/ \therefore (z)(y)(x)[Hx \supset ([Gy \cdot \sim Ky] \supset [(Fz \supset Hz) \cdot Gy])]$

3. $(\exists x)Hx$ $/ \therefore (\exists y)(\sim Ky \cdot Gy) \supset (z)(Fz \supset Hz)$
4. $(\exists y)(\sim Ky \cdot Gy)$ $/ \therefore (w)(Fw \supset Hw)$
5. Fw $/ \therefore Hw$
6. $Fw \supset ((\exists y)Hy \supset Gz)$ 1, UI, x/w
7. $(\exists y)Hy \supset Gz$ 5, 6, MP
8. $(\exists y)Hy$ 3, RBV x/y
9. Gz 7, 8, MP
10. $Gz \supset ((y)(Gy \supset Ky) \lor Hw)$ 2, UI x/w
11. $(y)(Gy \supset Ky) \lor Hw$ 9, 10, MP
12. $(\exists y)(\sim Ky \cdot \sim \sim Gy)$ 4, DN
13. $(\exists y)\sim(\sim Gy \lor Ky)$ 12, TE, transp.
14. $\sim(y)(Gy \supset Ky)$ 13, QN, CE
15. Hw 11, 14, canc
16. $Fw \supset Hw$ 5–15, CP
17. $(w)(Fw \supset Hw)$ 16, UG w/w
18. $(\exists y)(\sim Ky \cdot Gy) \supset (w)(Fw \supset Hw)$ 4–17, CP
19. $(\exists x)Hx \supset ((\exists y)(\sim Ky \cdot Gy) \supset (w)(Fw \supset Hw))$
                                           3–18, CP
20. $(\exists x)Hx \supset ((\exists y)(\sim Ky \cdot Gy) \supset (z)(Fz \supset Hz))$
                                         19, RBV w/z

This "surrogate conclusion" may now be transformed into the original conclusion, as follows:

21. $(\exists x)Hx \supset (z)((\exists y)[\sim Ky \cdot Gy] \supset (Fz \supset Hz))$
                                   20, QS ("z" quantifier)
22. $(z)[(\exists x)Hx \supset ((\exists y)[\sim Ky \cdot Gy] \supset (Fz \supset Hz))]$
                                   21, QS ("z" quantifier)
23. $(z)[(\exists x)Hx \supset (y)([\sim Ky \cdot Gy] \supset (Fz \supset Hz))]$
                                   22, QS ("y" quantifier)
24. $(z)(y)[(\exists x)Hx \supset ([\sim Ky \cdot Gy] \supset (Fz \supset Hz))]$ 23, QS ("y" quantifier)
25. $(z)(y)(x)[Hx \supset ([\sim Ky \cdot Gy] \supset (Fz \supset Hz))]$ 24, QS ("x" quantifier)
26. $(z)(y)(x)[Hx \supset (\sim Ky \supset [Gy \supset (Fz \supset Hz)])]$
                                   25, exp.
27. $(z)(y)(x)[Hx \supset (\sim Ky \supset [Gy \supset [Gy \cdot (Fz \supset Hz)]])]$
                                   26, abs.
28. $(z)(y)(x)[Hx \supset ([\sim Ky \cdot Gy] \supset [Gy \cdot (Fz \supset Hz)])]$
                                   27, exp.
29. $(z)(y)(x)[Hx \supset ([Gy \cdot \sim Ky] \supset [(Fz \supset Hz) \cdot Gy])]$
                                   28, transp., transp.

Ch. 20, Ex. II

(1)

1. $(x)Fx$
2. $(y)Fy$ 1, RBV x/y
3. $(x)Fx \supset (y)Fy$ 1–2, CP
4. $(\exists x)(Fx \supset (y)Fy)$ 3, QS

(6)

1. $(x)Fx \cdot (\exists y)Gy$ / ∴ $(\exists z)(Fz \cdot Gz)$
2. Gy 1, sev., y/y
3. Fy 1, sev., UI, x/y
4. $Fy \cdot Gy$ 2, 3, conj.
5. $(\exists z)(Fz \cdot Gz)$ 4, EG, y/z
6. $(\exists z)(Fz \cdot Gz)$ 2–5, EI
7. $[(x)Fx \cdot (\exists y)Gy] \supset (\exists z)(Fz \cdot Gz)$ 1–6, CP

(10)

1. $(\exists x)Fx \cdot (\exists y)Gy$
2. $(z)(Fz \supset Hz) \cdot (w)(Gw \supset Kw)$
3. $Ft \cdot Gu$ / ∴ $Ht \cdot Ku$
4. $Ft \supset Ht$ 2, sev., UI, z/t
5. Ht 3, sev., 4, MP
6. $Gu \supset Ku$ 2, sev., UI, w/u
7. Ku 3, sev., 6, MP
8. $Ht \cdot Ku$ 5, 7, conj.
9. $(Ft \cdot Gu) \supset (Ht \cdot Ku)$ 3–8, CP
10. $(u)[(Ft \cdot Gu) \supset (Ht \cdot Ku)]$ 9, UG, u/u
11. $(t)(u)[(Ft \cdot Gu) \supset (Ht \cdot Ku)]$ 10, UG, t/t
12. $[(z)(Fz \supset Hz) \cdot (w)(Gw \supset Kw)] \supset$
    $(t)(u)[(Ft \cdot Gu) \supset (Ht \cdot Ku)]$ 2–12, CP
13. $(t)(u)[(Ft \cdot Gu) \supset (Ht \cdot Ku)]$
14. Fz / ∴ Hz
15. $(u)[(Fz \cdot Gu) \supset (Hz \cdot Ku)]$ 13, UI, t/z
16. Gy 1, sev., y/y
17. $(Fz \cdot Gy) \supset (Hz \cdot Ky)$ 15, UI, u/y
18. $Hz \cdot Ky$ 14, 16, conj., 17, MP
19. Hz 18, sev.
20. Hz 16–19, EI
21. $Fz \supset Hz$ 14–20, CP
22. $(z)(Fz \supset Hz)$ 21, UG, z/z
23. Gw / ∴ Kw
24. Fx 1, sev., x/x
25. $(u)[(Fx \cdot Gu) \supset (Hx \cdot Ku)]$ 13, UI, t/x
26. $(Fx \cdot Gw) \supset (Hx \cdot Kw)$ 25, UI, u/w
27. $Hx \cdot Kw$ 24, 23, conj., 26, MP
28. Kw 27, sev.
29. Kw 24–28, EI
30. $Gw \supset Kw$ 23–29, CP
31. $(w)(Gw \supset Kw)$ 30, UG, w/w
32. $(z)(Fz \supset Hz) \cdot (w)(Gw \supset Kw)$ 22, 31, conj.
33. $(t)(u)[(Ft \cdot Gu) \supset (Ht \cdot Ku)] \supset$
    $[(z)(Fz \supset Hz) \cdot (w)(Gw \supset Kw)]$ 13–32, CP
34. $[12] \cdot [33]$ 12, 33, conj.
35. $[(z)(Fz \supset Hz) \cdot (w)(Gw \supset Kw)] \equiv$
    $(t)(u)[(Ft \cdot Gu) \supset (Ht \cdot Ku)]$ 34, BE
36. $[1] \supset [35]$ 1–35, CP

Ch. 21, Ex. I

(2) $(x)Dx \supset (\exists y)Py$
$(x)Px$ $/ \therefore (\exists x)Dx$
Shown invalid by: $Dx : x$ is both round and square
$Px : x$ is vertebrate if human

(7) $(x)[(Ax \lor Ox) \supset (Ex \cdot Fx)]$
$(x)(Ex \supset Nx)$
$(x)(Fx \supset Ex) \supset (y)(By \supset Ey)$ $/ \therefore (x)[(Ax \lor Bx) \supset (Nx \cdot Fx)]$
Shown invalid by: $Ax : x$ is a lizard
$Ox : x$ is a snake
$Ex : x$ is a reptile
$Fx : x$ has scales
$Nx : x$ is cold-blooded
$Bx : x$ is a cow

So interpreted, the first premiss says 'Lizards and snakes are scaly reptiles', which is true; the second premiss says 'Reptiles are cold-blooded', which is true; the antecedent of the third premiss says 'Everything with scales is a reptile'. This is false (fish and armadillos are counterexamples), and so the third premiss is true because it is a conditional with a false antecedent. Finally, the conclusion says 'Lizards and cows are scaly and cold-blooded', which is false because cows are neither.

(10) $(x)(Sx \supset Fx)$
$(x)(Fx \supset Lx)$
$(\exists x)Lx \supset (\exists y)Ay$ or else $(x)(Lx \supset Ax)$
$(\exists x)\sim Sx$ $/ \therefore (\exists y)\sim Ay$
Shown invalid by: $Sx : x$ is a cat
$Fx : x$ is a mammal
$Lx : x$ is warm-blooded
$Ax : x$ is vertebrate if human

Ch. 21, Ex. II

(3) $(Fc \supset (\exists y)Gy) \cdot (Fd \supset (\exists y)Gy)$ and then
$(Fc \supset (Gc \lor Gd)) \cdot (Fd \supset (Gc \lor Gd))$

(6) $(\exists y)((Fc \cdot Gy) \lor (Fy \cdot Gc)) \lor (\exists y)((Fd \cdot Gy) \lor (Fy \cdot Gd))$ and then
$[((Fc \cdot Gc) \lor (Fc \cdot Gc)) \lor ((Fc \cdot Gd) \lor (Fd \cdot Gc))] \lor$
$[((Fd \cdot Gc) \lor (Fc \cdot Gd)) \lor ((Fd \cdot Gd) \lor (Fd \cdot Gd))]$

(9) $(Fc \cdot Fd) \supset Gd$

Ch. 21, Ex. III

(4) Shown invalid for $\{a, b\}$ by:

Fa	Fb	Ga	Gb	Ha	Hb
F	T	F	T	T	T
T	F	T	F	T	T

Ch. 21, Ex. IV

(4) $(x)(Fx \lor Sx)$ $/ \therefore (x)Fx \lor (x)Sx$
$(Fa \lor Sa) \cdot (Fb \lor Sb)$ $/ \therefore (Fa \cdot Fb) \lor (Sa \cdot Sb)$
Shown invalid for $\{a, b\}$ by:

Fa	Fb	Sa	Sb
T	F	T	F
F	T	F	T

Also shown invalid by: $Fx : x$ is alive
$Sx : x$ is not alive

(7) 1. $(x)(Fx \supset Sx)$
2. $(\exists x)(Fx \cdot Wx \cdot \sim Gx) \cdot (\exists y)(Fy \cdot Gy \cdot \sim Wy)$
3. $(\exists x)(Sx \cdot \sim Fx)$ $/ \therefore (\exists x)(Sx \cdot Wx \cdot Gx)$
1a. $(Fa \supset Sa) \cdot (Fb \supset Sb) \cdot (Fc \supset Sc) \cdot (Fd \supset Sd)$
2a. $[(Fa \cdot Wa \cdot \sim Ga) \lor (Fb \cdot Wb \cdot \sim Gb) \lor (Fc \cdot Wc \cdot \sim Gc) \lor$
$(Fd \cdot Wd \cdot \sim Gd)] \cdot [(Fa \cdot Ga \cdot \sim Wa) \lor (Fb \cdot Gb \cdot \sim Wb) \lor$
$(Fc \cdot Gc \cdot \sim Wc) \lor (Fd \cdot Gd \cdot \sim Wd)]$
3a. $(Sa \cdot \sim Fa) \lor (Sb \cdot \sim Fb) \lor (Sc \cdot \sim Fc) \lor (Sd \cdot \sim Fd)$
$/ \therefore (Sa \cdot Wa \cdot Ga) \lor (Sb \cdot Wb \cdot Gb) \lor (Sc \cdot Wc \cdot Gc) \lor$
$(Sd \cdot Wd \cdot Gd)$

Shown invalid for $\{a, b, c, d\}$ by:

Fa	Fb	Fc	Fd	Ga	Gb	Gc	Gd	Sa	Sb	Sc	Sd	Wa	Wb	Wc	Wd
F	T	T	F		T	F	T	F	T	T	T		F	T	F
					F									T	
					F										F

or any of 48 other, similar combinations.

Ch. 21, Ex. V

(2) $(\exists x)((Wx \cdot Px) \cdot Ix) \supset (y)((Py \cdot \sim Wy) \supset \sim Iy)$
False when: $Px : x$ is a number
$Wx : x$ is even
$Ix \ : x$ is greater than 10

(6) $[(\exists x)(Tx \cdot (Fx \cdot Ax)) \cdot (y)((Fy \cdot Ay) \supset By)] \supset (z)((Fz \cdot Tz) \supset Bz)$
False when $Tx : x$ is an automobile
$Fx : x$ is red
$Ax : x$ is a Chevrolet
$Bx : x$ was made by General Motors

Ch. 21, Ex. VI

(1) $(x)(Ox \supset Dx) \lor (y)(Oy \supset \sim Dy)$
False for $\{a, b\}$ when

Oa	Ob	Da	Db
T	T	F	T
T	T	T	F

(3) $(\exists x)(Px \cdot Hx) \lor (\exists y)(Py \cdot \sim Hy)$
False for $\{a\}$ when

Pa	Ha
F	T
F	

Ch. 22, Ex. I

(1) $(x)[x$ is a person $\supset (\exists y)(y$ is a person $\cdot\ x$ loves $y)]$
$(x)[Px \supset (\exists y)(Py \cdot Lxy)]$

(4) $(\exists x)[x$ is a person $\cdot\ (y)(y$ is a person $\supset y$ loves $x)]$
$(\exists x)[Px \cdot (y)(Py \supset Lyx)]$

(8) $(x)([x$ is a person $\cdot\ (y)(y$ is a person $\supset x$ loves $y)] \supset x$ loves $x)$
$(x)([Px \cdot (y)(Py \supset Lxy)] \supset Lxx)$

Ch. 22, Ex. II

(2) $(\exists x)[x$ is a person $\cdot\ (\exists y)(y$ is an elephant $\cdot\ x$ gave y to Edna$)]$
$(\exists x)[Px \cdot (\exists y)(Ey \cdot Gxy\underline{e})]$

(6) $(x)([x$ is a person $\cdot\ (\exists y)(y$ is an elephant $\cdot\ x$ gave y to Edna$)] \supset$
$(\exists z)[z$ is a wombat $\cdot\ x$ gave z to Clyde$])$
$(x)([Px \cdot (\exists y)(Ey \cdot Gxy\underline{e})] \supset (\exists z)[Wz \cdot Gxz\underline{c}])$

(9) $(\exists x)(x$ is a person $\cdot\ (y)[y$ is a person $\supset (\exists z)x$ gave z to $y]) \supset$
$(\exists w)(w$ is a person $\cdot\ (\exists t)w$ gave t to $w)$
$(\exists x)(Px \cdot (y)[Py \supset (\exists z)Gxzy]) \supset (\exists w)(Pw \cdot (\exists t)Gwtw)$

Ch. 22, Ex. III

(2) $(x)([x$ is a person $\cdot\ (y)(y$ is a person $\supset\ \sim x$ loves $y)] \supset$
x is a complete failure$)$
$(x)([Px \cdot (y)(Py \supset\ \sim Lxy)] \supset Fx)$

(6) $(x)[(x$ is a person $\cdot\ (\exists y)$ Edna gave y to $x) \supset\ \sim x$ is a complete failure$]$
$(x)[(Px \cdot (\exists y)G\underline{e}yx) \supset\ \sim Fx]$

(10) $(x)([x$ is a person $\cdot\ (\exists y)((y$ is a person $\cdot\ x$ loves $y) \cdot (z)\{x$ owns $z \supset$
x gives z to $y\})] \supset [\sim x$ is a complete failure $\cdot\ (w)(w$ is a person $\supset$
$\sim w$ will have x arrested$)])$
$(x)([Px \cdot (\exists y)((Py \cdot Lxy) \cdot (z)\{Oxz \supset Gxzy\})] \supset [\sim Fx \cdot (w)(Pw \supset$
$\sim Hwx)])$

Ch. 22, Ex. IV

(1) false	(5) true
(2) true	(6) true
(3) false	(7) false
(4) false	(8) true

Ch. 22, Ex. V

(3) $(\exists x)(y)[(y$ is a man $\cdot\ y$ admires something$) \supset y$ admires $x]$
$(\exists x)(y)[(y$ is a man $\cdot\ (\exists z)y$ admires $z) \supset y$ admires $x]$
$(\exists x)(y)[(My \cdot (\exists z)Ayz) \supset Ayx]$

(6) $(\exists x)(y)[y$ is a man $\supset y$ desires x from somebody$]$
$(\exists x)(y)[y$ is a man $\supset (\exists z)(z$ is a person $\cdot\ y$ desires x from $z)]$
$(\exists x)(y)[My \supset (\exists z)(Pz \cdot Dyxz)]$
is preferred; however

($\exists x$)($\exists z$)[z is a person · (y)(y is a man $\supset$ y desires x from z)]
($\exists x$)($\exists z$)[Pz · (y)($My \supset Dyxz$)]

could also be acceptable.

(9) ($\exists x$)[x is a man · (y)(y is a person $\supset$ x desires something from y)]
($\exists x$)[x is a man · (y)(y is a person $\supset$ ($\exists z$)x desires z from y)]
($\exists x$)[Mx · (y)($Py \supset$ ($\exists z$)$Dxzy$)]

Ch. 22, Ex. VI

(1) There is a person x and an object y such that x gave y to everyone. This would be true, for example, in the case of Thelma and her ugly vase. In the course of 16 years she gave it to everyone and still didn't get rid of it. (The "gift" and "giver" quantifiers are both specific with respect to the universal "receiver" quantifier.)

(5) Each member is such that something or other was given by him to someone or other. This would be true, for example, if at Christmas time the members each drew someone's name out of the hat and then gave *that* person a gift. (The "gift" and "receiver" quantifiers are both distributed with respect to the universal "giver" quantifier: each giver has his own gift and his own recipient.)

(8) There is a person z such that each member gave him (or her) something or other. This would be true, for example, if on Zelda's birthday the members showered her with presents, each of them giving her something. (The "receiver" quantifier is specific with respect to the universal "giver" quantifier; but the "gift" quantifier is distributed with respect to the "giver" quantifier: there is one recipient—Zelda—but each giver has his own gift for her.)

Ch. 22, Ex. VII

(1) ($\exists x$)[(x is a dog · x belongs to Clyde) · ($\exists y$)(y is a person · x bit y)]
($\exists x$)[(Dx · Kxc) · ($\exists y$)(Py · Bxy)]

(2) ($\exists y$)[y is a person · ($\exists x$)((x is a dog · x belongs to Clyde) · y bit x)]
($\exists y$)[Py · ($\exists x$)((Dx · Kxc) · Byx)]

(5) (x)[x is a person $\supset$ (y)([y is a dog · y belongs to x] $\supset$ $\sim y$ bit Clyde)]
(x)[$Px \supset$ (y)([Dy · Kyx] $\supset \sim Byc$)]

(9) ($\exists x$)[x is a person · ($\exists y$)(y is brother to x · ($\exists z$){(z is a dog · z belongs to Clyde) · z bit y})]
($\exists x$)[Px · ($\exists y$)(Fyx · ($\exists z$){(Dz · Kzc) · Bzy})]

(12) ($\exists x$)[x is a person · (y)(y is brother to x $\supset$
(z){(z is a dog · z belongs to Clyde) $\supset$ z bit y})]
($\exists x$)[Px · (y)($Fyx \supset$ (z){(Dz · Kzc) $\supset$ Bzy})]

Ch. 22, Ex. VIII

(3) ($\exists x$)[x is father to Arthur · ($\exists y$)(y is a present · x brought y to Arthur)]
($\exists x$)[Pxa · ($\exists y$)(Gy · $Bxya$)]

(6) ($\exists x$)[x is father to Arthur · ($\exists y$)(y is a present · x brought y to x)]
($\exists x$)[Pxa · ($\exists y$)(Gy · $Bxyx$)]

(9) $(\exists x)[x$ is father to Galahad $\cdot$ $(\exists y)(y$ is a dog $\cdot$ $[(\exists z)\{z$ is father to Arthur $\cdot$
$(\exists w)[w$ is brother to $z \cdot y$ belongs to $w]\} \cdot$ Arthur brought y to $x])]$
$(\exists x)[Pxg \cdot (\exists y)(Dy \cdot [(\exists z)\{Pz\underline{a} \cdot (\exists w)[Fwz \cdot Kyw]\} \cdot B\underline{a}yx])]$

Ch. 22, Ex. IX

(1) $(\exists x)(x$ is a spreading chestnut tree $\cdot$ $(\exists y)[y$ is a village smithy $\cdot$
y stands under $x])$
$(\exists x)(Tx \cdot (\exists y)[Sy \cdot Uyx])$

(10) $(\exists x)(x$ is a cavern $\cdot$ $(\exists y)[y$ is a canyon $\cdot$ x is in $y]$ $\cdot$
$\quad(\exists z)[z$ is a miner $\cdot$ z is a forty-niner $\cdot$ z was excavating for a mine $\cdot$
$\quad\quad z$ dwelt in x $\cdot$
$\quad\quad\quad(\exists w)(w$ was daughter to $z \cdot w$ was Clementine $\cdot w$ dwelt in $x)])$
$(\exists x)(Cx \cdot (\exists y)[Ky \cdot Lxy] \cdot (\exists z)[Mz \cdot Fz \cdot Ez \cdot Dzx \cdot (\exists w)(Hwz \cdot Qw \cdot Dwx)])$

Ch. 22, Ex. X

(2)
1. $(\exists x)(Px \cdot (y)(Py \supset Lyx))$	$/ \therefore (x)(Px \supset (\exists y)(Py \cdot Lxy))$	
2. $Pz \cdot (y)(Py \supset Lyz)$	1, x/z	
3. $(y)(Py \supset Lyz)$	2, sev.	
4. $Pw \supset Lwz$	3, UI, w/y	
5. Pw $/ \therefore (\exists y)(Py \cdot Lwy)$		
6. Lwz	4, 5, MP	
7. Pz	2, sev.	
8. $Pz \cdot Lwz$	7, 6, conj.	
9. $(\exists y)(Py \cdot Lwy)$	8, EG, z/y	
10. $Pw \supset (\exists y)(Py \cdot Lwy)$	5–9, CP	
11. $(x)[Px \supset (\exists y)(Py \cdot Lxy)]$	10, UG, w/x	
12. $(x)[Px \supset (\exists y)(Py \cdot Lxy)]$	2–11, EI	

(5)
1. $(x)[(Px \cdot (y)(Py \supset (\exists z)Sxzy)) \supset (\exists w)Sxwg]$		
2. $(x)[Px \supset \sim(\exists y)Sxyg]$ $/ \therefore (x)[Px \supset \sim(y)(Py \supset (\exists z)Sxzy)]$		
3. Px $/ \therefore \sim(y)(Py \supset (\exists z)Sxzy)$		
4. $Px \supset \sim(\exists y)Sxyg$	2, UI, x/x	
5. $\sim(\exists y)Sxyg$	3, 4, MP	
6. $(Px \cdot (y)(Py \supset (\exists z)Sxzy)) \supset (\exists w)Sxwg$	1, UI, x/x	
7. $\sim(\exists w)Sxwg$	5, RBV, y/w	
8. $\sim(Px \cdot (y)(Py \supset (\exists z)Sxzy))$	6, 7, MT	
9. $\sim Px \lor \sim(y)(Py \supset (\exists z)Sxzy)$	8, TD	
10. $\sim(y)(Py \supset (\exists z)Sxzy)$	3, 9, DN, canc.	
11. $Px \supset \sim(y)(Py \supset (\exists z)Sxzy)$	3–10, CP	
12. $(x)[Px \supset \sim(y)(Py \supset (\exists z)Sxzy)]$	11, UG, x/x	

(9)
1. $(x)[(Px \cdot (\exists y)[Dyx \cdot Axy]) \supset Bx]$
2. $(x)[Wx \supset (y)(Py \supset Dxy)]$
3. $(x)[(Px \cdot Hx) \supset \sim Bx]$ $/ \therefore (x)[(Px \cdot (\exists w)[Ww \cdot Axw]) \supset \sim Hx]$

4. $Px \cdot (\exists w)[Ww \cdot Axw]$ $/ \therefore \sim Hx$
5. Hx (IP)
6. $(Px \cdot Hx) \supset \sim Bx$ 3, UI, x/x
7. $\sim Bx$ 4, sev., 5, conj., 6, MP
8. $Ww \cdot Axw$ 4, sev., w/w
9. $Ww \supset (y)(Py \supset Dwy)$ 2, UI, x/w
10. $(y)(Py \supset Dwy)$ 8, sev., 9, MP
11. $Px \supset Dwx$ 10, UI, y/x
12. Dwx 4, sev., 11, MP
13. $Dwx \cdot Axw$ 8, sev., 12, conj.
14. $(\exists y)(Dyx \cdot Axy)$ 13, EG, w/y
15. $Px \cdot (\exists y)(Dyx \cdot Axy)$ 4, sev., 14, conj.
16. $(Px \cdot (\exists y)[Dyx \cdot Axy]) \supset Bx$ 1, UI, x/x
17. Bx 15, 16, MP
18. $Bx \vee (A \cdot \sim A)$ 17, disj.
19. $A \cdot \sim A$ 7, 18, canc.
20. $A \cdot \sim A$ 8–19, EI
21. $\sim Hx$ 5–20, IP
22. $(Px \cdot (\exists w)[Ww \cdot Axw]) \supset \sim Hx$ 4–21, CP
23. $(x)[(Px \cdot (\exists w)[Ww \cdot Axw]) \supset \sim Hx]$ 22, UG, x/x

Ch. 22, Ex. XI

(2) Using the abbreviations $Cx : x$ is a head, $Hx : x$ is a horse, $Ax : x$ is an animal, and $Bxy : x$ belongs to y, the translation is
$(x)[(Cx \cdot (\exists y)(Hy \cdot Bxy)) \supset (\exists z)(Az \cdot Bxz)]$ $/ \therefore (x)[Hx \supset Ax]$
Shown invalid by: $Cx : x$ is a person
$\quad\quad\quad\quad\quad Hx : x$ is a college
$\quad\quad\quad\quad\quad Ax : x$ is a high school
$\quad\quad\quad\quad\quad Bxy : x$ graduated from y
So interpreted, the argument says: 'All college graduates are high school graduates; therefore all colleges are high schools'.
For $\{a, b\}$ the interpretation is:
$[\{Ca \cdot ([Ha \cdot Baa] \vee [Hb \cdot Bab])\} \supset ([Aa \cdot Baa] \vee [Ab \cdot Bab])] \cdot$
$[\{Cb \cdot ([Ha \cdot Bba] \vee [Hb \cdot Bbb])\} \supset ([Aa \cdot Bba] \vee [Ab \cdot Bbb])]$
$/ \therefore (Ha \supset Aa) \cdot (Hb \supset Ab)$
Shown invalid for $\{a, b\}$ by:

Aa	Ab	Ca	Cb	Ha	Hb	Baa	Bab	Bba	Bbb
		F		F	T	F		F	

and many other assignments.

Ch. 22, Ex. XII

(2)　　　　 1. Oac
　　　　　　 2. Och $/ \therefore Yha$
Supp.　 3. $(x)(y)(z)[(Oxy \cdot Oyz) \supset Oxz]$—'older than' is transitive
Supp.　 4. $(x)(y)[Oxy \equiv Yyx]$—'older than' is the converse of 'younger than'
　　　　　　 5. $(y)(z)[(Oay \cdot Oyz) \supset Oaz]$ 3, UI, x/a
　　　　　　 6. $(z)[(Oac \cdot Ocz) \supset Oaz]$ 5, UI, y/c

7. $(Oac \cdot Och) \supset Oah$ 6, UI, z/h
8. Oah 1, 2, conj., 7, MP
9. $(y)[Oay \equiv Yya]$ 4, UI, x/a
10. $Oah \equiv Yha$ 9, UI, y/h
11. Yha 8, 10, equiv.

(4)

1. Fcz
2. Fzm
3. $(x)(y)(w)[(Fxy \cdot Fyw) \supset Gxw]$
4. $(x)(y)[Gxy \supset Axy]$ $/ \therefore Dmc$
Supp. 5. $(x)(y)[Axy \equiv Dyx]$—'ancestor of' is the converse of 'descendant of'
6. $(y)(w)[(Fcy \cdot Fyw) \supset Gcw]$ 3, UI, x/c
7. $(w)[(Fcz \cdot Fzw) \supset Gcw]$ 6, UI, y/z
8. $(Fcz \cdot Fzm) \supset Gcm$ 7, UI, w/m
9. Gcm 1, 2, conj., 8, MP
10. $(y)[Gcy \supset Acy]$ 4, UI, x/c
11. $Gcm \supset Acm$ 10, UI, y/m
12. Acm 9, 11, MP
13. $(y)[Acy \equiv Dyc]$ 5, UI, x/c
14. $Acm \equiv Dmc$ 13, UI, y/m
15. Dmc 12, 14, equiv.

(7)

1. Seb
2. $Sle \cdot Mlb$ $/ \therefore B$
Supp. 3. $(x)(y)(z)[(Sxy \cdot Syz) \supset Sxz]$—'studies less than' is transitive
Supp. 4. $(x)(y)[Sxy \supset \sim Syx]$—'studies less than' is asymmetric
Supp. 5. $(x)(y)[Sxy \equiv Myx]$—'studies more than' is the converse of 'studies less than'
6. $(y)(Sby \equiv Myb)$ 5, UI, x/b
7. $Sbl \equiv Mlb$ 6, UI, y/l
8. Sbl 2, sev., 7, equiv.
9. $(y)(z)[(Sly \cdot Syz) \supset Slz]$ 3, UI, x/l
10. $(z)[(Sle \cdot Sez) \supset Slz]$ 9, UI, y/e
11. $(Sle \cdot Seb) \supset Slb$ 10, UI, z/b
12. Slb 2, sev., 1, conj., 11, MP
13. $(y)[Sly \supset \sim Syl]$ 4, UI, x/l
14. $Slb \supset \sim Sbl$ 13, UI, y/b
15. $\sim Sbl$ 12, 13, MP
16. $Sbl \lor B$ 8, disj.
17. B 15–16, canc.

Ch. 22, Ex. XIII

(2) Supplied premisses:
     (a) 'All algebra classes are math classes'
     (b) 'If something fails something, then it doesn't pass it.'
     Txy : x took y

1. $(\exists x)(Ax \cdot Tpx \cdot Fpx)$ $/ \therefore \sim (x)[(Mx \cdot Tpx) \supset Ppx]$
Supp. (a) 2. $(x)(Ax \supset Mx)$

Supp. (b) 3. $(x)(y)(Fxy \supset \sim Pxy)$

4. $Ax \cdot Tpx \cdot Fpx$	1, x/x
5. $Ax \supset Mx$	2, UI, x/x
6. Mx	4, sev., 5, MP
7. $(y)(Fpy \supset \sim Ppy)$	3, UI, x/p
8. $Fpx \supset \sim Ppx$	7, UI, y/x
9. $\sim Ppx$	4, sev., 8, MP
10. $(Mx \cdot Tpx)$	4, sev., 6, conj.
11. $(Mx \cdot Tpx) \cdot \sim Ppx$	9, 10, conj.
12. $\sim \sim (Mx \cdot Tpx) \cdot \sim Ppx$	11, DN
13. $\sim [\sim (Mx \cdot Tpx) \lor Ppx]$	12, TE
14. $\sim [(Mx \cdot Tpx) \supset Ppx]$	13, CE
15. $(\exists x) \sim [(Mx \cdot Tpx) \supset Ppx]$	14, EG, x/x
16. $\sim (x)[(Mx \cdot Tpx) \supset Ppx]$	15, QN
17. $\sim (x)[(Mx \cdot Tpx) \supset Ppx]$	4–16, EI

(6) Supplied premisses:
(a) 'Bachelors don't have wives'
(b) One's sister-in-law is either one's wife's sister or one's brother's wife'
Lxy : x is a sister-in-law of y

1. Kc	
2. $(\exists x)(Lxc \cdot Hcx)$ / $\therefore$ $(\exists x)Bxc$	
Supp. (a) 3. $(x)(Kx \supset \sim (\exists y)Wyx)$	
Supp. (b) 4. $(x)(y)[Lxy \supset ((\exists z)(Wzy \cdot Sxz) \lor (\exists w)(Bwy \cdot Wxw))]$	
5. $Lxc \cdot Hcx$	2, x/x
6. $Kc \supset \sim (\exists y)Wyc$	3, UI, x/c
7. $(y)[Lxy \supset ((\exists z)(Wzy \cdot Sxz) \lor (\exists w)(Bwy \cdot Wxw))]$	4, UI, x/x
8. $Lxc \supset ((\exists z)(Wzc \cdot Sxz) \lor (\exists w)(Bwc \cdot Wxw))$	7, UI, y/c
9. $(\exists z)(Wzc \cdot Sxz) \lor (\exists w)(Bwc \cdot Wxw)$	5, sev., 8, MP
10. $(\exists z)(Wzc \cdot Sxz)$	(IP)
11. $Wzc \cdot Sxz$	10, z/z
12. Wzc	11, sev.
13. $(\exists y)Wyc$	
14. $(\exists y)Wyc$	11–13, EI
15. $\sim (\exists y)Wyc$	1, 6, MP
16. $(\exists y)Wyc \cdot \sim (\exists y)Wyc$	14, 15, conj.
17. $\sim (\exists z)(Wzc \cdot Sxz)$	10–16, IP
18. $(\exists w)(Bwc \cdot Wxw)$	9, 17, canc.
19. $Bwc \cdot Wxw$	18, w/w
20. Bwc	19, sev.
21. $(\exists x)Bxc$	20, EG, w/x
22. $(\exists x)Bxc$	19–21, EI
23. $(\exists x)Bxc$	5–22, EI

Ch. 23, Ex. I

(2) ∼[*e* is a man in the town · (*x*)([*x* is a man in the town · *x* ≠ *e*] ⊃
   e is richer than *x*)]
   ∼[*Me* · (*x*)([*Mx* · *x* ≠ *e*] ⊃ *Rex*)]

(6) (*x*)[*x* is a person ⊃ (∃ *y*)(*y* is a person · *x* ≠ *y* · *x* hates *y*)]
   (*x*)[*Px* ⊃ (∃ *y*)(*Py* · *x* ≠ *y* · *Hxy*)]

(11) (*x*)[(*x* is a person · *x* ≠ Clyde) ⊃ (*x* ≠ Harvey ⊃ ∼*x* drinks as much as
   Clyde)]
   (*x*)[(*Px* · *x* ≠ *c*) ⊃ (*x* ≠ *h* ⊃ ∼ *Dxc*)]

(16) (*x*)[(*x* is a person · *x* ≠ Thelma) ⊃ (∃ *z*)(*z* is a person · *z* ≠ *x* ·
   (∃ *y*)[*y* is a present · *x* received *y* from *z*])]
   (*x*)[(*Px* · *x* ≠ *t*) ⊃ (∃ *z*)(*Pz* · *z* ≠ *x* · (∃ *y*)[*Gy* · *Rxyz*])]

(19) (*x*)[*x* is a present ⊃ ∼ Harvey received *x*] · (*y*)[(*y* is a person · *y* ≠ Harvey) ⊃
   ∼(*z*)(*z* is a present ⊃ ∼*y* received *z*)]
   (*x*)[*Gx* ⊃ ∼ *Rhx*] · (*y*)[(*Py* · *y* ≠ *h*) ⊃ ∼(*z*)(*Gz* ⊃ ∼ *Ryz*)]

(22) Clyde is a man in town ·
   (*x*)[(*x* is a man in town · *x* ≠ Clyde) ⊃ Clyde is uglier than *x*] ·
   (*y*)(*y* is a man in town ⊃ ∼*y* is dumber than Clyde)
   Mc · (*x*)[(*Mx* · *x* ≠ *c*) ⊃ *Ucx*] · (*y*)(*My* ⊃ ∼ *Dyc*)

(25) ∼[Clyde is a man in town ·
   (*x*)(*x* is a man in town ⊃ ∼*x* is handsomer than Clyde)]
   ∼[*Mc* · (*x*)(*Mx* ⊃ ∼ *Hxc*)]

Ch. 23, Ex. II

(4) (*x*)[*x* is on the committee ⊃ ((*y*)(*y* is on the committee ⊃ *y* = *x*) ⊃
   ∼*x* is chairman)]
   (*x*)[*Ox* ⊃ ((*y*)(*Oy* ⊃ *y* = *x*) ⊃ ∼ *Cx*)]

(7) (*x*)[*x* is a person ⊃ (*y*)(*z*)([*y* is father to *x* · *z* is father to *x*] ⊃ *y* = *z*)]
   (*x*)[*Px* ⊃ (*y*)(*z*)([*Fyx* · *Fzx*] ⊃ *y* = *z*)]

(13) (∃ *x*)[*x* is carnivorous · *x* is a liger ·
   (*y*)([*y* is carnivorous · *y* is a liger] ⊃ *y* = *x*)]
   (∃ *x*)[*Cx* · *Lx* · (*y*)([*Cy* · *Ly*] ⊃ *y* = *x*)]

(14) (∃ *x*)[*x* is a liger · (*y*)(*y* is a liger ⊃ *y* = *x*) · *x* is carnivorous]
   (∃ *x*)[*Lx* · (*y*)(*Ly* ⊃ *y* = *x*) · *Cx*]

(19) (∃ *x*)[*x* is an axolotl in the tank · (∃ *y*)(*y* is an axolotl in the tank · *x* ≠ *y* ·
   (*z*)(*z* is an axolotl in the tank ⊃ (*z* = *x* ∨ *z* = *y*)) ·
   (*x* is dead ∨ *y* is dead) · ∼(*x* is dead · *y* is dead))]
   (∃ *x*)[*Ax* · (∃ *y*)(*Ay* · *x* ≠ *y* · (*z*)(*Az* ⊃ (*z* = *x* ∨ *z* = *y*)) ·
   (*Dx* ∨ *Dy*) · ∼(*Dx* · *Dy*))]

(21) Recall (Ch. 18) that any expression occurring in the antecedent of a conditional and ranging into the consequent must be translated as universal
   quantification over a conditional matrix: expressions which would otherwise be translated by existential quantifiers must be "shifted out" to
   capture the whole conditional. Thus, (21) must translate as
   (*x*)(*y*)[(*x* is an axolotl in the tank · *y* is an axolotl in the tank · *x* ≠ *y* ·
   (*z*)[*z* is an axolotl in the tank ⊃ (*z* = *x* ∨ *z* = *y*)]) ⊃
   (*x* is invisible ∨ *y* is invisible)]
   (*x*)(*y*)[(*Ax* · *Ay* · *x* ≠ *y* · (*z*)[*Az* ⊃ (*z* = *x* ∨ *z* = *y*)]) ⊃ (∼ *Vx* ∨ ∼ *Vy*)]

(23) ($\exists x$)[x is an axolotl in the tank · ($\exists y$)(y is an axolotl in the tank · $x \neq y$ · (z)(z is an axolotl in the tank $\supset$ ($z = x \lor z = y$)) · (x is longer than $y \lor y$ is longer than x) · (x is longer than $y \supset y$ is smarter than x) · (y is longer than $x \supset x$ is smarter than y))]

($\exists x$)[Ax · ($\exists y$)(Ay · $x \neq y$ · (z)($Az \supset (z = x \lor z = y)$)) · ($Lxy \lor Lyx$) · ($Lxy \supset Syx$) · ($Lyx \supset Sxy$))]

Ch. 23, Ex. III

(1)
1. $x \neq x$ (IP)
2. $x = x$ 1, SI
3. $x = x \cdot x \neq x$
4. $x = x$ 1–3, IP, DN
5. (x)($x = x$)   4, UG, x/x

(4)
1. $x \neq x$
2. $x = x$ 1, SI
3. $x \neq x \supset x = x$ 1–2, CP
4. $x = x$ 3, CE, DN, dup.
5. ($\exists y$)$x = y$ 4, EG, x/y
6. (x)($\exists y$)$x = y$ 5, UG, x/x

(7)
1. Fx
2. $x = x$ 1, SI
3. $x = x \cdot Fx$ 2, 1, conj.
4. ($\exists y$)($y = x \cdot Fy$)   3, EG, x/y
5. $Fx \supset (\exists y)(y = x \cdot Fy)$ 1–4, CP
6. (x)[$Fx \supset (\exists y)(y = x \cdot Fy)$]   5, UG, x/x

Ch. 23, Ex. IV

(2)
1. (x)[$Px \supset Dxm$]
2. $m = j$
3. $Fj \cdot Lj$ / ∴ ($\exists x$)[$Fx \cdot Lx \cdot (y)(Py \supset Dyx)$]
4. (x)[$Px \supset Dxj$]   1, 2, Id. (m/j in 1)
5. $Fj \cdot Lj \cdot (x)(Px \supset Dxj)$ 3, 4, conj.
6. $Fj \cdot Lj \cdot (y)(Py \supset Dyj)$ 5, RBV, x/y
7. ($\exists x$)[$Fx \cdot Lx \cdot (y)(Py \supset Dyx)$]   6, EG, j/x

(5)
1. ($\exists x$)[$Cx \cdot Rx \cdot (\exists y)(Cy \cdot Ry \cdot x \neq y)$]
2. $Cb \cdot Db$
3. (x)($Rx \supset \sim Dx$)
4. $Ca \cdot Cc \cdot (x)[((Cx \cdot x \neq b) \supset (x = a \lor x = c)]$
    / ∴ ($\exists x$)[$Cx \cdot Rx \cdot (\exists y)(Cy \cdot Ry \cdot y \neq x \cdot (z)[(Cz \cdot Rz) \supset (z = x \lor z = y)])$]

The strategy here is first to prove that neither of the Republican councilmen is Brown (easily done, since he is a Democrat), next to prove that Andrews and Carlyle are the two Republicans, which involves proving that Andrews and Carlyle are not the same man, as well as proving that they are Republicans. From this it can be proven that Andrews and Carlyle are the only two Republican councilmen, from which it may be inferred by

Existential Generalization that there are exactly two Republican councilmen. First, the proof that neither Republican is Brown:

5.	$Cx \cdot Rx \cdot (\exists y)(Cy \cdot Ry \cdot x \neq y)$	1, x/x
6.	$Cx \cdot Rx$	5, sev.
7.	$(\exists y)(Cy \cdot Ry \cdot x \neq y)$	5, sev.
8.	$Cy \cdot Ry \cdot x \neq y$	7, y/y
9.	$x \neq y$	8, sev.
10.	$Rx \supset \sim Dx$	3, UI, x/x
11.	$Ry \supset \sim Dy$	3, UI, x/y
12.	$\sim Dx$	6, sev., 10, MP
13.	$\sim Dy$	8, sev., 11, MP
14.	$x = b$	(IP)
15.	$\sim Db$	12, 14, Id. (x/b in 12)
16.	$Db \cdot \sim Db$	2, sev., 15, conj.
17.	$x \neq b$	14–16, IP
18.	$y = b$	(IP)
19.	$\sim Db$	18, 13, Id. (y/b in 13)
20.	$Db \cdot \sim Db$	2, sev., 19, conj.
21.	$y \neq b$	18–20, IP

Next, the proof that each of the councilmen who is a Republican is
identical with either Andrews or Carlyle:

22.	$(x)[(Cx \cdot x \neq b) \supset (x = a \lor x = c)]$	4, sev.
23.	$(Cx \cdot x \neq b) \supset (x = a \lor x = c)$	22, UI, x/x
24.	$(Cy \cdot y \neq b) \supset (y = a \lor y = c)$	22, UI, x/y
25.	$x = a \lor x = c$	6, sev., 17, conj., 23, MP
26.	$y = a \lor y = c$	8, sev., 21, conj., 24, MP

Then the proof that Andrews and Carlyle are (thereby) both Republicans:

27.	$x = a$ / $\therefore$ $Ra \cdot Rc$	
28.	$y \neq a$	9, 27, Id. (x/a in 9), sym.
29.	$y = c$	28, 26, canc.
30.	Ra	6, sev., 27, Id. (x/a in 6)
31.	Rc	8, sev., 29, Id. (y/c in 8)
32.	$Ra \cdot Rc$	30, 31, conj.
33.	$x = a \supset (Ra \cdot Rc)$	27–32, CP
34.	$x = c$ / $\therefore$ $Ra \cdot Rc$	
35.	$y \neq c$	9, 34, Id. (x/c in 9), sym.
36.	$y = a$	35, 26, canc.
37.	Ra	8, sev., 36, Id. (y/a in 8)
38.	Rc	6, sev., 34, Id. (x/c in 6)
39.	$Ra \cdot Rc$	37, 38, conj.
40.	$x = c \supset (Ra \cdot Rc)$	34–39, CP
41.	$(Ra \cdot Rc) \lor (Ra \cdot Rc)$	25, 33, 40, dilem.
42.	$Ra \cdot Rc$	41, dup.

And the proof that Andrews and Carlyle are not the same man:

→43. $c = a$	(IP)
→44. $x = c$	(IP)
45. $y \neq c$	9, 44, Id. (x/c in 9)
46. $y = a$	26, 45, canc.
47. $y = c$	43, 46, Id. (a/c in 46)
48. $y = c \cdot y \neq c$	47, 45, conj.
49. $x \neq c$	44–48, IP
50. $x = a$	25, 49, canc.
51. $x = c$	43, 50, Id. (a/c in 50)
52. $x = c \cdot x \neq c$	51, 49, conj.
53. $c \neq a$	43–52, IP

Next, the proof that there are no Republican councilmen besides Andrews and Carlyle (that is, that every Republican councilman is identical with one or the other of that pair):

→54. $Cz \cdot Rz$ / ∴ $z = a \lor z = c$	
→55. $z = b$	(IP)
56. $Rz \supset \sim Dz$	3, UI, x/z
57. $\sim Dz$	54, sev., 56, MP
58. $\sim Db$	55, 57, Id. (z/b in 57)
59. $Db \cdot \sim Db$	2, sev., 58, conj.
60. $z \neq b$	55–59, IP
61. $(Cz \cdot z \neq b) \supset (z = a \lor z = c)$	22, UI, x/z
62. $z = a \lor z = c$	54, sev., 60, conj., 61, MP
63. $(Cz \cdot Rz) \supset (z = a \lor z = c)$	54–62, CP
64. $(z)[(Cz \cdot Rz) \supset (z = a \lor z = c)]$	63, UG, z/z

And, finally, the proof is completed by:

65. $Cc \cdot Rc \cdot a \neq c \cdot (z)[(Cz \cdot Rz) \supset (z = a \lor z = c)]$	4, sev., 42, sev., 53, sym., 64, conj.
66. $(\exists y)(Cy \cdot Ry \cdot a \neq y \cdot (z)[(Cz \cdot Rz) \supset (z = a \lor z = c)])$	65, EG, c/y
67. $Ca \cdot Ra \cdot (\exists y)(Cy \cdot Ry \cdot a \neq y \cdot$ $(z)[(Cz \cdot Rz) \supset (z = a \lor z = c)])$	4, sev., 42, sev., 66, conj.
68. $(\exists x)[Cx \cdot Rx \cdot (\exists y)(Cy \cdot Ry \cdot y \neq x \cdot$ $(z)[(Cz \cdot Rz) \supset (z = a \lor z = c)])]$	67, EG, a/x, sym.
69. [68]	8–68, EI
70. [68]	5–69, EI

Ch. 23, Ex. V

(2)   1. $(\exists x)[Fx \cdot (y)(Fy \supset y = x) \cdot x = a]$
       2. Fb / ∴ $a = b$

3. $Fx \cdot (y)(Fy \supset y = x) \cdot x = a$ 1, x/x

4. $(y)(Fy \supset y = x)$ 3, sev.

5. $Fb \supset b = x$ 4, UI, y/b

6. $b = x$ 2, 5, MP

7. $b = a$ 3, sev., 6, Id. (x/b in 3)

8. $a = b$ 7, sym.

9. $a = b$ 3–8, EI

(4) 1. $(\exists x)[Fx \cdot (y)(Fy \supset y = x) \cdot (\exists z)(Gz \cdot (w)[Gw \supset w = z] \cdot z = x)]$

2. Ga / $\therefore$ $(x)(Fx \supset x = a)$

3. $Fx \cdot (y)(Fy \supset y = x) \cdot (\exists z)(Gz \cdot (w)[Gw \supset w = z] \cdot z = x)$ 1, x/x

4. $(\exists z)(Gz \cdot (w)[Gw \supset w = z] \cdot z = x)$ 3, sev.

5. $Gz \cdot (w)[Gw \supset w = z] \cdot z = x$ 4, z/z

6. $(w)[Gw \supset w = z]$ 5, sev.

7. $(y)(Fy \supset y = x)$ 3, sev.

8. $z = x$ 5, sev.

9. Ft / $\therefore$ $t = a$

10. $Ft \supset t = x$ 7, UI, y/t

11. $t = x$ 9, 10, MP

12. $Ga \supset a = z$ 6, UI, w/a

13. $a = z$ 2, 12, MP

14. $a = x$ 8, 13, Id. (z/x in 13)

15. $t = a$ 11, 14, Id. (x/a in 11)

16. $Ft \supset t = a$ 9–15, CP

17. $(x)(Fx \supset x = a)$ 16, UG, t/x

18. $(x)(Fx \supset x = a)$ 5–17, EI

19. $(x)(Fx \supset x = a)$ 3–18, EI

(7) 1. $(\exists x)(\exists y)[Fx \cdot Fy \cdot x \neq y \cdot (z)(Fz \supset [z = x \lor z = y])]$

2. $(\exists x)[Fx \cdot Gx \cdot (y)([Fy \cdot Gy] \supset y = x)]$

   / $\therefore$ $(\exists x)[Fx \cdot {\sim} Gx \cdot (y)([Fy \cdot {\sim} Gy] \supset y = x)]$

The first premiss of this argument says that there are exactly two F's. The second premiss says that there is exactly one F which is G. The conclusion is that there is exactly one F which is $\sim G$. As a first step, it is necessary to prove that the F which is G is the same as one or the other of the F's mentioned in the first premiss:

3. $(\exists y)[Fx \cdot Fy \cdot x \neq y \cdot (z)(Fz \supset [z = x \lor z = y])]$

     1, x/x

4. $Fx \cdot Fy \cdot x \neq y \cdot (z)(Fz \supset [z = x \lor z = y])$

     3, y/y

5. $Fx \cdot Fy \cdot x \neq y$ 4, sev.

6. $(z)(Fz \supset [z = x \lor z = y])$ 4, sev.

7. $Fw \cdot Gw \cdot (y)([Fy \cdot Gy] \supset y = w)$ 2, x/w

8. $(y)([Fy \cdot Gy] \supset y = w)$ 7, sev.

$$9. \ Fw \supset [w = x \lor w = y] \qquad\qquad 6, \text{UI}, z/w$$
$$10. \ w = x \lor w = y \qquad\qquad\qquad 7, \text{sev.}, 9, \text{MP}$$

Next, it must be shown that whichever of the two F's w is, the other one is the unique F which is $\sim G$. Once this is done, it will follow by EG that there is exactly one F which is $\sim G$. The easiest way to proceed is with a proof by cases (Appendix L) on line 10:

$$11. \ w = x$$
$$12. \ Gx \qquad\qquad\qquad\qquad\qquad 7, \text{sev.}, 11, \text{Id. } (w/x \text{ in } 7)$$
$$13. \ Gy \qquad\qquad\qquad\qquad\qquad (\text{IP})$$
$$14. \ [Fy \cdot Gy] \supset y = w \qquad\qquad 8, \text{UI}, y/y$$
$$15. \ y = w \qquad\qquad\qquad\qquad\qquad 5, \text{sev.}, 13, \text{conj.}, 14, \text{MP}$$
$$16. \ x \neq w \qquad\qquad\qquad\qquad\qquad 5, \text{sev.}, 15, \text{Id. } (y/w \text{ in } 5)$$
$$17. \ x = w \qquad\qquad\qquad\qquad\qquad 11, \text{sym.}$$
$$18. \ x = w \cdot x \neq w \qquad\qquad\qquad 16, 17, \text{conj.}$$
$$19. \ \sim Gy \qquad\qquad\qquad\qquad\qquad 13\text{--}18, \text{CP}$$
$$20. \ Ft \cdot \sim Gt \qquad / \therefore \ t = y$$
$$21. \ t \neq y \qquad\qquad\qquad\qquad\qquad (\text{IP})$$
$$22. \ Ft \supset [t = x \lor t = y] \qquad\quad 6, \text{UI}, z/t$$
$$23. \ t = x \lor t = y \qquad\qquad\qquad 20, \text{sev.}, 22, \text{MP}$$
$$24. \ t = x \qquad\qquad\qquad\qquad\qquad 21, 23, \text{canc.}$$
$$25. \ Gt \qquad\qquad\qquad\qquad\qquad 12, 24, \text{Id. } (x/t \text{ in } 12)$$
$$26. \ Gt \cdot \sim Gt \qquad\qquad\qquad\qquad 20, \text{sev.}, 26, \text{conj.}$$
$$27. \ t = y \qquad\qquad\qquad\qquad\qquad 21\text{--}26, \text{IP, DN}$$
$$28. \ [Ft \cdot \sim Gt] \supset t = y \qquad\qquad 20\text{--}27, \text{CP}$$
$$29. \ (t)([Ft \cdot \sim Gt] \supset t = y) \qquad 28, \text{UG}, t/t$$
$$30. \ Fy \cdot \sim Gy \cdot (t)([Ft \cdot \sim Gt] \supset t = y) \qquad 5, \text{sev.}, 26, \text{sev.}, 29, \text{conj.}$$
$$31. \ (\exists x)[Fx \cdot \sim Gx \cdot (t)([Ft \cdot \sim Gt] \supset t = x)]$$
$$\qquad\qquad\qquad\qquad\qquad\qquad\qquad 30, \text{EG}, y/x$$
$$32. \ (\exists x)[Fx \cdot \sim Gx \cdot (y)([Fy \cdot \sim Gy] \supset y = x)]$$
$$\qquad\qquad\qquad\qquad\qquad\qquad\qquad 31, \text{RBV}, t/y$$
$$33. \ w = x \supset (\exists x)[Fx \cdot \sim Gx \cdot (y)([Fy \cdot \sim Gy] \supset y = x)]$$
$$\qquad\qquad\qquad\qquad\qquad\qquad\qquad 20\text{--}32, \text{CP}$$

which concludes the first "case": if x is w—that is, the F which is G, then y is the unique F which is $\sim G$, and so there is exactly one F that is $\sim G$. Next we consider the other "case":

$$34. \ w = y$$
$$35. \ Gy \qquad\qquad\qquad\qquad\qquad 7, \text{sev.}, 34, \text{Id. } (w/y \text{ in } 7)$$
$$36. \ Gx \qquad\qquad\qquad\qquad\qquad (\text{IP})$$
$$37. \ [Fx \cdot Gx] \supset x = w \qquad\qquad 8, \text{UI}, y/x$$
$$38. \ x = w \qquad\qquad\qquad\qquad\qquad 5, 36, \text{conj.}, 37, \text{MP}$$
$$39. \ x = y \qquad\qquad\qquad\qquad\qquad 34, 38, \text{Id. } (w/y \text{ in } 38)$$
$$40. \ x = y \cdot x \neq y \qquad\qquad\qquad 5, \text{sev.}, 39, \text{conj.}$$
$$41. \ \sim Gx \qquad\qquad\qquad\qquad\qquad 36\text{--}40, \text{IP}$$

42. $Ft \cdot \sim Gt$ $/ \therefore t = x$	
43. $t \neq x$	(IP)
44. $Ft \supset [t = x \lor t = y]$	6, UI, z/t
45. $t = x \lor t = y$	42, sev., 44, MP
46. $t = y$	43, 45, canc.
47. Gt	35, 46, Id. (y/t in 35)
48. $Gt \cdot \sim Gt$	42, sev., 47, conj.
49. $t = x$	43–48, IP
50. $[Ft \cdot \sim Gt] \supset t = x$	42–49, CP
51. $(y)([Fy \cdot \sim Gy] \supset y = x)$	50, UG, t/y
52. $Fx \cdot \sim Gx \cdot (y)([Fy \cdot \sim Gy] \supset y = x)$	5, sev., 42, 51, conj.
53. $(\exists x)[Fx \cdot \sim Gx \cdot (y)([Fy \cdot \sim Gy] \supset y = x)]$	
	52, EG, x/x
54. $w = y \supset (\exists x)[Fx \cdot \sim Gx \cdot (y)([Fy \cdot \sim Gy] \supset y = x)]$	
	34–53, CP

which concludes the second "case." The desired conclusion now follows
from 10, 33, and 54, by Dilemma and Duplication; and there is nothing
left to do except sweep up.

55. $(\exists x)[Fx \cdot \sim Gx \cdot (y)([Fy \cdot \sim Gy] \supset y = x)]$	
	10, 33, 54, dilem., dup.
56. [55]	7–55, EI
57. [55]	4–56, EI
58. [55]	3–57, EI

Ch. 23, Ex. VI

(2) Supplied premisses:
    (a) Nothing is both fat and skinny.
    (b) Nothing is both smart and dumb.

	1. $Fa \lor Ia$	
	2. $Sj \lor Dj$ $/ \therefore a = j \supset (Fa \supset Da)$	
Supp. (a)	3. $(x)(Fx \supset \sim Sx)$	
Supp. (b)	4. $(x)(Ix \supset \sim Dx)$	
	5. $a = j$ $/ \therefore Fa \supset Da$	
	6. Fa $/ \therefore Da$	
	7. $Fa \supset \sim Sa$	3, UI, x/a
	8. $\sim Sa$	6, 7, MP
	9. $\sim Sj$	5, 8, Id. (a/j in 8)
	10. Dj	9, 2, canc.
	11. Da	5, 10, Id. (j/a in 10)
	12. $Fa \supset Da$	6–11, CP
	13. $a = j \supset (Fa \supset Da)$	5–12, CP

(4) Supplied premisses:

(a) All and only parents are fathers or mothers.

(b) All and only siblings (sisters or brothers) have the same parents.

(c) No fathers are mothers.

(d) No females are brothers.

(e) Maude is a female.

(f) Nothing has more than two parents.

(g) 'Son of' is a partial converse of 'parent of'.

(h) 'Older than' is asymmetric.

$$1. \ (\exists x)(Sxb \cdot (y)(Syb \supset y = x) \cdot Obx)$$

$$2. \ Fym \cdot Omj \quad | \ \therefore \ Kbf \supset [(b = j \cdot (\exists x)(Mxm \cdot Mxb)) \supset f \neq y]$$

Supp. (a) 3. $(x)(y)(Pxy \equiv (Fxy \lor Mxy))$

Supp. (b) 4. $(x)(y)((Sxy \lor Bxy) \equiv (z)(Pzx \equiv Pzy))$

Supp. (c) 5. $(x)[(\exists y)Fxy \supset \sim(\exists z)Mxz]$

Supp. (d) 6. $(x)(y)(Wx \supset \sim Bxy)$

Supp. (e) 7. Wm

Supp. (f) 8. $(x)(y)(z)(w)[(Pyx \cdot Pzx \cdot Pwx) \supset (y = z \lor y = w \lor z = w)]$

Supp. (g) 9. $(x)(y)(Kxy \supset Pyx)$

Supp. (h) 10. $(x)(y)(Oxy \supset \sim Oyx)$

The actual derivation will not be given. As a point of reference, it took the author 94 steps.

Ch. 23, Ex. VII

(3) The translation of this argument is:

1. $(x)(\exists y)(Myx \cdot Lxy)$

2. $(x)(\exists y)(Myx \cdot (z)(Mzx \supset z = y))$

$\therefore (x)(\exists y)(Lxy \cdot (z)(Lxz \supset z = y))$

The interpretation of this argument for the universe $\{a, b\}$ is:

1. $[(Maa \cdot Laa) \lor (Mba \cdot Lab)] \cdot [(Mab \cdot Lba) \lor (Mbb \cdot Lbb)]$

2. $[\{Maa \cdot ([Maa \supset a = a] \cdot [Mba \supset b = a])\} \lor$
$\{Mba \cdot ([Maa \supset a = b] \cdot [Mba \supset b = b])\}] \cdot$
$[\{Mab \cdot ([Mab \supset a = a] \cdot [Mbb \supset b = a])\} \lor$
$\{Mbb \cdot ([Mab \supset a = b] \cdot [Mbb \supset b = b])\}]$

$\therefore [\{Laa \cdot ([Laa \supset a = a] \cdot [Lab \supset b = a])\} \lor$
$\{Lab \cdot ([Laa \supset a = b] \cdot [Lab \supset b = b])\}] \cdot$
$[\{Lba \cdot ([Lba \supset a = a] \cdot [Lbb \supset b = a])\} \lor$
$\{Lbb \cdot ([Lba \supset a = b] \cdot [Lbb \supset b = b])\}]$

Shown invalid for $\{a, b\}$ by:

Laa	Lab	Lba	Lbb	Maa	Mab	Mba	Mbb	$a = a$	$a = b$	$b = a$	$b = b$
T	T	T	T	F	T	T	F	T	F	F	T

and many other assignments. Also shown invalid by:

Mxy : x is mother to y,

Lxy : x is younger than y.

Ch. 24, Ex. I

(2) (∃ x)(x is a man · x shook hands with the author of b̲)
    (∃ x)(Mx · the author of b̲ is such that x shook hands with him)
    (∃ x)(Mx · [(ιy)y authored b̲]x shook hands with y)
    (∃ x)(Mx · [(ιy)Ayb̲]Sxy)

(5) Despite its form, 'the Holy Roman Empire' is not a description but a proper
    name. If we abbreviate this name as 'h̲', the statement will translate succes-
    sively as:
    ~ h̲ was holy · ~ h̲ was Roman · ~ h̲ was an empire
    ~ Hh̲ · ~ Rh̲ · ~ Eh̲

(8) The king of the fairies is such that Oberon is he.
    [(ιx)x is king of the fairies]Oberon is x
    [(ιx)Kx]o̲ = x

Ch. 24, Ex. II

(1) The author of h̲ is such that the husband of a̲ is he.
    [(ιx)x authored h̲]the husband of a̲ is x
    [(ιx)x authored h̲][(ιy)y is husband to a̲]y is x
    [(ιx)Axh̲][(ιy)Hya̲]y = x

(5) The king of the Boohoos is a member of the tribe and is taller than every
    other member of the tribe.
    [(ιx)x is king of the Boohoos](x is a member of the tribe · x is taller than
        every other member of the tribe)
    [(ιx)Kx](Mx · (y)([My · y ≠ x] ⊃ x is taller than y))
    [(ιx)Kx](Mx · (y)([My · y ≠ x] ⊃ Txy))

    or, if we are worried about 'the tribe',
    The king of the Boohoos is a member of a tribe and is taller than every other
    member of the tribe.
    The king of the Boohoos is such that (∃ y)(y is a tribe ·
    he is a member of y · he is taller than every other member of y)
    [(ιx)Kx](∃ y)(Ty · x is a member of y ·
        (z)([z is a member of y · z ≠ x] ⊃ x is taller than z))
    [(ιx)Kx](∃ y)(Ty · Mxy · (z)([Mzy · z ≠ x] ⊃ Txz))

(10) The butler at Carfax is such that he has two sisters and one of them is mar-
    ried to the owner of Carfax.
    [(ιx)x buttles at Carfax](x has two sisters and one of them is married to the
        owner of Carfax)
    [(ιx)Bxc̲](x has two sisters and the owner of Carfax is such that one of them
        is married to him)
    [(ιx)Bxc̲](∃ y)(∃ z)(y is sister to x · z is sister to x · y ≠ z · the owner of
        Carfax is such that y is married to him ∨ z is married to him)
    [(ιx)Bxc̲](∃ y)(∃ z)(Syx · Szx · y ≠ z · ∨ [(ιw)w owns Carfax](y is married
        to w ∨ z is married to w))
    [(ιx)Bxc̲](∃ y)(∃ z)(Syx · Szx · y ≠ z · [(ιw)Owc̲](Myw ∨ Mzw))

Ch. 24, Ex. III

(2) The author of *Ivanhoe* is such that Scott is he.
[$(\imath x)x$ authored *Ivanhoe*]Scott is x
[$(\imath x)Ax\underline{i}]\underline{s} = x$
$(\exists x)(Ax\underline{i} \cdot (y)(Ay\underline{i} \supset y = x) \cdot \underline{s} = x)$

(5) [$(\imath x)x$ buttles at Carfax] the sister of x is lovely
[$(\imath x)x$ buttles at Carfax][$(\imath y)y$ is sister to x]y is lovely
[$(\imath x)Bx\underline{c}$][$(\imath y)Syx$]$Ly$
$(\exists x)(Bx\underline{c} \cdot (z)(Bz\underline{c} \supset z = x) \cdot $[$(\imath y)Syx$]$Ly)$
$(\exists x)(Bx\underline{c} \cdot (z)(Bz\underline{c} \supset z = x) \cdot (\exists y)(Syx \cdot (w)(Swx \supset w = y) \cdot Ly))$

(8) [$(\imath x)(x$ is a man $\cdot$ x loves everybody)]x loves somebody
[$(\imath x)(x$ is a man $\cdot$ x loves everybody)]($\exists y)(y$ is a person $\cdot$ x loves $y)$
[$(\imath x)(x$ is a man $\cdot$ $(z)(z$ is a person $\supset$ x loves $z))$]($\exists y)(Py \cdot Lxy)$
[$(\imath x)(Mx \cdot (z)(Pz \supset Lxz))$]($\exists y)(Py \cdot Lxy)$
$(\exists x)[(Mx \cdot (z)(Pz \supset Lxz)) \cdot (w)([Mw \cdot (z)(Pz \supset Lwz)] \supset w = x) \cdot$
$(\exists y)(Py \cdot Lxy)]$

Ch. 24, Ex. IV

(2)
1. $[(\imath x)Axi]s = x$
2. $[(\imath x)Axi]Bx$ $/ \therefore Bs$
3. $(\exists x)(Axi \cdot (y)(Ayi \supset y = x) \cdot s = x)$ 1, DT
4. $(\exists x)(Axi \cdot (y)(Ayi \supset y = x) \cdot Bx)$ 2, DT
5. $Axi \cdot (y)(Ayi \supset y = x) \cdot s = x$ 3, x/x
6. $Azi \cdot (y)(Ayi \supset y = z) \cdot Bz$ 4, x/z
7. $(y)(Ayi \supset y = x)$ 5, sev.
8. $Azi \supset z = x$ 7, UI, y/z
9. $z = x$ 6, sev., 8, MP
10. $s = x$ 5, sev.
11. $s = z$ 9, 10, Id. (x/z in 10)
12. Bz 6, sev.
13. Bs 11, 12, Id. (z/s in 12)
14. Bs 6–13, EI
15. Bs 5–14, EI

(4)
1. $[(\imath x)Axc]x = v$
2. Aac $/ \therefore v = a$
3. $(\exists x)(Axc \cdot (y)(Ayc \supset y = x) \cdot x = v)$
   1, DT
4. $Axc \cdot (y)(Ayc \supset y = x) \cdot x = v$ 3, x/x
5. $(y)(Ayc \supset y = x)$ 4, sev.
6. $Aac \supset a = x$ 5, UI, y/a
7. $a = x$ 2, 6, MP
8. $x = v$ 4, sev.
9. $a = v$ 7, 8, Id. (x/v in 7)
10. $v = a$ 9, sym.
11. $v = a$ 4–10, EI

(7)   1. $(x)[Kxb \supset (\exists y)Syx]$
       2. $(x)[Kxb \supset (y)(z)([Syx \cdot Szx] \supset y = z)]$
       3. $(x)[(\exists w)(Kwb \cdot Sxw) \supset Wx]$
       4. $(x)[(Wx \cdot (\exists w)(Kwb \cdot Sxw)) \supset \sim Ix]$
       5. $(\exists x)(Kxb \cdot (y)(Kyb \supset y = x))$ $/ \therefore [(\imath x)Kxb][(\imath y)Syx] \sim Iy$

Premiss 5 assures us that there is exactly one king of Belsnavia. Thus, the strategy is to prove that the king has exactly one son, and that that son is not industrious, then to use DT on these quantified formulae to get the desired conclusion. First, the proof that the king has at least one son:

$\longrightarrow$ 6. $Kxb \cdot (y)(Kyb \supset y = x)$ 5, x/x
       7. $Kxb \supset (\exists y)Syx$ 1, UI, x/x
       8. $(\exists y)Syx$ 6, sev., 7, MP

then the proof that the king has no other sons:

$\longrightarrow$ 9. Syx 8, y/y
$\longrightarrow$10. $(\exists z)(Szx \cdot z \neq y)$ (IP)
       $\longrightarrow$11. $Szx \cdot z \neq y$ 10, z/z
       12. $Kxb \supset (y)(z)([Syx \cdot Szx] \supset y = z)$ 2, UI, x/x
       13. $(y)(z)([Syx \cdot Szx] \supset y = z)$ 6, sev., 12, MP
       14. $(z)([Syx \cdot Szx] \supset y = z)$ 13, UI, y/y
       15. $[Syx \cdot Szx] \supset y = z$ 14, UI, z/z
       16. $z = y$ 11, sev., 9, conj., 15, MP, sym.
       17. $A \cdot \sim A$ 16, disj., 11, sev., canc.
       18. $A \cdot \sim A$ 11–17, EI
       19. $\sim (\exists z)(Szx \cdot z \neq y)$ 10–18, IP
       20. $(z) \sim (Szx \cdot z \neq y)$ 19, QN
       21. $(z)(Szx \supset z = y)$ 20, TD, CE, DN

then the proof that the son of the king is not industrious:

       22. $(\exists w)(Kwb \cdot Syw) \supset Wy$ 3, UI, x/y
       23. $(w)[(Kwb \cdot Syw) \supset Wy]$ 22, QS
       24. $[Kxb \cdot Syx] \supset Wy$ 23, UI, w/x
       25. Wy 6, sev., 9, conj., 24, MP
       26. $(Wy \cdot (\exists w)(Kwb \cdot Syw)) \supset \sim Iy$ 4, UI, x/y
       27. $Wy \supset ((\exists w)(Kwb \cdot Syw) \supset \sim Iy)$ 26, exp.
       28. $(\exists w)(Kwb \cdot Syw) \supset \sim Iy$ 25, 27, MP
       29. $(w)((Kwb \cdot Syw) \supset \sim Iy)$ 28, QS
       30. $(Kxb \cdot Syx) \supset \sim Iy$ 29, UI, w/x
       31. $\sim Iy$ 6, sev., 9, conj., 30, MP

Now to put them all together:

       32. $Syx \cdot (z)(Szx \supset z = y) \cdot \sim Iy$ 9, 21, 31, conj.
       33. $(\exists y)(Syx \cdot (z)(Szx \supset z = y) \cdot \sim Iy)$ 32, EG, y/y
       34. $[(\imath y)Syx] \sim Iy$ 33, DT
       35. $Kxb \cdot (y)(Kyb \supset y = x) \cdot [(\imath y)Syx] \sim Iy$
                                                               6, 34, conj.
       36. $(\exists x)(Kxb \cdot (y)(Kyb \supset y = x) \cdot [(\imath y)Syx] \sim Iy)$
                                                               35, EG, x/x
       37. $[(\imath x)Kxb][(\imath y)Syx] \sim Iy$ 36, DT

and the proof is complete, except for sweeping up.

Ch. 24, Ex. VII

(1)   1. $[(\imath x)(Ex \cdot Px \cdot Nx)]x < 3$
       2. $(x)(x < 3 \supset x < 4)$ $/\therefore (\exists x)(Ex \cdot Nx \cdot x < 4)$
       3. $(\exists x)((Ex \cdot Px \cdot Nx) \cdot (y)((Ey \cdot Py \cdot Ny) \supset y = x) \cdot x < 3)$
                                                                 1, DT
  → 4. $Ex \cdot Px \cdot Nx \cdot (y)((Ey \cdot Py \cdot Ny) \supset y = x) \cdot x < 3$ 3, x/x
       5. $x < 3$ 4, sev.
       6. $x < 3 \supset x < 4$ 2, UI, x/x
       7. $x < 4$ 5, 6, MP
       8. $Ex \cdot Nx$ 4, sev.
       9. $Ex \cdot Nx \cdot x < 4$ 7, 8, conj.
     10. $(\exists x)(Ex \cdot Nx \cdot x < 4)$ 9, EG, x/x
     11. $(\exists x)(Ex \cdot Nx \cdot x < 4)$ 4–10, EI

(6)   1. $[(\imath x)(Ex \cdot Px \cdot Nx)]x < 3$
       2. $3 < 4$
       3. $(x)(x < 3 \supset x < 4)$
       4. $P3 \cdot N3 \cdot {\sim}E3$ $/\therefore (\exists x)(\exists y)(Px \cdot Nx \cdot x < 4 \cdot Py \cdot Ny \cdot y <$
                                 $4 \cdot x \neq y)$
       5. $(\exists x)(Ex \cdot Px \cdot Nx \cdot (y)((Ey \cdot Py \cdot Ny) \supset y = x) \cdot x < 3)$
                                                                    1, DT
  ┌→ 6. $Ex \cdot Px \cdot Nx \cdot (y)((Ey \cdot Py \cdot Ny) \supset y = x) \cdot x < 3$
  │   5, x/x
  │   7. $Px \cdot Nx$ 6, sev.
  │   8. $x < 3$ 6, sev.
  │   9. $x < 3 \supset x < 4$ 3, UI, x/x
  │   10. $x < 4$ 8, 9, MP
  │→11. $x = 3$ (IP)
  │| 12. Ex 6, sev.
  │| 13. $E3$ 11, 12, Id. ($x/3$ in 12)
  │| 14. $E3 \cdot {\sim}E3$ 4, sev., 13, conj.
  │   15. $x \neq 3$ 11–14, IP
  │   16. $Px \cdot Nx \cdot x < 4 \cdot P3 \cdot N3 \cdot 3 < 4 \cdot x \neq 3$ 7, 10, 4, sev., 2, 15, conj.
  │   17. $(\exists y)(Px \cdot Nx \cdot x < 4 \cdot Py \cdot Ny \cdot y < 4 \cdot x \neq y)$
  │   16, EG, $3/y$
  │   18. $(\exists x)(\exists y)(Px \cdot Nx \cdot x < 4 \cdot Py \cdot Ny \cdot y < 4 \cdot x \neq y)$
  │   17, EG, x/x
  └─────────────────────────────────
      19. [18]   6–18, EI

(9)   1. $[(\imath x)Sx1]Px$
       2. $(x)((Nx \cdot Px) \supset (Fxx \cdot (z)(Fzx \supset z = x)))$
       3. $(x)[(Nx \cdot Ox) \supset (\exists y)(Ny \cdot Ey \cdot Syx)]$
       4. $N1 \cdot O1$ $/\therefore (\exists x)(Nx \cdot Ex \cdot (\exists y)[Fyx \cdot (z)(Fzx \supset z = y) \cdot$
                                             $[(\imath w)Sw1]y = w])$
       5. $(\exists x)(Sx1 \cdot (y)(Sy1 \supset y = x) \cdot Px)$ 1, DT

6. $Sx1 \cdot (y)(Sy1 \supset y = x) \cdot Px$ 5, x/x
7. $(N1 \cdot O1) \supset (\exists y)(Ny \cdot Ey \cdot Sy1)$ 3, UI, $x/1$
8. $(\exists y)(Ny \cdot Ey \cdot Sy1)$ 4, 7, MP
9. $Ny \cdot Ey \cdot Sy1$ 8, y/y
10. $(y)(Sy1 \supset y = x)$ 6, sev.
11. $Sy1 \supset y = x$ 10, UI, y/y
12. $y = x$ 9, sev., 11, MP
13. $Ny \cdot Ey$ 9, sev.
14. $Nx \cdot Ex$ 12, 13, Id. (y/x in 13)
15. $(Nx \cdot Px) \supset (Fxx \cdot (z)(Fzx \supset z = x))$ 2, UI, x/x
16. $Fxx \cdot (z)(Fzx \supset z = x)$ 6, sev., 14, sev., conj., 15, MP
17. $Sx1 \cdot (y)(Sy1 \supset y = x) \cdot y = x$ 6, sev., 12, conj.
18. $(\exists w)(Sw1 \cdot (y)(Sy1 \supset y = w) \cdot y = w)$ 17, EG, x/w
19. $[(\imath w)Sw1]y = w$ 18, DT
20. $[(\imath w)Sw1]x = w$ 12, 19, Id. (y/x in 19)
21. $Fxx \cdot (z)(Fz \supset z = x) \cdot [(\imath w)Sw1]x = w$
     16, 20, conj.
22. $(\exists y)(Fyx \cdot (z)(Fzx \supset z = y) \cdot$
     $[(\imath w)Sw1]y = w)$ 21, EG, x/y
23. $Nx \cdot Ex \cdot (\exists y)(Fyx \cdot (z)(Fzx \supset$
     $z = y) \cdot [(\imath w)Sw1]y = w)$ 14, 22, conj.
24. $(\exists x)(Nx \cdot Ex \cdot (\exists y)(Fyx \cdot (z)(Fzx \supset$
     $z = y) \cdot [(\imath w)Sw1]y = w))$ 23, EG, x/x
25. [24]   9–24, EI
26. [24]   6–25, EI

Ch. 24, Ex. VIII

(2) $(\exists x)[x$ is a man $\cdot$ x lives in Albuquerque $\cdot$ $(y)((y$ is a man $\cdot$ y lives in Albu-querque $\cdot$ $y \neq x) \supset x$ is older than $y) \cdot (\exists z)(z$ plays for the Celtics $\cdot$ $(\exists w)[w$ plays for the Celtics $\cdot$ $w \neq z \cdot$ $\sim z$ is taller than $w \cdot (k)([k$ plays for the Celtics $\cdot$ $k \neq w \cdot k \neq z] \supset z$ is taller than $k)] \cdot x$ is shorter than $z)]$
$(\exists x)[Mx \cdot Lx\underline{a} \cdot (y)((My \cdot Ly\underline{a} \cdot y \neq x) \supset Oxy) \cdot (\exists z)(Cz \cdot$
$(\exists w)(Cw \cdot w \neq z \cdot \sim Tzw \cdot (k)([Ck \cdot k \neq w \cdot k \neq z] \supset Tzk)] \cdot Sxz)]$

(5) $(\exists x)(x$ is Danish $\cdot$ x is a prince $\cdot$ the mother of x is such that her second husband is such that his (the prince's) father is such that he (the hus-band) is a brother to him (the father) $\cdot$ he (the prince) is Hamlet)
$(\exists x)(Dx \cdot Px \cdot [(\imath y)y$ is mother to $x][(\imath z)z$ is second husband to $y][(\imath w)w$ is father to $x]z$ is brother to $w \cdot x =$ Hamlet)
$(\exists x)(Dx \cdot Px \cdot [(\imath y)Myx][(\imath z)Szy][(\imath w)Fwx]Bzw \cdot x = \underline{h})$

(9) $(x)(x$ is a person $\supset \sim$(the composer of $\underline{d}$ is such that x is acquainted with him))
$(x)(Px \supset \sim[(\imath y)Cy\underline{d}]Axy)$
or, less plausibly,
The composer of $\underline{d}$ is such that $(x)(x$ is a person $\supset \sim x$ is acquainted with him)
$[(\imath y)Cy\underline{d}](x)(Px \supset \sim Axy)$

Appendix M, Ex. I

(2) A = Every marsupial is an opossum.
 E = No marsupial is an opossum.
 I = given
 O = Some marsupial is not an opossum.

(5) A = given
 E = No counterclockwise ocean current is a phenomenon of the Northern Hemisphere.
 I = Some counterclockwise ocean current is a phenomenon of the Northern Hemisphere.
 O = Some counterclockwise ocean current is not a phenomenon of the Northern Hemisphere.

Ex. IV

Note: In this and the following two exercises, it must be understood that 'non' governs the *entire* term, not merely the first part of it.

(3) Every Born-Again Baptist is a non-disbeliever in total immersion.

(5) No combat soldier is a non-believer.

(10) No hangover symptom is a non-result of dehydration of the brain lining.

Ex. V

(5) No non-believer is a combat soldier.

(10) No non-result of dehydration of the brain lining is a hangover symptom.

Ex. VI

(5) Every non-believer is a non-combat soldier.

(10) Every non-result of dehydration of the brain lining is a non-hangover symptom.

Ex. VII

(1) Isn't: contains four terms (sophomore, honors student, philosophy student, philosophy honors student).

(4) Isn't: minor premiss given first.

(7) Isn't: major premiss and conclusion are not SFCP's.

Ex. VIII

(2) AAA-2	(8) AAI-3	(15) EAO-2
(5) AAA-4	(11) EIO-4	

Ex. IX

(2) Invalid—middle term not distributed, in violation of Distribution Condition.

(5) Invalid—minor term distributed in conclusion but not in premiss, in violation of D.C.

(8) Valid.

(11) Valid.

(15) Valid.

Ex. X

(8) Invalid—middle term distributed twice, in violation of M.D.C.
(11) Valid.
(15) Invalid—minor term distributed in premiss but not in conclusion, in violation of M.D.C.

SELECTED BIBLIOGRAPHY

This short bibliography makes no pretensions to completeness. It is intended only to provide a choice of starting places for the reader who is interested in pursuing logic beyond the scope of the present book. Larger bibliographies are included in most of the works cited below.

HISTORICAL AND SURVEY

Eaton, Ralph M., *General Logic*. New York: Charles Scribner's Sons, 1959. A somewhat dated but still useful survey of traditional and modern logic. First published in 1931.

Kneale, William, and Martha Kneale, *The Development of Logic*. Oxford: The Clarendon Press, 1962. A thorough and well-written history of logic from ancient Greece through the first half of the twentieth century.

Prior, A. N., *Formal Logic*. Oxford: The Clarendon Press, 1962. An excellent reference book, covering the logic of truth-functions and quantification (developed from axioms), syllogistic, and a few more advanced topics. Uses Polish notation throughout.

INTERMEDIATE AND ADVANCED TEXTS

Whitehead, Alfred North, and Bertrand Russell, *Principia Mathematica*, vol. I. Cambridge: Cambridge University Press, 1950. A classic. First published in 1910 and slightly revised in 1925, this is the fountainhead of modern logic. Although its terminology is archaic, it remains an invaluable sourcebook in the philosophy of logic. Volumes II and III exist, but offer little to the casual student of logic. An abridged paperback edition of vol. I is available.

Quine, W. V., *Mathematical Logic*. Cambridge, Mass.: Harvard University Press, 1951. Covers substantially the same territory as vol. I of *Principia Mathematica*, but in a more succinct and readable manner. Includes axiomatic developments of truth-functional and quantificational logic, the logical development of basic concepts of mathematics, and certain other topics.

———, *Methods of Logic*, 3d ed. New York: Holt, Rinehart and Winston, Inc., 1972. A widely used intermediate-level text.

Thomason, Richmond H., *Symbolic Logic*. New York: The Macmillan Company, 1970. A very good intermediate-level text. Unlike the present text, it is concerned with logic as a subject of study in its own right rather than as an instrument for the evaluation of reasoning. For this reason it can give the student a different perspective on the nature of logic.

Leblanc, Hugues, *Techniques of Deductive Inference*. Englewood Cliffs, N.J.: Prentice-Hall, Inc., 1966. A fairly advanced text in pure formal logic. Leblanc has an unusual talent for writing both clearly and briefly, and this book contains far more material than its size would indicate.

Mendelson, Elliott, *Introduction to Mathematical Logic*. New York: Van Nostrand Reinhold, 1964. An excellent, but advanced and difficult text. The fact that it is titled "Introduction" will help the beginning student to realize how far logic reaches beyond the present elementary text.

Rosser, J. Barkley, *Logic for Mathematicians*. New York: McGraw-Hill, 1953. A fairly advanced text. The style and terminology make it more suited to the reader with some mathematical sophistication.

SPECIALIZED TOPICS

Bird, Otto, *Syllogistic and its Extensions*. Englewood Cliffs, N.J.: Prentice-Hall, Inc., 1964. A brief but comprehensive treatment of syllogistic logic.

Hughes, G. E., and M. J. Cresswell, *An Introduction to Modal Logic*. London: Methuen & Co., Ltd., 1968. "Modal logic" is what happens when the operators 'it is possibly true that' and 'it is necessarily true that' are added to regular logic; it is a field of increasing philosophical importance. This is a lucid and comprehensive survey of its essentials.

Rescher, Nicholas, *Many-Valued Logic*. New York: McGraw-Hill, 1969. "Many-valued logic" is what happens when formulae are permitted to take more than the two values 'T' and 'F'. This is a basic textbook on the subject.

INDEX OF OPERATORS

INDEX

/